A History of East Central Europe

VOLUMES IN THE SERIES

*Published

VOLUME IX

East Central Europe
between the Two World Wars

A HISTORY OF EAST CENTRAL EUROPE

VOLUME IX

EDITORS

PETER F. SUGAR
University of Washington

DONALD W. TREADGOLD
University of Washington

East Central Europe
between the
Two World Wars

BY JOSEPH ROTHSCHILD

UNIVERSITY OF WASHINGTON PRESS
Seattle and London

NOTABLE

Copyright © 1974 by the University of Washington Press
Second printing (paper), with corrections, 1977
Third printing (paper), 1979
Fourth printing (paper), 1983
Fifth printing (paper), 1988
Sixth printing (paper), 1990
Seventh printing (paper), 1992
Printed in the United States of America

Library of Congress Cataloging-in-Publication Data
Rothschild, Joseph.
    East Central Europe between the two World Wars.
    (A history of East Central Europe, P.F. Sugar and D.W. Treadgold, editors, v.9)
    Bibliography: p.
    1. Europe, Eastern—History.   I. Title   II. Series: Sugar, Peter F. A history of East Central Europe, v. 9
DR36.S88 vol. 9 [DR48] 914.9s [320.9′49] 74–8327
ISBN 0–295–95357–8 (pbk.)

The paper used in this publication meets the minimum requirements of American National Standard for Information Sciences—Permanence of Paper for Printed Library Materials, ANSI Z39.48–1984. ∞

For Nina and Gerson

FOREWORD

THE systematic study of the history of East Central Europe outside the region itself began only in the last generation or two. For the most part historians in the region have preferred to write about the past of only their own countries. Hitherto no comprehensive history of the area as a whole has appeared in any language.

This series was conceived as a means of providing the scholar who does not specialize in East Central European history and the student who is considering such specialization with an introduction to the subject and a survey of knowledge deriving from previous publications. In some cases it has been necessary to carry out new research simply to be able to survey certain topics and periods. Common objectives and the procedures appropriate to attain them have been discussed by the authors of the individual volumes and by the coeditors. It is hoped that a certain commensurability will be the result, so that the eleven volumes will constitute a unit and not merely an assemblage of writings. However, matters of interpretation and point of view have remained entirely the responsibility of the individual authors.

No volume deals with a single country. The aim has been to identify geographical or political units that were significant during the period in question, rather than to interpret the past in accordance with latter-day sentiments or aspirations.

The limits of "East Central Europe," for the purposes of this series, are the eastern linguistic frontier of German- and Italian-speaking peoples on the west, and the political borders of Rus/Russia/the USSR on the east. Those limits are not precise, even within the period covered by any given volume of the series. The appropriateness of including the Finns, Estonians, Latvians, Lithuanians, Belorussians, and Ukrainians was considered, and it was decided not to attempt to cover them systematically, though they appear repeatedly in these books. Treated in depth are the Poles, Czecho-Slovaks, Hungarians, Romanians, Yugoslav peoples, Albanians, Bulgarians, and Greeks.

There has been an effort to apportion attention equitably among regions and periods. Three volumes deal with the area north of the Danube-Sava line, three with the area south of it, and four with both areas. Four treat premodern history, six modern times. The eleventh consists of a historical atlas and a bibliography of the entire subject. Each volume is supplied with a bibliographical essay of its own, but we all have attempted to keep the scholarly apparatus at a minimum in order to make the text of the volumes more readable and accessible to the broader audience sought.

The coeditors wish to express their thanks to the Ford Foundation for the financial support it gave this venture, and to the Institute of Comparative and Foreign Area Studies (formerly Far Eastern and Russian Institute) and its three successive directors, George E. Taylor, George M. Beckmann, and Herbert J. Ellison, under whose encouragement the project has moved close to being realized.

The whole undertaking has been longer in the making than originally planned. Two of the original list of projected authors died before they could finish their volumes and have been replaced. Volumes of the series are being published as the manuscripts are received. We hope that the usefulness of the series justifies the long agony of its conception and birth, that it will increase knowledge of and interest in the rich past and the many-sided present of East Central Europe among those everywhere who read English, and that it will serve to stimulate further study and research on the numerous aspects of this area's history that still await scholarly investigators.

Peter F. Sugar
Donald W. Treadgold

Seattle

PREFACE

THE study of East Central Europe between the two world wars is not only intrinsically important for the historical record but is also currently relevant to America's national concern and interest. The relaxation in the techniques of Soviet control over the East Central European area, and the partial withering of the substance of that control in and over a number of the area's states, elicit and, in turn, are accelerated by the revival of certain political patterns that had been suppressed during the 1940s and 1950s. The experiences and memories of the interwar period of political independence have reasserted themselves and are helping to shape the current and future expectations of these countries' societies and elites. Hence a policy of building bridges to these countries requires an awareness of their interwar histories.

Furthermore, both individually and collectively, the several states of interwar East Central Europe present a good body of historical experience for the comparative study of the political and socioeconomic problems that confront developing multiethnic societies in general. Though the strategies adopted for the attempted resolution of these problems by the local East Central European elites at the time proved unsuccessful (quite apart from the fatal intervention of World War II), an analysis of the problems and the strategies as such should have value for scholars, students, and, perhaps, rulers concerned with understanding and mastering similar issues in other societies.

Though I have attempted a comprehensive study of interwar East Central Europe, I have deliberately avoided symmetry in my analyses of its several countries. Certain problems characteristic of the entire area, or much of it, are discussed in detail for only one or two countries, and only synopses of these issues are given in the chapters on other countries. For example, my extended probe of the Romanian Iron Guard is intended to serve paradigmatically for such Right-Radical movements in general. Parallel phenomena in other countries, e.g., the Hungarian Arrow Cross and the Croatian Ustaša, are mentioned as political factors where appropriate, but I do not analyze them for their ideological, sociological, or psychological significance. Similarly, Bulgaria functions as my paradigm for the economics of peasant agriculture, Hungary for the impact of the depression on a transitional economy, Czechoslovakia and Yugoslavia for political problems arising from multiethnicity, and Poland for the structure and program of a "government party." Again, the Jewish question is studied in some detail only in Hungary, Poland, and Romania, which are exemplars, respectively, of heavily assimilated, unassimilated, and mixed Jewish communities; it is only given passing mention elsewhere. Had I attempted to plumb such issues to equal depths for each country, the book would have become repetitious and its size would have exceeded its editorial perimeters. Since it is intended to be read as a whole, the reader will have no difficulty in applying the case studies to related phenomena in other countries.

An additional caveat appears in order here: there are no separate chapters for Austria or Greece, though they are discussed whenever necessary. Great as had been Habsburg Austria's pre-World War I position in East Central Europe, the small interwar Austrian Republic was not politically or economically or spiritually a part of the area. Her domestic and foreign attention was absorbed by the problematics of Anschluss —whether to initiate, resist, or accommodate to it—and her involvement with East Central Europe was quite secondary. Greece, in turn, though diplomatically engaged in Balkan issues, regarded herself as a Mediterranean, not an East Central European, country in terms of cultural, economic, and political perspectives. For each of the countries to whom I have devoted separate chapters, the narrative is carried through the moment of its loss of effective territorial sovereignty during or on the eve of World War II: 1939 for Czechoslovakia, Albania, and Poland; 1940 for the three Baltic states of Estonia, Latvia, and Lithuania; 1941 tor Yugoslavia; and 1944 for Hungary, Romania, and Bulgaria.

The decision to keep footnotes to a minimum was the editors' and publisher's. Any reader desiring source references for factual statements made in this book is welcome to write to me directly. Three former students, Andrew Dzirkalis, Benjamin Lopata, and Jonathan Sunshine, are cordially thanked for their conscientious bibliographical assistance. I also wish to express my warm appreciation to the John Simon Guggenheim Memorial Foundation, the American Council of Learned Societies (Joint Committee on Slavic and East European Studies of ACLS and SSRC), and the Columbia University Institute on East Central Europe for their financial generosity.

After my manuscript was delivered to the editors came the dismaying news of the premature death of my teacher, colleague, and friend Henry

L. Roberts. Professor Roberts first drew me to the study of East Central Europe as an undergraduate in Columbia College and thereafter sustained this interest by his encouragement and example. He was a scholar of wide erudition, subtle judgment, and absolute integrity. My debt to his intellect is immeasurable, my affection for his person abiding.

The American equivalents to the metric measures used in this book and in interwar East Central Europe are:

1 kilometer (km.) = 0.62 mile
1 square kilometer = 0.386 square mile
1 hectare (ha.) = 2.47 acre
1 cadastral yoke = 0.575 hectare = 1.42 acre

JOSEPH ROTHSCHILD

Columbia University
New York City

CONTENTS

MAPS

East Central Europe
between the Two World Wars

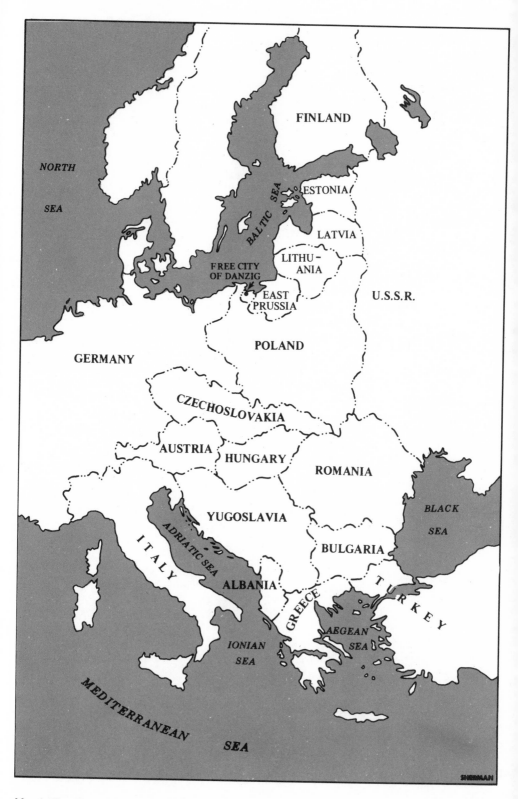

Map 1. East Central Europe, 1921-38

Chapter One

INTRODUCTORY SURVEY

1

AT THE beginning of the nineteenth century, East Central Europe contained no sovereign national states. Rather, it was organized into, and divided among, the Habsburg, Ottoman, and Russian supranational empires and the Prussian kingdom, whose population was binational (German and Polish) but whose political image was specifically German. In the century between the peace conferences of Vienna (1815) and Paris (1919), the supranational empires succumbed and were replaced in East Central Europe by a dozen sovereign states, all of which were established in recognition and partial fulfillment of the principle of nationality. Even with the creation of these states, a number of the area's nations had still not received political recognition in the form of independent statehood. The principle of nationalism had thus proved a powerful but ambiguous lever for the political reorganization of this geographic zone. In other parts of Europe during this time span, the national principle had promoted the consolidation of numerous small political units into a lesser number of larger states, e.g., the unifications of Germany and Italy and the solidification of the Swiss federation. In East Central Europe it had tended to have the opposite effect, to fragment a few large units into many smaller ones. This tendency may well prove prophetic of the dominant effect of nationalism in twentieth-century Europe in general, as the Basque, Catalan, Breton, Provençal, Flemish, Scottish, Ukrainian, and other peoples also assert their various claims to national distinctiveness and perhaps to separate statehood. In East Central Europe, the ultimate thrust to this process was provided by the generally unanticipated military and political collapse of the area's four partitioning but mutually warring empires—Russian, Ottoman, Austro-Hungarian, and German—in the closing phases of World War I.

The political and economic problems ensuing from this fragmentation-effect of East Central European nationalism later induced

3

among many conservative observers of the interwar scene, and especially among the revisionist apologists for the losers of World War I, a real or pretended nostalgia for the vanished prewar imperial order. They would repeatedly allege that the territorial settlements of 1919-21 had simply and cynically reversed the prewar roles of master and subject peoples without any greater distribution of "ethnic justice." Indeed, the dubious corollary to this argument was that since the new master nations were politically and culturally less experienced and sophisticated than their predecessors, and since East Central Europe was ethnically too variegated and mixed ever to be organized into neat and viable nation-states, therefore the interwar arrangements allegedly were, on balance, pragmatically worse than the prewar ones and morally no better.

If, however, one acknowledges the national principle of the nineteenth and twentieth centuries as embodying a valid concept of political justice—indeed, it was probably the dominant such concept during this historical epoch—then the above argument is defective even on statistical grounds. The interwar territorial settlements, for all their weaknesses, freed three times as many people from nationally alien rule as they subjected to such rule. Furthermore, the new subjection, while deplorable, was usually committed not arbitrarily but in the considered interest of other, economic or strategic, priorities. These priorities were, alas, incompatible with the general one of nationalism. Ignorance and revisionist propaganda should not be allowed to obscure these facts, especially as the moralistic rhetoric of most revisionist propagandists was a red herring and they were more interested in geopolitical domination than in the fate of minorities.

The real failure of the interwar territorial settlements lay not in any alleged hypocrisy in applying the principle of ethnic justice, but rather in the impossibility of reconciling this principle with the other major political aims of the peacemakers: the permanent diminution of German and containment of Russian power, and the restoration of international order in Europe. This general, continental failure was, in turn, exacerbated by the failure of the new or restored states of interwar East Central Europe to instill a sense of political nationality, such as the Swiss had, in their linguistically and religiously heterogeneous ethnic groups. Thus the settlements of 1919-21 have become the classic exemplar both of the triumph of nationalism and of its political limitations. Their strength lay in their acknowledgment of its legitimacy; their weakness, in the discrepancy between the resultant arrangements and the real distribution of power in Europe.

2

Germany and Soviet Russia presented the two basic revisionist threats to the interwar territorial and social settlement. Though many East Central European governments were more mesmerized by the Bolshevik danger, Germany proved to be the primary menace and for that reason we focus on it first. The defeat of Germany in 1918 was deceptive. Neither in absolute nor in relative terms had Germany been weakened to anything like the extent that was often assumed in the 1920s. In absolute terms, Germany's industrial and transportation resources had been left largely intact because World War I had not been fought on her territory. In relative terms, a territorial settlement predicated on the national principle, such as now ensued in 1919-21, ipso facto left Germany as Europe's second largest country after Russia; outside Europe it insidiously undermined the British and French empires without comparable effect on a Germany now disencumbered of colonies. Indeed, relative to East Central Europe, Germany had gained through the replacement of the Habsburg Empire as a neighbor, which for all its debilities had still been a major power, by a large number of frail and mutually hostile successor states in the Danubian area to her southeast, and through the substitution of Poland and the Baltic states in lieu of Russia as her immediate eastern neighbors. Her own central continental position was only enhanced by these developments. The very existence of the newly independent but highly vulnerable states of East Central Europe, legitimated by the victorious Western Allies, proved on balance a political and diplomatic asset to Germany. It (a) initially buffered her against a spillover of the Bolshevik Revolution, (b) then tempted Soviet Russia to collaborate with her throughout the 1920s and again in the partition of this area in 1939-40, and (c) ultimately frustrated efforts at Soviet-Western cooperation to halt Nazi Germany in the late 1930s, as the West was then inhibited by its commitments to these states from paying the Soviet Union's price for such cooperation, namely, the sacrifice of East Central Europe's effective independence to Soviet hegemony.

The governments of Weimar Germany pursued a "Prussian" policy of directing the brunt of their revisionist pressure against interwar Poland, in the hope of recovering at least a substantial part, if not all, of the prewar Reich frontiers there. Hitler, on the other hand, contemptuously dismissed as inadequate such a limited program. Setting his sights on the conquest of all East Central and Eastern Europe, he temporarily froze the German-Polish revisionist issue with the bilateral Non-Aggression Statement of January 26, 1934, and launched his program of virtually limitless conquest by first following the "Austrian" pattern of establishing hegemony over the Danube Valley. Austria and Czechoslovakia, rather than Poland, thus became his initial international victims.

It has often, and correctly, been pointed out that the Nazi concept of race was politically incompatible with the existence of independent East Central and East European states. Less attention has, however, been given to the at least equally sinister concept of space in Hitler's politico-ideological armory. While racial rhetoric was occasionally used by certain Nazis (other than Hitler) to flatter the supposedly "young" and "vigorous" peoples of East Central Europe into deserting their allegedly "decadent" and "enfeebled" Western allies and patrons, the political language of space always implied conquest and peonization of the peoples to Germany's east and southeast. Indeed, the capacity for such spatial expansion was defined as the test and measure of racial vitality.

Given his maximalist program of expansion and conquest, Hitler was tactically correct in identifying Czechoslovakia, rather than Poland, as the keystone of Germany's "encirclement" that would have to be dislodged first to collapse that arch. Territorial revisionism against Poland was likely to be more limited in its political effect since it would have to be coordinated with Soviet Russia; it implied shared influence rather than exclusive domination. Against Czechoslovakia, Hitler's ally would be a Hungary conveniently revisionist but too weak to present a serious obstacle to further German expansion. Furthermore, the German officer corps, heavily "Prussian" in its political commitments and interests, might be satisfied with the defeat of Poland and thereafter reluctant to be used for further Danubian, Balkan, and Russian conquests toward which it was historically conditioned to be either indifferent or even unfriendly. Finally, Czechoslovakia, unlike Poland, could be conveniently tarred with the phony but propagandistically effective brush of serving as "Bolshevism's Central European aircraft carrier" by virtue of the Czechoslovak-Soviet Pact of May 16, 1935, which supplemented the Franco-Soviet Mutual Assistance Treaty of May 2, 1935. Though this pair of agreements had been a response to Hitler's reintroduction of German conscription on March 16 in violation of the Versailles Treaty, and though they were soon to be tested and found wanting by Hitler's remilitarization of the Rhineland on March 7, 1936—again in violation of treaty obligations—which rendered all of France's military commitments to her several East Central European allies strategically worthless, nevertheless the German propaganda assault on Czechoslovakia proved successful. Its victim stood isolated, friendless, and shunned amidst all its neighbors at the time of the Munich tragedy in September, 1938.

East Central European anti-Communism and fear of Soviet ambitions thus benefited and were manipulated by Germany—to such an extent, indeed, that the international politics of the 1930s were fatally skewed by fundamental misjudgments as to the source of the immediate threat to the area's independence. A number of the local states owed all or much of their territory to Russia's weakness in 1917-21; the ruling elites in all of them feared Communism. Hence, they were understandably reluctant on the eve of World War II to grant the Soviet army access to their territories as their contribution to collective security against Nazi Germany. Once in, it was feared the Soviets were unlikely ever to depart, least of all from territories that had once been parts of the Russian Empire. The Western governments, in turn, sharing many of these ideological and political anxieties and committed to the principle of the integrity of small states, were reluctant to press them into such a hazardous concession. Stalin, on the other hand, could scarcely be impressed by the West's assertion against the Soviet Union in mid-1939 of a principle that it had indecently sacrificed to Hitler at Munich less than a year before.

A circular dilemma thus arose: the East Central European governments were unwilling to accept Soviet assistance against the Nazi threat lest it either provoke the German invasion that collective security was intended to deter or lest it simply become a Soviet occupation; the West now refused to cap its abandonment of Czechoslovakia in 1938 by coercing Poland and Romania into abdicating their sovereignty to the Soviet Union in 1939; Stalin was unwilling to expose his country to the risk of bearing the brunt of a war against Germany unless he could at least reduce that risk by forestalling Hitler in a military occupation of East Central Europe. Underlying the failure to resolve this dilemma were a set of interlocking misjudgments: Stalin was skeptical of the West's readiness finally to stand up to Hitler, underestimated Britain's military competence, and overestimated French military prowess. The Western governments, on the other hand, deprecated the Soviet Union's military value and presumed that ideological incompatibility would prevent any Nazi-Soviet rapprochement. All miscalculated; the upshot of the unresolved dilemma was the Hitler-Stalin Pact of August 23, 1939 and World War II, in which the Wehrmacht quickly disposed of the Polish and French armies and thus destroyed that continental second front for which Stalin was to implore his allies when that same Wehrmacht was later turned against him. A moral of this sad tale is that the balance of power is never automatic but requires rationality, perceptiveness, and perhaps even wisdom for its proper recognition.

East Central European fears of Russia and of Communism persisted into the years of war and German occupation. Then, because of these fears, a number of the original resistance movements were eventually to compromise themselves by collaboration with the occupier.

3

The ease with which Germany, and later Russia, regained control over interwar East Central Europe was based on more than just ideological manipulation, important as that was. They also capitalized on the abdication of the other Great Powers and on the profound politico-demographic and socioeconomic weaknesses and conflicts within the area itself. On the morrow of the peace settlements the United States withdrew into isolation, the United Kingdom turned to a policy of encouraging the revival of Germany so as to "correct" a supposed, but actually illusory,

French continental preponderance, Italy entertained her own dreams of hegemony in the Balkan Peninsula and the Danube Valley, and France adopted a self-contradictory stance of making far-ranging political and military commitments to several states in East Central Europe but simultaneously undermining these with defensive and isolationist strategic and economic postures. France, though granting them some loans, traded very little with her East Central European protégés, protected her own agriculture from their surpluses, and sought to veto their industrialization programs for refining their own mineral resources owned by French concessionaires. Simultaneously, her Maginot strategy—a function of the multiple trauma of having been bled white during the war and then deserted by one ally (the United States) and persistently restrained by the other (the United Kingdom) after its close—eroded the credibility of her alliance commitments in East Central Europe. That credibility was finally flushed away with her passive acceptance of Hitler's remilitarization of the Rhineland, after which he could direct the bulk of the Wehrmacht against selected East Central European victims without fear of French counteraction in western Germany.

Thus, East Central European hopes of achieving security by bringing the weight of benevolent, if distant, Great Powers to bear against the area's rapacious and immediate neighbors proved abortive. During the 1920s, only Germany's and Russia's temporary postwar and post-revolutionary exhaustion had provided East Central Europe with a respite despite their ominous diplomatic collaboration. In the 1930s, though both countries were rapidly reviving, their ideological and political enmity again gave a brief reprieve to the lands between them, until their fateful reconciliation at the area's expense in 1939.

Given this constellation of predatory, indifferent, and ineffective Great Powers, a constellation that it could neither prevent nor even control, East Central Europe might nevertheless have achieved at least minimal power-credibility if it had been able to achieve internal regional solidarity and some system of mutual assistance. But this alternative, too, was negated by the multiple divisions and rivalries that were born of competing territorial claims, ethnic-minority tensions, socioeconomic poverty, mutually irritating national psychologies, and sheer political myopia. These factors transformed the area's internal relations into a cockpit and facilitated Hitler's program of conquest. It is scarcely an exaggeration to suggest that as a general rule in interwar East Central Europe, common borders entailed hostile relations. Thus, the "blame" for the demise of the region's independence must be charged to its own fundamental weaknesses, the instability of its institutions, and its irresponsible governments, as well as to the active and passive faults of the Great Powers.

Simply to list the area's internal irredentist disputes may convey an impression of their cumulative complexity, though not of their bitter and well-nigh paralyzing intensity. Lithuania and Poland quarreled over Wilno (Vilnius, Vilna), which the former claimed on historical, the latter on ethnic-demographic and strategic grounds. Poland and Czechoslovakia were mutually alienated by: (a) their dispute over Teschen (Těšín, Cieszyn), where the former's sounder ethnic-demographic claims clashed with the latter's economic needs; (b) their contrasting perceptions of Russia's and Hungary's proper roles in the European balance, each regarding the other's *bête noire* with some benevolence; (c) the conviction of each that the other had doomed itself by greedily incorporating too many unabsorbable, and hence inflammable, ethnic minorities; and (d) their contrasting social structures and national psychologies, namely, Polish gentry versus Czech bourgeois. Czechoslovakia was also under revisionist pressure on historical and ethnic-demographic grounds from Hungary. Hungary, in turn, as the biggest territorial loser of World War I, nursed territorial claims on historic and/or ethnic-demographic grounds against all four of her interwar neighbors: Czechoslovakia re Slovakia and Ruthenia; Romania re Transylvania; Yugoslavia re the Vojvodina and perhaps Croatia; Austria re the Burgenland (this last less intensely than the others). Yugoslavia herself coveted the Slovene-populated portion of Austria's Carinthian province, and she and Romania were, in turn, also the objects of Bulgarian irredentist resentments respectively over Macedonia and Southern Dobruja. In addition, Bulgaria directed similar pressures against Greece over parts of Macedonia and Thrace. Bulgaria's revisionist rationale was the characteristic combination of historical, ethnic-demographic, economic, and strategic arguments. As regards Albania and Austria, finally, the major problem was not so much irredentist aspirations harbored by and against them—though these, too, existed —but that their very existence was challenged and their survival seemed doubtful during the interwar era.

As though these quarrels within the region were not enough, a number of its states were under even more ominous pressures from the Great Powers. Weimar Germany remained unreconciled to the loss of the Pomeranian "Corridor" and of southeastern Silesia to Poland, and Hitler was to add to these revisionist grievances his further claims to Czechoslovakia's highly strategic, German-populated, Sudeten perimeter and to all of Austria. Less pressing was Germany's suit against Lithuania for the retrocession of the city and district of Klaipėda (Memel). The Soviet Union remained openly unreconciled to interwar Romania's incorporation of Bessarabia and harbored designs on Poland's eastern borderlands with their heavy Belorussian and Ukrainian ethnic concentrations; her attitude toward the Baltic states was more complex but still ambivalent. Italy craved Yugoslavia's Dalmatian littoral on the Adriatic Sea, in particular, and schemed to fragment the entire Yugoslav state into its ethnic-regional components, in general. She also aspired to control

Albania directly and to intimidate Greece into subservience. Indeed, Italy's ambitions also included the establishment of diplomatic protectorates over Austria, Hungary, and Bulgaria, to redouble the pressure on Yugoslavia. But, in contrast to Germany and the Soviet Union, she lacked the economic and military muscle to sustain her political designs.

Thus, each state of interwar East Central Europe had one or more enemies from within the area, and each of the "victor" states among them also had a Great Power enemy—Poland even had two. The numerous "internal" enmities, alas, rendered the region even weaker than it need have been with respect to the "external" ones, and all efforts at reconciling the former were aborted by rampant chauvinism; the spirit of the age was not supranational, as had been naively predicted during the war, but ultranational. Indeed, it appears that the only really potent internationalistic ideology in the area at that time was neither Marxism, on the left hand, nor dynastic loyalism, on the right, but anti-Semitism based on both conviction and expedience. This, in turn, provided an ideological bond and precondition for eventual collaboration with the Nazis, including the administration of wartime genocide.

Meanwhile, in the interwar era itself, efforts on the part of the newly victorious states to consolidate the international settlement of which they were the beneficiaries proved halting, partial, and unimpressive. Czechoslovakia, Romania, and Yugoslavia formed an alliance termed the Little Entente. This alliance was directed exclusively against a Hungary that, while admittedly stridently revisionist, was nevertheless weaker than any of the three members singly, but it was inoperative against the three Great Powers, each of which threatened one of the alliance partners. The Little Entente thus was a case of "overkill" against a shared secondary danger and "every man for himself" vis-à-vis each of the primary ones. Furthermore, by ostracizing Hungary, it made her more receptive to collaboration with Germany and Italy in their maneuvers to fragment seriatim the member states of the Little Entente and thus the interwar East Central European settlement in general. Similarly, the Balkan Entente, formed by Greece, Romania, Turkey, and Yugoslavia, provided only for mutual defense against revisionist Bulgaria and also ignored Great Power claims on individual partners. Though the two alliances were linked through two of their members, Romania and Yugloslavia, they contributed little to the coherence or unity of East Central Europe.

It is, of course, psychologically understandable that the several partners were reluctant to pull each other's chestnuts out of Great Power fires if they were not directly burned themselves. Thus, for example, Romania and Yugoslavia were unwilling to irritate a powerful Germany by supporting Czechoslovakia in a quarrel that was not theirs, and Czechoslovakia and Yugoslavia refused to underwrite Romania's possession of Bessarabia against Soviet objections. Yet such behavior could scarcely impress anyone. Nevertheless, while deprecating this deliberate impotence of these small-state alliances under the pressure of the revisionist Great Powers, one does well to recall that the real culprits of appeasement were not these small states, but the other Great Powers, whose abdication was the more culpable as their responsibility was greater.

It is, parenthetically, of some interest and relevance that foreign economic relations and foreign political relations often failed to synchronize in these several interwar East Central European constellations. Just as France, as noted above, traded little with her political protégés, Poland and the Little Entente states, so the Little Entente partners traded more with their Hungarian enemy and with Austria than with each other, and two of them, Czechoslovakia and Yugoslavia, traded far more with their respective Great Power nemeses, Germany and Italy, than with their allies. The economies of Romania and Yugoslavia were too similar to stimulate much exchange between them; each exported agricultural surpluses and mineral resources. Industrial Czechoslovakia, on the other hand, though in theory complementary to their economies, in practice imported little of Romania's and Yugoslavia's agricultural produce in order to protect and mollify her own politically potent peasantry. Romania and Yugoslavia, in turn, refused her their mineral exports, in which Czechoslovakia was interested, and favored free currency countries and later Germany, which was prepared to absorb their agricultural surpluses as well as their ores and oils. Similarly, Italy's foreign trade did not correspond with her diplomatic preferences, being less with her clients Austria, Bulgaria, and Hungary than with their Little and Balkan Entente enemies, until the mid-1930s. Then the latter abided by the League of Nations' sanctions against Italy for her invasion of Abyssinia in 1935, and the former together with Germany filled the resultant trade gaps.

Nazi Germany, which pursued the politically most adept foreign trade policy of any Great Power, was the chief beneficiary of this sanctions episode as she stepped in to rescue, to her own and their benefit, the economies of those Balkan states which had loyally abided by Anglo-French political wishes to interrupt their trade with Italy and had then been left in the economic lurch by these Western Powers. The entire affair suffused East Central Europe with a feeling that the West regarded Germany's economic hegemony over the area as inevitable and natural, and this feeling accelerated the decision of a number of the local regimes to accommodate themselves accordingly to the German drive.

4

An important, and often the main, component of the several revisionist-irredentist territorial disputes in interwar East Central Europe was the ethnic one: specifically, one state's interest in politically "redeeming," or at least culturally sustaining, a minority of its own nationality that happened to be geographically located in another state, and, on the other hand, that host state's indignant repudiation of what it chose to regard as illicit pressures upon its territorial integrity or internal sovereignty. Admittedly, the existence of ethnic minorities was nothing new in the region. But as the interwar states, unlike the Austrian half of the old Habsburg Empire, preferred to regard themselves as explicit and specific national states, the lot of the numerous and vocal interwar ethnic minorities was emotionally more demeaning and politically more hopeless than had formerly been the case. Thus, for example, the Czechs or Poles or Slovenes of the old Habsburg Empire had not been obliged to view themselves as minorities in an explicitly German state. Though they might have felt ethnically aggrieved at particular times, they could always quite realistically anticipate a future imperial government's reversal of its schedule of ethnic favoritism. Even the more consistently excluded minorities of the empire's Hungarian half awaited a change with the next royal succession. But in the nation-states of the interwar era, a minority seemed fated, short of a war and a redrawing of frontiers, to remain a minority forever, not simply in the neutral statistical sense, but also in terms of political if not civil deprivation. Hence it tended to seek succor from its ethnic and cultural "mother country" against the pressures of the "host" state, and thus the dispute was internationalized. The Jews, of course, being without a state of their own, lacked this option and hence felt particularly exposed politically.

The "host" government, in turn, was committed to the cultivation of the specific national culture of its state-nation throughout its territory; otherwise, it reasoned, the achievement of national independence would have been purposeless. Its apprehensions of "subversion" tended quickly to become as exaggerated, albeit sincere, as the minority's fears of "extinction." The resultant reciprocal recriminations would become particularly truculent, the protagonists' respective stances particularly rigid, and the quarrel particularly dangerous if, as was often the case, the minority and the interested "mother country" to which it appealed represented one of the region's prewar dominant powers—Germany, Hungary, Bulgaria (Macedonia), Russia (Ukraine)—still unreconciled to its recent defeat and loss.

The determination of a newly independent state to "nation-ize" not only its cultural and political patrimonies but also its economic wealth was often a key motive behind such seemingly social and "class" programs as land reform and etatist industrialization. These were politically easiest where "alien" landlords and entrepreneurs could be expropriated for the benefit of "native" peasants and bureaucrats. Such an amalgamation of ethnic and social policy was facilitated by the fact that ethnic, religious, and class differences and identities often coincided or at least overlapped.

In Poland, the Baltic states, and the former Habsburg lands, the large estate owners were Poles, Germans, and Magyars, while the entrepreneurial class was heavily German and Jewish and only in part native. In the Balkans the entrepreneurial class was Greek, Italian, and Jewish and only incipiently native, while in several regions the landlords were still Muslim or Magyar. Another indirect way of implementing ethnic policy in the absence of explicit legislative authorization to that effect, which was generally avoided for legal reasons or because of public relations, was through silent but relentless administrative discretion. All in all, the importance of ethnic consciousness in the new, or restored, or enlarged victor states of interwar East Central Europe is illustrated, *en reverse*, by the observation that none of them experienced the sharp social and class violence that on the morrow of World War I wracked the losers—first Russia, then Germany, Austria, Hungary, and Bulgaria.

Standing politically midway between state-nations and ethnic minorities were those peoples who were officially defined as belonging to the former but felt themselves not only culturally distinct from, but also politically and economically exploited by, the dominant part of that same state-nation. The most vivid interwar examples of these groups were the Slovaks with respect to the Czechs, and the Croats with respect to the Serbs. In each case the aggrieved group became increasingly disenchanted with and suspicious of the formal ideology of "Czechoslovak" and "Yugoslav" nationality, which appeared to it to be a manipulative device screening, respectively, Czech and Serb domination. Whereas in the Czechoslovak case there was a correspondence between the Czechs' political control and their superior economic and cultural resources vis-à-vis the Slovaks, in Yugoslavia there existed a "crossed" relationship between Serb political domination on the one hand, and the more advanced and developed Croatian economic and cultural levels on the other. Many commentators, expressing acknowledged or unconscious Marxist assumptions, have termed the latter case "anomalous." But the statistics belie this judgment, for the world abounds, for better or worse, with cases of economically and culturally marginal regions that exercise political dominion over more productive and modern ones. One need mention only the traditional political power of provincial France and of the United States' southern and agrarian states, the preponderance of Poles from the eastern *kresy* during the Piłsudski era, and the more recent hegemony of Pakistan's western and Nigeria's northern regions.

A third, and far less incendiary, category of ethnic tensions in interwar East Central Europe consisted of those cases where nations of common stock and language had earlier been partitioned for extensive periods of time among different political units. Upon being finally reunited after World War I, their diverse and even divergent past experiences tended to generate a certain amount of friction. However, that friction was nowhere near as intense or long-lasting as was often gloatingly and maliciously claimed by propagandists for the erstwhile master (now revisionist) powers. In fact, these nations—the Poles, who had been partitioned among the Austrian, German, and Russian empires; the Romanians who had been separated between their Danubian Principalities and historic Hungary; the Lithuanians of old Russia and East Prussia—quickly asserted their political unity toward the outside world despite some lingering internal conflicts. (An analogous post-World War II case adjacent to our area is the Ukrainians.)

All in all, the rather complicated structure of the ethnic minority question both reflected the attempted but fragile interwar European power-balance and, due to the ensuing political tensions, also helped to overturn it. These chronic tensions, and particularly the manner in which Nazi Germany manipulated them, then elicited a sharply different approach to the entire problem at the close of World War II. Whereas at the end of the first world conflagration there had been vast frontier changes but relatively little mass population movement in East Central Europe, after the second one there were fewer frontier changes, the major exceptions being in the case of the Soviet Union's western borders and Poland's eastern and western ones, but enormous population migrations and expulsions, following on the wartime Nazi genocide of the area's Jewish and Gypsy minorities and persecution of several indigenous nations. Hitler, having on the one hand rendered the numerous German minority in East Central Europe odious to the Slavic peoples, and having on the other hand demonstrated the ease with which minorities could be eliminated, thereby provoked the colossal enforced *Völkerwanderung* of 1944-46. In the course of this migration a millennium of German eastward expansion by peasant, burgher, miner, monk, and soldier was reversed and the political achievements of Henry the Lion, Frederick the Great, and Bismarck were undone. While proclaiming that he only wished to save Europe from the supposedly corrosive "Internationals" (Communist, Jewish, Jesuit, Masonic, plutocratic, etc.), Hitler had in fact persuaded the six million Volksdeutsche of East Central Europe to serve him as an all-too-truly subversive Pan-German "International," to their ultimate misfortune.

5

While ethnic tensions constituted interwar East Central Europe's most vivid and sensitive political problem and were, indeed, often exploited so as to obscure social and economic weaknesses, these weaknesses proved just as chronically debilitating and difficult to correct. By virtually every relevant statistical index, many of which will be analyzed in the later chapters devoted to individual countries, East Central Europe was less productive, less literate, and less healthy than West Central and Western

Europe. A potentially rich region with poor people, its interwar censuses record not so much a distribution of wealth as a maldistribution of poverty. The main component of this sad spectacle was the so-called peasant question, in both its economic and its ideological manifestations.

Interwar East Central Europe was preponderantly unproductively agricultural. While far higher proportions of its population were engaged in farming than was the case in Western Europe, the productivity of its agriculture in terms both of yield rates per unit of agricultural area and of yield rates per agricultural worker was far lower. The result was a vicious cycle of rural undercapitalization, underproductivity, underconsumption, underemployment, overpopulation, and pervasive misery. Despite strenuous, if often misapplied, efforts to correct these imbalances and to increase the area's wealth through industrialization, in 1938 East Central Europe still produced only 8 percent of the industrial output of all Europe minus the Soviet Union, and of this small share, a third was recorded by Czechoslovakia. Except for that country, whose western half comprised the area's most thoroughly industrialized region, the fate of the several states' economies was annually determined by the single, hazardous, factor of weather.

Problems ancillary to, and aggravating, this low productivity in the agricultural sector were weak transportation, disruption of prewar trade patterns, economic nationalism and competitive striving for autarky (especially prominent and destructive in the Great Depression of the early 1930s), competition of Argentine and North American grains in the markets of Western Europe, and drastic reduction of opportunities for overseas emigration to the United States. The swelling surplus peasant population of East Central Europe vegetated at bare subsistence levels on its holdings, subdividing them into ever smaller and less rational plots. Its very existence and condition of underemployment discouraged any investment in agronomic technology. Even then, it was scarcely permitted to consume an adequate proportion of its relatively low food output as governmental fiscal, tariff, and investment policies consistently forced the undernourished peasants to sell at a pittance far more than any authentic surplus of their produce in order to raise cash for the payment of taxes, debts, fees, and a few astronomically priced (because protected and cartel-lized) essential industrial products.

Where governments did arrange land reforms for the ostensible benefit of the peasantry, the motivation and hence the application was primarily political—either, as mentioned above, to expropriate ethnically "alien" landlords or to immunize a restless peasantry against the feared attractions of Communism—and was not adequately supplemented with equivalent interest in correcting the economic and agronomic malaise of agriculture. The peasant's standard of living was falling precisely at a time when his expectations and self-esteem were rising. His travels and other experiences as a mobilized soldier in World War I had not only sophisticated his material wants, but had also shown him how heavily governments and urban populations depended on his docility and labor. He now responded to his interwar lot by vacillating among resentment, mistrust, despair, and rage. In particular the combination of his disasterous impoverishment during the Great Depression of the early 1930s, when the industrial-agricultural price scissors opened drastically against him, followed in the decade's second half by his economic rescue—in the Danubian and Balkan countries, if not in Poland and Czechoslovakia—through Nazi Germany's bulk purchase at high prices of his produce, served to radicalize the East Central European peasant—occasionally toward the Left but more frequently toward the "new" Right. This trend suggests that a reexamination of the traditional claims and postures of peasantist ideologues and politicians is in order.

Against these ideologues' claims, in the tradition of Rousseau and Jefferson, that the peasant's proximity to nature, his rustic life-style, and his sustained work habits allegedly made him a "naturally" democratic, tolerant, peaceable, cooperative citizen,[1] we may offer the suggestion that the East European peasant's characteristic political behavior, as expressed by long periods of submissiveness interspersed with periodic bouts of *jacquerie* violence, indicates profound, albeit understandable, apathy, alienation, and rancor. Excluded from the general progress of Europe, he felt himself to be both the guardian and the victim of anachronistic values and institutions, whose very anachronism undermined and negated the potential power of the peasantry as the area's most numerous class. The peasant's political stance in the restored or enlarged "new" states of the interwar era was problematic and uneasy. Grateful, on the one hand, for land reform, he also resented that one of its side-effects had been to intensify the control of the state apparatus over his village. This control he felt to be exploitative rather than benevolent, exercised in its own interest by a culturally alien urban bureaucracy which would either neglect or suppress but neither probe nor solve the social tensions accruing from the economic malaise of the countryside.

Against its ideologues' rhapsodic presentation of peasantism as a supposed humanistic alternative to allegedly crassly materialistic capitalism and socialism, we may legitimately note their naiveté about both the "soulless" industrialism espoused by these two competing ideologies as well as about their own favored "peasantist way of life." For the hard fact is that the peasants could achieve prosperity only by transforming that way of life into an integrated, productive relationship with urban market

1. See, for example, Milan Hodža, *Federation in Central Europe* (London: Jarrolds, 1942), passim; David Mitrany, *Marx against the Peasant* (New York: Collier Books, 1961), passim; Ghiţa Ionescu and Ernest Gellner, eds., *Populism* (New York: The MacMillan Co., 1969), Ch. 4.

needs and industrial capacities. Furthermore, the ideological celebrators of peasantism appear to have misread or misrepresented the real views of their claimed constituents. For the peasant's actual attitude toward industrialization was less one of hostility than one of ambivalence: he was both fascinated and afraid. He realized that it alone held out the promise of salvation from rural poverty and overpopulation. But he also dreaded industrialization as a threat to his values and traditions. More specifically, he shrewdly suspected that its immediate costs in terms of restricted consumption and increased prices and taxes would be unloaded onto his shoulders, or rather squeezed from his belly.

The general peasant resentment and mistrust of urban society extended also to the proletariat, the area's other interwar "outsider" class. The East Central European Socialist parties and workers, in turn, feared and shunned the peasant masses as incarnating an allegedly reactionary, clericalist threat to economic and social progress. It was, indeed, true that the only political parties other than explicitly peasantist ones that the East Central European peasantry occasionally supported were explicitly Christian-denominational ones in the 1920s and then also Right-Radical ones in the depression decade of the 1930s. More generally, the area's still young and small urban proletariat, in its anxiety to avoid being weakened or manipulated from any quarter, tended to isolate itself from social alliances with any older and larger classes even on the rare occasions where these were available as would-be allies.

The potential political power placed in the peasantry's hands by the universal suffrage introduced throughout interwar East Central Europe, except in Hungary, was soon blunted by the emergence of a specific political ruling class. This class initially coopted peasant political leaders and eroded the peasantist component of their political commitments; later, alarmed by escalating social and political unrest, it simply replaced the formally democratic political institutions with authoritarian ones everywhere except in Czechoslovakia. This political ruling class was not, contrary to conventional assumptions, the bourgeoisie, which was quite weak and either dependent on state subsidies or else ethnically "alien" and hence vulnerable. Rather it was the bureaucracy, which was allied with, and recruited from, the intelligentsia.

The conduct of peasant political leaders and the strategies of peasantist political parties will be analyzed and compared in detail in the chapters on individual countries. Briefly, the leaders ran the gamut from "bearer of the national conscience" or "peasant Gracchus," through "statesman," "pragmatist," and "power-broker," to sheer "betrayer-of-trust" and "office-seeker," or, alternatively, "opposition demagogue." None adequately benefited their village constituencies, which were nevertheless pathetically loyal to them. In many cases, the peasant politician's class pride was accompanied and corroded by a residual political inferiority complex. This led him to overvalue the sheer fact of his admission into the councils of government, where his often vague programs and generalized aspirations were promptly and easily neutralized by cabinet colleagues who appealed to his sense of "realism" or "patriotism." There were always plausible reasons, for example, why indirect taxes on necessities consumed in the village were more "feasible" than direct taxes on the incomes of the urban entrepreneurial, professional, and bureaucratic classes, or why the "national interest" required that the resultant revenue be spent on the army and on subsidized industry rather than reinvested in agriculture or in rural amenities. While prominent peasant "tribunes" were often thus coopted at the top, their party machines were always infiltrated at the less visible middle echelons by the same political class of lawyers and bureaucrats that had already captured control of other political parties and of the state apparatus as such. To the limited extent that this type was at all responsive to peasant needs, it served the interests of the more prosperous stratum of the peasantry.

International peasantist solidarity was articulated by the so-called Green International, an appellation intended to symbolize its supposed historic role as an alternative to the "Red" International of Communists and the "White" International of capitalists and landlords. Its institutional expression was an International Agrarian Bureau established in Prague by several East Central European peasantist parties. Organizationally and financially, it was controlled by the Czechoslovak Agrarians, who sought to give it a Slavophile flavor, to the irritation of its Romanian member. Despite high rhetoric, it never had much political influence; its constituent peasantist parties either failed to master domestic power in their respective countries or, in the few cases where they did so, became absorbed in the desperate but vain pursuit of purely domestic solutions to area-wide problems. In or out of power, these parties were quite nationalistic. The one authentic internationalist exception here was the Bulgarian peasant leader Aleksandŭr Stamboliski—and he was soon murdered for his pains by domestic supernationalists. The Green International's particular irrelevance, and peasantism's general inadequacy, were later exposed by the Great Depression.

6

The Communist parties, which came to power after World War II thanks to the Soviet armies' conquest of the area, were politically weak during the interwar era. Though they might attract many genuine idealists, and though their cadres usually bore persecution with courage, and though they benefited from the irascible habit of many local regimes of labeling all opposition as communistic, these parties were often discredited by their "antinational" identification with: Russia (perceived as a historic foe and potential threat in Poland, Romania, and the Baltic states); the local ethnic minorities (popularly suspected as subversive); and atheism (especially damaging in the Roman Catholic countries). They were also hampered by their often inappropriate and vacillating approaches to issues of territorial revisionism, to the agrarian question, and to the peasantry as a class (was it a solid bloc or internally differentiated?)—a weakness which, in turn, flowed from their organizational, financial, and moral dependence on the Comintern. Occasional lapses from slavish imitation of the vagaries of the Moscow party-line resulted in drastic purges, which racked the Polish, Yugoslav, and Bulgarian Communist parties with particular severity. Hence, zombie-like obedience and the ritual discharge of assigned tasks became both a necessity for survival and a kind of psychological compensation for the Communist cadres' lack of real political influence.

On the other hand, the Communists could capitalize on the pervasive discontent with poverty and oppression, on the peasants' resentful alienation from the bureaucratic state apparatus, and on the related failure of the peasantist parties and leaders. Here their appeals to social justice and revolution, while eliciting no immediate response, nevertheless sustained an awareness of them as representing a political alternative. Under Nazi occupation the Communists finally enjoyed the advantage of long experience at underground organization, survival, and action. Ultimately, however, their conquest of power was determined less by local factors than by the decisive intervention of the Soviet Union. The one exception was in Yugoslavia, where they fought independently and won a revolutionary national and civil war.

7

Trends and styles of governmental activity passed through several similar sequences in the interwar East Central European countries. Yet throughout these changes and phases the bureaucratic "political class," to which allusion has been made above as coopting peasantist leaders, formed the effective and, except in Czechoslovakia and Hungary, the virtually autonomous ruling class of interwar East Central Europe. Both its civilian and military components were recruited from the so-called intelligentsia which, in turn, was simply identified by its possession of academic diplomas. The intelligentsia and, through it, the bureaucracy might be descended from the gentry, the middle class, or the peasantry; in the last-mentioned case, it tended to sever its cultural and political ties with the village despite sentimental and propagandistic professions of attachment. It might rule in association with the landed and entrepreneurial classes, but it was never a mere tool of the aristocracy or bourgeoisie. Universal suffrage did not protect the peasant masses from the intimidation or manipulation of this political class of bureaucrats and intelligentsia, and election results generally reflected its overall priorities, if not always its particular preferences. Indeed, in the area's more primitive regions, universal suffrage functioned as the bureaucracy's tool for breaking the traditional power of "feudal" notables over their dependent peasant clientèles.

Given the high prestige of formal academic education in the "new" interwar states of East Central Europe, the investment in higher education tended to be disproportionately large relative both to their investments in primary education as well as to the absorptive capacities of their still basically agrarian, or at most transitional, societies. The failure of industrialization to develop with sufficient rapidity and depth to absorb the surplus peasant population was paralleled by its analogous failure to absorb the surplus academic proletariat into economically or socially functional employment. Politics and state-service remained the only career-lines for these university alumni, who were heavily biased in their studies toward law or humanities and away from science and technology. Thus, land-hunger among the peasantry was matched by office-hunger among the intelligentsia. The result was a proliferation of political parties more concerned with patronage than with policy ("program" parties fared badly), and a swollen, nepotistic, underpaid, callous, routine-ridden bureaucracy that was open to corruption. All this deepened the peasant's alienation from, and contempt for, the state, the city, and politics, which consistently confronted him as an impenetrable and hostile maze of linked fiefdoms and privileged connections.

The tenacious but essentially stagnant power of this bureaucratic class largely accounts for the peculiar syndrome of immobility and instability in interwar East Central European politics—a syndrome to which, as has been indicated, Great Power pressures and ethnic tensions also contributed. Changes in cabinets were frequent, in constitutions occasional, but the fundamental political reflections of social transitions were suffocated by these bureaucracies, and the social transitions themselves were often deliberately braked and slowed. When the resulting tensions, aggravated by the depression, became so acute as to erode the reliability of the parliamentary regimes of the 1920s as shields for the bureaucracy's ongoing power, it initiated or endorsed *coups d'état* that replaced the old regimes with royal, military, or political dictatorships or semidictatorships. The exception to this trend was Czechoslovakia, the area's economically most mature society.

This East Central European shift from parliamentary to authoritarian institutions was also facilitated and supposedly vindicated by the impressive performance of the Great Power dictatorships, especially of Nazi Germany, in energizing their economies and consolidating their societies. Over the great esteem in which German culture had traditionally been held in East Central Europe was now superimposed a new fascination, which was grudging or enthusiastic as the case might be, but always respectful, with the Nazi political model. The imposing domestic and diplomatic successes of the Nazis, which contrasted vividly with the apparent stagnation and decadence of France, projected the impression that authoritarian dictatorship was the wave of the future. States of lesser power, especially new or restored states, generally take as their model the political institutions and values of the seemingly strongest and most successful Great Power of the day. On the morrow of World War I, this appeared to be France; after the depression, it became Germany. Furthermore, and with specific reference to East Central Europe, Nazi Germany's policies rendered territorial revisionism realistically "thinkable" and ethnic xenophobia, especially anti-Semitism, psychologically "respectable."

But the East Central European dictatorships would not or could not emulate the totalitarian dynamism of Hitler's example. Their commitments were essentially bureaucratic and conservative, at most technocratic and oligarchical. Projecting no mass ideology, they either failed or refused to elicit mass support. Despite their sonorous rhetoric of "the strong hand," they proved petty, brittle, often irresolute, and generally demoralizing.

Various Right-Radical movements, drawing their political elan even more emphatically from the Nazi example, atavistic in their ideology but modern in their methods, claimed to supply the dynamism, the commitment to radical change, and the capacity to mobilize the masses, that these authoritarian regimes lacked or spurned. Noisiest in the countries with prominent and vulnerable Jewish minorities, the Right-Radical leaders, while themselves usually educated and urbanized, appealed to the supposedly primitive, instinctive, and healthy revulsion of the peasant and proletarian "folk-masses" against the allegedly decadent, "judaized," secular culture of their bureaucratic and bourgeois exploiters. Indeed, the appeal and the appeals of Right-Radicalism nicely reflected the contemporary condition of interwar East Central Europe as an agricultural society in a crisis of transition and fragmentation: though not yet sufficiently developed and integrated to have moved beyond this demagoguery, it no longer was adequately stable and patriarchal to remain immune to it. The local Right-Radical movements were, however, inhibited in their political offensives by the very fact that the authoritarian regimes which they sought to challenge already embodied a number of their professed ideological values, i.e., were already undemocratic, ultranationalistic, and militaristic, and often mouthed Right-Radical rhetoric even while repelling Right-Radical bids for power. An even greater irony was the fact that Hitler's regime, eager to extract maximal economic resources from East Central Europe for its own projected war effort, eventually endorsed the local forces of order and rationality, i.e., the authoritarian governments, against the counterproductive, albeit ideologically closer, enthusiasts of turmoil and upheaval, i.e., the Right-Radicals.

8

To the extent that the area's dictatorships scored any permanent successes, it was in the limited, albeit important, area of etatist economic investment, which did not, however, extend into radical social change or political mobilization. In all cases, excepting Poland and Czechoslovakia, this was achieved through Nazi German assistance in the form of bilateral exchange of local agricultural surpluses and raw materials for industrial equipment, investments, and technical support. While such German economic aid was scarcely altruistic and was clearly designed to achieve regional hegemony and supplement the Reich's war economy, neither was it utterly exploitative or negative. Contrary to frequent allegations at the time and since, Germany did not flood East Central Europe with cuckoo clocks, aspirin, and thermometers in exchange for grains, minerals, and timber; rather she supplied capital goods for industry, encouraged the diversification of vulnerable one-crop agricultures, and supplied a steady market at reasonable prices. Nazi Germany's economic policy and behavior thus effectively supplemented her ideological, political, military, and diplomatic prowess in attracting Danubian and Balkan Europe to herself in the second half of the 1930s. Though the Serbs recoiled at the last moment, the Yugoslav governments had also climbed on this bandwagon.

In Poland, the equivalent etatist economic success was scored in the late 1930s without German assistance, through enforced local savings and investments. Czechoslovakia, on the other hand—or, more precisely, its western provinces of Bohemia and Moravia-Silesia—had already reached a substantial industrial plateau and made no analogous economic leap.

Though promising and perhaps indispensable, these etatist investment successes of the late 1930s were too little and too late to absorb more than a puny fraction of the surplus rural population into industrial employment or to spark self-sustaining economic growth. Hence they failed to transform the general economic physiognomy of interwar East Central Europe as an area of low industrialization, poor urban-rural imbalances, acute shortages of capital, and chronic agricultural poverty. Furthermore, as these etatist policies were generally predicated on attitudes of economic nationalism, they also aggravated the understandable but nevertheless irrational craving for state-autarky and thus contributed to the further fading of the fragile flower of intra-area cooperation, already withered by the arid winds of ethnic and irredentist enmity.

The searing trauma of the depression had, of course, been the catalyst of the twin decisions to industrialize and to pursue "beggar-my-neighbor" economic policies. It is difficult, even in retrospect, to appreciate and impossible to exaggerate the tremendous impact of this experience on the peoples and governments of interwar East Central Europe. As the world prices of agricultural commodities fell earlier, more steeply, and remained longer at deeper troughs than the prices of industrial products, the depression taught the dire lesson of the economic impotence of agricultural-exporting countries relative to industrial ones. Particularly hard hit were those extensive regions of East Central Europe that practiced an exclusive cultivation of grain for export, for grains are a commodity for which demand is notoriously inelastic while its supply is highly variable. Hence, as prices dropped, the peasants desperately sought to compensate by increasing production, thereby merely further depressing prices to their own impoverishment. In combination with governmental protection of infant native industries, with absurdly deflationary fiscal and monetary policies, and with exorbitant indirect taxes on necessities such as salt, matches, and kerosene, purchasable only from state monopolies, this price trend put virtually all industrial commodities —plows for production as well as textiles for consumption—out of the reach of the peasants and pushed them into bare subsistence and often into outright starvation. Economic despair then prompted political radicalization which, in interaction with the judiciously orchestrated German drive for hegemony in the area, reopened the whole question of East Central Europe's international, domestic, political, and economic order. Apropos the author's earlier judgment of the futility of the Green International, one may note that on no occasion did the area's agrarian countries negotiate as a bloc with any industrial grain-importing country.

The agricultural price disaster was paralleled and compounded by the West's abrupt, and probably unnecessary, withdrawal of all its capital credits to East Central Europe in the midst of the depression. Unnecessary—because, while the sums involved were critical for the area's stability (even though they had often been applied unwisely), they were a relatively small fraction of the Western creditors' total international investments. Industrial output, capital formation, and employment now all fell precipitously, with calamitous political repercussions. This politico-economic myopia of the West, which had already been foreshadowed by France's earlier and persistent refusal to support her alliances in the area with adequate trade relations, virtually invited Nazi German penetration. Germany, in turn, did not intend to integrate East Central Europe into the world economy, but the reverse: she wished to tie it to her own and thus create a large and autarkic *Grossraumwirtschaft* supplementing and facilitating her projected political and military conquest of Europe.

A particularly powerful instrument of this economic strategy was the blocked currency device, whereby the high prices paid by Germany for her huge purchases of agricultural goods and raw materials from East

Central European countries were held in blocked accounts at the Reichs-
bank and could only be "cleared" by East Central European purchases
of German commodities. Though sometimes the local governments
grumbled at being obliged to take German equipment when they would
have preferred being paid in convertible currencies, on balance they
appreciated being rescued by Berlin from the economic and political
disaster of otherwise unsaleable agricultural surpluses. Nazi Germany
thus acquired control over the area's economy by first dominating its
exports, then through these its imports, and finally rendering it utterly
dependent on continuing German purchases, supplies, spare parts, and
infrastructure. In this way she achieved a position approaching both
monopsony and monopoly. By 1939, on the eve of World War II,
Germany's economic hegemony over East Central Europe was more
categorical than it had been in 1913, demonstrating that the political
advantages that accrued to her from the replacement of the Habsburg
Empire by several smaller states were paralleled by economic opportunities.

Thus, the combination of Nazi Germany's ideological, diplomatic, political, and economic drives paved the way for her military conquests. In one
form or another all the states of the area eventually succumbed to her
offensives, either as resisting victims (Poland, Yugoslavia), or as passive
victims (Austria, Czechoslovakia, Albania), or as calculating satellites
(Hungary, Romania, Bulgaria), or as ephemerally "independent" depen-
dencies (Slovakia, Croatia).

9

If the preceding discussion has emphasized interwar East Central
Europe's internal weaknesses and external vulnerabilities, and hence
appears to signal a negative judgment, this would be an erroneous impression of the author's intention and ultimate conclusion. That impression arises partly from the fact that the most positive political achievement
of the area's states during this interwar era is so obvious as easily to pass
notice: they legitimated their sovereign existence in the world's eyes
beyond Nazi or Stalinist capacity to obliterate. (The three Baltic states are
here an exception, but even they are granted distinct republican status
within the Soviet Union.) Thus, contemporary Communist historians,
otherwise highly critical of their countries' interwar social and economic
policies, join the "bourgeois" émigré scholars and politicians in valuing
highly the sheer fact of interwar state-independence and judging it a
historic advance over the area's pre-World War I political status. (Here,
again, the Baltic states are treated as a negative exception.) No Communist, Soviet or local, would any longer indulge in Molotov's contemptuous dismissal of interwar Poland as "this ugly offspring of the Versailles
Treaty" (speech of October 31, 1939). Nor do respectable German writers

repeat their interwar predecessors' persistent derision of the alleged Polish "Saisonstaat" or the Czechoslovak "staatliches Missgebilde." Thus, despite major and avoidable failings (too little area-wide solidarity, too much over-politicization of human relations, too little strategic government intervention in the economy, too much petty government interference with the society), thanks to the political performance of the interwar era it is impossible today to conceive of East Central Europe without its at least formally independent states. In retrospect, one must assign greater responsibility for the catastrophes of 1939-41 to the malevolence, indifference, or incompetence of the Great Powers than to the admittedly costly mistakes of these states.

Furthermore, any reader's mistaken impression of an overall negative judgment on the part of this author will hopefully be rectified by a perusal of the chapters on individual countries that follow. Finally, to the extent that political and economic history, being the least happy phases of the interwar East Central European experience, tend to leave a sorry impression, the survey of cultural achievements in Chapter 10 should serve as a felicitous corrective.

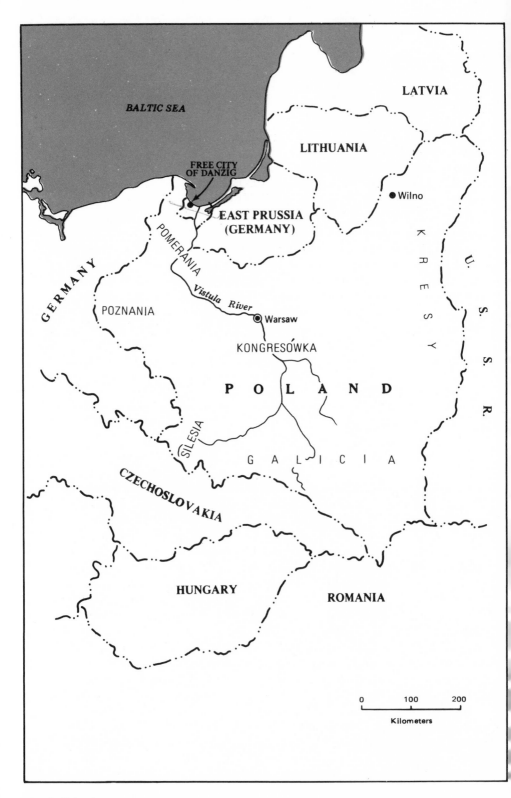

Map 2. Poland

· *Chapter Two* ·

POLAND

1

THE Polish Commonwealth, before its decline in the second half of the seventeenth century, had been one of the major European powers, second only to France in population and to Russia in territory. When her fortunes thereafter waned, she lacked the asset of a peripheral geographic position such as had permitted Spain and Sweden, for example, to withdraw into hard and relatively immune shells once their bids for expansion had been defeated. Poland's location being more central and pivotal, she was doomed to obliteration as a state in the second half of the eighteenth century, rather than the gentler lot of a mere reduction in power and size.

Before its partition at the hands of Austria, Prussia, and Russia, this Polish Commonwealth had been a multiethnic state governed through quasi-federalistic and decentralistic constitutional arrangements by a nobility of Polish and polonized Lithuanian, Belorussian, Ukrainian, German, and even Tatar, Armenian, and apostate-Jewish stock. Its political principles had required neither linguistic nor ethnic uniformity: Latin was the language of state functions, and caste rather than race was the criterion of access into the ruling establishment. Indeed, even religious uniformity was not highly valued until the last century preceding tne partitions. Thus, at a time when the rest of Europe had been convulsed by the post-Reformation religious wars and persecutions of the sixteenth and seventeenth centuries, Poland had enjoyed the widest degree of religious toleration and freedom of any state on the continent. Such latitudinarianism, while morally admirable and culturally interesting, may well have been a political hindrance in an age when language and religion were the mortar and bricks of nation-building.

Political life in the restored Polish state after 1918 was heavily colored by a craving to avoid repeating the errors that had weakened the old commonwealth; there was, however, no unanimity in identifying those errors. Did historic Poland's mistake lie, for example, in having first tolerated wide religious dissent in an age when nationalism was closely tied to a specific religion, or in later having alienated her Eastern Orthodox and Protestant subjects through Roman Catholic exclusivism? Politically, had Poland been originally too generous, or subsequently too restrictive, toward her non-Polish populations? Was it a misjudgment to have contested the rise of Muscovy, or to have failed to smother her when she was still vulnerable? Did the Poles blunder in refusing to elect a Habsburg to their throne, which would have identified that dynasty's interests with the fate of their commonwealth? Or did they err in saving Vienna from the Ottomans, which simply rescued and revived one of their own later partitioners? Interwar political and ideological stances were heavily influenced by the virtually universal Polish awareness of such historical problems and of their ambiguity. By and large, the parties of the Right and Center interpreted Polish history as validating their preference for an ethnically and religiously homogeneous modern society with a centralistic state apparatus and a foreign policy particularly alert to the assertedly primary threat of German eastward expansionism. The Left and the Piłsudskist movement, supported in part by the ethnic minorities, read that same history as a prescription for pluralism and federalism and as a lesson that Poland's main external foe was Russia.

In the century and a quarter between independent Poland's annihilation in 1795 and her restoration in 1918, the former gentry-nation had transformed itself into the Polish *społeczeństwo*, a term conventionally but inadequately translated as "society." *Społeczeństwo* signified, in fact, the more complex notion of the organized, politicized, albeit still stateless, community of all Poles, led now by an intelligentsia that preserved, at the same time as it modified, the values and the style of the old szlachta, or gentry. Indeed, the new intelligentsia was not only psychologically strongly anchored to the former szlachta, but also heavily descended from it, as that class had protected itself from the degeneration that might otherwise have followed the loss of statehood by transforming itself into the leading fraction of the intelligentsia. Bourgeois and peasant sons who also entered the intelligentsia assimilated to its gentry-derived norms. Thus, whereas among the neighboring Czechs the native medieval nobility had vanished and a new bourgeoisie allied with a prospering peasantry furnished the political leadership, among the Poles the ancient szlachta lived on through the newly ascendant intelligentsia.

Though Polish economic and political patterns were to develop along different lines in the three partitioning empires among whom the nineteenth-century *społeczeństwo* was divided, the fact that the intelligentsia preserved a uniform code of values and style and a network of social connections across the partition-borders was to prove immensely important. It sustained Polish historical and political consciousness during the era of subjugation, and it also facilitated the eventual political reintegration, which proceeded more rapidly than the economic reintegration, of the several parts of the restored, independent state after 1918. The intelligentsia then not only mastered the state apparatus, but effectively controlled all political parties no matter how contrasting their programs. It was thus a sociological, rather than an organizational, entity. Not deliberately dictatorial, the intelligentsia simply took for granted its supposedly unique qualification for public affairs. The independence movement had allied it with the peasantry and proletariat in 1918, but thereafter the intelligentsia blocked, deflected, and captured the claims of the other classes to power and, though a numerical minority, charged itself with the task of reunifying the reborn Polish state and presiding over its subsequent development. Not until the mid-1930s did the peasants and workers challenge and repudiate this political and psychological domination on the part of the intelligentsia, which was by now heavily bureaucratized, over the state and over their own movements.

2

During the long era of the partitions, the three separated segments of the Polish nation had developed different political and economic patterns. The Poles of Prussia had achieved a high level of economic development during the nineteenth century, which in Poznania and Pomerania was based on a prosperous agriculture and an ancillary processing industry, and in Silesia on mining and heavy industry. They had also reached a high level of national consciousness. Though economically integrated into the German imperial market, they had resisted political assimilation and in the process had developed a remarkable degree of national solidarity that transcended class lines. In restored Poland their social stance was more "bourgeois-capitalistic" and their economic patterns often healthier than the socialist, or peasantist, or aristocratic ones prevailing in the generally poorer areas that had been recovered from the Austrian and Russian empires. In the ex-Prussian western regions both the peasantry and the bourgeoisie were economically enterprising and innovative. In the southern and eastern regions, the peasantry was generally more primitive, and the Polish middle class was heavily composed of members of the professions and of bureaucrats, allowing the specifically *economic* bourgeoisie to remain preponderantly Jewish. Even the landscape reflected these differences; in the ex-German areas frequent small towns which were the loci of agricultural marketing and processing industries and collieries and foundries dotted the countryside, while in much of the rest of Poland the endless vista of fields, forests, and villages interspersed with an occasional city, which functioned mainly as an administrative and garrison center, prevailed.

Politically, these western Poles manifested a strong regional identity combined with a somewhat contemptuous and resentful pride toward their compatriots. Though passionately anti-German, they regarded themselves as the sole bearers in restored Poland of such positive, "Prussian," cultural virtues as industriousness, efficiency, perseverance, and punctuality. Convinced that they alone worked hard and effectively, these westerners came to feel themselves exploited by the southern and eastern Poles, whom they viewed as economic parasites and political schemers. Their view was somewhat analogous to the one that the Transylvanian Romanians took of their Regateni brethren in interwar Romania. There, too, intense nationalism was combined with resentment of the allegedly slovenly "Levantine" style of their fellow nationals from the other regions, and passionate anti-Magyarism did not preclude appreciation for the relatively high standards of competence which had been inculcated and acquired in old Hungary (see Chapter 6, section 3). The western Poles' sense of grievance was fed by the economic dislocations consequent upon their severance from Germany, by the subsequent chronic financial turmoil of the first half of the 1920s, and, finally, by the sacrifices required during a long German-Polish tariff war that lasted from June 15, 1925, to March 7, 1934.

In Galicia, the Austrian share of partitioned Poland, the Poles were overwhelmingly agricultural and the Jews controlled most of what little commerce and industry existed. Politically, the Polish nobility and intelligentsia had been favored by the Habsburgs, both locally and in Vienna. Hence, in the first years of the restored Polish state, only this region was capable of supplying a large reservoir of trained civil servants, until Polish universities began to graduate a steady flow of new bureaucrats and managers in the mid-1920s. But though politically, administratively, and culturally privileged, Galicia was economically poor and demographically overpopulated relative to the primitive level of its agronomic technology. Since the turn of the century, the hitherto exclusive political hegemony of its conservative Polish gentry had come under sustained challenge by peasantist, socialist, and Ukrainian nationalist movements.

The area that reverted to restored Poland from Russian rule consisted of two quite different parts: (a) the Kongresówka, created by the Congress of Vienna in 1815 as a political adjunct of the Tsarist Empire with a certain degree of administrative autonomy, which was whittled away in the course of the nineteenth century, and with a solidly Polish population; and (b) the *kresy*, or eastern borderlands, which had been administered as integral parts of Russia since Poland's partition and where the Polish ethnic element consisted of a relatively thin upper crust of aristocracy and gentry exercising economic and cultural "stewardship" over a socially and ethnically still "immature" Belorussian and Ukrainian peasantry. Though basically agricultural, the Kongresówka also boasted a fairly highly developed industry, which was second only to ex-German Silesia's. The *kresy*, on the other hand, were well-nigh exclusively agricultural and economically backward, with the Jews monopolizing the indispensable minimum of commerce and handicrafts. In both regions the tsarist authorities had consistently sought to weaken the Polish szlachta as punishment for its insurrections of 1830-31 and 1863-64 by such measures as peasant emancipation, cultural russification, and administrative repression. The Poles, in turn, had developed a tenacious and ramified political life—partly conspiratorial and revolutionary and partly pragmatic—characterized by a wide spectrum of ideological hues.

3

Independent Poland's political parties both reflected and in part bridged these regional differences. There was a great multiplicity and duplication of parties, and by 1926 there were twenty-six Polish and thirty-three ethnic minority parties, with thirty-one of the total having achieved legislative representation. Given their number and their propensity to splits, fusions, and general instability of organization, it seems preferable to depict their policies and clientèles in broad, rather than in detailed, strokes, identifying only the largest and most stable parties.

The Polish Right, stemming from the mid-nineteenth century rise of integral nationalism, and politically allied with Roman Catholicism, which it perceived as the protector of Polish nationhood, rejected the multiethnic and federalistic traditions of the old prepartition commonwealth. Insisting that Poles alone be masters in the restored state, it wished to exclude the ethnic minorities—though they numbered over 30 percent of the population—from effective participation in political power. It also wanted, if possible, culturally to polonize all of them except the Jews, whom it viewed as unassimilable and hence to be preferably expatriated. Thus an integral Polish society would be achieved. Basically bourgeois in its appeal, the Right endorsed private enterprise, called for rapid industrialization linked to the polonization of the entire economy, and insisted on constitutional and administrative centralization. Its leading ideologist was Roman Dmowski; its main organizational expression, the National Democratic movement (Narodowa Demokracja). Interwar Poland's geographically most universal party, the National Democrats were particularly strong in ex-Prussian western Poland, in the Kongresówka, and among the Polish urban islands in the Ukrainian peasant sea of eastern Galicia.

Frequently allied with these National Democrats, though ostensibly preferring to regard themselves as centrist rather than rightist, were the Christian Democrats (Chrześcijańska Demokracja). This party was a more specifically clericalist movement, professing the Christian-social ideology of *Rerum Novarum*. It was popular with the proletariat and petite bourgeoisie of industrial Silesia.

Further toward the political Center stood the National Labor Party (Narodowa Partia Robotnicza), which was nonsocialist and had strong support among the nationalistic Polish workers of the light industries of Poznania and Pomerania. It enjoyed less solid but still significant popularity with a similar constituency in the Kongresówka.

The most quintessentially centrist party, in terms of its policies as well as its pivotal location on the parliamentary seesaw, was the Piast Peasant Party (Stronnictwo Ludowe "Piast"). Its support came mainly from the Polish peasantry of Galicia. Quite nationalistic, hence intermittently allied with the Right, it was reluctant to promote a truly radical land reform lest Belorussian and Ukrainian peasants in the eastern areas benefit at the expense of the Polish element, and lest the principle of private property be jeopardized. Hence the Piast Party preferred to gratify the expectations of its constituency through such devices as patronage, public works, and other state favors. This required it to strive to be always a government party; indeed, under its dexterous leader Wincenty Witos, Piast was the leading "broker" party that manipulated coalitions during the first years of interwar Poland.

A second peasant party, the Wyzwolenie (Liberation) Party (Stronnictwo Ludowe "Wyzwolenie"), was authentically leftist but politically less effective than Piast. It was sympathetic toward the grievances and aspirations of the ethnic minorities, anticlerical, and committed to radical land reform. Just as the Piast Party was basically Galician, so the Wyzwolenie was also something of a regional party, its home being in the Kongresówka. Not until the depth of the agrarian depression, on March 15, 1931, was a united Peasant Party (Stronnictwo Ludowe) formed through a merger of the Piast, Wyzwolenie, and interim groups that had split away from one or another of these two parent parties in the mid-1920s and were known collectively as the Stronnictwo Chłopskie.

The classic bearers of the ideology of the Polish Left were the Socialist Party (Polska Partia Socjalistyczna) and, originally, the Piłsudskist movement. (At that time the Communists, identified with a historic and contemporary foe of Poland, and obliged by that foe to advocate the cession of Poland's *kresy* to the Soviet Union, were viewed suspiciously as a party of the "East" rather than of the "Left" by most Poles.) The Socialists and the Piłsudskists, who had been one movement before World War I and were still closely linked by many ideological, personal, and sentimental ties throughout the 1920s, identified with the old commonwealth's multiethnic, federalistic, and latitudinarian religious traditions, as well as with the anti-Muscovite insurrections of 1794, 1830-31, and 1863-64 which had been intended to recover an independent Polish state. Hence, not only the proletariat but much of the state-oriented intelligentsia endorsed these two unimpeachably patriotic movements of the Left in interwar Poland. The Socialists enjoyed substantial urban support in all regions except those of ex-Prussian western Poland, while the Piłsudskists did not, until 1927, function as a distinct party, but rather as coteries within several parties, which they sought to win over to Marshal Józef Piłsudski's policies. Though the Socialists and the Piłsudskists differed over socioeconomic policies and legislative-executive relations, they were initially at one in repudiating the integral nationalism, ethnic chauvinism, and clericalism of the Right.

It follows that the ethnic minorities, who sought to maximize their bargaining power by organizing a quite cohesive parliamentary bloc during the 1920s, long expected more favorable treatment from the Left than from the Right-Center coalition. After 1930, however, the Ukrainians became profoundly alienated from a by-now unresponsive Piłsudski, and toward the end of the decade the Jews were deeply troubled by his heirs' reluctant, but nonetheless shameful, concessions to popular anti-Semitism.

Finally, mention must be made of the political stance of the surviving upper aristocracy, who were fearful of the Left's espousal of land reform and alienated by the Right's raucous chauvinism and bourgeois political outlook. Though they had served the governments of the partitioning empires until 1918, though they declined thereafter to adapt themselves to the rules of the parliamentary game in independent Poland, and though the peasant and worker masses would in any event have used the power of universal suffrage to exclude them from government, they were nevertheless viewed and wooed by Piłsudski as the bearers of an allegedly suprapartisan tradition of public service, that went back to the days of the old commonwealth. He felt that this tradition was desperately needed by a Poland deeply lacerated by the incessant strife of parties and factions. Soon after seizing power in May, 1926, to stem the apparent disintegration of the body-politic, Piłsudski arranged a rapprochement with this aristocracy that supposedly embodied the state and whose political ideology was conservative rather than rightist in the integral-nationalist sense. By then exasperated with all political parties, whom he held collectively responsible for the travails of the state, Piłsudski was undeterred by the consideration that this move implied and signaled an early break with the Left which had hitherto been his ally.

4

Interwar Poland's foreign and domestic stances were to a large extent determined by the historic vision of Józef Piłsudski—and by the Right's deliberate frustration of that vision. Piłsudski's moral authority in interwar Polish politics derived from his successful leadership of the political and military struggle, before and during World War I, to achieve the resurrection of an independent Poland. Then, as chief of state and commander in chief of the armed forces in the immediate postwar years

1918-22, he sought through military efforts to carve out for the restored state the wide eastern frontiers and, in consequence, the multiethnic population that had characterized the old commonwealth before its partition. This program implied a federalistic constitutional structure.

The Right, meanwhile, which before the war had been less concerned with independent *statehood* than with the economic and cultural strengthening of Polish *society* was concentrating its diplomatic efforts on persuading the Allied statesmen at the Paris Peace Conference, who recognized the Rightist leader Dmowski as head of the Polish delegation, to grant Poland generous frontiers vis-à-vis Germany. Simultaneously, the Right was using its domestic political power to achieve the adoption of a highly centralistic constitution on March 17, 1921, which implied that the proportion of the state's non-Polish population would be small enough to be effectively assimilated.

Between Piłsudski's and Dmowski's visions, Polish policy fell between two stools. The former, though not entirely successful in his endeavor to recover all the Lithuanian, Belorussian, and Ukrainian lands that had been lost by the old commonwealth to Muscovy, nevertheless did manage, thanks to Russia's momentary postwar and postrevolutionary prostration, to incorporate into Poland extensive eastern territories of a non-Polish ethnic complexion. Simultaneously, the centralistic constitution and generally chauvinistic stance of Dmowski's adherents alienated these large minorities, rendering them unabsorbable even on a political level. Cultural assimilation, which might have been possible a half century earlier, was now out of the question. Russia, meanwhile, was wounded without being permanently crippled by these territorial losses to Poland. Since Germany's enmity was inevitable—being utterly unreconciled to having been obliged to yield to interwar Poland a "corridor" to the Baltic Sea through Pomerania, as well as the rich industrial region of Silesia—it seems, in retrospect, unwise for Poland to have gratuitously saddled herself, in addition, with Russian resentment and with an unsolvable ethnic-minority problem—a triple complex which entailed an acrobatic and basically hopeless foreign policy. At the time, however, in the first euphoric years of independence, the gravity of this problem was not appreciated, as most Polish—and most European—political leaders entertained exaggerated impressions of the extent to which Russia had been weakened—supposedly permanently—by war and revolution. Furthermore, in justice to Piłsudski, one might now well share his skepticism that even a generously treated Russia would have reciprocated in kind once her leaders were persuaded that their interests indicated otherwise.

5

The ethnic, social, and demographic difficulties confronting the restored Poland are suggested by the results of her two censuses of September 30, 1921, and December 9, 1931. Spokesmen for the ethnic minorities criticised the categories and the actual tabulations as being skewed. Indeed, the official distinction between "Ukrainian" and "Ruthenian" (in 1931) as well as between "Belorussian" and "local" *(tutejsi)* nationality (in 1921 and 1931) appears to have been an artificial, dubious, and politically motivated Polish attempt to reduce the statistical visibility of the Ukrainians and the Belorussians. However, on balance, the census returns can be used with profit. It should be noted that in 1921 ethnicity was defined by the respondent's national identification, whereas a decade later it was inferred from his native tongue *(język ojczysty)*, "in which he conventionally thinks and communicates with his family." This change may have figured in the sharp drop in the number of Germans recorded between the two censuses, though emigration also played a role here. A less significant variation is that the 1921 census included in its various subcategories the barracked military personnel, whereas the 1931 census did not. In the latter year they numbered 191,473. Furthermore, as the frontiers were not finally delimited until 1922, the population statistics for Silesia and the Wilno (Vilnius, Vilna) region were interpolated into the 1921 census from 1919 data. Thereafter, the area of interwar Poland from 1922 up to her peremptory incorporation of Czechoslovakia's fraction of Silesia (the Teschen, or Cieszyn, or Těšín district) at the time of the latter country's "Munich" travail and truncation in September-October, 1938 (see Chapter 3, section 11), was 388,634 square kilometers. Within that territory resided a highly heterogeneous population (see tables 1 and 2).[1]

It may be useful at this point to indicate a number of internal correlations as well as problems within these official data. The Polish population was overwhelmingly Roman Catholic with only a very small Protestant minority. The Lithuanians were even more exclusively Roman Catholic, but four-fifths of the Germans were Protestant. The bulk of Jews-by-religion also regarded themselves as Jews-by-nationality and spoke Yiddish or Hebrew, yet a significant minority indicated Polish as their native tongue and identified correspondingly in national terms. While the other three major minorities were concentrated geographically—Germans in the west, Belorussians and Ukrainians in the east—the Jews were concentrated in a different but equally vivid sense. Four-fifths of them were urban, and in 1931 they furnished 25.2 percent of the inhabitants of the twelve largest cities with populations of over a hundred thousand, though only 9.8 percent of the general population. (This concentration would be even more strikingly illustrated if the four large cities of ex-Prussian western Poland, which had few Jews, were subtracted, and Jewish urban

1. All statistics are from the official statistical yearbooks of the Main Bureau of Statistics of the Polish Republic (Główny Urząd Statystyczny Rzeczypospolitej Polskiej), entitled during the 1920s *Rocznik Statystyki* and in the 1930s *Mały Rocznik Statystyczny*.

proportions were then recalculated for Galicia, the Kongresówka, and the *kresy* together.)

TABLE 1

POPULATION BY ETHNICITY

	1921 (Nationality)		1931 (Native Tongue)	
	Number	Percentage	Number	Percentage
Polish	18,814,239	69.2	21,993,444	68.9
Ukrainian ⎫ Ruthenian ⎭	3,898,431	14.3	3,221,975 1,219,647	10.1 3.8
Local	49,441	0.2	707,088	2.2
Belorussian	1,060,237	3.9	989,852	3.1
Jewish; Yiddish ⎫ Jewish; Hebrew ⎭	2,110,448	7.8	2,489,084 243,500	7.8 0.8
German	1,059,194	3.9	740,992	2.3
Lithuanian	68,667	0.3	83,116	0.3
Russian	56,239	0.2	138,713	0.4
Czech	30,628	0.1	38,097	0.1
Other	29,193	0.1	50,271	0.2
Total	27,176,717	100.0	31,915,779	100.0

TABLE 2

POPULATION BY RELIGION

	1921		1931 (available only by rounded hundreds)	
	Number	Percentage	Number	Percentage
Roman Catholic	17,365,350	63.8	20,670,100	64.8
Greek Catholic (Uniate)	3,031,059	11.2	3,336,200	10.4
Eastern Orthodox	2,846,855	10.5	3,762,500	11.8
Lutheran and Calvinist	1,002,216	3.7	835,200	2.6
Other Protestant	12,416	0.1 ⎫	145,400	0.5
Other Christian	65,586	0.2 ⎭		
Mosaic	2,845,364	10.5	3,113,900	9.8
Other and Unknown	7,871	0.0	52,500	0.1
Total	27,176,717	100.0	31,915,779	100.0

TABLE 3

AVERAGE ANNUAL RATE OF POPULATION INCREASE

(IN PERCENTAGES)

Region	1921-31	1931-39
Central Provinces	1.7	1.2
Eastern Provinces	3.0	1.4
Western Provinces	1.0	1.1
Southern Provinces	1.3	1.1
All of Poland	1.7	1.2

The census returns for the Slavic eastern minorities present problems. Since the adherents to the Eastern Orthodox and Uniate (Greek Catholic) confessions came almost exclusively from among Belorussians, Ukrainians, and Russians, it is somewhat discrepant that the sum of the worshippers in these two churches (table 2) should substantially exceed the sum of these three ethnic minorities (table 1), and it appears that many Belorussian and Ukrainian adherents to the Orthodox and Uniate rites were persuaded or pressured to declare themselves Polish by ethnicity. In addition, Roman Catholic Belorussians often identified themselves as believing in "the Polish faith" and were accordingly recorded as Polish by ethnicity as well. Being politically still somewhat immature—though not as much so as Polish propagandists of the Right often alleged—such eastern-minority peasants might have been ready to have their nationality or language, but not their religion, recorded incorrectly. The majority of Belorussians were Eastern Orthodox, the minority Roman Catholic; and Ukrainians were Uniate in ex-Habsburg eastern Galicia, and Orthodox in the ex-tsarist *kresy*. It should also be noted that the rate of population increase (table 3) was highest in the eastern provinces where these two ethnic groups were concentrated and constituted the rural majorities. Hence, some skepticism is elicited by the statistics purporting that the combined percentage of Ukrainians, Ruthenians, "locals," and Belorussians in Poland as a whole rose between 1921 (18.4) and 1931 (19.2) by as little as 0.8 percent (table 1).

Throughout the entire country, the socioeconomic pressures accruing from this high rate of population increase were aggravated by the interwar throttling of emigration outlets. Furthermore, the failure of industrialization to develop sufficiently to absorb the bulk of this increase meant that approximately four-fifths of the population remained confined to the villages. The census recorded 17.1 percent of the population as urban and 82.9 percent as rural in 1921, and 20.4 percent as urban and 79.6 percent as rural in 1931. Here the official census definition of an urban locality was one with a population of ten thousand or more.

6

Before commencing a chronological analysis of interwar Poland's politics, this is a suitable point to scan her society's relations with the ethnic minorities. Polish culture had historically been magnetic and absorptive. The old commonwealth's assimilation of non-Polish gentries has been mentioned. Somewhat surprisingly, this power of Polish culture to attract other people continued even after the loss of independent statehood. Still more surprisingly, it first waned (initially unperceived) during the second half of the nineteenth century among the allegedly still primitive eastern neighbors (Lithuanians, Ukrainians, later the Belorussians), while it remained potent in the west, among the supposedly more advanced, heavily germanized, Silesians, Kashubs, and Mazurians, and the border-Germans proper, who continued to be culturally and linguistically repolonized and polonized throughout the nineteenth and early twentieth centuries. This imposing magnetism of Polish culture, even in the absence of a Polish state, seduced many interwar Poles, especially on the Right, into underestimating the new recalcitrance of the still young nationalisms of the country's ethnic minorities, and hence into rejecting a federalistic in favor of a centralistic constitutional structure.

Of the four important minorities, the Belorussians and Ukrainians were as overwhelmingly agricultural and rural in social structure as the Jews were commercial, artisanal, and urban, while the Germans were mixed. The two Slavic minorities were also consciously autochthonous in the regions of their settlement, while the Jews and Germans were somewhat on the defensive, the former having been invited to Poland in medieval times and the latter having come as modern colonists. While the three Christian minorities intially enjoyed the patronage of neighboring powers of their own ethnicity and might in theory realize their national aspirations through yet another truncation or even partition of the Polish state (ignoring for the moment the realities of Stalin's own hostility toward Ukrainian nationalism), the Jews' political dilemma was more problematical. Having no contiguous "mother country" into which to be incorporated, and hence no clear ethnic interest in the territorial fragmentation of Poland, their political stance oscillated between general ethnic-minority solidarity against Polish domination on the one hand, and occasional efforts to come to a particular arrangement with the ruling Poles on the other—an arrangement by which they would hope to trade their endorsement of the state's territorial and political integrity and of its governments in return for special recognition of their cultural peculiarities and educational needs. Alas, as rightist ideology permeated Polish society ever more deeply, the governments, in turn, somewhat reluctantly acceded to popular anti-Semitism and rebuffed such overtures for an authentic accommodation. Hence many Jews sought a third alternative, Zionism.

Already at the moment of Poland's rebirth, the Jews had been caught in the crossfire of Polish, Ukrainian, Bolshevik, and White Russian armies and bands: 1919 was a traumatic year in East European Jewish history. Later, they were held responsible for inducing the Paris Peace Conference to impose on Poland the Minorities Protection Treaty of June 28, 1919, which was intended to shelter the minorities against coerced assimilation by guaranteeing them legal equality as well as civil and political rights. Poland resented this treaty as implicitly denigrating her sovereignty, since the established powers, many of whom also housed substantial ethnic minorities, did not commit themselves to the same international legal obligations as they enjoined upon the new states. The frequent petitions filed against Poland under the terms of this treaty at the League of Nations, both by the minorities themselves and by interested (malevolently interfering, in the Polish view) states, embittered the Poles. And, as neither the treaty nor the League had enforcement teeth, eventually the minorities became cynical. Finally, on September 13, 1934, Poland unilaterally refused further cooperation with the international bodies that monitored the treaty, pending the universalization of its obligations to all states.

The vast bulk of Polish Jewry was culturally unassimilated, and the pattern of its economic structure was almost the reverse of the general society's (table 4). The high, and allegedly provocative, prominence of Jews in the developing urban economic sectors of commerce, industry, culture, and communications, and their virtual absence from agriculture can be illustrated even more vividly through the proportions of adher-

TABLE 4

POPULATION BY ECONOMIC SECTORS (INCLUDING DEPENDENTS). 1931 CENSUS

	Total		Jewish		Non-Jewish	
	Number	Percentage	Number	Percentage	Number	Percentage
Agriculture, forestry, fishing	19,346,900	60.6	125,100	4.0	19,221,800	66.7
Mining, industry	6,177,900	19.3	1,313,300	42.2	4,864,600	16.9
Commerce, insurance	1,943,200	6.1	1,140,500	36.6	802,700	2.8
Communications, transportation	1,153,100	3.6	139,400	4.5	1,013,700	3.5
Education, culture	338,100	1.0	72,600	2.3	265,500	0.9
Domestic services	441,100	1.5	22,500	0.7	418,600	1.5
Other	2,515,500	7.9	300,500	9.7	2,215,000	7.7
Total	31,915,800	100.0	3,113,900	100.0	28,801,900	100.0

ents to the various religions engaged in the several economic sectors (table 5). In other words, whereas table 4 gives the total Jewish and Gentile populations across the various economic sectors, table 5 gives the religious distribution within these sectors. (Economic identification by linguistic criteria would have been more helpful than by religious ones for reconstructing the separate economic profiles of the other minorities and of the Polish majority, but unfortunately it was not available.)

TABLE 5

Economic Sectors by Religion. 1931 Census

(in percentages)

	Agriculture, Forestry, Fishing	Mining, Industry	Commerce, Insurance	Communications, Transportation	Education, Culture	Domestic Services	Other
Roman Catholic	62.8	69.9	36.6	81.7	68.9	77.7	77.9
Uniate	15.2	3.1	1.2	2.7	4.0	8.7	3.8
Eastern Orthodox	17.9	2.1	1.2	2.1	2.3	5.4	3.2
Protestant	2.6	3.2	2.1	1.1	3.0	2.8	2.7
Mosaic	0.7	21.3	58.7	12.1	21.5	5.1	11.9
Other	0.8	0.4	0.2	0.3	0.3	0.3	0.5
Total	100.0	100.0	100.0	100.0	100.0	100.0	100.0

Lest, however, an erroneous impression be here conveyed, that a thoroughly affluent and powerful Jewish minority dominated the modern nerve-centers of interwar Poland, the following considerations should serve as correctives: (a) the census category of "Mining and Industry" included many small and technologically obsolescent sweatshops and handicraft establishments; (b) Jews, like the other minorities, were emphatically underrepresented in the public services, which the Poles understandably wished to monopolize in a Polish state; (c) the Jewish community maintained an extensive school system with only a pittance in state financial support; (d) poor Jews were numerous—one-third of the Jews were on charity—and just as poor as poor Gentiles; (e) the Jews were originally invited into Poland by medieval rulers precisely to develop its commerce and trade, which the szlachta then disdained—hence, their overrepresentation in this sector was historically as much a result of Polish as of their own preferences.

From his seizure of power in 1926 until his death in 1935, Piłsudski had sought to honor the nonexclusivist traditions of the old commonwealth in its age of glory. His epigoni, however, not only encouraged economic discrimination against Jews, including boycotts which occasionally degenerated into quasi-pogroms, but also tolerated explicitly political anti-Semitic violence, especially at the hands of nationalistic university students. Here the supposedly "strong" government of 1936-39 showed itself suspiciously weak in failing to curb or apprehend the culprits. While it refrained from racially anti-Semitic legislation, this regime did indulge in administrative policies intended to weaken and damage the Jews' role in the economy and the free professions, even to a degree that was irrational from the perspective of Poland's own interests. Experienced Jewish entrepreneurs, who often employed Poles and extended credit to them, were taxed into oblivion on behalf of clumsy and unprofitable state monopolies. In a country desperately short of physicians, engineers, and other professionals, Jews were virtually excluded from such academic studies. Their proportion of the entire university student body was reduced through a *numerus clausus* from 20.4 percent in the academic year 1928-29 to 9.9 percent in 1937-38; the latter percentage was about the same as the Jewish proportion of the entire population but far under the Jewish proportion of the urban population, which classically furnishes the academic youth. Within the university walls, the rightist student body was allowed to impose ghetto benches and other humiliations, including frequent beatings, on their Jewish classmates.

The economic and social context partly explains, but does not justify, this malevolence. Poland's slow recovery from the depression threw Polish workers, craftsmen, peasants, entrepreneurs, and intelligentsia into severe competition with the highly visible Jews for the limited supply of employment, credit, entrepreneurial, and professional opportunities. There was real, if misplaced, anxiety lest the Poles become a nation of peasants, proletarians, and officials while the Jews flooded commerce and the free professions. Nevertheless, thoughtful members of the Polish elite became concerned that the specifically anti-Semitic violence might eventually degenerate into a broader rightist assault on all political rivals and, indeed, on public order *per se*. As war clouds darkened the horizon in 1938-39, even some government leaders indicated misgiving lest anti-Jewish excesses identify Poland with, and undermine her vis-à-vis, Nazi Germany.

Interwar Poland's German minority, being economically prosperous and socially well-balanced, and enjoying more political support from the Weimar Republic—and later in a different way from Nazi Germany —than the other minorities were given by any external power, complained primarily about educational discrimination. Especially in Silesia was it subject to a vigorous effort at cultural polonization. The manner in which land reform, industrial investment, and bureaucratic recruitment were administered also aggrieved the Germans, many of whom emigrated to Germany. In the 1930s, those who remained divided politically into Nazi (the majority), bourgeois-nationalist, Catholic, and Socialist groups. As the Polish government was then cultivating good relations with Berlin under the rubric of their joint Non-Aggression Statement of January 26, 1934, it did not support the Catholic and Socialist parties against the pressure of the Nazi-controlled one. By the same token, the latter cooperated with the Polish government rather than with other minority parties and, being unable to win parliamentary representation under new and restrictive electoral laws of 1935, it thereafter accepted two appointive senatorial seats from the hands of the Polish president.

The poor and heavily illiterate Belorussians were regarded by the Polish authorities as having the lowest degree of political consciousness of all the state's minorities. At the beginning of the interwar era, when the still embryonic Belorussian nationalist awakening was expected to develop primarily into a sense of differentiation from Russia, the Polish Left and the Piłsudskists had even nursed it along. By the second half of the 1920s, however, this potential accommodation had soured as the Belorussian peasants became offended by the economic hegemony of old Polish landlord-families and the physical intrusion of new Polish colonists (osadnicy) into their territory. In 1931, 37 percent of the arable land in the Belorussian areas of Poland was owned by Poles, and the region's extensive timber resources were also exploited in a predatory manner. Many Belorussians now became enamoured of the supposedly better political and economic lot of their conationals in the Soviet Union's Belorussian Soviet Socialist Republic. Their fascination with the neighboring Communist model, in turn, alarmed the Polish authorities, who attempted to repress politically this Belorussian nationalist movement that now appeared even more concerned about differentiating itself from Poland than from Russia. Yet even this Polish repression of the late 1920s was still intermittent and inconsistent; though severe against explicit political expressions of Belorussian "subversiveness" and brutal in the villages, it left the central Belorussian cultural institutions in Wilno unmolested. In the 1930s, finally, the repression was extended to cultural expressions as well; Belorussian schools were polonized or closed, and the youth given the unhappy choice of studying in Polish or remaining illiterate. As is generally the case in such circumstances, Belorussian nationalism was only strengthened and rendered yet more subversive by the efforts to destroy it. By the time of Poland's destruction in September, 1939, the loyalties of its Belorussian citizens were divided between aspirations for independence and hopes for unification with their Soviet Belorussian brethren.

The Ukrainians were the largest national group in interwar Europe to whom the doctrines of political self-determination and unification had not yet been applied. They were then divided between the Soviet Union, Poland, Czechoslovakia, and Romania, not as dispersed minorities, but as compact local majorities in the regions of their settlement. The fraction of the Ukrainian nation that was assigned to interwar Poland was over-whelmingly agricultural. But even in the midst of a solidly Ukrainian rural countryside, the populations of the southeastern towns consisted of Polish officials and garrisons, and of Polish and Jewish professionals and merchants. The land-hungry Ukrainian peasants craved the estates owned by Polish landlords. Thus, the Ukrainian problem in interwar Poland was social, economic, and cultural as well as political—a complex which the Polish Right, preferring to dismiss Ukrainian nationalism as either immature or a German machination, declined to acknowledge.

The Ukrainians were aggrieved and alienated by linguistic pressure and cultural polonization, economic exploitation and Polish colonization, as well as by restrictions on their access to higher education and public careers, and their gerrymandered underrepresentation in the legislature. In the 1930s, Polish-Ukrainian relations sporadically degenerated into quasi-guerrilla warfare, characterized on the one side by assassinations of Polish politicians, officials, and colonists, and on the other by dragonnade-like military brutalization and "pacification" of Ukrainian villages. But as interwar Poland was not a police-state, the conscience of the Polish intelligentsia restrained the political authorities from stripping the minorities of their rights altogether. Thus, through all the vicious cycle of provocation and revenge, the Ukrainians managed to develop an active intelligentsia and a lively cooperative movement, which functioned as a school of politico-administrative self-education as well as a bulwark of economic self-defense. They also succeeded in easing pressure to trans-form their ecclesiastical institutions into funnels of polonization. Though Poland's Eastern Orthodox (i.e., Ukrainian, Belorussian, Russian) dio-ceses did assert their autocephalous organization with respect to the Moscow Patriarchate in the early 1920s at the urging of the Polish au-thorities, they resisted heavy pressure in the late 1930s to polonize their sermons, prayerbooks, and calendars. The Uniate Church functioned even more emphatically as an explicit expression of Ukrainian national consciousness in interwar Poland.

In the mid-1930s, as Stalin moved to destroy Ukrainian national culture and imposed the hated kolkhozi on the Ukrainian peasantry in the Soviet Union, and as Warsaw achieved diplomatic détentes with both Berlin and Moscow, the Ukrainian nationalist movement in Poland was for the time being deprived of the patronage of any major state. This would appear to have been a likely moment to reconcile the isolated Ukrainians to the Polish state. The Poles, however, failed to seize it. Instead of viewing the situation as an opportunity to bid for their Ukrainians'—and, analog-ously, their Belorussians'—allegiance, they myopically interpreted it as a license to ignore and repudiate their minorities' aspirations.

Statistics may also help to explain, though not to excuse, why so many Poles, especially on the political Right, succumbed to the temptation to dismiss the two Slavic, eastern minorities as too immature and primitive to merit serious consideration as authentic nations. The census tabulations for illiteracy indicate considerably higher rates in the provinces where these two minorities were concentrated than in Poland as a whole (see table 6). Similarly, the economic structure of their Orthodox and Uniate denominations show higher absorption in agriculture and lower representation in more "advanced" economic sectors than the general average (see table 7).

TABLE 6

ILLITERACY ABOVE THE AGE OF TEN
(IN PERCENTAGES)

Region	1921	1931
Provinces of Ukrainian concentration:		
Wołyń	68.6	47.8
Stanisławów	46.0	36.6
Tarnopol	39.2	29.8
Lwów	29.2	23.1
Provinces of Belorussian concentration:		
Wilno	58.3	29.1
Nowogródek	54.6	34.9
Polesie	71.0	48.4
Poland	33.1	23.1

TABLE 7

RELIGIONS BY ECONOMIC SECTORS (INCLUDING DEPENDENTS). 1931 CENSUS*

	Total	Roman Catholic	Uniate	Eastern Orthodox	Protestant
Agriculture, forestry, fishing	60.6	58.8	88.1	92.4	59.2
Mining, industry	19.3	20.9	5.8	3.4	23.7
Commerce, insurance	6.1	3.4	0.7	0.6	4.8
Communications, transportation	3.6	4.6	1.0	0.7	1.6
Education, culture	1.0	1.1	0.4	0.2	1.2
Domestic services	1.5	1.7	1.1	0.6	1.5
Other	7.9	9.5	2.9	2.1	8.0
Total	100.0	100.0	100.0	100.0	100.0

*Tabulations for Jews were presented in table 4.

Of course, except for the Jews, who have been analyzed earlier, religion does not quite correspond with ethnicity. Here, for example, the Roman Catholic Belorussians and Germans cannot be separately identified as such. Also, about a third of the Protestants were Poles, though almost all the rest were Germans. On the other hand, the Uniates and Orthodox were entirely composed of Poland's eastern Slavic minorities and hence table 7, even when interpreted conservatively, does demonstrate that these were overwhelmingly relegated to the relatively poor and backward agricultural sector. This was the result of long historical neglect far more than of interwar Poland's policies. Indeed, illiteracy rates of these peoples declined dramatically under Polish rule (table 6).

It must be acknowledged that even a rich and long-established state —and interwar Poland was neither—might well have been baffled by the staggering problems presented by her ethnic minorities: their number, their size, their recalcitrance, their external support, and, in the eastern regions, their poverty. Poland was doubly handicapped by having simultaneously to cope with the postpartition reintegration of the long-severed parts of the Polish state-nation as she vainly sought for a consistent and feasible approach toward the minority problem. Her search for a solution was fatefully compromised by the apparent incompatibility between her frontiers and her institutions. Piłsudski's military efforts had incorporated non-Polish populations whom Dmowski's domestic arrangements could not digest. The Right, which by the 1930s had ideologically saturated Polish society, viewed all expressions of nationalism on the part of minorities as treasonable and to be stifled. Believing that the old quasi-federalistic commonwealth had too long been suicidally indulgent toward the non-Polish and non-Catholic populations, the Right insisted that restored Poland either assimilate or expel her minorities. But they were too numerous, already too conscious, and still too rooted for either of these alternatives to be practicable at that time. They were simply alienated by the whole sterile paraphernalia of discriminatory devices which this program entailed: skewed census tabulation, boycott, *numerus clausus*, colonization, biased land reform, prejudicial tax assessment, and violence.

7

Already in reborn Poland's first and most important assertion of sovereignty, the drafting of its constitution, the chasm between Piłsudski and the Right proved crippling. The resurrection of an independent Poland at the close of World War I was made possible by that war's singular outcome, which Piłsudski had uniquely anticipated: the defeat of all three of her partitioning powers—first of Russia by Germany, then of Germany and her Austrian partner by the Western Powers. Piłsudski and his Legionnaires had fought as associates of the Central Powers until Russia's defeat had been assured in the spring of 1917. Then, insisting on

Polish priorities, they had refused further collaboration and were interned until the war's end. This audacious, skillful, and successful conduct had won such high moral authority for Piłsudski that he was promptly acknowledged as chief of state and commander in chief of the armed forces upon his return to Warsaw from German confinement on November 10, 1918. Thus, for the moment, he eclipsed his rightist rival Dmowski, who had endorsed the Russian and Western war efforts and whose wartime activities had been diplomatic and political rather than military and political. The Polish Right had traditionally been more interested in the development of a modern society than in independent statehood; hence it liked to see in the Russian Empire—Piłsudski's *bête noire*—both a shield against what it feared was the more pressing menace of Germany to Polish society, and a vast market for that society's nascent industries.

To the disappointment of his friends of the Polish Left, who hoped at one stroke to achieve land reform, nationalization of industry, social security, secularization of culture, and the democratization of society, Piłsudski now refrained from instituting a radical-reform dictatorship and insisted, instead, that fundamental social changes could only be initiated by an elected legislature. Accordingly, he arranged for the early election of a unicameral Constituent Assembly, which on February 20, 1919, proclaimed itself the sovereign authority while unanimously confirming Piłsudski as chief of state, which became an office of reduced authority, and commander in chief, which remained a position of great power. Piłsudski's apparent self-restraint during this period may be interpreted either as a manifestion of an impressive sense of democratic responsibility, or as an intended (but unsuccessful) maneuver to free himself from all partisan and ideological affiliation and thereby render himself the umpire among the several political phalanxes whom he hoped would emerge deadlocked from the elections to the Constituent Assembly.

The Right, however, emerged from these elections as the strongest phalanx but not sufficiently dominant to give Poland stable governments. Thus, whatever may have been Piłsudski's hopes and intentions, the elections were politically premature and inaugurated seven-and-a-half years of party anarchy and fragile coalitions until Piłsudski closed this painful era with his reseizure of effective power by a *coup d'état* in May, 1926.

The effectiveness of the Constituent Assembly as a potential vehicle for national integration was seriously compromised *ab initio* by the circumstance that its election was confined to areas under Polish control at the beginning of 1919 and was later extended, on a staggered schedule, to the ex-Prussian provinces and some northeastern localities. Thus, the large Belorussian and Ukrainian minorities of the east, whose incorporation into Poland was not settled until 1921, were unrepresented in the constitution-drafting process—just as neighboring Czechoslovakia excluded her numerous German and Magyar minorities from the same process (see below, Chapter 3, section 4). Furthermore, these Polish elections, held so early in what had recently been a major battle area for over three years and in regions politically separated for over a century, were characterized by much passion and confusion, a truly stunning plethora of lists, considerable administrative incompetence (but not pressure), and frequent irregularities in such matters as eligibility, tabulation, and verification. The system was proportional and complicated, and it appears that somewhat over 70 percent of the eligible electorate (men and women over twenty years of age) participated. Table 8 gives approximate coherence to the quite disjointed results. Even here, the tabulation for "Seats" is somewhat arbitrary since the various parliamentary clubs divided and merged several times during the nearly four years that this Constituent Assembly remained in session. (The Christian Democrats and the Communists had not yet differentiated themselves, respectively, from the National Democrats and the Socialists in 1919 and are thus included in the latter parties' data.)

TABLE 8

ELECTIONS TO THE CONSTITUENT ASSEMBLY

Party	Number of Votes	Percentage of Total Vote	Seats
Right:			
National Democrat	2,361,006	42.3	141
Center:			
National Labor (NPR)	206,571	3.7	25
Piast	450,578	8.1	89
Populist Federation	239,325	4.3	45
Left:			
Wyzwolenie	1,029,799	18.5	36
Socialist	515,062	9.2	36
National Minorities:			
German lists	148,204	2.7	7
Jewish lists	508,614	9.1	11
Miscellaneous:			
Progressive Democrat	29,646	0.5	. . .
Other	92,165	1.6	42
Total	5,580,970	100.0	432

The Constituent Assembly's main achievement was to rally the nation to a rare moment of solidarity during the summer crisis of the Polish-Soviet

War of 1920, when Piłsudski's armies, having been repulsed in their attempt to conquer the Soviet Ukraine in the spring, stood embattled before Warsaw and finally triumphed. Its chief failure was the mishandling of its most specific task, the drafting of the constitution. Here the Right feared that Piłsudski, whom it detested as a former Socialist and as the current protagonist of federalistic notions for "coddling" the ethnic minorities, would become president, since he was the spectacular hero of Poland's resurrection to independent statehood; and so it decided to tailor the constitution to its own apprehensions. It used its powerful position in the assembly to endow the country with an emasculated presidency and an omnipotent legislature. Poland's basic institutions of government were thus shaped *ad personam*—a fatal political procedure. Particularly crippling for any presidential ambitions which Piłsudski might have entertained was Article 46, which, while making the president titular head of the armed forces, prohibited his exercising command in wartime. Ironically, just as the Right in 1919-21 violated its own general belief in a strong executive and, for fear of Piłsudski, proceeded to cripple the presidency as an institution, so in May, 1926, the Left, out of resentment against the policies of the legislature's dominant Right-Center coalition, was to help this same Piłsudski stage a military *coup d'etat* against the parliamentary institutions which the Left, in principle, championed.

Though the constitution was formally adopted on March 17, 1921, and the Polish-Soviet War was concluded with the signing of the Treaty of Riga just one day later, the Constituent Assembly, still fearful of allowing the newly acquired eastern minorities to share political power, extended its own existence for another year and a half and postponed the first elections for a regular parliament until November, 1922. This time the Belorussians and Ukrainians òf the former Russian Empire participated while the Ukrainians of ex-Austrian eastern Galicia abstained. Of those eligible, 67.9 percent voted in the election of November 5 for the Sejm, the lower but more powerful house, and 61.5 percent in that of November 12 for the Senate. The results failed to correct the fragmentation and paralysis of the parliamentary system. To convey, albeit inadequately, an impression of the deputies' penchant for political permutations and combinations, the allocation of Sejm seats is given in table 9 for the beginning and the close of the legislature's five-year term. In the Senate, party alignments were firmer and, except for a major defection from the Piast Party, seat allocations did not change much.

8

The next four years witnessed the accelerating degeneration of Polish parliamentary life and of governmental stability. Piłsudski's response to the constitutional engineering of the Right was to decline nomination to the presidency. The new Sejm and Senate, sitting jointly as the National

TABLE 9

Parliamentary Elections, November, 1922

Party	Sejm, November 5, 1922 Number of Votes	Percentage of Total Vote	Seats Nov. 1922	Seats Oct. 1927*	Senate, November 12, 1922 Number of Votes	Percentage of Total Vote	Seats Nov. 1922
Right:							
National Democrat et al.	2,551,582	29.1	126	120	2,173,756	39.1	39
Christian Democrat			43	40			8
Center:							
National Labor	473,676	5.4	18	16	291,779	5.3	3
Populist-Bourgeois	289,609	3.3	...	...	58,916	1.1	...
Piast	1,199,714	13.7	70	50	739,718	13.3	17
Left:							
Wyzwolenie	1,138,004	13.0	51	23	611,376	11.0	8
Stronnictwo Chłopskie	...	...	...	29	...	...	...
Socialist	906,537	10.3	41	41	468,147	8.4	7
Communist	121,448	1.4	2	5	51,094	0.9	...
National Minorities:							
Joint list	1,796,763	20.5	89	80	1,100,707	19.8	27
Separate lists	95,041	1.1	...	3	41	0.0	...
Miscellaneous:							
State list for *kresy*	86,611	1.0	...	...	58,291	1.0	...
Other	103,713	1.2	4	37	6,713	0.1	2
Total	8,762,698	100.0	444	444	5,560,538	100.0	111
Invalid	58,977	...	...	...	36,858	...	...

*Included for purposes of comparison.

Assembly, thereupon elected Gabriel Narutowicz on December 9, 1922, in an exceedingly bitter contest requiring five ballots. The winning balance of 289 versus 227 was supplied by a coalition of the Left, the Center, and the National Minorities. A week later, on December 16, 1922, the new president was assassinated by a rightist fanatic because he owed his margin of victory to non-Polish votes. The murder deepened the chasm between the Right and Piłsudski, who never forgave the National Democrats for what he regarded as their moral responsibility for the murder of Poland's first president.

On December 20, 1922, the same Left-Center-National Minorities coalition, by a vote of 298 to 221, elected to the presidency the founder of Poland's cooperative system, Stanisław Wojciechowski. The victorious coalition broke up soon thereafter when Wincenty Witos took his Piast Peasant Party into partnership with the Right in the spring of 1923. In any event, Wojciechowski's election was already something of a concession by the other parties to the Right, which considered him the least objectionable candidate outside its own ranks.

Wojciechowski's office was weak in the manner of the French presidency under the Third Republic. Elected for a seven-year term, the president had neither legislative initiative nor a veto, and he could dissolve the Sejm only with the assent of three-fifths of the total number of 111 Senators in the presence of at least half the 444 Sejm deputies, the Senate thereby dissolving itself simultaneously. In fact, these provisions for dissolution by the president were a dead letter, and their ineffectiveness became an important factor that contributed to the crisis of 1926. Equally inoperative was the power of the Sejm to dissolve itself by a two-thirds vote.

In effect, executive power rested within the cabinet, which was dependent on a Sejm majority. The large number of parties and their tendency toward splits, excessive maneuvering for office, and frequent change of partnerships rendered such majorities highly unstable. Ministerial upheavals were consequently frequent. The cabinet that Piłsudski ousted by his coup of May, 1926, was Poland's fourteenth since November, 1918—not counting reshuffling of portfolios within any one cabinet.

This instability tended to weaken the ministers in relation to both party leaders and individual deputies. The minister, frequently so transient as to be unable to familiarize himself adequately with the work of his department, was often bullied by his party's leaders into transforming both its policy and its personnel into a party rampart. Individual deputies, acting as messengers for powerful interests and constituents, shamelessly applied pressure on both ministers and civil servants. The government, in turn, would try to secure a deputy's support through judicious use of state credits, import and export licenses, land leases, forest concessions, and the administration of the alcohol and tobacco monopolies. Ironically, the deputies, who on the one hand habitually exceeded their authority by chronic interference with administration, would simultaneously shirk their basic legislative and budgetary responsibilities through excessive recourse to delegated legislation and to ex post facto legalization of economic and fiscal departures by the cabinet. A raucous and intensely partisan press aggravated the general political debasement and maximized the timidity of the ministers.

While corruption and venality were probably not as extensive as the public thought them to be, the very belief in their pervasiveness proved fatal to the prevailing political order. By 1926 the Sejm, though elected by universal suffrage, was out of touch with a public that craved stronger and more disciplined and responsible government. The beneficiary of this decline in the prestige of the legislature in particular, and of parliamentary politics in general, was Piłsudski, who in May and July of 1923 had followed up his earlier refusal of the presidency by resigning from his military functions and withdrawing into intensely political retirement.

Piłsudski had been provoked into resigning from all his public offices by the formation, on May 28, of a Right-Center coalition government in which the Piast leader Wincenty Witos was prime minister but the National Democrats held the most important portfolios and set the political tone. Its refusal to assuage the peasants' hunger for radical land reform and its failure to stem a disastrous inflation provoked serious unrest and brought this cabinet down on December 14, 1923. It was replaced by a supraparty ministry led by the financial expert Władysław Grabski, who was close to the National Democrats.

A mixture of politicians and experts, the Grabski cabinet governed largely through delegated legislation, thus indicating the legislature's declining authority and prestige. It drastically revised the currency and banking systems, replacing the hopelessly inflated mark with the gold-based złoty; it resolutely collected taxes and energetically promoted industrialization. But it was undermined by a decline in the world market price for three major Polish exports—coal, lumber, and sugar—and by Germany's launching a politically motivated tariff war against Poland on June 15, 1925. Under these circumstances, Grabski's program of combining industrial expansion with financial stabilization proved untenable, and another run on the złoty, together with public unrest, forced his resignation on November 14, 1925. His fall was widely interpreted as a failure not only of democracy but even of semidemocracy, for democracy was assumed to have already been abdicated with the legislature's grant of wide decree powers to Grabski at the beginning of his tenure.

Another inflationary spiral now uncurled and unemployment increased starkly. Public disillusion was profound; the great sacrifices of the past two years appeared to have been in vain. But though he was the beneficiary of this atmosphere of crisis and frustration, Piłsudski's time had not yet come; the political parties decided on one more try at a broad parliamentary coalition. On November 20, 1925, a cabinet headed by the foreign minister of the outgoing Grabski cabinet, Count Aleksander Skrzyński, took office.

Inauspicious was the manner in which the Skrzyński cabinet was formed. The parliamentary leaders of the five member parties—National Democratic, Christian Democratic, Piast Peasant, National Labor, and Socialist (the Wyzwolenie Peasant Party was the one major Polish group to decline participation or support)—distributed the portfolios and then invited Skrzyński as a nonparty man to head this cabinet. The prime minister, who also retained the foreign affairs portfolio, was thus virtually an outsider in his own government. He owed his position to the fact that the party leaders did not trust each other sufficiently to agree on an oustanding political figure as prime minister, and to the expectation that his good reputation in the West (he had accommodated Poland's foreign policy to the Locarno system) would facilitate Poland's quest for loans and credits there. Known as the government of "national concord," this five-party coalition was a particularly inept one, composed as it was of parties with diametrically contradictory fiscal and economic theories in a situation of immediate and intense fiscal-economic crisis. The National Democrats had insisted on holding the ministries of Finance and Education, which were crucial for economic and ethnic-minority policy, as their price for entering the cabinet. The Socialists on the other hand were determined to force pump-priming and welfare spending on the government through their Ministry of Public Works and that of Labor and Welfare. Though the assignment of the War Ministry to one of his protégés had briefly purchased Piłsudski's toleration, this cabinet was wracked by too many internal contradictions to take a strong position on any controversial issue or to avoid eventual schism.

In March and April, 1926, the złoty currency broke. Many banks failed as deposits were withdrawn in panic. A third of the industrial labor force stood unemployed, and this did not include youths entering the labor market for the first time or the several million "superfluous" village poor. Demonstrations of unemployed and riots, with attendant loss of lives, took place in many towns. Calls for a dictatorship became ever more general and open, and even those who opposed this drastic remedy were demanding early constitutional revision so as to strengthen the president and give him effective power to dissolve the legislature.

The National Democratic finance minister insisted on a thoroughly deflationary policy toward the crisis. He severed the automatic correlation of wages to prices (the abolition of the cost-of-living bonus), dismissed 18,000-25,000 railroad workers, and sharply reduced (by about 35 percent) compensation payments to the sick, the disabled, and the aged. He also raised all taxes, except for those on real property, by 10 percent and instituted a head tax of five złoty per person. The price of gas, electricity, oil, salt, tobacco, matches, and alcohol was raised so as to render these state enterprises and monopolies economically viable.

The Socialists also wished to balance the budget but not at the shameless expense of workers, employees, and civil servants. They were caught in a double embarrassment. Initially they suggested cutting down expenditures by reducing police and army outlays but dropped the latter proposal at the request of their former comrade Piłsudski, whom many among them still considered one of their own. Initially, also, they had agreed to a three months' reduction in the cost-of-living bonus of state employees, but, embarrassed by the Communist pressure on their left and by the outraged response of those affected, they refused toward the end of March to extend this concession. Then they also demanded immediate massive investments in construction and industry so as to break the unemployment curve, as well as a heavy capital levy and a substantial increase in the real property tax. When the National Democrats refused to consider such a policy, the marshal (speaker) of the Sejm summoned an extraordinary conference of political leaders on April 18, 1926, which proved abortive. The discussion was more formal than genuine since each side had for days been warning that it would not retreat. Failing to force the substitution of their own fiscal-economic program for the Right's, the Socialists withdrew their ministers from the government on April 20.

The next day Skrzyński offered President Wojciechowski the resignation of his entire cabinet, but he was persuaded to delay this step until the budget estimates for May and June had been accepted by the Sejm and Senate in order to avoid a governmental vacuum at the critical time of the workers' May Day demonstrations. The Right and Center leaders, who had been negotiating with each other for a renewal of their coalition of 1923, urged Skrzyński to replace the departing Socialists with members of their own parties and to carry on the government on such a reconstructed basis. At that time, however, Skrzyński was convinced that Poland could not be governed against both Piłsudski and the Socialists. He therefore provisionally reassigned the Socialists' erstwhile portfolios on a nonparty and "acting" basis, and, with May Day as well as the national holiday of May 3 peacefully behind him and the May-June budget estimates passed, he then resigned on May 5, 1926, opening the parliamentary era's last and most severe cabinet crisis.

The Right and Center leaders chose to disregard the skepticism of Skrzyński and other reflective men concerning the feasibility of governing Poland against both Piłsudski and the Left, and to disregard also the fact that the legislature in which they commanded an arithmetic majority no longer mirrored the political mood of a public exasperated by chronic crises. Their formation of another Witos-led coalition cabinet on May 10, and their simultaneous intimations of a radical purge of their enemies out of the state apparatus, provoked Piłsudski's and the Left's violent riposte of May 12-14, 1926. By then Piłsudski believed that he had given the party system more than enough time to correct itself and that he could no longer be accused of a premature or unnecessary or merely self-serving grab for power.

9

In addition to this unhappy record of parliamentary degeneration, two other sets of problems—army organization and foreign policy—helped pave the path to Piłsudski's *coup d'etat*. He and his fellow ex-Legionnaires were constantly at odds with military veterans from the former Austro-Hungarian armies and with rightist politicians over the proper organization of the armed forces' high command and its appropriate relations with the government. Here Piłsudski's enemies insisted on the primacy of the war minister, who was answerable to the Sejm and thus represented the principle of civilian, constitutional control over the armed forces. Piłsudski, on the other hand, argued that since Polish cabinets were discouragingly unstable and the tenure of war ministers all too brief, the armed forces must be protected from partisan political influences through a command structure assuring the autonomy and superiority of the Inspector General, the officer designated to be commander in chief in the event of war. This arrangement was also dictated, he believed, by Poland's precarious geopolitical situation. Furthermore, Piłsudski's argument for the autonomy of the military command was rooted in his fear that restored Poland might neglect the military establishment the way the society and Sejms of the old commonwealth had during the century preceding the partitions.

The quarrel proved profoundly divisive and many responsible persons otherwise well disposed toward Piłsudski, including some of his Socialist admirers, were disturbed by his insistence on an organization of the military that appeared to them to confuse the necessary apoliticism of the army with its impermissible exemption from parliamentary accountability, and hence to be incompatible with the political and constitutional principles of democracy. On the other hand, the Right-Center's determination, signaled by Witos as he formed his last cabinet in May, 1926, to frustrate Piłsudski's return to active service and to purge his former Legionnaires out of the army clearly provoked the opposite results.

International developments during 1925 and 1926 starkly emphasized Poland's vulnerabilities and thus also facilitated Piłsudski's coup by undermining the prestige of the party-dominated parliamentary system. Warsaw's inability to raise substantial Western loans during the economic crisis of 1923-26 testified to Germany's success in weakening international confidence in Poland. The multilateral Locarno Treaties of October 16, 1925, which acknowledged Germany's insistence on a differentiation between the legal and political validity of her western borders and that of her eastern frontiers, were also a defeat for Poland. Not only did Locarno legitimate by implication, as it were, Germany's anti-Polish territorial revisionism, but it also exposed the unreliability of Poland's French ally, then striving for an independent understanding of her own with Germany, and it emphasized Britain's indifference to Poland's security interests vis-à-vis Germany. Moreover, Germany's rapprochement with France and Britain at Locarno did not prevent her continued cooperation with Russia to Poland's detriment. Indeed, half a year after Locarno, these two historic enemies of Poland reaffirmed their Rapallo rapprochement of April 16, 1922, with the Berlin Treaty of April 24, 1926. Though overtly only a nonaggression and neutrality agreement, this pact nevertheless appeared in fact to confirm Poland's isolation. It thus contributed to the general sense of political malaise in Poland, to the increasing suspicion of prevailing policies, personalities, and institutions as bankrupt, and hence to the widespread readiness that was born of hope and despair to look to Piłsudski for salvation.

10

Though Piłsudski won his *coup d'etat* after three days of street fighting in Warsaw between May 12 and 14, 1926, and thus achieved political control of the Polish state, the episode was a personal psychological disaster for him. He had anticipated that the entire army would rally to him, its creator and victorious former chief, and that this cohesion of the military would morally oblige the politicians to yield without fighting. Instead, the army had split between those units, usually commanded by his fellow Legion veterans, that followed him and those that, from political or legal motives, remained loyal to the constitutional Right-Center government. Piłsudski, in fact, owed his victory in large part to the refusal of the Socialist-affiliated railroad workers to transport troop reinforcements to Warsaw for his enemies—a political debt that chagrined him and that he never acknowledged. He was also helped by the judicious decision of the Witos government to yield after three days, even though it still held a number of strong military and political cards in the country at large, lest full-scale civil war invite German and/or Russian intervention or related insurrection by the ethnic minorities.[2] That he, the restorer of the Polish state, the father of its army, the protagonist of a strong presidency, should lead a revolt against the state authorities, sunder the unity of the army, and overthrow a constitutional president—for Wojciechowski refused to legitimate the coup by remaining in office—were facts that would haunt Piłsudski for the remaining nine years of his life. This was not merely a case of a remorseful personal conscience, but of a violated political model.

2. Joseph Rothschild, *Piłsudski's Coup d'Etat* (New York: Columbia University Press, 1966), chs. 4-8.

Piłsudski liked to see himself as the educator of the Polish people to civic virtue, away from the antistate attitudes inherited from the era of partition, and he now had set a pedagogically ominous example. Convinced that this regeneration of the nation required his own control, or at least supervision, of her state apparatus, he wanted categorical and ultimate power—but he had wanted it legally and consensually. The fact that his coup was bitterly contested had exposed as vain Piłsudski's hope to be accepted as a suprapolitical guardian of the national interest, as the olympian nemesis of all transgressors and malefactors. To the politicians of the Right and the Center and to their sympathizers in the officer corps, he remained a partisan, unacceptable figure, who might seize and hold power but could not harmonize the nation to a collective, cathartic effort at rededication.

This contradiction between his preferred self-image and his actual role accounts for the inconsistent cat-and-mouse game that Piłsudski was henceforth to play with the country's established constitutional, parliamentary, and political institutions. He permitted all of these institutions to survive and formally honored them, yet also sought to manipulate and eviscerate them. The result was a peculiar lockstep of intimidating, undermining, and cajoling the parliament and political parties that he had inherited and that he habitually blamed for the nation's ills. Piłsudski would not establish an overt dictatorship, yet he could not tolerate authentically autonomous loci of power. Thus his style came to require splintered parties, a submissive legislature, and an obedient president. Yet he remained pathetically aware of the contradiction between this campaign of emasculating the nation's institutions of government and his desire to educate that nation to political maturity. This awareness accounts for the tortured quality, the combined brutality and hesitancy, of Piłsudski's reluctant yet inevitable vendetta against parties, legislature, and constitution over the next years.

11

These contradictions in Piłsudski's perception of his proper role in Poland's political life quickly surfaced with his assumption of power. He began his nine years of hegemony by declining the presidency, now vacated by the upright and embittered Wojciechowski, and arranging for the election to that office of the electrochemist Professor Ignacy Mościcki, a choice intended to symbolize a new technocratic approach to Poland's problems in place of the allegedly obsolete, and slovenly partisan, political habits of the past. Simultaneously, he did not follow through with the universally expected new parliamentary elections, fearing a leftist victory at a time when there was as yet no organized Piłsudskist political party. He shrewdly permitted the 1922-27 legislature, with its now chastened Right and Center majority, which had analogous reasons to fear early elections, to live out its term, simultaneously extracting from it a series of constitutional amendments to strengthen the authority of the executive.

Piłsudski was capitalizing on a dual trend within a Polish society deeply riven by six years of economic and political turmoil: (a) the masses still viewed him as a man of the Left and hence looked to him for salvation, and (b) the vested interests needed him as an alternative to social revolution. Piłsudski's manifest unwillingness to be identified with any party's ideology, his vividly signaled preference for supposedly apolitical, technocratic approaches to the nation's problems, his early flattery of the surviving aristocracy as the alleged bearer of state-service traditions stemming from the golden age of the old commonwealth, his self-congratulation on the morrow of his coup for having made a political revolution without socially revolutionary consequences, but also his colorful denunciations of injustice and exploitation, were designed to satisfy all expectations, no matter how contradictory. These approaches also enabled him to keep a free hand for himself, and, most subtly, to isolate the National Democrats by peeling away their erstwhile, and somewhat reluctant, aristocratic and peasantist allies.

Assigning himself to the two offices of war minister and inspector general of the armed forces, Piłsudski identified his own considerable personal popularity with the genuinely revered army, regarded by the public not only as the nation's defence against rapacious neighbors, but also as a model of proper administration. The other cabinet portfolios, including the premiership, in the fourteen cabinets that held office during the nine years of Piłsudski's rule were rotated at his command, and the function of their ministers was to implement Piłsudski's intentions and to supply the technical expertise that he lacked in the nonmilitary fields. Until 1930, his favorite and frequent prime minister was the mathematician Professor Kazimierz Bartel, who gave his name to a style of government, the *bartlowanie*, characterized by tempered firmness and the avoidance of definitive deadlock in relations with the parties and the legislature. Thereafter, and coinciding with the sharpening of social tensions during the depression, a more self-consciously tough and truculently antiparliamentary "command" style was to emerge, with the rise to ministerial office of the so-called colonels. The "colonels" were Legion veterans whose sole political *raison d'être* was personal dedication to their old commander, Piłsudski.

The Piłsudski-Bartel style of government from 1926 to 1930 was not only intrinsically interesting, but also anticipated Gaullism. Bartel would argue and sincerely believe that his regime was by no means an aloof bureaucratic one and that the nation's social and political interests were adequately represented in it, in consultative roles. Cooperation among the "objective" technocratic experts in the government, the "independent" theoretical experts from the universities, and the "subjective" but informed and politically articulate interest groups was Bartel's idea of good government. He also acknowledged the ultimate veto power of the political forces in the form of the parliamentary censure vote. Let, however, the "subjective" political forces and parties claim direct policy-making and executive power, and Bartel would become indignant. The ministers were chosen for their technical expertise and as such enjoyed Bartel's and Piłsudski's confidence. Simultaneously, the "colonels" served as Piłsudski's personal eyes and ears throughout the state apparatus. Though not yet the ministers that they were to become in the 1930s, they were put in second-ranking yet crucial posts of the government departments and public agencies to supervise them politically for Piłsudski. In both its *bartlowanie* and its "colonel" incarnations, the Piłsudskist regime claimed to embody a *sanacja* (regenerative purge) against the debilitating former *partyjnictwo* (partisan corruption and chaos).

While sincere, this commitment to *sanacja* was more of a general stance, even a frame of mind, than a specific program. *Sanacja*, in fact, came to imply a buttressing of the Piłsudskist executive in relation to the multiparty legislature, a superordination of the Piłsudskist state over the allegedly politically immature society, purging that state's apparatus of its incompetent and/or inconvenient personnel, and the cultivation of a mystique of Piłsudski as the nation's heroic father, wise guide, and benevolent protector. Formally, *sanacja* implied three things. First, it suggested immunization of the army from political influences; this meant in practice the transformation of the army into Piłsudski's own instrument and a reflection of himself. Second, it suggested the healthy cleansing and professionalization of the state apparatus; this came to mean its infusion with a technocratic-managerial (and again antipolitical) stance. Third, there was the laudable but vague admonition, expressed by Piłsudski himself during the first night of his coup, that "there must not be too much injustice in the state toward those who labor for others, there must not be too much wickedness, lest the state perish"; this eventually came to mean the strategy of seeking to form an allegedly nonpolitical phalanx of all classes and parties supposedly prepared to elevate general state interests above particular partisan and social ones. (Piłsudski's traditional National Democratic enemies were presumed to be unequal to this test.) Piłsudski's resumption of power thus took the form of an uneasy yoking of excessively specific purposes to exceedingly general ones: on the one hand, the purging of the army and polity of certain undesired personnel; on the other hand, the regeneration of moral excellence in the service of the state. Though he would attempt to make a virtue of his and the new regime's freedom from ideological preconceptions, to the distress of his recent supporters on the Left, Piłsudski and Poland were to pay a heavy price for this absence of a clear, long-run, middle-range political program in the *sanacja*.

The strategy alluded to in the preceding paragraph, that of fashioning an allegedly nonpolitical, or rather suprapolitical, phalanx to assist the regime in supposedly elevating state interests above partisan ones, was Piłsudski's organizational anticipation of new parliamentary elections. Having committed himself after the coup to a major effort at exercising his power through legal, constitutional channels, Piłsudski had thereby accepted an obligation to put that power to an electoral test sometime after the expiration of the legislature's mandate in November, 1927. This challenge, in turn, made it necessary to weld his diversified following into a cohesive and disciplined camp in preparation for these elections. This camp, however, could not be like the other political parties. For one thing, no serious social and ideological agreement was possible among the post-coup Piłsudskists, who represented a great variety of political views. Hence, a vague, general program was essential for the new organization. On the one hand, this vagueness was a condition imposed by diversity. On the other, it could be turned into a lure to induce defections from the traditional parties. Yet another factor rendering a typical political party unfeasible was that Piłsudski's own political views, which were seconded and lent some theoretical refinement by Bartel's concept of proper administration of government, were by now passionately antipartisan and statist. His own political machine therefore had to be a kind of state-party, capable both of expressing his *sanacja* notions and of subsuming within itself the widest possible spectrum of old and new, genuine and self-styled Piłsudskists.

The party that came into being was given the awkward but candid name of the Nonpartisan Bloc for Cooperation with the Government, generally referred to by its Polish initials as the BBWR (Bezpartyjny Blok Współpracy z Rządem). The core of the BBWR consisted of Piłsudski's ex-Legionary paladins, who were intellectually reinforced and "modernized" by the sponsors and practitioners of the new cult of technocracy. To this inner core were assimilated converts from all the earlier political orientations in Poland—conservative, Socialist, peasantist, centrist, Catholic, even from the ethnic minorities—regardless of whether they came out of conviction, prudence, opportunism, anxiety, or resignation. This great variety of the BBWR's membership could be accommodated on only one common political ground: the appeal of strong executive government after a decade of confused parliamentary instability. Its apologists desperately tried to surround this perfectly obvious and quite respectable, if somewhat prosaic, fact with an aura of ideological profundity and historical necessity. They claimed, in the fashion of the day, that the BBWR represented the positive answer of national solidarity to the

Marxist challenge of class conflict, that it signified the healthy rejection by resurrected Poland of the fatal prepartition tradition that had elevated opposition per se into a virtue, and that it symbolized the victory of responsibility over demagoguery, of service to the state over the spirit of party. The fact was that in political practice the mission of the BBWR was simply to support Piłsudski. Precisely because this was its only intended function, and because its ideological poverty was otherwise so drastic and its ability to express social claims so deficient, the BBWR was able to split but not to replace the political parties, to win the adherence of office-seekers but not to attract the youth, to channel policy problems into the inner councils of the regime but not to articulate, refine, or adjudicate them in the course of its inevitably hollow and formal internal discussions.

At the apex of the regime, whither these problems were directed for solution, a statist-managerial theory of government held sway. Both the technocratically inclined supporters of Bartel and the inner core of Piłsudskist colonel-praetorians were convinced that Poland's problems were not solvable by ordering the interests and claims of the various sectors of her civil society through political parties competing in the public and parliamentary arenas. In their view, the immaturity of Polish society for such a performance had been too glaringly exposed during the first few years of her recovered independence. No, Poland's primary need was to emancipate the state from, and to elevate it above, civil society and to grant the state apparatus, rather than any part of the society, priority of claim and jurisdiction. Poland was to be purged, cleansed, and modernized through state direction, not political competition. She was to be administered, rather than governed. Interest of state, not of class or party, would alone determine the government's political, social, and economic policies.

Alas, this cult of the state was both intellectually and politically dubious. In practice, it was useless because it had no program and no direction. The concept of "interest of state" was, under certain circumstances, an adequate guide to foreign policy, but it was not sufficiently refined to be serviceable for the resolution of serious domestic socioeconomic policy problems. It might spotlight obvious national goals, such as industrialization, but could not indicate cost-free paths to their realization. Hard political choices still had to be made. Decision-making was simply transferred from the faction-ridden legislature to the inner councils of the regime. While one might acknowledge that the men who ultimately made the regime's policy decisions in these inner councils believed themselves to be ideologically neutral, while one could credit them with being motivated by a high sense of public service and duty to the state, while one could concede that the BBWR as an organization was probably too docile to impinge significantly on their evaluation of policy imperatives, it was futile to pretend that they were not making political choices among political options, that they were simply applying a manifest "interest of state."

Though the BBWR could win elections and thus enable Piłsudski to retain legal control of the state apparatus, it proved in a deeper sense a political failure due to Piłsudski's political misanthropy. On the morrow of the 1926 coup, he could have exploited the collective national catharsis to rally the Polish people around himself, activate them politically, elicit rededication, demand sacrifices, and accomplish much. But, distrusting the spontaneity of the masses, he chose to do the opposite. He imposed political passivity on the nation and reserved the responsibility of governing to himself, to the technocratic elite recruited by Bartel, and to his own immediate coterie of "colonels." The function of the BBWR was to insulate the regime from antagonistic social and ideological pulls and pressures, not to draw the nation into political activism. Though a number of "new" recruits were accepted and were promoted quite high up in the *sanacja* hierarchy, the regime managed tragically to isolate itself. Piłsudski and his entourage succeeded in asserting their monopoly over the state apparatus and its power structure, but they lost control and leadership over Polish society to the allegedly corrosive political parties.

The achievements of his regime, which were undeniable despite their immolation in the 1939 catastrophe, were a series of structural and diplomatic reclamations achieved within and by the state apparatus. Among them were: the postcoup constitutional amendments that strengthened the executive; the revival of military morale; the professionalization of the civil bureaucracy; the reintegration of all preponderantly Polish-populated areas, including the once disaffected western regions, into one political system; the balancing of budgets; and the raising of Poland's international prestige and self-confidence. But no fundamental social problem was solved or even seriously tackled in Piłsudski's lifetime.

Given his reluctance to take the nation into genuine confidence and political partnership, Piłsudski might have done better to establish an explicit dictatorship on the morrow of the coup rather than lead the country through a demoralizing pseudo-parliamentary charade. This dictatorship need not have been "leftist" to achieve some positive "revolutionary" corrections. However, such a solution was precluded both by Piłsudski's own scruples, fears, and hopes, and by a general national craving to demonstrate that the reborn Poland was, despite the coup, sufficiently mature to emulate successfully the Western model of constitutional parliamentary government. Hence, the coup fell between two stools. It was a potentially revolutionary action whose revolutionary potential was immediately denied and repressed by its instigator, abetted by the "responsible" political and economic interests.

12

This semiparliamentary style of government which Piłsudski launched on the morrow of his coup in 1926 was to prove a failure by 1930. The elections of March, 1928, whose politico-historical function was to proclaim the nation's judgment on Piłsudski's seizure and subsequent utilization of power as well as on the earlier period of legislative and party hegemony that had largely elicited his coup, gave Piłsudski an inconclusive victory. True, the BBWR and its satellites emerged as by far the largest constellation, but it failed to achieve an absolute legislative majority. Furthermore, to Piłsudski's intense irritation, the parties of the Left also gained by riding—illegitimately, in his view—on Piłsudski's coattails as a prewar Socialist. On the other hand, nemesis struck specifically the Right and Center parties of the Witos coalition, and not all the "old" parties across the entire pre-BBWR political spectrum, as Piłsudski had hoped. The results thus indicated considerably stronger public approval of the coup itself than of Piłsudski's subsequent efforts to restructure the pattern and style of Polish political life to his own mold. Moreover, in the context of the incipient mutual alienation of the Piłsudski camp and the parliamentary Left, the failure of either to win a clear and unequivocal majority was ominous, despite their parallel successes relative to the Right and the Center. The capacity of the Polish political system either to accommodate itself, or to offer effective resistance, to the Piłsudski experiment was thrown into doubt.

Heightening this uncertainty were the polymorphous nature and the disparate constituency of the Piłsudski camp. It indeed enjoyed some support in almost every sector of the society, but most of the workers, peasants, petite bourgeoisie, Roman Catholic clergy, and ethnic minorities had remained outside it. Would the backing of the conservative stratum, on the one hand, and of the technical intelligentsia, on the other (assuming, for the moment, their reliability), prove sufficient to compensate for the soft and spotty support of the intermediate social classes in a country finding itself in the socioeconomic transitional stage that characterized interwar Poland? In the context of Piłsudski's reluctance to institute an explicit dictatorship as the capstone to his coup, and his entourage's technocratic, managerial outlook, and given his decision, instead, to try to rule through and within the established constitutional and parliamentary machinery, the prospects for an affirmative answer to this question were rendered doubtful by the inconclusive outcome of the 1928 elections.

The statistical results are given in table 10. Turnout was 78.3 percent of eligible voters in the Sejm elections of March 4, and 63.9 percent in those for the Senate a week later, on March 11. This time the Ukrainians of eastern Galicia joined those of the former Russian Empire in participating. The disproportionate rise in invalid votes, many of which were

TABLE 10
PARLIAMENTARY ELECTIONS, MARCH, 1928

Party	Sejm, March 4, 1928			Senate, March 11, 1928		
	Number of Votes	Percentage of Total Vote	Seats	Number of Votes	Percentage of Total Vote	Seats
Right:						
National Democrat	929,266	8.2	37	589,905	9.2	9
Monarchist	53,623	0.5	...	4,661	0.1	...
Center:						
Christian Democrat }	910,707	8.0	19 }	493,399	7.7	5
Piast }			21 }			3
National Labor	228,162	2.0	14	143,806	2.3	3
Left:						
Wyzwolenie et al. }	1,675,538	14.7	40 }	717,512	11.2	7
Stronnictwo Chłopskie }			26 }			3
Socialist	1,495,641	13.1	65	714,956	11.2	10
Communist	266,528	2.3	7	101,781	1.6	...
Other Left	118,325	1.0	8	...	...	...
National Minorities:						
Joint list	2,130,678	18.7	65	1,337,098	20.9	23
Separate lists	802,060	7.0	19	290,653	4.6	1
BBWR et al.	2,739,301	24.0	122	1,987,325	31.1	46
Miscellaneous	58,389	0.5	1	9,435	0.1	1
Total	11,408,218	100.0	444	6,390,531	100.0	111
Invalid	320,142	...	...	116,931	...	...

intended for the Communists, over 1922 indicates the political "engagement" of the bureaucracy. This "engagement" did not yet amount to terror; nevertheless there was modest chicanery involved in the elections of 1928.

Though now reduced and isolated, Dmowski's National Democrats quickly consolidated their forces and strengthened their ideological militancy; they were destined to reemerge in the later 1930s as the Piłsudski camp's most dynamic ideological adversary. In the meantime, the National Democrats in this new legislature were soon joined in their current hostility to the Piłsudskist regime, albeit from different ideological perspectives, by centrist, leftist, and National Minority opposition. All objected to the regime's conservative socioeconomic policies, or to its cavalier contempt for legislative prerogatives, or to its occasional violations of civil legality. The Sejm majority could only frustrate the government, lacking as it did sufficient cohesion to replace it, and soon became locked in a futile struggle with Bartel.

This situation eventually provoked the exasperated Piłsudski into inaugurating the tougher "colonels" regime in September, 1930, which action was accompanied by the brutal beating and inhumane incarceration of a number of opposition leaders and the quite vigorous application of police pressure in the new elections of November, 1930. Though superficially these tactics of intimidation proved successful—the BBWR now received absolute parliamentary majorities—Piłsudski paid a heavy price for his recourse to atrocities that, unlike his coup four years earlier, were almost universally condemned as a gratuitous abuse of power, not a necessary or purgative seizure of it. Already rapidly losing the nationalistic youth to Dmowski's Right-Radical nostrums, Piłsudski had now repelled the influential intelligentsia of virtually all political hues, sacrificed the support of many of his prestigious conservative allies, driven an ultimate chasm between himself and his earlier Socialist and Left-peasantist partners, and even shaken the confidence of some of his immediate coworkers. Moreover, he was simultaneously destroying whatever credit he may still have possessed, thanks to his onetime sponsorship of federalism, with the Slavic minorities by seeking to break the Ukrainian nationalist movement through brutal military repression of the disaffected eastern districts between mid-September and the end of November, 1930.

Thus, the November, 1930, elections were a success only in terms of numbers for the regime. The turnout was 74.8 percent of those eligible in the balloting on November 16 for the Sejm, and 63.4 percent on November 23 for the Senate. A joint opposition list was run by five Center and Left parties, among whom the three peasant groups were soon to merge into the united Peasant Party on March 15, 1931 (see section 3). The results are shown in table 11.

TABLE 11

Parliamentary Elections, November, 1930

Party	Sejm, November 16, 1930			Senate, November 23, 1930		
	Number of Votes	Percentage of Total Vote	Seats	Number of Votes	Percentage of Total Vote	Seats
Right:						
National Democrat	1,443,165	12.7	63	882,215	13.0	12
Monarchist	1,816	....	....	....	....	....
Center:						
Christian Democrat	430,074	3.8	14	160,444	2.4	2
Piast			15			2
National Labor			10			3
Left:						
Wyzwolenie	1,965,864*	17.3	15	882,636*	13.0	4
Stronnictwo Chłopskie			18			..
Socialist			24			5
Communist	232,000	2.1	4			..
Communist "front"	23,000	0.2	1			..
National Minorities	1,719,445	15.1	33	1,045,119	15.4	7
BBWR et al.	5,366,821	47.4	247	3,725,783	54.8	76
Miscellaneous	151,610	1.4	....	100,991	1.4	....
Total	11,333,795	100.0	444	6,797,188	100.0	111
Invalid	482,618	....	....	unavailable		....

*Figures for individual parties are not available.

13

The depression was now to strike Poland with devastating rigor and superimpose additional socioeconomic problems upon her chronic political ones. In the economic realm, restored Poland had been seriously handicapped by the heritage of over a century's separation of her several regions and their diverse development, followed by the catastrophic devastation during World War I. Trade among the divided parts of Poland had been minimal before the recovery of independence; afterward their economic integration lagged behind their political and administrative integration and, indeed, was not really completed by 1939. Galicia and the *kresy* remained far poorer, less industrialized, and crippled by more primitive agricultural patterns than pertained in western Poland and the Kongresówka.

The first years of recovered independence had been economically darkened, as described earlier, by chronic dislocations, inflation, unemployment, and turmoil, which cumulatively undermined the then reigning parliamentary-party system and facilitated Piłsudski's bid for power. On the morrow of his coup, the Polish economy was suddenly blessed with a windfall. A lengthy British coal miners' strike from May to December, 1926, gave a massive and lasting spurt to Polish coal exports; this was sufficient to pull the entire industrial economy into a few years of prosperity. Agricultural prices and exports were also relatively high between 1926 and 1929. These favorable indicators, in turn, attracted foreign capital, enabling Poland to stablize her złoty and to outflank Germany's tariff war and credit boycott. The Piłsudski-Bartel regime was thus initially the political beneficiary of an economic revival flowing from a happy conjunction of international developments with its own technocratic, yet fiscally conservative, policies; the whole was lubricated by the general impression of strength and confidence that Piłsudski projected.

Alas, during the 1930s the Piłsudski-"colonel" regime faced dimmer economic vistas, which exposed the precarious and dependent quality of the preceding recovery. The currency had indeed been stabilized, but mass purchasing power remained deficient; the budgets had indeed been balanced, but at too low a level. With the onset of the world agricultural crisis at the turn of the decade, the international prices for Polish agricultural commodities fell so drastically, that any increases in their production and export were thereafter utterly swallowed up by the decline in their value. Misery and near-starvation now stalked the Polish countryside.

As an overwhelmingly agricultural country, Poland experienced the depression most painfully in that economic sector, which was plagued by acute overpopulation, underemployment, underconsumption, and inequality and fragmentation of land distribution. Admittedly even a radical land reform and redistribution could not have satisfied the land-hunger of the fecund peasant population in the absence of simultaneous and rapid industrialization. Yet even a moderate reform was inhibited by political considerations, which included an awareness that in the *kresy* and eastern Galicia land reform would benefit Belorussian and Ukrainian peasants at the expense of Polish landlords. In the end, Poland opted for a minimal reform that, next to Hungary's, was the least extensive of any in interwar East Europe. The maximum beyond which large owners were obligated to sell their excess land was generously set at 180 hectares (444.8 acres), except in the eastern regions where it was extended to 300 hectares (741.3 acres). Furthermore, estates "that were devoted to highly specialized or unusually productive agricultural enterprises of national importance"—a definition so vague as to be open to the most subjective interpretations—were exempt from this ceiling. Thus, it is hardly surprising that the total amount of land transferred during the entire interwar era from large estates to peasants—2,654,800 hectares—was but 20 percent of all land in holdings larger than fifty hectares, or 40 percent of all agricultural land in such holdings of over fifty hectares. If these calculations are augmented by the 595,300 hectares received by peasants in exchange for the surrender of usufructs, then the total land distribution to peasants still comes to only 23 percent of all the land and 54 percent of agricultural land in holdings larger than fifty hectares.

Peasants also benefited from the consolidation of 5,423,300 hectares of hitherto fragmented strips into unified farms; but this land had already been in peasant ownership, albeit irrationally organized. However, renewed parcelization through inheritance within the prolific peasantry negated the effects of such officially sponsored consolidations. Similarly, the 548,700 hectares that were realized for agriculture through drainage and other reclamations were not transferred out of large estates. Due to the minimalistic nature of the reform, the structure of land ownership remained highly inegalitarian.[3]

Contrary to conventional expectations, the productivity of large estates was not significantly greater than that of small plots since the latifundists had little incentive to replace cheap and plentiful peasant labor with modern agronomic technology. There was, however, great regional variation in productivity, with western and central Poland boasting substantially higher yields per hectare than the southern and eastern areas. Yet the national average remained considerably below that of Europe in general and even of Central Europe. Interwar Polish agriculture suffered

---

3. It would be possible, but awkward, to demonstrate the generalization statistically as the two censuses of 1921 and 1931 were not strictly comparable in this regard: the first registered all land by various size-categories, the second only agricultural land; the size-categories were also slightly altered from the one census to the other; finally, the second census was taken only in the middle, rather than at the close, of the interwar era. Cf. Mieczysław Mieszczankowski, *Struktura Agrarna Polski Międzywojennej* (Warsaw: PWN, 1960), chs. 1, 2, and 10.

from lack of capital, and was hampered by primitive market transportation, poor processing facilities, inadequate use of fertilizer (virtually none was used in the east), low technical competence on the peasant's part, and uneconomic but politically sustained distribution of ownership. But the most devastating hindrance was the lack of that external and essential *deus ex machina*: rapid industrialization to syphon off its surplus population. Estimates of the proportion of interwar Poland's agricultural population that was surplus even at the prevailingly low levels of agronomic technology vary from a fourth to a half,[4] but even the lower estimate indicates economic pathology.

More interesting, but also more difficult to evaluate, is interwar Poland's industrial performance. Here one begins with the observation that except for coal, timber, and the largely untapped water-power potential, she was rather poorly endowed in natural resources, especially metals. Furthermore, the industries with which she entered the interwar era were (a) geared to what were now, after 1918, unfriendly foreign markets in Russia and Germany, and (b) heavily destroyed and looted between 1914 and 1918. They required not only extensive physical reconstruction, but also commercial reintegration into either the internal Polish market, which was weak, or new and different foreign markets, which tended to close themselves off, especially in the general world flight into autarky during the depression.

It would be possible but superfluous to illustrate statistically the painful blows inflicted on the Polish economy by the depression. Foreign capital was withdrawn, production declined, unemployment soared, and the peasant's purchasing-power vanished. Poland's recovery from the depression was initially slowed by Piłsudski's cleaving—from mixed motives of state-prestige, fear of repeating the politically fatal inflationary trauma of 1923-26, and simple economic philistinism—to the gold standard long after other countries had abandoned it. This unfortunate monetary policy imposed an unnecessarily prolonged stagnation of production upon the Polish economy.

After Piłsudski's death, however, the administrative technocrats whom Bartel had earlier recruited were joined by economic technocrats whom the "colonels" now sponsored. Etatism replaced orthodoxy as the economic ideology of the regime, vast investments for "social overhead" and direct production were sunk into state-owned enterprises, and industrialization proceeded apace in the last three interwar years before the Nazi assault and occupation interrupted these promising developments. The experience of this abbreviated period of state capitalism in the late 1930s served as a useful exercise from which helpful experience was ac-

4. Cf. P. N. Rosenstein-Rodan, "Agricultural Surplus Population in Eastern and South Eastern Europe," summarized by N. Spulber, *The Economics of Communist Eastern Europe* (Cambridge, Mass.: MIT Press, 1957), p. 276, versus Wilbert E. Moore, *Economic Demography of Eastern and Southern Europe* (Geneva: League of Nations, 1945), p. 64.

cumulated for the rapid industrialization of the post-1945 era.

While impressive, this belated spurt of industrialization was running a hare-and-tortoise race against the older, remorseless, population growth. The employment opportunities it opened up scarcely made a dent in the vast army of rural paupers. It came too late to stem an erosion of living standards over the span of the decade as a whole—and Polish living standards were already among the lowest in Europe to begin with. Finally, despite the patriotic and nationalistic rhetoric with which it was promoted, it failed to rescue the post-Piłsudski "colonels" from their political isolation.

14

This political isolation of the regime deepened throughout the 1930s. The flawed—because "pressured"—elections of 1930 had given the BBWR a legislative majority adequate to pass the *sanacja* camp's ordinary legislation, but not the two-thirds majority required to amend the constitution. Such amendments to strengthen the executive still further were deemed essential by Piłsudski, who regarded the more modest postcoup revisions of August, 1926, as inadequate. Declining to decree a new constitution by fiat—he always showed greater respect for the letter than the spirit of legality—Piłsudski had his paladins maneuver a new constitution through the legislature by utilizing an extended series of parliamentary tricks and formal casuistries. This exercise in sharp practices was politically and morally at least as demoralizing as straightforward dictation would have been.

Coming into formal effect on April 23, 1935, the new constitution provided for a massive extension of presidential powers, including the suspensive veto, the dissolution of the legislature, the dismissal of the cabinet and of individual ministers, the authority to issue ordinances with the force of law, the appointment of a third of the senators, and the nomination of one of two possible candidates to succeed the incumbent president in peacetime and the direct appointment of his own successor in wartime. Not unsuited to the Poland of that day, it was to become a partial model for Gaullist France's charter of 1958. Piłsudski's new constitution was immediately devitalized by his death on May 12, 1935, and by his "colonel"-heirs' supplementing it with electoral ordinances of July 8 that were blatantly designed to ensure that the regime would always win, thus humiliating the electorate. It was one of the many ironies of interwar Poland's history that both its constitutions were drafted with Piłsudski specifically in mind: that of 1921 to cripple the presidency which the Right feared he would occupy; that of 1935 to extend this office to suit his style and authority. In each case the drafters miscalculated: in the first, he declined to serve; in the second, he died, and this legacy was transmitted to inadequate heirs.

In protest against the manifest intent of the new electoral regulations to produce a rubber-stamp legislature through a transparently rigged system of screening and selecting candidates, the Polish opposition parties boycotted the elections of September 8 and 15, 1935. Even the government's own publications conceded that only 45.9 and 62.4 percent respectively of the eligible Sejm and Senate electorates had participated in this "plebiscite of silence," and the opposition claimed that these official figures were exaggerated. Interestingly, the turnout was higher in the *kresy* and in Silesia, i.e., in the areas of Belorussian, Ukrainian, and German population concentration, than in the country as a whole. Perhaps these ethnic minorities were indifferent to an internal Polish quarrel among antagonists who were by now almost equally unfriendly to the minorities' interests; perhaps they were more vulnerable to official intimidation or seduction. In any event, the Germans, Jews, and Ukrainians (but not the Belorussians) appear to have made quiet arrangements with the regime to assure themselves at least some representation. The new legislature was nevertheless totally dominated by the BBWR, which furnished 153 of the statutory 208 Sejm deputies under the new constitution, and 45 of the 64 elected Senators. The latter were elected indirectly by a narrowly limited group of supposedly distinguished citizens (holders of advanced degrees, of certain decorations, of local office, and of important positions in officially recognized professional, economic, and cultural organizations) under the recent electoral ordinances. Thanks, presumably, to previous arrangements, the ethnic minorities then received presidential appointments to a few of the 32 remaining Senate seats as a minimal redress of their electoral underrepresentation and as a reward for their participation.

That the regime's intention had been to destroy the political parties and produce a nonpolitical parliament was confirmed when its own BBWR was dissolved on October 30, 1935, avowedly to demonstrate that henceforth there was no longer any need for "an organization of a political character intervening between the legislature and the country." The naiveté of this attitude was soon exposed, as the locus of political struggle simply moved out of the halls of parliament into the streets and villages —to the regime's thorough disadvantage—and as the *sanacja* camp, deluded by its formally consolidated grip on the state apparatus, henceforth indulged in the luxury of internal quarrels, which Piłsudski's authority had hitherto prevented.

The first of these two developments, the shift in the locus of political conflict, was an aspect and a consequence of a general radicalization within all political camps. This radicalization, in turn, was in part a response to the depression and specifically to the regime's initially slow and helpless reaction to the depression, in part an expression of increasing interethnic tensions, and in part a repudiation by the peasantry and proletariat of the hitherto unchallenged hegemony of the intelligentsia.

Openly fascistic trends came to the fore within the rightist camp led by the National Democrats; peasants engaged in desperate food-delivery strikes against the cities and forced the hitherto moderate political leadership of their centrist movement to move sharply leftward; the underground Communists made gains among indigent peasants, unemployed workers, the younger intelligentsia, and the Belorussians; to avoid being outflanked, the Socialists sponsored a series of massive strikes; as for the ethnic minorities, Ukrainian extremists resorted to assassinations, the bulk of the Germans turned Nazi, and ever more Jews opted for Zionism; finally, the regime itself became more radical in both its economic (étatist) and its political responses. Radicalization was truly universal, but all camps, including those of the opposition, remained mutually divided. Indeed, their very radicalization widened the gaps among them.

Piłsudski's heirs were split as to the proper course and content of the more radical policies that they agreed were needed. Distressed by the isolation of their state apparatus from the nation's most energetic social forces, they quarreled over the correct direction in which to steer in order to close this gap. The virtually byzantine intricacy of their internal divisions and maneuvers over this crucial and charged issue can be simplified—hopefully without distortion—by dividing their camp into three lobbies. The first was the generally older generation of Piłsudski's original comrades from the prewar underground struggles against Tsarist Russia, who recommended a reconciliation with the Socialist movement of which Piłsudski had been a founder and early leader at the turn of the century. The second was a more daring coterie who pushed for a swing toward the Right in order to tap for the regime the impressive energies of the by-now partly fascistic Polish youth; in other words, to trump the National Democrats by adopting their ideology and constituency. The third was the technocrats and protagonists of an "organized economy" who believed that sheer physical modernization would prove both necessary and sufficient to solve the country's and the regime's problems. These three lobbies were led, respectively, by Piłsudski's closest personal friend, Colonel Walery Sławek, by Colonel Adam Koc, and by President Ignacy Mościcki. The chief of the armed forces, Marshal Edward Rydz-Śmigły, oscillated between the second and the third, finally opting for the latter. By the outbreak of World War II this third group had blocked the first two but had not yet achieved its own conclusive victory. In retrospect, one doubts whether its sheer technocratic gambit could have succeeded without an accompanying dynamic political ideology of leftist or rightist variety: rapid industrialization always entails social mobilization.

Thus, by the late 1930s, the strategy of isolation with which Piłsudski had hoped politically to cripple the Right on the morrow of his coup had been turned against his own camp. Piłsudski's personal charisma and authority had obscured this trend during his own lifetime, but now his epigoni were left stranded by the *sanacja*'s ideological poverty and lack of social bases. Hence, at the end they were reduced to the "blackmail of patriotism," to trying to smother the opposition parties' boycott by transforming the last parliamentary elections of November 6 and 13, 1938, into a plebiscite of endorsement of the recent annexation of the Cieszyn region from Czechoslovakia (see Chapter 3, section 11). As a result of this demagogic appeal to national pride, 67.1 percent and 70.0 percent, respectively, of the Sejm and Senate electorates voted. This time the regime's lists took 166 of the 208 Sejm seats and almost all the 64 elective Senate positions, and it also used the occasion to purge out of the legislature those of its own cadre who wished a reconciliation with the Left. That these results did not truly reflect public opinion was exposed by the stunning successes of the Socialists and the Right in the subsequent municipal-council elections of December 18, 1938. In short, as interwar Poland entered its last year, the regime's "ownership" of the state was counterbalanced, and indeed outweighed, by the various opposition parties' ideological saturation of the society and their political leadership of its classes.

With the sharpening of the German danger in 1939, the government undertook conciliatory gestures toward its domestic foes. Its awareness of the strength of public feeling undoubtedly influenced its stubborn resistance to Hilter's pressure. *Per contra*, the challenge of the semifascist Right, which was the most dynamic of the opposition parties, was handicapped by the fact that the regime was already nationalistic, militaristic, and authoritarian. But it was not totalitarian. Though badgered, the opposition parties operated legally, except for the Communists who were obliged to resort to the subterfuge of "fronts"; though harassed, the trade unions and press remained independent and active; outspoken enemies of the regime continued to teach at the universities and to publish their criticisms; the autonomy of the judiciary from the administration was preserved; and the administration, while rigid, was technically competent. Interwar Poland's faults and weaknesses were many, and serious: the imprudent imbalance between frontiers and institutions, the alienation of the ethnic minorities, rural overpopulation and industrial backwardness, the political decline from the original semidemocracy to Piłsudski's semidictatorship and then to his heirs' spasmodic authoritarianism. But in no way did they justify her neighbors' decision to inflict a fifth partition on her in September, 1939. With their heroic resistance in that campaign and under the next years of occupation, the Polish people demonstrated that they had overcome the most demoralizing error of the old commonwealth in its last century of decadence: the lack of a readiness to make personal or partisan sacrifices for the sake of the nation as a whole. In World War II Poland, in again fighting for her own freedom, was again fighting for Europe's.

Chapter Three

CZECHOSLOVAKIA

1

THE medieval Kingdom of Bohemia, the ancestral core of modern Czechoslovakia, had developed into a unified state at a time when not only Germany and Italy but even France and Spain were still disunited and internally fragmented. Geographical factors, which were both advantageous and disadvantageous, contributed to this early and perhaps premature development of an explicitly articulated Bohemian political entity. A string of mountains (the Sudeten, Giant, Ore, and Bohemian ranges) provided natural frontiers and at the same time landlocked the country. Ethnic geography, in turn, rendered Bohemia the westernmost Slavic salient amidst surrounding Germans.[1] Reinforcing such geographical contributions to the formation of Bohemian statehood and Bohemian consciousness were certain historical experiences, of which the most enduring were the fifteenth-century Hussite Wars and their repercussions. As interpreted by subsequent generations of national intellectual leaders, these induced in the Czechs the self-image of a small but stubborn nation that taught all Europe the virtues of religious freedom, moral integrity, and social equality and was capable of martial valor but preferred leaders of intellectual and ethical, rather than of military or political, distinction. Be that as it may, the Hussite Wars also, alas, overstrained medieval Bohemia and isolated her within Europe, thus contributing to her eventual defeat and absorption into the empire of the Habsburgs. This process was completed with the exceedingly destructive Thirty Years' War of 1618-48.

---

1. Propagandists of its Sudeten German minority, on the other hand, have argued that Bohemia is politically and historically as much a German land as any other part of the former Holy Roman Empire, within which it is the Czechs who were a small, tolerated minority. When used here in reference to pre-1918 history, the term "Bohemia" is intended to connote the historic provinces of the Bohemian Crown: Bohemia proper, Moravia, and Silesia (specifically southern Silesia after the wars of 1740-63). Relative to post-1918 development, it will be used to refer only to the first-named, westernmost province of modern Czechoslovakia.

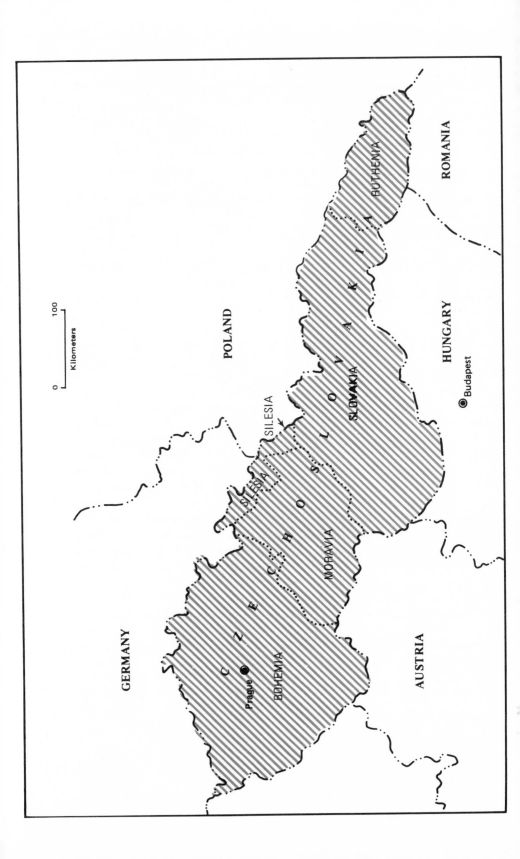

Within this Habsburg Empire, Bohemia occupied an anomalous position: it was economically the most valuable, but politically the most suspect of its rulers' possessions. Precisely because its people were relatively recalcitrant and of dubious loyalty—they failed, for example, to resist the Prussian-French-Bavarian invasion of 1741—Bohemia's economic exploitation by the dynasty could the more easily be justified. Yet, with the development of modern nationalist ideologies in the nineteenth century, the Habsburg regimes veered to the quite different, but still plausible, assumption that Czech nationalism—precisely because it was not affected by any "brother" states outside the imperial frontiers—was less dangerous to the empire's integrity and security than, say, German, Italian, Romanian, or South Slav nationalism. Furthermore, Bohemia was central and vital, rather than peripheral and expendable, from the perspective of the imperial government, and the economic resources in the hands of its Czech population were second only to those of the Habsburgs' German subjects by the second half of the nineteenth century. Therefore, the central authorities in Vienna now intermittently found themselves taking a relatively tolerant view of Czech aspirations. For this they were denounced by their German subjects, particularly by the Sudeten Germans who lived along the interior rim of Bohemia and whose own nationalism had meanwhile grown to such a virulent racist intensity that its primary loyalty was more to the Pan-German Volk than to the Habsburg dynasty.[2]

During the half-century between the Ausgleich of 1867 and the eruption of World War I in 1914, the Austrian imperial government became something of an umpire between its German and Czech subjects, and the status of the latter was rather different from the supposed repression and deprivation that Masaryk and Beneš were later to allege to the West. Indeed, in the first part of the war, the Czechs did their duty, albeit with less fervor than their German fellow citizens. Also, as (unintended) schools of political and administrative preparation for subsequent independent statehood, the Vienna Reichsrat and the imperial civil service provided invaluable experience for the Czechs in the last decades before 1914.

The Bohemian nobility had been decimated and eventually destroyed during the two centuries of chronic foreign and domestic war between the burning of Jan Hus (1415) and the battle of White Mountain (1620).

2. The term "Sudeten Germans," popularized by the Nazis, appears to have been first used in 1902 in the pages of the Prague weekly *Deutscher Volksbote* by deputy Franz Jesser. Although the Sudeten Mountains proper cover only a fraction of the part of Bohemia once populated by Germans (the northeastern sector), this term eventually became the conventional reference to all Germans in interwar Bohemia and Moravia-Silesia; and since 1945 it has been used as well for those formerly settled in Slovakia and Ruthenia, who until then had carried the separate appellation of *Karpatendeutsche*. The beginnings of the German settlements in Bohemia date back to the High Middle Ages, when Germans came as miners and burghers. Their colonization was greatly expanded after Bohemia's absorption into the Habsburg realms.

Czech nationalism and the Czechoslovak state were reborn in the nineteenth and twentieth centuries as the offspring of the bourgeoisie and intelligentsia, which, in turn, had emerged from the ever-resilient Czech peasantry in the process of Bohemia's substantial industrialization. Thus, the modern Czech political style—in contrast, for example, to those of the Hungarian and Polish "gentry nations"—came to be characterized by bourgeois rather than by aristocratic traits: practicality and rationality, instead of audacity and romanticism. And the existence of a disciplined proletariat and an organized peasantry side by side with the experienced bourgeoisie made for a more balanced society and a more integrated polity than existed among these neighbors.

2

The territorial consolidation of Czechoslovakia and the delimitation of its frontiers, which included provinces and regions of disparate historical, cultural, and economic development, were the products of extremely intricate diplomatic maneuvers. Despite the vigorous development of their nationalism during the half-century before the outbreak of World War I, the Czechs by-and-large did not entertain the concept of a fully independent Czech state, let alone a Czechoslovak state, in 1914. Fearing that a disintegration of Austria-Hungary would only result in their own incorporation into a Greater Germany, the Czechs' aspirations were initially directed toward a federalistic reform of the empire, entailing a substantial degree of autonomy for themselves. Hence their political activities within the Habsburg Empire had a different cutting edge than, say, those of the Piłsudskist Poles in the Russian Empire. Yet all this was to change precipitously during the World War; by its end the Czechs not only had an Allied commitment to an independent state of their own, but, through a combination of skillful diplomacy and luck, they had managed to emerge from the subsequent Paris Peace Conference with virtually all their serious territorial claims realized. Their state included not only the historic Czech lands of Bohemia and Moravia intact, but also the Slovak and Ruthenian territories of historic Hungary, which had not been part of the old Bohemian kingdom, as well as the most valuable part of the Duchy of Těšín (Cieszyn, Teschen) Silesia. The duchy, though indeed formerly under the medieval Bohemian crown, was by the twentieth century predominantly Polish in ethnicity.

This was a remarkable achievement, and credit for it goes to a small, and initially scarcely representative, trio of Czech and Slovak exiles: T. G. Masaryk, Edvard Beneš, and Milan Štefánik. These men succeeded during the war in persuading the leaders of the Allied Powers that the replacement of Austria-Hungary by a series of independent national states was not only inevitable but also desirable from the Allied and general European perspectives. Only during the last year or two of the war did Czech public opinion at home, which was finally exasperated by deprivation, weariness, governmental chicaneries, and the growing suspicion that the war aims of the Central Powers were inimical to even the more moderate national aspirations of the Slavic peoples of East Central Europe, come to appreciate and to endorse the radical independence-oriented activities of Masaryk and his group in the West. Yet, as late as the last week of October, 1918, when imperial authority had indeed disintegrated, a group of leading Czech politicians traveling from Prague to consult with the exile leaders in Geneva interrupted their journey at Vienna for consultations with the now powerless Habsburg officials. In so doing they symbolized the tenacity of this traditional pull upon the Czech political consciousness.

The very fact, however, that the impressive Czech success scored at the peace conference was largely a function of the exile group's persuasiveness and energy in the chancelleries and corridors of the major Allied governments, saddled the new Czechoslovakia's political leaders, and in particular Beneš, with a heavy psychological mortgage that left them ever afterward with an exaggerated sense of dependence on the West and inadequate confidence in the nation's own resources. Though by war's end there were three infantry divisions and one cavalry brigade of Czech and Slovak Legionnaires in Russia, two infantry divisions in Italy, and one in France, which were formed largely of one-time Austro-Hungarian prisoners and deserters, and though the Legions in Russia were to become a potential (but not seriously played) Allied trump during the subsequent Russian civil war, which strengthened Czech bargaining power in the capitals of the Allies, nevertheless the strictly military contribution of these Czech and Slovak units to the Allied defeat of the Central Powers had not been of such an order or such an intensity as to shake Beneš' conviction, born of his own diplomatic experiences during and immediately after the war, that ultimately Czechoslovakia's fate and salvation rested less with her own forces than with her powerful patrons. (Even against Béla Kun's improvised and ramshackle Hungarian Communist army in 1919, Czechoslovakia called Allied units to her rescue.) This dependent stance of the new state's political elite entailed both irony and tragedy, for there is good reason to suppose that twenty years later, at the time of the Munich surrender, the worth of Czechoslovakia's armed forces was greater than her political leaders' confidence in them, and the nation's readiness for self-reliance greater than the government's willingness to test it.

In yet another sense the very success of the Czechs at the peace conference in gaining virtually all their territorial demands was to tempt nemesis against their new state. A large and truculent German minority along the strategic northern, western, and southern border regions could potentially call on the assistance of the powerful German Reich against the policy and eventually even the integrity of the Czechoslovak state. Poland and Hungary were tacit allies in coveting substantial and valuable Czechoslovak territories. Of the great and small powers on whose friendship Masaryk and Beneš had counted, the United States soon withdrew into isolation, and the United Kingdom into indifference; and even France occasionally speculated about boundary-revision in favor of Czechoslovakia's direct enemies. Though they were helpful in containing Hungary, neither Yugoslavia nor Romania were prepared or able to pull Czechoslovak chestnuts out of any German fires. All in all, Czechoslovakia was born a territorially satisfied but politically rather isolated state, and desperately isolated she was destined to be again two decades later at the time of the Munich crisis when all her neighbors except Romania, with whom she shared her shortest border, lodged irredentist demands against Czechoslovakia. Her diplomatic situation—but not her military response to it—was reminiscent of Hussite Bohemia's at the end of the Middle Ages.

The Czechoslovak claims as presented to the Allied Powers at Paris in 1919 had rested upon two radically different, indeed mutually incompatible, principles: (a) historic frontiers as against Sudeten German and Polish nationalism in Bohemia, Moravia, and Czech Silesia; and (b) nationality as against Hungary's historic frontiers in Slovakia and Ruthenia. Not only did this contradiction corrode the logic of the Czechs' case, but their moral credit was damaged by their apparent truculence against the Poles in Těšín in January, 1919. Their political plausibility was further undermined by their unimpressive military performance against Béla Kun's Hungarian troops in Slovakia in May and June of that year. Aggressiveness plus weakness are ever a dubious combination. Furthermore, in the summer of 1919 the peace conference at Paris was made aware by the turbulent Slovak leader Father Andrej Hlinka that relations between Czechs and Slovaks—the "state-nation" of the new republic—were by no means as cordial as hitherto claimed by the Czech spokesmen. Thus, although the Allied leaders did proceed to grant and confirm the various Czech demands, one senses that at the very moment of doing so they were already skeptical of the long-run viability of these new territorial arrangements.

It was in defense of the historic Bohemian-Moravian boundaries that the Czechs had first to assert themselves against a Sudeten German movement for secession and subsequent affiliation to Austria and/or Greater Germany. Approximately three-and-a-quarter million Germans, the largest such Volksdeutsche community in any non-German state, had been settled for centuries in a circular belt of mountainous territories inside the rim of these frontiers and were intensely conscious of the fact that formerly they had been the dominant state-nation. They now insisted, virtually unanimously across their entire political spectrum, that the Wilsonian principle of self-determination of peoples be applied and that they be allowed to opt out of the new Czechoslovakia. On October 29, 1918, the day after the declaration of the independent Czechoslovak Republic, the Bohemian-German deputies of the old imperial Reichsrat in Vienna proclaimed "Deutschböhmen" as a province of Austria, and the next day their Moravian and Silesian compatriots likewise proclaimed their "Sudetenland" an Austrian province. Provisional governments of these two would-be provinces were established respectively in Liberec (Reichenberg) and Opava (Troppau), and repeated appeals for endorsement were sent to President Wilson. In review of the fact that the western and northern districts of these self-proclaimed provinces adjoined the German Reich (Bavaria, Saxony, Prussian Silesia) rather than Austria, from which they were separated by the broad Czech heartland, it appears that the long-run assumption behind these proclamations was Austria's own early incorporation into Greater Germany. This assumption was shared by the new Austrian National Provisional Assembly when it both accepted the adhesion of these Bohemian-Moravian Germans and on November 12 declared Austria "a constitutent part of the German Republic." Vienna thus had the will but lacked the power to help the Sudeten Germans avoid incorporation into Czechoslovakia.

For the German government itself, on the other hand, the fate of the Sudeten Germans, who had not belonged to the Bismarckian-Wilhelminian empire, had at this moment of defeat and revolution a relatively low priority. Hence, it gave them no serious support when Czech Legion troops, newly returned home from France and Italy, proceeded to occupy the German-populated areas and thus reassert the territorial integrity of the historic Bohemian lands during the next weeks. The provincial capitals of "Deutschböhmen" and "Sudetenland" fell to the Czechs on December 16 and 18, respectively, and all remaining localities by Christmas. The absence at this time of military resistance by the local Germans to this Czech occupation was a function not only of weakness but also of confidence that the Allied Powers at the peace conference would order plebiscites whose results would prove decisive. Three months later, when it was clear that such expectations were erroneous, the local Germans belatedly staged massive protest demonstrations, with scattered marches on gendarmerie barracks, on March 4, 1919, the day of the opening of the new Austrian National Assembly in whose election they had not been allowed to participate by the triumphant Czech authorities. In the course of dispersing them, fifty-two Germans were killed and eighty-four wounded by the Czech gendarmes and troops.

For the Czechs, the principle of the integrity of the historic Bohemian-Moravian frontiers was not negotiable. They refused to acknowledge the self-declared German provincial governments within these frontiers. Echoing the celebrated words of Prince Windischgrätz to the

Hungarians in 1848, the Czech minister Alois Rašín now curtly informed the deputy chief of the "Deutschböhmen" movement, Josef Seliger, that "I don't negotiate with rebels." On December 22, 1918, two days after his return to the country from his wartime endeavors in the West and in Russia and one day after his installation as Czechoslovakia's first president, Masaryk, in a solemn address to the National Assembly at the ancient Prague Hradčany (Royal Castle), insisted that the German-populated areas would, come what may, remain in the new state. Inviting the Germans to recognize this inevitable fact and to help build the new state, Masaryk reminded them of their one-time status as "immigrants and colonists." Though historically valid, this expression, which was uttered rather vehemently, was scarcely the most tactful one to use when discussing the Germans' political rights within the new democratic republic, and Masaryk sought to soften it by visiting the Prague German Theater the next day where he spoke soothingly of full equality for all nationalities in Czechoslovakia.

At Paris, meanwhile, concerned lest the German demands for self-determination make a positive impression on the peace conference in general and on the American delegation in particular, the new Czechoslovakia's foreign minister, Beneš, was promising that it was his government's intention "to make of the Czecho-Slovak Republic a sort of Switzerland, taking into consideration, of course, the special conditions of Bohemia."[3] He thereby, alas, gave later German propagandists, who habitually cited only the first clause of this statement, ammunition with which they would attempt to shame Czechoslovakia before the world when Hitler launched his pre-Munich propaganda offensive against her in the 1930s. At Paris in 1919 Beneš had also argued that a strong Czechoslovakia within her historic western borders not only would be an element of stability in the midst of anarchy, but also would simultaneously serve as a bulwark against both the Bolshevik tide rolling in from the east and the German *Drang* toward the east—the historic borders being happily also strategically strong and economically rational ones. The American delegation was initially unimpressed, the British reserved; the French, however, were at that time enthusiastic, and as they were the best organized and most purposeful of the Great Power delegations, they carried the day for Beneš and the Czechs.

To appreciate fully how their current discomfiture and impotence struck the Sudeten Germans, how allusions to them as "colonists," "immigrants," "rebels" enraged them, one must bear in mind that they were traditionally the most Pan-Germanist of all the Germans of the Habsburg Empire, far surpassing in nationalistic intensity, for example, those of the

---

3. Note of May 20, 1919, as republished in Elisabeth Wiskemann, *Czechs and Germans: A Study of the Struggle in the Historic Provinces of Bohemia and Moravia* (London: Oxford University Press, 1938), pp. 92-93.

Austrian Alpine provinces proper. They regarded themselves as historically conditioned and destined to rule over the inferior Czechs in Bohemia, to control the imperial government in Vienna, and, in alliance with the Reich Germans to the north, to organize all Central Europe against the West and the Slavs. During the Great War they had expended their blood and their treasure with desperate abandon in the cause of Germandom, sustaining casualties that were proportionately greater than those of any other group in the Habsburg Empire, and indeed, in the German Empire as well.[4] Now, overnight, their dream was shattered, and their first response was an instinctive refusal to live as a minority in a land where they had once held a privileged status. Sudeten German Social Democrats were, if anything, initially even more vehement in their insistence on seceding into a Greater Germany than were the bourgeois nationalists, for to them this option bore the further ideological legitimacy of the Marxist radical German democratic vision of 1848. As late as June, 1919, the Social Democrats called a general strike in protest against the Treaty of St. Germain which officially and definitively confirmed the Sudeten lands to Czechoslovakia.

As time passed, the Germans reluctantly took stock of the new situation. Always politically energetic and shrewd, they now insisted that, the bulk of their territories having been assigned to Czechoslovakia, any partial arrangements that would lower their numbers and lessen their political weight within this state (for example, the rumored cession by Czechoslovakia of the extreme western Egerland district to Germany or other minor border rectifications) were not permissible. They now recalled that, long before they had become Pan-Germans, they had been "Böhmer"—provincial German patriots characterized by a particularly tenacious and parochial sense of identity with their land and with each other.[5] Finally, their economic elite sobered and bethought itself of the unwelcome consequences should it have to compete with the German Reich's industry in a Greater German market unprotected by Bohemian tariffs. Furthermore, as a "victor" state, Czechoslovakia, in contrast to Germany and Austria, escaped heavy reparations obligations. More dramatically, the Sudeten German elite could draw an instructive contrast in the spring and summer of 1919 between the reassuringly bourgeois government of Prague and the alarmingly "red" ones of Vienna, Munich, and Berlin. This comparison lost nothing in vividness with the great in-

4. The ratios were: Sudeten Germans killed in battle, 34.5/1000 of population; Austrian average killed in battle, 27.7/1000 of population; Reich Germans killed in battle, 27.8/1000 of population. Quoted in S. Harrison Thomson, "The Germans in Bohemia from Maria Theresa to 1918," *Journal of Central European Affairs* 2 (July, 1942): 178.
5. There was no exact equivalent to this autonomous "Böhmisch" self-identification among, say, the Germans of historically Polish Poznania or Pomerania. The reader should note that neither the Pan-German nor the Bohemian ideology was necessarily loyal to the Habsburgs.

flation and political turmoil of 1923 in Germany and Austria. The Sudeten Germans now decided to bide their time, meanwhile fighting tenaciously for their rights, privileges, and powers within a Czechoslovakia whose western half had been restored to its historic frontiers.

When it came to delimiting the borders of the eastern half of the new state, the provinces of Slovakia and Ruthenia, the arguments were reversed: history and economic factors were the weapons of the Hungarians, and it was the Czechs who now turned to the theory of national self-determination. Another difference is that the Hungarians were initially willing and able to offer much more serious military resistance to the Czechs than were the Germans and Austrians.

Among the Slovaks, the Protestant minority (16 percent) had traditionally felt close to the Czechs, and its fraternal sentiments had been reinforced since the end of the nineteenth century by the influence of Masaryk's western-oriented, as contrasted to Pan-Slavic, Czecho-Slovak ideology, whose main Slovak organ was the revue *Hlas* (Voice). The first serious Czech political claims to Slovakia came during World War I. Masaryk's group articulated them in the Western capitals, and, in an address of May 30, 1917, to the new Habsburg emperor Charles, the Czech delegation to the Vienna Reichsrat demanded a federal reorganization of his entire realm, that would unite the Czech and Slovak-populated lands at the expense of millennial Hungary. The political lead was taken by the Czechs since the Slovaks were politically impotent in old Hungary, both in the gerrymandered central parliament at Budapest as well as in the local administration. In 1910, for example, there were only 184 Slovak speakers out of 3,683 judicial functionaries in the Slovak-populated counties of northern Hungary, and only 164 Slovaks out of the other 6,185 civil servants. Furthermore, since the Ausgleich of 1867 the Hungarian rulers had imposed on the Slovaks a rigorous policy of linguistic and cultural assimilation (but not racial exclusion) that had by the outbreak of World War I achieved such success among the nonpeasant strata of the Slovak population as to deprive it of much of its potential national elite.

At the postwar Paris Peace Conference, Beneš skillfully and indefatigably presented the Czech—or Czechoslovak—case in general and in detail. He argued that Czechs and Slovaks were two branches of the same nation, that the Slovaks wanted separation from Hungary and affiliation with the Czechs in a new state, and, finally, switching back from ethnic and political to strategic and economic criteria, that the new border should be drawn far enough south to incorporate significant parts of the rich plains and a generous stretch of Danubian shoreline into the new Czechoslovakia. Encouraged by a pro-Czechoslovak declaration issued on October 30, 1918, by about one hundred Slovak intellectuals and politicians gathered at Turčiansky Svätý Martin (Thurócz Szent-Márton), Beneš even urged the Czech authorities in Prague to "assist" his arguments by confronting the peace conference with a *fait accompli* in the form of military occupation of the Slovak territories being claimed. Twice, however—in November, 1918, and in May-June, 1919—the resilient Hungarians were able to force back the Czech contingents attempting to implement this strategy, and eventually it was to be French diplomatic endorsement in Paris rather than military performance locally that won the day for the Czechoslovak argument.

As in the Sudeten German case, so here, too, among the roughly seven hundred thousand Magyars who were now incorporated together with the Slovaks into the new Czechoslovakia, it was the Social Democratic workers who initially resisted most vigorously. The society and governments of rump Hungary were never reconciled to the loss of the Slovak-populated northern counties of their historic kingdom and remained doggedly determined throughout the interwar era to recover them and the neighboring Ruthenian-populated counties to the east. As political relations between Czechs and Slovaks also soon soured, the Slovak link of the general peace settlement of 1919 proved to be a source of chronic friction.

The easternmost province of interwar Czechoslovakia, Subcarpathian Ruthenia, or the Carpatho-Ukraine, had held no political interest for the Czechs as long as Russia remained in the war and was regarded by them as having primary claims of cultural wardship over this retarded but strategically important Slav-inhabited corner of old Hungary. At war's outbreak Ruthenia was populated by approximately six hundred thousand people, of whom two-thirds were miserably poor peasants and mountaineers speaking several Ukrainian dialects, with the remaining third divided roughly evenly between Hungarian officials and Jewish merchants and innkeepers. For a thousand years it had been an integral part of Hungary, supplying that country's most faithful peasant soldiers and itinerant agricultural laborers and, in turn, being treated by the Hungarian gentry as a primeval deer forest. With over half of them illiterate on the eve of the war, the depressed and exploited Ruthenian peasants lacked the resources for effective political action; indeed, the real pressure for extricating them from under Hungarian rule came during the war from their numerous (about three hundred thousand) brothers in the United States. But the American Ruthenians' stand against their old homeland's Hungarian past did not by itself answer the question of Ruthenia's political future.

This answer was eventually supplied in 1918 by a process of elimination: Russia was in the grip of civil war, hence the new Ukrainian state's future appeared dubious; as Ukrainian-speakers, the Ruthenians were unwilling to be assigned to Poland or Romania; the American Ruthenians' preference for a new state composed of the Bukovina, eastern Galicia, and Ruthenia was discouraged by President Wilson. At this point, late in October, 1918, their leader Grigory Žatković met with Masaryk, who was then traveling in the United States, and worked out with him an agreement to affiliate Ruthenia with Czechoslovakia, reserving for her extensive autonomous rights and institutions. A referendum among American Ruthenian parishes, culminating in a congress at Scranton on November 19, then approved this option, and on May 8, 1919, it was endorsed by the Central National Council back home in Užhorod (Ungvár). In Ruthenia the sentiment for continued association with Hungary, which earlier had more adherents at home than in America and which the first postwar Hungarian government had sought to encourage with a law of December 25, 1918, promising the Ruthenians autonomy, had meanwhile withered, partly under the impact of Béla Kun's Hungarian Communist regime. The Great Powers were also suitably impressed by this logic of events and duly assigned Ruthenia to Czechoslovakia, specifying that the province be granted autonomy (September 10, 1919). Žatković himself came from America to be its first governor but resigned on March 16, 1921, and returned home a few weeks later, embittered at finding his supposed autonomous authority to be a dead letter and at learning that his province's western boundary was so drawn as to leave almost one-fifth of Czechoslovakia's Ruthenians outside it, in Slovak administrative districts.

Though the chance to attach Ruthenia to their state was for the Czechs a windfall from the unforeseen fact that the war destroyed both the Habsburg and the Tsarist empires, the Prague authorities quickly came to appreciate Ruthenia's strategic significance for interwar Czechoslovakia, as a land bridge to her Little Entente ally Romania and as a potential political magnet for the Ukrainians in rival Poland. (The fact that Ruthenia is the only Ukrainian-speaking area south of the Carpathian Mountains is, of course, also of great strategic interest [military and political] to Moscow and probably accounts for Stalin's decision to take it from his Czechoslovak ally in 1944.)

If Ruthenia was the acquisition for which Beneš found it easiest to elicit Great Power endorsement at the Paris Peace Conference, Těšín was the most troublesome one. This corner of old Silesia was small but important, thanks to its coal and industry and its transportation network. The Polish claim to it was ethnographic. The Czech claim was based on a combination of historical, economic, and strategic considerations: it had belonged to the Bohemian Crown since the fourteenth century; it contained Czechoslovakia's only potential high quality coal reserves (of which Poland had a surplus); through it passed the railroad connection between the Czech provinces and Slovakia and on to Ruthenia and Romania.

Though Polish and Czech nationalism were in one sense allied during World War I—both aspiring to the restoration of their lost independence—Polish and Czech war aims and political strategies had not been synchronized and, indeed, were implicitly at variance. Their respective assessments of the Habsburg and Tsarist empires clashed: the former was the Czechs' bugbear but was regarded benevolently by the Poles, and the reverse attitudes pertained toward Russia. Their views of each other's postwar frontiers and destinies were also incompatible. Each wished to see the other confined to ethnographic frontiers, lest this neighbor become a source of irredentist instability in postwar Europe, while reserving for itself the right to claim historic or strategic or economically rational frontiers. The Czechs, for example, were convinced that Poland blundered in annexing her Belorussian- and Ukrainian-populated eastern *kresy*, while the Poles were skeptical about Czech-Slovak fraternity. Interwar alienation between Czechoslovakia and Poland thus went much deeper than the Těšín (Cieszyn, Teschen) dispute, this being rather its most vivid and tangible example.

Early in 1919, the Poles appeared to have the stronger hand in that dispute. For varying reasons, the American, British, and Italian delegations to the conference at Paris accepted the Poles' ethnographic claims, and the Czechs had somewhat discredited themselves and embarrassed their French patrons by attempting—and failing—to impose a *fait accompli* via a sudden military occupation of Těšín at the end of January. The Poles resisted successfully, and the Czechs here, as they had in Slovakia on two occasions, paid the price of lowered credibility for this combination of aggressiveness and weakness. In 1920, however, the diplomatic situation shifted to the Czechs' favor. The pro-Polish American delegation lost influence when the Senate repudiated President Wilson, Curzon replaced Balfour in the office of the British Foreign Secretary, and the Poles' desperate straits in July, 1920, at the time of the Soviet advance on Warsaw, obliged them to become docile over Těšín, whose coal mines and railroad junction the Allies now assigned to Czechoslovakia. The Poles considered this loss to have been the result of despicable blackmail at a moment of great danger and never forgave the Czechs. (Two decades later, at the time of the 1938 Munich crisis, the Polish and Czech roles were to be reversed in an otherwise remarkably similar situation.) Masaryk and Beneš, if left to their own judgment, might have been more accommodating toward Polish sensibilities, but they were obliged—or claimed they were obliged—to trim their sails to the strong wind of the Russophile and Polonophobe Czech National Democrats in the Prague government. Beneš, indeed, had at the time no independent political strength in the Czechoslovak party system and felt himself under constant pressure to protect his political flanks by great stubbornness in the conduct of foreign policy. Vis-à-vis Poland, this degenerated into the ludicrous pettiness of a wrangle that extended until 1924 over Javořina (Jaworzyna), a village of three hundred souls in the Tatra Mountains to which Czechoslovakia's claim was weak but successfully realized.

Czechoslovak and Polish considerations of national prestige had become so involved in these border quarrels and so irritated by the failure to solve them amicably or at least promptly, that the two neighbors never during the interwar period overcame their mutual mistrust. Even in the face of revived German and Russian pressures in the later 1930s, which might have been expected to bring home to them a realization of their common stake and destiny, they remained hostile.

Three more small Czechoslovak territorial acquisitions require mention to conclude this survey of the establishment of the new state's frontiers. From Austria, Czechoslovakia received the railroad junction, but not the town, of Gmünd (Cmunt) and a short stretch of the Morava River at Feldsberg. From Germany she acquired the small Hlučín (Hultschin) valley near Opava with a population of about forty-five thousand poor peasants who were Czech-speaking but notoriously cantankerous.

In sum, the frontiers of interwar Czechoslovakia were eminently defensible from a topographical point of view: seven-ninths of their length ran along mountain ridges, one-ninth was river banks, and only the last one-ninth was artificial. On the other hand, only one-tenth of the total international frontier was conterminous with linguistic frontiers. The state's area was 140,493 square kilometers.

3

The several territories incorporated within the new Czechoslovakia's frontiers had never before been united as a sovereign state or even as a distinct administrative entity within another state. Lacking ethnic, religious, cultural, historical, or physical unity, the new Czechoslovakia was faced with the task of compensating for the absence of such unity by creating political unity through the application of that political and administrative skill which the Czech elite possessed in generous measure. The challenge was formidable but the resources that Prague could apply to its attempted solution were also impressive.

Czechoslovakia was, first of all, the richest of the "successor states" that emerged from the destroyed Habsburg Empire. Its territories had not been overrun or ravaged during the war, and they contained in toto over two-thirds of the industries but only one-fourth of the population and one-fifth of the area of the old empire. It is true that a considerable fraction of this industrial capacity was in Sudeten German hands, and that Czechoslovak industry was henceforth to be deprived of the former secure internal imperial market and subjected instead to the competitive vagaries of several international trade, currency, and tariff systems. Nevertheless, there is no denying that Czechoslovakia emerged from the war with a unique economic advantage, especially as she was also blessed with sufficient rich agricultural land to render her theoretically capable of a greater degree of self-sufficiency than any other state in Central

Europe. Her war industry was bigger than Italy's, and even in the late 1930s, after frantic endeavors by all her neighbors to develop their heavy industries, Czechoslovakia was still producing half the steel and pig iron of all East Central Europe, i.e., as much as the other states of the area combined. Additional assets were the high rates of literacy and education among the Czech and German sectors of the population, and the availability of a well-trained, honest, and efficient though slow-moving Czech bureaucracy, which was numerous enough to staff Slovakia and Ruthenia as well as the western, historic provinces. Even Czechoslovakia's wedge-like geographical thrust into the core of Germanic territory might, under certain circumstances, be construed as an advantage since it gave her general European strategic significance—and her mountain-ringed borders were emphatically defensible. The problem confronting the country's political elite was whether all these assets could be exploited to prevail over Czechoslovakia's congenital weaknesses.

The most vivid of these infirmities was Czechoslovakia's dubious distinction as ethnically the least homogeneous of all the new states of Europe. Her German, Magyar, and Polish minorities were numerous, settled in strategic border areas, and at best reluctantly acquiescent in their minority status in this state. Unlike, for example, the Belorussian and Ukrainian minorities of Poland, for them this status was doubly painful as they had been the master nations of the prewar imperial system. In addition to chronic tensions with these minorities, the Czechs soon learned that relations with their "brother" Slovaks and Ruthenians were to be troubled and complicated.

Even the generally rosy economic prospectus was not without thorns: industrialized and fertile Bohemia is geographically part of the Elbe Basin system but connected with its navigable section by only one gorge; Moravia, Slovakia, and Ruthenia, on the other hand, belong to the Danube system, which is much better fitted for navigation, but being poorer, they had much less economic use for its facilities. Silesia is topographically part of the Oder system. The railroad and road networks of Bohemia and Moravia-Silesia had been designed to connect them with Vienna, while those of Slovakia and Ruthenia had focused on Budapest; consequently, the transport connections between these formerly Austrian and formerly Hungarian parts of Czechoslovakia were poor. Initially, indeed, the only main railroad line between them was the one running through the disputed Těšín area, and by the end of the interwar period there were only four additional secondary connections. This paucity of communications tended to confirm and exacerbate the inherited imbalances in overall economic and social levels between the wealthy western (ex-Austrian) and poor eastern (ex-Hungarian) parts of the country. The latter remained an area deficient in both industrial and agricultural capital and costly to administer. Even in the relatively advanced western provinces, many of the industrial enterprises were small and dependent on rather primitive technology, their economic survival being a function of highly specialized production, traditional family dedication, and extensive recourse to low-paid artisanal work done at home. Thus, though Bohemia and Moravia were, indeed, highly industrialized and utilized an impressive array of modern technology in such sectors as heavy industry and shoe manufacture (e.g., the famous Škoda and Bat'a works), other sectors of industry lacked the attributes of modern industrialization as their plants were dispersed and obsolescent and they conserved types of production that were elsewhere extinct.[6]

To supplement the preceding discussion and to provide auxiliary information for the political analysis that follows, some statistics are here in order. While the Czechoslovak tabulations on ethnicity were on occasion challenged as biased by spokesmen for the German and Hungarian minorities, the author's own chief difficulty arises from the official refusal to register separate categories for "Czech" and "Slovak." It should also be noted that the total number of Jews is not included in the Hebrew and Yiddish-speaking column since many Jews listed Czech, German, or Magyar as their mother tongue and nationality. Here the table on religion (table 14) is more accurate than the table on ethnicity (table 13).

The author is aware of the hazards involved in all efforts toward a valid identification of the nationality of individuals in ethnically mixed areas such as interwar East Central Europe. "Spoken tongue" was for long the internationally preferred criterion of demographers and statisticians, but in this part of the world, where so many people were bilingual, the problem was whether "mother tongue" or "colloquial language" was the "spoken tongue." For Jews, as mentioned, either language criterion could be misleading and for everyone else "colloquial language" tended to absorb minorities into the dominant culture. Theoretically, the subjective self-identification of census-respondents might be taken as definitive, but this, too, creates dilemmas as between "origins" and "political identification." Furthermore, among poor and premodern populations, such as those that still existed in substantial numbers in all the states of East Central Europe during the period under review, many respondents were unclear about their nationality. In addition, a deliberate abdication

6. "Two causes favor the survival of the small firm. Firstly, the small are usually old-established family concerns, privately owned; the larger ones are all under the control of banks and have no motive to acquire the small firms, which earn what profits they do earn by some small monopoly or trade secret. The wide distribution of industry, and the high specialization, make this sort of undertaking more prevalent than elsewhere. Secondly, the solitary position of these works makes them exempt from any efforts at collective bargaining. . . . The unions indulge in a practice which British trade unions regard as contrary to the whole spirit of trade unionism: they allow smaller and weaker firms to pay lower wage-rates. . . . Hard-working, but not enterprising, saving and not risking money they [the Czechs] do not take naturally to capitalism." Doreen Warriner, "Czechoslovakia and Central European Tariffs," *The Slavonic Review* 11 (January, 1933): 317, 325, 327.

by the census authorities of all claims to control respondents' replies would, in localities of mixed population, have allowed various forms of pressure to be inflicted by dominant social elements upon the dependent ones. While conceding that in a state where several nationalities coexist uneasily the census inevitably becomes a political measure, the author nevertheless considers the Czechoslovak tabulations credible and useful. Tables 12 through 18 give the calculations from the two interwar censuses of February 15, 1921, and December 1, 1930.[7]

TABLE 12

POPULATION BY PROVINCE

	1921		1930	
	Number	Percentage	Number	Percentage
Bohemia	6,670,582	49.00	7,109,376	48.27
Moravia	2,662,884	19.56 ⎱	3,565,010	24.20
Silesia	672,268	4.94 ⎰		
Slovakia	3,000,870	22.04	3,329,793	22.61
Ruthenia	606,568	4.46	725,357	4.92
Total	13,613,172	100.00	14,729,536	100.00

TABLE 13

POPULATION BY ETHNICITY (MOTHER TONGUE)

	1921		1930	
	Number	Percentage	Number	Percentage
Czechoslovak	8,760,937	65.51	9,688,770	66.91
Ruthenian (Ukrainian)	461,849	3.45	549,169	3.79
German	3,123,568	23.36	3,231,688	22.32
Magyar	745,431	5.57	691,923	4.78
Polish	75,853	0.57	81,737	0.57
Hebrew & Yiddish	180,855	1.35	186,642	1.29
Other	25,871	0.19	49,636	0.34
Total (Citizens)	13,374,364	100.00	14,479,565	100.00
Resident Foreigners	238,808		249,971	
Total Population	13,613,172		14,729,536	

7. All statistics are from the official yearbooks of the State Statistical Office of the Czechoslovak Republic, *Statistická Ročenka Republiky Československé* (Prague: Státni Úřad Statistický).

The preponderance of the resident foreigners were, in descending numerical order, citizens of Poland, Austria, Germany, and Hungary. Hence, had they been included in their respective ethnic categories in table 13, the resulting computations would have slightly lowered, by less than 1 percent, the Czechoslovak proportion of the total population and slightly raised the Polish, German, and Magyar ones.

TABLE 14

Population by Religion

	1921		1930	
	Number	Percentage	Number	Percentage
Roman Catholic	10,384,833	76.29	10,831,696	73.54
Greek Catholic (Uniate)	535,543	3.93	585,041	3.97
Bohemian Brethren	233,868	1.72	297,977	2.02
Lutheran	535,382	3.93	586,775	3.99
Calvinist	207,906	1.53	219,108	1.49
Other Protestant	13,163	0.09	25,898	0.17
Eastern Orthodox	73,097	0.54	145,598	0.99
Czechoslovak National	525,333	3.86	793,385	5.39
Old Catholic	20,255	0.15	22,712	0.16
Israelite	354,342	2.60	356,830	2.42
Other Confessions	2,824	0.02	8,252	0.05
Without Confession	724,507	5.32	854,638	5.80
Unknown	2,119	0.02	1,626	0.01
Total	13,613,172	100.00	14,729,536	100.00

The cross-correlations between ethnicity (table 13) and religion (table 14) require some explanation. Most Czechs, Slovaks, Germans, and Magyars were Roman Catholic, but a substantial minority of each was Protestant (Bohemian Brethren in the case of Czechs, Lutheran in the case of Slovaks and Germans, and Calvinist in the case of Magyars). The Czechoslovak National Church was an antipapal, nationalistic, modernistic secession of Czechs from Roman Catholicism, dating from 1919-20, while the Old Catholics had rejected the dogma of papal infallibility in matters of faith and morals since its proclamation in 1870. The Ruthenians (Ukrainians) were overwhelmingly Uniate with a small minority Eastern Orthodox.

Table 15 gives population by economic sector. The proportions of Czechoslovakia's population engaged in the agricultural and industrial sectors were respectively the lowest and highest of any state in interwar East Central Europe. In other words, her economic level and profile were the area's most modern. That this generalization, while valid, tends however to hide the profound disparity in levels of development between the country's western, ex-Austrian provinces on the one hand, and the eastern, ex-Hungarian half on the other, is exposed when the percentages for economic sectors as well as for urbanization and literacy are given by province (tables 16, 17, and 18). The comparison of illiteracy

TABLE 15

POPULATION BY ECONOMIC SECTORS (INCLUDES DEPENDENTS)

| | 1921 | | 1930 | |
	Number	Percentage	Number	Percentage
Agriculture, forestry, fishing	5,385,790	39.57	5,101,614	34.64
Industry, handicrafts	4,601,098	33.80	5,146,937	34.94
Commerce, banking	787,243	5.78	1,094,063	7.43
Communications, transportation	664,298	4.88	814,468	5.53
Free professions, civil service	590,670	4.33	715,841	4.86
Military service	159,853	1.18	193,463	1.31
Domestics	173,428	1.27	183,814	1.25
Other	1,250,792	9.19	1,479,336	10.04
Total	13,613,172	100.00	14,729,536	100.00

TABLE 16

ECONOMIC SECTORS BY PROVINCES
(IN PERCENTAGES)

| | Bohemia | | Moravia-Silesia | | Slovakia | | Ruthenia | |
	1921	1930	1921	1930	1921	1930	1921	1930
Agriculture, forestry, fishing	29.69	24.06	35.27	28.56	60.63	56.82	67.63	66.29
Industry, handicrafts	40.55	41.78	37.79	40.82	17.43	19.07	10.41	11.94
Commerce, banking	6.87	8.91	5.30	6.67	4.14	5.44	4.66	5.73
Communications, transportation	5.58	6.18	4.97	5.46	3.53	4.73	2.47	3.18
Free professions, public services	6.08	6.32	5.44	5.95	5.01	6.31	4.35	5.21
Other	11.23	12.75	11.23	12.54	9.26	7.63	10.48	7.65
Total	100.00	100.00	100.00	100.00	100.00	100.00	100.00	100.00

TABLE 17

Population by Urban/Rural Residence*
(In percentages)

	1921		1930	
Region	Urban	Rural	Urban	Rural
Bohemia	22.3	77.7	26.2	73.8
Moravia	21.9	78.1 ⎫	24.5	75.5
Silesia	15.9	84.1 ⎭		
Slovakia	11.1	88.9	14.5	85.5
Ruthenia	11.1	88.9	15.4	84.6
Czechoslovakia	18.9	81.1	22.6	77.4

*Urban = town of 10,000+ inhabitants

rates and the calculation of illiteracy reduction between 1921 and 1930 is somewhat marred by a change in the officially defined base-age from six years in the first census to ten in the second.

TABLE 18

Illiteracy
(In percentages)

	1921 (Above Age Six)	1930 (Above Age Ten)
Bohemia	2.10	1.24
Moravia	2.65 ⎫	1.49
Silesia	3.12 ⎭	
Slovakia	14.71	8.16
Ruthenia	50.03	30.88
Czechoslovakia	7.02	4.06

4

We shall now sketch the constitutional anatomy of interwar Czechoslovakia and scan the spectrum of political parties which fleshed it out. The constitution under whose terms the country's variegated population was to be governed was drafted and approved by a self-appointed Constituent National Assembly consisting of 201 Czechs designated by the political parties in proportion to their relative strengths at the last imperial Austrian Reichsrat elections in 1911, and 55 (later 69) Slovaks coopted by these Czechs (the Slovak districts having been too disfranchised in old

Hungary to make feasible a similar representative selection from the old Hungarian parliament). The state's ethnic minorities were thus excluded (but also exluded themselves) from the constitution-making process, and when they finally did agree (and were permitted) to enter the political arena, they found themselves confronted with a series of institutional *faits accomplis*. Certain politically sophisticated Sudeten Germans had wished to end their original boycott of the newborn Czechoslovak state and enter the Constituent National Assembly promptly with the signing of the Treaty of St. Germain on September 10, 1919, in order to fight within it for such federalistic constitutional devices as cantonization and the concurrent veto by regions. But now the Czechs and Slovaks were determined that the constitution be shaped by themselves alone and as nearly unanimously among themselves as possible.

After slightly more than a year of deliberations, during which a brief provisional constitution of November 13, 1918, had interim validity, this Czechoslovak goal was achieved with the adoption of the nation's definitive constitution on February 29, 1920. Of the 155 roll-calls required to pass the Constitution's various articles and clauses, 105 were unanimous and the remaining 50 saw the parties of the Left and Center defeat those of the Right, who, in any event, had almost certainly been overrepresented in this postwar body due to the decision to use the 1911 Austrian Reichsrat returns as the base.

The Czechoslovak craving to achieve near-unanimity had been so general and the anxiety to shun the specters of red and/or white terror (which vividly haunted neighboring Hungary in 1919) so pervasive, that the final constitutional document must be regarded as an ideological compromise rather than as a victory of the Center and Left. One of the less inspired of its internal compromises was the decision to have a Senate of 150 seats and simultaneously to ensure that it would be largely a powerless reflection of the 300-member Chamber of Deputies. In time, senatorial office became a dignified pension for veteran party war horses. More impressive was the subtle compromise on the presidency: the president was to be elected, like the French one, by the two legislative houses sitting jointly as the National Assembly, but he was given considerable executive powers in keeping with the American and Weimar models. In its curbing of the agencies of direct and plebiscitary democracy, on the other hand, as well as in its overall parliamentary and centralistic bias, the Czechoslovak constitution was quite British. Finally, the wide powers that were officially assigned to the political parties and their executive committees clearly indicated the Austrian parentage of the Czechoslovak constitutional system.

The combination of (a) compulsory universal adult voting in parliamentary elections, (b) "fixed-order" lists of candidates arranged by the respective parties within a general system of proportional representation, and (c) the rule, enforced by the Electoral Court, that a deputy or senator must vacate his seat on the demand of his party (since in Czechoslovak theory, the electorate's mandate had been conferred on the party, not the candidate) added up to a formidable assignment of power to the several party leaderships. In their hands the general electorate as well as the parliamentary backbenches were politically and legally reduced to mere auxiliaries and dependents. The party leaders' effective sovereignty was limited only by the extent to which they might chose to permit some free discussion in the secrecy of the parliamentary party clubrooms before committing themselves to particular positions in public debate. (Membership in a parliamentary party club was legally compulsory for every deputy and senator; independency was proscribed.) It must, of course, be conceded that, in view of the large number of political parties, the remarkable cohesion and stability of Czechoslovak coalition cabinets might not have been maintained without this rather drastic system of discipline. Thus, though this political efficiency of the coalition system conveyed prestige on the country's parliamentary system, the fact that in order to achieve it the "real" business of politics was withdrawn from the public arena detracted therefrom. Furthermore, the craving and the need for compromise within the government coalitions resulted in ever-increasing encroachment by the cabinet as a whole on the separate departments, as regards administrative and personnel as well as policy matters. Here again the results were mixed: a desirable degree of coordination and unity of administration at the cost of slow and difficult procedure.

The political stability of the cabinets should not be obscured by the fact that formally there were seventeen successive cabinets in the years 1918-38. Most of these were "arranged," technical reshuffles. No coalition ever broke up except as a result of a deliberate decision on the part of the leaders who composed it, preparatory to new elections. And no vote of censure was ever passed, nor was any government-sponsored bill ever rejected.

Czechoslovak politics crystallized around "ideological" parties, whereas Polish politics polarized toward "charismatic" personalities. Thanks to the country's complicated ethnic, religious, and cultural structure, thanks also to its Austrian and Hungarian political inheritances, and thanks, finally, to its proportional electoral system, the number of parties tended to be large and any one party's size correspondingly limited. In the elections of 1920, twenty-three parties competed and seventeen achieved parliamentary representation; the equivalent figures for the remaining three general elections of the interwar period were, respectively, twenty-nine and sixteen in 1925, nineteen and sixteen in 1929, and sixteen and fourteen in 1935. This enumeration does not even include the many mini-parties that, in the poorer regions such as Ruthenia, either did not enter slates for elections or rode "piggy-back" on the lists of others. The balance, furthermore, among those parties that achieved parliamentary representation in these four elections was such that a minimal numerical majority (quite apart from the question of a politically feasible and effectively working majority) required the cooperation of no less than five parties. The one exception was a brief period after the 1920 elections, when four would have been theoretically adequate. No party ever amassed more than a fourth of the popular vote. The profiles of the more important parties follow. The Czech and Slovak ones are discussed first, then those of the ethnic minorities; the spectrum in each case proceeds from Right to Left.

A. CZECH AND SLOVAK PARTIES

1. The "oldest" Czech political party in terms of ideological pedigree, if not of organization, was the National Democratic Party, heir to the Young Czech movement of the nineteenth century to which it added some smaller and later affiliates. It was nationalistic to the point of being chauvinistic, panslavist, conservative, and anticlerical,[8] and it moved steadily toward the Right throughout the interwar period, putting forward a joint slate with the Czech fascists in the 1935 elections. Supported by the upper bourgeois commercial and industrial strata as well as by the nationalistic segment of the intelligentsia, the National Democratic Party never achieved much electoral strength outside its original base of Bohemia. Thanks, however, to its traditional prestige, its skilled leadership, its penetrating influence within the senior civil service, its control of much of the quality press, its strong organization in the capital city of Prague, and its ornamentation by a number of distinguished cultural figures, this party's effective weight was greater than the election figures would tend to suggest. Its forceful leader Karel Kramář was one of the architects of the independence movement, his pro-Russian "domestic" prewar and wartime activities having paralleled in intensity and courage, if not in effectiveness, the "external" ones of his Western-oriented (and luckier) rival, Masaryk.

2. The Small Traders and Artisans Party was a secession from the National Democrats in protest against the latter's capture by the upper bourgeoisie. Its clientele is indicated by its name. Opposed to the technology of mass production, to the cooperative movement, to department stores and related phenomena of economic rationalization, it was already a political beneficiary of some of the rooted economic tensions that stemmed from the uneven levels and patterns of development of Czechoslovak economic life even before the Great Depression sent new and frustrated recruits its way.

---

8. In Poland, where the Roman Catholic Church was a traditional crucible and guardian of national identity, the National Democratic Party was politically friendly to it. Among the Czech National Democrats, on the other hand, the Church was suspect as a Habsburg Trojan horse.

3. Also on the secular Right was the Fascist movement, which went under several labels until its partial merger with the National Democrats to form the National Union from 1934 to 1937. Although small and kept from power by the stability of the coalition pattern among the "respectable" parties, it had some significance thanks both to the benevolence extended it by the National Democrats and certain senior elements in the civil service, and to the celebrity of its leaders and patrons. Among the latter were the Siberian Legion hero and later acting chief of staff, General Rudolf Gajda, the talented poet Viktor Dyk, and the erratically brilliant politician Jiří Stříbrný, who like so many European Fascists of his generation (e.g., Déat, Moseley, Mussolini) was a renegade from socialism (see below).

4. Oscillating between Right and Center on the political spectrum were the Catholic, or so-called Populist (People's), parties. Except for a brief and early period in 1920-21, the Czech and Slovak organizations remained distinct and generally went separate political ways. The Slovak People's Party was the chief institutional and political repository of Slovak autonomist aspirations against Czech centralism and, except for a brief period from 1927 to 1929 when it supplied two cabinet ministers, it remained in opposition to the Prague governments. Its founder and leader was Msgr. Andrej Hlinka, who had earned his reputation as a Slovak national hero by his prewar resistance to the forced magyarization of his people and who sustained it in the postwar years by his eloquent, tenacious, suspicious, and provincial opposition to all influences emanating from the more secular and cosmopolitan Czech lands. Proud, refractory, and naive, Hlinka in his parochialism eventually became the dupe of more modern and more totalitarian elements that used his cassock as a shield. Czechs often alleged that Hlinka's autonomist demands did not really speak for a majority of the Slovak people since his party never won a majority of their votes. Nevertheless, the centralist parties that consistently participated in the Prague governments also failed to achieve a collective majority of Slovak votes and appeared to draw their support in this province from resident Czechs and Jews, the Slovak Protestant minority, and those Slovak Catholics whose pragmatic appreciation of the political-bureaucratic system convinced them of the utility of being known as voters for the government parties. The fact that a disparate agglomeration of opposition parties (Hlinka's, the Communists, the Magyar slates) consistently accumulated a majority of votes cast in Slovakia suggests the vanity of Czech claims that the province was satisfied with its status.

5. The Czech Populists, in contrast to their Slovak coreligionists, consistently preferred to be a government party. This choice may have been motivated in part by a need to demonstrate their nationalist respectability in postwar Czechoslovakia after having adopted a somewhat damaging

Austrophile stance before and during World War I. Tightly led by Msgr. Jan Šramek, this clerical party drew some support from all Czech classes but was relatively strongest among the peasants and small-town workers of Moravia. It could not, of course, share in the national cult of Jan Hus, but it was nevertheless relatively advanced (in the old Austrian style of Christian socialism) on social and economic matters.

6. The largest and pivotal Czechoslovak party was the Agrarian Party (formally: The Republican Party of Agriculturists and Small Peasants). So strongly organized, so deeply entrenched in the provincial and local government apparatus, so thoroughly involved in the cooperative and banking systems, so indispensable to any and every cabinet coalition, and so strategic in its choice of ministerial portfolios was this party, that despite its name and without losing contact with the original constituency indicated by that name, the Agrarian Party in effect became a general political "holding company" for middle-class interests at large. It was the government party with the most evenly distributed support throughout the country, and even ethnic minority and Slovak and Ruthenian elements saw advantages in giving it, rather than their own specific parties, electoral support. Utilizing the land reform program whereby extensive properties were transferred from German, Magyar, and ecclesiastical magnates to Czech and Slovak (and Ruthenian and even German) peasants to secure its patronage over the countryside, the Agrarian Party simultaneously extended its political infrastructure in the urban areas through judicious leverage on the tax, tariff, and credit systems. It always managed to contain, if not to resolve, the internal tensions between its original peasant and its later bourgeois clienteles, but in the process of containing them it moved steadily rightward, against working class interests, in the 1930s. In Antonín Švehla, their leader during the happier decade of the 1920s, the Agrarians gave Czechoslovakia her shrewdest and her most responsible (in Max Weber's sense of that word) democratic political leader, and by providing a political home for such prestigious Slovaks as Masaryk's "Hlasist" disciple Vavro Šrobár and the ideologue of international "peasantism" Milan Hodža, the Agrarians complemented, to some extent, their organizational virtuosity with intellectual respectability.

7. Of the two Czechoslovak Socialist parties, the National Socialists, which bore no ideological relation to its German namesake, had been organized in 1897 as an explicitly patriotic, evolutionary Czech alternative to the avowedly internationalistic, Marxist Social Democrats. Originally the most articulately anti-Austrian, anticlerical, and antimilitarist Czech political formation, the National Socialists became the postwar party with the widest ideological spectrum. However, its membership and electoral appeal were still confined largely to Czechs, and its organizational base anchored in the rail, postal, and white collar unions. The formal member-

ship of Edvard Beneš, who was foreign minister from 1918 to 1935 and president from 1935 to 1938, lent the party some additional prestige, but the real leaders were its founder Václav Klofáč, the first Czech parliamentarian to have been arrested by the Austrian authorities in World War I, and, until his apostasy to fascism in 1926, the demagogue Jiří Stříbrný.

8. As the National Socialists expelled their fascist elements and the Social Democrats demonstrated their national respectability, a political reconciliation became possible between them, though they did not merge. Tracing their organizational history back to 1878—further than any other Czech party—the Social Democrats were, during the interwar decades, a typical Central European Socialist party: patriotic, yet suspicious of the military establishment and eager for international disarmament; anticapitalist, yet receptive to technological innovations; class-oriented, yet ready to participate in coalition governments. One of this party's major services to interwar Czechoslovakia was that of keeping open the channels of dialogue with the ethnic minorities through its fraternal relations with their Socialist parties.

9. The Communists finally parted ways with the Social Democrats in the autumn of 1920, after repeated urgings from Moscow and under considerable provocation from the Socialist party's right wing. They took with them a majority of that party's members and, at first, of its voters, but only a minority of its leaders and members of parliament. Unlike the several ethnically distinct Socialist parties, the various Communist groups amalgamated into one party for the entire republic, the only such transethnic party in all Czechoslovakia, in October, 1921. It was indeed a mass party but not a revolutionary one, despite attempts to "bolshevise" it through repeated purges. The country's only party able to attract equal support in urban and rural areas, in the advanced and in the backward regions, on the basis of social as well as of ethnic discontents, the Communists—whether under the original leadership of the old Austrian Social Democratic war horse Bohumír Šmeral, or later that of the Moscow-backed younger apparatchik Klement Gottwald—consistently failed to translate their considerable electoral and organizational strength into serious revolutionary or effective parliamentary action. Never declared illegal or driven underground in interwar Czechoslovakia (in sharp contrast to its sister parties in the other states of East Central Europe), the Communist Party drew its sustained strength less from any unbearable conditions of exploitation, than from a generalized complex of alienations that reflected rigid social barriers between the working class and the lower middle class, and estrangements between juxtaposed ethnic communities. In addition to these sources of support, in the late 1930s it gained patriotic respectability, thanks to its emphatic denunciation, first of nazism and appeasement in general, and then of the Munich capitulation in particular.

B. ETHNIC MINORITY PARTIES

As mentioned earlier, the Sudeten Germans were originally well-nigh unanimous in deploring their incorporation into Czechoslovakia, but in time a process of adjustment to this situation occurred both among the German Social Democrats as well as within the bourgeois political camp. Late in 1922 the latter, loosely aggregated as the Deutscher Verband (German Union), split into the potentially cooperative Arbeitsgemeinschaft (Association for Work) and the continuingly irreconcilable Kampfgemeinschaft (Association for Struggle). In interwar Czechoslovak political rhetoric, the first tendency received the appelation "activism," which denoted a readiness to take an active part in the political life and institutions of the republic, while the intransigent position was referred to as "passivism," or "negativism."

1. Mention must be made first of the two members of the Kampfgemeinschaft, the German Nationalist Party and the German National Socialist Party. The latter was affiliated with the Hitler movement in the Reich and until the 1930s less troublesome for the Czechs than the former.

2. Within the Arbeitsgemeinschaft, as it moved toward "activism" in the mid-1920s, three distinct orientations were discernible:

a. a group of liberal Democrats, endorsed by industrialists increasingly eager to avoid Reich competition, supported also by German-speaking Jews, numerically relatively weak but fortunate in the skilled parliamentarians who represented it in the legislature;

b. the Christian Social Party, whose correct and then cordial relations with its ideological analogue on the Czech spectrum, the Catholic People's Party, added to its distrust of the *Los von Rom* anti-Catholic pedigree of the National and National Socialist parties in its own German community;

c. the Bund der Landwirte (League of Farmers), which became the first German party to turn to "activism," thereby presumably reflecting a lower level of nationalistic resentment among peasants than among townsmen, and a greater interest in the agricultural tariffs toward which the Prague government was being steered by its Agrarian leaders.

3. Beyond these several bourgeois parties stood the German Social Democrats. Initially the most fervent partisans of Anschluss to a Greater Germany, they then shifted, moving with the European "spirit of Locarno" (1925) and propelled by a compact among Czech and German trade union federations (1927), toward "activism," and finally responded to the rise of Hitler with full commitment to the defense of the democratic Czechoslovak Republic. The German Communists, after splitting from the Social Democrats in January, 1921, fused into the unified Communist Party of Czechoslovakia in October of that year.

4. Among the Magyar minority in the eastern half of the country, the

structural differentiation of parties resembled an embryonic version of that among the more numerous Germans in the western provinces. Here, too, there were Christian Social (Catholic), National Agrarian (Calvinist) and Social Democratic parties, but "activism" never achieved the resonance that it did among the Germans. This was partly a reflection of the fact that the governments of Hungary consistently showed a more intensive irredentist interest in the fate of their fellow Magyars in Slovakia and Ruthenia than did the governments of the Weimar Republic in that of the Sudeten Germans of Bohemia and Moravia-Silesia. Hence the Magyar minority problem was all along for Prague what the German one became only after 1933: a dual domestic *and* foreign policy issue. Furthermore, the consistent irredentism and revisionism of Hungarian policy toward Czechoslovakia had ideological as well as national motivations: the gentry rulers of Horthyite Hungary had little wish to see bourgeois democratic Czechoslovakia succeed and prosper lest the example undermine their own neobaroque system. To a small degree, indeed, this situation did elicit a backlash. The spectacle of "feudal" peasant conditions in Hungary enabled the Czechoslovak Agrarian Party to organize, in 1924, an affiliate among the Magyar peasants of Czechoslovakia, who, like the Sudeten German peasants, also appreciated Prague's mid-decade agrarian protectionism. The Czechoslovak Social Democratic and especially the Communist parties also drew considerable Magyar votes. Also, the bloody pogroms of the white terror which had established the Horthy regime alienated many hitherto fervently Magyarophile Jews into opting for Czechoslovak or explicitly Jewish political identification. All this was, however, relatively unimportant in the overall context of general Magyar intransigence with respect to Czechoslovakia.

5. The small Polish minority of Silesia was obliged by its small size to participate in elections on joint lists with other slates: Jewish, Czech Social Democratic, or Slovak Populist. Similarly, in primitive Ruthenia political organizations were either affiliates of the main Czechoslovak parties or sundered into intensely local and scarcely comprehensible factionalism.

5

The political history of interwar Czechoslovakia up to the Munich disaster of 1938 was unique in East Central Europe not only for its uninterrupted constitutional and civil libertarian continuity, but also for a pattern of extraordinary stability, mentioned above, within and among the political parties. Once the Communists and Socialists had parted in 1920, and the Czech and Slovak Populists in 1921, no later crisis or election brought any drastic shifts in the positions or the relative strengths of the Czechoslovak political parties. Even the virtual absorption of the Sudeten German political community into the Henleinist incarnation of nazism in the mid-1930s had no organizational or electoral impact upon the traditional balances that prevailed among the non-German parties. Instead of the radical discontinuities that marked her neighbors' politics, Czechoslovakia's was characterized by palpable but nevertheless second-ary shifts along her partisan spectrum. These shifts ran from a brief nationalist, to a brief socialist, to a long agrarian-dominated phase, and culminated in the telescoping of domestic and international crises at the close of our period; each shift along the spectrum occurred within the prevailing pattern of coalition adjustments.

The first, nationalist phase of Czechoslovak politics was both a general expression of the euphoria of newly recovered independence, and a particular consequence of proportioning party representation within the Constituent National Assembly to the results of the 1911 Reichsrat elec-tions. This formal discounting of popular reactions to the World War and the Russian Revolution undoubtedly gave exaggerated representation to the National Democrats, until it was corrected in the first general elections of April, 1920. In any event, the achievements of this early nationalistic phase, in which the prestigious National Democratic leader Karel Kramář was premier and his party colleague Alois Rašín was the policy-making pacesetter as finance minister, were: the establishment of favorable fron-tiers; the maintenance of public order amidst the chaos of the other successor states; the avoidance of inflation (which likewise was lacerating the country's neighbors) through vigorous deflationary and control measures; the passage of land-reform legislation for gradual implemen-tation; the "Czechization" of public administration.

While the municipal and communal elections of June 15, 1919, in the historic provinces did not formally alter the balance of parties within the Constituent National Assembly, they did indicate that the national politi-cal mood was now to the left of 1911. Accordingly, Kramář resigned the premiership, remaining, however, as formal head of the Czechoslovak delegation to the Paris Peace Conference. In that capacity he threw himself into a futile and embarrassing crusade on behalf of European intervention (utilizing, he hoped, the Czechoslovak Siberian Legions) to crush the Bolshevik experiment in Soviet Russia.

Meanwhile, his cabinet constellation was succeeded on July 8, 1919, by a "red-green," i.e., Socialist-Agrarian, one headed by the Social Democratic veteran Vlastimil Tusar. Its legislative achievements were the institution of secular democracy, not socialism. The constitution was adopted; church-state relations regulated; secular education provided; state con-trol over railroads, mines, and hydroelectric power authorized. Less explicitly and more subtly, the Tusar experiment established a number of patterns and precedents: the restless urban masses, who had staged hunger- and price-protests against Kramář as recently as May, were mollified when a Socialist became premier; the Socialist parties, in turn, accustomed themselves to governmental responsibility in lieu of the oppositional heritage of Habsburg days; there was established the tradition that the most popular party furnish the prime minister, who need not be the cabinet's—or even his own party's—most prestigious figure. Tusar, for example, owed his designation to (a) the Social Democrats' recent victory in the local government elections, and (b) the fact that four better-known party comrades declined, pleading lack of administrative skill or Jewish origins.

The general parliamentary elections of April 18 and 25, 1920, which were postponed in Ruthenia, Těšín, Hlučín, and a few smaller frontier districts, confirmed the public's leftward shift along the political spectrum. The suffrage age was twenty-one years for the Chamber of Deputies and twenty-six for the Senate. The results are given in table 19.[9] Of a total of 285 elected deputies, 139 belonged to Socialist parties; within the Czechoslovak contingent of 203, there were 104 Socialists.

TABLE 19

PARLIAMENTARY ELECTIONS, APRIL, 1920

	Chamber of Deputies, April 18, 1920			Senate, April 25, 1920		
Party	Number of Votes	Percentage of Total Vote	Seats	Number of Votes	Percentage of Total Vote	Seats
Czech National Democrat	387,552	6.2	19	354,561	6.8	10
Czech Small Trader	122,813	2.0	6	107,674	2.1	3
Czech and Slovak Populist	699,728	11.3	33	622,406	11.9	18
Czech Agrarian ⎫ merged 1922	603,618	9.7	28	530,388	10.1	14
Slovak Agrarian ⎭	242,045	3.9	12	181,289	3.5	6
Czech National Socialist	500,821	8.1	24	373,913	7.1	10
Czech Progressive Socialist	58,580	0.9	3	3,050	0.1	....
CzSl. Social Democrat	1,590,520	25.7	74	1,466,958	28.1	41
German Nationalist and Nazi	328,735	5.3	15	300,287	5.7	8
German Democrat	105,446	1.7	5	118,103	2.3	3
German Christian Social	212,913	3.5	10	141,334	2.7	4
German Farmer	241,747	3.9	11	210,700	4.0	6
German Social Democrat	689,589	11.1	31	593,344	11.4	16
Magyar Christian Social	139,355	2.2	5	100,658	1.9	2
Magyar Agrarian	26,520	0.4	1	40,302	0.8	1
Magyar Social Democrat	108,546	1.8	4	no list	....	....
Jewish list	79,714	1.3	....	59,913	1.1	....
Other (five lists)	61,790	1.0	....	21,931	0.4	....
Total	6,200,032	100.0	281*	5,226,811	100.0	142

*The Czechoslovak Siberian Legions elected 4 additional deputies: 2 National Socialists, 1 Social Democrat, and 1 Agrarian.

9. In supplementary elections held on March 16, 1924, in Ruthenia (which in 1920 had been partly under Romanian military administration), nine additional deputies (four of whom were Communists) and four additional senators (two of whom were Communists) were elected by, respectively, 254,200 and 212,516 voters. Of the thirty-three Populist deputies elected in 1920, twenty-one were Czech and twelve Slovak; of the eighteen Populist senators, twelve were Czech and six Slovak. Of the fifteen German rightist deputies, ten were Nationalist and five Nazi.

Accordingly, a minor reshuffle of Tusar's cabinet was arranged on May 25; this slightly increased its Social Democratic contingent at the expense of the National Socialists and Agrarians. But developments over the summer were to prove fatal to that cabinet; the left wing of Tusar's own Social Democratic party became increasingly mutinous over his neutrality vis-à-vis the current Polish-Soviet War, and his cabinet's would-be moderate stand on ethnic problems was rejected by Czech (National Democratic), German, and Polish jingoists alike. It may, finally, be assumed that the Agrarians were consequently increasingly uncomfortable at being the only Czech bourgeois party in this "red-green" government. But as no other political constellation was then feasible, the Tusar cabinet gave way on September 15 to one of nonpartisan experts headed by a civil servant, Jan Černý.

Informal but effective contact between this ministry of officials and the parties of the legislature was maintained by a consultative committee of five (hence its name, "pětka") designated by the main Czechoslovak parties: National Democratic, Populist, Agrarian, National Socialist, and Social Democratic. The "pětka" thus allowed coalition-stability to be maintained even in the temporary absence of an overt coalition government. The "pětka" furthermore implied the continuing primacy of national solidarity over ideological or class solidarity, since, like the Czechoslovaks, the ethnic minority parties were not prepared at this time to hazard a government based on the latter option. (The number of parties participating in the "pětka" arrangement varied from time to time but the system as such draws its name from the original five.)

The continuing ethnic estrangement had been illustrated during one of the last effective political actions over which the Tusar cabinet presided: the reelection of T.G. Masaryk as President of the Republic at the first session of the regular National Assembly on May 27, 1920. Masaryk had been unanimously designated president by the exclusively Czech and Slovak Constituent National Assembly as one of its first acts on November 14, 1918. Now, with the constitution adopted and general elections having taken place, he requested the formal confirmation of this decision in the prescribed constitutional manner, i.e., by a joint session of the two houses of the legislature. This chagrined the Czech party leaders who disliked the implication that the all-national, regular, National Assembly had rights of scrutiny or review over the earlier decisions of its exclusively Czechoslovak, revolutionary predecessor. But Masaryk insisted, and his demand was then met at a rancorous session of the National Assembly. The session opened with the German and Magyar members protesting when they heard their first names entered in Czech versions in the official protocol (e.g., Jiří in lieu of Georg or György), and then went on to reelect Masaryk by 284 exclusively Czech and Slovak votes out of a total of 411. The German bourgeois parties cast 61 votes for Dr. August Naegle, rector of the German University in Prague; the German Social Democrats and the Magyars accounted for the bulk of the 60 blank ballots and the absentees; and the Czech Communist Alois Muna received 4 (technically invalid) votes, while 2 went to his comrade Antonín Janoušek, who a year earlier had headed a short-lived Slovak Soviet Republic under the protection of Béla Kun's Hungarian one. As the balloting proceeded, angry shouts were exchanged between Slovak autonomists (the People's Party) and Slovak centralists (the Hlas group), and when it was over and Masaryk arrived to take his oath, many of the Germans, who recalled his earlier allusion to them as colonists and immigrants, left the Chamber in a huff. All in all, it did not augur well for future ethnic symbiosis under the new constitution and within its newly functioning institutions.

Thus, the nonpartisan, officials' cabinet of Černý was the only alternative once the Czechoslovaks had fallen out among themselves. It was in office for a full year, from September 15, 1920, to September 26, 1921, during which time Czechoslovak-Sudeten German relations remained bad—indeed, they worsened, with the legislature in frequent uproar and the country in chronic turmoil over school, language, and other ethnically relevant administrative policies. On the other hand, during this year the permanent military and diplomatic stances of interwar Czechoslovakia were determined (the Little Entente, reliance on France, patronage of Austria, support for the League of Nations); the institutions and policies of social and industrial regulation were developed (shop councils, railroad councils, state registry of vital statistics); the "pětka" system of extragovernmental interparty consultations was formalized; and a Communist bid for power was contained, simultaneously ending the country's leftward political drift and permanently replacing the Social Democrats with the Agrarians as the strongest party.

Various pressures, maximized by the Polish-Soviet War of mid-1920, had, as mentioned earlier, precipitated the festering tensions between the left and right wings of the Social Democratic Party and thus contributed to the Tusar cabinet's fall. As Czech public opinion in general, and working class opinion in particular, were generally pro-Russian—or, rather, anti-Polish—in this struggle, it became increasingly probable during the late spring and summer of 1920 that the Communist-oriented wing of the Social Democratic Party would have a majority at the party congress scheduled for September 25, there being no apparent incompatibility between the workers' pride in their new Czechoslovak state and their attraction to the Communist International. To avert this development, an anti-Communist group of party leaders, which included Tusar and his fellow Social Democratic ministers, undertook a preemptive stroke. First they surreptitiously transferred legal ownership over the party's property (presses, headquarters, etc.) to their persons. They then engineered a rump meeting of the party executive on September 14, which they cajoled into postponing the congress from September 25 to December 25 and resolving that the left wing had excluded itself from the party since Social Democratic principles and Comintern loyalties were declared mutually exclusive. Tusar and his colleagues resigned their ministerial portfolios later that day, advising President Masaryk to replace them with Černý and his fellow officials.

The understandably outraged left wing of the party accepted this challenge, confirmed the originally scheduled date of the congress, attracted to it a majority (338 out of 527) of the already designated delegates, and, claiming to represent a majority of the membership, proceeded to occupy the party headquarters and printing plant. The right-wing leaders, in legal possession of the deeds, resorted to the scarcely socialistic parry of requesting the authorities to enforce the property laws by evicting the technical trespassers, the leftist majority, from the said premises. The Černý government complied with alacrity; the police were dispatched, and a general strike—which in the Kladno area took on near-insurrectionary proportions but at no time seriously threatened the republic—was provoked and smashed (December 9-16). When the dust had settled the account stood as follows: Tusar and his colleagues had sacrificed the power of their Social Democratic Party on the altar of the Czechoslovak political system; a large, morally indignant but politically isolated Communist Party had been born; the bourgeois parties henceforth steeled themselves against further "red," i.e., social reform, legislation. In January and March, 1921, the Slovak and Sudeten German socialist left-wings also seceded from their parties. In October all three leftist sections then amalgamated, to form the Communist Party of Czechoslovakia.

By September, 1921, the Černý interlude had served its purpose; the political parties were ready to resume more overt direction of the government. The Czechoslovak Social Democrats, though still formally the largest party in the legislature (they had lost only eighteen of their seventy-four deputies in the recent schism), were reluctant to 'bait' the Communists by furnishing the prime minister. So it was agreed that this office be filled by the prestigious foreign minister, Beneš, who, though nominally a deputy elected on the National Socialist slate, would for this purpose function as a nonpartisan official. The ministries of finance, Slovak affairs, and interior were also carefully assigned to nonpartisan experts; Černý, who had already headed the last-mentioned ministry during his own stormy premiership, remained in that post.

Beneš' mixed cabinet of politicians and officials held office from September 26, 1921, to October 7, 1922. It consolidated the initiatives of its predecessors in foreign and domestic affairs: an attempted Habsburg restoration in Hungary was repudiated under the pressure of Czecho-slovak mobilization in October, 1921; strikes of miners and metalworkers were handled peacefully in February and April, 1922; land reform and social insurance legislation were implemented; religious instruction in public schools regulated; the currency definitively stabilized and the budget balanced. Politically more pregnant developments were the di-vorce in November, 1921, of the briefly wedded Czech and Slovak People's parties, as Msgr. Šramek declined to go into opposition in sup-port of Msgr. Hlinka's demands for the reactivation of three Roman Catholic secondary schools in Slovakia, and the more promising division of the Deutscher Verband into the Kampfgemeinschaft of irreconcil-ables and the Arbeitsgemeinschaft of potential "activists."

The "pĕtka" system of extraparliamentary consultations and clearances had again proven its resiliency in holding Beneš' coalition together in the face of the Slovak Populist defection. Indispensable, it nevertheless ex-tracted a price: several ministries soon became the specific fiefs of certain parties, and their civil servants were expected to behave as virtual party functionaries; pressing problems on which compromise was difficult were shelved; some member parties became chronic government parties and grew insensitive to the ideological and moral costs of participation-at-any-price, while certain opposition parties became chronic nay-sayers and potential subversives. Finally, the ubiquity and secretiveness of the "pĕtka" system came to be regarded—rightly or wrongly, cynically or remorsefully—as symptomatic of fundamental ills in the constitutional parliamentary life of the republic.

Just as the local elections of June, 1919, which signaled a national shift to the left of Kramář's first government, had elicited the replacement of that government by Tusar's, so a palpable waning of Social Democratic strength in mid-1922 permitted the party leaders to phase out Beneš' interim and hybrid cabinet and supersede it on October 7, 1922, with an unambiguously political one headed by the Agrarian leader Antonín Švehla. Known as "the ministry of all the talents" because the chiefs of the five key Czechoslovak parties, who had remained in the background under Beneš, now accepted portfolios, Švehla's was regarded as the first cabinet that was not born in a crisis or with the specific function of manag-ing an impending crisis.

However, the pugnacious National Democrat Alois Rašín now resumed direction of the finance ministry. In conformity with the conservative national trend and for personal reasons of national pride, he was deter-mined to raise the exchange value of the already stabilized Czechoslovak currency. Applying needless deflationary pressures which caused much unnecessary unemployment for the sake of prestige, Rašín soon became the country's most hated man and was assassinated early in 1923 by a young fanatic who declared himself to be an anarcho-communist destined to avenge the suffering poor.[10]

Though exaggerated in implementation, Rašín's deflationary policies did contribute to the insulation of Czechoslovakia from the great inflation which lacerated Germany, Austria, and Poland in 1923 and which, indeed, drove capital seeking security out of these countries into her. Similarly, though the unemployment provoked was painful, the stabilization of Czechoslovakia's fiscal affairs was not achieved at the cost of destroying an entire class—again in contrast to some neighboring states—since the Sudeten German bondholders had been ruined less by Czech policies than by the Central Powers' loss of World War I.

As an expression of its intention to give administrative meaning to the theory of a united country, the Švehla government refreshed a long-standing commitment to dèvelop a nationwide, centralistic, prefectural system and implemented it in Slovakia during 1923. But the Czech National Democrats and Populists, fearful lest administrative districts with German majorities result, vetoed its application in the historic provinces. An Agricultural Chambers Act of April, 1923, also fell between two political stools. Benefiting the peasantry, it did not resolve and perhaps even aggravated Agrarian-Socialist differences over grain tariffs.

These tariffs remained an open issue and eventually were a key factor in the decision to hold early general elections for both legislative houses in November, 1925, even though constitutionally the Chamber of Deputies' term did not expire until April, 1926, and the Senate's until April, 1928. Other reasons for consulting the electorate were: a desire to test the secession of the Communists and Slovak Populists from the formerly united 'parent' parties with whom they had run on joint slates in the elections of April, 1920; a wish to test the fusion of the Czech and Slovak Agrarians, which had likewise occurred since 1920, and a similar organizational strengthening of the Small Traders and Artisans Party. The small Progressive Socialist Party of the 1920 elections having split, it was desirable to ascertain whether its erstwhile constituency would follow two of its three deputies into the Czechoslovak Social Democratic Party; again, it was appropriate to consult the populations of the Těšín and Hlučín districts which, not having yet been legally annexed, had not voted in 1920; furthermore, local elections in September, 1923, had indicated a drift of disaffected Slovaks from the various 'centralistic' parties (espe-

10. Rašín was shot on January 5 and died on February 18, 1923, at the age of fifty-five. Rašín's assassination was one of a rash sweeping Central Europe at this time. In addition to an abortive attempt on Beneš' life not long afterward and one on that of Prince-Regent Alexander of Yugoslavia on June 29, 1921, there were also the murders of the Yugoslav minister of the interior Milorad Drašković, on July 21, 1921, of the German vice chancellor Matthias Erzberger, August 29, 1921, of the German foreign minister Walther Rathenau on June 24, 1922, and of the Polish president Gabriel Narutowicz on December 16, 1922.

cially from the Socialists) to Hlinka's 'autonomist' Populists, a trend that invited verification by general elections. But the most spectacular development prompting the elections of November, 1925, was a Church-State crisis precipitated by the 510th anniversary of the burning at the stake of the Czech national martyr and Roman Catholic heretic Jan Hus on July 6.

With approximately three-fourths of the country's population adhering to it, the Roman Catholic Church was strong enough in interwar Czechoslovakia to prevent the pursuit of a radically secular domestic course; but, since its Czech, though not its Slovak, laity was mildly anticlerical, the Church was not powerful enough to impose its own political ascendancy. Negatively identified in Czech nationalist historiography as the perfidious agent of old Bohemia's destruction through civil war and foreign subjugation, the Roman Catholic Church was further suspect for its aloofness from the Czech national renaissance of the nineteenth and early twentieth centuries, and for the preponderance of cosmopolitan and/or German aristocrats among its senior ecclesiastical dignitaries in the Czech lands during the Habsburg rule. Though in Slovakia, too, the senior hierarchy was Magyar (or magyarized) rather than consciously Slovak, nevertheless here the less secularized, less urbanized, less modern Slovak peasantry had remained more pious than the bulk of the nominally Catholic Czech laity.

Msgr. Jan Šramek, the energetic and somewhat dictatorial leader of the Czech People's Party, had labored assiduously, subtly, and with incipient success during independent Czechoslovakia's first years to rehabilitate political Catholicism's patriotic respectability. Insisting on remaining in the government even at the cost of Msgr. Hlinka's defection from the once-joint party, Šramek had "from inside" achieved some amelioration of the land reform in regard to church estates, a compromise matrimonial law which, though permitting divorce and civil marriage, also recognized religious marriage ceremonies as valid and sufficient without supplementary civil ones, quite generous state salaries (so-called *congrua* payments) to the clergy of officially recognized religions, and compulsory religious instruction for all children of parents who in the census declared an affiliation to a recognized religious cult (there were ten such cults in the historic provinces and eight in Slovakia and Ruthenia).

Now, in the summer of 1925, Šramek's carefully tended plant of Roman Catholic-Czech nationalist reconciliation was to be tested by a sudden storm as the government prepared for the first official celebration of the Hus anniversary. The anniversary had been made a national holiday by statutory legislation in the spring, and the Papal Nuncio, supported by the Archbishop of Prague, had lodged vehement protests and urged the Czech Populists to leave the coalition. On the appointed day of July 6, his "last warning" having been rebuffed as Masaryk, Švehla, and Beneš attended the controversial ceremonies (allegedly as private persons), Nuncio Msgr. Marmaggi angrily quit Prague for Rome. It was an excessive reaction, and Šramek showed considerable political shrewdness in remaining in the cabinet. (He had shown the same shrewdness in February when he had emphatically dissociated himself from a pastoral letter by the Slovak bishops threatening with ecclesiastical punishment any Catholic belonging to a socialistic party or organization or even to the secular Sokol [Falcon] gymnastic society.) Šramek's sobriety in this charged situation helped to contain the subsequent anticlerical reaction; indeed, it was the National Socialist rather than his own Czech Populist party that suffered defections as a result. It also helped to win for Czechoslovakia favorable concessions from the overextended Vatican in an eventual *modus vivendi*; an agreement of December, 1927, permitted the Czechoslovak government to screen for political acceptability Vatican nominees to episcopal appointments in the republic, and the Vatican furthermore committed itself to a redrawing of diocesan and monastic-province boundaries. The effect of the latter provision was to bring all parishes and monastic establishments in Czechoslovakia under the jurisdiction of superiors also resident in the country, thus ending the subordination of Slovak and some Těšín-Silesian parishes to the Archbishops of Esztergom (Hungary) and Breslau (Germany).

Šramek was also politically vindicated by the outcome of the elections of November 15, 1925, which saw Catholic, Agrarian, and Communist triumphs at the expense of the moderate Socialists, while the intransigent nationalist electoral strength in all ethnic camps remained relatively stable (see table 20). In this complex election, the Catholics and the Agrarians had gained across the entire ethnic board. The Communists' emergence as the country's second largest party, while also impressive, was ideologically marred for 'pure' Marxists by being inversely related to the degree of industrialization in the various regions. Thus, whereas the Communist share of all ballots cast for professed "worker," i.e., Communist and Socialist, parties in the 1925 Chamber elections was 36.1 percent in the republic as a whole, it was 30 percent in the Czech- and German-populated western provinces, 60 percent among Slovaks, 70 percent in Ruthenia, and 90 percent in the specifically Magyar districts of southern Slovakia and Ruthenia. It appears that the Communist victory over the Socialists owed at least as much to ethnic factors, and particularly to the so-called revolution of rising expectations in the backward areas, as to the fact that, for Czech voters, the Communists were the most 'available' opposition party.

As the 146 Chamber seats of the five "pětka" parties, representing 44.9 percent of the popular vote, fell just short of a majority in the 300-member lower house, the Czechoslovak Small Traders Party, which had more than doubled its performance over 1920, was now coopted with

TABLE 20

Parliamentary Elections, November 15, 1925

	Chamber of Deputies			Senate		
Party	Number of Votes	Percentage of Total Vote	Seats	Number of Votes	Percentage of Total Vote	Seats
Czech National Democrat	284,601	4.0	13	256,360	4.2	7
Czech Small Trader	286,058	4.0	13	257,171	4.2	6
Czech Populist	691,095	9.7	31	618,033	10.1	16
Slovak Populist	489,111	6.9	23	417,206	6.9	12
CzSl. Agrarian	970,940	13.7	45	841,647	13.8	23
Czech National Socialist	609,153	8.6	28	516,250	8.5	14
CzSl. Social Democrat	631,403	8.9	29	537,470	8.8	14
German Nationalist	240,918	3.4	10	214,589	3.5	5
German Nazi	168,354	2.4	7	139,945	2.3	3
German Democrat	no list	....	....	no list	....	....
German Christian Social	314,438	4.4	13	289,055	4.7	7
German (and Magyar) Farmer	571,765	8.0	24	505,597	8.3	12
German Social Democrat	411,365	5.8	17	363,310	6.0	9
Magyar Christian Social	98,337	1.4	4	85,777	1.4	2
Jewish lists	115,781	1.6	....	51,513	0.9	....
Polish list	29,884	0.4	1	25,746	0.4	....
Ruthenian Autonomist	35,699	0.5	1	30,767	0.5	....
Communist	934,223	13.2	41	774,454	12.7	20
Other (eleven lists)	224,286	3.1	....	171,827	2.8	....
Total	7,107,411	100.0	300	6,096,717	100.0	150

its 13 seats into the government coalition. Thus, the quintet of Czechoslovak parties was expanded to a sextet. But this maneuver could not resolve the inner political tensions of Švehla's second cabinet, which he formed on December 9, 1925, and within which the now buoyed Agrarian and Populist partners inevitably demanded their due rewards at the expense of the cramped Socialists: agricultural tariffs, Socialist relinquishment of the education ministry, more generous *congrua* payments to clergy, and more active pursuit of the negotiations with the Vatican. Other intracoalition quarrels involved the length of military service, taxes on alcohol, and the question of which party would supply the Senate's presiding officer. Under these stresses and with Švehla in bad health, the government accomplished little other than passage of the official language laws on February 3, 1926, before it disintegrated on March 18.

Černý now once again formed a stop-gap cabinet of nonpartisan officials, while Švehla deputized his Agrarian colleague Hodža, a Slovak Hlasist, to sound out the moderate German and Slovak opposition parties on the possibility of an entirely new type of coalition, one structured on bourgeois ideological and class lines rather than on Czechoslovak national ones. Indeed, unofficially it was precisely such a combination that sustained Černý's interim cabinet whenever it required a parliamentary vote over the next half year. Hodža's patient and skillful negotiations bore fruit.

On October 12, 1926, Černý made way for Švehla's third cabinet in which, for the first time, two German parties, the electorally successful Christian Socials and Farmers, each accepted a portfolio. The Slovak Populists at first simply supported the cabinet, pending Msgr. Hlinka's return from an extensive American tour, after which they supplied two ministers from January 15, 1927, on. The Czech National Democrats found it difficult to swallow their nationalist pride by conceding the right of Germans to furnish ministers of the Czechoslovak Republic and to sit at their sides as colleagues. Initially, therefore, the National Democrats only agreed to give conditional support from the floor in debate and in confidence votes, but on April 28, 1928, they overcame their scruples and entered the cabinet, which thus now incorporated every significant bourgeois party in the country except the isolated German and Magyar irreconcilables. On the other hand, all Socialist parties in all ethnic camps were for the first time in opposition.

6

The late 1920s were now to test the viability and sagacity of a coalition government in which the Czech bourgeois parties shared power with their ideological colleagues from the Slovak and German ethnic communities. In the retrospect of five decades, the entry of the two Sudenten German "activist" parties into the Czechoslovak cabinet may appear a pathetically ephemeral phenomenon. At the time, however, it was hailed as virtually a chiliastic event, as the domestic confirmation of the "spirit of Locarno"—that supposed healer of all of non-Soviet Europe's international wounds. There is, indeed, no doubt that Berlin, which during the life of the Weimar Republic consistently gave higher priority to Prussian irredentist claims on Poland than to the nationalist aspirations of the formerly Austrian Sudeten Germans, whom it regarded as strong and numerous enough to fend for themselves, encouraged this reconciliation in Czechoslovakia. But the Sudeten Germans were also moved by more compelling considerations than Berlin's blessing. The run-away inflation of 1923 in Germany and Austria, contrasting so vividly with Czechoslovak stability and prosperity, had for the moment cooled the ardor of many for the Greater Reich, and the possibilities of Czechoslovak protection for their agriculture and industry and of concessions to religion interested still more of them. Indeed, as early as 1924, the Arbeitsgemeinschaft parties, the German Democrats, Christian Socials, and Farmers, had signaled their availability for a grand bourgeois coalition. At the time, however, the Czechoslovaks were still unreceptive, wishing first to conclude three policy courses without Sudeten German participation: land reform legislation, official language legislation, and "Czechization" of the bureaucracy. Now, with these matters out of the way by 1926, and with the strong Communist electoral performance in the recent elections acting as a prod toward a closing of interethnic bourgeois ranks, the new coalition at last became mutually feasible.

No exceptional declarations of loyalty were exchanged between the Czechoslovak and the German coalition partners. The latter entered the cabinet as, in Švehla's words, "equals among equals." Dr. Franz Spina, leader of the German Farmers, explained that, "(we) no longer fight against this state, but to assure our rights within it," and his watchword soon became "No cabinet without Germans." While the intransigent Kampfgemeinschaft leveled charges of national sell-out, Professor Bruno Kafka of the German Democrats suggested that the Sudeten Germans henceforth emulate the Czechs' strategy in the Austrian Empire at the turn of the century. That strategy had dictated that some parties were formally 'governmental,' others 'oppositional,' but all worked together when Czech/Bohemian issues were before the imperial Reichsrat. It must have been a somewhat disquieting prescription to any listening Czechs, yet it certainly failed to convince the German Nationalists and Nazis.[11]

For the immediate future, however, doubts and suspicions were muted in an aura of confidence. Paralleling the reconciliation of the Czechoslovak and German government parties was a new harmony among the equivalent Socialist parties, which was facilitated by their being together in opposition. The German Social Democrats explicitly distinguished their opposition to the current Prague government from the Nationalists' and Nazis' continuing rejection of the Czechoslovak state per se. On January 1, 1927, the headquarters of the trade union federations associated with the Czech and with the German Social Democratic parties were linked, and on September 18, 1928, a similar development occurred in the "class enemy's" camp, when the German and Czechoslovak Chambers of Industry formed a joint Directing Committee. When Masaryk was reelected president of the republic on May 27, 1927, by 274 votes out of 432 valid ballots, three-fourths of the German deputies and senators supported him; in 1920 none had. Indeed he would not now have been reelected but for this German support. The Communist Šturc received 54 votes, and among the 104 blank ballots were those of the German and Magyar irreconcilables as well as those of the Slovak Populists and some Czech Populists and National Democrats who resented Masaryk's liberalism. In compensation, he had the solid support of the parliamen-

11. Perfectly bilingual, Spina was Professor of Slavistics at the German University in Prague. In the government, he was minister of labor and public works. The other German in the cabinet, the Christian Social leader Dr. Robert Mayr-Harting, who was Professor of Law at the same university, was given the justice ministry. Illustrative of the Sudeten German Nationalists' attitude toward Czechoslovakia are the following remarks by two of their leaders. On October 27, 1922, Dr. Rudolph Lodgman von Auen, on the floor of the Chamber of Deputies, stated: "He who does not believe that it is the supreme duty of the German deputies to commit high treason against this state, is in error." And in 1921, Dr. Lehnert told Sudeten German recruits for the Czechoslovak army: "Your conscience need not be bothered at swearing a false oath of loyalty. You can deceive and cheat (belügen und betrügen) this state at will, for we don't regard its laws as valid."

tary Socialist opposition. All this cross-national fraternization moved one Czech commentator to the ecstatic conclusion that the Sudeten population had become "veritable Czechoslovaks of the German tongue."[12]

Such raptures aside, what did "activism" and its improved political atmosphere achieve? The Catholics in both national camps were gratified by the increased *congrua* allocations and the *modus vivendi* with the Roman Church; the Agrarians, by the grain tariffs. One ironic success was the cultural salvation of the small German communities of Slovakia and Ruthenia; before 1918 they were rapidly succumbing to the pressure of magyarization, but now they were permitted a renaissance under the more generous interpretation of the intrinsically more liberal Czechoslovak language laws. The Germans also achieved the disfranchisement of the armed forces, thus ending the political use of Czech garrisons to tip the ethnic balance in mixed areas, and somewhat increased influence (but no real equality) in the civil service. All the coalition partners could congratulate themselves on the general prosperity and high employment of the next few predepression years; they celebrated in June, 1927, with a comprehensive tax reform very partial to business interests. An attempt to extend this bourgeois euphoria into an assault on the social welfare and social security systems dating from the era of Socialist participation in the government collapsed under tenacious resistance and Švehla's reluctance to embitter the entire working class.

On the politically sensitive matter of standardizing the administrative system, the government, pulled in opposite directions by its Slovak and German members, chose to mollify the former. The problem arose because the ex-Austrian half of Czechoslovakia had inherited a system of provincial administrative units, whereas the formerly Hungarian lands had a system of counties. Early in 1920, it had been decided to establish a general prefectural system that was closer to the old Hungarian than to the old Austrian model, though more centralistic than either, but only in Slovakia had this program been implemented (in 1923). Now, however, Hlinka made the participation of his Slovak People's Party in the cabinet conditional on the extension to Slovakia of the old Austrian system of provinces; he regarded this as a stepping-stone toward eventual Slovak autonomy. The Czechs assented and the Germans acquiesced.

The necessary legislation was passed in July, 1927, and went into effect the next year. Under it, four provinces with relatively impotent provincial diets and executives came into existence: Bohemia, Moravia-Silesia, Slovakia, and Ruthenia. The attachment of Silesia, i.e., Těšín, to Moravia was designed to preclude the possibility of a German-Polish coalition that would force the Czechoslovak element into a politically secondary role in a separate Silesian province. For the Germans, who would have enjoyed

12. F. Damiens, "Les Minorités en Tchécoslovaquie," *Le Monde Slave* 7, no. 5-6 (May-June, 1930), p. 247.

majorities in a number of the twenty-one prefectures formerly scheduled, the four-province system was a complete rebuff and relegated them to permanent minority status in each unit. The two German government parties that reluctantly consented were to be punished by their constituents in due course at the next parliamentary elections. Since it was scarcely in the long-run interest of the Czechoslovak parties to see "activism" thus discredited among the Germans, this entire episode was something of a defeat for all concerned. Not the least of the losers were the Slovaks, who soon learned that their supposed incipient autonomy was utterly illusory. Having burned its fingers on this administrative problem, the bourgeois coalition drew back from the even hotter issue of consolidating the country's several educational systems; nor did it deal capably with the pressing and politically sensitive question of housing and construction.

Although the legal competence of the newly authorized provincial diets was restricted to cultural and economic issues, and although one third of their members were to be safely nominated by the central government, nevertheless the first elections to the diets, on December 2, 1928, aroused considerable political curiosity as an interim test of the two-year-old Czech-Slovak-German bourgeois coalition. Voter turnout was light and, on balance, all the government parties except the Czechoslovak Agrarians were punished. On the other hand, the extreme opposition parties, the Communists and the German intransigents, also lost, while those who were "positivist" in principle but currently not in the government did well. The latter category refers to the three Socialist parties and a new group, the German Work and Economy Association (DAWG), consisting of a fusion of Professor Bruno Kafka's Democrats and an "activist" big-business splinter from the Nationalists led by one Alfred Rosche. On balance, therefore, the results suggested that both the Czechoslovak and the German electorates, without repudiating interethnic political collaboration, demanded more positive government policies and more convincing results, particularly in the socioeconomic field.

Msgr. Šramek had been presiding at cabinet meetings since March 8, 1928, when Švehla took a medical leave. But as his Czech Populists had done far less well than the Agrarians in the provincial elections, the latter party now decided to reclaim the full exercise of the premiership. Accordingly, on February 1, 1929, Švehla retired and was succeeded by Defense Minister František Udržal. Udržal was eager for fresh parliamentary elections to confirm his own and his party's primacy before the ominous clouds of the world agricultural crisis burst over Czechoslovakia, but initially he was restrained by the other coalition partners who required time to recover from their recent buffeting at the provincial elections. A crisis over Slovakia soon provided Udržal with sufficient leverage to have his way.

At the approach of the republic's tenth anniversary in 1928, the official organ of the Slovak People's Party had published an article entitled "Vacuum Juris," claiming that the Slovak leaders who had declared Slovakia's union with the Czech lands on October 30, 1918, at Turčiansky Svätý Martin (see section 2), had, in a secret clause, limited that adherence to a ten-year probationary period, at the end of which a legal vacuum would come into existence as the Slovaks recovered their sovereignty and hence the right to renegotiate their constitutional and political status. No conclusive proof of this assertion was offered then or later. The article's author was Vojtech Tuka, a professor of law in old Hungary, a man who, though of Slovak origins, had as late as 1920 still given his nationality as Magyar, but who had since gained Msgr. Hlinka's confidence and risen to the vice-presidency of the Slovak People's Party. After some delay, the authorities responded. Tuka's parliamentary immunity was suspended, he was arrested early in 1929, tried over the summer, and sentenced on October 5, 1929, to fifteen years' imprisonment for espionage, communicating military secrets to a foreign power (Hungary), planning Slovakia's secession from the republic, and organizing armed bands for this purpose. The cross-grained Hlinka had throughout defended his sinister protégé Tuka with so much heat and so little discernment—even to the point of demanding a political promise of a juridical acquittal—as to convince the other parties that the current coalition's days were numbered.

Udržal now forced the pace and created a cabinet crisis by transferring the defense ministry, which he had retained when he became the premier, to a fellow member of his Agrarian Party. To the other government parties' charge that this was a unilateral disturbance of the established coalition balance, Udržal retorted that it simply restored the situation that had pertained before Švehla's sick-leave. Negotiations proved unavailing, and it was decided to hold new parliamentary elections on October 27, 1929. By this time even the Czech Populists, who had been most reluctant to face early parliamentary elections after the battering they took in the provincial ones, were agreeable; they believed that political Catholicism had been revivified by the impressive and emotional ceremonies of the St. Václav Millennium on September 28, commemorating the assassination of the nation's patron saint-king in 929. Hlinka, in turn, truculently insisted on placing Tuka's name in a place of honor high up on the Slovak Populists' list of candidates.

Just as the parliamentary elections of 1920 had been a setback for the hitherto dominant National Democrats, and those of 1925 had brought defeat to the "pětka" coalition of the preceding years, so, too, those of 1929—again deliberately scheduled by an adequate, in terms of numbers, but internally fraying government coalition—also witnessed the aggregate rejection by the electorate of the prevailing cabinet constellation.

This time the interethnic bourgeois coalition of seven parties was defeated and lost its collective parliamentary majority. But also, once again, the well-entrenched Czechoslovak Agrarians emerged relatively unscathed from the rebuff administered to their partners. As shown in table 21, all Catholic parties lost: the Czech and German ones because their working-class constituents of 1925 were now punishing them for their acquiescence in the conservative socioeconomic governmental policies of the intervening years, the Slovak one because Hlinka had miscalculated his people's reaction to Tuka's Hungarian-subsidized demagogery. The various moderate Socialist parties gained over 1925. However, the Communists lost (in urban rather than in rural districts) and slipped from second to fourth place, indicating that the general prosperity of recent years, while scarcely dissolving all social and political discontents, nevertheless funneled them away from extremist expressions. In the German community, this meant that the dissatisfaction with the late coalition partners did not lead to an utter disillusionment with "activism" per se, such as would have been grist for Nationalist, Nazi, or Communist mills. Similarly, among the Czechs neither Communists nor Fascists benefited from the disillusionment with recent government policies, despite the fact that the latter ran under the attractive lable of "League Against Fixed-Order Lists"—a clever bid to capitalize on the popular resentment against the party-bosses' rigid control of the voters' choice and the backbenchers' freedom. The seemingly marginal gains by the Czech National Democrats were due to local alliances with small groups in Slovakia and Ruthenia, not to any greater popularity in their Czech homeland.

TABLE 21

PARLIAMENTARY ELECTIONS, OCTOBER 27, 1929

	Chamber of Deputies			Senate		
Party	Number of Votes	Percentage of Total Vote	Seats	Number of Votes	Percentage of Total Vote	Seats
Czech National Democrat	359,547	4.9	15	325,023	5.0	8
Czech Small Trader	291,209	3.9	12	274,085	4.3	6
Czech Populist	623,340	8.4	25	559,700	8.7	13
Slovak Populist	425,051	5.7	19	377,498	5.9	9
CzSl. Agrarian	1,105,498	15.0	46	978,291	15.2	24
Czech National Socialist	767,328	10.4	32	666,607	10.3	16
CzSl. Social Democrat	963,462	13.0	39	841,331	13.0	20
Against Fixed-Order Lists	70,850	1.0	3	51,617	0.8	1
German Nationalist	189,187	2.5	7	166,718	2.6	....
German Nazi	204,110	2.8	8	171,181	2.6	4
German Chr. Soc. and allies	348,066	4.7	14	313,544	4.9	8
German Farmer and DAWG	396,454	5.4	16	359,002	5.6	9
German Social Democrat	506,761	6.9	21	446,940	6.9	11
Magyar Chr. Soc. and Nationalist	257,372	3.5	9	233,772	3.6	6
Jewish-Polish bloc	104,556	1.4	4	27,823	0.4	....
Communist	753,220	10.2	30	644,896	10.0	15
Other (three lists)	18,968	0.3	....	12,473	0.2	....
Total	7,384,979	100.0	300	6,450,501	100.0	150

It now required six weeks of negotiations before Udržal could form his second cabinet on December 7, 1929, consisting of eight Czech and German parties commanding a total of 206 Chamber votes. The two moderate Czechoslovak Socialist parties, the National Socialists and the Social Democrats, now reentered the cabinet after a four-year lapse; the German Social Democrats joined them for the first time, their Czech comrades refusing to enter without them. The German Farmers and their new DAWG allies remained in the government, while the German Christian Socials were out (quite against their own will) but remained loyally aloof from the German intransigents. It was a characteristically insensitive blunder to exclude this sincerely and loyally "activist" German party merely on grounds of arithmetic convenience in the distribution of cabinet portfolios and because its leader, Mayr-Harting, had been less adept than the Farmers' Spina at administering his ministry. Hlinka's Slovak Populists now resumed their preferred posture of opposition, while their Czech analogue remained in the cabinet together with the other Czech standard coalition parties—National Democrats, Small Traders, and, of course, Agrarians. In sum, therefore, Czechoslovakia was to enter the depression era with a doubly mixed government—bourgeois/socialist and Czechoslovak/German—that had no comprehensive or united policies for coping with the coming pressures and dislocations.

7

Before proceeding to the painful analysis of Czechoslovak politics under the pressures of the depression, it appears appropriate to interrupt the chronological survey at this point for an examination of relations among Czechs, Slovaks, and Ruthenians in the interwar republic. As mentioned above, these relations had ran counter to early hopes of Slavic solidarity even before being subjected to redoubled stresses by the depression.

Though ethnically and linguistically related, Czechs and Slovaks had been politically separated for a thousand years, since the absorption of the Slovak lands into the Hungarian kingdom in the ninth or tenth century. This absorption, moreover, had at no time left them with the autonomous or semi-independent status of Transylvania or Croatia. Again, though the majority of both Czechs and Slovaks were Roman Catholic, the latter, not having experienced the Czechs' Hussite catharsis, were also left without its critical residue of modernism, secularism, and anticlericalism. The Slovaks were, rather, a pious, provincial, and heavily illiterate peasant people, who remained politically submissive to the Hungarian authorities until well into the nineteenth century.

After the Austro-Hungarian Ausgleich of 1867, Slovakia was subjected to two new Hungarian policies; both corroded her somnolent traditions. First of all, an inflexible program of linguistic magyarization sought the cultural decapitation of the Slovak nation; only the uneducated peasantry was left unaffected. While the Hungarians' goal here was clearly the dubious one of ultimately denationalizing an entire people, it should be recalled that their intolerance was exclusively cultural and linguistic, not racial and ethnic. A magyarized Slovak found all careers and opportunities—public, professional, and especially ecclesiastical—open to him. This accessibility of the Roman Catholic ecclesiastical hierarchy to able magyarized Slovaks was an ambivalent phenomenon. On the one hand, it provided a career ladder for "upward-mobile" Slovak talent; on the other hand, it ironically emphasized the political disadvantage that accrued to the Slovaks as a result of professing the same religious faith as the Magyars' state church. Unlike the Orthodox and Uniate Romanian population of Hungarian Transylvania, for example, the Catholic Slovaks did not benefit from the defensive barrier of a different church to protect them from magyarization in general and from the use of Roman Catholic institutions as a particular weapon in this very process. Secondly, a vigorous Hungarian drive for economic autarky promoted the Slovak area's development into a center of extractive and primary industry, while the finishing industries were concentrated around Budapest.

The first Hungarian policy, that of magyarization, came to meet with some resistance during the last two decades before World War I, largely, though not entirely, under the inspiration of Masaryk's Czecho-Slovak program. Even the most anti-Czech Slovaks concede that their nation had been rescued from the threat of cultural extinction by the Czechs' utilizing World War I as the lever to pry Slovakia away from Hungary. The second policy, that of industrialization, was to have a bitter denouement in interwar Czechoslovakia, as the Prague governments allowed the more highly developed industries of the Czech provinces to destroy nascent Slovak industries. Prague's land-reform legislation on the other hand, by dealing with the extremely unequal prewar distribution, benefited the Slovak peasants at the expense of the Magyar estate-owners.

The disagreements and tensions between Czechs and Slovaks that quickly surfaced in the interwar republic astonished the Czechs more than the Slovaks. The latter, though content to be out of Hungary, from the very first approached the new Czechoslovak state with a ballast of parochial mistrust and, indeed, entered it only in the expectation of an autonomous political status that would permit them to protect themselves from the Czechs' modernism. Autonomous status had, they believed, been guaranteed them by the terms of the Pittsburgh Agreement, negotiated in the American city of that name on May 30, 1918, by representatives of several American-Czech and American-Slovak fraternal organizations with the assistance of Masaryk, who was then traveling in the United States as head of the Czecho-Slovak National Council in exile and who also appended his signature.[13] Whatever may have been the Czechs' original intentions apropos of autonomy for Slovakia, the tenacious and skillful Hungarian efforts of 1918 and 1919 to retain it, as well as the lingering awe in which many Slovak peasants continued to hold their former Magyar masters (half-fearfully expecting their return at any moment), quickly convinced Prague that autonomy was not a feasible political proposition. Supported by a numerically small but culturally advanced contingent of Slovak centralizers, largely from the Slovak Lutheran minority, the Czechs promptly and sanguinely accepted the 'responsibility' of their 'mission' and despatched their gendarmes, their bureaucrats, their teachers, their judges—as well as their tax-collectors and recruiting sergeants—to replace the departed Hungarians in Slovakia. And when these agents of modernization met with the sullen resentment inevitably accorded by a traditionalist peasantry to 'godless' intruders, the baffled and exasperated Czechs concluded, equally inevitably, that the Slovaks were a mulish, benighted, and priest-ridden people.

As only a handful of old Hungary's civil servants stationed in the Slovak areas in 1918 remained to serve the new Czechoslovak state, and as the Slovak intelligentsia was then still small, the Czechs were obliged to fill the administrative gap. They expanded and "Slovacized" the educational system, thus protecting the Slovaks from further magyarization and dramatically reducing their illiteracy rate. A Slovak press and Slovak cultural activities were encouraged, the franchise was democratized, social legislation enlightened, the administration was honest, the land re-

13. The polemics generated by this document are long, repetitive, and bitter. The Czechs later rationalized their failure to fulfill its autonomy clause by alleging four types of arguments: (a) ethnological—there was no Slovak nation, only a Slovak branch of the Czechoslovak nation; (b) pragmatic—due to centuries of Hungarian misrule, the population of Slovakia was insufficiently mature for self-government; (c) juristic—the Constitution of the Republic had normative precedence over all other political documents; (d) casuistic-—Masaryk had merely witnessed a local programmatic statement drafted by two sets of American citizens, who could not possibly bind the future sovereign Czechoslovak state. At the time of the Tuka trial in 1929, Masaryk was even to repudiate the document itself as a kind of fraud, allegedly because the American-Slovak organization whose leaders signed it in 1918 was not chartered under American law until 1919. This was a rather unbecoming descent on Masaryk's part into legalistic hypocrisy, since he had himself composed the final draft and had then once more signed the formal calligraphic copy in Washington on November 14, 1918, the day he was designated President of Czechoslovakia and at a time when he wanted to impress the American government with such evidence of American-Slovak endorsement of his Czechoslovak cause. The Prague government had on November 11 accepted as binding all engagements undertaken by Masaryk abroad. Morally his signature of the Pittsburgh Agreement was such a commitment, for he would scarcely have been asked to sign, or bothered to redraft, a statement intended as no more than a local agreement of American citizens on a program of joint aspirations. While the Czechs' constitutional argument ("c", above) carries weight, one must recall that the Slovaks in the Constituent National Assembly had been coopted by the Czechs and were in many ways unrepresentative.

form beneficial, the towns were demographically demagyarized and slovacized. And yet the Slovaks resented the apparent paternalism, the frequent tactlessness, and the sheer numbers of the Czech bureaucrats who flooded into their country to administer these programs. By 1930 there were 100,274 Czech "immigrants" in Slovakia (exclusive of military personnel), of whom 21,828 worked in the state administration and free professions. Although Slovaks were being phased into these services as rapidly as the educational system graduated them, the Czechs were not withdrawn and hence came to be resented as superfluous and parasitical. It was also frequently alleged, especially of the teachers, that only second-raters came from advanced Bohemia and Moravia to these "hardship posts" in poor Slovakia (and Ruthenia).

The Slovaks also had economic grievances: their infant industry no longer enjoyed old Hungary's subsidies and protection vis-à-vis Bohemian and Moravian-Silesian competition, which now destroyed much of it, and their mountaineer population no longer had its traditional access to the Hungarian plain for seasonal agricultural labor. Czechoslovakia's tax rates were also higher in the former Hungarian than in the former Austrian provinces, until the two fiscal systems were unified in 1929. Though the public services in Slovakia were heavily subsidized by the Czech and German areas, and though the Prague governments invested considerable "social overhead capital" in new railroads, highways, and electric power in Slovakia, the gap between Czech and Slovak living standards nevertheless widened in the interwar period, due in large part to the much higher Slovak birthrate. By 1937 Slovakia's per capita income was only half of Bohemia's and Moravia-Silesia's. Oddly enough, however, fewer Slovaks emigrated from their overpopulated and poor land to the wealthier and more promising western provinces than there were Czechs coming in the opposite direction. Most Slovaks were little interested in exploiting the economic opportunities open to them in the republic at large and yearned for cultural isolation and political autonomy at home. They vehemently rejected the official theory (and census practice) of a "Czechoslovak" nation, and the "centralizers" among them were scorned as both political and religious renegades. The Czechs, in turn, preferred working with the more cosmopolitan Slovak Protestant minority which thus achieved a prominence in public and political life disproportionate to its small numbers but indicative of its high educational attainments. While Msgr. Hlinka was thus the more authentic voice of the Slovak nation, the cohort of Šrobár, Hodža, et al. wielded the effective governmental power.

The Tuka scandal of 1928-29 had for a time appeared to sober the Slovak Populists. Characteristically, Hlinka, after having stubbornly backed Tuka through the trial and having insisted on placing Tuka's name at the top of the party's list of candidates in the Košice district at the subsequent parliamentary elections, then dropped him when the election results of 1929 revealed this nomination to have damaged the Populists. Košice repudiated Tuka, and Slovakia as a whole gave Hlinka's party considerably fewer votes than in 1925 (see tables 20 and 21).

This clearing of the air was, alas, not to survive the onset of the depression, which brought particularly severe economic hardship to Slovakia (specifically through a Czechoslovak-Hungarian trade war), and sharply revived the autonomy movement. Not only did Hlinka himself become more strident in the 1930s, but a still more radical generation now moved to the fore in his own party. Less provincial and more totalitarian than he, these young "Nastupists" (after their revue *Nástup* [Forming Ranks]) attacked the foreign as well as the domestic policies of the Prague governments, urged Slovak solidarity with Nazi Germany and Fascist Italy, and eventually insisted on full independence—no longer mere autonomy—from the Czech lands. A few days before his death on August 16, 1938, Hlinka once again counselled his people to seek a constitutional transformation that would somehow preserve the republic and at the same time give Slovakia autonomy within it; yet from the time of Austria's Anschluss to Germany in mid-March, he had, in fact, been undermining this frequently articulated goal of his by synchronizing ever more closely the tactics of his Slovak People's Party with those of the Sudeten German Henleinists, who were by then in the service of Nazi Germany.

8

The easternmost province of Ruthenia presented interwar Czecho-slovak governments with problems often analogous to those of Slovakia. Here, however, the obligation to confer autonomy was legal as well as moral. Not only had Masaryk in 1918 made a commitment to this effect to the American Ruthenians (see section 2), but with her signing of the international Minorities Protection Treaty on September 10, 1919, Czechoslovakia again committed herself to grant wide autonomy and specified institutions of self-government to Ruthenia. This pledge was solemnly reiterated in the constitution of February 29, 1920. None of these undertakings was ever formally disavowed, though Žatković's cre-dentials in America were no better than the subsequently challenged ones of the American-Slovaks who signed the Pittsburgh Agreement, but neither were they honored until a law conferring limited autonomous powers was passed on June 26, 1937, and finally implemented under the pressure of the Munich disaster on October 8, 1938. Prague periodically rationalized this long postponement by citing the province's extreme backwardness and poverty. Ruthenia was, indeed, one of the most primi-tive corners of East Central Europe, but no more so in the 1920s and 1930s than in 1918 and 1919, when Masaryk and Beneš had dangled autonomy as a bait before the Ruthenians and the peace conference to persuade them to affiliate the province to Czechoslovakia. Nor was Ruthenia's backwardness as such the only Czech motive for postponing the fulfillment of commitments to autonomy; Prague was also disturbed by the specifically *political* "backwardness" of strong subversive tendencies there: Communist, Ukrainian, and, most alarmingly, Magyarophile. It was these tendencies that provoked concern lest autonomy might be incompatible with the integrity of the republic (the "saving clause" of the Minorities Protection Treaty).

The Ruthenians had, indeed, for centuries manifested that blind loyalty to their Hungarian lords which is often characteristic of abjectly exploited peasantries in stagnant "feudal" relationships. As with the Slovaks, most of their potential elite had been magyarized, and it was among the many Ruthenian immigrants in America rather than at home that national consciousness had been born.

The Ruthenians' benefits from and grievancies against the interwar Czechoslovak governments again paralleled those of the Slovaks. The staggering prewar illiteracy was radically reduced, magyarization reversed, and public utilities developed and heavily subsidized by the Czechs. But the other side of this coin was again problematical: the symbiotic economic relationship with prewar Hungary was painfully interrupted; the local population growth devoured the expected economic benefits of land reform (hardly Prague's fault); and a numerous, paternalistic, honest, but listless Czech bureaucracy overran the province. Here, too, the local branches or affiliates of the centralistic Czechoslovak political parties developed a statistical but illusory superiority over the autonomists. If the Ruthenians as a whole gave Prague less trouble than the Slovaks, it was because they were fewer in number, poorer, less nationally conscious and less united, and because they appreciated that Czech tutelage was still preferable to the contemporary Hungarian, Polish, and Romanian treatment of minorities.

9

Interwar Czechoslovakia's second decade was dominated by the related problems of the depression and nazism. The first of these scourges did not lacerate her industry and industrial exports until a year or so after many other industrial countries had been hit, but it lasted longer in Czechoslovakia than elsewhere. The third of her population that was dependent on agriculture had already been affected by the slightly earlier world agricultural crisis of the late 1920s. And because the paramount Agrarian Party always kept an attentive ear cocked toward its original peasant constituency, agricultural problems inevitably had serious political repercussions. The Agrarian-led coalition's response was redoubled protectionism. This policy not only set Czechoslovakia's agricultural tariffs at a high level; it also fixed them by law, thus rendering them virtually nonnegotiable internationally—even with her diplomatic allies of the Little Entente. The result was a trade war with Hungary from 1930 onward and an unhelpful—though scarcely unique—Czechoslovak rigidity in the various international consultations of these years, seeking to alleviate East Central Europe's aggregate agricultural surplus crisis. Nor were the economic or political aspects of the domestic farm problem solved by protectionism.

Industrial production, exports, and unemployment began to worsen precipitiously in 1931 and reached their nadir during the middle years of the decade. By all these indices, the Sudeten German areas were the worst hit, and this immediately had serious political repercussions. As early as the communal elections in the autumn of 1931, the Nazis and Communists scored significant gains in the Sudeten districts. The Prague government took this as a warning and tried its best to counteract the accelerating erosion of the economic bases of German "activism," but its best efforts were clumsy and politically utterly inadequate after Hitler came to power on January 30, 1933, and promptly launched an impressive and successful attack on unemployment and its attendant hardships in Germany.

It was not primarily Prague's fault that the sector of the national economy owned by Sudeten Germans happened to be more vulnerable than the Czech sector to the "beggar my neighbor" international spirit of the depression, though its policies in the predepression years had certainly not been calculated to correct this imbalance. The Czechs, understandably, had consistently disclaimed responsibility for: the Sudeten Germans' earlier heavy losses on Habsburg imperial war bonds (1914-18); the fact that local Sudeten banks had most of their assets on deposit with the central banks of Vienna on the day Finance Minister Rašín froze all fiscal transactions and separated the new Czech currency from the depreciating but still circulating imperial one (February 25, 1919); the Sudeten Germans' subsequent nationalistic and mistrustful decision to transfer much of their remaining liquid wealth to banks in the German Reich, where it was again dissolved in inflation (1923); the fact that this same German and Austrian inflation temporarily destroyed the traditional Sudeten export markets; the Sudeten Germans' failure during the subsequent years of revived prosperity to modernize and rationalize their technologically old and obsolescent plant; and now, finally, the fact that Sudeten German industry happened to be more dependent on exports—particularly to the Reich—than the newer, heavier, more internally geared Czech-owned industry, and hence, ironically, more vulnerable than the latter to Germany's autarkic policies during the depression. Indeed, the Czechs did not maliciously instigate these Sudeten German economic frailties, but they were never averse to benefiting from them. Czech banks replaced Viennese banks in financing; hence they partly controlled much Sudeten industry in the later 1920s. When the Central Bank of Sudeten German Savings Banks collapsed in 1932, the Czechs rescued it at the cost of its economic independence. When Sudeten German banks received one billion crowns in subsidies out of a total of three-and-a-half billion disbursed during the depression by the Czechoslovak state, they were obliged to accept government limitations and control. As evidence of their benevolence, the Czechs would point to their heavy "pump priming" for public works in the Sudeten areas during the depression, while the Germans retorted that this was a device to settle colonies of Czech workers on hitherto "clean" German landscapes. Thus, the statistics, which indicate that the Sudeten German districts were particularly hard hit by the depression but also that the Czechoslovak government concentrated much of its relief work in those same areas, in no way resolve the political problematics of this situation.

At the end of 1930 the four deputies of the Rosche-Kafka DAWG group of German "activists" left the governing coalition, followed in April, 1932, by the twelve Czech Small Traders. They were alarmed by the higher taxes which the coalition majority agreed were necessary to maintain state solvency amidst a stumbling economy. By February, 1934, on the other hand, it was the National Democrats' turn to quit the cabinet over the devaluation of the crown by one-sixth (from 44.58 to 37.15 gold milligrams). Theoretically, this last defection, by removing the most "Manchesterian" party from the governing coalition while still leaving it with an arithmetically comfortable parliamentary majority, might have permitted a vigorously unorthodox attack on the depression. But except for an exchange between the Agrarians and the Socialists of a state grain monopoly and export institute for new collective bargaining arrangements in July, 1934—hardly innovative measures—the coalition government limped along without a strategy and postponed essential but painful decisions lest its internal bourgeois-socialist tensions explode. Prime Minister Udržal, who was indeed a sadly "flappable" heir to the masterful Švehla but as much the victim as the manipulator of this paralysis, had been jettisoned by his own Agrarian Party on October 24, 1932, in favor of the cooler and supposedly tougher Jan Malypetr. Nothing much was changed. Though Malypetr was hailed as the country's first "new," i.e., entirely postwar, political figure, and thus allegedly free of the bad "Viennese" habits of his predecessors, he was already sixty years old on becoming premier and his style was as inevitably shaped by the necessity to balance coalitions in the Czech political system as were those of his elders and peers.

In the fatigue and unimaginativeness with which her governments approached the depression, Czechoslovakia was hardly unique. But she was exceptional in Central Europe for the stability manifested by the established Czechoslovak (but not the Sudeten German) political parties in the face of the depression's turmoil, and for the resultant constancy of her commitment to constitutional parliamentarism while all around her neighbors were succumbing to totalitarian, military, or royal dictatorships. There was indeed a Czechoslovak Fascist movement, which leaned more toward the Italian than toward the German model. The National Democrats in time patronized it, and even some right-wing Agrarians eventually itched to flirt with it; but, despite the turbulent leadership of the talented ex-Socialist agitator Stříbrný and the daredevil military hero Gajda, fascism's intended Czech social clientele remained on the whole immune to its demagogic blandishments. The Communists, too, though increasing their membership and their electoral support among the Czech population in the early 1930s, never received a mandate to overthrow the Republic and made no serious attempts to capitalize on the depression for revolutionary purposes. Among the Sudeten Germans, furthermore, the Communists now lost supporters to the Henleinists, indicating that their reputation with the ethnic minorities had rested all along on unstable and "un-Marxist" foundations which were vulnerable to erosion at the hands of the first nationalistically more demagogic alternative to make an appearance.

The octogenerian Masaryk's last reelection to the presidency on May 24, 1934, saw him receive 327 of the 418 valid ballots; 38 went to the Communist Klement Gottwald, and 53—including those of Hlinka's Slovak Populists, the Czech Fascists, and some Czech National Democrats—remained blank. But this formally overwhelming endorsement of the republic's founder by most of the Sudeten German deputies and senators was doubly deceptive: it was personal rather than political, and it was at the hands of a body of men elected to their functions in the still happily "activist" year of 1929. The parliamentary elections of May 19, 1935, were to demonstrate the continuing relative stability of Czech and Slovak political alignments despite the depression. But this stability was undermined now in the German community by an avalanche toward nazism in the form of Konrad Henlein's Sudetendeutsche Partei which won two-thirds of all German votes (and more votes even than the Czechoslovak Agrarians) and broke the backs of the "activist" parties. Indeed, the Henleinists had done proportionately better than the Nazis in the Reich at the last reasonably meaningful interwar German elections, those of March 5, 1933, when Hitler was already Chancellor but his party could do no better than 44 percent. As in all three previous Czechoslovak parliamentary elections, the outgoing coalition had failed to achieve an ongoing majority. The results are shown in table 22.

Throughout the preceding decade, the Czech leaders in Prague had enjoyed a choice of either bourgeois or socialist Sudeten German "activists" available for coalition-building. The very availability of these options had, of course, given them considerable leverage and maneuverabil-

TABLE 22

PARLIAMENTARY ELECTIONS, MAY 19, 1935

	Chamber of Deputies			Senate		
Party	Number of Votes	Percentage of Total Vote	Seats	Number of Votes	Percentage of Total Vote	Seats
Cz. Nat. Dem. and Fascist (Stříbrný)	456,353	5.6	17	410,095	5.6	9
Czech Small Trader	448,047	5.4	17	393,732	5.4	8
Czech Populist	615,877	7.5	22	557,684	7.7	11
Sl. Populist, Sl. Nat., Ruthenian Autonom., and Polish	564,273	6.9	22	495,166	6.8	11
CzSl. Agrarian	1,176,593	14.3	45	1,042,924	14.3	23
Czech National Socialist	755,880	9.2	28	672,126	9.3	14
CzSl. Social Democrat	1,034,774	12.6	38	910,252	12.5	20
Czech Fascist (Gajda)	167,433	2.0	6	145,125	2.0	....
German Nazi SdP (Henlein)	1,249,530	15.2	44	1,092,255	15.0	23
German Christian Social	162,781	2.0	6	155,234	2.1	3
German Farmer	142,399	1.7	5	129,862	1.8	....
German Social Democrat	299,942	3.6	11	271,097	3.7	6
Magyar Chr. Soc. and Nationalist	291,831	3.5	9	259,832	3.6	6
Communist	849,509	10.3	30	740,696	10.2	16
Other (two lists)	16,190	0.2	....	973	0.0	....
Total	8,231,412	100.0	300	7,277,053	100.0	150

ity. Now, on the morrow of the 1935 elections (in which, incidentally, Henlein, following Hitler's example, had himself declined to stand as a candidate for the supposedly decadent parliament), the Henleinists announced that henceforth they alone were the legitimate political spokesmen of the Sudeten German community and that the "activist" parties' further membership in the governing coalitions could no longer be regarded as genuine German participation. Though on that same day (May 20, 1935) Henlein cabled Masaryk a declaration of loyalty to the constitution (again emulating Hitler's earlier formal statements toward the Weimar Republic), it was indeed true that, given the election results and given the Henleinist movement's inclusivist, "folkish," ideology as well as its subsidization from the Reich, Czechoslovakia could henceforth not easily be governed "against" the Sudetendeutsche Partei, notwithstanding Malypetr's technical reconstitution and enlargement of his previous cabinet by adding to it the Czech Small Traders (June 3, 1935) and German Christian Socials (July 2, 1936). All this renders appropriate here a brief analysis of the origins and nature of Henlein's "movement-party."

10

As noted earlier the nationalism of the Sudeten Germans had already been particularly vehement and intense in the nineteenth century—far more so, for example, than that of the Habsburgs' Alpine German subjects. In the twentieth century, their youth continued, in the Wandervogel tradition, to cling to a mystic-organicist, romantic-reactionary ideology, and rejected rationalism, democracy, and industrialism. Purportedly grounded in esthetic and moral objections to modern urban culture, this "bündische" attitude made for receptivity to Nazi ideology on the one hand, while on the other it exuded a certain initial elitist contempt for the "vulgarity" of the "plebeian" masses who swelled the rank and file of the Nazi political movement at the end of the 1920s and the beginning of the 1930s.

The Sudeten affiliate of the Nazi movement, the Deutsche National-sozialistische Arbeiterpartei (DNSAP), had led a relatively stable political existence during the 1920s; it had elected five, seven, and eight deputies in that decade's three Czechoslovak parliamentary elections, and had actually conducted a less "secessionist" and more "autonomist" style of propaganda than had the older, classic Nationalist Party. During the depression, it grew rapidly, at the expense first of the Nationalists, then also of the "activist" bourgeois parties, and eventually even of the Communists and German Social Democrats. This growth was accompanied by a fierce internal struggle against the elitist, corporativist "bündische" youth movement already alluded to, a clash that the Czechoslovak authorities affected—perhaps inadvertantly—by banning as treasonable some of the German paramilitary "cultural" organizations (e.g., Volkssportverband, Studentenbund) within which this Nazi-Bündisch struggle was raging.

By the time the dust had settled somewhat, in October, 1933, many veteran leaders of both factions were either in Czech custody or had fled to the Reich, the Nazi and Nationalist parties had dissolved themselves to evade destruction at the hands of the police, and a comparative newcomer, the hitherto relatively unpolitical gymnastic instructor Konrad Henlein, had founded the Sudetendeutsche Heimat-front as a supposedly suprapartisan rendezvous for all *volk*-inclined Sudeten Germans. Henlein's pedigree in the Turnverband, the gymnastic movement, rendered him originally closer to the "bündische" than to the Nazi orientation and more concerned than the latter with preserving the supposedly special cultural character of Sudeten Germandom within the larger German *Schicksalsgemeinschaft*. Hitler's charisma and subsidies from the Reich were to transform him into a docile pawn of Berlin's foreign policy by the later 1930s, and his reward was to be the prestigious designation as Reichsstatthalter (Regent) of the Sudetengau after Munich; but it appears that Henlein was never the particular Sudeten favorite of Nazis in the Reich, who preferred his far more radical and sinister associate Karl Hermann Frank, their state secretary and SS police chief in the Protectorate of Bohemia-Moravia during World War II.

Though embedded in the murky and ominous "folkish" rhetoric then characteristic of nazism, Führer Henlein's formal pledges of allegiance to constitutional methods and to the Czechoslovak Republic were initially accepted at face value—or at least on a trial basis—by Czech and German "activist" leaders. Not only the former Sudeten German Nationalist and Nazi parties, but also the Artisans and the Liberals (the Rosche group) dissolved themselves into his Heimatfront. The Christian Socials declined to follow suit only after agonized self-searching. Professor Spina of the German Farmers originally entertained "Hugenbergian" illusions of manipulating and taming the popular, yet supposedly clumsy, Henlein, but was also outmaneuvered. (The embarrassment of the German government parties in the face of the depression-driven revival of truculent nationalism had already been emphasized by their absenting themselves from earlier parliamentary votes of February 21 and 23, 1933, on lifting the immunity of four Nazi DNSAP deputies accused of treasonable activities.) Among the Czechs, too, the right wing of the Agrarian Party patronized Henlein. Furthermore, on the eve of the 1935 elections even Masaryk deprecated as premature and hopefully unnecessary the warnings now coming from all the German "activist" parties and all the Czech parties other than the Agrarians, namely, that the survival of the democratic republic required the banning of the Heimatfront. Accordingly, Henlein was only required to rename it as a Partei (party). The label he now selected, Sudetendeutsche Partei, tended to identify the entire ethnic community with his political movement. Once the elections were over, Henlein's immense victory served, of course, as a political guarantee against further threats of proscription.

The leaders of the German "activist" parties now desperately pleaded with the Czechs not to abandon them in favor of a reactionary *modus vivendi* with Henlein and to restore their credibility with the Sudeten community through some concessions on outstanding grievances. There existed, indeed, a current of Czech (and, of course, Slovak) right-wing opinion that regarded the Henleinists as potential allies against "socialism," and it was this notion, far more than the Czech Fascist movement per se, that represented the main internal threat to Czechoslovak democracy in the 1930s. Not until after Munich, however, did it achieve primacy. In the meantime, serious and formal Czech promises were given to the German "activists" early in 1937 to increase German representation in the civil service, the German share of welfare and cultural expenditures, the allocation of public contracts to German firms with German workers, and the use of German translations of official communications. The Henleinists were unnecessarily alarmed by this agreement; an understandably suspicious Czech public, the cumbersome Czech party system, and a resentful Czech bureaucracy, as well as the scarcity of qualified and loyal bilingual Germans, effectively crippled its implementation until outside events overtook it altogeher. Thus the breathing spell which Czechoslovakia had given herself with the earlier crackdown on subversive German organizations went for nought.

A year later the sands ran out on "activism": on February 20, 1938, Hitler declared the Reich to be the protector of all Germans subject to another sovereignty; on March 13 he annexed Austria; on March 16 Henlein announced that he would close his party's membership rolls as of May 31, thus eliciting an avalanche of new applications; on March 22 and 24 the German Farmers and Christian Socials withdrew from the cabinet, dissolved themselves, and merged into the Sudetendeutsche Partei (Spina simultaneously retiring from politics). Only the weakened German Social Democrats and Communists remained aloof, although the former now prudently replaced their Jewish, aging, and ailing chairman, Dr. Ludwig Czech, with the gentile, youthful, and vigorous Wenzel Jaksch. The cabinet seat that Dr. Czech simultaneously resigned was not, however, filled by any other German Socialist as the Czechoslovak Agrarian Party allowed itself to be blackmailed by a Henleinist veto against such continuity. At the municipal elections of May and June, 1938, the Henleinists took over 91.4 percent of the German vote (and even if the German Communist ballots are considered, over 85 percent). All this occurred in an atmosphere of enthusiasm mixed with intimidation in the Sudeten areas. The Czechoslovak authorities, anxious to avoid charges of provocation, failed to protect the minority of German democrats from terrorization at the hands of the now openly Nazi Henleinists, and permitted, as charged by Jaksch on the floor of the legislature on May 12, "the authority of the state (to be) completely undermined." The Agrarian Party, which held the interior ministry and hence controlled the gendarmerie—and some of whose leaders had always been peculiarly prone to appease the Henleinists—bore particular responsibility for this abdication and defeatism.

11

By now Czechoslovakia's Sudeten problem had been transformed by Nazi aggressiveness, British naiveté, and French weakness into an international issue. Gone were the Weimar days when Reich governments regarded Sudeten German nationalist agitation as something of a nuisance-diversion from their own anti-Polish revisionist priorities. The "Austrian" Hitler had replaced the "Prussian" Stresemann. The first provable Nazi subsidy to Henlein can be traced to September, 1934, and it swelled into a steady flood from the spring of 1935 on. Political directives soon followed, and by the end of 1936 at the latest Henlein had ceased to be an independent, party policy-making agent. But while the general fact of the Sudetendeutsche Partei's subordination to Nazi Germany's foreign policy by this date is established, there remains some uncertainty as to precisely when that policy specifically and irrevocably committed itself to the territorial truncation of Czechoslovakia.

Until the spring of 1938, Prague received repeated feelers, both from Berlin as well as from Henlein, hinting at a readiness to call off revisionist pressure and autonomist and irredentist agitation in return for a reversal of Czechoslovakia's foreign policy and its synchronization with Germany's. (There was a curious echo here of Kramář's pre-1914 insistence that the Habsburgs could appease their Czech subjects only by exchanging the alliance with Germany for a rapprochement to Russia.) Given the nature of nazism, for Czechoslovakia to accede would have involved more than merely loosening her many ties to France and repudiating her formal alliance with the Soviet Union. Eventually domestic ideological and constitutional coordination to Hitlerian totalitarianism would have been a required corollary to such a diplomatic volte-face. For Beneš, who had meanwhile succeeded Masaryk in the presidency but retained close control over foreign affairs and especially over relations with Hitler and Henlein, this was too high a price to pay for those improved relations with the German Reich and the Sudeten German minority which he otherwise seriously sought.

Though his later capitulation to "Munich" in September, 1938 (and again to "Moscow" in February, 1948) has understandably damaged Beneš' historical reputation, he was impressively perspicacious about the political implications of Nazi rhetoric in the pre-Munich years. A trained sociologist and a man of considerable discernment, Beneš had seen through Henlein earlier than had Masaryk or any other leading Czech figure. Long before Henlein had escalated his demands from mere administrative decentralization within the republic (October 21, 1934), through federalization by racial units (June 21, 1936), to complete political autonomy and the application of Nazi ideology for the Sudeten Germans (April 24, 1938), Beneš had consistently but unavailingly urged upon his colleagues that Czechoslovakia's salvation required the prompt banning of the Sudetendeutsche Heimatfront (Partei) combined with maximum concessions to the "activist" elements. What Beneš lacked, in the final recourse, was not analytical keenness but moral toughness.

Despite the by-now open sedition of the Sudeten German leaders and the dubious loyalty of the Slovak Populist leaders, Czechoslovakia entered the pre-Munich crisis with some strong but, alas, unplayed domestic cards. Constitutionally and politically, the government was solid, being able to count on the massive parliamentary majority of the six nonfascist Czech parties plus the German Social Democrats and the Communists. The succession of the internationally rather prestigious Slovak Agrarian Hodža to the premiership on November 4, 1935, in place of Malypetr had raised the authority of that office and, as Hodža was the first of his people to hold it, had somewhat assuaged Slovak sensibilities. A few weeks later, on December 14, 1935, Masaryk, now eighty-five years old, had abdicated the presidency (he died on September 14, 1937), simultaneously recommending Beneš as his successor. Despite some preliminary opposition by the right wing of the Agrarians, the National Democrats, and the Small Traders, this wish was heeded and Beneš was elected on December 18, by 340 votes that included those of the German "activists," of the Communists (in accordance with the Comintern's new popular-front line), and of the Slovak Populists (in alleged response to Vatican urgings). The National Democrats' candidate, the botanist Professor Bohumil Němec, received 24 votes, while the Henleinists and Czech Fascists cast 76 blanks. Though this potential Czech détente with the Slovak Populists was, alas, frittered away over the next three years,[14] the Czech population nevertheless entered the critical summer of 1938 resolute and confident. Indeed, at the time of the partial Czechoslovak mobilization from May 20 to 31, 1938, it was the Sudeten Germans who were suddenly chastened, and international observers agreed that from then on through the pre-Munich tensions the Czech people were more pugnacious than either the Sudeten or the Reich Germans.

The public's confidence in the armed forces appears to have been warranted. Though it had not made the vivid contribution of, say, the Polish Legions to the re-creation of the state and hence enjoyed less prestige and power, the Czechoslovak military establishment was thoroughly competent and professional. During World War II, Hitler once avowed that only two states, the Reich and Czechoslovakia, had really seriously planned and prepared for war, and at the postwar Nürnberg trials Keitel and von Manstein testified that in 1938 the Czechoslovak fortifications could have offered formidable resistance to the Wehrmacht. The Czechoslovaks excused their failure to use their impressive military capacity, despite Munich, by saying that their plans had been utterly and unexpectedly undermined by the sudden desertion of their French ally. This is not altogether convincing, for the possiblity of effective French military assistance had already been discounted by the Czechoslovak General Staff since Germany's unresisted remilitarization of the Rhineland on March 7, 1936. The important new military development of 1938 had been the turning of Czechoslovakia's Austrian flank with the Anschluss of March 13; but even here the terrain emphatically favored the defense, and the Czechs had responded energetically over the summer to extend and deepen their fortifications.

Given its naturally defensible and well-fortified frontiers, its technologically advanced armaments industry, its disciplined and literate population, Czechoslovakia's potential military position in September, 1938, was

14. Beneš had apparently made some sweeping pre-election promises to the Slovaks: a wide degree of autonomy within a year; a guaranteed percentage of Slovaks in the central administration; more denominational schools, state contracts, and public expenditures in Slovakia. These promises, together with the alleged Vatican hints, prompted the Slovak Populists (except Hlinka himself) to vote for Beneš' presidential candidacy. As Beneš subsequently found himself unable or unwilling to honor these commitments, the episode eventually played into the hands of the anti-Czech "Nastupist" Slovak radicals.

not as apparently hopeless as Poland's, or even Finland's, a year later. Hence, Beneš' capitulation to Munich (for which, incidentally, he never accepted responsibility but consistently blamed the Great Powers exclusively) was not a rational calculation of military and political odds, but a profound failure of psychological and political nerves. Indeed, in the light of what he ultimately did in September, 1938, it would have been more coldy rational for Beneš to draw the logical conclusion from French inertness in March, 1936, and to abandon this unreliable ally in favor of the then beckoning Germans before she abandoned him. This course was, as mentioned, rendered impossible by the laudable revulsion of Beneš and the Czech people to nazism, as well as by persisting illusions about the international system. There are, in the final analysis, certain ultimate historical decisions that determine the moral even more than the material fate of future generations; such decisions the political leaders of even a small nation cannot "rationally" or "logically" abdicate to their Great Power patrons without simultaneously surrendering their own integrity.

12

The material losses sustained by Czechoslovakia as a consequence of Munich and the various denouements thereto were staggering. The country lost three-tenths of its territory, one-third of its population, and four-tenths of the national income, including 66 percent of the coal and 80 percent of the lignite reserves, 80 percent of textile production, 70 percent of iron and steel as well as of electric power capacity. Her main railroad lines were severed. In effect, the country ceased to be economically or strategically viable. The lion's share of this loot went, of course, to Germany, but Poland and Hungary also took advantage of Czechoslovakia's humiliation at Munich to present their long-standing revisionist claims. The former now reciprocated the blackmail of 1920 by seizing Těšín (Cieszyn) after a twelve-hour ultimatum of September 30, 1938, while the latter was awarded the southern plains of Slovakia and Ruthenia at the hands of Germany and Italy acting as arbitrators on November 2. Though the rationale for the truncation of Czechoslovakia was "ethnic justice," it appears that of the almost five million people transferred to German, Polish, and Hungarian jurisdiction, over one-and-a-quarter million were Czechs, Slovaks, and Ruthenians, while approximately half-a-million Germans and Magyars still remained in the rump state. These facts give eloquent testimony to the impossibility of drawing ethnic frontiers in interwar East Central Europe.

Worse even than the material loss was the psychological one. The public's confidence in the international system and in its own leaders was snuffed out; the elite's morale, broken. Even the shattering defeat at White Mountain in 1620, when battle had been accepted by the Czechs, was less demoralizing than this humiliating acquiescence to Munich in

1938. Last, but scarcely least, of this episode's many hard lessons is that the sacrifice of Czechoslovakia did not save the peace.

Beneš resigned the presidency on October 5 and left his country on October 22, 1938. As the French government, unable to forgive the man whom it had betrayed, refused him any contacts, Beneš went on to exile in Britain, where the government also kept him at arm's length until well into World War II. His formal successor at home was the elderly and apolitical jurist Dr. Emil Hácha. Slovakia, where the Populists proceeded to make themselves the only legal party and to organize a clerico-fascist regime, was granted extensive autonomy on October 6, and two days later, Ruthenia was granted the same. The state's name now became hyphenated to Czecho-Slovakia. The surviving political leaders drew the logical inference from Munich that, their rump state being henceforth utterly dependent on Hitler's benevolence, they had best offer him their willing collaboration. Accordingly, the constitution of 1920 was nullified, the Czech party system consolidated into two formally distinct but mutually consulting groupings (National and Labor), the Communists banned, the remaining German minority given privileged status, the Jews restricted, censorship extended, and democracy vilified in public propaganda. An extraterritorial road connecting Silesia and Austria was put at Germany's disposal, and the remaining heavy armaments also transferred to her. Finally the new Czecho-Slovak foreign minister, František Chvalkovský, beseechingly promised Joachim Ribbentrop, on October 12, 1938, full policy compliance with, and reliance on, Germany "if Germany will allow this."

For a brief period it appeared that this obsequiousness might work. In the autumn arbitration proceedings concerning the new frontier with Hungary, for example, Ribbentrop was less vindictively hostile to the Czecho-Slovak case than was Ciano. The Germans had also initially backed that relatively moderate wing of the Slovak People's Party which was prepared to accept autonomy within what was left of the general state (Msgr. Jozef Tiso, Karol Sidor), rather than the radicals who craved total independence (Vojtech Tuka, Ferdinand Ďurčanský). Indeed, since the Czecho-Slovak rump state (also known as "the second republic") was a true satellite and utterly dependent on the Reich, it would appear to have been in Berlin's interest to stabilize and sustain it.

Hitler, however, acting for reasons and from motives that remain somewhat unclear, chose otherwise. On February 12, 1939, he lamented to the Slovak radical leader Tuka that an opportunity to arrange for full Slovak independence had been allowed to slip by at the time of the Munich crisis. A month later, Hitler took advantage of an internal crisis between the Prague central government and the Slovak autonomous one to impose the Slovak radicals upon the moderates and hence to elicit a declaration of full Slovak independence under German protection (*de facto* vis-à-vis Hungary). Simultaneously, he utilized Hácha's suppliant visit to Berlin to browbeat that old man into accepting German military occupation of, and a politico-administrative German Protectorate over, Bohemia and Moravia. Operationally, the resultant military occupation was a mere police action, all effective Czech defenses having been surrendered after Munich and any (unlikely) urge to offer "quixotic" resistance at this point having just been allayed by Hácha's capitulation. Hungary, meanwhile, upon being denied Slovakia, consoled herself by reannexing Ruthenia.

On balance, these frenzied actions of March 13-16, 1939, were a blunder on the part of Hitler. Politically, he gained no greater control over the territories now under his formal protection than he had in fact enjoyed since Munich, while internationally he finally aroused even the hitherto complacent British government from its illusions of appeasement. The German occupation of the Czech rump state on March 15, 1939, thus led directly to the British guarantee of March 31 to Poland, with consequences fateful for the world and fatal to Hilter and his Third Reich.

13

The political life and death of interwar Czechoslovakia invite a number of conclusions. This was the most prosperous, progressive, and democratic state of East Central Europe, and precisely therein lay its fatal flaw. Masaryk and Beneš had committed its political system to two ideological propositions that were then incompatible: (a) there must be a democracy, with all citizens of whatever ethnic community enjoying equal political and civil rights; yet (b) the state must have and express a specifically Czechoslovak national culture. But the sheer numbers, cultural level, and economic power of the non-Czechoslovak ethnic minorities produced early tension and an eventual contradiction between these two propositions. The interwar decades were simply too late (and perhaps too early) for multinational states in East Central Europe. "Activism" was an illusion rendered plausible only by the temporary European prosperity of the mid-1920s. To argue that "activism," and hence the Czechoslovak political system, would have prospered but for the fortuitous bad luck of the depression with its cataclysmic consequences in the Reich and in the Sudetenland is unconvincing. It is, after all, precisely under the stresses of adversity that the viability of political systems is tested. Furthermore, economic depressions cannot be regarded as extraneous intrusions into political life. Hence, in the first half of the twentieth century, only two solutions to the ethnic tensions of Czechoslovakia were realistic: the territorial truncation of the state, or the expulsion of the disloyal minorities. In time, if the virulence of nationalism becomes attenuated in East Central Europe, multinational political entities may again become feasible.

The Czech political elite aggravated such inevitable, historically determined difficulties with gratuitous political blunders. To compound its strife with the ethnic minorities by alienating as well the admittedly difficult Slovaks was a fatal error, since the Czechs alone accounted for barely more than half of the state's population. The political structure, though indeed democratic, was stagnant: the parties clutched their administrative fiefdoms and adjusted their coalitions, but they accepted no dynamic momentum between a "government" and an "opposition." Though the electorate four times denied the outgoing coalition an ongoing majority, the political consequences were relatively trifling, the chronic government parties considering themselves more-or-less immune to effective electoral retribution. A still graver fault was the system's oligarchical and paternalistic rigidity. Rhetoric apart, neither the party leaders nor the three presidents seriously sought to involve the younger generations in political responsibilities.

None of these weaknesses, however, negated interwar Czechoslovakia's constitutional and civil-libertarian strengths. Nor did they warrant —though they may have facilitated—her brutal destruction at the hands of ruthless neighbors and faithless friends.

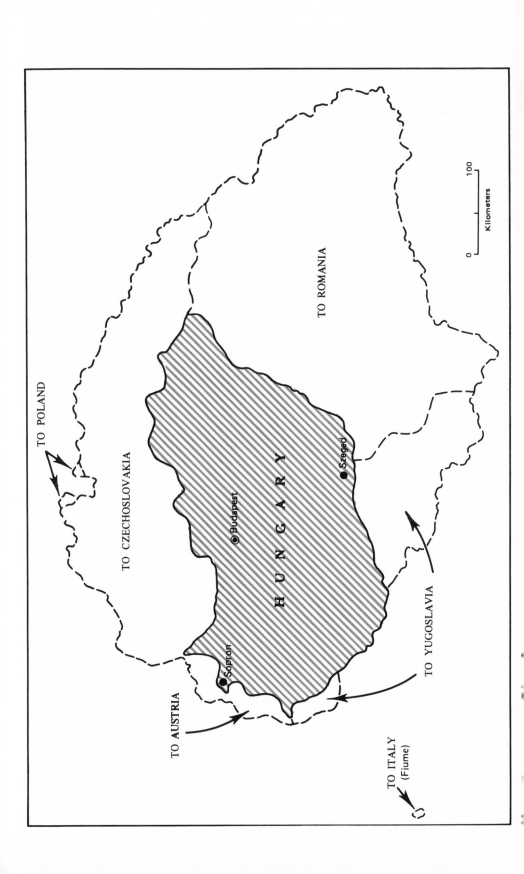

TO POLAND

TO CZECHOSLOVAKIA

TO ROMANIA

H U N G A R Y

●Budapest

●Szeged

Sopron●

TO AUSTRIA

TO YUGOSLAVIA

TO ITALY
(Fiume)

0   100
Kilometers

Chapter Four

HUNGARY

1

THE coming of the Magyars into Europe and their establishment of the
Hungarian kingdom on the Pannonian Plain and in the Carpathian
Mountains in the ninth century was once bewailed by the nineteenth-
century Czech historian František Palacký as "the greatest misfortune to
befall the Slavic world in thousands of years," for it geographically severed eastern, southern, and western Slavs from each other. The subsequent internal political and social history of this Hungarian state consisted
of a tenacious and—until well into the twentieth century—a successful
struggle by the mettlesome Magyar nobility to assert and maintain its
dominant position against royal authority, against the non-Magyar
nationalities residing in the kingdom, and against other social classes,
including the dispossessed Magyar peasantry that had virtually no rights.
The Magyar nobility drew its strength and resiliency for this ceaseless
defense of its position from its control of the land and of the governmental administrative apparatus. The nobility, in short, was "the political
nation" of the Kingdom of Hungary; it neither acknowledged claims to
representative power by other nationalities, which constituted about half
the population by the beginning of the twentieth century, nor did it
permit any middle class to intervene between itself and "its" peasantry.
Even the "mercantilistic" commercial and industrial expansion of the
Ausgleich era was guided by the nobility-saturated bureaucracy in directions and toward structures that complemented rather than challenged
the social sources of the nobility's political power.

But the very perspicacity and perseverance of the Magyar nobility in
identifying and defending its historic prerogatives and styles had, by the
last decades before World War I, misled it into chronic and often trivial
constitutional disputes with its Austrian partner in the Habsburg Empire
and into consuming its political energies in short-run domestic manipulations and repressions. The bulk of even the ethnically Magyar population

137

was refused enfranchisement with the chauvinistic argument that any extension whatsoever of political participation would endanger Magyar supremacy. The rhetoric of "national survival" was thus used as a figleaf for social and political privilege. At the same time, the urban economic and much of the intellectual leadership was abdicated to the bourgeoisie, which was heavily Jewish. Despite her impressive historical, geographic, hydrographic, and economic unity, the political structure of millennial Hungary became increasingly isolated, narrow, and brittle.

World War I was to provide an acid test of the Dual Monarchy's and Hungary's viability. Though the king-emperor's subjects did their duty and half the adult male population of the empire responded to mobilization, yet the appalling rate of casualties—out of the 8,321,050 men mobilized, as many as 5,051,424 were killed, wounded, missing, or prisoners of war—as well as the general decline in food and industrial production eroded morale. By the end of 1918, weariness and hopelessness had sapped even the dominant German-Austrian and Magyar peoples of the empire. Though by a calculation strictly proportional to population Hungary would have been obliged to furnish only 40.96 percent of the manpower in the imperial armed forces, her contribution in fact came to 43.43 percent, or 3,614,179 troops, and accounted for three-fourths of all her males fit for service; of this number 2,138,496 suffered casualties.[1] By the last year of the war her contingents consisted of raw recuits, recovered wounded, and prisoners returned from defeated Russia, while the level of both her agricultural and industrial production was half that of 1913.

Yet the Magyar nobility, true to character, stubbornly refused to contemplate either defeat or any compromise with other nationalities and classes, which might conceivably stave off the worst territorial and political consequences of defeat. As late as the Peace of Bucharest, which was imposed in May, 1918, on a temporarily prostrate Romania, the Hungarians had forced the cession to themselves of a belt of valuable forested area. In September of that final year of the war the veteran premier and strongman of old Hungary, Count István Tisza, rebuffed a delegation of the monarchy's South Slav subjects with the snarled imprecation, "even if we go under, we shall still summon enough strength to grind you to pieces first."[2] At the very end, with the war manifestly lost, Hungary's Magyar

1. Statistics from Zoltán Szende, *Die Ungarn im Zusammenbruch 1918* (Oldenburg i. O: Schulzesche Hofbuchdruckerei, 1931), p. 18.
2. Tisza's intelligence was as impressive as his obduracy was perverse. The previous year, when the Russian Revolution appeared to signal the victory of the Central Powers and, in any event, the defeat of Hungary's most feared foe, Tisza, who as a true noble of the *ancien régime* was as concerned with intra-societal as with international tensions, had cautioned prophetically: "Do not be too pleased with this turn of events; it is a two-edged sword which may yet bring disaster to the world. Think what a seductive and distracting thought it must be for every rascal that he may live to become the ruler of a State! Every butcher's assistant will be asking himself why Russia should be the only country in which a workingman may become dictator." Albert Kaas and Fedor de Lazarovics, *Bolshevism in Hungary* (London: Grant Richards Ltd., 1931), p. 18.

rulers still expected to save their country's historic boundaries and their own dominant position within them, not through significant reform or serious compromise, but merely by abandoning the German wartime ally and the Austrian constitutional partner and pretending to the West that Hungary had all along been a victim of Teutonic bondage.

By now, however, even the Magyar regiments—not to mention the troops furnished by the kingdom's other nationalities—were no longer reliable as protectors of the established but frayed political and social systems, though they would have been ready to defend the historic frontiers. Furthermore, the politicians who had succeeded Tisza in the premiership, Count Móric Esterházy and Sándor Wekerle, lacked their imposing predecessor's mastery and resolution, and King Charles IV was too pliant to commit himself to any consistent course of action. It was under these circumstances of incipient disintegration and persisting illusion that Count Mihály Károlyi, a lone dissenter from the inherited ideology of the Magyar nobility, was elevated into power on October 31, 1918, by a virtually bloodless revolution of the Budapest workers and masses upon whom the garrison was unwilling to fire.

The head of one of Hungary's most ancient and wealthy magnate families, Károlyi had been brought up in an atmosphere where there was neither concealment nor denial of the fact that the country was governed by and for its nobility. Hence, he understood the real motives behind and methods of the traditional political style and social system better than many of the Liberal and Socialist critics who now joined him in forming a revolutionary government. A man of great sincerity and consistency, Károlyi had succeeded to the leadership of the opposition Kossuthist Party of Independence shortly before the eruption of World War I. As such, he was committed not only to exchanging Hungary's political affiliation with Germany for an understanding with France and to asserting her autonomy vis-à-vis Austria (policies that, at least toward the end of the war, were also accepted by a ruling establishment which now adopted a stance of saving Hungary by deserting its partners), but eventually also to a democratization of Hungary's internal political and social life and to a reconciliation with her Romanian, Ruthenian, Slovak, and Southern Slav nationalities. Indeed, for him these several commitments were interrelated, for only if the Magyar rulers were reconciled to their peasants and their non-Magyar peoples could they hope successfully to confront Berlin and Vienna.

Alas, though this policy in theory entirely conformed with the Wilsonian ideology of 1918, though its legislative and administrative implications were assiduously worked out by Károlyi's indefatigable minister of nationalities, the liberal sociologist Oszkár Jászi, though the Slovak leader Milan Hodža briefly negotiated a possible *modus vivendi* in Budapest in November, and though the Ruthenians, German Schwabs, and Slovaks were formally granted autonomous status on December 25, 1918, and January 28 and March 8, 1919, respectively, yet the Károlyist experiment came too late to be acceptable to the border nationalities or to impress the chancelleries of the victorious Allied Powers. While Károlyi's good intentions were well known in the Western countries which he had frequently visited in prewar days (his connections to Poincaré were particularly good), their governments were by war's end too far committed to their Czech, Romanian, and Southern Slav clients' claims to total independence and separation from Hungary to be in a position to endorse Károlyi's bid for a federalistic reorganization of the millennial kingdom. Furthermore, Károlyi's position in his own Magyar nation and society was tentative.

Károlyi had been swept into office on October 31 only after the publication of the Imperial Manifesto on October 16, 1918, authorizing the federalistic self-determination of the nations through national councils in the empire's Austrian half, after Tisza's concession on October 17 on the floor of the Hungarian parliament that the war was lost, and after the Hungarian government's decision on October 22 to recall Hungary's troops from the Balkan, Italian, and Eastern fronts, on which they were serving with Austrian and German contingents, back into the kingdom. The above sequence of events refutes the later charges of his revilers (reminiscent of Germany's *Dolchstosslegende*) that Károlyi's assumption of office had corroded an ongoing war effort. At the time, all of his later detractors—the nobility, persons in high finance, the political Right, the Church—pledged loyalty to Károlyi in the hope that his credit with the victors would save their Hungary.

Though he now sought to extend that credit by proclaiming Hungary a republic and dissolving the wartime legislature on November 16, 1918, Károlyi failed to develop either an organization or a policy that would have allowed him to capitalize on his current indispensability and on the hopes reposed in him by less dubious supporters than the above, by the intelligentsia, the workers, the peasantry. He, too, banked excessively on the presumed leniency of the Allies and neglected to develop a structured, extraparliamentary political party of his own, thus rendering himself organizationally dependent on the Socialist cadres and trade unions, who were utterly myopic and hostile toward the potentially decisive aspirations of the peasantry for the partition and distribution of the nobility's vast estates. Károlyi privately distributed his own lands among his peasants early in 1919, but this fine personal gesture proved politically stillborn. A general land-reform program prepared by his minister of agriculture, which would have provided for the limitation of landed property to 500 cadastral yokes, the expropriation and distribution to peasants of land beyond this maximum, and the eventual indemnification of the former owners at 1913 prices, was vetoed by the Socialists as being politically reactionary and economically retrogressive. The nobility, of course, was also opposed but cleverly held its fire. Contradicting the Socialists' agronomic arguments stands the fact that most Hungarian latifundia were then cultivated so extensively and wastefully that they were *not* more productive than medium-sized peasant plots and failed to realize their economic potential.

Károlyi also promoted a new electoral law of November 22, 1918, extending the suffrage to adult citizens literate in any language spoken in Hungary; but he then repeatedly postponed elections to a Constituent Assembly until such time as the country would be cleared of Allied occupation troops. He eventually fell before the elections were held. Even his major success, the orderly demobilization of the armies, was at best a dubious achievement for it left him without reliable military contingents. Károlyi, in short, was a decent and enlightened man overcome by the external pressures of the war's victors and his own inability to order his internal priorities or master his options.

The eventual fall of Károlyi was also a marked defeat for the largest and the only really organized and disciplined party of his coalition, the Socialists and their trade union affiliates. Thanks to the rapid development of military industries, the Hungarian proletariat had multiplied during the war. Trade union membership rose from 51,510 at the end of 1914 to 721,437 four years later. A series of massive strikes and workers' demonstrations in the course of 1918 had fed the party's sense of power, even though it was not represented in the gerrymandered parliament. Though originally furnishing only two of Károlyi's ministers—and later four after a cabinet reshuffle of January 18, 1919—the Socialists really formed the structural spine of his government by making their party and union cadres available to take on many of the tasks of the former political elite. Indeed, they may well have stretched themselves so thin by this involvement in public administration, that they let political work among the masses pass by default to the Communists and the Right Radicals. They were overly bureaucratized and ideologically underdeveloped, and their ingrained "class" suspicion of the peasantry and their failure to produce leaders capable of denying and yet productively rechanneling the apocalyptic expectations of the urban masses at war's end proved to be the Socialists' ultimate political failings.

As regards the other constituents of Károlyi's government, his own Party of Independence was exclusively a parliamentary club, devoid both of organizational bases and, apart from its leader's conscience, of socioeconomic awareness. The Democrats were a small and heavily Jewish (assimilationist) contingent of bourgeois liberals. The Smallholders had no clear program and were politically unreliable on the burning land-reform question, while the Radicals owed their standing entirely to the intellectual superiority of Jászi and a handful of others over the tarnished apologists of the *ancien régime* and the leaden oracles of Socialist orthodoxy. Only Jászi appears to have grasped the connection between the hope of persuading the other nationalities to remain in some sort of constitutional-federalistic relationship with Magyar Hungary—a hope shared by all, including the Socialists—and the land reform rejected by the doctrinaire Socialists. Budapest could scarcely even begin to compete with Prague, Belgrade, and Bucharest for the ear of old Hungary's Ruthenian, Slovak, Southern Slav, and Romanian peasant subjects unless it, too, promised to these peoples the distribution of the (largely absentee) Magyar nobles' estates. Jászi further alarmed the Socialists by recommending the recruitment of a peasant army to be rewarded with land for its defense of the revolution. With the rejection of his interrelated constitutional, social, and political program, Jászi resigned in January, 1919. A governmental reshuffle then followed, in which Károlyi was elevated from the premiership to the presidency of the republic. The most important ministerial portfolios were handed over to the Socialists, who thereby accepted paramount public responsibility for the further fate of the revolution.

The Socialists had for some time been experiencing the hitherto unfamiliar sensation of pressure from the left, from a group of Hungarian prisoners of war recently released and returned from Soviet Russia where their observations and experiences during 1917 and 1918 had converted them into Communists. A numerically modest but politically significant fraction of the approximately half-million Hungarian war prisoners held in Russia, they had participated to considerable effect in the Russian Revolution and Civil War. At a conference in Moscow on November 4, 1918, they had resolved to found a Hungarian Communist Party and to send approximately two hundred of their agitators back to Hungary to radicalize the new Károlyist experiment. An additional three hundred were despatched in March, 1919.

The leader of this group, the prewar provincial Socialist functionary and journalist Béla Kun, who since April 14, 1918, had been head of the Federation of Foreign Groups of the Bolshevik Communist Party, accordingly returned to Hungary under the pseudonym of Colonel (Medical) Sebestyén on November 16, 1918, and promptly set his considerable talents as an agitator and Soviet subsidies to the task of "deepening" the revolution. The Communist Party of Hungary was promptly refounded in Budapest on November 20 or 24, 1918, by the returnees from Russia and some local leftist Socialists and Social Revolutionaries, and its paper, *Vörös Ujság* (Red Gazette), began publishing incendiary diatribes against the Károlyist and Socialist moderates with the first issue of December 7.

Whereas the veteran prewar Socialists and trade unionists were relatively immune to this Communist propaganda, the newer generation of formerly apolitical wartime recruits, the demobilized and idle soldiers, as well as the younger intelligentsia, were more receptive, and by December

12 Communist pressure, applied through the restive Budapest garrison, had forced the resignation of Károlyi's defense minister, Lieutenant Colonel Albert Bartha. Though they failed to gain a foothold in the Socialist-controlled Workers' Councils that was comparable to their strong leverage on the Soldiers' Councils, the Communists nevertheless benefited from the chronic turmoil and the repeated postponements of elections to a Constituent Assembly. By February, 1919, they had from ten to fifteen thousand members in the capital and another twenty to twenty-five thousand in provincial towns[3] and with Soviet moneys had managed to acquire approximately thirty-five thousand of the rifles left behind by the German army of Field Marshal August von Mackensen, which at Allied insistence had been disarmed on its way home through Hungary from the Balkans. Accordingly, on February 3 and 6, *Vörös Ujság* openly incited an armed uprising against the Károlyist-Socialist "counterrevolutionary" regime.

The now-aroused Socialists thereupon met in an Extraordinary Congress on February 9 and resolved to expel "Communist splitters" and "intruders" from their own and their trade unions' ranks and to enforce discipline. Though the Communist leaders were somewhat sobered by this unexpectedly tough response, the momentum of putschist violence that they had set into motion was for the moment out of their control. On February 20 a clash between the police and a demonstration of the unemployed marching on the offices of the Socialist daily *Népszava* (People's Voice) resulted in the killing of several policemen and the wounding of many more. The Károlyist-Socialist government steeled itself to retaliate, and in the following days the key Communist personnel, including Kun, were arrested on charges of conspiracy against public order and incitement to riot. The Communist headquarters and press facilities were also seized. But the Socialist leaders, petrified lest they fall into the disreputable trap of "Noskeism," namely, becoming the allies and tools of the "old" forces of order, failed to follow up and exploit this riposte. Guilt-ridden, they insisted on the parallel arrest of a rather amateurish counterrevolutionary contingent of magnates, retired officers, and clerics. Kun, meanwhile, became the beneficiary of a wave of public sympathy as the news spread that he had been roughed up by the police after his arrest and that he had been forewarned of his impending imprisonment but had declined a chance to go into hiding. As Lenin now also undertook to hold the Socialist members of the Hungarian Red Cross Mission in Moscow hostage for the Communists jailed in Budapest, the Károlyist-Socialist government quickly arranged that the conditions of Kun's detention be extraordinarily loose and unrestrictive.

3. There exist many, widely varying, estimates of Communist membership strength at this time. The statistics above are from Ferenc T. Zsuppán, "The Early Activities of the Hungarian Communist Party," *Slavonic and East European Review* 43 (June, 1965): 320.

The Allied Powers were also providing grist for Kun's mills by repeatedly reinterpreting the Belgrade Armistice of November 13, 1918, to
Hungary's disadvantage, and hence to Károlyi's and the Socialists' embarrassment. By authorizing Czechoslovakia, Romania, and Yugoslavia to
send not only their troops but also their civil authorities into those parts of
millennial Hungary's territories which they claimed, by repeatedly shift-
ing the armistice demarcation lines to the benefit of these hostile neighbors of Hungary, and by maintaining an economic blockade to enforce
Hungarian compliance, the war's victors aroused and outraged Magyar
nationalist feeling. Kun was able to capitalize on this outrage in a double
sense: the Károlyi-Socialist reliance on French generosity having proven
as abortive as the older Ausgleich association with Austria and Germany,
it was time, Kun could argue, to base the fight for Hungary's national
survival and greatness on a revolutionary alliance with Bolshevik Russia;
furthermore, his own and his associates' activities in the Russia of 1917-18
had provided them with highly pertinent experience for the work of
harnessing national and revolutionary energies to the dual task of repelling foreign invasion and domestic reaction. Inexorably, this dual appeal
to patriotism and revolution impressed minor Socialist functionaries and
the rank and file as well as a significant fraction of the leadership, not to
mention the ideologically illiterate but fervently patriotic troops and
masses. The new republican army was readily receptive to Kun's radical
prescription. It had been recruited simply by age classes (eighteen
through twenty-two), with no attempt to attract contingents for social or
ideological reliability; for example, peasants rewarded with land or veteran trade unionists, as recommended by Oszkár Jászi and Vilmos Böhm.
Thus when the military representative of the victor states in Budapest, the
French lieutenant colonel Vyx, presented on March 20, 1919, one more
Allied demand for the evacuation of still another belt of Hungarian
territory claimed by the Romanians, he was the catalyst rather than the
cause of the disintegration of the already profoundly undermined
Károlyi regime.

That the Vyx *démarche* was unacceptable was a virtually unanimous
Hungarian reaction. Károlyi advised the government that, its reliance on
the generosity of Allied statesmen having proved a broken reed, an
all-Socialist government now be formed. Such a government could
appeal—hopefully with Communist endorsement—over the heads of the
Allied governments to the working classes and Socialist parties of Europe
for a repudiation of this latest example of imperialism and vindictiveness
against Hungary. But such half-measures could no longer arrest the
momentum of events in Hungary, nor could they satisfy the conviction of
the masses that only explicit Communist power and Soviet Russian military support, which was erroneously assumed to be readily available,
would now suffice for Hungary. The Socialist leadership, no longer

capable of resisting this pressure, assented on March 21, 1919, to the immediate merger of its party with the Communists and to the joint formation of a Soviet Hungarian government which would defy Paris and rely on itself and on Moscow. Only two Socialist leaders declined to participate. Thus, exactly a month after his incarceration at the hands of Károlyi and the Socialists, Kun emerged from his jail cell as the apparent master of Hungary; the cautious, cowed, and compromised Socialists were seemingly in his train, while the hapless and betrayed Károlyi had resigned the presidency preparatory to going into exile on July 4, 1919.

2

Kun's Soviet government vaulted into office on a wave of "national bolshevik" enthusiasm that transcended class and ideological lines. The Vyx memorandum was rejected, the army expanded beyond the size authorized by the armistice, and the Ruthenian, Slovak, and German Schwab nationalities again assured of cultural and economic autonomy. (Kun, a native of Transylvania, declined to extend similar promises to the Romanians whom he apparently despised.) With these bold initiatives, the belligerent Kun initially achieved more than had the compliant Károlyi. The native conservative and reactionary forces, which had again been flexing their muscles toward the close of the Károlyi episode, for the time being reverted to indulgent passivity to see if Kun's attack on "Allied bourgeois imperialism" might effectively secure Hungary's historic frontiers. The victors in Paris, meanwhile, after having consistently dealt with Károlyi through ultimata and ignored his prophetic pleas for leniency lest otherwise his people be driven to desperation and Bolshevism, now promptly despatched the South African-British general Jan Smuts to Budapest. Arriving on April 4, Smuts substantially modified the Vyx ultimatum to Hungary's advantage and indicated that, in the event of Kun's compliance with the revised stipulations, the Allied blockade against Hungary would be raised, the Soviet government would be invited to negotiate peace terms in Paris (i.e., a kind of international recognition of Kun), and the final peace frontiers might be more favorable to Hungary than the current armistice lines.

Kun was, however, trapped by the nationalistic expectations of an integral restoration of Hungary's millennial frontiers, which his earlier propaganda had aroused, as well as by his commitments to Lenin to synchronize Hungarian policy with Soviet Russia's, and, finally, by his own belief in the imminence of world revolution. Instead of accepting the Smuts proposals, he determined to spin out the discussions in the hope of obtaining still more concessions and simultaneously maximizing discord among the Allied Powers while at the same time awaiting the arrival on Hungary's borders of the eagerly expected Russian Red Army and/or "the German proletarian revolution." But Smuts was not to be drawn into

Kun's strategy and left Budapest the day after his arrival without resuming negotiations. On the plausible assumption than an immediate settlement on the basis of the Smuts terms would have disintegrated his regime, and in the fallacious expectation of eventual external help, Kun had decided to risk drifting into renewed war.

Though Kun was, in his own way, a Hungarian patriot, he was also a committed Communist. For him, the defense of the state's territory made sense only on the assumption that the area and time gained thereby would be utilized for the application of Marxism-Leninism. Hence there soon arose a certain dichotomy between his regime's original appeal to nationalism and its eventual prosecution of "class struggle" within Hungarian society. Ambivalences in regard to the respective Communist and Socialist expectations concerning their merger also quickly surfaced. *Kto kogo?* Who had captured whom in this fusion? The Communists, indeed, supplied the ideological momentum, the apocalyptic audacity, and the important psychological and political ties to Soviet Russia, but they were heavily dependent on the Socialists' administrative experience, organizational competence, and traditional ties of comradeship to the workers. Lenin, who regarded party purity as more essential than working class unity, was originally skeptical of Kun's decision to merge with the Socialists, and a significant fraction of Hungarian Communists never overcame their suspicion that a naive Kun had abdicated ideological principle in order to achieve organizational cohesion. The Socialists had agreed to the "merger of the working class parties" in order to save Hungary; the Communists, in order to advance the world revolution by expanding the Soviet system westward. Both depended on external political and military assistance, and their hope for this insinuated itself into their policy judgements—most vividly in their joint decision not to accept Smuts' offer of a kind of Hungarian Brest-Litovsk. But in daring this much, they were also obliged to brace themselves for a renewed foreign onslaught and to mobilize Hungary's resources for resistance to the bitter end. Here, too, however, a degree of ideologically prompted wishful thinking distorted their calculations.

Convinced that the war years had provided the Hungarian public with a political and psychological proto-socialist (or proto-communist) experience in the form of etatism, militarism, spartanism, polarization, and collectivism, and that the loss of the war had ruined the credit and self-confidence of the former political elites, the merged Communist-Socialist leadership chose to disregard Rosa Luxemburg's famous warning against Marxists "accepting power for the mere reason that all other parties have failed." These leaders now proceeded to implement their program with a reckless disregard for their own marginality in the Hungarian society of the day; here the Communists behaved with chiliastic fervor, the Socialists with fatalistic desperation. Titles and ranks were abolished, church and state separated, education secularized, out-of-wedlock children legitimated, and divorce facilitated. Revolutionary tribunals were authorized to administer politicized justice. Housing, transportation, banking, medicine, and culture (including private art possessions) were socialized. Industrial and commercial establishments with more than twenty employees, and land not personally cultivated by the owner, were taken over by the state. Labor was proclaimed compulsory, proletarian males between seventeen and forty-five years of age were declared eligible for military service, and factories instructed to furnish half their working force for a new Red Army. The Dictatorship of the Proletariat was officially proclaimed on June 25, 1919, "in order to bring the bourgeoisie to its senses . . . and if necessary to suffocate its counter-revolution in blood."

The regime itself, however, was provoking what it chose to denounce as "counterrevolutionary" resistance. Massive food requisitions for the army and the cities, paid for in worthless "white" (as contrasted to old Habsburg "blue") currency, alienated the peasants who quickly learned that the chronic "revolutionary" chaos in the factories, exacerbated by the Allies' blockade, had virtually eliminated the possibility of acquiring industrial commodities in exchange for their agrarian produce. Even more damaging was the fact that, in spite of having witnessed at close hand Lenin's politically successful neutralization of the Russian peasants' land hunger through the redistribution of the nobles' estates, Kun chose to persist in the rigidly doctrinaire course set earlier by the Hungarian Socialists. The estates were nationalized, but parcelization was refused on economic and technical grounds, namely, the alleged productive superiority of larger over smaller units of production. Moreover, the former owners and bailiffs were generally appointed as managers of their supposedly nationalized estates; hence the peasants could see no significant change in the social ecology of their villages.[4] Not surprisingly, grain production per acre fell in 1919 to less than a third of the already relatively low prewar ratio as the enraged regime and the obdurate peasantry locked themselves into a vicious circle of coercion and recalcitrance. By thus deliberately repudiating Lenin's model for handling the problem, and by gratuitiously choosing to consider the peasantry as incorrigibly reaction-

4. "The proprietor remained in the same country-house, drove about with the same carriage-and-four, was addressed by the workmen as 'your honor.' . . . The Feudalist managers of the big estates, now 'whitewashed' in red, handed over as little as possible of their produce and reckoned the rest under management expenses. . . . The Communist experiment would in any case have failed, owing to its internal weaknesses, especially in the matter of workmen's discipline, but it need not have left such a hateful memory behind and injured so gravely the whole cause of progress, if the Soviet Government had pursued a less doctrinaire and dishonorable agrarian policy." Arnold Dániel, "The Agrarian Problem in Hungary," *The Slavonic Review* 1 (June, 1922): 164, 166.

ary, the Kun regime sacrificed not only the possibility of general toleration on the part of the peasantry but also the potential specific support of
the partly ideologized peasant war prisoners returning from Russia.

Chronic recourse to forced requisitions and worthless currency, excessive egalitarianism and persistent shortages, bureaucratic hypertrophy
combined with arbitrariness and incompetence—all this alienated the
urban as well as the rural population. As the "best" trade unionists were
recruited for the army and their most experienced leaders into the government, and the families of the conscripts were left to fend for themselves, the urban masses became disillusioned and restive while the middle classes and intelligentsia were offended by persistent incursions into
their homes, property, and professional work. Finally, all classes of
Magyar society, both urban and rural, came to resent the anticlerical
excesses as well as the large number and high visibility of Jews in the Kun
government and administration. (Thirty-two of the Kun regime's
forty-five commissars were Jewish.)

The regime had provided itself with a brief but spectacular reprieve in
the late spring, by resorting to the same force that had brought it to
power, nationalism. Though the eastern portion of old Hungary, which
was now occupied by the Romanians, was by far the most valuable of the
lost territories, the Hungarians decided to assert themselves most vigorously against the Czechoslovak intrusion in the north. They lacked adequate artillery to recross the Tisza River against the Romanians, and they
were reluctant to become embroiled with French units who were inter-
mingled with the Serbian army holding the Vojvodina triangle of old
Hungary to the south. The Czechs, moreover, were legally and morally
the most compromised of the three hostile neighbors, having themselves
violated the Allied-imposed armistice line at the expense of Hungary late
in April; strategically they were the most vulnerable, being operationally
divided between wings commanded by French and Italian generals. On
May 20 a Hungarian counteroffensive was launched into Slovakia and
met with quick successes. By the end of the first week in June, two-thirds
of Slovakia had been reconquered, and ground contact between the
Czechoslovak and Romanian armies had been severed; only a sharp
ultimatum of June 8 from Clemenceau to Kun halted the Hungarian
advance and stemmed the Czech rout.

The Magyar population of the reconquered towns originally welcomed
the Red Army, but the Slovak people were unenthusiastic. Neither
Magyar nor Slovak allegiance was consolidated by a Slovak Soviet Republic which was proclaimed on June 16 by certain Czech and Slovak Communists from Kun's entourage in Budapest, even though—or perhaps
because—its political propaganda and national policies were federalistic
and latitudinarian (it published its statements in all the languages and

dialects of the area). The arrival of Red bureaucrats and "white" currency from Budapest only increased the local disenchantment.

It had been Kun's intention that his Red Army's offensive into Slovakia be synchronized with a Communist *coup d'etat* in Vienna, to which he had committed considerable funds and attention. Though he might have reasoned that Hungary already had sufficient enemies without alienating a benevolently neutral Austria as well, it appears that Kun believed that the maintenance of his own personal authority vis-à-vis both Socialists and Communists in Hungary required a spectacular external breakthrough. But the alert Austrian police aborted the planned Vienna coup, and the credit for the military triumph in Slovakia was quite properly given to the steely nerved commander in chief, the veteran Socialist trade union functionary Vilmos Böhm, and to his talented chief of staff, Lieutenant Colonel Aurel Stromfeld, a career officer of the old Habsburg army who, like many of his colleagues, put his professional services at the regime's disposal out of patriotic motives. The troops were likewise animated by nationalism, but it was an ominous note that, of the various regiments of peasant soldiers, those recruited from the territory of rump Hungary performed far less effectively than those who hailed from Magyar localities now under foreign occupation and intended for at least partial reconquest in the current counteroffensive. The former's direct experience with the land policy of the Communists and Socialists appears to have sapped much of their devotion.

The first ultimatum of June 8 from Paris to halt the Hungarian advance was quickly followed on June 13 by a second one ordering a Hungarian evacuation of the freshly overrun Slovak territory. Conceding now to Clemenceau what two and a half months earlier he had refused to Smuts, Kun complied categorically, thereby prompting the resignation of Stromfeld and other nationalistic officers. Though an attempted coup on June 24 by elements of the political Left and Right was suppressed, the psychological impact of these swift and devastating events was profoundly corrosive. The abject acceptance of Clemenceau's terms cost Kun his last shreds of acceptability and irreparably disillusioned the army and the people, for whom the Dictatorship of the Proletariat, proclaimed by a frantic Kun the day after the coup had failed (see above) was not an acceptable substitute for revolutionary national fervor. Escalation of the struggle against "internal enemies" and "traitors" with terror now availed Kun nothing and merely exacerbated the tension, suspicion, and defeatism which gripped Hungary in July, 1919. Nor could he save his regime with a last desperate military attack on the Romanians, launched in the night of July 19-20 to compel compliance with a promise given, but not kept, in Clemenceau's ultimatum of June 13, that upon Hungarian evacuation of Slovakia the Allies would also oblige Romanian withdrawal from some "surplus" territory to the west of Hungary's armistice line with that country. After three days of relative success, the Hungarian attack disintegrated under the multiple impact of treason in the officer cadre, demoralization in the ranks, and hysteria within the government. Even the hitherto militant miners and metalworkers abandoned Kun.

Having sacrificed the confidence of the nation, the Communist regime now lost confidence in itself. Rather than fulfill their own heroic rhetoric of a final stand at the barricades, Kun and his immediate entourage fled to Austria on August 1 in a special train with diplomatic immunity, leaving many other functionaries of the regime to their own fates. Like Wekerle's and Károlyi's, so now Kun's authority had simply withered away, and his final ouster from power was again relatively bloodless in its immediate setting. The Socialists, having tacked with the wind in the crises of October, 1918, and March, 1919, which had brought Károlyi and Kun, respectively, to power, now once again maneuvered desperately, but this time in vain, to avoid being shipwrecked with their associates. On August 2 they formed a government headed by that pair of leaders who had remained aloof from their fusion of March 21 with Kun—the trade unionists Gyula Peidl and Ernö Garami—and sought Allied endorsement for its moderation and respectablity. But the swing of the political pendulum was not to be halted by and for the Socialists. On August 6 the traditional ruling elite of old Hungary evicted the Peidl government. In the classic pattern of counterrevolutions, the white terror that now ensued dwarfed in ferocity the red excesses that had preceded and supposedly warranted it. Also historically characteristic was the sudden shift toward the virulent right of those traditionally apathetic strata of the old lower middle class and the unskilled proletariat who had only recently been politicized toward an extreme but superficial radicalism by Communist and Socialist propaganda and actions.

Though its errors of policy and administration contributed substantially to the manner and speed of the Kun regime's downfall—and especially to the execrated memories which survived it—the questions which pose themselves are whether, in the absence of the eagerly expected European revolution and/or Russian military assistance, any Communist-Socialist government in the Hungary of 1919, no matter how locally rational its policies and functional its administration, could long have survived? And if Kun knew, as he had reason to know, how remote were the possibilities of direct Russian and of European revolutionary aid to a Hungary defying the Allies, was not his drive to power here ideologically irresponsible? Or is it just possible that by briefly but intensely focusing the Allies' attention upon Hungary and deflecting certain of their military supplies from the Russian anti-Bolshevik white armies to those of Hungary's neighbors, Kun gave Lenin that timely and critical assistance which the latter was unable to reciprocate?

For the interwar world-Communist movement, the fact that a Communist government had managed to establish and to maintain itself for 133 days in a country *not* geographically adjacent to Russia was an enormous psychological and political boon, one that appeared to confirm the direction as well as the inevitability of Communism's expansion. For Hungarian society, per contra, a final tragedy of the Kun episode was that, by the manner of its rise and fall, it appeared to discredit by association the Károlyi experiment that had preceded and given birth to it, and hence allowed the counterrevolutionary white regime that followed it to equate liberalism with Communism. Social and political democratization could thus be resisted henceforth as allegedly treasonable to the Hungarian way of life.

3

Though the Right now restored itself to power, it could not—any more than could Károlyi or Kun—avoid paying the Allies' bill for Hungary's lost war. The political Right had initially sought to oust Kun by an independent coup in Budapest at the height of the original Romanian and Czech military threats in the second half of April, but its rather amateurish plot, organized by a Count Zsigmond Perényi, was handily unraveled. The Budapest workers' emphatic rallying to Kun's call for resistance to the bitter end against the foreign invaders had then prompted the counterrevolutionaries to transfer their base to the provinces and their headquarters to border towns under Allied protection. The first such counterrevolutionary government was organized on May 5 at Arad, in the Romanian zone of the armistice administration, by Count Gyula Károlyi, a cousin and political enemy of the "red" Count Mihály Károlyi. Later that month he transferred its operations to the town of Szeged. In Szeged the military presence of the French and Serbs was more congenial than that of the Romanians in Arad, and a Captain Gyula Gömbös, whose Right-Radical and anti-Semitic agitation had earlier resulted in his being purged from the republican army, was assembling certain military contingents on behalf of an Anti-Bolshevik Committee. Gömbös was supplied with funds, information, and manpower by the Hungarian political emigration in Vienna and eastern Austria, whose leader was Count István Bethlen. In a daring robbery and kidnapping raid on Kun's embassy in Vienna on May 2, these elements had seized 135 million crowns; this substantial sum, which had been intended to subsidize Communist activities in Austria, now became available to underwrite the counterrevolution. The approving Serbian authorities, with the hesitant acquiescence of the French, winked at this Vienna-Szeged traffic and facilitated the gathering of a counterrevolutionary army at Szeged. Due to Romanian chicaneries, it required two weeks, from May 9 to 23, to complete the transfer of Gyula Károlyi's government from Arad to Szeged. Once installed there, Károlyi quickly absorbed the Anti-Bolshevik Committee and recruited the Transylvanian nobleman Count Pál Teleki to be his minister of foreign affairs, and the last commander in chief of the Habsburg navy, Admiral Miklós Horthy, to serve as his war minister. Gömbös, who had sponsored Horthy's selection, was assigned as his undersecretary.

Horthy arrived in Szeged on June 6. He and Teleki promptly went to Belgrade to negotiate continued Serbian connivance with their counterrevolution. The British were also friendly. But the French, who were alienated by the crass anti-Semitism and the suspected Germanophilism of many Szeged leaders and considered the entire operation to be excessively reactionary, were now reserved and insisted on the formation of a multiparty government as well as the removal of Gömbös from the war ministry. Accordingly, on July 12, Gyula Károlyi gave way to Dezsö Ábráham at the head of a wider cabinet in which Horthy, offended at the purge of his deputy Gömbös, declined the war ministry but under which he served as commander in chief of the Szeged counterrevolutionary army.

That army never went into battle. It remained at Szeged until Kun had given way to Peidl (August 1-2). Then, as the Romanians continued their advance from the east, into which they had, so to speak, been "provoked" by Kun's abortive final attack on them, Horthy slipped his Szeged army across the Danube into western Hungary, out of the path of the Romanian march but into a position to secure the counterrevolution in Transdanubia. Though Clemenceau had indicated that with the fall of Kun the Romanian army would be halted, the Hungarian counterrevolutionaries preferred to use that army to assist in the ouster of the Peidl Socialist-trade union government. Nothing loath, the Romanians entered Budapest with "white" connivance on August 4, two days later facilitated the putsch against Peidl, and remained until November 14, meanwhile thoroughly looting the capital and the countryside. Not until November 16 did Horthy enter "sinful" Budapest at the head of his twelve-thousand-man Szeged army, which had at no time engaged either Kun's or the Romanians' troops and had confined its heroics to pogroms and a "white" terror in western Hungary.

In Budapest, meanwhile, the counterrevolutionary government established on August 6, and headed by István Friedrich, had designated King Charles's *homo regius* for Hungary, the Habsburg archduke Joseph, to be governor and Admiral Horthy to be its commander in chief. The Szeged government, which also stood on the principle of legitimacy and in which Horthy held the identical commission, had then formally dissolved itself on August 22, its members making for the capital to infiltrate and take over the Friedrich cabinet. Ministerial reshuffles followed in rapid sequence as a tugging match ensued between the traditional Hungarian political elite, whose instinctive inclination was for a total reversion to its former ascendancy, and the Allied Powers, who insisted on concluding peace with a reasonably representative and non-Habsburg government. The archduke was obliged to withdraw on August 24, and Friedrich had to reshuffle his cabinet on August 27 and September 12 and to commit himself to the early election of a National Assembly on the basis of a wide, secret, and equal suffrage (decree of November 17)—the only Károlyist innovation briefly to survive the counterrevolution. Under Western pressure, Friedrich was nevertheless obliged to give way on November 25 to a more moderate and broader government headed by Károly Huszár, in which the Socialists were finally granted one ministerial portfolio (welfare and labor) and one undersecretaryship (commerce). At last Hungary received an invitation on December 1 to send a delegation led by the polyglot Count Albert Apponyi to Paris to receive the peace terms, which were then duly transmitted on January 15, 1920.

The campaign for the elections to a National Assembly took place early in 1920, in the midst of a white terror and an atmosphere of intimidation that in effect made nonsense of the theoretically broad suffrage. Whereas even the victorious counterrevolutionaries subsequently conceded, after three years of investigation, that the so-called red terror of the Soviet regime had claimed a maximum of 587 victims (some of whom were, in fact, common criminals and others of whom had fallen in the act of attempting putsches), and that most of these were killed in Kun's last, hysterical, disintegrating weeks after the retreat from Slovakia, the subsequent white terror was, by all accounts, a systematic, ferocious hunt, combining "spontaneous" pogromist bestialities with a deliberate assault on those strata and institutions that had recently challenged and might once again seek to challenge the traditional arrangements of Hungarian political life. In other words, it was a reaction against the Károlyi as well as the Kun episodes.

Executed mainly by déclassé elements of the lumpen gentry, who enjoyed the personal protection of Admiral Horthy and were organized into bodies bearing such vivid and portentous designations as "Association of Awakening Magyars," "Blood Pact of the Double Cross," "Hungarian Scientific Race-Protecting Society," "Hungarian Association for National Defense," the white terror killed five to six thousand victims, many of whom were Jewish. Countless were the beatings, tortures, rapes, castrations, and incarcerations, and many outstanding elements of Hungary's intelligentsia were driven into exile. ("Horthy" thus became as much the "horrible example" with which the Russian Bolsheviks would frighten their peoples to illustrate what was in store for them should the whites ever return, as "Károlyi-Kun" came to serve the Hungarian Horthyite regime as a handy alarm to warn against the allegedly inevitable degeneration of even moderate reforms.) Perhaps the colossal destructiveness to human life during World War I had psychologically anes-thetized the public to such a mindless carnage.

Against this background, it was a listless nation that trooped to the polls on January 25, 1920, to elect an overwhelmingly counterrevolutionary, agrarian, professedly "Christian" (in contradistinction to "Jewish" Bol-sheviks) National Assembly. The Communists were, of course, excluded from the elections, and the disillusioned Socialists, having at last roused themselves on January 15 into quitting the counterrevolutionary gov-ernment, were cowed (or shamed) into abstention. Later supplementary elections in certain eastern and southern areas currently under foreign occupation altered somewhat the balance of parties within the counter-revolutionary coalition; for example, the anti-Habsburg Free Electors were strengthened vis-à-vis the pro-Habsburg Legitimists in regard to the constitutional problem. But the collective weight of this coalition was not lessened by these shifts within it. Budapest, the pacemaker of 1918 and 1919, was, for the time being, neutralized.

On January 29 and 30, respectively, Premier Huszár and Archduke Joseph prematurely declared that the election results warranted the king's restoration (that is, before the later by-elections had strengthened the Free Electors), whereupon the Allied Powers at the Paris Peace Conference warned on February 2 that the Habsburg problem was an international, not a domestic Hungarian, issue and that they would regard restoration of that dynasty as incompatible with peace. Hence, when the Hungarian National Assembly formally convened on February 16, it acknowledged that Hungary's commitment to the Habsburgs' Pragmatic Sanction of 1723 as well as the Austro-Hungarian Ausgleich of 1867 had indeed lapsed in 1918, but it decided to shelve the dynastic issue for the time being and on March 1 elected Horthy to be regent of the kingdom by a vote of 131 to 7 for Count Albert Apponyi. It also declared invalid all legislation and enactments of the Károlyi and Kun regimes. The legal powers of the regent (a title graced in the sixteenth century by János Hunyadi and in the nineteenth by Lajos Kossuth) were, in general, identical with the royal prerogatives, except that he could not create new titles of nobility nor exercise the Apostolic Crown's patronage rights over the Roman Catholic church. He was thus supreme chief of the armed forces (subject to parliamentary allocations to cover their costs), had a suspensive veto on legislation (which Horthy never found it neces-sary to exercise), appointed and dismissed the premier, and could con-vene, adjourn, and dissolve the legislature regardless of its own wishes.

The Huszár cabinet, having done its duty, now resigned, and on March 15, 1920, the Legitimists (Christian National Union) and Free Electors (Smallholder coalition) formed a new cabinet under Sándor Simonyi-Semadam for the painful task of weighing and then accepting the Allies' severe peace terms. The terms were formally signed by Hungary and the victors on June 4 at the Trianon Palace in Versailles.

The extent of the Trianon disaster for Hungary is graphically, but only partially, conveyed by a series of statistics extrapolated from her last prewar census of 1910, as shown in table 23[5]. Were one to consider

TABLE 23

TRIANON LOSSES AND RESIDUES (PER 1910 DATA)

	Area (sq. km.)	Population (total)	Magyars (linguistic)
Historic Hungary (without Croatia-Slavonia)	282,870	18,264,533	9,944,627
Lost to:			
Austria	4,020	291,618	26,153
Czechoslovakia	61,633	3,517,568	1,066,685
Poland	589	23,662	230
Romania	103,093	5,257,467	1,661,805
Yugoslavia	20,551	1,509,295	452,265
Italy	21	49,806	6,493
Total Losses	189,907	10,649,416	3,213,631
Residual Hungary	92,963	7,615,117	6,730,996

Croatia-Slavonia, which had been constitutionally affiliated with the Hungarian Crown since 1102, as part of historic Hungary, then its area, total population, and Magyar population as of 1910 (42,541 square kilometers, 2,621,954 people, 105,948 Magyars) would be added to the statistics for both prewar historic Hungary as well as her postwar losses to Yugoslavia. But even omitting Croatia-Slavonia from the Trianon calculations, and thus avoiding the knotty legal problem as to whether its medieval union to the Kingdom of Hungary as *partes adnexae* was "real" or "personal," the peace terms left truncated Hungary with only one-third of her historic territory, two-fifths of her prewar population, and two-thirds of her Magyar people. Indeed, the area lost to Romania alone was larger than the rump Hungarian state, which now bore the dubious distinction of being Europe's main loser from World War I and which was reduced from a Carpatho-Danubian to an exclusively Danubian entity. Whereas four-fifths of Hungary's historic frontiers had been

5. All statistics, unless otherwise specified, are from the official statistical yearbooks of the Central Royal Hungarian Office of Statistics, *Annuaire Statistique Hongrois* (Budapest: A Magyar Kir. Központi Statisztikai Hivatal).

natural, i.e., coterminous with mountain crestlines and with rivers, scarcely one-fourth of her new borders—sections along the rivers Danube (Czechoslovakia) and Drava (Yugoslavia)—could be considered natural, and even the first of these two stretches ran right through a heavily Magyar-populated countryside.

Crude comparisons with the losses suffered by the prewar Austrian half of the Habsburg Empire would be misleading, for unlike those other realms, Hungary had for centuries been a centralized and coherent state, one characterized by an extraordinary degree of constitutional, geographic, hydrographic, and economic unity (but also by much ethnic diversity—her eventual Achilles heel). That Trianon restored to Hungary her complete sovereign independence after four centuries among the Habsburg domains was small compensation for the destruction of her historic integrity, especially in light of the fact that, whereas ethnicity was supposedly the victors' main (though admittedly not exclusive) criterion in their considerations of postwar borders, several million Magyars were assigned for strategic or economic reasons to other states and their usually hostile governments. And these states' own interwar political and ethnic tensions were to be at least as acute as old Hungary's had been, but without the compensation of her economic and geographic unity. To be distributed among several sovereign states and to see large fractions of their nation existing as irredentas across international frontiers was for the Magyars, unlike the Germans, an utterly new and psychologically unacceptable condition. Nor did they have the consolation the Austrians had of being able to draw cultural succor from a great neighboring Reich of their own people. Their land truncated and isolated, the Hungarians reacted to Trianon with far greater outrage than did the Austrian Germans to the Treaty of St. Germain.

The loss in economic resources imposed on Hungary by the Trianon frontiers was staggering: 58 percent of her railroad and 60 percent of her road mileage; 84 percent of her timber resources and 43 percent of her arable land; 83 percent of her iron ore, 29 percent of her lignite, and 27 percent of her bituminous coal. As regards manufacturing, the calculation of losses is complicated by the fact that it had been the traditional policy of old Hungary's governments to concentrate finishing, food-processing, chemical, and machine-building industries around Budapest. Therefore, many such factories now remained to her. Their potential productive capacity was intact, but they were severed from their supplies of raw materials as well as from some of their traditional markets; hence, they were vulnerable to the possible (and eventual) autarkic or punitive policies of the neighboring states.

While the Trianon frontiers were drawn with considerable disregard for topographic, economic, demographic, and administrative and historical considerations, it remains to be proven whether they were made particularly vindictive in order to punish Hungary for her recent flirtation with Bolshevism. It is more likely that the terms that finally emerged from the protracted deliberations of the victors, whose main attention was focused on Germany and Russia, were so punitive to Hungary because they were the product of separate committees designated to evaluate the validity of her neighbors' separate claims on her. Had a single committee for the new Hungarian frontiers been appointed, it assuredly would not have preserved historic Hungary intact; but it might well have prevented the severance of over three million Magyars from their own country.

To ensure, finally, that Hungary should remain powerless to act on the indignation that these territorial amputations would inevitably arouse, the disarmament provisions of the Trianon Treaty restricted her to an army of thirty-five thousand volunteers and to gendarmerie and police units of twelve thousand men each. She was also prohibited from maintaining an air force, tanks, heavy artillery, and a general staff and from resorting to universal military service. The combined armed forces maintained by her three neighbors who had emerged as the chief beneficiaries of Trianon (Czechoslovakia, Romania, and Yugoslavia) numbered about half-a-million.

Passionate revisionism was the general—indeed, the virtually universal —response of Hungarian society to Trianon. For a brief moment in 1920 there appeared to be hope that a sudden shift in France's diplomatic posture in favor of Hungary might permit the revision of the treaty virtually before the ink had dried. Hungary, under Count Pál Teleki, who succeeded Simonyi-Semadam as premier on July 19, while temporarily retaining the foreign affairs portfolio which he had held in the preceding ministry, did its best to encourage this incipient French development by proposing concessions to French capital in Hungary in exchange for frontier revision, and by volunteering Hungarian military assistance to France's protégé Poland in that country's desperate struggle with Bolshevik Russia in the summer of 1920. Teleki was thus offering Hungary as a cornerstone for French policy in southeastern Europe in return for scrapping Trianon. But the Poles won the battle of Warsaw in August without Hungarian aid, and Hungary's friends in the French government, Alexandre Millerand and Maurice Paléologue, failed to convice their colleagues of the soundness of a diplomatic about-face that would entail sacrificing France's strong standing in Czechoslovakia, Romania, and Yugoslavia. Hungary thus had no option but silently to ratify, on November 13, the Trianon Treaty which she had signed on June 4, 1920. Only after it went into effect on July 26, 1921, did the Yugoslavs finally evacuate the Pécs area of south-central Hungary.

The experienced, resourceful, and resilient Hungarian ruling elite drew the obvious inference from this failure to achieve instant revision with one diplomatic stroke. Considering also the extensive damage that the war and the subsequent Romanian plunder had inflicted on Hungary, the elite decided that a period of domestic consolidation on constitutional, political, cultural, and economic levels would have to precede an eventual resumption of diplomatic and possibly military efforts to achieve revision.

4

This period of domestic recuperation preparatory to redoubled revisionism is known in Hungarian history as the Bethlen era, after its resourceful leader Count István Bethlen. His first order of business was the dynastic-constitutional question. Constitutional issues were intertwined with revisionist aspirations as a result of a peculiar Hungarian theory of public law. Rooted in medieval formulations, it held that the integrity of the historic frontiers was a function of their delimiting the "Lands of the Holy Apostolic Crown of St. Stephen [István]." In interwar Hungarian eyes, therefore, Hungary could sustain the historico-juridical basis of all her revisionist claims only if she remained a kingdom. And as complete, rather than merely partial, revision remained the ultimate goal of her ruling elite, both the Legitimist and the Free Elector factions of that elite could easily agree on the need to retain a formally royalist constitution.

The main institutional expression of the Free Elector position, the new and somewhat misnamed Smallholder Party (itself a coalition) which had emerged as the National Assembly's largest party in the staggered elections of 1920, was not republican or even peasantist, still less "leftist," in ideology as much as it represented an "1848" reaction against the discredited solution of "1867" to the Hungarians. It was thus easily infiltrated and captured by forces whose social origins and economic interests had little in common with its founding Smallholders, but who shared, and were able to manipulate, these founders' aversion to the allegedly disastrous Habsburg dynasty.[6] The next step was the merger, arranged in July, 1920, by the politically dexterous Count István Bethlen, of this Smallholder Party with the more truly conservative and largely Legitimist Christian National Union. The result was what came conventionally (if unofficially) to be called the Government Party, based on a set of reciprocal waivers: both the dynastic restoration issue and serious land reform would be indefinitely postponed and Hungary would remain a kingdom with a regency, a country whose constitutional and social institutions would vividly illustrate her commitment to integral revisionism in foreign policy and thorough restitution of the prewar social system in

6. In Hungarian usage, the term "smallholder" applies to an owner of less than 100 cadastral yokes of land. Hence it does not designate the great mass of poor peasants, still less the army of landless agricultural laborers.

domestic affairs. Since the Allies in general and the neighbor states in particular had in any event vetoed a Habsburg restoration, the original Smallholder founders had manifestly traded away a substantial concession (land reform) in return for an illusory one (the dynasty) in this domestic politico-social exchange.

The bargain demonstrated its viability in 1921. In that year two attempts by King Charles to recover his throne through sudden and dramatic returns to Hungary from his Swiss exile—once at Easter and again late in October—were repudiated, though on the first occasion the king may well have had clandestine French encouragement, while on the second some fighting at the outskirts of Budapest was required before the Legitimists' easily aroused nostalgia for their crowned sovereign yielded to political realism. An Act of Dethronement was passed, under external pressure, after an intense debate of November 3-6, 1921, and the ruling establishment was spared further embarrassment from this direction by Charles' premature death at the age of thirty-five on April 1, 1922, at Funchal in the Madeira Islands. The first of the abortive royal putsches had, incidentally, been followed on April 14, 1921, by Teleki's yielding the premiership to his fellow Transylvanian, Bethlen. The former's conduct during that brief crisis had initially been somewhat ambiguous, and since he had all along considered himself but a "chair-warmer" for Bethlen, the true creator and leader of the Government Party, the change was a logical development. That party having been severely strained and somewhat fragmented by the king's ventures, Bethlen definitively restructured it with all but the most incorrigible Legitimists in February, 1922.

The second part of the bargain upon which the Government Party was based, the restoration of the traditional land-holding system, was facilitated by the fact that the Kun regime had never proceeded to partition the large, noble-owned, estates which it had formally "socialized" on paper. During the so-called revolutions of 1918-19, the peasants had no sense of real change in agrarian or agronomic arrangements on the land, and hence they lacked leverage with which to resist the return to the latifundist system of extensive cultivation carried on by large armies of itinerant and domiciled agricultural laborers. A sham agrarian reform was authorized by Law XXXVI of December 7, 1920 (amended in 1936), but it transferred only a little over a million cadastral yokes (about six hundred thousand hectares) of generally inferior land to about seven hundred thousand recipients (i.e., an average of less than one hectare per recipient). The original proprietors received full compensation, and the new ones were burdened with prohibitive redemption payments that ruined most of them again within a few years. Scarcely half the land involved had been contributed by large estates, hardly any of it was used to create medium or small farms of real durability, and half of it was squandered into a large number of nonviable dwarf-holdings. The law was administered so as to discredit the very idea of substantial land reform and scarcely modifies the above generalization that Hungary reverted to the full restoration of her prewar agricultural system.

The ruling elite, in turn, for whom the restoration of that system was a logical parallel to revisionism in foreign goals, sought, with persistence and considerable success, to persuade the agricultural proletariat, the dwarf-holders, and the other masses, that all their economic hardships and social grievances were rooted in the Trianon peace terms. Indeed, in a style reminiscent of the prewar arguments for a Magyar monopoly of political power as a screen for the nobility's socioeconomic prerogatives (see section 1), so now, again, the prevailing and genuinely popular revisionist-irredentist atmosphere of interwar Hungary was exploited to camouflage the elite's deliberate decision to sustain the nation's traditional feudal-bourgeois institutions.

Bethlen paralleled his finessing of the Smallholders with the virtual bribery of the Socialists in an agreement of December, 1921, according to which, in return for amnesty and Bethlen's permission that their party resume full legal activity, organize the industrial workers in its trade unions (whose confiscated funds were now restored), and freely publish its newspapers, the Socialists committed themselves to abstain from political or organizational activity among agricultural laborers, peasant dwarf-holders, and public employees, to refrain from political strikes and from "antinational propaganda," and to adopt an "expressly Hungarian attitude" toward foreign affairs, i.e., to support the regime's anti-Trianon revisionism.

The stage was now set for Bethlen's masterstroke in this triumphal counterattack on behalf of Hungary's "historic classes." The two-year term of the National Assembly having expired on February 16, 1922, Bethlen issued a decree on March 2; of dubious legal validity but of decisive political authority, it abolished the relatively wide and secret "Friedrich suffrage" that had characterized the elections of 1920, and reverted to Hungary's traditional, restricted, and, in the countryside, open ballot for the elections of a new, quinquennial legislature. An interesting pretext offered for the abolition of secret voting in the villages was that the upright peasants were alleged to have repudiated it as falsely implying that they were ashamed to have other people know their views. In fact, of course, as the forthcoming and subsequent elections were vividly to demonstrate, the open rural ballot facilitated the exercise of sufficient coercion (short of terror) and corruption (including voting the dead) to assure the Government Party a permanent and safe majority, one easily produced by the potent rural trinity of landlord, gendarme, and village notary. (Even in the cities, where the vote was indeed secret, a candidate's nomination papers required a large number of open signatures.)

Held between May 28 and June 12, 1922, the elections returned 169 Government Party and allied deputies and 20 unreconciled Legitimists —the latter's partial opposition to Bethlen being based exclusively on constitutional, and by no means on social or economic, grounds—versus 56 oppositionists of the Center and Left, of whom 25 were Socialists. As anticipated, the Government Party enjoyed its greatest successes in the 201 provincial election districts where the balloting was open. There 149 of its seats were won and it received over 67 percent of the votes, in contrast to only 18 percent in the forty-four urban districts (Budapest and ten additional cities) where the secret ballot obtained. The Legitimist magnates, of course, utilized the open ballot on their own estates to wrest some seats from the Government Party machine.

As subsequent Hungarian elections during the decade of Bethlen's premiership served no apparent political function other than the periodic renewal of the Government Party's backbenches, it appears appropriate at this point to interrupt chronology and cite their more-or-less "arranged" results in table 24.

TABLE 24

PARLIAMENTARY ELECTIONS IN THE BETHLEN ERA

Party	Seats		
	1922 (May-June)	1926 (December)	1931 (June-July)
The Regime Phalanx:			
Government Party	143	170	158
Christian Social (allied with G.P.)	2	35	36
Independents endorsing G.P.	24	4	15
Christian National (Legitimist)	20	. . .	. . .
Center and Left Opposition:			
Socialist	25	14	14
Other Parties of C. and L.	20	9 ⎫	11
Independents of C. and L.	11	3 ⎭	
Right-Radical Opposition:	. . .	10	11
Total	245	245	245

On the eve of the 1926 elections, Bethlen had constitutionally further consolidated the restoration with the re-creation of an Upper House (Act XXII of November 15, 1926), to consist of four types of members: hereditary, ex-officio, elected (by autonomous corporations), and appointed (by the regent on the nomination of the cabinet). Adult male members of the Habsburg family who resided in Hungary belonged to the hereditary category; senior judges and crown attorneys, keepers of the crown and the banners, the commander in chief of the armed forces, the president of the National Bank, and Roman Catholic and Lutheran bishops and heads of other religious cults were ex-officio members; representatives elected by the members of the former House of Magnates, by municipalities, counties, chambers of agriculture, commerce, and industry, and by the stock exchange, the Academy of Sciences and the universities belonged to the third category; and up to forty eminent citizens could be appointed, for life. The total membership of this Upper House was to be 244 (raised to 248 in 1940) and, though it had little influence on legislation until its powers were extended by Law XXVII of 1937 to virtual equality with the Lower House, except in money matters, it was intended to serve as a kind of "historico-political conscience" of the nation. Indeed, in the 1930s and 1940s it came to be a relative breakwater of "whiggish" decency and humanity against the totalitarian tide of the radical Right during that era.

In the first interwar decade, the Government Party in the Lower House proved a sufficently docile instrument in Bethlen's hands to render superfluous any political reliance on the Upper House. Since the open ballot virtually eliminated the electorate as a serious factor in public life and rendered the Government Party the only ladder to positions of power, and since its leader enjoyed full discretion to select that party's parliamentary candidates, it followed that any leader who enjoyed the regent's confidence could, as premier, govern Hungary without fear of opposition or of censure. Since the Government Party was but a sounding board for its leader's policies, which, despite Bethlen's conservative rhetoric, could be of startling tactical elasticity when industrial and commercial or fiscal innovations were in order, its very programmatic latitudinarianism and pliancy came to compensate in part for the system's exclusiveness and severity toward other parties. The one possible chink in the leader-premier's political armor was his legal dependence on the regent's confidence. Bethlen, whose experience, skill, culture, and authority vastly impressed the more limited Horthy, enjoyed this trust for a full decade. His successors of the 1930s and 1940s, however, were painfully to learn that, while no backbench mutiny could force the leader-premier's ouster against the regent's will, neither could backbench support save him from the regent's dismissal; and the regent's choice of successor, by virtue of his potential power to call new elections and hand-pick the candidates, could always be imposed on the Government Party machinery.

One must bear in mind that, as such, the Government Party was but one arm of a cohesive ruling establishment whose other instrumentalities included the civil and military bureaucracies, the clergy, the banks, the professions, and the manor houses. During the Bethlen era of the 1920s, that establishment continued to be dominated by Hungary's "historic classes"; their reflexes were conservative rather than totalitarian, they were even capable of liberalism on questions of intellectual and civil freedom, and their preferred stance toward the masses of peasants and workers was one of paternalism and aloofness rather than mobilization and manipulation. Yet the very pervasiveness and comprehensiveness of Bethlen's organizational and political triumphs at the beginning of the decade in reknitting this establishment and shaping its political institutions and style had screened and harnessed, but scarcely dulled and still less deadened, the vitality of the counterrevolution's other, Right-Radical, elements. These elements had allowed themselves to be coopted into Bethlen's system but remained a potentially powerful counterelite to his historic one should the latter ever appear to lose its grip.

Such were the institutional arrangements of the Bethlen era. Though the system's goals were unashamedly those of external and internal restoration, its leader recognized that their realization would require a substantial dose of international diplomatic, fiscal, and general confidence in Hungary. Hence Bethlen curbed the white terrorists and pogromists, while his able minister of education and cults, Count Kunó Klebelsberg, conducted an imaginative, if somewhat extravagant, policy of compensating for Hungary's current military prostration by encouraging the demonstration on the international scene of her continuing cultural and scientific vigor. A small but significant breakthrough in Hungary's drive for foreign goodwill had been achieved when a plebiscite, arranged under Italian auspices with the assent of the other Allied Powers, was held in the city and hinterland of Sopron (Oedenburg) on December 14-16, 1921, and resulted in the return to Hungary of a slice of the Burgenland province lost to Austria under the terms of Trianon. This was the first, and for a long time the only, alteration of that treaty. Interwar Hungary's area was now stabilized at 93,073 square kilometers. Less than a year later, having continued to demonstrate her overtly reputable and pacific domestic and foreign policies, Hungary was admitted to the League of Nations on September 18, 1922. This was a necessary stepping-stone to her securing a League-sponsored Reconstruction Loan of 250 million gold crowns (equivalent at that time to $50 million) in July, 1924.

The year 1926, on the other hand, saw a brief set-back, with the exposure of a scandal involving the forgery of French francs on the premises of the Hungarian Cartographical Institute. Implicated were some very high political and governmental personages, who pleaded "patriotic," i.e., irredentist, motives. The scandal was handled in a manner that protected some of the principal culprits. Again at the turn of the year 1927-28 the Hungarian government was somewhat embarrassed by the so-called St. Gotthard incident, which exposed illicit armaments imports from Mussolini's Italy, with which Bethlen had recently concluded a Treaty of Friendship and Cooperation (April 5, 1927). The treaty, based on common hostility toward Yugoslavia, did, indeed, end Hungary's long political isolation but was of dubious value in her current endeavors to win the goodwill of the other Western powers.

Hungary, of course, consistently utilized her seat in the League of Nations as a sounding board for revisionism and for protests against her neighbors' treatment of their Magyar populations. Just as consistently, these neighbors cited the "sanctity of international treaties" and rejected such "intolerable interference" in their internal affairs. Soon the Hungarians developed a series of alternative strategies for the prosecution of revisionism within and outside the League. When feeling diplomatically weak, they would emphasize their neighbors' often neglected obligations under the Minorities Protection Treaty; when feeling stronger, they would press for limited border rectifications so as to redeem at least some of the Magyars immediately across the Trianon frontiers. Both these tactics rested on the plausible rationale of ethnicity. Ultimately, however, the Hungarian goal remained the integral restoration of all the lands of the Holy Crown within their historic frontiers. But the pursuit of this final goal, as well as of other, more limited, objectives, required some ordering of priorities.

Though the territory that had been lost to Romania was geographically the most extensive as well as economically and demographically the most valuable of Hungary's Trianon bereavements, and though some of inter-war Hungary's leading political figures, such as Bethlen and Teleki, had genealogical ties to this severed Transylvanian land, and though Hungarian national psychology was particularly contemptuous of Romanians, yet territorial Hungarian revisionism in that direction was rather surprisingly muted. Bethlen and Horthy conceded that the Transylvanian Romanians were true Romanians who had opted against Hungary of their own free will, but argued that they ought now to treat the Magyars amongst them better. A sobering consideration, presumably, was the fact that until the very end of the interwar era, no Great Power was available to underwrite Hungarian irredentism against Romania.

Hungarian revisionist aspirations against Yugoslavia, on the other hand, were nurtured by Italian protection and by the enticing spectacle of Croatian-Serb animosities in that country. Yet Hungary's policy here oscillated for a long time between the options of (a) working to dismember Yugoslavia by aggravating Croatian disaffection (the "Zagreb line"), or (b) seducing Yugoslavia as a whole away from her Czechoslovak and Romanian allies by relinquishing Hungarian claims to Croatia and offering to abide by plebiscites in the other areas lost to Yugoslavia (the "Belgrade line"). Here again, the Hungarian leaders conceded that Croatia had not historically been considered an integral part of the Holy Crown and that its secession in 1918 had been freely decided.

Thus, by a process of political elimination, Hungary came to concentrate her revisionist pressure on Czechoslovakia, despite the fact that the Magyar minority in that country enjoyed the widest civil and cultural liberties. Indeed, its educational opportunities were not only far superior to those granted by old Hungary to her Slovak and Ruthenian minorities, but they even compared favorably with those available in Trianon Hungary to Hungarians. Such considerations, however, carried no weight in interwar Budapest, where Czechoslovakia was correctly judged to be the keystone of the Versailles-Trianon-St. Germain arch in Central Europe and was also thought to be peculiarly fragile in consequence of its internal ethnic and political tensions. Considering Czechoslovakia an utterly artificial and nonviable political structure, and refusing to take seriously the possibility that the Slovaks' and Ruthenians' alienation from the Magyars might run deeper than their disenchantment with the Czechs, the Hungarian political leaders had independently opted for a policy of relentless revisionism against Czechoslovakia long before Hilter's Germany came along to urge this course on them. The very fact that the political institutions and style of interwar Czechoslovakia were, in a sense, a living refutation of the values of counterrevolutionary Hungary served as an additional goad to Budapest's vendetta.

It is an interesting hypothetical question whether the Hungarian public's outrage against Trianon would have died down in time had the regime decided not to exploit it. In Germany, for example, the admittedly more totalitarian Nazi regime was able, when it so chose, to dampen popular clamor against the so-called Polish Corridor between 1934 and 1939. This, of course, did not mean that the issue had vanished or that the irredentist feelings were unreal. Alternatively, might the Hungarian leaders have achieved more in the long run—and better sustained their country's international reputation—if, instead of promoting chronic tumult over Hungary's truncation, they had adopted the stance of the French after the loss of Alsace-Lorraine in 1870: *n'en parler jamais, y penser toujours.* From hindsight, it appears obvious that a fatal blunder was committed by the ruling elite's leading Hungary into a position where her Great Power patrons became Fascist Italy and Nazi Germany, where she herself was subsidizing clerico-fascist paramilitary bodies in neighboring Austria, and where the major thrust of her foreign policy was directed against Czechoslovakia, which was generally regarded as the most democratic and progressive state in Central Europe. To a certain extent, this complex of missteps was inadvertent, and in the later 1930s Bethlen and Teleki were to try desperately but vainly to retrace at least that part of it which had led to exclusive dependence on the Axis Powers. Yet it had all followed logically (or psychologically) from the original commitment to subordinate every other consideration to the cause of revisionism, and to use that commitment as a pretext to stifle domestic reform.

5

Supplementing his program of political and diplomatic consolidation was Bethlen's effort to fortify the country economically—an effort that was, however, eventually destined to be aborted by the depression. Though interwar Hungary remained a preponderantly agricultural country, Bethlen was quite aware that national pride, national interest, recent national history, and current international politico-economic competitiveness required the development of her industrial and commercial capacity. Like his predecessors of the post-Ausgleich era, he was more than willing to underwrite such a policy provided the capitalist elite administering it would politically concert with, rather than challenge, the traditional noble landed and bureaucratic elites. Since Hungarian capitalism was highly oligarchic, centralized, and Jewish, Bethlen's political preconditions presented no difficulties as the relatively small number of powerful families to whom they were addressed had no interest in refusing them. He had, after all, earlier smitten the Bolsheviks and checked the pogromists and was now offering to coordinate the state's economic policy with these families. (Such "businesslike" political and economic cooperation between Magyar nobles and Jewish capitalists had no bearing on social anti-Semitism, which Bethlen, Horthy, and others carried in fairly strong doses.)

Hungary's society provided a feasible platform for Bethlen's economic program. Though not as modern as the western provinces of Czechoslovakia, it was nevertheless quite advanced within East Central Europe in general and relative to the country's Balkan neighbors in particular. In a sense, interwar Hungary's stage of development was roughly comparable to Poland's: it was still basically agricultural but there were significant industrial sectors. A statistical demonstration of this, based on the two interwar censuses taken on the last day of 1920 and of 1930, is given in table 25.

The large category of "Rentiers and retired" in 1930 was politically important for it included the many highly nationalistic former officials repatriated since 1920 from the territories lost by Hungary under the Trianon Treaty.

Illiteracy rates and urban-rural population ratios are also important indicators of a country's level of modernity. Hungary's official statistics recorded illiteracy above the age of six at the impressively low, and declining, percentages of 15.2 in 1920 and 9.6 in 1930. It was estimated to have been reduced to 4 percent by the eve of World War II. This compares well with other East Central European countries. As regards urban-rural ratios, a caveat is in order. The great Hungarian plain was dotted with a number of localities that were large enough to be defined as towns, but whose inhabitants remained almost exclusively involved in agriculture. Hence, this indicator is not strictly comparable to the equivalent ratios for other East Central European countries, which lacked the peculiarly Hungarian phenomenon of the agricultural town. Nevertheless, making due allowances for this consideration, Hungary's level of urbanization was high in comparison to the area's other countries. With an urban locality officially defined as one of more than ten thousand inhabitants, the census recorded 40.3 percent of the population as urban and 59.7 percent as rural in 1920, and 42.5 percent as urban and 57.5 percent as rural in 1930.

TABLE 25

POPULATION BY ECONOMIC SECTORS (INCLUDING DEPENDENTS)

	1920		1930	
	Number	Percentage	Number	Percentage
Agriculture	4,454,241	55.7	4,499,393	51.8
Mining	117,653	1.5	115,041	1.3
Industry	1,524,755	19.1	1,883,257	21.7
Commerce, banking	407,321	5.1	469,059	5.4
Communications, transportation	356,632	4.4	338,875	3.9
Free professions, civil service	372,460	4.7	434,782	5.0
Military service	124,702	1.6	72,541	0.8
Rentiers, retired	197,095	2.5	360,901	4.2
Domestics	175,652	2.2	197,179	2.3
Other	259,691	3.2	317,291	3.6
Total	7,990,202	100.0	8,688,319	100.0

Despite her immense losses at Trianon, Hungary's remaining economic assets were not inconsiderable, but their exploitation emphatically required international economic cooperation since they were largely a residue of the prewar concentration of many industries around Budapest, which were now, as mentioned earlier, politically separated from their original raw-material sources and markets. Thus, computed on the basis of value of production, the following percentages of prewar capacity remained in Trianon Hungary: machinery industry, 90.1; printing, 89.5; clothing, 76.7; electric power, 60.4; leather, 57.8; stoneware and earthenware, 57.7; chemical, 56.8; food processing, 55.7; iron and metallurgical, 50.3. All in all, 55.5 percent of the prewar production value of industry, 49.2 percent of the factories, 50.9 percent of the industrial labor force, and 51.3 percent of the mechanical power remained.[7] Given favorable conditions, these capacities could be extended, just as it proved possible to compensate for major losses in known reserves of coal, iron, and timber by the extraction of other types of raw materials, such as bauxite, whose existence was unsuspected at the signing of Trianon. Furthermore, though the transportation network was overly centralized upon Budapest, the density of Hungary's railroad system was already high and also subject to further improvement.

As regards agricultural assets, Trianon Hungary retained the following percentages of her prewar areas (excluding Croatia-Slavonia): vineyards, 68.4; arable land, 42.9; pasturage, 30.5; meadows, 25.1; gardens, 25.0; marshlands, 54.0; uncultivable land, 39.0.

To realize and extend the productive potential of these residual economic assets, and to liquidate the dislocations accruing from the Kun chaos and the Trianon truncations, Hungary's rulers opted for a two-stage policy. Initially, they stimulated an inflation so as to shift the costs of the war and of postwar reconversion onto the shoulders of wage and salary earners. Then they solicited international financial investments in an expanding economy with a disarmed labor force. During the inflationary phase, real wages sank by 1923 to half their prewar value and were paid in local currency that had fallen to a level at which 16,300 paper crowns were equivalent to 1 gold crown, while prices were calculated according to foreign currencies. Over six hundred new enterprises were launched on this inflationary tide between 1921 and 1923, while the magnates and gentry, in their turn, paid off estate-mortagages amounting to one and a half billion crowns with depreciated money. By 1924 the inflation had served its purpose and had begun to threaten its beneficiaries. Hence, it was halted. On February 21, 1924, Hungary's remaining reparations were definitely fixed and scheduled over the next twenty years; on May 24 a new National Bank to serve as the country's sole issuing bank was founded with a capital of 30 million gold crowns; on July 2-4 came the League-sponsored Reconstruction Loan of 250 million gold crowns (84 percent of which was realized) at 7.5 percent interest; and on August 3 a schedule of relatively high protective tariffs (averaging 27 percent), which had been virtually drafted by the National Federation of Manufactures and the National Agricultural Federation, was enacted, to become effective on January 1, 1925.

The Reconstruction Loan was used primarily to pay Hungary's share of the Habsburg Monarchy's debts, to consolidate the state budget, and to achieve financial stability. (A new currency, the pengö, equal to 0.26315789 grain of fine gold, received parliamentary authorization on

7. Statistics in this and the next paragraph are from I. T. Berend and Gy. Ránki, "The Development of the Manufacturing Industry in Hungary (1900-1944)," *Studia Historica Academiae Scientiarum Hungaricae*, no. 19 (1960), pp. 47-49, and Ladislaus von Buday, "Landwirtschaftliche Produktion in Ungarn," *Ungarische Jahrbücher* 1 (1921): 177.

November 3, 1925.) Only a small fraction went into productive investments. It was followed during the remainder of the decade by some eighty additional foreign loans, which totaled over 3 billion pengös and placed approximately 415 million pengös credit annually at Hungary's disposal. By 1930 her per capita foreign debt was Europe's heaviest. Interest, however, being high and terms short, as much as 40 percent of the value of these loans was swallowed up in service charges and amortization. Nor could the Bethlen-Horthy system, given its deliberately obsolete and socially ambivalent structure, invest the remainder prudently: 25 percent was absorbed by ostentatious consumption on estates and in the civil service. Thus, only 20 percent was available for investment in production, and 15 percent for useful social overhead.[8] Internally accumulated capital was not invested rationally either; had it been, Hungary's dependence on foreign money markets would have been drastically reduced. Alternatively, had the external loans been used discerningly, a really impressive growth rate could have been achieved. Foreign trade policy was equally improvident, the balance being consistently passive and covered by borrowing. In a real sense, therefore, Hungary's rulers invited her exploitation and maximized her vulnerability by soliciting foreign credits that were too high, relative to the current productive capacity of her economy—a capacity kept limited by sociopolitical considerations. The constantly revolving supply of foreign credits screened this precariousness of Hungary's apparent economic recovery during the rest of the 1920s, the halcyon days of the Bethlen system; but when nemesis struck with the Great Depression, it was to destroy Bethlen together with "his" prosperity.

Statistics illustrate the apparently promising, if slow, recovery of the first interwar decade. Thus, if the value of manufacturing output (at constant prices) in the last peace year of 1913 is set at 100, then in 1924, at the end of a decade of turmoil and at the beginning of stabilization, it was 65.4, and in 1929, on the eve of the depression, it was 112.3. Even at the time, however, it was patent that this trend was lopsided, being concentrated overwhelmingly in light industry (textile, clothing, leather, paper, etc.). Heavy industry, and especially machine building, still lagged, and the lag was not overcome until the rearmament industrialization of the late 1930s. Furthermore, thanks to a deliberate policy of rationalization in industry—and only in industry—the size of the industrial labor force rose

8. Statistics in this and the following two paragraphs are from I. T. Berend and Gy. Ránki, "Capital Accumulation and the Participation of Foreign Capital in the Hungarian Economy After the First World War," in *Nouvelles études historiques publiées à l'occasion du XII*e *Congrès Internationale des Sciences Historiques par la Commission Nationale des Historiens Hongrois* (Budapest: Akadémiai Kiadó, 1965), 2: 284; Emmerich Kolbenheyer, "Die Strukturwandlung der Wirtschaft Ungarns seit dem Kriege und die deutsch-ungarischen Wirtschaftsbeziehungen," *Ungarische Jahrbücher*, 17 (1937): 235-40; and M. Incze, "The Conditions of the Masses in Hungary During the World Economic Crisis of 1929-1933," *Acta Historica* 3 (1954): 22, 51.

more slowly than its output and utterly failed to absorb the surplus agricultural manpower; this, in turn, kept the purchasing power of the internal market low. The bureaucracy, on the other hand, remained not only swollen but also expensive. The cost of collecting taxes in interwar Hungary was 19.8 percent of the yield, as compared to 5.4 percent in Germany. Agricultural production and exports were also high (though the harvests of 1928 and 1929 were poor), but their value remained totally dependent on the international price of grain cereals, which collapsed at the turn of the decade.

Again, statistics can illustrate but scarcely convey a full sense of the devastation that the depression inflicted on Hungary. By 1931, wholesale agricultural prices had fallen to 78.5 percent of their 1929 level, and by 1933 to 62.7 percent. The decline in grain prices, together with the simultaneous Czechoslovak drive for agricultural autarky, brought disaster to the Hungarian countryside and, by slashing its purchasing power, affected industry as well. The production of agricultural machinery virtually ceased, and the general value of industrial production in 1933 had slipped to 61 percent of the 1929 level. Yet certain branches, such as textiles, leather, paper, and food processing, were much less affected, since the very absence of foreign exchange initially enabled them to fill the whole of the shrinking domestic market. Tax yields fell, and foreign credit melted away as the preponderantly short-term foreign loans were called home, further deepening the crisis. With the possible initial (but only initial) exception of Hungary's most miserable class, the seasonal agricultural laborers who were paid in kind and with a percentage of their harvest, all sectors of society were hurt as average incomes fell by 23 percent between 1929 and 1933. By the latter year, 18 percent of Budapest's population was officially classified as destitute, and the national incidence of tuberculosis was 15.2 percent. Whereas in 1929 the ratio of employed wage-earners to dependents had been 100:215, by 1933 it had slid to 100:303 and 24.5 percent of all industrial plants were idle for more than fifty days. Yet, though utilization of available industrial capacity declined drastically in the depression years, vigorous efforts were applied to intensify technical rationalization, regardless of the immediate social and political effects on labor. Among the industrial workers and artisans, the unemployment rate rose from 5 percent in 1928 to 35.9 percent in 1933, the length of unemployment tended to last hundreds of days, and unemployment insurance was nonexistent; the workers were in a turmoil. The villages, too, where penury hardened and enforced idleness gripped half the rural population as landlords now laid off agricultural laborers while smallholders could no longer market their produce, witnessed extraordinary political and extrapolitical ideological ferment. This was most vividly illustrated by the mushrooming of various millennarian and pentecostal sects bearing such revealing designations as

"Seedless Ones," "Starvers," "Tremblers," "Devil Chasers," "Whitsun-Waiters," and "Sabbatians." In some regions, the peasants resorted to a semiconcealed system of infanticide and abortion.

Given Hungary's recent political history, and given the fact that Fascist Italy and Nazi Germany were now the only Great Powers to absorb a good part of her otherwise unmarketable agricultural produce and, in the case of Germany, a significant fraction of her surplus agricultural manpower, it was virtually a foregone conclusion that all this crisis and turbulence would redound to the benefit of Right- rather than Left-Radicalism in the process of undermining confidence in the Bethlen system and its values.

6

As the depression thus eroded the economic basis of the Bethlen system, Hungary entered a period of political confusion, in which Conservatives and Right-Radicals vied for power with mounting ferocity. The Right-Radicals, it will be recalled, while deferring the public leadership of the counterrevolutionary governments of the 1920s to the Bethlenite conservatives, had never surrendered their political ideology. They had not dissolved their reserve network of secret and quasi-secret patriotic societies, nor had they abdicated their claims to governmental power should the Bethlen system ever founder, as had now occurred with the depression. The very contradictions of that system and of its leaders' multiple commitments now appeared to deprive the Bethlenite leaders of the instruments and the will to tackle the crisis. They had come to power fervently preaching nationalism, and had then accepted peace terms that even Kun had rejected; since then they had ceaselessly beaten the revisionist drum, but had cooperated with the League of Nations which treated the postwar frontiers as hallowed; they affirmed their monarchist convictions, but had chased their crowned king out of the country and put the royal question into cold storage; their rhetoric alluded to Jews as distasteful and subversive upstarts, yet their economic policy was one of alliance with Jewish business. In contrast, the Right-Radicals claimed to operate with an altogether simpler, more natural, and more effective set of ideological commitments and political expectations: categorical revisionism, racial nationalism, anti-Semitism, anti-capitalism (specifically, "finance" capitalism), anti-intellectualism, and social radicalism in the service of the organic solidarity of the Magyar race. The last-named meant attracting the masses through land reform, social amelioration, and denunciations of the inherited privileges of the historic classes. In foreign affairs, the Right-Radicals were ready to sever Bethlen's unrewarding ties to the League "gabble-shop" and the "effete" democracies and to align Hungary unreservedly with Hitler's Germany. Indeed, their leader Gyula Gömbös had been in intimate contact with the Nazi movement since its beginning in 1921.

As early as October, 1930, Right-Radical agitation had led to an ominous defection from the Government Party of a small group of deputies who restyled themselves the Independent Smallholders, but Bethlen had still managed to carry off the parliamentary elections of June-July, 1931, which he quickly arranged half a year before they were legally compulsory, upon learning of the collapse of the Vienna Kreditanstalt in May—a collapse which he knew would buffet Hungarian society and whip up a high fury. But his will appears to have drained away together with his luck, and he no longer felt sure of Regent Horthy's undiminished support. Hence, when the financial and political storm provoked by the Vienna bankruptcy lashed Hungary over the summer, he unexpectedly resigned on August 19, 1931, handing the premiership over to his fellow aristocrat Count Gyula Károlyi, the original organizer of the Arad-Szeged counterrevolutionary government in 1919 and, since December 10, 1930, minister of foreign affairs.

Gyula Károlyi sought to maintain the essentials of the Bethlen system while changing its tone: puritanical thrift would replace cavalier extravagance, and sobriety succeed amoral cynicism. His attempt was in vain: Károlyi's style was even more infuriating than his predecessor's to the depression's most restless victims—the hungry workers, the destitute peasants, the discharged civil servants, the superfluous academic proletarians. To these people the Right-Radical panacea of "breaking the chains of finance capitalism" was far more appealing than Károlyi's budgetary orthodoxy. Even the bulk of the Government Party, for once in its history, was provoked into a mutinous state. Károlyi succumbed after little more than a year, and on October 1, 1932, the Right-Radical leader Gyula Gömbös stepped into the premiership at the head of the first ministry (other than Kun's) in all Hungarian history in which not a single titled aristocrat held office. An era had come to an end.

International complications also played a secondary role in the fall of Gyula Károlyi. He was a Francophile and felt obliged to yield office when the Stresa Conference (September 5-20, 1932) saw Germany and Italy defeat France's bid for economic hegemony in Central Europe (the Tardieu Plan) and thus demonstrate the need for Hungary's premier to be *persona grata* in Berlin and Rome. This was, ironically, the counterpart to Bethlen's fall having been catalyzed by the Kreditanstalt bankruptcy, which had been instigated by the French as punishment for the German-Austrian Customs Union project (Curtius-Schober Plan) of March 21, 1931.

Like Hindenburg vis-à-vis Hitler a few months later, so too did Horthy now attempt to tie Gömbös' hands in the very act of designating him to head the government. Setting himself firmly against a dissolution of the year-old "Bethlen" parliament and against new land-reform legislation, the regent also obliged his new premier to balance the Right-Radical element in the cabinet by assigning the strategic ministries of agriculture, commerce, and interior to conservative Bethlenites. Yet the analogy to the German transfer of power is hardly complete; though Horthy's ideological reflexes indeed tended toward the old school, he personally liked and felt indebted to Gömbös, who in 1919 had sponsored Horthy's designation to command the Szeged counterrevolutionary army and in 1921 had been instrumental in aborting King Charles' second attempt to recover his throne. Indeed, a renewed wave of Habsburg-restoration propaganda, which was launched, apparently with French connivance, upon the archduke Otto's coming of age in 1933, only refreshed Horthy's appreciation of the stoutly anti-Legitimist Gömbös.

A professional officer by training, a truculent Magyar racial chauvinist by conviction, a self-declared "National Socialist" as early as 1919, Gömbös had left the army in 1920 to devote himself entirely to politics —first as organizer of Right-Radical secret societies and as a deputy in the Smallholder wing of the Government Party, and then as head of the Race-Protecting Party which he founded in 1923 as a secession from the Government Party, now too tamely conservative for his tastes. A few weeks after founding the Race-Protecting Party, Gömbös was implicated in a bizarre plot to synchronize a Right-Radical coup in Budapest with Hitler's beerhall putsch in Munich. Claiming to have been victimized by *agents provocateurs*, Gömbös was let off with the indulgence habitually reserved in Trianon Hungary—as in Weimar Germany—for political offenders on the Right. Bethlen nevertheless arranged the parliamentary elections of 1926 to demolish the Race-Protecting Party, whereupon Gömbös, having demonstrated his nuisance value, dissolved it two years later, was coopted back into the Government Party, and on October 10, 1929, was appointed defense minister at Horthy's instigation and with the clandestine assignment of preparing the expansion of Hungary's armed forces beyond the Trianon limits.

A man of vast ambition and limitless energy, sentimentally attached to the Magyar lower classes whom he regarded as the victims of Jewish and aristocratic exploitation, and ideologically convinced that the future belonged to the totalitarian movements, Gömbös as premier initially found himself blocked from launching as many Right-Radical innovations as his supporters expected and his enemies feared. Nevertheless, he remained determined to grind down the conservatives' constraints upon his freedom of action. Starting out with, and resourcefully utilizing, the emphatic backing of his secret societies, the nationalistic academic youth, the ruined lower-middle classes, the patriotic refugees from the lost territories, the officer cadre, the resentful reserve officers, and the recently reconstituted Independent Smallholder Party (several of whose leaders had once been Gömbös' comrades in the Race-Protecting Party), he slowly but inexorably advanced his own protégés into the middle and upper ranks of the civil and military bureauracies and intimidated the opposition through the more drastic extension of techniques of surveillance and pressure (telephone tapping, opening of letters, informers, press manipulation, etc.). Meanwhile, with somewhat breathtaking tactical elasticity, Gömbös had assured himself adequate confidential funds through an agreement with leading Jewish circles, concluded immediately upon his assuming the premiership, whereupon he publicly announced the revision of his views on the Jewish question and his readiness henceforth to view as brothers those Jews who identified their destiny with that of the Magyar people (speech of October 11, 1932). But the rhetoric of anticapitalism was too valued a political device to be similarly muted in return for such subsidies.

The new financial resources facilitated Gömbös' drive to bring the backbenchers of the Government Party under his own control, and by the spring of 1935 he felt strong enough to use the Bethlenite political and administrative machinery against its designer. Parliament was dissolved, and the Government Party was radically purged before and via new elections that saw only twenty-five of its outgoing deputies returned. The detailed results of these elections, shown in table 26, were somewhat more complex than those of the Bethlen era, as there now emerged a nascent conservative opposition in reaction to Gömbös' radicalization of the regime phalanx.

TABLE 26

PARLIAMENTARY ELECTIONS, MARCH 31, TO APRIL 11, 1935

Party	Seats
The Regime Phalanx:	
Government Party	170
Christian Social (allied with G. P.)	14
Independent Smallholder	25
Conservative, Center, and Left Opposition:	
Bethlenites and Independents	12
Legitimist	3
Liberal	7
Socialist	11
"Pure" Right-Radical Opposition:	
Arrow Cross	2
National Radical	1
Total	245

As tradition dictated, the Government Party won 154 of its seats in the 201 rural constituencies where the open ballot prevailed. On the other hand, it is indicative of the genuine attraction of Right-Radicalism for the urban masses that the Socialist share of Budapest's votes, which were cast by secret ballot, declined from 42.8 percent in 1922 to 25.4 percent in 1935. The Gömbös elections of 1935 were a major, though not total, victory for Right-Radicalism in the country, in the parliament, and in the Government Party.

Shortly before the elections, Gömbös, who had retained the defense portfolio upon his designation as premier, was unexpectedly presented with a welcome opportunity to seed his own praetorians into senior military commands when a large number of incumbents were provoked into resigning by a critical League of Nations inquest into Hungarian responsibility for the assassinations of King Alexander of Yugoslavia and French Foreign Minister Louis Barthou on October 9, 1934. The new men were, in every case, more Right-Radical and pro-German than their predecessors, and Hungary was eventually to pay a bitter price for Gömbös' fatal politicization of the armed forces. More immediately portentous was the fact that with this maneuver Gömbös had seriously alienated Horthy, who took his prerogatives as supreme chief of the armed forces most seriously and who, as an old sea dog and member of the gentry class, tended toward Anglophilia. His disenchantment with Gömbös was further aggravated by the latter's reviving interest in rural social problems and their alleviation through land reform.

Horthy, accordingly, now drew closer again to Bethlen. This automatically rendered Gömbös' control over the Government Party—and hence of parliament—somewhat less categorical than the raw election results might suggest, and a new political polarization emerged in the mid-1930s. On one side stood the "revolutionary" and mass-supported axis of Right-Radicalism; on the other, the emerging elite coalition of "old-school," civil libertarian Conservatives and Liberals, the Socialists, soon again the Jews, and others with a vested interest in the preservation or restoration of the traditional securities and decencies of civilized public life and hence also in maintaining ties with the Western democracies. Bethlen, as this coalition's leader, recovered from his discredit of 1931 and came to enjoy within these strata the reputation of a wise elder statesman, concerned for human rights at home and Hungary's good name abroad. In due time, even some Independent Smallholders otherwise prone to Right-Radicalism were propelled toward this coalition precisely by fear of tying Hungary's destiny to Nazi Germany's.

Gömbös, however, also gained much public popularity by projecting an impression of disciplined vigor in the purposeful pursuit of social justice and national pride. He even went so far as to enforce magyarization upon the German Schwab minority. He probably held the more powerful political levers in his contest with the "effete" and "parasitical" aristocratic coterie gathered around Bethlen, but he became seriously ill with a prolonged kidney disease and died on October 6, 1936, before being able to consolidate his partial victories of the previous year. His premiership therefore enters Hungarian history as a transitional period, during which he took Hungary so far along the paths of Right-Radicalism and of association with Nazi Germany as to render impossible any later retraction.

After him, Horthy was to appoint seven premiers; from each he hoped for a return to the Bethlenite virtues in domestic and foreign policy, and by each he was disappointed in this expectation—partly as a result of their mediocrity and myopia, but more in consequence of the phenomenal growth of Germany's power and the popularity of this process among the Hungarian masses. German aggrandizement was a double-edged process for Hungary: it facilitated her recovery from the depression and then her demolition of Trianon, which Bethlen and Horthy also craved, but simultaneously it harnessed her as a satellite to Germany. Though the recalcitrant regent managed to dismiss seriatim all the premiers in whom he lost confidence as a result of their domestic and external accommodation to Nazi demands, he never found one capable of squaring the political circle, of reaping the harvest from the German alliance without paying its inevitable price. The Bethlen-Horthy coalition slowed, but never reversed, the course set by Gömbös, with whom they shared, after all, some ultimate goals.

Gömbös had been the first head of government of any country to call on Hitler after he became German chancellor. Cordial Italo-Hungarian relations, based on joint antipathy toward Yugoslavia and on the Budapest elite's fascination with Mussolini's fascism, had long pertained, but the German Nazi movement's Danubian ambitions appeared to jeopardize Hungary's interests, notwithstanding Gömbös' well-established personal connections with it. Gömbös, accordingly, had on his own initiative paid a secretly arranged visit to Hitler on June 17, 1933. The two men had agreed that: (a) Hungary would continue to concentrate her revisionist ambitions against Czechoslovakia (Romania and Yugoslavia enjoyed Hitler's benevolent interest at this time); (b) Germany would not politically support the Schwab minority in Hungary; (c) Gömbös would urge Dollfuss (and Mussolini) to admit the Austrian Nazis into the Austrian government and not to align Austria's policy with France's. This agreement was a compromise insofar as points of friction (the ultimate future of Austria, Hungary's eventual claims on Romania and Yugoslavia) were avoided.

The next year brought a more significant breakthrough as Germany's new economics minister, Hjalmar Schacht, reversed former Food Minister Alfred Hugenberg's autarkic agricultural policies and launched a phenomenal expansion of German trade (in blocked currencies) with southeastern Europe. This reversal enabled Hungary once again to dispose of her agricultural surpluses and thus save her latifundia system.

Simultaneously she became technically dependent on German industrial materials, machinery, and spare parts, and her entire economy was locked into Germany's for both markets and supplies. But it was once again an expanding economy, and the masses, newly reemployed and even benefiting from seasonal labor in the Reich, accepted the proposition that Nazi Germany had saved them from the "parasitical tyranny of Jewish finance-capitalism." The ruling circles, especially the military, were also impressed and captivated by Nazi Germany's obvious energy and apparent invincibility. Italy's influence, in turn, had waned with her involvement in the Abyssinian war in October, 1935, after which she ceased to balance Germany in the Danubian area.

7

From the mid-1930s onward, the domestic contest between Hungary's Right-Radicals and Bethlenites was subsumed within the larger struggle between Nazi Germany and her foes for the control of Europe. The German reaction to Horthy's designation of Kálmán Darányi, hitherto minister of agriculture, to succeed Gömbös as premier on October 10, 1936, was cool. A compromise choice known to be acceptable to Bethlenites as well as to Right-Radicals, Darányi was thus suspect in German eyes as a would-be backslider from the policies launched by Gömbös. To signal its displeasure, Berlin now undertook active sponsorship and subsidization of political agitation by the Schwab minority in Hungary. But the Germans' concern was groundless. Regardless of Darányi's personal preferences—and these proved friendlier to Nazi Germany than had been originally suspected by either Horthy or Hitler—Hungary had passed the point of return in its commitments. The military caste, recruited heavily from magyarized Schwabs, had been vigorously politicized by Gömbös and was now at last tasting the pleasures of some secret rearmament under German technical and financial auspices; it was no more willing to tolerate an about-face than were the other classes and strata of Hungarian society that had benefited from recent policy developments. Indeed, increasing credence was given to a favorite Right-Radical argument of the decade's second half, which insisted that Hungary must assure herself of continuing and extended German support for her immediate and long-range revisionist aspirations by synchronizing her internal political institutions and styles ever more closely with those of Nazi Germany.

It was in this spirit of "ingratiation through imitation" that a series of anti-Semitic laws was adopted, the first coming shortly after the Anschluss of Austria had made Hitler's Reich and Hungary direct neighbors. Though falling short of authorizing the genocide of Hungary's Jews—a catastrophe that awaited the outright German occupation of 1944—these measures slowly squeezed them out of their traditional strongholds in the economy, the free professions, and the intelligentsia. The Magyar beneficiaries of these anti-Jewish measures, chiefly the lower middle class and the academic proletariat, were, of course, only confirmed thereby in the rightness of Right-Radicalism. In turn, the main opposition to this legislation had characteristically come from the old-fashioned aristocracy in the Upper House of parliament.

The pace at which Hungary was implementing the Right-Radical ideology was, indeed, still too cautious even under Gömbös and Darányi to satisfy the apocalyptic expectations of her totalitarian extremists. These, accordingly, founded a series of "pure" Right-Radical secret societies and parties, the most significant of which was the Arrow Cross movement of Ferenc Szálasi, a former General Staff officer who left the army for politics early in 1935 but retained close connections with the younger military cadres. Propagating a nebulous but intransigent creed of absolute anticapitalism, antisocialism, anti-Semitism, Magyar racism, and populist authoritarianism, Szálasi attracted the fervent support of students, unskilled workers, and agricultural laborers and provoked the apprehensive enmity of all strata with vested interests, including even the "government" Right-Radicals. In April, 1937, the Darányi government brought Szálasi to court on charges of "agitation against the political and social order and against religious toleration." He was sentenced to three months' imprisonment and three years' deprivation of civil rights, but the effort only made him a popular martyr and he was released within a few days, whereupon he promptly visited Germany to study its Nazi revolution. By October of that year Szálasi had brought virtually all the "pure" Right-Radical groups under his own charismatic leadership and had made the Arrow Cross movement a real political force. Darányi thereupon attempted to reverse gears, sought to entice Szálasi into a working arrangement, and was then ousted when news of this maneuver reached the outraged ears of Horthy's Conservative-Liberal (Bethlenite) entourage.

The new premier was Béla Imrédy, who had been hitherto president of the National Bank and minister without portfolio with the task of coordinating economic policy. Designated premier by Horthy on May 13, 1938, on the advice of Bethlen and other conservatives precisely on account of his excellent British connections and presumed Western sympathies, Imrédy, like his predecessor Darányi, initially elicited a frigid German response and promptly proceeded to have Szálasi resentenced to three years at hard labor and five years' loss of civil rights for subversion. This time, the Arrow Cross leader did spend two years in jail, but his political reputation among his followers was only enhanced. In his absence, the Germans achieved perhaps greater direct influence over the Arrow Cross than they might have otherwise, since Szálasi, though ideologically a sincere Nazi, was less of a German stooge than were his lieutenants.

Developments quickly rendered the ambitious Imrédy, like his predecessor, far more amenable to German wishes and influences than had originally been expected by either his supporters or his detractors. The Munich crisis exposed the general unreliability of Western promises to small Central European states, and for Hungary, in particular, its aftermath brought significant territorial reacquisitions under German-Italian patronage, thereby transforming Imrédy and many other Hungarians in and out of government into convinced collaborators with the Axis Powers. On the heels of Hungary's post-Munich territorial aggrandizement, Imrédy dropped Foreign Minister Kálmán Kánya, in whom the Germans had little confidence due to his known reluctance to put all Hungarian eggs into their basket, and appointed Count István Csáky who, on assuming office in mid-December, 1938, described his foreign policy as "quite simply that of the . . . Axis all along the line."

The territory recovered by Hungary under the terms of Ribbentrop's and Ciano's so-called First Vienna Award of November 2, 1938, consisted of 12,103 square kilometers from southern Slovakia and southern Ruthenia, an area termed the Felvidék by Hungarians. This was about one-fifth of the land lost to Czechoslovakia under the Trianon terms. Hungary's new frontier with her northern neighbor was drawn primarily with regard to ethnic, rather than economic, criteria; this meant that it severed a number of recovered Hungarian towns from their Slovak hinterlands. Less than half a year later, Hitler's destruction of rump Czecho-Slovakia in mid-March, 1939, allowed Hungary to reannex the rest of Ruthenia (but not Slovakia, which stood under German protection); thus, an additional 12,171 square kilometers and a joint border with Poland were acquired.

The Magyar population of these recovered territories, having lived for two decades in bourgeois, progressive, Czechoslovakia as a frustrated but vibrant minority and having survived land reform and other socioeconomic innovations, tended now to be appalled by the "feudal" conservatism of the Horthy-Bethlen coalition in Hungarian politics and emphatically reinforced Imrédy's incipient bias toward Right-Radicalism. Having now also suddenly lost the protection of the Czechoslovak tariff system against the agricultural competition of the great Hungarian plain proper, these reintegrated Magyars were eager to compensate themselves for this new economic vulnerability through rapid self-enrichment at the Jews' expense. Hence, they vehemently urged the more-than-willing Imrédy to sharpen the anti-Semitic restrictions of the previous year. Imrédy now even toyed with land-reform notions and launched an imitative fascist organization of his own, named the "Movement of Hungarian

Life." Once again, however, such untoward and unexpected adaptability on the part of the prime minister to Right-Radicalism provoked the palace-centered Conservative-Liberal coalition into resistance. On February 16, 1939, Horthy replaced Imrédy with Count Pál Teleki, who, it will be recalled, had served a brief term in the premiership as *locum tenens* for Bethlen in 1920-21 and had more recently been minister of education and cults in Imrédy's late cabinet.

With each new prime-ministerial succession crisis following upon another German triumph in Europe, the noose around Hungary tightened and her rulers' area of maneuver shrank. Teleki's supposed mission, for example, was to extricate his country from its excessive and unilateral dependence on the Axis and to effect a rapprochement with the West. Yet, merely to earn German toleration, he felt himself constrained to take Hungary into the Anti-Comintern Pact (February 23, 1939), out of the League of Nations (April 11, 1939), and then into the Tripartite (Axis) Pact (November 20, 1940)—all the while retaining the notorious Csáky as his foreign minister. Though he would not grant semisovereign, extraterritorial rights to Hungary's Schwab minority nor permit Nazi propaganda in its school textbooks, Teleki reassured Hitler of his own anti-Semitic reliability by personally supervising the final legislative passage and administrative application of Imrédy's recent round of restrictive measures. A conservative Transylvanian aristocrat of the "old school" and a justly renowned professional geographer, Teleki was, on the other hand, also a man who had been compromised in the white terror of 1919-20 as well as in the forged-francs scandal of 1926. He was thus an ambiguous, even dubious, figure, and the policy to which he was committed, that of exploiting German power in order to undo Trianon while at the same time avoiding identification in Western eyes as Germany's associate, was beyond his or his country's capacity to sustain, quite apart from its inherent lack of integrity (in all senses of this word).

To capitalize on the territorial reacquisitions of 1938 and 1939, Teleki held new elections in the old Trianon territory on May 28-29, 1939. Though the suffrage remained restricted, the influence of the state bureaucracy and the estate owners was for the first time somewhat curbed by the universality of the secret ballot, which had been extended to the countryside during the Darányi ministry by Law XIX of 1938. On the other hand, a more ominous and competing influence was for the first time brought to bear in the form of lavish German subsidies to the Arrow Cross and related Nazi-type formations, countervailing Teleki's efforts to destroy these groups through "traditional" legal and police harassments. The results shown in table 27 include the thirty-six deputies who were coopted from the recently regained northern territories and were not actually elected at the polls. Evaluation of the results requires an awareness that the sympathies of the Government Party's backbenchers were now divided between Teleki and Imrédy and that the Independent Small-holders were Right-Radical but pro-West.

TABLE 27

PARLIAMENTARY ELECTIONS, MAY 28-29, 1939

The Regime Phalanx:	
Government Party	183
Christian Social (allied with G. P.)	4
Coopted from the Felvidék and Ruthenia	36*
Conservative, Center, and Left Opposition:	
Independent Smallholder	14
Liberal	5
Socialist	5
"Pure" Right-Radical Opposition:	
Arrow Cross	31
Other Nazi-type Parties	18
Total	296

*26 from the Felvidék, 10 from Ruthenia.

The popular vote was even more Right-Radical than these parliamentary results suggest. The Arrow Cross received one-fourth of all ballots cast nationally, and in Budapest it polled, together with its allies, 72,400 votes to the Socialists' 34,500 and the Government Party's 95,500; even the proletarian heartland of "red" Csepel Island sent two Nazi deputies to parliament. The Arrow Cross had always been popular with the unskilled and semiskilled workers, but now, in addition to German funds, the connivance of "new" elements in the bureaucracy, and the martyr's halo of its imprisoned leader Szálasi, it also enjoyed the secret support of the underground Communist movement as well as the widespread popularity earned by its authentic commitment to land reform and concern for social equity. Though the Government Party absorbed the thirty-six deputies from the recovered territories, including a few "tame" Slovaks and Ruthenians, this very success pushed its own center of gravity further toward Right-Radicalism. Indeed, only a third of its deputies were genuinely committed to Teleki, and he could scarcely have controlled it but for the regent's reserve powers.

The ironic aftermath of the joint German and Hungarian destruction of Czechoslovakia was a momentary divergence of their paths, priorities, and interests. Hungary's still unsatiated craving for integral restoration of its historic territories now met not only with Germany's protection of newly independent Slovakia, but also with competitive German and Anglo-French wooing of the other two objects of Hungary's irredentist ambitions, Romania and Yugoslavia. Hitler's pact with Stalin on August 23, 1939, stunned the anti-Communist Hungarian ruling strata, and the next month's joint German-Soviet partition of Hungary's historic friend and fellow "gentry nation," Poland, deeply offended them. The Hungarian government refused a German request for the strategic use of its Kassa-Velejte railroad line in the September campaign, despite a German bribe-offer of Galician territory; it permitted a Hungarian volunteer legion, "The Ragged Guard," 6,000 strong, to fight on the Polish side; and it allowed between 100,000 and 140,000 Poles to use and cross its territory on their way to France to continue the war after their defeat in Poland. Yet, in terms of the larger picture, European geography, Western weakness, their own revisionism, and their people's Right-Radicalism severely restricted the Hungarian rulers' capacity to adopt alternatives to continued sailing in the German wake.

The eruption of World War II did, on the other hand, somewhat ease Teleki's domestic difficulties. The Liberals and Socialists understood and assisted his delicate efforts to retain openings to the West by virtually abandoning all opposition to the government so as not to embarrass it. Indeed, this passive collaboration was to cost them dearly after the war. While the Right-Radicals, on the other hand, remained incorrigible and vociferous, their furious momentum was somewhat checked by the full employment that Germany's economic assistance to Hungary facilitated, by the conscription of their youthful militants into the armed forces where the government had them under surveillance, and by the fact that the interest of a Germany at war now dictated that her allies and satellites be administered by orderly, productive regimes rather than by ideologues and enthusiasts who were prone to turmoil and fanaticism. The Arrow Cross, furthermore, suffered from the delusion that Germany wished a "great" Hungary to police the entire Carpatho-Danubian area on behalf of their common cause, whereas the Reich, in fact, desired no "great" partners regardless of ideological loyalty. The nazified German Schwab minority in Hungary, by analogy, preferred to receive real concessions from the Budapest governments rather than ally itself in pointless opposition with the Arrow Cross.

In mid-1940, immediately after the fall of France, the Soviet Union proceeded to collect the remaining gains accruing to her under the secret terms of the previous year's pact with Nazi Germany. On June 26 she delivered an ultimatum to Romania, requiring the prompt surrender of Bessarabia and northern Bukovina. Bulgaria thereupon also extracted the return of Southern Dobruja from Romania. The Teleki government, which since war's outbreak had been promising both sets of belligerents not to press Hungary's revisionist claims on Romania unless the latter yielded fractions of her territory to other parties, now threatened to fight unless Transylvania were also returned to Hungary—and here the Romanians suddenly stiffened. As in the previous year's Hungarian-Slovak controversy, so now once again Germany found herself obliged to adjudicate a quarrel between two of her clients.

Though Hitler had formerly favored the Romanians, who treated their Volksdeutsche minority better, and whose political institutions and style were more "modern" (i.e., para-totalitarian), he nevertheless had now to take into account that with war's outbreak the German public recalled with warm nostalgia their Hungarian ally of the First World War, and that the Romanian authorities had recently assassinated the leader of that country's Nazi-type Iron Guard. By the summer of 1940 Hitler would much have preferred to remain aloof from this quarrel, but he could scarcely risk its escalating into war lest the Romanian oil fields be destroyed and/or further Soviet intervention ensue. Hence the German arbitration, with the help of Italy, that now took place was a genuine effort to solve the difficult Transylvanian problem and not, as is often alleged, a Machiavellian maneuver to leave both contenders so dissatisfied that for the duration of the war Germany would be able to play them off against each other. The latter development indeed occurred, but it does not appear to have been originally intended.

Under the terms of the so-called Second Vienna Award of August 30, 1940, Hungary regained 43,492 square kilometers of northern and eastern Transylvania, or two-fifths of her Trianon loss to Romania, with a population of roughly two and a half million, of whom over one million were Romanians. About half a million Magyars still remained in the part of Transylvania that was left to Romania—yet another eloquent testimony to the virtual impossibility of drawing "clean" ethnic borders in this part of Europe.[9] Romania retained the disputed province's most valuable economic resources, while Hungary gained control of the strategic Carpathian crestline and passes. Hitler's initial reluctance to intercede in this affair was, ironically, paralleled by Teleki's unhappiness at owing these gains to German arbitration rather than to Hungary's own military or diplomatic efforts. Stalin, in turn, resented his exclusion from the episode, and especially the guarantee that the Axis Powers now gave

9. These gross, crude, rounded statistical estimates reflect the difficulty of reconciling the significant discrepancies between the Romanian and Hungarian censuses. For the part of Transylvania ceded back to Hungary by Romania under the terms of this Second Vienna Award, the respective claims are:

	1930 Romanian census	1941 Hungarian census
Magyar	911,550	1,347,012
Romanian	1,176,433	1,066,353
Other	307,164	163,926
Total	2,395,147	2,577,291

rump Romania, a guarantee underlined by the stationing of a German division in that country.

Whereas the Magyar population in the territories reannexed in 1938-39 from interwar Czechoslovakia had, as noted above, tended to reinforce Right-Radicalism in Hungary and within the Government Party, the Transylvanian Magyars who returned "home" in 1940 buttressed the Conservative-Liberal political phalanx. Of the sixty-three parliamentary seats now assigned to recovered Transylvania in the Lower House, twelve were theoretically reserved for Romanians but left vacant until such time (never reached) as Romania might guarantee equivalent representation to her Magyar minority, three were alloted to Germans, while the forty-eight Magyars designated to fill the bulk of the seats were hand-picked Teleki men.

Whatever his personal chagrin, and regardless of his insistence that all of Hungary's recent territorial reacquisitions were hers by historic right and put her under no moral obligation to anyone, Teleki had to demonstrate his gratitude for this latest enlargement of Hungary under German patronage. On September 18, 1940, he released Szálasi from jail; on October 8 he indicated further anti-Semitic legislation and concessions to the German Schwab minority; and on November 20 he brought Hungary into the Axis' Tripartite Pact. This last step provoked the first criticism of Teleki from his own Conservative supporters and his Center-Left well-wishers, who attacked it as an excessive concession and a dangerous departure from Hungary's formal neutrality. Teleki, accordingly, once again sought to redress the balance by signing a Treaty of Eternal Friendship with Yugoslavia on December 12. At the time, this was intended to be interpreted in the West as a symbol of continuing Hungarian independence, yet it was assumed to entail no substantive risks since Yugoslavia was herself expected to adhere presently to the Tripartite Pact. But nemesis was shortly to overtake Teleki's "balancing act" across the diplomatic tightrope. On March 25, 1941, the Yugoslav government indeed signed the Tripartite Pact, but was promptly ousted by a *coup d'etat* during the night of March 26-27. Hitler immediately determined to annihilate Yugoslavia and demanded Hungarian facilities and assistance in the coming campaign.

Teleki might have been prepared to reconcile even this project with his pledge of eternal friendship to Yugoslavia had he been given some sign of

---

For the part of Transylvania remaining with Romania in 1940, the Romanian census of 1941 can only be compared with the last pre-Trianon Hungarian one of 1910:

	1941 Romanian census	1910 Hungarian census
Magyar	363,206	533,004
Romanian	2,274,561	1,895,505
Other	695,131	618,634
Total	3,332,898	3,047,143

British "understanding" for a policy that he preferred to view as one of independent—nay, even competitive—action parallel to Germany's, rather than of collaboration with her. His somewhat casuistic reasoning ran as follows: Hungary had never renounced her irredentist aspirations to the Vojvodina; if she were now to refrain from reannexing these ancient Hungarian counties in the aftermath of Yugoslavia's impending destruction, then Germany would join them to the Reich; Hungary, accordingly, would technically honor her recent pledges to Yugoslavia by avoiding hostile contact with the latter's army and advancing only in the Wehrmacht's wake. In sum, Hungary would not precipitate the demolition of Yugoslavia, but she would benefit from it and simultaneously preventively snatch those parts to which she had historic claims from under Germany's grasp. When Britain, understandably, failed to show the expected appreciation for this overly nice distinction between competitive and collaborative cooperation with Germany, Teleki at last despaired of his policy of balance, which was always uneven, and committed suicide during the night of April 2-3, 1941. On April 6 came the collective assault on Yugoslavia, in which the Hungarian military, unlike the deceased premier, collaborated enthusiastically; on April 8 came the inevitable British severance of relations with Hungary; between April 11 and 14, Hungary reoccupied 11,475 square kilometers, or slightly more than half, of her Trianon loss to Yugoslavia, with a population of approximately a million, of whom one-third were Magyars and the remainder a mixture of Germans, Jews, Romanians, and Serbs. New anti-Semitic measures once more followed this "victory."

Thanks to her association with Germany, Hungary had now achieved four extensions of territory since 1938. As a result, the Trianon core had almost doubled in area, and, ironically, the nationally "integral" Magyar Hungary of 1920-38 was once again saddled with substantial minorities (see section 9). This development might well have eventually led to a return of the ethnic and political tensions of Ausgleich Hungary but for the fact that all these territorial gains had to be relinquished at the end of World War II.

In selecting Teleki's successor, Horthy was yet again prompted by the same considerations that had preceded the designations of Darányi, Imrédy, and Teleki. This time his choice fell on the career diplomat László Bárdossy, who had become foreign minister upon Csáky's death on January 27, 1941, and was not affiliated with any political party. But once more the same futile cycle of an opening bid for greater independence followed by closer accommodation to Nazi Germany in foreign and domestic policy repeated itself. On June 23, 1941, the day after the German attack on the Soviet Union, Bárdossy, seconded by the chief of the General Staff, strongly urged Hungary's participation in this venture—even though she had no tangible war aims in Russia—lest otherwise she be outclassed by Romania in the competition for Hitler's favor. The cabinet refused on that occasion, but four days later Bárdossy stampeded it and the regent into war by alleging that on June 26 Soviet planes had bombed several localities in the Felvidék and Ruthenia; at the same time he suppressed evidence that suggested that these raids were a staged German provocation, and withheld news of reassuring Soviet overtures. On November 29 Great Britain gave Hungary an ultimatum to withdraw from the Russian campaign; when this was ignored, she declared war on December 6. A few days later, on December 12, Hungary herself, out of loyalty to Germany, declared war on the United States (which did not reciprocate until June 5, 1942). Thus did Bárdossy finally burn Hungary's diplomatic bridges, whereupon the regent once more, and again too late, dismissed his premier and replaced him on March 10, 1942, with Miklós Kállay, a veteran Bethlenite politican whose explicit but virtually hopeless task it was to extricate Hungary from Germany's suffocating embrace.

Kállay began his tenure by bringing to heel the excessively Germanophile and right-radicalized Hungarian military establishment through leaking news of its massacre of over two thousand Vojvodinian Serbs and one thousand Jews the previous January. He was then handed a convenient pretext to reject German demands for more Hungarian troops on the Russian front—the Germans dangling more of Transylvania as bait—when Croatia, Romania, and Slovakia publicly proclaimed their anti-Magyar friendship in May, 1942. This act virtually reconstituted the Little Entente within the Axis coalition and allowed Hungary to claim that her army was needed to man her own new frontiers. To judge from the ethnicity of Hungarian prisoners of war, it would appear, furthermore, that the army corps that Budapest had despatched to the Russian front contained disproportionately large numbers of her several new non-Magyar minorities, quite apart from the separate Jewish labor battalions. In September, 1942, Kállay replaced a pro-German defense minister who had tolerated scandalously inhuman conditions in these semipenal Jewish labor units with an anti-German one under whom conditions improved. At the turn of the year, the Hungarian corps was decimated by the Soviets at Voronezh and then virtually abandoned by its German ally during the retreat from Stalingrad. This gave Kállay an excuse to withdraw the remnants into Hungary by April, 1943, after which date only a few garrisons remained in Russia and the bulk of the Hungarian army was manning the Carpathian passes against possible Romanian or Russian assaults. Just as Hungary and Romania competed for Germany's favor when the Axis tide had been running strong, so now, as that tide ebbed, they were competing to be the first to desert her by shirking their obligations. Each rationalized its desire to end its military commitments in Russia with the argument that its security against the other required the recall of its army homeward.

In such noncombatant war efforts as industrial production, the export of food and raw materials to Germany, and the facilitation of the Wehrmacht's communications and supply systems, Kállay's government also saw to the quiet sabotage of Hungary's contribution to the common Axis effort. Hungarian production and delivery figures increased so markedly after the German occupation in March, 1944, that the low figures before that date must be imputed to official "sabotage." Only one-fifth of the country's electric power had been allocated to war production, and only one-fourth of the stipulated food delivery quotas had been despatched to Germany during Kállay's tenure.

As for internal political and social coordination to Nazi German measures and styles, Kállay's Hungary—to the rage of the Arrow Cross —remained a decent contrast to neighboring Croatia, Romania, and Slovakia. Parliamentary life not only survived but was even revitalized, the Center and Left opposition parties as well as the trade unions remained free, and political journalism was diverse and intense. Although overt criticism of Germany was taboo, covert friendliness toward Britain and the United States was permitted. Though economically and politically molested, the Jews were not consigned to extermination, while Poles and escaped Allied war prisoners were protected. Civil rights endured. From the spring of 1943, Kállay was in sympathetic contact with the formal opposition coalition known as the Popular Front. Composed of Independent Smallholders, National Peasants, Socialists, and Liberals, the front stood for withdrawal from the war, land reform, rejection of nazism, and decent treatment of the ethnic minorities. Similarly, Kállay came to a secret arrangement with the English and Americans: their planes were not fired upon when flying over Hungary and, in turn, did not bomb her. Hungary, indeed, was virtually a neutral in 1943 as regards the war between the Axis and the Western Powers.

Ultimately, however, the Kállay-Horthy endeavor to extricate their country from the German embrace was no more successful than the Teleki-Horthy strategy of avoiding it. The Nazi totalitarian model was becoming more popular among the masses; Arrow Cross membership rose from 0.3 percent of the population in 1938 to 4.0 percent in 1944, and its influence increased even more. The ruling establishment remained politically trapped by its own passionate irredentism, fervent anti-Communism, and anachronistic sociopolitical outlook. Its whiggish Anglophilia, its conservative repugnance toward Hitler as a revolutionary upstart (reciprocated by him), its even greater horror of Soviet encroachment into Danubian Europe, and its determination to retain the allegedly rightful territorial gains of 1938-41 did not provide a basis for realistic maneuver in the conditions of World War II. The spectacle of the impressive German response to Italy's attempt to switch sides in July, 1943, compared with the clumsy Allied reaction, also petrified the Hungarians; Italy appeared to have achieved nothing by her audacious stroke except to ensure her own physical destruction. Kállay's maneuvers, too, now simply alienated Germany without winning effective Western support; for it was illusory to expect the British and Americans to prefer Hungary over their Soviet, Yugoslav, and Czech allies.

Hitler, finally weary of Kállay's trimming, occupied Hungary on March 18-19, 1944, forcing Horthy to dismiss the premier and reactivate the country's military and economic war effort, which act now elicited intensive Allied bombing. For the Jews, the "final solution" was promptly inaugurated, but for Magyar society Horthy was able to stave off for another seven months the ultimate Arrow Cross revolution with a pair of premiers, the diplomat Döme Sztójay (until August 24) and then General Géza Lakatos, who were acceptable to the Germans. At the same time, he preserved the formal structure of the established Hungarian polity, though the Popular Front with its constituent parties and unions was dissolved. But when Horthy, emulating Romania's audacious leap of August 23, 1944, from the Axis to the Allied side, also finally steeled himself at Bethlen's urging to a bungled attempt to quit the war through an armistice with the Soviets on October 15, the Germans, with the connivance of his own army, deposed and deported him and transferred governmental authority to Szálasi's Arrow Cross movement. With that event, the traditional rule and role of Hungary's historic elite were ended, and her lower classes achieved political power. In this social dimension, therefore, the war year 1944 was a prelude to the postwar consolidation of the Communist dictatorship in 1948.

8

It remains now to discuss two postdepression and war-time trends in Hungary. The first, that of economic modernization, was facilitated by her alliance with Nazi Germany and, like the rise to political power of her lower classes in 1944, is also relevant to her development after World War II. The second, that of the reemergence of the ethnic-minority problem, complicated her wartime relations with Germany but was automatically resolved at the close of World War II when she was forced to surrender the territories briefly recovered during 1938-41, and most of the Jewish remnant that survived the Holocaust emigrated.

Accelerated trade with Germany and production in preparation for war pulled Hungary out of the depression in the late 1930s. The renewed military production was initially for export (to Italy, China, Greece, Latin America, Portugal, the Netherlands, Turkey, and Bulgaria), and after 1938 for her own expanding armed forces. In that year Hungary openly repudiated the Trianon restrictions on her armed forces by reintroducing universal military training and budgeting a standing army of eighty thousand. New, war-related bauxite, chemical, and oil industries were developed and, while the workers' educational, hygienic, and welfare conditions remained poor, their unemployment shrank rapidly toward the vanishing point. The structure of the country's economy and of her foreign trade also improved, as industry's share of the national product and of exports rose with the remarkable development of such finished-goods industries as telecommunications equipment, railway carriages and railbuses, electrical instruments, and pharmaceuticals, in which Hungary achieved international significance in the 1930s. Whereas in 1929, 40.22 percent of her imports had consisted of finished products and only 37.46 percent of raw materials, already by 1937 her own industry had developed to such an extent that finished products accounted for only 26.83 percent of her imports but raw materials to feed that industry had risen to 42.53 percent. (Semifinished items were 22.32 percent of imports in 1929 and 30.64 percent in 1937.) The equivalent comparison for exports is less revealing since Hungary classified both her processed foods as well as her industrial products under the category of "finished goods." Hence, the formal export percentages for finished products remained overtly stable between 1929 (33.35) and 1937 (30.56), but in fact a shift from food to manufactures did occur.

Though suggesting a more balanced and productive economy, none of this indicates that Hungary had ceased to be economically vulnerable. Whereas foreign ownership of Hungarian industry lessened in the interwar years and Jewish ownership was destroyed during the war, the economy as a whole became increasingly dependent on Germany and the industrial plants continued to be overconcentrated at Budapest. In 1938, on the eve of the war and of the territorial gains of 1938-41, Hungary accounted for 2.2 percent of Europe's population but only 0.9 percent of the continent's volume of industrial production, and the per capita value of her industrial production was only 32 percent of the European average.

The war years finally brought an economic boom. Whereas the number of workers employed in manufacturing had risen from 223,043 to only 288,512 during the two interwar decades (i.e., by 29.3 percent), in the next six years, from 1938 to 1943, this figure rose to 466,077 (a 61.5 percent increase over 1938) for enlarged Hungary and to 391,838 (a 35.7 percent increase over 1938) in its Trianon core. The machine, chemical, and iron industries absorbed the bulk of this growth in manpower. The value of industrial production (at constant prices) rose 37.5 percent in the Trianon core during these same wartime years, as compared to 28 percent for the whole interwar period, and in this area, too, heavy industry advanced more than light. While much of this growth was financed through inflation, the real wages of industrial workers nevertheless did not deteriorate until Hungary became a battlefield in 1944.

While it is true that German needs distorted this economic growth and that Germany accumulated enormous debts which ultimately had to be written off by Hungary after the war, these years nevertheless taught her the lesson, pregnant for the future, that massive state capitalist investments were an alternative and a more rapid means of modernization than was free enterprise. On March 5, 1938, the then Premier Darányi had proclaimed an investment and rearmament program of one billion pengös over a two-year period, and Hungary never turned back from this approach. The percentage of her total national income accounted for by state budgetary expenditures rose from 33.1 in 1938-39 to 67.4 in 1943 and 71.7 in 1944. Finally, while it is also true that in the destructive fighting, looting, and evacuation of 1944-45 Hungary lost 40 percent of her national wealth and 24 percent of her industrial capacity, nevertheless her residual industrial capacity was still greater than it had been in 1938. More important, the experience and memory of rapid industrialization could not be extirpated.[10]

The countryside, by contrast, remained relatively static in terms of its agrarian structure, though it, too, witnessed changes in its agricultural output away from overdependence on grains and toward industrial crops. Though the percentage of the population that derived its income from agriculture declined from 55.7 in 1920 to 51.8 in 1930 and then to 48.7 on the same territory in 1941 (i.e., excluding the recent reannexations), the structure of land distribution remained unhealthily polarized between big estates on the one hand, which were often entailed and relatively tax-free, and dwarf-holdings and a landless agricultural proletariat on the other. According to the detailed agricultural census of 1935, 48.1 percent of the agriculturally productive land was held in estates larger than a hundred cadastral yokes (57.5 hectares), and 29.9 percent in estates of over a thousand yokes (575 hectares). Less than 1 percent of the population owned over half the cultivable area, while three million peasants, who accounted for two-thirds of the agricultural and one-third of the national population, were either totally landless or owned nonviable dwarf-holdings of less than 5 yokes (2.9 hectares) which constituted but one-tenth of the cultivable area. Two-thirds of the country's villages, containing 70 percent of its rural people and 30 percent of its total population, were still without electricity on the eve of the war.

This timeless, traditional, rural culture gave Hungary's historic ruling

10. The statistics in the four preceding paragraphs are from I. T. Berend and Gy. Ránki, "The Development of the Manufacturing Industry in Hungary (1900-1944)," *Studia Historica Academiae Scientiarum Hungaricae*, no. 19 (1960), passim, and the same authors' "The Hungarian Manufacturing Industry, Its Place in Europe," *Studia Historica Academiae Scientiarum Hungaricae*, no. 27 (1960), pp. 31-35.

classes the impressive political cohesion and moral self-assurance that allowed them to retain their power so long, so stubbornly, and so effectively. They, in turn, guarded it by so structuring Hungarian society that each social class came to lead its own form of life, guided by its own codes of behavior and honor, its own set of eligible occupations, its own fetishes concerning titles, rank-orders, styles of address, and modes of conduct. For example, gentlemen paid their bills belatedly; the middle classes, promptly.

Though the system as a whole was organized so as to impede, if not eliminate, social mobility, the ruling elite was also prepared to protect itself from substantive challenges by catering to symbolic gratifications within this caste system. Thus, the Horthy regime "recognized" so many spurious pretensions to noble status that by 1944 one out of every five Hungarians was asserting some such claim and one out of seventy was reputed an aristocrat. A compulsory code of dueling persisted till that year. (Horthy, indeed, proposed in 1935 to settle Hungary's political differences with Czechoslovakia by challenging Masaryk or Beneš to a duel; though drafted, this anachronistic and ludicrous challenge was not delivered.) Even the Roman Catholic and Calvinist ecclesiastical institutions preferred to uphold rather than to question this highly structured system that distributed wealth and privilege so unequally. They preached no "social gospel," and whatever interest in the exploited classes and concern for their distress was expressed in interwar Hungary came either from a Marxist or a pagan-romantic (Right-Radical and Populist) rather than from a Christian ideological perspective.

Precisely because of their self-consciousness as an historic elite, the ruling classes were reluctant to resort to totalitarian mobilization through mass violence and racist propaganda. These were the devices of upstarts and rabble-rousers, not of "gentlemen" and "upholders of law and order." Thus it came about that this elite, which had earlier fastidiously declined to fuse landed with urban economic activities and had thereby invited the strong Jewish role in modern Hungarian society, had then, in a moment of panic that signaled its coming obsolescence, permitted interwar Europe's first quasi-official pogroms, ultimately sought to redeem itself in its own death throes by establishing Axis Europe's last arena of protection for Jews from the genocidal terror of its Nazi partner and its own lower class Arrow Cross counterelite. Hence, also, the seeming anomaly that this Hungarian historic ruling class, which had organized interwar Europe's first white counterrevolution and had been the most persistent oracle of revisionism, ended by being Hitler's most reluctant associate as well as the only one to tolerate an independent Socialist movement and to sustain free parliamentary institutions through the dark years of World War II.

9

Trianon Hungary was one of the few states of interwar East Central Europe that was ethnically integral and in which no significant section of the population wished to belong to another state. Austria, though also ethnically homogeneous, was politically torn by substantial sentiment for Anschluss to Germany. Most of the area's other countries were plagued by separatism on the part of minorities and/or divisiveness within the alleged state-nation. This exceptional Hungarian ethnic and political unity was one of the ironic blessings of the Trianon Treaty's truncation of the body of historic Hungary. The statistics are given in tables 28 and 29.

In perusing the first of these two tables, the reader should be aware of the fact that many of those whose primary tongue was not Magyar were nevertheless able to speak Magyar as a second language—575,615 out of 833,475 in 1920, and 509,891 out of 687,207 in 1930. Hence, those able to speak Magyar as either their preferred or their secondary language composed 96.8 percent of the total population in 1920 and 98.0 percent in 1930.

TABLE 28

Population by Ethnicity (Language)

| | 1920 | | 1930 | |
	Number	Percentage	Number	Percentage
Magyar	7,156,727	89.5	8,001,112	92.1
German	551,624	6.9	478,630	5.5
Slovak	141,918	1.8	104,819	1.2
Romanian	23,695	0.3	16,221	0.2
Croatian	36,864	0.5	27,683	0.3
Serbian	17,132	0.2	7,031	0.1
Bunyevci, Šokci	23,228	0.3	20,564	0.2
Other	39,014	0.5	32,259	0.4
Total	7,990,202	100.0	8,688,319	100.0

TABLE 29

Population by Religion

| | 1920 | | 1930 | |
	Number	Percentage	Number	Percentage
Roman Catholic	5,105,375	63.9	5,634,003	64.9
Greek Catholic (Uniate)	175,655	2.2	201,093	2.3
Calvinist	1,671,052	21.0	1,813,162	20.9
Lutheran	497,126	6.2	534,165	6.1
Eastern Orthodox	50,918	0.6	39,839	0.5
Israelite	473,355	5.9	444,567	5.1
Other	16,721	0.2	21,490	0.2
Total	7,990,202	100.0	8,688,319	100.0

Magyars were either Roman Catholic or Calvinist by religion, and almost all Jews (Israelites) were also Magyar-speakers. Germans and Slovaks were Roman Catholic or Lutheran. Croats, Bunyevci, and Šokci were also Roman Catholic, while Serbs and some Romanians were Eastern Orthodox. But the anomaly that the number of Uniates was so much larger than the number of recorded Romanians suggests that many more Romanians were miscounted as Magyars of the Uniate faith.

It might be presumed that interwar Hungarian public opinion would infer from Trianon and from the disaffection of old Hungary's national minorities that had made Trianon possible, that the prewar militant magyarization policy toward these minorities had been a political blunder. Quite the contrary lesson was, however, drawn: old Hungary's mistake had supposedly been insufficient vigor in pressing magyarization; hence, the failure to achieve an adequately comfortable Magyar majority when the test came in 1914-18. Supplementing this interesting, if dubious, analysis was the understandable political emotion: Trianon Hungary might be a poor cripple, but at least let it now be all-Magyar. Hence, the separate political and cultural facilities made available to interwar Hungary's ethnic minorities were stingier than their equivalents in any other country of East Central Europe; even when granted on paper, they were still further cramped in administrative practice and whittled away by public pressures. The Roman Catholic clergy pressed magyarization in the school system even more energetically than did the civil service, and responded to utterly legal efforts by the Catholic ethnic minorities to found minority-language schools as though these endeavors were somehow heretical or at least subversive. A more subtle reinforcement of magyarization even beyond legal requirements arose from the ambition of many minority parents for their children to "get ahead"; such parents preferred Magyar schools over minority, or even over mixed, schools. As no secondary or teachers' training schools were permitted the minorities, it was obvious that their capacity to sustain and replenish their cultures was to be drained dry. By the mid-1930s, for example, German Schwabs reaching adulthood still spoke their dialects but could scarcely read and write High German. There was also considerable social pressure, which was virtually irresistible among public employees, to magyarize personal names.

The pressure of magyarization, it must be recalled, was cultural rather than racial. Hence, it was sincere in the sense that anyone who accepted it and magyarized himself or his children in speech, name, and political outlook was accepted as assimilated—at least until the anti-Semitic legislation of the late 1930s. Magyarized individuals of Slovak or Schwab descent, for example, filled many senior positions in the Church and army, respectively. Furthermore, while anyone who resisted magyarization was, indeed, subject to political and cultural handicaps, he was not subject to the kinds of civic and fiscal chicaneries (prejudicial court proceedings, overtaxation, biased application of social and economic legislation) that some of Hungary's neighbors often inflicted on their ethnic minorities.

In terms of both numbers and political sensitivity, the German Schwab minority was the most problematical, especially in the 1930s when militant nationalism rose among both Magyars and Schwabs as the Nazi government of the Reich took an ominous interest in the Auslanddeutsche. Though prepared to pursue international revisionism in tandem with Germany, Hungarian government and public opinion, even in their Right-Radical expressions, were most reluctant to make domestic concessions to the German minority. Here, at least, was one issue on which the heavily Jewish journalistic profession could without reservations identify with and encourage spontaneous Magyar sentiments. The German Schwabs, on the other hand, were electrified by nazism, and after the Austrian Anschluss of March, 1938, they virtually openly confessed their primary loyalty to the Reich. They now abandoned their veteran ethnic association, Ungarländisch-Deutscher Volksbildungsverein (UDV), founded by the former counterrevolutionary minister of nationalities (1919-20), Professor Jakob Bleyer, in 1923 to cultivate Schwab cultural identity in the context of exclusive political loyalty to Hungary, and flocked instead to the new and Nazi-subsidized Volksbund der Deutschen in Ungarn, founded in November, 1938, by Dr. Franz Basch, former secretary of the old, rival, organization. The UDV now disintegrated. It had, indeed, lost credibility by developing beyond loyalty to docility; Bleyer had agreed to refrain from youth activities and to allow half its officials and two-thirds of its executive directorate to be government nominees, yet even this had not softened the general pressure of magyarization. When the 1930 census revealed a German ethnic decline of 73,000 from 1920, despite a natural increase of about 40,000 among the Schwabs, at last even Bleyer was troubled; but he died on December 5, 1933, before he could effect a probable turn to greater political assertiveness.

To counter Basch's pro-Nazi and pro-Reich Volksbund, the Hungarian governments sought to organize a rival Treuebewegung among their Germans, the leadership of which was entrusted to a Msgr. József Pehm, who was destined to become better known after World War II under his later, magyarized name as Cardinal Mindszenty. Simultaneously, they sought to "buy off" and "defuse" the Volksbund politically by "assigning" it two parliamentary seats under the Government Party's mantle in the elections of 1939; this shrewd maneuver provoked a falling-out between the Baschists and the opposition Hungarian Right-Radicals. Though persistent Reich pressure did oblige the wartime Hungarian governments to ease their hitherto intense magyarization pressure on the Schwabs, no concessions that infringed on Hungarian state sovereignty were made until 1943, when Volksdeutsche youths serving in the Hungarian army were combed out by Reich German recruiting teams for service in the Wehrmacht or the SS.

During these war years, indeed, the Schwabs had suddenly ceased to be Hungary's largest minority, thanks to the territorial extensions of 1938-41. After the last of these, in April, 1941, the population of enlarged Hungary showed the ethnic profile given in table 30. Note that the 1941 census supplemented the traditional linguistic criterion, defined as "the language that the respondent considers as his own and that he speaks best and most willingly," with the new psychological and political criterion of "nationality." This criterion had hitherto been avoided by Hungarian statisticans, presumably because of its subjective nature, and was now described as "without prejudice and without regard to language, the nationality to which the respondent feels and believes that he belongs." Some interesting variations, reflecting the strong pressure on non-Magyar speakers to declare themselves Magyar-by-nationality, emerge between the two criteria (see table 30).

TABLE 30

1941 POPULATION BY ETHNICITY

	Language		Nationality	
	Number	Percentage	Number	Percentage
Magyar	11,367,342	77.5	11,881,455	80.9
German	719,762	4.9	533,045	3.6
Slovak	268,913	1.8	175,550	1.2
Romanian	1,100,352	7.5	1,051,026	7.2
Ruthenian	564,092	3.8	547,770	3.7
Croatian	127,441	0.9	12,346	0.1
Serbian	164,423	1.1	159,000	1.1
Bunyevci, Šokci	77,484	0.5	54,585	0.4
Slovene	69,586	0.5	20,336	0.1
Gypsy	57,372	0.4	76,209	0.5
Yiddish	126,312	0.9 ⎫	139,041	1.0
Hebrew	5,659	0.0 ⎭		
Other	30,835	0.2	29,210	0.2
Total	14,679,573	100.0	14,679,573	100.0

For Jews, finally, the census criterion of religion must be compared to the linguistic and nationality ones. The figures given in table 31, however, do not show as Israelite the approximately one hundred thousand persons of Christian confession who were regarded as racial Jews under the anti-Semitic legislation of 1938-42 that preceded Hungarian Jewry's final tragedy in 1944.

TABLE 31

Population by Religion in 1941

	Number	Percentage
Roman Catholic	8,073,689	55.0
Greek Catholic (Uniate)	1,701,544	11.6
Calvinist	2,785,701	19.0
Lutheran	729,288	5.0
Eastern Orthodox	559,944	3.8
Unitarian	57,909	0.4
Baptist	36,422	0.2
Israelite	724,306	4.9
Other	10,770	0.1
Total	14,679,573	100.0

The role and position of the Jewish ethnic minority in Trianon Hungary, as well as its ultimate fate, can be briefly summarized. In 1930, before the restrictive measures of subsequent years, Jews constituted 5.1 percent of Hungary's population (20 percent of Budapest's) and the following high percentages in various professions: physicians, 54.5; lawyers, 49.2; articled clerks, 34.9; journalists, 31.7; engineers, 30.4; pharmacists, 18.9; white collar employees in mining, 47.6; white collar employees in industry, 43.9; white collar employees in commerce, 42.0; white collar employees in agricultural management, 27.0. In addition, apostates from Judaism formed substantial proportions in these professions and in academia, for such assimilation had long been a trend much encouraged by the Hungarian ruling establishment and accepted by large numbers of Jews. In the two interwar decades close to thirty-five thousand Jews accepted baptism, and an average of over a thousand per annum contracted mixed marriages. The offspring of these marriages were almost invariably raised as Christians. Apart from their numerical proportions in various professions, Jews were estimated to control one-fourth of the national income, four of the country's five leading banks, and more than four-fifths of its industry.

Though the number of Jews in old Hungary had quadrupled from a quarter of a million in the mid-nineteenth century to a million by the eve of World War I, due to a high rate of natural increase as well as to substantial immigration from Galicia, Russia, and Romania, the "Jewish question" was officially and politically a taboo subject in Ausgleich Hungary. The preponderantly agrarian Magyar ruling elite was happy to have the Jews develop the country's industry and commerce and needed the Magyar-speaking Jews to give Hungary its very narrow Magyar statistical majority (51.4 percent in 1900). Law XVII of December 22, 1867, had emancipated the Jews to full legal equality, and Law XIII of May 16, 1896, had conferred on Judaism full acknowledgement as a "received" religion, equal in status to others. Most Jews reciprocated with fervent Hungarian patriotism.

The situation was different in truncated, frustrated, impoverished Trianon Hungary: the very fact that the "Jewish problem" had not been permitted on the prewar political agenda now exacerbated its controversial character and maximized the popular conviction that there must be something darkly sinister about a community that supplied not only the country's leading capitalists but also most of the functionaries of the recent Communist regime. Furthermore, in Trianon Hungary the racial Magyars had their own vast demographic majority and no longer needed the Jews as statistical recruits to the cause of Magyardom. Indeed, there was now a strong temptation to make them the scapegoats for the country's recent disasters. Finally, the Jews' recent branching-out from business to the free professions toward the end of the Ausgleich era had brought them into much more direct and more resented competition with the Magyar déclassé gentry than had pertained in earlier decades. The direction of the postwar and post-Kun white terror resulted from this, as did a *numerus clausus* of 6 percent on Jewish admission to university studies, adopted by the counterrevolutionary parliament through Law XXV of September 22, 1920. This law, however, was rather loosely administered and then amended by the Bethlen administration later in the decade, when, on coming to a *modus vivendi* with the Jewish business community, the government also chose to treat outwardly emancipated Jews as Hungarians in applying this law. The universities—and hence the professions—thus continued to be heavily penetrated by Jews; at the same time, however, they became hotbeds of anti-Semitism as the Magyar academic proletariat turned toward the radical Right. Meanwhile, the military and civil bureaucracies, were quietly purged of Jews even in the Bethlen years, but these careers had never attracted Jews on anything like the scale of the liberal and learned professions. Nevertheless, the surplus Magyar civil servants who crowded into Trianon Hungary from the lost peripheral areas were particularly susceptible to anti-Semitism.

The depression and the Nazi example accelerated anti-Semitic trends in the 1930s. Even the hitherto indifferent but now economically insecure landed nobility was infected. The first legal example of this revival was Law XV of 1938, entitled "Concerning the More Effective Safeguarding of a Balanced Economic and Social System." It established new professional chambers for the press and theater which supplemented the traditional ones for medicine, the bar, and engineering, and restricted Jewish membership in all of them and in "other types of white collar employment" to 20 percent. This was almost quadruple the proportion of Jews in the general population, but it was far less than their traditional quotas in these fields. Compliance was required within five years, and fifteen thousand Jews were to be affected. Early the next year came the more drastic and complicated Act IV of 1939, "Concerning the Restriction of the Participation of Jews in Public and Economic Life," which for the first time extended the definition of a Jew beyond the individual's confessional status and made the religion of his grandparents the criterion. Baptisms of Jews performed after 1919 were not recognized. This law categorically excluded Jews from state service and from parliament's Upper House (except for two ex-officio rabbis who were not expelled until 1940), reduced their quotas in the professional chambers from 20 to 6 percent, reactivated the university *numerus clausus* of 6 percent (12 percent at commercial academies), and authorized the expropriation of Jewish-owned land. Only 5 percent of all business establishments and no more than 12 percent of any one firm's employees might be Jewish. No Jews could qualify as publishers, theater directors, responsible editors of journals, or managers of state monopolies. Four years were permitted for implementation, and about three hundred thousand Jews were affected. Interesting and characteristic was the fact that the government's original draft of this law was harsher but was softened by the Upper House, which had even sought to establish a privileged category of "Honorary Christians" as a compromise between the old, confessional, and the new, racial criteria of Jewish identification.

Still more repressive was the legislation passed after the eruption of World War II. Law XV of 1941, "Concerning the Protection of Race," approximated Germany's Nuremberg Laws of 1935 by prohibiting marriages and extramarital sexual relations between Jews and non-Jews. The latter offense was subject to from three to five years' imprisonment for the Jew involved. The genealogical-racist classification of Jews by grandparentage was also tightened. Law VIII of 1942 abrogated the Jewish community's legal status, deprived it of subsidies, and prohibited conversion to Judaism. Laws XIV and XV of the same year prescribed auxiliary military labor service (semipenal) for Jews while excluding them from regular military organizations, and prohibited Jewish acquisition of real estate while categorically expropriating Jewish-owned farm and forest land. So much for the pregenocidal legislation.

In July, 1941, the Hungarian government deported 40,000 Jews of "doubtful nationality" to the area of German-occupied Poland. Of these, 13,000 were summarily executed and the remainder perished in due time. In January, 1942, the Hungarian army massacred 1,000 Jews (and over 2,000 Serbs) in the corner of interwar Yugoslavia that had been recently reannexed to Hungary. In the spring of that year, 60,000 Jews were shipped for labor service to the Russian front (under Law XIV); of these only 20,000 returned. All this was the work of the Hungarian authorities and preceded the German occupation of March, 1944. After that event came the final holocaust of Hungarian Jewry, in which the

Right-Radical elements of Hungary's society and puppet government served as Eichmann's enthusiastic accomplices, while the weaker conservative circles endeavored to protect at least the magyarized, urbanized fraction of the country's Jewish population from final extermination. Of the 725,000 persons of "Israelite faith" residing within the recently expanded Hungarian borders of 1941, only 260,500—mainly from Budapest—survived to the war's end. (This does not take into account the additional, but statistically undetermined, destruction inflicted on the 100,000 Christians who were reclassified as racial Jews under the legislation of 1939-41.) The proportion surviving, though all too small, was larger than in most other East Central European Jewish communities. The credit for this goes to the now often maligned and ridiculed "feudal," "whiggish," and "obsolete" ruling elite of old Hungary, stiffened on this issue by the admonitions and pleas of several foreign governments and diplomats.

Map 5. Yugoslavia

· Chapter Five ·

YUGOSLAVIA

1

By VIRTUALLY every relevant criterion—history, political traditions, socioeconomic standards, legal systems, religion and culture—Yugoslavia was the most complicated of the new states of interwar East Central Europe, being composed of the largest and most varied number of pre-1918 units. From the Austrian half of the late Habsburg Empire, Yugoslavia inherited Slovenia and Dalmatia; from the Hungarian half, the formerly quasi-autonomous subkingdom of Croatia-Slavonia and the explicitly Hungarian districts of the Vojvodina; and from the joint Austro-Hungarian administration, the province of Bosnia-Hercegovina. Macedonia and the Sanjak of Novibazar had been Ottoman imperial territories until the Balkan Wars of 1912 and 1913. Finally, there also entered into the new Yugoslavia the two hitherto independent kingdoms of Montenegro and Serbia. The latter had emerged in the half-century preceding World War I as the most plausible candidate for the role of Piedmont to a South Slav union but insisted now that the memory of her former independence be preserved by formally designating the new state as "The Kingdom of Serbs, Croats, and Slovenes," rather than the more colloquial "Yugoslavia." Yugoslavia will, however, be used here for convenience.

Thus, unlike Czechoslovakia, the new Yugoslav state did not emerge in its entirety from the deceased Habsburg Empire; unlike Romania, it was not simply an enlargement of a prewar core kingdom; unlike Poland, it was not a restored, but an altogether new, state; unlike interwar Hungary, it lacked ethnic homogeneity. Its several parts had over the centuries been subsumed within Byzantine, Ottoman, Hungarian, Germanic, and Italian cultural zones. Indeed, the so-called Illyrian Provinces along the Adriatic and in the northwest had for a brief interval even been attached to Napoleonic France. Each part had interwoven the culture of its particular zone with indigenous South Slav institutions and styles. The ancient and

201

tenacious Theodosian line that divided the Western, Roman (Catholic and Protestant) world from the Eastern, Byzantine (Orthodox and Ottoman) one ran right through the new Yugoslavia.

Geography added to the effects of historical fragmentation in hampering the development of Yugoslav unity. The new state was one of contrasting regions, of internal mountain barriers, of fragmented communications within and among the several regions. Hence, even had the country been populated by only one ethnic and cultural community, great political skill on the part of its rulers would have been required to fuse it together. Populated as it was by sundry antagonistic communities of widely divergent cultures, who worshiped in several different religions, had inherited eight legal systems from their former sovereignties, and wrote the basic Serbocroatian language in two orthographies (not to mention their several other Slavic and non-Slavic languages), Yugoslavia was bound to be subjected to profound centrifugal pressures which were to overwhelm her elite. Furthermore, areas of mixed population, such as the Vojvodina, Bosnia, or Macedonia, functioned less as bridges than as barriers, aggravating rather than easing these centrifugal pressures.

Statistical demonstration of the ethnic complexity of interwar Yugoslavia's population is rendered difficult by the official policy of lumping Croats, Serbs, Macedonians, and Serbocroatian-speaking Muslims together into one "Serbocroat" category in the two official censuses of January 31, 1921, and March 31, 1931. The religious and regional statistics can, however, be used to estimate the several groups within that catch-all category, provided one bears in mind the following factors: (a) the Macedonians (albeit heavily Orthodox in religion) as well as the Bosniaks (Serbocroatian-speaking Muslims of Bosnia-Hercegovina and the Sanjak) felt themselves to be distinct from the Serbs and Croats; (b) most Montenegrans acknowledged ethnic classification as Serbs, and most Dalmatians as Croats; (c) virtually all Slovenes and Croats were Catholic; (d) Germans and Magyars were either Catholic or Protestant; and (e) Yugoslavia's Albanians were overwhelmingly Muslim but regarded themselves as distinct from the Bosniak (Serbocroatian-speaking) and Macedonian (Turkish-speaking) Muslims.[1]

When the statistics given in tables 32, 33, and 34 are correlated, these percentages of nationalities appear reasonable: Serbs (with Montenegrans), 43.0; Croats, 23.0; Slovenes, 8.5; Macedonians, 5.0; Bosniaks, 6.0; non-Southern Slavs (including Albanian and Turkish Muslims as well as

1. From 1929 Yugoslavia followed most other states of East Central Europe in publishing an official, statistical yearbook, *Statistički Godišnjak* (Belgrade: Opšta Državna Statistika). Since the categories used therein were often cruder than, and different from, those of other states' official yearbooks and since there are occasional internal inconsistencies, these yearbooks, though forming the basic statistical source for this chapter, have been supplemented by further statistical data not published officially but supplied by later Yugoslav authorities to the authors of Werner Markert, ed., *Jugoslawien* (Cologne: Böhlau, 1954).

German, Magyar, Romanian Christians, and Jews), 14.5. This variegated population inhabited a realm of 247,542 square kilometers.

TABLE 32

POPULATION BY ETHNICITY (MOTHER TONGUE)

	1921 Number	1921 Percentage	1931 Number	1931 Percentage
Serbocroat	8,911,509	74.36	10,730,823	77.01
Slovene	1,019,997	8.51	1,135,410	8.15
Czech ⎱	115,532	0.96	52,909	0.38
Slovak ⎰			76,411	0.55
German	505,790	4.22	499,969	3.59
Magyar	467,658	3.90	468,185	3.36
Romanian and Vlach	231,068	1.93	137,879	0.98
Albanian	439,657	3.67	505,259	3.63
Turkish	150,322	1.26	132,924	0.95
Gypsy	. . . .	. . . .	70,424	0.51
Other*	143,378	1.19	123,845	0.89
Total	11,984,911	100.00	13,934,038	100.00

*Included Polish, Russian, Ukrainian, Italian, Yiddish, each of whom had less than 50,000 speakers.

TABLE 33

POPULATION BY RELIGION

	1921 Number	1921 Percentage	1931 Number	1931 Percentage
Eastern Orthodox	5,593,057	46.67	6,785,501	48.70
Roman Catholic	4,708,657	39.29	5,217,847	37.45
Greek Catholic (Uniate)	40,338	0.34	44,671	0.32
Muslim	1,345,271	11.22	1,561,166	11.20
Lutheran ⎱	229,517	1.91	175,279	1.26
Calvinist ⎰			55,890	0.40
Israelite	64,746	0.54	68,405	0.49
Other and Unknown	3,325	0.03	25,279	0.18
Total	11,984,911	100.00	13,934,038	100.00

TABLE 34

Population by Historic Units (1921)*

	Number	Percentage
Serbia and Macedonia	4,133,478	34.50
Montenegro	199,227	1.66
Bosnia-Hercegovina	1,890,440	15.77
Dalmatia	620,432	5.18
Croatia-Slavonia	2,642,996	22.05
Slovenia	962,624	8.03
Vojvodina (and Mur districts)	1,535,714	12.81
Total	11,984,911	100.00

*This category was abolished in 1929.

In 1931 there were but 3 Yugoslav cities with populations of over 100,000 and another 4 with more than 50,000. The percentage of the population residing in localities of over 20,000 people rose slowly from 8.1 in 1921, to 9.3 in 1931, to 10.6 in 1941, while the percentage of those dependent on agriculture scarcely declined between 1921 and 1931 from 78.9 to 76.5 (in 1938 it was estimated as 74.8). Interwar Yugoslavia's average annual rate of population growth, 1.45 percent, was one of Europe's highest; the total population in 1940 was estimated at 15,919,000. Due to the lamentably slow growth of industrial and other types of nonagricultural employment and the contraction of emigration outlets, most of this increase vegetated in the villages in deteriorating conditions of underemployment, underproduction, underconsumption, and general misery. Demographic pressure and socioeconomic impoverishment tended to increase along a north-to-south scale: the northern Slovenes, Croats, Germans, and Magyars, though largely Roman Catholic in religion, enjoyed lower rates of population growth and more advanced production patterns than did their Orthodox and Muslim fellow citizens to the south. Over time, this pattern exacerbated political resentments and apprehensions.

2

The particular political traditions of each of interwar Yugoslavia's component regions and peoples must now be examined and their leading political parties described. The course and outcome of World War I had permitted the political realization of that "Yugoslav dream" whose ideological roots lay in nineteenth-century romanticism and nationalism. Disillusioned and frustrated by the repression of their political and cultural aspirations within the Habsburg Empire, and fearful lest Italy's territorial ambitions be satisfied at their expense, the Habsburgs' Southern Slav (Slovene, Croatian, and Serbian) elites came to seek safety through the union of their areas with the independent kingdom of Serbia, whose international prestige had soared in the course of the war thanks to its army's impressive performance against the Central Powers.

Ironically, Serbia's government had long been unenthusiastic about such a merger: its main territorial interests were directed toward achieving Serbian outlets to the Aegean and Adriatic seas, not to the protection of Slovene and Croatian ports from Italian encroachments; it was reluctant to merge its Orthodox people, and the Muslim Bosniaks whom it expected to annex, with the largely Catholic Southern Slavs to the north of the Una-Sava-Danube river line; finally, it could not initially bring itself really to contemplate the disappearance of the seemingly eternal Habsburg Empire. Nikola Pašić, Serbia's perennial premier and her strongest political personality, had little sympathy for the type of broad Yugoslav state desired by the Slovenes and Croats. His outlook was fiercely, even provincially, Serb, and it was now reinforced by the consideration that most of the Habsburg Southern Slavs were, after all, fighting on what for Pašić was not only the losing, but also the wrong, side. Serbia, furthermore, did not need them, while they needed her; hence she had no reason to surrender her initiative to them or to merge her existence with theirs. Not until mid-1917, after it had lost its special patron upon the fall of the Tsarist regime and the United States had entered the war as an enthusiast for national unifications, did the government of Serbia reluctantly accommodate itself to the Western-favored Yugoslav idea. Even then, it still considered itself to be the sole legitimate institutional and diplomatic representative of that idea. The corollary was that whatever South Slav state might emerge from the war would be regarded as but a chronological extension and geographic expansion of old Serbia.

In terms of political power, these Serbian hopes were largely fulfilled by the circumstances of Yugoslavia's creation at the end of the war. Fears of Italian invasion and of social revolution amidst the disintegration of the Habsburg Empire panicked the political elite of that empire's Southern Slav communities into a precipitous dash for protection and cover to Serbia's army, dynasty, and bureaucracy. No attempt was made to elicit popular endorsement for this step. Nor was any effort made to use such potential assets as the Habsburg army's still intact Croatian regiments, with their established traditions of military prowess, or the effective Croat-Slovene control of the Habsburg navy as bargaining levers in negotiating the terms of this union with Serbia. Of all the political leaders of the defunct empire's Southern Slavs, only Stjepan Radić of the Croatian Peasant Party protested this overly hasty and ill-prepared *fait accompli* of virtually unconditional merger without eliciting guarantees from Serbia on such issues as federalism and/or decentralization. The others were too depressed by their relative paucity of military and administrative power and by their lack of formal international diplomatic standing, and too impressed by their optimistic assumption that Serbia's own tradition of universal suffrage would provide a sufficient guarantee for their constituencies in the new state, to engage in any serious bargaining over the terms of the union.

Though the other Southern Slavs of the Vojvodina, Bosnia-Hercegovina, and Montenegro joined their Slovene and Croatian brethren in merging with the prewar kingdom of Serbia, the protests and warnings of Stjepan Radić were soon confirmed as serious frictions quickly developed between these peoples, on the one hand, and the Serbian armies and bureaucracies that were supposedly protecting them, on the other. Already on December 5, 1918, there were clashes in the streets of Croatia's capital, Zagreb, between local elements and Serbian troops, and by the end of May, 1919, Radić had collected 167,667 signatures on an appeal to the Western Powers to authorize the recovery of Croatia's independence.

While the behavior of the Serbian troops in these newly adhering areas was correct, the military authorities moved swiftly to "decapitate" the former Habsburg regiments of their Croatian officers and in some cases to "exile" the truncated units to provincial garrisons in old Serbia. The election of a constituent assembly was, meanwhile, deferred until after the peace conference's delineation of the new state's frontiers—that is, until November, 1920. Thus, for its first two formative years, Yugoslavia was administered by old Serbia's army and bureaucracy according to old Serbia's constitutional and political models. Neither a ministry for the new territories nor special departments in the existing ministries to supervise the transition to Serbian administration were organized. Compared to the record of the other interwar states of East Central Europe, these were two barren and unproductive years in Yugoslavia.

The government and people of old Serbia entered the new Yugoslavia conscious of being the victor of a desperate war, and they viewed Slovenia and Croatia as the liberated and seceded parts of the loser, parts incapable of defending themselves against other covetous neighbors. The Serbs further felt entitled to impose themselves and their institutions upon Yugoslavia by virtue of the fact that their little kingdom had been bled white by the war, suffering a relatively greater loss of men and wealth than any other participant in that worldwide slaughter, while the Southern Slav areas of the Habsburg Empire, whose regiments had been deployed mainly against Italy, escaped comparatively unscathed. Serbia's per capita battle casualties were two-and-one-half times those of France and three times those of the United Kingdom and Italy. Direct and indirect war losses, resulting from both battle casualties and a devastating typhus epidemic, amounted to one-fifth of her population, one-fourth of her cattle, one-third of the horses, and half the pigs, sheep, and goats, as well as much destruction of farm implements, transportation, and housing. All this carnage was superimposed on the already substantial Serbian casualties of the two Balkan Wars of 1912 and 1913, which the Habsburg Slavs had been altogether spared. From this situation came the short-sighted but not surprising determination of the Serbs to compensate themselves for these truly staggering sacrifices at the expense of the alleged beneficiaries, the less marred parts of the new state, and their deafness to the Croatian complaints of being reduced to second-class citizens.

Such immediate postwar expectations and grievances were superimposed on long-established cultural and political differences and conflicts. While ethnicity and race linked Slovenes, Croats, Bosniaks, and Serbs and while a common language was shared by Croats, Bosniaks, and Serbs, yet history, religion, social organization, and political styles all divided these core Southern Slav communities of interwar Yugoslavia, not to mention here the major non-Slavic minorities such as the Albanians, Turks, Magyars, and Germans, nor the Slavic Macedonians whose distinct identity was denied during the interwar decades by the dominant Serbs.

In the ensuing conflict among these various ethnic communities, the Orthodoxy of the Serbs, Montenegrans, and Macedonians affected their political styles and strategies less than did the Catholicism of the Croats and Slovenes. The majority of the Catholic peoples formed a clerical, social, and political community of a type characteristic to Central Europe, while the Orthodox peoples viewed their religion simply as defining their nationality. The Serbs, with their political experience of successful nineteenth-century insurrections by a socially homogeneous people to carve its independent and populistic kingdom out of the decaying Ottoman Empire, tended toward a positive, proud, and possessive view of the state; they were prone to assertive, even aggressive, and sometimes violent, strategies to achieve their political aims, and they were inclined to be rough and ready in dealing with recalcitrant elements. *Samo Sloga Srbina Spasava* (Only Solidarity Saves the Serb) was their historic aphorism and current watchword. By 1918 they had many decades of experience at organizing their own state, raising their own armies, determining their own policies. Only Serbia could contribute to the new Yugoslavia a political elite knowledgeable in the art of ruling, not merely of opposing, as well as a comprehensive government apparatus that included democratically elected legislatures, experienced civil, diplomatic, and military services, and a native dynasty. The Montenegran political tradition, in turn, was similar but still primitive, clannish, and patriarchal. The Macedonians' anti-Ottoman revolts had been abortive, whereas the Serbs' and Montenegrans' had been successful; hence, their political pattern tended to be one of violence, subjugation, and resentment, rather than violence, independence, and assertion.

The Muslim communities of Bosnia-Hercegovina, which were racially and linguistically Serbo-Croatian, were traditionally very conservative and therefore unsympathetic to the secularizing Ottoman reform movement of the nineteenth century. Lacking experience in government and administration and considering themselves too weak numerically to challenge the state apparatus, they early developed a "clientele strategy" of supporting whomever was ruling them, be these rulers Ottoman, Habsburg, Serb, Axis, or Communist, in return for favors and concessions.

The Slovenes, in turn, as a small but modern community, had learned the arts of bargaining and maneuvering coalitions in the politically and ethnically intricate setting of the prewar Vienna Reichsrat, and, being generally literate and pragmatic, had become highly skilled in local government and general administration. Their need for the protection of the Serb-officered army against Italy, and the Serbs' desire, in turn, politically to detach the Slovenes from the Croats, provided the ingredients for informal but effective political arrangements between the Slovenes and Serbs. The linguistic distinctiveness of the Slovene language also served as a barrier to any massive influx of Serbian officials into Slovenia; at the same time it presented no obstacle to the steady insinuation of educated Slovenes who, unlike the Serbs, tended to be bilingual in Slovene and Serbocroatian, into the central ministerial bureaucracies of Belgrade. The hard-bargaining Slovenes, in short, were administratively overprivileged in interwar Yugoslavia. While they liked to depict their role as that of mediators, their Croatian neighbors and fellow Catholics were understandably prone to view it less loftily as self-serving.

Finally, the assumptions and styles underlying the Croatian political tradition proved particularly baffling to the Serbs. Having been perennially used and deserted by both the Habsburg dynasty and the Hungarian political elite in the course of the nineteenth-century political maneuverings, the Croats had developed an almost morbid mistrust of governments and of power *per se*; they were determined not to be outwitted this time by the Serbs. As a subkingdom of prewar Hungary, relegated to permanent underrepresentation and subjected to cultural magyarization, Croatia had spawned a political tradition and a political elite that placed a high value on defensive obstructionism in the parliament and administration, while acceptance of the responsibilities of power and of office had come to evoke suspicions of cooptation and incipient betrayal. To the Serbs, with their rough-and-ready habits of rulership, constitutional problems were basically political and most political issues were fairly simple; for the Croats, with their ingrained sense of being the underdog, political energies had to be constrained within a legal and contractual framework that would necessarily be intricate and complex. The political history of interwar Yugoslavia is largely a history of mutual mystification and frustration of these two peoples.

Croatia and the Vojvodina also contained sizeable communities of Serbs who were descended from earlier waves of Serb migration from the Ottoman lands to the Habsburg Empire. Designated the "prečani" Serbs, i.e., those "beyond" (to the north of) the Una, Sava, and Danube rivers, they numbered about one-fifth of all Serbs. They were torn between a craving, on the one hand, to identify with their brethren of the prewar kingdom, the "srbijanci" Serbs, whose political power would rescue them from the status of a permanent minority within the northern provinces, and, on the other hand, a sense of sharing with the Slovenes and Croats a "Western" culture and socioeconomic level superior to that of the srbijanci Serbs. The political behavior of the prečani Serbs in interwar Yugoslavia was to oscillate between the options implied by these two views. Initially they emphatically pursued Pan-Serb solidarity; later, propelled in large part by the refusal of the srbijanci Serbs to concede to them sufficient political patronage, they tortuously experimented with, and eventually adopted, the strategy of "ex-Habsburger" solidarity.

This theme of cultural superiority and inferiority is, of course, notoriously dubious and risky and must be treated with great circumspection. It proved to be even more incendiary for interwar Yugoslav than for Czechoslovak politics. In the latter country, at least, the political hegemony of the Czechs corresponded with their higher levels of literacy, urbanization, and productivity over the Slovaks. In Yugoslavia, on the other hand, the former subjects of the late "Central European" Habsburg Empire considered themselves more advanced, in terms of all such cultural and socioeconomic criteria, than the "Balkan" Serbs to the south, by whom they were politically dominated to their lasting ire. The Serbs of the prewar Serbian kingdom, in turn, repudiated the cultural pretensions of the northerners and dismissed their political legacies as Austrophile, formalistic, and irresponsible. They viewed themselves as "doers" and these others as "carpers."

The politics of ethnicity were aggravated by the tensions arising from class cleavages and the resultant ideologies. During the mobilizations and campaigns of World War I, the peasant-soldiers of East Central Europe had "seen the world," had developed a greater sense of their own strength by observing how essential the food they produced was to the cities and regimes that commandeered it. They had been impressed by the new ideologies of Wilsonism, Bolshevism, and peasantism with their slogans: freedom, republicanism, and democracy. To the politically still unripe peasant masses, freedom meant release from conscription, requisitions, rents, and domination by townfolk; republicanism meant the elemental populist force that had recently toppled, with apparent ease, the hitherto seemingly eternal dynasties of the Habsburgs, Hohenzollerns, and Romanovs; democracy meant the repudiation of the exploitative past and the reversion of power from the allegedly parasitical bourgeoisie and bureaucracy to truly productive peasant, or peasant and worker, elements. Uncertain whether it desired a nostalgic return to traditional, tested village ways, or to commit itself to new methods of production with their revolutionary social consequences, the peasantry was angry and mistrustful. A regime might for an interval repress or pander to these smoldering peasant resentments and thus silence them into seeming docility, but in the long run they would prove unappeasable, short of a genuine socioeconomic revolution, and hence fatal to all regimes that approached them cynically or superficially.

In the new Yugoslavia, the peasants of the former Habsburg territories immediately clamored for land reform, while those of Serbia and Montenegro required cheap credit to restore their war-ravaged lands and herds. The government responded with an Interim Decree of February 25, 1919 that abolished the serfdom still practiced in Bosnia-Hercegovina and Macedonia, as well as the semiservile colonate system of Dalmatia; provided for the distribution of large estates among landless and poor peasants in Croatia-Slavonia and the Vojvodina; granted grazing and wood-gathering privileges on state lands and forests to all peasants; and authorized indemnification to the previous feudal rentiers and landlords. Though it achieved an immediate alleviation of political pressures, the decree was not followed up in subsequent years with equally essential massive capital and overhead investments in agriculture. In a country where over three-fourths of the population was engaged in agriculture and the bulk of state revenue was extracted from the peasants, the ministry of agriculture was habitually allocated only 1 percent of the budget. In interwar Yugoslavia the neglected village, with its vegetating, unemployable, undernourished, disease-ridden, semiliterate, surplus population, presented a more refractory and a more explosive problem than did the urban slum.

Around such ethnic and social tensions did the country's political parties structure themselves, develop their programs, and recruit their clienteles. They are listed here according to their ethnic affiliations.

1. The Radical Party, founded in 1881 and led by the venerable Nikola Pašić, had since 1903 been the dominant government party in old Serbia and remained so during the first decade of Yugoslavia's existence. Originally the political expression of the nationalistic, egalitarian, and self-reliant peasantry of old Serbia, it retained the electoral allegiance of this constituency despite the rapid *embourgeoisement* of its leadership and policies in interwar Yugoslavia. Coopting and, in turn, being coopted by, business, bureaucratic, and military interests, and well-organized for electoral, bargaining, and administrative purposes, the Radical Party,

like the Czechoslovak Agrarian Party, quickly became its country's leading *Interessengemeinschaft*, the political instrument of the čaršija, the Establishment-clique of businessmen, bureaucrats, professionals, politicians, the army, and the royal palace. Yet its electoral base remained south of the Una-Sava-Danube line. The one exception was the Vojvodina in the northeast; it generally gave about half its legislative mandates to a local party which in 1919 merged with the Radicals.

Precisely because they were initially skeptical of Yugoslavia and anxious lest this large and amorphous state enervate their beloved Serbia, the Radical leaders were at first willing to consider granting a considerable degree of administrative self-government to the northern, Catholic areas. They abandoned this strategy only when it became clear, by 1921, that such limited autonomy for a truncated Croatia would not satisfy that region's political elite, which cherished its own claims to Bosnia-Hercegovina, and that, in any event, this elite at that time lacked political "clout" and reliability.

2. The Democratic Party traced its origins to a secession, in 1901, of somewhat more progressive and doctrinaire elements from the still patriarchal and already opportunistic Radicals of old Serbia. Interested in such issues as women's emancipation, protection of labor, and state regulation of the economy, its current leader, Ljubomir Davidović, promptly joined forces in the new Yugoslavia with the political chieftain of the correspondingly advanced prečani Serbs, Svetozar Pribičević, on a platform that was more "Yugoslav," more unitarist, but also more etatist than that of the Radicals. Yet, as both parties were self-consciously Serbian, and as the prečani contingent of the Democrats in particular feared isolation within Croatia, the Radicals and the Democrats perforce worked out a troubled but effective political symbiosis in the first years of the new state. At the same time, the very fact that the Pribičević wing of the Democrats were such doctrinaire centralizers made them a convenient stalking-horse for the Radicals' agile leader Pašić, who was always able to prove to the disgruntled Croats and Bosniaks that the most vehement champions of a unitary state and deriders of regional autonomy came from outside old Serbia proper.

3. The Agrarian Party of Jovan Jovanović, founded in 1919 by the merger of like-minded and high-minded splinter groups in Serbia, Bosnia, Dalmatia, and Slovenia, made a trenchant argument, but little political headway, with their denunciations of the Radicals for allegedly betraying their original peasant constituency.

4. The Croatian Peasant Party was founded in 1904 by the brothers Ante and Stjepan Radić, of whom only the latter survived into the interwar era. In the prewar legislatures of Croatia and Hungary it had been underrepresented, thanks to the restricted suffrage, but in Yugoslavia it quickly developed into the chief political expression of the Croatian

people: a national, mass party that retained a specifically agrarian ideology as it overwhelmed and absorbed the prewar bourgeois parties and groups. Committed to a program of Croatian state rights, land reform for the benefit of Slavic peasants at the expense of Hungarian and German landlords, decentralized and populistic administrative arrangements, as well as to such less tangible propositions as peasantism, pacifism, internationalism, and plebiscitary democracy, Stjepan Radić quickly emerged as the oracle of the Croatian people, the idol of its peasantry. Just as promptly, however, he proved himself an erratic tactician and sterile strategist who generally opted for the politics of abstention, boycott, and withdrawal. Yet his constituents never held Radić accountable for his failure to achieve power or results, and they consistently lionized him for articulating their frustrated rages. The Croats of interwar Yugoslavia appeared to prefer the role of the righteously indignant "outsider" over that of an effective "insider."

5. The Slovene People's Party, the Populists, founded in 1905 and led since shortly before World War I by Msgr. Dr. Anton Korošec, enjoyed a position of power in its homeland that was analogous to that of the Radicals in Serbia. But whereas the Radical and the Croatian Peasant leaders expended themselves after 1918 in exclusively political struggles, the clerical chiefs of the Slovene Populists remained consistently, albeit paternalistically, attentive to the economic and cultural as well as the political aspirations and needs of their village and small-town constituencies. Through their comprehensive cooperative movement, the Populists supplied Slovenia with a resource sadly lacking in the rest of interwar Yugoslavia: ample and cheap agricultural credit. Through their systematic program of Catholic popular education, they nurtured a relatively homogeneous and advanced Christian-Social culture. Not in principle either a government or an opposition party, the Slovene Populists used their solid political base, their administrative competence, and their parliamentary sophistication (the heritage of the prewar Austrian Reichsrat) to exploit the tensions between Serbs and Croats so as to achieve virtual self-administration for their region and a strong base in the central bureaucracy for its native sons.

6. Muslim interests were articulated by the Yugoslav Muslim Organization (JMO) of the Bosniaks, led by Dr. Mehmed Spaho, and by the weaker Džemijet party of the Macedonian (Turkish-speaking) and Albanian Muslims. Buoyed by the example of the Kemalist victories of the early 1920s in Turkey, the Yugoslav Muslims generally traded their parliamentary weight for economic and cultural favors.

7. The Communists, organized during 1919, emerged from the local and general elections of 1920 with the country's third strongest parliamentary representation and as the only major party whose appeal transcended ethnic and regional particularism. They alone affirmed the

existence of a Yugoslav nation at a time when official nomenclature was still committed to the distinctiveness of its Serbian, Croatian, and Slovene parts. Running well in both the most advanced and the poorest areas, and best of all where national unrest and economic distress reinforced each other (the Vojvodina, Dalmatia, Montenegro, Macedonia), the Communist Party was first administratively prevented from taking its controlling seats on the Belgrade and Zagreb municipal councils; then, by an interim decree of doubtful legality, it was deprived of its trade union and other ancillary organizations; finally, it was altogether banned on August 2, 1921, after an abortive attempt to assassinate Prince-Regent Alexander on June 29 and a successful one on Interior Minister Milorad Drašković on July 21—for both of which the Communist leadership disclaimed responsibility. Driven underground and subjected to severe repression, the party, which had claimed sixty thousand members on the eve of the ban, continued to attract the most idealistic and talented elements of the younger intelligentsia and proletariat while simultaneously lacerating itself with doctrinaire and sterile feuds within the leadership. Thanks to their myopic habit of denouncing all militant opposition as "Communist-inspired," the Yugoslav regimes inadvertently strengthened the real Communists as many disaffected people concluded that the best way to express their alienation from the regime's system was to support the Communist movement. It quickly reduced its repudiated Social Democrat parent to political impotence. Finally, the tiny parties of the German, Magyar, and Romanian ethnic minorities generally confined their attention to governmental policies affecting the educational and cultural resources allocated to their communities.

3

As these parties sought, in the early 1920s, to endow Yugoslavia with a viable political system—commencing with the drafting of a constitution—they exacerbated rather than assuaged the tensions and differences among their ethnic and social constituencies. After two years of government by an overwhelmingly Serb administration, "supervised" by an unrepresentative Provisional National Assembly (March, 1919-November, 1920) that had been mustered through cooptation on the basis of prewar election returns and from which Macedonian and Montenegran autonomists as well as the ethnic minorities has been excluded, elections to a Constituent Assembly were at last held on November 28, 1920. During these two years, Stjepan Radić, whose Croatian Peasant Party had been gerrymandered out of the Provisional National Assembly, had become deeply alienated and embittered. He had been twice imprisoned for lengthy terms at the instigation of the prečani Serb leader Svetozar Pribičević, who had been successively minister of the interior and of education in these early years, for his persistent agitation against the failure to safeguard Croatian state rights when Yugoslavia was founded in November-December, 1918. Pribičević, alarmed by the Communist conflagration of 1919 in neighboring Hungary and frightened by the burgeoning energies of Croatian nationalism, had pursued a severe administrative policy toward both movements (frequent arrests, confiscations, dismissals, etc.); in so doing he had poisoned Serbo-Croatian relations from the very outset of Yugoslavia's existence. Moderates were undermined and extremists strengthened on both sides. In addition, the Croats were disturbed by what they considered to be the indifferent response of the Serb-dominated government to suspected Italian designs on Croatia's Adriatic littoral. The Serbs, in turn, were outraged when the Croatian Peasant Party's "republican pacifist" ideology expressed itself in subversive advice to Croatian soldiers to desert. The political atmosphere of the municipal elections on March 21, 1920, in Croatia and August 22 in Serbia and Macedonia, as well as of the long-awaited general elections to the Constituent Assembly on November 28 was charged.

Based on universal suffrage of all males over twenty-one, with the exception of military personnel on active duty as well as the Germans and Hungarians of the Vojvodina, and with constituencies apportioned by prewar census figures (thus somewhat favoring Serbia which had lost so much population during the war), the Constituent Assembly elections were comparatively free. Though in the preceding *campaign* the authorities had manifestly favored the Serbian Radicals and the Democrats, actual administrative pressure to skew the *results* was applied, if at all, only in Macedonia and Montenegro. Approximately 65 percent of those eligible voted, the turnout being highest in the former Habsburg areas and lowest in those most recently still Ottoman. Twenty-two parties competed, of which sixteen won seats.

The overall results, given in table 35, indicate that over half the elected deputies belonged to parties committed to unitarist constitutional theories (Radicals, Democrats, Agrarians), while less than a third were members of federalistic and regional parties (Croats, Slovene Populists, Muslims). To the two Marxist parties, with a sixth of the deputies, this constitutional issue was not a matter of principle. About one-third of the deputies belonged to parties that favored a republic (Communists, Social Democrats, Croatian Peasants, minor parties).

While the Serbian (prečani and srbijanci), Slovene, and Muslim political elites had remained relatively stable since prewar days, the leadership of the Croats had shifted decisively from the bourgeois parties to the Peasant Party. Though his style and rhetoric were at this time still too rustic and antiurban to enable Radić to capture the Croatian urban vote, he had swept the rural districts with a vigorous campaign for Croatian autonomy. Now he and his followers boycotted the Constituent Assembly in protest against the government's refusal to place on the assembly's agenda the question of the validity and the terms of Croatia's adhesion to Serbia in 1918. Declaring themselves the "Croatian National Representation," the fifty Peasant Party deputies assembled in Zagreb on December 7, 1920, and eventually shamed most of the Croatian bourgeois deputies into also withdrawing from the Belgrade legislature when that body's Serb leadership proved unwilling to make any autonomist, federalistic, or even decentralistic concessions to regional particularism. Pašić's Radicals, who would once have been willing to cooperate with Croatian moderates against the Davidović-Pribičević Democrats, had meanwhile come to despair of finding a reliable partner among the Croats and had made their own terms with the Democrats.

TABLE 35

ELECTIONS TO THE CONSTITUENT ASSEMBLY, NOVEMBER 28, 1920

Party	Number of Votes	Percentage of Total Vote	Seats
Serbian Radical	284,575	17.7	89
Serbian Democrat	319,448	19.9	94
Serbian and Slovene Agrarian	151,603	9.4	39*
Croatian Peasant	230,590	14.3	50
Slovene Populist and Croatian Clerical	111,274	7.0	27
Bosniak Muslim (JMO)	110,895	6.9	24
Džemijet Muslim	30,029	1.9	8
Communist	198,736	12.4	58
Social Democrat	46,792	2.9	10
Croatian bourgeois (four lists)	81,728	5.1	14
Other (nine lists)	41,865	2.5	6
Total	1,607,535	100.0	419

*Serbs received 30 seats and Slovenes, 9.

The most crucial and divisive test that the Constituent Assembly faced was to determine whether Yugoslavia would be a unitary or a federal state. To a limited extent the problem hinged on a legal question: was Yugoslavia a new entity created jointly by all its constituent parts, or was it an extension of old Serbia with certain postwar annexations? Politically, on the other hand, the problem presented itself as follows: did the profound cultural and historical variations among the country's regions suggest a federal political structure, or did they seem to require the centralistic containment of their centrifugal energies? Finally, were these differences truly intrinsic and ingrained, or were they the relatively superficial residue of foreign rule for which no permanent structural accommodations need be made in an independent Yugoslavia? In each of these formulations the non-Serbs preferred the first variant, the Serbs the second.

Pašić, the dominant personality of the Radical-Democratic coalition and premier since December 30, 1920, when he returned home from Paris where he had led the Yugoslav delegation to the peace conference, proposed a constitution that would be legislatively unitarist but allow for decentralized administration. Thanks to Radić's politically dubious policy of boycott and to Pašić's wily political "purchase" of the Muslims with especially generous offers of compensation for the feudal holdings that their begs and aghas were about to lose under the land-reform program, and of some Slovene Agrarians (not Populists) with promises of prestigious diplomatic assignments, the Radical-Democratic constitutional draft was successfully pushed through the assembly's committees and formally adopted by that body on June 28, 1921. Supporting it were 223 Radical, Democratic, Muslim, and Slovene Agrarian votes, against 35 Serbian Agrarian, Social Democratic, and miscellaneous negative votes; 161 deputies were either absent (Croats) or abstained (Communists, Slovene Populists, other Serbian Agrarians, miscellaneous). All in all, the deputies who adopted the constitution formed an adequate but politically fragile majority of the assembly and represented less than half the popular vote cast in its election.

The leading protagonists all emerged from this discordant episode having paid a heavy price. Radić, through his boycott, lost the chance to amend and affect the constitutional draft in committee or to persuade the Muslims and Slovene Agrarians to withhold their assent. Pašić, Davidović, and Pribičević, by overplaying their hands, refusing all compromises, and humiliating Croatia, scored a pyrrhic parliamentary victory but deepened the rifts among the country's communities. Pribičević myopically helped Pašić to consolidate the hegemony of the srbijanci Serbs at the eventual expense of his own prečani constituency. With such an inauspicious birth, the constitution itself—henceforth termed, after the saint's day on which it was adopted, the Vidovdan (St. Vitus Day) Constitution[2]—could not elicit the respect that such fundamental charters require for their proper functioning. Interestingly enough, Article 126 required that amendments be passed by three-fifths majorities of future National Assemblies; this was a substantially higher margin than the simple majority that the government had declared adequate for its original adoption.

In partial exoneration of Pašić's conduct on this occasion, one might argue that Yugoslavia itself was at the time still such a new and untried state, that no impressive majority was available for any constitutional plan whatsoever, and that his Vidovdan charter at least had the negative virtue of being congenial to the country's largest community, the Serbs. The

2. This was also the anniversary of the historic Battle of Kossovo in 1389, when medieval Serbia had succumbed to the Ottoman onslaught into the Balkans, and of the assassination of the Habsburg Archduke Franz Ferdinand in 1914, an event regarded by the Yugoslavs as a valiant act of liberation. Ironically, it was to be the same day on which, in 1948, Tito's Yugoslav Communist Party would be expelled from Stalin's Cominform.

opposition to the new constitution was, furthermore, incoherent. The Serbian Agrarians (who were in principle committed to unitarism and now opposed Pašić on quite different grounds), the Communists, the Croats, and the Slovenes could scarcely have agreed on an alternative document. Furthermore, the formal democratic procedures and guarantees of civil liberties outlined and specified in the constitution were well-nigh impeccable: a sovereign unicameral National Assembly, the Skup-ština, of 315 deputies elected for a four-year term by universal, direct, and secret suffrage of all males over twenty-one, with roughly proportional representation of parties; royal approval of legislation but no express veto; freedom and equality of religion and other human rights.

Despite its unpromising political origins, the Vidovdan Constitution need not have proven fatal had not its unitarist legislative provisions been exacerbated by the exceedingly centralistic, frequently brutal, and not always honest administrative and political habits of the bureaucracy and party elite of old Serbia. That bureaucracy and elite proved simply incapable of expanding their outlook from Serbian to Yugoslav horizons, and their license came less from this constitution than from the administrative law of April 28, 1922, which organized the country into thirty-three tightly and centrally controlled departments. The dominance of the Serbs, in turn, was also not the inevitable consequence of the unitarist constitution but was facilitated by the political disunity and dilettantism of the other communities. Indeed, though in the long run their urge for hegemony proved counterproductive, the Serbs' performance was quite remarkable for its self-confidence.

That considerable room for political maneuver remained open even after adoption of the constitution is indicated by the fact that each of the partners in the loveless Serbian marriage of convenience, the Radicals and the Davidović faction of the Democrats, soon made separate overtures to Radić with the clear implication of being prepared to abandon its current mate for a suitable association with him. Radić, however, had meanwhile organized all the Croatian parties into one Croatian Bloc in October, 1921, and he now overplayed his hand. He demanded immediate constitutional revisions, instead of settling for interim yet genuine political concessions, and he solicited the Great Powers early in 1922 to press Belgrade on behalf of Croatian state rights at their forthcoming Genoa Conference. Resented by the Serbs and ignored by the Powers, Radić's petition proved a fiasco. Nevertheless, he still believed, and not without reason, that time was on his side: within the Radical Party, Pašić was being challenged by the milder Stoyan Protić; within the Democratic Party, relations between Davidović and Pribičević were strained; the JMO Muslim auxiliaries to the ruling coalition were quarreling over the above-mentioned departmental organization law, which administratively fragmented their Bosnian redoubt; the outlawing of the Communists in

August, 1921, had left the Croatian Peasants as the only legal opposition party with a strong organization and a purportedly radical program, yet with growing influence among the nationalistic Croatian bourgeoisie.

Buoyed by these developments, Radić spun out his contacts with Davidović and missed an opportunity for a deal with Pašić. Groping for alternatives to his futile appeals for outside intervention and his equally unproductive boycott stance, Radić nevertheless decided to await new parliamentary elections before committing himself. He therefore declined to participate in the legislature until and unless the government fell. Davidović, in turn, did not dare risk an open break with Pribičević and Pašić without the assured support of Croatian votes on the chamber floor. Pašić thus remained master and could look forward to new elections in which to strengthen his own hand at the expense of his divided and faithless partners. Accordingly, he had the king dissolve the Constituent Assembly on December 16, 1922, and schedule new elections for March 18, 1923. He then promptly launched a double-barreled campaign charging the Pribičević faction of the Democrats with alienating Croatia through excessive centralism, and the Davidović wing of the same party with breaches of coalition solidarity through its negotiations with Radić.

Though the rhetoric of the electoral campaign was quite vitriolic, the balloting was free and peaceful. Once again, since the electoral districts were configured according to the 1910 census returns, Serbia was given a demographic bonus. The non-Slavic minorities were now enfranchised. Almost three-fourths of those eligible cast their ballots, thus producing a total vote one-third larger than in the 1920 elections. Though the number of competing parties had also risen, from twenty-two to thirty-three, the number of those achieving parliamentary representation slipped slightly to fourteen. The basic issue of the elections of 1923 was the viability of the Vidovdan Constitution.

As can be seen from the results given in table 36, formally about half the deputies again belonged to parties committed in principle to unitarist constitutional arrangements (the Radicals, Democrats, Agrarians). In practice, however, the Agrarians had to be considered part of the parliamentary opposition to Pašić, and the Davidović wing of the Democrats was seeking an "opening" toward Radić. Furthermore, the Agrarians' Slovene contingent had obviously been punished by that region's electorate, to the benefit of the Populists; presumably it had allowed itself to be bought too cheaply by Pašić to vote for the Vidovdan Constitution, while the faction of the Bosniak JMO that had gone into opposition over the controversial departmental organization law gained overwhelmingly at the expense of its collaborationist wing. Their Džemijet coreligionists in the south, meanwhile, profited from the outlawing of the Communist Party and from the increasing reluctance of the Albanians and Turks to vote for Serbian tickets. Radić's Croatian Peasant Party electorally destroyed its bourgeois competitors, and in the process hastened its own *embourgeoisement*. Pašić's Radicals, in turn, doubled their vote and inflicted major defeats on their Democratic and Agrarian rivals. Davidović's recent vacillation between Radić and Pašić meant that by election time he could neither disavow responsibility for controversial governmental actions nor claim the prestige of real power; the tough-minded electorate of old Serbia punished him accordingly. The 1923 elections thus sharpened the differences among the ethnic communities on the one hand and accelerated the internal political consolidation of each of them on the other. Within each ethnic community, the strongest, most cohesive, and reputedly most nativist party gained at the expense of smaller, looser, and more ecumenical ones.

TABLE 36

SKUPŠTINA ELECTIONS, MARCH 18, 1923

Party	Number of Votes	Percentage of Total Vote	Seats
Serbian Radical	562,213	25.8	108
Serbian Democrat	400,342	18.4	51
Serbian and Slovene Agrarian	164,602	7.6	11*
Croatian Peasant	473,733	21.8	70
Slovene Populist and allies	126,378	5.8	24†
Bosniak Muslim (JMO)	122,494	5.6	18
Džemijet Muslim	71,453	3.3	14
Montenegran Federalist	8,561	0.4	2
Independent Labor (Communist "front")	24,321	1.1	0
Social Democrat	48,337	2.2	2
Croatian bourgeois (four lists)	32,398	1.5	2
German	43,415	2.0	8
Romanian	7,070	0.3	1
Other (sixteen lists)	91,734	4.2	1
Total	2,177,051	100.0	312

*10 Serbian and 1 Slovene.
†21 Slovene Populist and 3 allies.

The realistic Pašić concluded that Radić's newly enhanced power merited greater regard and that Pribičević's treatment of Croatia had proven counterproductive. A solid political machine that was anchored in the villages but mobilized all classes and dominated the national political effort was something the Radicals could recognize and respect, for it matched their own organizational and historical pattern. Pašić, accordingly, now formed an all-Radical interim cabinet supported by the Džemijet Muslims and the Germans. He left four portfolios vacant as a lure and opened negotiations with the three parties that had formed a loose bargaining alliance on the morrow of the elections: the Croatian Peasants, the Slovene Populists, and the Bosniak JMO.

Radić, who was as mercurial as Pašić was cool, characteristically defamed the latter and the king in public while the negotiations were proceeding in confidence. Though begun in a conciliatory spirit and initially marked by some substantive progress, these talks came to naught during the late spring. Radić's demands for a Croatian subrepublic with its own army within the Yugoslav kingdom baffled Pašić. The Radical cadres, for their part, resented Radić's unrestrained allusions to their leaders as "gypsies," "vlachs," "asses," "capitalists," "bandits," which he alternated with flattering appeals to the "uncorrupted" Serbian peasantry. They also held him morally responsible for an abortive attempt to assassinate Păsić on June 28, 1923, the second anniversary of the Vidovdan Constitution. Finally, they were outraged by his open appeal on July 18 for Italian assistance to the Croats in their struggle against the Belgrade government. This last gaucherie had come at a time of acute Italian-Yugoslav tension over the northern Adriatic port of Fiume (Rijeka), an issue on which most Serbs already felt themselves to be running risks for the Croats. At the same time an Italian-financed conspiracy by Croatian émigrés and Macedonian terrorists against the Yugoslav state was being exposed. As his own former secretary was implicated in this plot, which had been organized by ex-Habsburg Croatian officers currently residing in Vienna and Budapest, and as his own parliamentary immunity from arrest was thus jeopardized, Radić fled abroad on July 21, 1923, using a false passport supplied by Hungarian authorities.

Radić's antics naturally provided Pašić with a convenient pretext to break off the discussions with the Croats and just as understandably disgusted the latter's Slovene and Bosniak partners in the negotiation. Even some of Radić's own followers were reported to be disconcerted. Though his tactics were erratic and his rhetoric revolutionary, Radić had remained strategically passive; he had evaded power and shirked responsibility as sinuously in these discussions with Pašić as in those of the previous year with Davidović, while maintaining his party's boycott of the Skupština. Pašić now assigned the four open cabinet portfolios to fellow Radicals, and his party then followed through on its recent electoral and political successes by recouping all the municipal losses it had suffered to the Communists in 1920 when the next series of local elections took place on August 19, 1923. The disillusioned Slovenes and Bosniaks, in turn, formed an opposition bloc with the Serb Democrats at the turn of the year on a platform of constitutional revision to achieve administrative decentralization. But the fragile unity of the Democratic Party quickly sundered on this issue when twelve prečani Serb deputies, led by Pribičević, seceded from Davidović in March, 1924, in protest against this "centrifugal" concession. Pašić astutely made four ministerial chairs available to Pribicević's new Independent Democratic Party. Provided the Croatian Peasants maintained their parliamentary boycott, his government could retain a tenuous majority even though the Germans were now repelled into opposition by the antiminority administration of Pribičević's education ministry.

In Radić's absence, though perhaps with his assent, his deputies were groping toward shrewder stances. Abstention had not only cost their party much political influence, but had also allowed the all-Serbian government to negotiate the Adriatic question with Italy over Croatia's head through the Pact of Rome of January 27, 1924. Toward the end of March, at about the same time as Pribičević's defection from Davidović and cooptation by Pašić, the first group of sixteen Croatian Peasant deputies took their parliamentary seats and joined the opposition bloc. This step would, if it were a harbinger of things to come, erode the Pašić-Pribičević cabinet's majority, but it also implied incipient reconciliation of the Croats to the Yugoslav state and acknowledgment of its political "rules of the game." Pašić wished to test this new situation with fresh parliamentary elections and, upon King Alexander's refusal to dissolve the current Skupština, he resigned in mid-July after first clearing himself with the Croats by arranging for the formal verification of their remaining parliamentary mandates.

Davidović now formed a cabinet on July 27, 1924, composed of his srbijanci wing of the Democrats, Spaho's Bosniak Muslims, and Korošec's Slovene Populists. He indicated that when the Croatian Peasants, who initially merely promised their 'benevolence,' were ready to join, three or four portfolios would be given them. At this point Radić returned home on August 11, after more than a year of controversial and futile efforts abroad to mobilize foreign leverage on behalf of Croatian aspirations, and wrecked Davidović's fragile coalition.

4

A dramatic effort to reverse the ominous polarization of Croats and Serbs was now mounted in the mid-1920s—an effort that proved, alas, abortive as Radić showed himself temperamentally incapable of governmental responsibility and as the death of Pašić led to the fragmentation of the main Serbian party. After a brief stopover in Vienna upon his flight from Yugoslavia the previous summer, Radić had arrived in London on August 18, 1923, and had been snubbed by both His Majesty's Government and the Establishment when he sought their intervention in Yugoslav affairs. He thereupon returned to Vienna on December 2, intending to convene there a "world congress of oppressed minorities," which was promptly barred by the Austrian government. During this Viennese interlude, Radić also consulted with two of his deputies from Zagreb and apparently assented to a more flexible and yet more consistent Croatian political line of working through and in the Skupština with the Davidović-Korošec-Spaho opposition bloc. At the same time, however, he also informally concerted with the Internal Macedonian Revolutionary Organization (IMRO) and with the Communist International (Comintern) on a program of Balkan federation and worker-peasant alliance. When the Austrian authorities demanded that he cease his political activities or leave, Radić vanished from Vienna on May 29, 1924, to resurface spectacularly in Soviet Russia on June 2. Jubilantly welcomed in Moscow, he requested that his Croatian Peasant Party be admitted to the Krestintern, the Peasant International analogue to the Comintern. His application was duly accepted on July 1, even though Radić had appended to it the following, quite un-Bolshevik, conditions: (a) his party would employ only peaceful means of struggle; (b) in Yugoslavia, the peasantry, not the proletariat, must be acknowledged as the "first political factor"; (c) Croatia's political goal was to become a peasant republic within Yugoslavia; (d) the Krestintern was understood to be independent of the Comintern.

Moscow's welcome was based on the consideration that Radić's was undoubtedly the most powerful party ever snared by the Krestintern. He, in turn, was happy to have snubbed the Prague-based Green International, which was dominated by the Czechoslovak Agrarian Party and hence in effect allied with the Yugoslav government through the Little Entente. The romance, however, soon cooled as the Bolsheviks came to recognize in Radić an incorrigible *narodnik* and he saw through their control of the ostensibly independent Krestintern. Quitting Moscow quite suddenly on August 4, Radić returned via Vienna and quietly slipped back into Zagreb on August 11, 1924. His uneasy but obedient party had, on August 3, endorsed his affiliation to the Krestintern and had then held its breath for the reactions of the international community and the Belgrade authorities. In Yugoslavia, meanwhile, the Slovene leader Korošec had emerged as the country's most prestigious alternative to Pašić. His rise was due less to the strength of his party than to his seriousness and skill, which contrasted so vividly with the erraticism of Radić and the feuding of Davidović and Pribičević.

Upon returning home, Radić endorsed his deputies' decision to support, without joining, the Davidović-Korošec-Spaho bloc that two weeks earlier had formed a government. Offering the provocative rationale that this was a fine transitional regime toward ultimate peasant-worker power, Radić further undermined it by intemperate and incendiary attacks on the bureaucracy, the army, and even the dynasty. Denouncing Pašić's Radicals as "an insurance consortium against the power of the law," Radić warned that any attempt to return them to power would provoke civil war. He again rejected the Vidovdan Constitution, attacked the country's French and Little Entente allies, demanded that the army be reduced to half its size and reorganized so that the Croatian recruits would be garrisoned in Croatia, and intimated that should Croatia be forced by

Serbian intransigence to secede from Yugoslavia, she was assured of immediate Soviet recognition and aid. By October 8, 1924, these antics had provoked the resignation of the war minister, General Stevan Hadžić, the king's *homme de confiance* within the Davidović cabinet, who refused to be further identified with a ministry that accepted such dubious support. Priding itself as a government of reconciliation, the Davidović-Korošec-Spaho coalition could not survive the general's defection. On November 6 it gave way to a resurgent Pašić-Pribičević cabinet which now easily persuaded the king to dissolve the Skupština on November 10, scheduled new elections for February 8, 1925, and at the turn of the year arrested Radić, who was now in hiding, with five of his associates under the provisions of the same law that had authorized the suppression of the Communist Party in 1921. The charge was seditious collusion with Comintern and other hostile, i.e., Bulgarian, Hungarian, and Macedonian, agents. Shortly before his arrest, Radić had denounced Davidović and the king for cowardice and undue deference toward Pašić and the Serbian generals. Yet he had surely played into the hands of the Radicals and the military. Indeed, it appears that Radić had given a convenient and plausible pretext for toppling Davidović to the Belgrade čaršija, which had been rendered uneasy by that premier's initial probings into the manipulations and irregularities of his predecessor's regime.

In the ensuing electoral campaign, each major party sought to induce defections from the ranks of its rivals by imputing corruption to their leaderships while simultaneously seeking to consolidate its own base of support. Pašić, who was, indeed, quite vulnerable to such allegations through the dubious behavior of his son, managed to turn them around when a financial scandal conveniently surfaced within the Croatian Peasant Party, inducing a few secondary leaders to desert Radić. (However, there was no significant palpable electoral effect.) Pašić also concentrated his campaign in the area south of the Una-Sava-Danube line and was relatively easy on Davidović, presumably so as not to weaken him too much to Pribičević's benefit. The adroit Pašić preferred to have these two balance each other rather than see either grow too strong. Pašić also vetoed Pribičević's motion to prosecute the arrested Croatian leaders, lest they be transformed into martyrs. He preferred to let his insinuations about 'Comintern collusion' fester within the uneasy Radić apparatus, though he knew them to be false or at any rate obsolete, especially as they also enabled Pašić to project himself in the West as the defender of the Balkans against Bolshevism. In any event, Radić's bluff was called: no outside power had protested his arrest, and no internal forces had responded with civil war to Pašić's return as premier. Pribičević, for his part, concentrated his campaign among the prečani Serbs in a style that was at once clumsy toward the Croats and brutal to Davidović. The latter, in turn, posed as the "national conciliator."

The 1925 elections were characterized by greater police pressure in areas of mixed population than those of 1920 or 1923. Nevertheless, 77 percent of the electorate voted. Thirty-three parties again competed but only ten won representation this time. The most significant casualty was the Džemijet Party, which was more-or-less forced to merge itself into the Serbian Radical Party.

TABLE 37

SKUPŠTINA ELECTIONS, FEBRUARY 8, 1925

Party	Number of Votes	Percentage of Total Vote	Seats
Serbian Radical }	1,040,616	43.4	141
Serbian Independent Democrat }			22
Serbian Democrat	285,741	11.8	37
Serbian Agrarian	117,922	4.8	4
Croatian Peasant	545,466	22.3	67
Slovene Populist	121,923	5.0	20
Bosniak Muslim (JMO)	132,296	5.4	15
Montenegran Federalist	8,873	0.3	3
Independent Labor (Communist "front")	16,330	0.6	0
Social Democrat	23,457	0.9	0
German	45,172	1.9	5
Hungarian	11,059	0.4	0
Other	88,742	3.2	1
Total	2,437,597	100.0	315

As can be seen from table 37, again Pašić and Radić were the big victors within their respective communities. The Serbs continued to reward the former for his consummate political skills, while the Croats still extended to the latter their indulgence, despite his seeming aversion to power and his futile flirtations with outsiders. Pribičević had not done as well as expected, despite administrative pressures on his behalf in the country's northern half. Davidović had held his own in old Serbia, thanks, in part, to a refusal by many former Džemijet voters to accept their leaders' enforced cooptation into the Radical Party, and had emerged, on balance, with his prestige as enhanced as Pribičević's had been clipped. The Agrarians, on the other hand, were almost annihilated. The Pašić-Pribičević coalition had been returned with an adequate parliamentary majority. As in past elections, opposition to the regime had expressed itself more vividly in ethnic than in social cleavages and solidarities. But a stunning reversal of the patterns of past coalitions was now to occur.

On March 27, 1925, three weeks after the convening of the new Skupština, Pavle Radić (Stjepan's nephew) appeared unexpectedly on its floor to make a speech that was as engaging in tone as it was sensational in content.

Drafted by his imprisoned uncle, it caught the rest of the Croatian leadership by surprise: it announced Croatian endorsement of the Yugoslav state ("we are at home here"), recognition of the ruling dynasty (the Croatian Peasant Party would delete the adjective "republican" from its name and program), and acceptance of the Vidovdan Constitution (with hopes for its legal emendation). Denying any Croatian hostility toward the Yugoslav army or obligations toward the Krestintern and Comintern, and repudiating secession, Pavle Radić also indicated that Pribičević, rather than Pašić, was now his party's particular *bête noire*.

This speech signaled a reversal of domestic alliances. Early in April, Pavle Radić had two conciliatory audiences with the king. The elected Croatian deputies soon took their seats in the Skupština, simultaneously hinting their readiness to be still more accommodating. Finally, on July 18, 1925, the charges against the six imprisoned Croatian Peasant leaders were quashed. On the same day they joined the Serbian Radicals in a two-party coalition government, which Stjepan Radić entered in person as minister of education on November 17. Radić's readiness to desert his former colleagues of the Davidović-Korošec-Spaho bloc had been signaled in his nephew's catalytic speech of March 27, in which "the clericals," by which term he certainly meant Korošec's Populists and possibly also Spaho's Muslims, had been reproached for their allegedly hypocritical *Realpolitik* at Croatia's expense. Pašić's dropping of Pribičević—Radić vetoed a tripartite coalition—embittered the prečani Serb leader, who felt himself treated as Schiller's "Moor who had done his work and could now go." Though Pašić remained mistrustful of Radić's erraticism, he nevertheless preferred to govern with a non-Serb partner since he believed his own Radicals to be the only truly valid Serbian party. Somewhat more intriguing is the evaluation of Radić's motives. Having earlier sabotaged the pliable Davidović, why did he now choose to be reconciled to the tougher Pašić? He appears to have erroneously persuaded himself that the Radicals, unlike the Democrats, had remained a true peasant party whose current coalition with his own had at last given Yugoslavia a government of the peasant class that alone had the moral strength to transmute ethnic tension into social harmony.

King Alexander, meanwhile, was eager to be reconciled to the Croatian people and had pressed the sober, and initially cautious, Pašić toward unusual generosity in responding to the original Radić feelers. In return for acknowledging the state, its dynasty, and its constitution, the Croatian Peasant Party was given: (a) control over administrative appointments in the country's northern half, expressly including the authority to purge Pribičević's incumbent protégés; (b) endorsement of its demands for certain innovative socioeconomic legislation, including changes in budgetary, judicial, procuratorial, educational, pensionary, and local governmental policies and systems; (c) standardization of tax collection and of land-reform implementation. On August 15, 1925, the Croatian nation showed its appreciation by giving a triumphal reception to the royal family on its first visit to Zagreb for the celebration of the millennium of the founding of the medieval Croatian state. Though he would soon reopen his feud with Pašić and the Radicals, Radić thereafter never again turned on the king.

Alas, Pǎsić's wariness concerning Radić's capacity to veer from the politics of opposition to the politics of participation was soon confirmed. Radić entered the coalition with his characteristic impetuosity and hyperbole; for example, he recommended that the Croats "free themselves from Rome" in order to be reconciled religiously to the Serbs, and that both communities adopt the Arabic script in order to be integrated with their Muslim fellows. And he soon proved as perverse within the government as he had formerly been outside it. He publicly referred to his fellow ministers as "swine," "gamblers," "gangsters," "tyrants," and "foreign agents"; he embarrassed the government's delicate relations with Italy, gratuitously demanded new elections, and stoked a campaign to destroy the premier through allegations, which were probably valid, of corruption against his son Radomir Pǎsić. This long train of erratic behavior aroused mistrust in all the non-Croatian political camps, especially as Radić's own party was now practicing nepotism as egregiously in its bailiwicks as the Radicals were in theirs. Indeed, Korošec now seized the opportunity, in a speech of February 8, 1926, to demand within Slovenia the same administrative power and autonomy vis-à-vis Zagreb as Radić had extracted for himself within the country's northern half in the previous spring's negotiations with Belgrade. All in all, Radić's highly developed talents for opposition proved a hindrance once he was in the government, especially a coalition government. Unable to resist the temptation to score demogogic advantages at the expense of his partners, Radić's participation seriously weakened the cabinet. In sum, the Pašić-Radić coalition proved as barren as previous combinations and achieved little for the peasantry. Though this was largely Radić's fault, Pašić also bears considerable responsibility. Despite Radić's erstwhile illusions to the contrary, neither Pǎsić nor his party were any longer truly interested in social or economic reform, nor were they amenable to taking up the burden of Croatia's anti-Italian anxieties in foreign policy.

On April 4, 1926, Pašić resigned the premiership until such time as his accused son purged himself of the charges of corruption. He hoped to control his successor, the pliant Nikola Uzunović, through the executive machinery of his Radical Party and eventually to resume the premiership. But he died on the eve of his planned comeback, on December 10, 1926. Radić, meanwhile, had fired so many demagogic attacks at his fellow ministers that they ousted him from his education portfolio on April 15. Yet, he consented to continued participation of his party colleagues in the cabinet, presumably realizing that the opposition bloc was now too skeptical of his reliability to welcome him back into its midst and that his own followers were reluctant to relinquish office. With the two strongest personalities of its constituent parties, Pašić and Radić, thus pulling wires from the outside, the Uzunović cabinet barely staggered through the rest of 1926. The ineffectual performance of these Croatian Peasant-Serbian Radical governments of 1925-26 discredited parliamentarism in the eyes of the public, to the ultimate benefit of the king. Though his perspective was often narrow, Pašić had been the one politician with sufficient authority to block a royal or military dictatorship, but the very totality of his mastery had thwarted the growth of able young heirs. After his death royal influence, which was often exercised through politically minded generals, expanded rapidly.

The Radicals had again scored successes in local elections of August 15, 1926, and January 23, 1927. Chagrined at being defeated in the ethnically mixed Vojvodina in the second series of these local elections, Radić charged fraud and announced that his Croats would retain their cabinet seats but would vote against the government's upcoming budget. Uzunović promptly resigned and on February 1, 1927, formed a Serbian Radical-Slovene Populist coalition government from which the Croatian Peasants were unceremoniously excluded, thus ending this vivid but sterile experiment in Croatian participation in government. Simultaneously, the party system in general began to disintegrate. In the absence of Pašić's commanding presence, the Radicals were now wracked by factionalism, with none of the surviving leaders any longer interested in a dialogue with Radić. The latter's Croatian Peasants were suffering from a small but painful trickle of defections of second-echelon leaders, as well as from the repudiation of Radić's latest feelers toward Korošec's Slovene Populists and Spaho's Bosniak Muslims. Of these two parties, the Slovenes, as mentioned, had joined Uzunović's coalition government while the Muslims had achieved an accord with Davidović's Serbian Democrats.

In the bitter recriminations that ensued from the making and breaking of these several *combinazione* came the first intimations of dictatorship. On February 26, 1927, a respected Croatian backbencher alleged that the real culprits manipulating the crisis were not the Radical parliamentary leaders but rather the "secret forces" of the royal palace and its favorite clique, the "White Hand" officers. Radić, whose strategy called for sparing the king and attacking the Radicals, disavowed his follower, but the fat was now in the fire with the airing of this hitherto taboo theme.

Domestic politics were also now thwarting Yugoslav foreign policy and this, in turn, further undermined the government's viability. The Croats persistently blocked Yugoslav ratification of the Nettuno Conventions of July 20, 1925, with Italy, which were intended to regulate the economic claims and consular privileges of each country's private citizens on the territory of the other. Since there were far more Italian investments in Yugoslavia—especially in Dalmatia—than vice-versa, the Croats objected that the negotiated arrangements were inherently quasi-colonial; the Serbs retorted that it was irresponsible to provoke a powerful Italy over a secondary issue. The Italians having long since ratified the agreements, Mussolini now disgustedly abandoned his intermittent interest in a détente with Yugoslavia and swung to a persistently hostile diplomacy, concluding "encircling" agreements with Albania on November 27, 1926, and with Hungary on April 5, 1927.

Personally bewildered and politically exhausted by these blows, Uzunović, who had reconstructed his cabinets four times and survived twelve crises in as many months, gave way on April 17, 1927, to a triumvirate of Velimir Vukičević (leader of a competing Radical faction), Vojislav Marinković (similarly a dissident factionalist within Davidović's Democratic Party), and Mehmet Spaho of the Bosniak Muslims. As neither of its two Serbian members controlled his own party, this "coalition of personalities" owed its existence to royal favor. To rescue it from parliamentary censure and ouster, the king quickly prorogued and then dissolved the Skupština, allowing Vukičević et al. to govern without legislative scrutiny for most of the spring and summer and then to "arrange" the next general elections on September 11, 1927.

Except in Serbia, where the fratricidal strife within the Radical Party provoked excitement, the electoral campaign was apathetic. The peasants were too busy with the harvest, too skeptical of the system, and too cynical about its corruption to pay much attention. Conversely, these elections were also marked by more chicanery and pressure than were those of 1920, 1923, and 1925. The Radicals were split between Vukičević's "opportunists," Uzunović's "loyalists," and a group of nostalgic "true Pašićites" led by Marko Trifković. The Vukičevićites concluded an electoral pact with the Slovene Populists, promising them the administrative unification of the Ljubljana and Maribor departments so as to unite all Yugoslav Slovenes into one governmental subunit in return for postelection parliamentary support. The Democrats were allied with the Bosniak Muslims and had sought to patch up their internal rivalry between Davidović and Marinković, though the latter's "disloyal" collusion with Vukičević since April rankled with the older leader. The Croatian Peasants and the Independent Democrats were now isolated from all their major former partners.

The percentage of the electorate that took the trouble to vote slipped from the 77 of 1925 to 69, declining most precipitously in the Croatian areas. The results for the twenty-seven competing electoral lists are given in table 38.

TABLE 38

Skupština Elections, September 11, 1927

Party	Number of Votes	Percentage of Total Vote	Seats
Serbian Radical	742,111	31.9	112*
Serbian Independent Democrat	199,040	8.6	22
Serbian Democrat	381,784	16.4	61
Serbian Agrarian	136,076	5.9	9
Croatian Peasant	367,570	15.8	61
Slovene Populist	137,993	5.9	21
Bosniak Muslim (JMO)	132,326	5.7	18
Montenegran Federalist	5,153	0.2	1
Independent Labor (Communist "front")	43,114	1.9	0
Social Democrat	24,102	1.0	1
Croatian bourgeois (four lists)	47,949	2.1	2
German	49,849	2.2	6
Hungarian	3,539	0.1	0
Romanian	4,654	0.2	0
Other (eight lists)	49,410	2.1	1
Total	2,324,670	100.0	315

*85 supported Vukičević, 10 Uzunović, and 17 Trifković.

Their internal feud had obviously been costly to the Radicals, but the results were nevertheless a personal victory for Vukičević who, though in no sense Pašić's designated dauphin, had brazenly maneuvered himself into control of the country's dominant party. The Uzunović coterie now immediately folded its tents, and Trifković's "true Pašićites," after briefly toying with overtures from Pribičević's Independent Democrats, soon also acknowledged Vukičević's leadership and merged again into his Radical Party. The Democrats, in turn, had gained at the expense of the Radicals, but within their party, too, the upstart Marinković had over-powered the veteran leader Davidović. The control that Korošec, Spaho, and Pribičević exercised over their relatively inelastic Slovene, Bosniak, and prečani Serb electorates had remained solid.

Fatigue and disillusionment among the Croats, on the other hand, had cost Radić substantially, more in terms of votes (one-third) than of seats, in comparison to 1925. The moderate Croatian bourgeois groups, the ex-treme nationalists, and the underground Communists who had backed him in previous elections now defected; once again Radić's base was reduced to the villages, where he remained politically impregnable. Though his various permutations—intransigent boycott, fishing for Western and Soviet support, oppositional alliances, governmental par-ticipation, attacks on his partners as well as his enemies—had all been equally barren, and though his party's ruling directorate had obviously come to be dominated over the past decade by men whose perspective was that of the intelligentsia and the bourgeoisie, nevertheless "his" peasants still backed Radić. Only now their support was an expression more of sheer loyalty than of expectations. So far they had no catastrophic economic grievances; harvests had been good and exports high since 1924, and the terms of trade had not yet precipitously turned against agricultural commodities, as they would with the coming depression. One might, indeed, argue that Radić's mercurial demagoguery had stolen potential Communist thunder among the Croatian peasantry.

5

Despite the atmosphere of seeming apathy in which they were held, the elections of 1927 were soon followed by a sharp revival of interethnic antagonism, which reached such intensity that it culminated the next year in lethal violence on the floor of the Skupština and shortly thereafter in the demise of the now paralyzed parliamentary system. Initially the Vukićević cabinet rested on a seemingly comfortable majority of 218 Radicals, Democrats, Slovenes, Bosniaks, and Germans in a 315-member chamber. Yet the campaign and the elections of 1927 had failed to clear the air and had only confirmed the resentments of the two excluded ethnic political camps, the Croats and the prečani Serbs. Accordingly, after a decade of ferocious enmity their respective leaders Radić and Pribičević were reconciled on the morrow of the elections and concluded what they termed a defensive entente of the country's "European" and "civilized" northern half against further exploitation by the "Balkan primitives" of the south. Not only did this geographical schema ignore the Slovenes' participation in the current as well as previous regimes, but the new-found indignation of Pribičević, who had been so ruthless from 1918 to 1925, over current administrative coercion, was also somewhat ironic. His motives would appear to have been a mixture: revenge on the Radicals for having "dumped" him in 1925; resentment of their monopolization of power and patronage; the realization that despite surface appearances they were now less united and hence more vulnerable than the Croatian Peasants; a conviction that the admittedly unstable Radić was not, after all, a traitor; and a genuine conversion to the view that administrative centralization had become counterproductive. In style and tactics Pribičević had always lacked a sense of proportion, and he now threw himself into a campaign of parliamentary obstructionism and civil agitation with the same reckless abandon as had earlier characterized his hounding of the Croats when he was in power.

Early in 1928 there appeared the first major cracks in the governing coalition as the internal feuds within its Radical and Democratic parties resumed. King Alexander sought to stabilize the situation by attempting to wean Radić away from his oppositional pact with Pribičević and bringing him into the government. (Simultaneously the king flattered the Croatian people by naming his second son after their medieval hero-ruler Tomislav.) Though tempted, Radić decided he was not being offered enough and made the prophetic but premature countersuggestion that the king install a military regime: "Your Majesty—only the sabre is honest." Vukičević thereupon reshuffled his government at the end of February, 1928, and the Radić-Pribičević team resumed its campaign to bring him to his knees by rendering the Skupština unworkable. Masters at the tactics of parliamentary obstruction, their vituperative attacks soon reduced the chamber to chaos. Particularly wounding was their standard allegation that intrigue, corruption, nepotism, brutality, and chicanery were the intrinsic vices of prewar Serbia's Byzantine and Ottoman heritage, and the implication that their own communities had been better off in the supposedly more civilized Habsburg Empire, The rage thereby provoked among the Serbian elite from south of the Una-Sava-Danube line, superimposed on the established frustrations engendered by the unresolved quarrel over the Nettuno Conventions, and now exacerbated by the first effects of the world agricultural crisis, all combined during the spring of 1928 into a highly combustible mixture.

During May and June, street demonstrations in the towns of Croatia, Dalmatia, and Slovenia against the Nettuno Conventions took on a serious antiregime character; on June 13 and 14, insults screamed between Serb and Croatian deputies on the use of the cyrillic or latin alphabets in the Skupština records brought that body's sessions to a halt; on June 14 and 17, a new Radical journal, which was probably subsidized by the government, editorialized on the need to liquidate Radić and Pribičević. On June 19, Radić, in the course of a heated exchange with the Radical backbencher Puniša Račić, alluded to the Radicals in general as "cattle," whereupon one of them predicted that blood would yet be shed on the floor of the chamber. Many of the Radical deputies elected in September, 1927, including Puniša Račić, were "new" men, handpicked by Vukičević from among Serbia's intensely nationalistic veterans of the Balkan and First World Wars as his personal cohort for capturing control of the party away from its elders. They had little knowledge of, and less patience for, the niceties of parliamentary procedure.

On the morning of June 20, 1928, Radić's fellow Croatian deputies, fearing violence, sought to dissuade him from attending that day's Skupština session, but he insisted on putting in an appearance though he promised to abstain from further debate. Puniša Račić demanded on a point of personal privilege the right to reply to Radić's allegations of the previous day. A Croatian deputy interrupted with a shouted insult. When the presiding officer failed to elicit an apology, Račić whipped out a revolver and shot the offender and four other Croats, including Radić. Two were killed on the spot, two recovered, and Radić eventually succumbed on August 8. The Croatian cause now had the most potent martyrs possible.[3]

Dedicated but impulsive, energetic yet muddled, innocent albeit crafty, learned and nevertheless anti-intellectual, Stjepan Radić had been a man of many convictions and had pursued several inconsistent strategies. His ideological commitments had been alternatively republican, monarchist, austrophobe, austrophile, slavophile, "western," Catholic, and anticlerical, and his political stances had run the gamut from pacificism through militancy, abstentionism, ministerialism, Western appeals, Krestintern leverage, ex-Habsburger oppositional solidarity, to a final recommendation for royal and military purge-rule. Yet all his fluctuations had been imbued with one constant style: demagogic flattery of, and subjective devotion to, the Croatian peasantry, which reciprocated with total loyalty to his person. Radić conceded to being carried away by "oceanic" feelings when addressing his peasants. The Croatian village was his intuitive element; away from it, he was a helpless Anteus. Vaguely refusing to state his ultimate terms in Belgrade, and incorrigibly subverting every interim arrangement for easing the Croatian-Serb dispute—including the very coalitions in which he participated—Radić had met his political match in Pašić, who was, by the 1920s, still capable of mastering power but no longer up to the mark of envisioning what to do with it. Radić, in short, became the prisoner as well as the master of his political style—a style that precluded either compromise or revolution and hence aggravated the Yugoslav political system's chronic paralysis.

Granted that Radić, together with Pribičević, bore a heavy share of responsibility for the political atmosphere that had made his murder possible, the Vukičević regime also now failed grievously in its response to this tragedy, treating it simply as the unfortunate outcome of a private vendetta and thus pouring salt into Croatian wounds. Radić's political heir, Vladko Maček, and his last ally, Pribičević, withdrew their delegations from the Skupština, challenging its right to continue representing the nation. Early in July, the Radical finance minister forced a reluctant cabinet to resign; the issue was not the Skupština shootings, but his inability to raise an Anglo-American loan due to the chamber's failure to

3. The assassin Račić, a native of Novibazar, had fought for Serbia as a volunteer in both Balkan Wars. Though a member of the "Union or Death" conspiratorial organization, he had testified against its leader Apis-Dimitrijević at the rigged Salonika Trial in 1917 and thus identified himself with Regent Alexander's "White Hand" counterconspiracy against Apis' "Black Hand." Elected to the Skupština with the "Vukičević levy" of September, 1927, he always considered his assassination of Radić to have been a patriotic act. After the shootings, he walked out of the Skupština building, cabled a manifesto to his Montenegran constituency, and then turned himself in to the police. Sentenced in July, 1929, to twenty years, which he served under remarkably easy conditions at Požarevac jail, Račić was released early in World War II but was recaptured and executed at war's end by Tito's Partisans. The editor of the incendiary journal that had agitated for Radić's liquidation and had justified it after the event was himself murdered on August 5, 1928, during an unwise visit to Zagreb.

ratify the Nettuno Conventions. No political leader proved sufficiently strong, responsible, or visionary to utilize the Skupština tragedy for a cathartic purge of the country's tempers.

Though King Alexander was later alleged by Radić's widow (and ultimately by some Titoist propagandists) to have been implicated in a plot to assassinate her husband, the victim himself had blamed only some Serbian army officers and Radical politicians. On his death-bed he had said that the shootings seven weeks earlier had "wiped out the constitution; now there is nothing left except the people and the king." In contrast to the Serbian politicians, indeed, Alexander had immediately recognized the assassinations as entailing a state, and not merely a cabinet, crisis that demonstrated that the political machinery inherited from prewar Serbia was inadequate for governing a Yugoslavia five times the size of old Serbia. The king's first reaction was the extraordinary one of offering to the Croats and the prečani Serbs the peaceful severance of their territories from Yugoslavia. Such a solution, he declared, would be preferable to the federalization that they had been demanding since the Radić-Pribičević reconciliation of 1927, and it had, he purported, a model in the peaceful separation of Norway from Sweden in 1905.

Whether or not the king expected his proposal to be entertained seriously is a moot point. Maček and Pribičević, fearing an Italo-Hungarian partition of the severed territories, declined it and reverted to their demands for a federalistic renegotiation of the constitutional and political bases of the Yugoslav state after new elections to identify representative negotiators within its several historic units. Apprehensive lest elections in the immediate aftermath of the assassinations degenerate into an explosion of tribal passions, and averse to federalization (which the Radicals, furthermore, categorically refused to consider), Alexander invited the same General Stevan Hadžić whose resignation as war minister under Radić's provocations had brought down the Davidović government in the autumn of 1924 to form a suprapartisan cabinet. Though in conformity with Radić's recent advice, this attempt to entrust the government to the supposedly "honest sabre" was premature. On July 27, 1928, the Slovene priest and politician Korošec formed a cabinet that essentially reconstituted Vukičević's coalition but in which for the first, and only, time in interwar Yugoslav history the premier was *not* a srbijanci Serb.

Korošec called for the Skupština, which had been adjourned early in July, to convene on August 1 in Belgrade. On that day its Croatian Peasant and Independent Democratic deputies (a Maček-Pribičević coalition) assembled as a counterparliament in Zagreb and resolved that the Skupština murders had "annulled" both the Vidovdan Constitution and Croatia's union with Serbia and had rendered necessary the renegotiation of both these arrangements. In Belgrade, meanwhile, Korošec managed to squeeze ratification of the Nettuno Conventions out of his rump Skupština by a vote of 158 "ayes" to 157 "nays" and absentees on August 13, 1928. Diplomatically, this was too belated and anticlimactic to mollify Mussolini: domestically, it only added to the Croats' sense of outrage. In other areas, Korošec was immobilized by re-emerging schisms within the Radical Party, his coalition's largest member, which aborted a trial plan for decentralization sponsored by this intelligent and energetic premier whose status as a Roman Catholic priest might possibly have given him some leverage in Croatia. The second half of 1928 thus degenerated into a chronic orgy of demonstrations, demagoguery, and cross-charges, both within the government and between the government in Belgrade and the "Aventine secession" in Zagreb, with each coalition expectantly awaiting the other's disintegration and with the opposition cheered by successes in communal and municipal elections in Bosnia-Hercegovina and Dalmatia on October 28. The tenth anniversary of the founding of the Yugoslav state on December 1 evoked clashes between students and police in Zagreb, in the course of which about a dozen persons were killed in the city's main square. When the cabinet Democrats, concerned to protect their flank from the oppositional Independent Democrats, thereupon demanded a purge of administrative cadres in Zagreb and the transfer of the interior ministry to themselves, and then compounded their pressure with demagogic public demands that the peasants be indemnified for the current poor harvest with substantial cash disbursements from the almost empty state treasury, Korošec resigned on December 30, 1928.

In the round of consultations that now ensued, the Zagreb coalition, having outlasted its Belgrade rival, adopted a tough stance. Maček regarded himself as the spokesman for a virtually independent Croatia and was conscious that Radić's murder had again rallied the Croatian nation, including the urban defectors of 1927, solidly behind his party; he refused to negotiate with anyone other than the king, of whom he demanded separate legislatures and separate administrations for Yugo-slavia's constituent parts, which were to be tied together only in a personal dynastic union. His partner Pribičević also recommended federalization, but under the aegis of another nationally elected con-stituent assembly. The Serbian Radicals rejected these formulae, offering none of their own. The king, who had made a hurried trip to Paris in November to assure a nervous French government of the viability of its Yugoslav protégé and perhaps to solicit its preliminary assent for drastic measures to prevent his country's feared disintegration, thereupon estab-lished a royal dictatorship on January 6, 1929, the Orthodox Christmas Eve. Announcing that "the time has come when there must no longer be any intermediaries between the people and the king," Alexander sus-pended the Vidovdan Constitution and the civil liberties it guaranteed, dissolved the Skupština, the trade unions, and those political parties that based themselves on religious or ethnic criteria, and replaced elected local authorities with his own appointees. The commander of the royal guard, General Petar Živković, was made premier and was directly and exclusively responsible to the king.[4] The king, in turn, proclaimed himself to be henceforth the source of all legislative and administrative authority.

The compounded problems of ethnic particularism, politico-administrative myopia, and economic vulnerability had finally overwhelmed the country's parliamentary experiment. Yugoslavia had proven too big and too diffuse, and it had come into existence too "suddenly" for the capacities of the Serb elite. The Croats, in turn, had behaved too negatively, too carpingly, too erratically to be of help. Clique government had provoked the opposition into irresponsibility which had then corroded the hopes for conciliation of even the most reasonable Serbs.

6

The decade that now closed with the proclamation of the royal dictatorship divides into four political phases: the constitutional and organizational struggles of 1918-21; then the period of polarization of the Serbs and the Croats, 1921-25; followed by that of the disintegration of the Serbian parties, 1925-27; and concluding with the restructured polarization of Croats plus prečani Serbs versus the others, 1927-28. During the entire decade no Skupština had lived out its allotted quadrennial lifespan. There had been twenty-four different cabinets, only one of which had been ousted by a direct parliamentary vote, all the others succumbing to internal maneuvers and intrigues. These frequent ministerial shuffles among and within a large number of parties arose out of contests over patronage rather than principle. No cabinet ever staked its life on a legislative program. The enemies of yesterday would be the coalition partners of tomorrow, including the accuser and accused in the many loudly trumpeted, but quietly buried, "corruption" cases. Commercial and industrial interests could generally depend on all parties to favor, or at least to heed, them, but bureaucratic patronage went primarily to Serbs from prewar Serbia, to Slovenes, and, for menial but sought-after jobs, to Bosniaks. Srbijanci Serbs furthermore monopolized the control of the armed forces, since northerners were suspect as ex-Austrians, and of the state banking system. Even when participating in cabinets, Croats and prečani Serbs felt themselves, in Radić's words, to be "not *in* the government, but attached *to* it." The bureaucracy was swollen, poorly paid, partially corrupt, and of a lower technical competence than that of Austro-Hungary. The least competent bureaucrats were often 'exiled' to the most sensitive areas, such as Macedonia and the Vojvodina, with disastrous political consequences. The first two elections were marred by

4. Živković was one of the conspirators behind the coup of 1903 against Serbia's last Obrenović rulers and subsequently Alexander's "White Hand" accomplice in the Salonika affair of 1917 that liquidated the "Black Hand" leader Apis-Dimitrijević.

gerrymandering, and the last two by police pressures. Tax assessments and collections were heavier in the ex-Habsburg lands than in the old-Serbian areas, and little progress was made toward unification of the several legal systems the new state had inherited.

All this political instability and legislative and administrative inadequacy was, of course, a general reflection of the country's retarded and uneven socioeconomic levels, and a particular index of the non-Serbs' disunity and inconstancy. The result was a legislature that was formally sovereign but ineffectual and a deadlocked political system in which power gravitated toward the čaršija clique. In a country where over three-fourths of the population was engaged in agriculture, the peasants had become well-nigh unrepresented, as even the nominally peasantist parties were infiltrated and captured—in both personnel and policy terms—by the bourgeoisie, the bureaucracy, and the intelligentsia. Police brutality, ethnic demagoguery, and credit manipulation ("the peasant in debt is the safest voter") kept the peasants in line. The workers, in turn, heavily employed in foreign-owned extractive industries, had no spokesman at all in this political system. Constitutional and ethnic politics absorbed so much energy and begat such ill-will that insufficient time and vigor were available for pressing social and economic problems. In turn,

> As the productive forces of the country were insufficiently developed, the state was not only the chief employer of all salaried people, but also the most important and the quickest source of enrichment. Thus, the conquest and retention of state power became the supreme objective of such a [čaršija] group for economic purposes as well as political. . . . The service for the state, business with the state, and abuse of state power were the primary sources of wealth.[5]

The question henceforth was to determine whether the Yugoslav experiment had gone awry simply in consequence of the institutional and political errors of 1921 and later years, or whether the unification of 1918 itself was fated to prove abortive. Except in Hungary, Italy, and the Communist world—and even here there were varying nuances at various times—European public and government opinion regarded the prevention of Yugoslavia's disintegration as a European desideratum. This explains the equanimity, and even relief, with which Alexander's dictatorship was accepted abroad; it also explains the West's earlier coolness toward Radić's centrifugal tactics. Nor had the Croats themselves categorically or ideologically repudiated the Yugoslav idea. Maček initially welcomed the royal coup for its abolition of the Vidovdan Constitution and promise of a clean slate. He only turned against it later when his party was dissolved with the others, and when Croatia, in common with all the historic units, was territorially fragmented in an administrative revolution

---

5. Jozo Tomasevich, *Peasants, Politics, and Economic Change in Yugoslavia* (Stanford: Stanford University Press, 1955), pp. 246-47.

that was intended by the king to replace his peoples' inherited ethnic-provincial loyalties with a new Yugoslav consciousness.

7

Capitalizing on the pervasive public disgust with parliamentary paralysis and ministerial instability, the royal dictatorship launched itself with a show of political energy and a series of overdue and well-received administrative reforms. Four ministries (religious cults, land reform, public health, post and telegraph) were merged into cognate ones (respectively, justice, agriculture, social welfare, and public works). Fifty diplomats and thirty-six generals were retired, and many government bureaus pruned of both their incompetents and their political undesirables. Graft and nepotism were at least reduced, and government showed more concern for economic life in the form of cadastral surveys, swamp drainage, and new investments in transportation networks. The closing down of almost one-third (250) of the country's newspapers and journals, many of which were specimens of "yellow journalism," and the dissolution of political parties—soon even those not based on ethnic or religious identity—were balanced by an amnesty for precoup political prisoners. The several regional penal and civil codes, educational systems, and tax structures were now finally unified, and the country was formally renamed the Kingdom of Yugoslavia on October 3, 1929. All in all, the new regime's first months were characterized by rigor and vigor, and while it may, indeed, have faked some of the flood of congratulations that now poured in from all parts, it was initially accepted with general relief. When the national Agrarian Bank was founded on August 15, 1929, to replace the several regional banks that had, in the regime's eyes, become instruments of ethnic particularism, the public oversubscribed, and indeed doubled, its anticipated share within two months. Even General-Premier Živković's quaint habit of unannounced early morning inspections of provincial government offices to monitor bureaucratic punctuality and efficiency was applauded by the peasantry, though derided by the elite.

Highest on the royal disctatorship's list of priorities was its determination to weld a national Yugoslav identity out of the country's several regions. Accordingly, the official renaming of the country as Yugoslavia was accompanied by a territorial-administrative reorganization of the thirty-three departments into nine banovinas (governorships), whose boundaries were deliberately drawn so as to obliterate historical borders and to fragment traditional provincial units, and whose very names were selected with the intention of expunging ethnic-regional loyalties. Like the French revolutionary regime a century-and-a-half earlier, the Yugoslav royal one now named its new administrative units after local rivers and other natural features and banished such historic, but supposedly centrifugal, terms as "Croatia" and "Serbia." The new units are listed in table 39.

TABLE 39

BANOVINAL ORGANIZATION OF OCTOBER 3, 1929

Banovina	Capital	Area (sq. km.)	Population (1931)
Drava	Ljubljana	15,849	1,144,298
Sava	Zagreb	40,535	2,704,383
Dunav (Danube)	Novi Sad	31,229	2,387,295
Primorje (Coast)	Split	19,653	901,660
Vrbas	Banja Luka	18,917	1,037,382
Drina	Sarajevo	27,845	1,534,739
Morava	Niš	25,466	1,435,584
Vardar	Skopje	36,673	1,574,243
Zeta	Cetinje	30,997	925,516
Belgrade (separate prefecture)		378	288,938
Total		247,542	13,934,038

A rough identification of the new banovinas in terms of historic provinces would run:

Drava—Slovenia
Sava—Croatia-Slavonia minus its easternmost district of Syrmia
Dunav—Vojvodina, Syrmia, north-central areas of Serbia
Primorje—most of Dalmatia plus western Hercegovina
Vrbas—northern Bosnia
Drina—eastern Bosnia and western areas of old Serbia
Morava—eastern part of old Serbia
Vardar—southern part of old Serbia plus Macedonia
Zeta—southern Dalmatia, Montenegro, Sanjak of Novibazar

The term banovina, drawn from ancient Croatian rather than Serbian public-law usage, was intended to flatter the Croats, and their historic province was far less fragmented by this territorial arrangement than were Serbia and Bosnia-Hercegovina. Nevertheless, the Croats resented the restriction of their people to majorities in only two of these nine new units (Sava and Primorje), while Serbian majorities were gerrymandered for six of the other seven, leaving a Slovene majority in the Drava banovina and a Muslim majority in none. Though sincere, this complaint had at best a symbolic relevance, for the banovinas, in fact, never became significant units of self-government or even of administrative power, let alone of local loyalty. Their configuration and their borders were relatively rational in economic and transportation terms, but they failed to assuage ethnic tensions or to ameliorate governmental arbitrariness.

By its third year, 1931, the royal dictatorship had dissipated its initial élan and lost its self-assurance. Lucky in the good harvests of 1929 and 1930, it thereafter appeared hesitant and helpless in the face of the economic and social problems posed by the depression. Simultaneously, the political challenges of mastering its peoples' unreconciled ethnic tensions and of containing other sources of opposition baffled it. As the regime reverted to the manipulative and repressive patterns of the past and fell back on many men of the past (Alexander recruited few new faces to Yugoslav politics), the public's original support soured. To compensate the Croats for the state's profoundly resented take-over of their hitherto autonomous Sokol sports-and-gymnastics movement on December 4, 1929, Alexander retired his army's equally venerated Serbian regimental flags on September 6, 1930, replacing them with new Yugoslav colors. But such attempts to demonstrate his ethnic evenhandedness by irritating the sensitivities of both peoples impressed neither. The Croats, whose political leader Maček had originally greeted the royal *coup d'etat* against the Vidovdan Constitution and the "Skupština of assassins" as tantamount to "release from a badly buttoned vest" and as "obliterating a boulder" that blocked the path to healthy political development and ethnic reconciliation, eventually came to see the dictatorship, for all its "Yugoslav" rhetoric, as but a disguised Serbian rule. And while its centralistic bias, in turn, conformed to the traditional political attitudes of the Serbs, the latter found it difficult to forgive the destruction of their traditionally autonomous and vigorous political parties, which, unaccustomed to the hazards of underground or clandestine existence, were fragmented to a far greater extent by the royal regime than were the more flexibly cohesive Croatian parties. The Muslims, finally, took deep offense at the administrative pulverization of "their" Bosnia-Hercegovina under the new banovinal arrangements.

For all his "Yugoslav" rhetoric and his wish, expressed to Maček on the eve of the royal coup, to be a king for the Croats as well as the Serbs, Alexander never fully transcended his suspicion of the bureaucratic and political veterans of the Habsburg Empire—a category that included prečani Serbs as well as Croats and Slovenes. On the one hand expecting loyal and obedient citizenship from them, he nevertheless doubted their suitability for sensitive administrative, and especially military, appointments. Though Mussolini inadvertently helped Alexander's effort to woo the Croatian and Slovene masses by repressing their respective minorities in Istria and Venezia Giulia in 1930, the king was unable, nor did he particularly try, to persuade any truly prestigious Croat or prečani Serb to join his regime. Even the initially helpful Slovene leader Korošec retired in disgust on September 26, 1930, thus exposing the new "Yugoslav" dictatorship's essentially "old Serb" personnel core, albeit without old Serbia's parliamentary and party institutions. A political show-trial of

Maček in the spring of 1930, on charges of abetting terrorism, had backfired; it ended in his acquittal, but a number of Croatian terrorists were jailed. The last shreds of confidence between the Croatian political elite and the regime were severed when Maček's adviser, the historian Professor Milan Šufflay, was murdered on February 18, 1931, by assassins who apparently enjoyed police protection.

While Croatian and Serbian flags, colors, heraldic emblems, anthems, and other historic symbols were banished from the state apparatus with overt impartiality, those of the Serbs were all preserved by and within the country's Orthodox Church which gave itself a new and very nationalistic internal constitution on November 16, 1931. The regime also irritated the Catholic Croats and Slovenes by establishing an Orthodox metropolitanate in Zagreb and by building Orthodox churches and chapels in Slovenia, presumably for the soldiers' use. In riposte, the two Catholic peoples bestirred themselves in Catholic Action and Eucharistic Congressional programs. The Croats now reversed the secularistic trends that their late leader Radić had championed and began to reclericalize their social life.

The opposition to the royal dictatorship thus ran the gamut from the Serbs, who were aggrieved primarily by its abolition of parliamentary and constitutional institutions, through the non-Serbs, whose ethnic sensibilities it offended, to the radicals and the youth, who rejected it as simply incompetent and reactionary. The style of opposition also ranged from Davidović's mere aloofness, Korošec's withdrawal, and Pribičević's emigration, through organizational and propaganda work at home and abroad on the part of the Croatian Peasant Party, to outright subversion and terrorism on the part of the Croatian and Left extremists. The regime responded myopically by denouncing all opposition, of whatever ideological hue or political style, as Communist-inspired. This was not only false but, ironically, won the real Communists considerable sympathy. Western public opinion was increasingly impressed, and the regime increasingly rattled, by documented allegations of tortures, provocations, imprisonments without trial, and other abuses that the opposition (mainly the Croatian Peasants) managed to present to the League of Nations and other international forums.

To assuage foreign sensitivities and thus facilitate his quest for Western, and in particular French, loans, to alleviate domestic discontent and thus take the revolutionary sting out of the political ferment aggravated by the depression, and to avert a repetition in Yugoslavia of Spain's republican revolution of April, 1931, Alexander resolved on a formal reform, which was, in fact, only superficial. On September 3, 1931, he issued a new constitution providing for a bicameral legislature. The Skupština, initially of 306 members and later expanded to from 368 to 373, was to be elected by universal, equal, direct, but *not* secret, male suffrage for a four-year term. A coequal Senate of up to 96 members was to be divided evenly between royal appointees and members elected indirectly by banovinal colleges; all senators were to serve six-year terms, half of each category being renewed every three years. Though enjoying formal immunity, this legislature would in fact be impotent since the government was to remain exclusively responsible to the monarch. The monarch, in turn, would also enjoy the right of preliminary sanction and veto on proposed legislation, as well as the role of arbiter in the event of disagreement between the legislature's two houses. Civil liberties were to be so subject to government regulation as to remain vulnerable to arbitrary chicaneries and intimidation. Even more ominous was the constitution's suspension, for a five-year period, of the traditional immunity and irremovability of judges. This measure was allegedly needed in order to purge incompetents, but it manifestly also facilitated the politicization of the courts and thus was likely to undermine any confidence the public might still have in the "blind" neutrality of justice.

The organization of political parties and the nomination of candidates was also subject to stringent regulations under the terms of this Alexandrine Constitution and of supplementary electoral decrees. Overtly ethnic, religious, or regional parties remained prohibited. To ensure truly "Yugoslav" parties, it was required that a party's central list of candidates be endorsed by sixty voters in each of the more than three hundred Skupština electoral districts. In addition, every candidate had to present two hundred signatures of persons from his own constituency as well as prove that he was running on the list of a party that met the above requirement of geographical ubiquity. Alexander's wish to reduce the number of political parties and to ensure the Yugoslavist ideology of those that survived is understandable, though his proscription of regional, ethnic parties in that country at that time was unrealistic. However, one must also acknowledge that for known opponents of his regime to collect all these signatures in the face of police surveillance and administrative pressure would be prohibitively difficult. As a final measure to ensure a "workable" legislature, the new arrangements provided that the party obtaining a plurality of popular votes would receive two-thirds of the Skupština seats, and any party achieving a majority of popular votes would obtain, in addition to this two-thirds bonus, its appropriate proportion of the remaining one-third of the seats.

The new constitution, with its supplementary electoral legislation, was intended to signal the end of a period of temporary dictatorship and the transformation of that dictatorship into a constitutional monarchy. In fact, the citizen remained insecure in his legal rights, and the king, as chief executive, commander in chief of the armed forces, and source of all sovereign authority, remained effectively beyond significant legal restraints. Curiously, Alexander did not seek to project an image of being outside or above the daily, and often unpopular, political activities of his governments, nor did he try to use the ministers as lightning rods to divert discontent away from himself. Quite the contrary. Having committed himself on the day of his *coup d'état* to removing the "intermediaries between the people and the king," he thereafter went out of his way to emphasize his personal responsibility for all the activities of his cabinets' members. Though in a quixotic sense courageous, this stance was scarcely judicious, and it partly undermined the supposed rationales for his regime's adoption of a formally new constitutional form late in 1931. None of the opposition camps had been consulted in this process, none were persuaded that the country's constitutional problems had thereby been resolved, and none participated in the charade of Skupština and Senate elections that were then held on November 8, 1931, and January 3, 1932. The elections were duly "won" by the regime, which claimed that 65.3 percent of the eligible electorate had voted in the direct Skupština elections and that 2,324,395 ballots had been cast for its list. The several opposition camps retorted that this statistic was false and insisted that an overwhelming majority of the electorate had heeded their clandestine appeals to boycott these blatantly rigged, open-ballot, elections. Of the 306 deputies "elected" on the government party's list, 219 were Serbs; 55, Croats; 25, Slovenes; 3, Bosniak Muslims; 2, Macedonian Muslims; 1, German; and 1, Magyar. Almost all were veterans of the precoup parliamentary parties, and a distressingly large proportion were truly unsavory types. All in all, the Alexandrine Constitution enjoyed still less legitimacy than had its Vidovdan predecessor, and not even the Serbs endorsed it. Ironically, even this freshly handpicked legislature of sycophants and opportunists was soon so irritated by the regime's bungling and arbitrariness that already by March, 1932, the king was vainly seeking support from Aca Stanojević and Maček, the still-powerful leaders of the formally illegal Serbian Radical and Croatian Peasant opposition parties. The play of political forces was manifestly not to be contained by Alexander's jejune institutional manipulations, and the moral victors of recent developments had clearly been the opposition camps.

On April 4, 1932, accordingly, General Živković, who since the royal coup had presided over three consecutive cabinets, which had been reshuffled thirteen times and been served by forty different men in ministerial capacities, was returned to the army by King Alexander and replaced as premier by the same Vojislav Marinković who had contested Davidović's leadership of the Serbian Democratic Party in the late 1920s (see section 4) and had then thrown in his lot with the royal dictatorship. Marinković, who now retained the foreign affairs portfolio (which he had held uninterruptedly since April 17, 1927) while serving as premier, was intended to project an image of "European" culture in contrast to Živković's "Balkan" style. He sought to politicize and civilianize the regime by assembling its functionaries and supporters into a new mass Yugoslav Radical Peasant Democratic Party; each adjective in this clumsy name was meant to appeal to the clientele of one of the major precoup parties. But he was by now an isolated and sick man and lasted only three months. He was replaced on July 2, 1932, by the former Serbian Radical Milan Srškić. This appeased veteran Radicals who had been unhappy over the premiership's going to an ex-Democrat.

Srškić, who had served as justice minister, interior minister, and general troubleshooter in the cabinets of his two immediate predecessors, supposedly combined their respective traits of toughness and adroitness. He was hated by the Bosniak Muslims for the obliteration of their province under the current banovina system which he had designed, by the Croats for his notorious centralism, and by many Serbs for his dictatorial political attitudes. An increased level of tension, agitation, and repression quickly followed his appointment. Students, rapidly radicalizing and led now by the new and clandestine Ujedinjena Revolucionarna Omladina (United Revolutionary Youth), rioted against the "perjured king" and for "the political and economic liberation of all South Slavs, from the Drava to the Black Sea [i.e., including the Bulgars] in a federal, socialist, worker-peasant republic." In June, 1932, certain army officers of the Maribor garrison in Slovenia had been tried as alleged Communists. At the other end of the political spectrum, Croatian nationalist extremists (Ustaši) launched an uprising in the hungry and restive Lika district of coastal Croatia that September. Its suppression by several thousand gendarmes and troops required two weeks, even though the rebel leaders were partially compromised in the eyes of the general Croatian public by their heavy dependence on Mussolini's Italy, whither most of them fled upon the insurrection's collapse. Slovenia, Bosnia, and other Croatian districts were also seized by peasant unrest. Conventional political opposition, in turn, accelerated as the regime's new party soon exposed itself as an organization of old men and exhausted policies.

'Respectable' Croatian, prečani Serbian, and Slovene opposition leaders articulated their grievances in two manifestoes, of which one was issued at Zagreb on November 7, and the other at Ljubljana on December 31, 1932. The former reiterated the Maček-Pribičević argument of 1928, that any ethnic or political reconciliation must be predicated on a constitutional renegotiation of the hurried unification of late 1918, while the latter demanded recognition of regional ethnic individuality and cultural autonomy. Democratic and populistic in rhetoric, they impressed public opinion and prompted the regime to a carrot-and-stick reaction. On November 23, it introduced draft-legislation (which formally became law on March 24, 1933) to ease the restrictive electoral laws of September, 1931, even though no new elections were due before 1935. Instead of being obliged to produce sixty endorsements from each of the country's electoral districts, a political party would henceforth have to furnish only thirty such signatures in half the total number of districts; however, the constituencies of its choice would have to be distributed through no less than six of the nine banovinas. The two-thirds bonus clause for the parliamentary representation of the winning slate was reduced somewhat, to three-fifths. The more palpable stick supplementing this somewhat ephemeral carrot was the arrest and internment early in 1933 of the Croatian opposition leaders Maček and Trumbić, the Slovenes Korošec and Kulovec, and Bosniak Muslims Spaho and Hrasnica. Immediately, many veteran Serbian Radical, Democratic, and Agrarian leaders vented their smoldering resentment over the regime's destruction of their parliamentary, partisan, and civic institutions by vehemently protesting, on February 14, 1933, this exercise in ethnic repression. The chairman of the government party's own Senate caucus, a renegade Croatian Peasantist, also issued a troubled statement, and latent frictions between the Roman Catholic hierarchy and the regime, which largely stemmed from the earlier etatization of all youth organizations, also now surfaced. Applications by the oppositional Serbian Radicals and the Social Democrats for relegalization of their parties were rejected by the regime in August, 1933, and February, 1934.

Though in July, 1933, the government party had simplified its hitherto unwieldy name to Yugoslav National Party, it was unable to deal with festering internal frictions and demoralization. The regime itself, too, now aggravated its own plight by adding internal discord and malaise to its earlier alienation of virtually all former political movements and its increasingly brutal treatment of political opponents and prisoners. On January 27, 1934, Srškić yielded the premiership to the former Serbian Radical workhorse Nikola Uzunović, who had presided over four consecutive cabinets during 1926-27, who had served as president of the government party since its formation in the spring of 1932, and whose current reappointment as premier by King Alexander was an implied but clear confession of fatigue and retreat.

The escalating spiral of domestic tension and alienation had driven the regime into a cul-de-sac from which it could extricate itself either by recourse to a radical "totalitarian" solution entailing categorical repression and energetic social mobilization, or by a withdrawal from its isolated position back into reconciliation with at least a part of its recalcitrant society. The replacement of Srškić by Uzunović indicated that the king would opt for the latter course. His tactical task now was to solve three interrelated but distinct problems: the Croatian-Serbian issue (federalism versus centralism); the issue of parliamentarism versus authoritarianism; and the economic crisis which was aggravating the tensions generated by the first two issues. That Yugoslavia was also likely to be confronted by increased regional and international tension along its borders in 1934 was suggested by the Austrian civil war of February 12-16, followed by the signature on March 17 of the Rome Protocols by the rightist governments of Italy, Austria, and Hungary, and then by the Austrian Nazis' assassination of Chancellor Engelbert Dollfuss on July 25, 1934.

8

Alexander's new, more conciliatory, course proved to be a case of too little and too late as the various oppositional groups, sensing his regime's isolation and disarray, became increasingly intransigent. The regime had hitherto misjudged both the Croatian and the Serbian communities. The former was now more militant than ever, and the latter was in unprecedented disarray. Both conditions portended increasing receptivity to radicalism of both the Right and the Left varieties unless the regime altered its repressive but palsied stance in one direction or the other.

On January 7, 1929, the day after the proclamation of the royal dictatorship, Dr. Ante Pavelić, secretary of the Party of Croatian State Rights and one of its two deputies in the now-dissolved Skupština, had fled abroad to found the Right-Radical Ustaša (Insurgent) movement, committed to a policy of Croatian independence to be achieved through insurrection and terror, and to an ideology of integral nationalism, elitism, and historical romanticism. Pavelić quickly established contacts with the more experienced Macedonian paramilitary organization IMRO, which was also militantly anti-Yugoslav, and soon drew subsidies and shelter from Italy and Hungary. In time three characteristic Ustaša "types" emerged: the politician-ideologue who was a member of the intelligentsia; the simple-minded, semieducated nationalist, who was often a "failure" in his personal life and full of unanalyzed resentments; and the criminal-mercenary.

Within a year of its birth, the Ustaša was locked in a spiral of terror and counterterror with the Alexandrine regime, characterized by assassinations, bombings, derailments, an insurrection, mass roundups, and trials. Through Pavelić's deputy Gustav Perčec, an ex-lieutenant in the Austro-Hungarian army, the Ustaša was in touch with the politically more old-fashioned circle of Habsburg-legitimist Croatian nationalists, led by General Stjepan Sarkotić, which had exiled itself to Vienna at war's end and committed itself to the restoration of an independent Croatian state. The Ustaša's relations with the older, larger, more moderate Croatian Peasant Party, in turn, were organizationally competitive but also, on occasion, politically complementary. Early in April, 1930, for example, as Maček and twenty-three other defendants were about to stand trial in Belgrade (see section 7), two of his deputies conferred with Pavelić and Perčec as well as with representatives of the Sarkotić circle in a suburb of Vienna to coordinate strategy. Although no agreement was reached on the troubled questions of whether the Croats should rely primarily on agitation or terror and whether their goal should be autonomy or independence, a rough but effective territorial division of foreign political endeavors emerged. The Croatian Peasant Party henceforth concentrated on arguing the case for Croatia to the American, British, and French governments and publics, and at the League of Nations, while the Ustaša deepened its connections with, and dependence on, the regimes of Italy and Hungary, assisted in the latter country and in Austria by the well-connected Croatian legitimist exiles. Both camps were effective in drawing the world's attention to the "Croatian problem." The self-exiled leader of the prečani Serbs, Pribičević, was also writing and lecturing to discredit the Alexandrine regime in the eyes of the French and Czech elites until his death in Prague on September 15, 1936. Hence, the need and the wish to restore Yugoslavia's credit abroad, as well as his belated awareness that the regime was falling between two stools at home and thus feeding grist into the mills of the radical, seditious opposition, prompted King Alexander's decision of the late summer of 1934 to soften drastically—indeed, to dismantle—the royal dictatorship.

That decision was, alas, aborted by Alexander's assassination at the hands of an Ustaša-IMRO squad shortly after he stepped ashore at Marseilles on October 9, 1934, to commence an official visit to France. The murder had been committed with the complicity of Italy and Hungary and facilitated by incompetent French police arrangements. The subsequent inquests into the assassination on the part of the French and the League of Nations, however, white-washed Mussolini's Italy, whose diplomatic support France still hoped to recruit against Nazi Germany, and sought to make Hungary the sole scapegoat. The Yugoslav authorities, in turn, were disillusioned by the French pressure on them to drop their demands for a thorough investigation; hence, they soon bid for improved relations with an increasingly powerful Germany and even with Italy. The Ustaša was thereupon put in 'cold storage' by Mussolini and its cadres relegated to remote villages in Sardinia, Sicily, and the Lipari Islands during the years of relative Axis-Yugoslav rapprochement, from 1937 to 1941.

Despite his belated recognition that the dictatorship had failed and his final intention, expressed on the eve of the fatal French trip, to inaugurate a more flexible and liberal course, Alexander must, on balance, be adjudged a man of limited vision and narrow horizons. While granting that he was motivated by the high ideal of Yugoslav unity, that his public style was free of theatricalities, and that he was personally courageous and even gallant, one must nevertheless recognize that he had a poor eye for talent, relied on an entourage of mediocrities, and never attempted seriously to understand, let alone to resolve, the historical, cultural, and socioeconomic complexities that prompted the opposition to his regime.

His political instincts were authoritarian and manipulative. Through the rigged trial that ended with the execution of the "Black Hand" leaders in 1917, he had established his personal control over the Serbian military establishment and had then discreetly separated it from politics. During the 1920s he had manufactured and exploited a number of ministerial crises in a persistent effort to undermine all strong parties. Only Pašić had proved a match for Alexander, but after the venerable Radical leader's death at the end of 1926 the political arena was open to royal domination. Nor ought one to assume, merely because he refrained from twisting the screws of that domination to full totalitarian intensity, that Alexander's dictatorship was benevolently paternalistic. Its repressive nature is suggested by the several thousand political prisoners incarcerated for varying terms during its six years' duration and, in even more sinister fashion, by the more than three hundred political victims who "died" in jail or in clashes with gendarmes, not to mention such less bloody, but also ominous, phenomena as the virtual closing of Belgrade University during 1932 in response to student ferment.

Convinced, in his patriotic but myopic fashion, that the national interest required the stifling of domestic conflicts, Alexander failed to learn in time that these conflicts were not amenable to his favored manipulative administrative 'solutions.' His regime was authoritarian but lacked a political ideology; its dilettantish administration oscillated planlessly between bureaucratic rigidity and opportunistic improvisation. On the morrow of his *coup d'état* of January 6, 1929, the Serbian masses had viewed Alexander as a potentially democratic answer to oligarchic corruption, and the Croatian nation had looked to him for relief from the paralysis of the Vidovdan system. By the eve of his assassination on October 9, 1934, the king had dissipated both these reservoirs of goodwill and had isolated himself from all his peoples without reconciling them to each other. His posthumous official appellation of "King-Unifier" was sadly undeserved.

Nevertheless, to the extent that the planners of the assassination expected Yugoslavia to disintegrate with the removal of its supposedly "one-man government," they miscalculated. Indeed, Alexander's murder shocked the Yugoslavs into an unexpected moment of solidarity. The Serbs recalled him as a scion of their native Karadjordjević dynasty and as their warrior prince during World War I, while the Croats and Slovenes, though devoid of such sentimental affections, could nevertheless not fail to be disturbed by Mussolini's hand in the affair. Once again, as in the closing phases of World War I, Italy's manifest designs on the eastern Adriatic littoral catalyzed a rapprochement among the several Yugoslav peoples. This moment of national catharsis might well have been seized by the regime to launch a program of genuine conciliation and reconciliation between itself and the society and among the society's ethnic groups, but the regime myopically allowed the strategic opportunity to slip by, failing to exploit the Ustaša's temporary isolation both at home and in the West or to probe certain overtures by some Croatian intellectuals and émigré Peasantist leaders. The minority of King Peter was the regime's specious excuse for postponing any substantive innovations or constitutional revisions until he reached his eighteenth birthday on September 6, 1941. Thus, the very same clique that over the past half-dozen years had consistently rationalized and lauded the royal abolition of the Vidovdan Constitution, which had at least been adopted by a popularly elected Constituent Assembly, now made a fetish of the Alexandrine Constitution, whose dubious legitimacy rested on a mere royal decree. The regime thus fatally played into the hands of those Croatian and Serbian extremists who were determined to abort the delicate seed of reconciliation.

In the immediate aftermatch of the assassination, Premier Uzunović had sought to strengthen his cabinet's authority by adding to it the ex-premiers Živković, Marinković, and Srškić—the first as war minister, the other two without portfolios. Nevertheless, already by the end of October, 1934, the cabinet started to unravel with the resignation of Justice Minister Božidar Maksimović, who was troubled over the furtive manner in which the late king's hitherto secret will, nominating a three-man regency headed by his cousin Prince Paul, had been hastily implemented by the regime without seeking the formal sanction of any public political body, not even the docile and handpicked legislature. Unable to resolve the internal divisions of his government between those wishing to pursue the possibility of a tentative overture toward the opposition, and a majority determined to hold rigidly to the hard line of recent years (which, ironically, Alexander had at last recognized as a liability just before his death), the weak Uzunović surrendered the premiership on December 20, 1934, to Foreign Minister Bogoljub Jevtić, a hard-liner in whose arms Alexander had expired at Marseilles. Jevtić quickly proclaimed his commitment to the integrity of the Alexandrine Constitution of 1931, thus rebuking any who might still hope for a milder course, and had the Skupština dissolved on February 6, 1935, to forestall criticism of his policy by the Uzunović faction of the government party. Though Maček himself was amnestied and released by the senior regent, Prince Paul (a cousin of Alexander), when the Jevtić cabinet was installed, there was no serious political follow-through such as the late king had intimated before his fatal trip to France.

The election campaign that now took place was waged by Jevtić under the abrasive slogan "For an integral Yugoslavia, against subversives and separatists," and was characterized by the mobilization of the state's administrative apparatus on behalf of the government party's candidates. The opposition parties were barred from access to the press, and their agents intimidated. Nevertheless, an Opposition Bloc headed by Maček and composed of the surviving cadres of his Croatian Peasants, the

Serbian Democrats, the Serbian Independent Democrats, and the Serbian Agrarians, and endorsed by the Bosniak Muslims, did manage, despite serious administrative and political obstacles, to nominate a sufficient number of candidates to meet the terms of the revised electoral law. Both the Croatian as well as the Serbian participants in this bloc were denounced by the extremists in their respective communities (the Ustaša and the government party) for alleged treason in forming their united list. The surviving oppositional Serbian Radicals and Slovene Populists abstained, thanks to the government's political bribery according to some allegations. The recently resigned Justice Minister Maksimović headed a list of defectors from Jevtić's government party, but the former premier Uzunović simply boycotted the campaign. Attempts by the Social Democrats and by one of General Živković's former aides to enter lists of candidates were banned, whereupon the former recommended abstention while the latter endorsed the Maček-led Opposition Bloc. A small, quasi-fascist "corporatist" bloc, led by a former justice minister (1931), Dimitrije Ljotić, was, on the other hand, permitted its own slate.

The government's first announced results of the elections of May 5, 1935, claimed that 72.6 percent of the eligible electorate had indeed cast a total of 2,778,172 (open) ballots, allegedly distributed as follows: the regime's Jevtić-led list received 1,738,390 votes (62.6 percent) and 320 seats; the Opposition Bloc's Maček-led list, 983,248 votes (35.4 percent) and 48 seats; the Maksimović and Ljotić lists, respectively 32,720 and 23,814 votes (1.2 and 0.8 percent) but no seats. These statistics elicited such an uproar that on May 22 the authorities announced the results of a "recount" (in 13 localities the voting had been interrupted on May 5 and resumed on May 12). One hundred thousand additional opposition ballots were now identified, slightly raising the rate of participation to 73.7 percent and yielding the following revised results from a total vote of 2,880,964: the Jevtić list received 1,746,982 votes (60.6 percent) and 303 seats; Maček list, 1,076,345 votes (37.4 percent) and 67 seats; the Maksimović and Ljotić lists, 33,549 and 24,088 votes (1.2 and 0.8 percent), respectively, but no seats.

This outcome was a statistical victory but a moral defeat for Jevtić. Five members of his cabinet had been defeated in their constituencies. In the areas where Croats and prečani Serbs were concentrated, the Maček list had outpolled the Jevtić list by 797,197 to 520,144. On June 2 the Opposition Bloc announced that it would boycott the Skupština, which was scheduled to open the next day, and meet as a rump assembly at Zagreb in protest against the still unrepresentative distribution of seats. The Roman Catholic archbishop of Zagreb supplemented their protest by personally itemizing the outrages and illegalities of the recent campaign to the Regent Prince Paul. On June 20, finally, five membres of Jevtić's own cabinet, including the key ministers of war (General Živković) and finance

(Milan Stojadinović), resigned in protest against the premier's clumsy rigidity. The specific provocation for their step had been Jevtić's inept handling of a turbulent Skupština session at which a Serbian deputy had charged the Croats in general, and Maček in particular, with collusion in the late king's assassination. Živković declared that the perilous foreign political situation and the interests of the all-national, and not just Serbian, army required that the country's inner divisions be soothed, not exacerbated, while Stojadinović believed the same imperatives to apply with regard to the economy and the exchequer. Prince Paul thereupon replaced Premier Jevtić, who was an experienced diplomat but out of his depth in the current domestic turmoil, with the financial expert Stojadinović on June 24, 1935.

9

Milan Stojadinović was to remain in power for three-and-a-half years and to prove himself Yugoslavia's strongest politician since Pašić, whose handpicked protégé he had been as a resourceful and young finance minister during 1922-26. Having withdrawn from the political limelight during the disreputable era of parliamentary anarchy that followed Pašić's death, and having then remained in the background through the royal dictatorship until his resumption of the finance portfolio under Jevtić in December, 1934, Stojadinović now inaugurated his premiership with a number of signs of greater political flexibility and pragmatism. Police terror was relaxed, the preliminary censorship of newspapers was abandoned, a statue of Radić was permitted to be unveiled in Zagreb, and about ten thousand political prisoners were amnestied. The oppositional Slovenian Populist and Bosniak Muslim leaders Korošec and Spaho were coopted into the cabinet, respectively as interior and transportation ministers. General Živković, whose recent intervention in the downfall of Jevtić had signaled his belated conversion to a policy of appeasing the Croats, was retained at the war ministry. Otherwise, most of the discredited warhorses of the royal dictatorship and of its official government party were now swept out in favor either of new technocrats or of politicians who had, like the new premier, remained aloof from the regimes of recent years. Stojadinović, indeed, managed to include representatives from most of the parties that had been prominent before the coup in his government, while nevertheless projecting an innovative image. He retained the foreign affairs portfolio in his own hands, a decision that signaled Yugoslav disillusionment with what was felt to be the weakness and unreliability shown by her French ally during and after the previous year's assassination crisis.

The vast majority of the government party's 303 backbenchers, though handpicked by the now-displaced Jevtić for the recent elections, docilely transferred their obedience to Stojadinović. Jevtić himself went into opposition. As was the case with similar parties in several neighboring countries, the very institutional weakness that rendered them incapable of overthrowing a government also prevented them from saving their preferred leaders once these had otherwise exhausted themselves. Within two months of assuming the premiership, Stojadinović went on to purge his government of a handful of recalcitrants and to restructure and rename the old government party, according to his own taste, as the Yugoslav Radical Union (Jugoslavenska Radikalna Zajednica, or JRZ), whose genealogy could be traced to a coalition of Serbian Radicals, Slovene Populists, and Bosniak Muslims, though its cadres were relatively young and its rhetoric emphatically "Yugoslavist."

Most of the Radical veterans, who viewed Stojadinović as an upstart, boycotted the JRZ, whose main function was obviously to furnish a personal base to the premier preparatory to his addressing himself to the country's manifold ethnic, economic, and diplomatic problems. In December, 1935, Stojadinović found it necessary and desirable to purge his JRZ of some senior ex-Radical veterans (including even Aca Stanojević, leader of the former oppositional Radicals against the royal dictatorship) who were still under the illusion that he could be treated as their "front man" rather than as their chief. There followed, on March 6, 1936, an abortive attempt by a disgruntled Serbian deputy associated with the Jevtić faction to assassinate the premier on the floor of the Skupština. Stojadinović behaved courageously and emerged from the incident politically strengthened, even though—or, perhaps, precisely because—it provided the occasion for the formation a few weeks later, on June 30, of a new, opposition front composed of purged and embittered old warhorses of the royal dictatorship led by ex-premiers Živković, who had been dropped from the cabinet the day after this assassination attempt, and Jevtić, of whom the public was manifestly tired. Meanwhile, the older but nonviolent Opposition Bloc led by Maček continued to boycott the Skupština; this also played into Stojadinović's hands. After a year of tactical maneuvering and in-fighting, he was at last ready to address himself to substantive problems.

On September 26, 1936, Stojadinović alleviated the problem of peasant indebtedness, which was chronic and still severely aggravated by the depression. He issued a decree providing that peasant debts antedating April 20, 1932, when a moratorium on repayment had gone into effect and such debts totaled 6.88 billion dinar, be halved and repayment of the remaining half be extended over a twelve-year period at 3 or 4.5 percent interest, depending on whether the debt was owed to private moneylenders or to banks and cooperatives. The privileged Chartered Agricultural Bank became responsible for the reduced peasant indebtedness to banks and credit cooperatives, and its obligations to these original creditors were spelled out in a rather complicated schedule. Stojadinović further sought to assist agriculture through programs of compulsory harvest insurance, silo construction and other rural public works, state monopolization of grain exports, development of veterinary and breeding institutions, credits for cooperative wine cellars, tax relief, and a general "cheap money" policy. Accompanied by splendid harvests in 1935 and 1936 and now by Germany's readiness to absorb virtually all of Yugoslavia's exportable agricultural output, these measures consolidated Stojadinović's standing with the peasantry. He went on to sweep the communal elections of December 6, 1936, in all regions of the country except the Sava and Primorje banovinas, whose Croatian peasants remained loyal to Maček. This development, combined with the recent purge and defection of so many ex-Serbian Radicals from his political camp, now served to confirm the premier's view that the time had come to address himself to the Croatian issue.

Stojadinović, like his mentor Pašić, preferred to solve the Croatian-Serbian problem through a political deal between the largest party in each ethnic camp rather than through a maneuver in which one of these two largest parties would seek to isolate the other by forming a coalition with splinter parties in that other's ethnic camp. Accordingly, on becoming premier in mid-1935 Stojadinović had made overtures to Maček, but the latter's price for an accommodation was still considered excessive: repudiation of the Alexandrine Constitution and of the results of the "Jevtić elections"; fresh elections for a Constituent Skupština, to be supervised by a neutral government with the reintroduction of the secret ballot and the abolition of the notorious three-fifths representational bonus to the plurality party. Stojadinović, announcing that, "we are not here to liquidate [the current political system] but to work," for the time being simply suspended further contacts with Maček. At the same time, he built up his own political machine and sought to ingratiate himself directly with the public at large, including Maček's Croatian peasant constituency, through such programs as the above-mentioned attack on peasant indebtedness. When negotiations were resumed in mid-January, 1937, however, Maček had just emerged trom the previous month's communal elections with his own political base still intact and hence was again recalcitrant. Stojadinović thereupon simply redoubled his "softening" and "outflanking" strategy. Later in January he demonstrated his self-confidence by allowing the son and son-in-law of the late Stjepan Radić to return home, undisturbed and uninterrogated, from foreign exile. More subtly and more ambitiously, Stojadinović sought direct leverage on Croatian public opinion through a concordat with the Vatican. Here, however, he was to miscalculate his opportunities and his risks on both his Croatian and his Serbian flanks.

Negotiations to draft a general Vatican-Yugoslav concordat to replace the six different administrative-juridical arrangements that Yugoslavia had inherited had been set in motion as early as 1922 but proved slow and complicated. The many Yugoslav cabinet crises and the deliberate pace of the Vatican bureaucracy would have entailed a protracted schedule even had there been none of the substantive problems that soon surfaced. The Yugoslav governments feared that certain prelates who were ethnically Magyar, or had been trained in prewar Hungarian seminaries, would promote Hungarian separatist propaganda in the Roman Catholic churches and schools of Croatia-Slavonia and the Vojvodina. Hence they solicited a governmental veto, which Rome was reluctant to concede, over the designation of bishops in Yugoslavia. The Roman Catholic hierarchy, on the other hand, sought guarantees that there would be no discrimination against the alumni of its schools in personnel recruitment for state employment. In turn, the government regarded this quest as an implied infringement on its sovereignty. The Eastern Orthodox bishops, meanwhile, who tended to view any church other than an autocephalous national one as somehow improper, were suspicious of these negotiations. The Vatican, finally, was sensitive to Mussolini's reluctance to see Yugoslavia gain the prestige and the cohesion that were presumed to flow from a concordat. Nevertheless, after many delays and travails, a concordat was finally signed in Rome on July 25, 1935.

Stojadinović, who had assumed the premiership barely one month before, now postponed presenting the concordat for legislative ratification for two years in the hope that passions would cool and he could consolidate an overwhelming political authority. In the interval, his government exchanged a series of clarifying letters with the resident Papal Nuncio in a vain effort to assuage Orthodox anxieties, which had by now centered on these features of the concordat: (a) the resurrection of a Roman Catholic diocese at Niš, deep in overwhelmingly Orthodox Serbia; (b) state recognition of the Catholic Action movement, which the Orthodox suspected of excessive missionary zeal; (c) an open-ended commitment by the state to subsidize as many seminaries and catechetical schools as the Roman Catholic Church might decide to build; (d) an unfortunately formulated Vatican commitment that Roman Catholic priests would abstain from political activities, provided that the state would ensure similar abstention by the clergies of other religions.

The Orthodox establishment whipped its public into an uproar, and Stojadinović's many Serbian political enemies, unreconciled to their earlier defeats at his hands, hoped to avenge themselves by capitalizing on this issue. The Croats, on the other hand, did not trouble to rally to him. Though the concordat was undoubtedly generous to their Roman Catholic Church, Croatian nationalism was not, in fact, as closely committed to political Catholicism as Stojadinović appears to have assumed. The late Stjepan Radić had been quite anticlerical,[6] and neither Maček's membership in the schismatic Old Catholic Church nor his canonically irregular matrimonial biography had barred him from succeeding to the leadership of the Croatian Peasant Party. All in all, the Croats were not prepared to have their secular political demands redeemed in the coinage of ecclesiastical favors. The otherwise shrewd Stojadinović had here made a commitment on which he could lose much and gain little.

Characteristically, Stojadinović followed up his long postponement of the issue with a sudden attempt to force it. Despite ominous confrontations between the police and illegal Orthodox demonstrations, his tightly disciplined JRZ pushed the concordat's ratification through the Skupština on July 23, 1937, by a vote of 166 to 128. That night the Orthodox Patriarch died, and a rumor that he had been poisoned by the regime quickly spread. The Orthodox Synod and the deceased's family ostentatiously refused the state funeral which was conventional in Serbia for such a dignitary. On August 8 the Synod suspended certain ecclesiastical privileges of the Orthodox ministers and deputies who had endorsed ratification and summoned them before tribunals preparatory to their excommunication. Two days later came the publication of Maček's statement to Serbian opposition leaders, in which he declared Croatian political disinterest in the concordat. Stojadinović thereupon beat a strategic retreat. In October he announced that he would not, for the time being, press the Senate for its supplementary ratification. Then, after conferring in Rome with Pope Pius XI and Vatican Secretary of State Eugenio Cardinal Pacelli (later Pope Pius XII), Stojadinović withdrew the concordat on February 1, 1938. The Orthodox Synod reciprocated on February 9, by rescinding its ecclesiastical penalties against the Skupština ratifiers.

Stojadinović was not a man to collapse after one setback. A political scramble now ensued between the sobered but still resilient regime and the exhilarated but still discordant opposition to determine which could consolidate its own position fastest and undermine the other's most. At the height of the concordat crisis Stojadinović had again asserted his mastery over the JRZ government party at its congress of September 7-10, 1937, and had then restructured his cabinet on October 4 to achieve even tighter personal control as well as to disembarrass himself of some ministers who were too closely identified with the concordat. In addition, he soon began to assume some of the trappings of Yugoslavia's fascist neighbors, such as youth parades, paramilitary guards, special salutes, and surveillance, in an effort to control the society through an extraparliamentary mass political base of his own. But he was personally too cold, too manifestly a mere, albeit a skillful, tactician to elicit the kind of

---

6. Radić would occasionally open a peasant rally with the pithy invocation, *Hvaljen Isus, dolje s popovima* (Praise be to Jesus, down with the clergy).

demogogic popularity in which his models basked. The conciliatory overtures with which Stojadinović had assumed office in 1935 had yielded to the manipulations of pseudo-fascism by 1937-38.

The opposition, in turn, which hitherto had only intermittently joined forces for election purposes, was at last driven to some sustained consolidation by the premier's rising dictatorial ambitions combined with his palpable weaknesses, as exposed during the concordat crisis. On October 8, 1937, five nonextremist opposition groups published an agreement in which they pledged to work together for a new, democratic constitution to be approved eventually by separate majorities of each of Yugoslavia's three state-peoples—the Serbs, the Croats, and the Slovenes—thereby avoiding the intrinsic defects and moral flaws which had discredited both earlier constitutions. Signed by Maček on behalf of the Croatian Peasants, Adam Pribičević (the younger brother of the late prečani Serb leader) for the Independent Democrats, Aca Stanojević of the antiregime Radicals, Ljuba Davidović of the Serbian Democrats, and Jovan Jovanović of the Serbian Agrarians, this manifesto elicited considerable popular support. The regime responded with its shopworn position that the constitutional question could not be reviewed until the boy-king reached his majority in another four years.

The supplementary Senate elections of February 6, 1938, though indirect, were carefully watched as an initial test of the respective strengths of the two camps in the aftermath of the concordat crisis and of the opposition's consolidation. They proved inconclusive. Of twenty-three seats being contested throughout all the banovinas except Zeta, Stojadinović's JRZ took seventeen and routed the Serbian contingent of the united opposition. In the Croatian-populated Sava and Primorje banovinas of Croatia-Slavonia and Dalmatia, however, Maček protégés won six of the eight seats. The results, in a sense, repeated those of the 1935 Skupština elections and, as at that time, the opposition again boycotted the chamber. Nothing daunted, Stojadinović turned to the third of the three substantive areas in which he had committed himself to innovative approaches, namely, to the appeal of his new foreign policy, as a lever to isolate the opposition in the public's eye.

For all their domestic caprices and failures, the parliamentary regimes of the 1920s as well as the royal dictatorship that followed had pursued a consistent and apparently successful foreign policy of anchoring Yugoslav security in the complementary Little Entente and French alliance systems. Stojadinović, on the other hand, was convinced that France's star was waning and that prudence required Yugoslavia to explore alternatives. Without any abrupt repudiation of France, he skillfully reoriented Belgrade's foreign policy toward the rising combination of Fascist Italy and Nazi Germany. After all, France and Britain were themselves assiduously appeasing these two Axis Powers, and Stojadinović could plausibly argue that Yugoslavia would be wiser to accommodate herself to them voluntarily than to leave herself out on a limb and ultimately be subjected to them. Germany, in turn, sought to ease and encourage Stojadinović's new course by absorbing Yugoslavia's otherwise unsalable agricultural surpluses. More than reasons of state, however, attracted Stojadinović to the dictatorships and their dictators: he also saw them as organizational, ideological, and personal models.

The incompetent French security arrangements at the time of King Alexander's assassination and, even more, the undignified French diplomatic performance in its wake, provided Stojadinović with convenient rationales for his deliberate drift away from that country. The shift was encouraged by his powerful interior minister and Slovene satrap, Msgr. Korošec, for whom French society was too "masonic," "Jacobin," and "Bolshevik." On becoming premier in the aftermath of the assassination crisis, Stojadinović had signaled his intention to explore new diplomatic options by retaining for himself the foreign affairs portfolio and then by replacing the veteran Yugoslav ambassadors to Paris, Berlin, and London. He also permitted hitherto banned Italian journals to circulate in Yugoslavia and tacitly accepted Italian penetration of Albania in return for Mussolini's de-activating his Ustaša clients.

As regards Germany, Stojadinović quickly drew the logical conclusions from Hitler's remilitarization of the Rhineland on March 7, 1936. Within three weeks of this pivotal event, he assigned to Krupp rather than to its French or Czech competitors a contract to convert the iron foundry at Zenica in Bosnia into a modern steel mill. The plant was inaugurated on October 2, 1937. Other German contracts, investments, and mass purchases followed in such a flood that, ironically, Stojadinović's new foreign policy, which had been intended to end Yugoslavia's overly exclusive diplomatic reliance on France, had by mid-1938 ended in her all-inclusive economic dependence on Germany. Belated endeavors to loosen the German economic stranglehold by persuading Italy and Britain to involve themselves more actively in Yugoslav investment and trade markets proved fruitless: Italy then lacked the economic stamina, and Britain the political discernment and the administrative and economic mechanisms, to challenge Germany's relentless penetration of the Balkans.

Such relatively sophisticated concerns about diversification of Yugoslavia's foreign trade partners did not, in any event, appear to trouble the general public. The peasant masses, in particular, were relieved that, after several years of deprivation during the depression, their crops were being purchased and their hunger for commodities was being satisfied by Germany at reasonable prices. Stojadinović therefore maintained his new course in foreign affairs, convinced that it entailed no serious domestic political costs. And, for all his strategic myopia and his moral callousness—he was stony beyond the requirements of mere prudence toward his country's Czechoslovak ally in 1938—he conducted it with tactical cleverness. Without sacrificing the formal French alliance or British goodwill, Stojadinović established cordial relations with Germany and Italy; without leaving the Balkan Pact, he effected a rapprochement with Bulgaria; and without burning his fingers over the Austrian Anschluss or the Munich crisis, he achieved, through Italy's mediation, an alleviation of Hungarian revisionist pressure on Yugoslavia. Indeed, he perceived Germany's liquidation of Austria, coming as it did on the heels of Italy's curbing of the Ustaša, as facilitating the burial of the Croatian problem, for now the legitimist (Sarkotić et al.) as well as the terrorist (Pavelić) factions of the Croatian political spectrum had had their wings clipped, leaving Maček supposedly isolated. If such was Stojadinović's view he seriously misjudged the tenacity and resilience of Maček's Croatian Peasant movement, just as he also misjudged the Serbian people's distress and disgust over the truncation inflicted on its Czech ally. But Stojadinović was so euphoric at having avoided being out on a limb during and after the Anschluss and Munich crises (March and September, 1938), that he decided to capitalize on his presumed reputation for diplomatic wisdom by dissolving the Skupština on October 10, half-a-year before its term expired, and scheduling new elections for December 11, 1938.

In the ensuing campaign Stojadinović employed various demagogic innovations, such as bands of green-shirted youths who graced his rallies with salutes and chants to the "Leader." While the police again systematically repressed the four Serbian partners of the Opposition Bloc, Regent Prince Paul interceded to assure mild treatment of the Croats. Maček, however, was too shrewd to succumb immediately to this obvious bid to peel him away from his associates. He played his cards close to the vest and, without spelling out his full program, stood on a warning he had issued on August 15, 1938, on the eve of the Munich crisis, to the effect that unless substantive constitutional and political reforms were implemented soon, "no Croat will defend this state" should it be sucked into the approaching European war.

The balloting on December 11, 1938, was again open. At its conclusion, it was announced that 74.5 percent of the electorate had participated, with the following astonishing distribution of 3,039,041 votes: the Stojadinović list received 1,643,783 votes (54.1 percent) and 306 seats; the Maček et al. list, 1,364,524 votes (44.9 percent) and 67 seats; the Ljotić list, 30,734 votes (1.0 percent) but no seats.

These results indicated a stunning decline, in both absolute and relative terms, in the regime's electoral support since the 1935 elections. In the Croatian and prečani Serb regions, the Maček list actually defeated Stojadinović's by a ratio better than two to one, or 943,964 to 429,332. Though Korošec once again had held his Slovenia for the regime, he was, as interior minister, blamed by Stojadinović for having failed to rig good general returns and retired from the cabinet on the morrow of the election, only to take on the presidency of the Senate, from which influential position he continued to have the ear of Regent Prince Paul. For his part, Stojadinović sought to brazen out the electoral fiasco and boldly reconstructed his cabinet on December 21, but it now lacked any Croats or Slovenes with even minimal political clout.

For all Stojadinović's dexterity in foreign affairs and the related alleviation of economic misery through his risky foreign trade policy, the political alienation of the Croats had remained unappeased. On the eve of the new Skupština's convocation in Belgrade on January 15, 1939, its freshly elected Croatian deputies assembled in Zagreb as a "Croatian National Representation" and, at Maček's direction, solemnly proclaimed void all commitments accepted or imposed by any body not representative of, or responsible to, the Croatian nation. Their resolution also alerted the governments of Europe, especially the Great Powers, to the instability of Yugoslavia's current system and warned them against underwriting it. It concluded with the omnious "hope" that the Croats would not be "forced" to resort to revolt and civil war in order to realize their due rights.

Prince Paul's latent anxieties were thoroughly aroused. Munich had, after all, just exposed the internal and international liabilities of ethnically riven states in the Europe of the day. For domestic reasons, however, he was averse to including the Serbian partners of the united opposition in any compromise. That coalition had, in any event, begun to crack on the morrow of the election over tactical questions; for example, characteristically, the Croatian deputies wanted to extend the Skupština boycott and the Serbs to ease it. In view of the opposition's moral political victory in the recent elections, its internal frictions, the assertiveness of its Croatian contingent, and the attendant international implications, Paul was prompted to initiate secret contacts with Maček. And when the latter objected to Stojadinović as a negotiating partner, Paul dropped his overly spectacular premier with alacrity, replacing him on February 6, 1939, with the pedestrian Dragiša Cvetković, a former mayor of Niš and hitherto minister of public health and social welfare in the Stojadinović regime, for which he had also organized its controlled, official trade union Jugoras. Cvetković was henceforth to prove himself the Prince Regent's reliable and obedient agent. Paul was at last free of the specter of a premier who might dominate him in the fashion of Mussolini's treatment of King Victor Emmanuel in neighboring Italy.

10

Formerly retiring and inconspicuous, the Prince Regent now emerged as Yugoslavia's pivotal political figure until the country was drawn into the war in the spring of 1941. An art collector by avocation and an Anglophile in his political and cultural sympathies, he was neither democratic nor even liberal, and he had been poorly prepared for the hard, "Balkan" responsibilities into which his cousin's assassination had catapulted him in the autumn of 1934. Yet he was less "Serb" and more "Yugoslav" in his thinking than Alexander had been, and this partly compensated for his initial inexperience. His "Yugoslav" as well as his conservative inclinations were encouraged by Korošec who, till his death on December 14, 1940, enjoyed considerable influence with the Prince Regent.

The Italian and German regimes were distressed by the dismissal of the trusted Stojadinović, for whom the Vojvodinian Volksdeutsche minority had been ordered by Berlin to vote *en bloc* in the recent elections. The Germans, however, were somewhat mollified when Stojadinović's ambassador to the Reich, Aleksandar Cincar-Marković, was designated foreign minister in Cvetković's new government. Italy, however, was determined to occupy Albania before the new Yugoslav regime could get its bearings and before it could repudiate Stojadinović's secret acknowledgment of Italy's "absolutely exceptional position" in Albania as quid pro quo for Mussolini's earlier curbing of the Ustaša; she did so on April 7, 1939. The Italians also now explored the possibility of subsidizing the Croatian Peasant movement and using it to subvert Yugoslavia. While the accounts by Ciano and Maček differ irreconcilably on the origin of these secret contacts, each ascribing the initiative to the other,[7] their existence is established.

Thus, in the spring of 1939, Maček was simultaneously heating three mutually incompatible irons in his political fire: (a) his established commitment to his Serbian partners in the Opposition Bloc to strive for a new, democratic, and democratically adopted constitution; (b) his negotiations with the Paul-Cvetković government for a reconciliation between the Croats and the regime; (c) his exploration of possible Italian support for Croatian independence. The scenario was in some ways reminiscent of the Croats' mid-nineteenth century shuttling between Budapest and Vienna. In the end, he consummated the second of these three choices.

After a period of exchanging "feelers," Maček and Cvetković began serious bargaining on April 2, 1939, in the chilling shadow of rump Czechoslovakia's extinction. Opposed from different directions by Maček's Serbian partners of the supposedly united opposition, by the Ustaša on his right flank, and by Serb ultranationalists in Cvetković's rear—all of whom charged betrayal—the negotiations proved difficult. Throughout, Maček maintained his pressure on the regime with minatory resolutions and mass meetings, though these latter appeared at times to play into Ustaša hands as much as into his own. In terms of historical

---

7. Compare Galeazzo Ciano, *The Ciano Diaries, 1939-1943* (New York: Doubleday & Co., 1946), pp. 48, 50, 87, 91, with Vladko Maček, *In the Struggle for Freedom* (New York: Robert Speller & Sons, 1957), pp. 187, 189-90.

analogies, his stand in the negotiations resembled that of the Hungarian Ferenc Deák vis-à-vis the Habsburgs in the mid-1860s: he argued that his nation had been deceived so many times by the regime, that this time any agreement must be detailed and self-enforcing, leaving nothing to "mutual goodwill" or to "pragmatic smoothing-out" at some later date. Hence, he insisted that all proposals be scrutinized by his legal experts as well as by his political entourage. The Prince Regent, in turn, repudiated the traditional Serbian anxiety that decentralization would weaken the state's international leverage. He believed that only substantial concessions to Maček might purchase Croatian loyalty to Yugoslavia and simultaneously neutralize the subversive Ustaša. Besides, an arrangement with Maček would allow Paul to detach the Croats from the general pressure for a liberalization of the regime. The ever-darkening war clouds over Europe also drove both Yugoslav principals on toward a domestic accommodation before the storm broke. Indeed, the final agreement, or Sporazum, was only hammered out on August 20, 1939, and formally published on August 26, less than a week before the outbreak of World War II.

In deserting his partners of the opposition for a separate accommodation with the regime, Maček had now repeated the maneuver of his mentor Radić in the summer of 1925, thereby provoking bitter Serbian taunts to the effect that the betrayal of allies appeared to be a habit with Croatian Peasants. (This collapse of Maček's popularity with the Serbs was hardly unwelcome to Prince Paul.) Maček's rationales were: (a) the weakness of these erstwhile Serb allies in the 1938 elections; (b) the Prince Regent's repugnance toward them; (c) the Ustaša threat on his own flanks; (d) the requirements of Yugoslav patriotism on the eve of the European war. Paul, for his part, also now marooned those Croats who, though few in number, weak, and disparaged as renegades by Maček, had collaborated with the regime through the preceding decade and enabled it to pretend to a "Yugoslav" veneer.

The Sporazum established an enlarged Croatian banovina, composed of the former Sava and Primorje ones plus eight fragments carved out of four adjacent banovinas: Dubrovnik (Zeta); Šid and Ilok (Dunav); Brčko, Travnik, and Fojnica (Drina); and Derventa and Gradačac (Vrbas). The population of the new banovina was estimated as 4,400,000 including 866,000 Orthodox Serbs and 164,000 Muslims, giving it an internal Croatian majority of 77 percent. It contained approximately 30 percent of both the territory and the population of Yugoslavia. It was to have its own legislative Sabor and an executive Ban to be appointed and dismissed by the king (regency); the Ban was to be responsible as well to the Sabor, but not to the central government. This puzzling arrangement apparently left the throne as the sole constitutional nexus between Croatia and the rest of the Yugoslav kingdom and was somewhat analogous to the difficult pattern of old Austria-Hungary. The banovinal government in Zagreb was to enjoy budgetary and administrative autonomy, and its sphere of competence was to encompass agriculture, commerce and industry, forestry and mining, public works, social welfare and public health, education, and justice. Reserved to the central government in Belgrade were foreign affairs and foreign trade, defense and security, transportation and communications, and, of course, the responsibility in the rest of Yugoslavia for all the above-enumerated functions which in Croatia alone were henceforth to be controlled by that banovina.

The regime had thus abandoned its persistent argument that any constitutional changes must await the young King Peter's majority, for the Sporazum altered the status of one part of the state. Like the Corfu Pact of July 20, 1917, between Pašić and Trumbić, the Sporazum of August 26, 1939, was essentially an agreement between a Serbian government and an unofficial but impressive Croatian political group. In terms of personal and regional power, however, the positions of the principals were virtually the reverse of their analogues of 1917; this time the Croatian signatory, Maček, enjoyed enormous authority in his community while the Serbian premier, Cvetković, was but a creature of his royal patron.

On the day of the Sporazum's publication, Maček and four of his Croatian Peasant colleagues entered the Cvetković central government—he as vice-premier, the others as ministers. Two days later Prince Paul, with Maček's assent, designated Dr. Ivan Šubašić as Ban of Croatia. A Croat who had served as a "Yugoslav" volunteer with the Serbian army in World War I, Šubašić had acted as confidential intermediary, first between King Alexander and Maček when the former was considering the relaxation of the dictatorship on the eve of his assassination, and then again between Paul and Maček in the preliminary phases of the recent negotiations. On January 14, 1940, finally, the Prince Regent paid a state visit to Zagreb, the first in a decade by a member of the royal house.

Though the terms of this Sporazum were more generous to the Croats than had been their Nagodba of 1868 with Hungary, it failed to reconcile Yugoslavia's major ethnic communities to each other and to the state. The Serbs, Slovenes, and Bosniaks resented the continued denial to them of the autonomy that had now been granted the Croats, while the prečani Serbs were bitter that it contained no clauses protecting their civil and political rights within the new Croatian banovina. The settlement did not, on the other hand, go far enough in its definitions of Croatian sovereignty or territorial extension to satisfy the Ustaša or to neutralize its growing appeal to Croatian public opinion—an appeal soon demonstrated in the local council elections of May 19, 1940. Many Ustaša activists simply took advantage of the Sporazum to return home from Italian exile and to intensify their subversion of both the Yugoslav state and Maček's authority. Even the part of the Croatian intelligentsia that remained within the

Peasant Party succumbed steadily to the attractions of xenophobia and authoritarianism.

On the day of the Sporazum's proclamation the Skupština was dissolved preparatory to supposedly democratic elections for this chamber as well as for the proposed Sabor of Croatia. But these elections were never held, nor was the technical, constitutional problem of how Croatia would henceforth participate in central-government legislation ever resolved. Hence, when the ultimate crisis struck interwar Yugoslavia in the spring of 1941, the Sporazum with its attendant institutional arrangements still lacked the moral legitimacy of a convincing public ratification, and the regime still appeared as the "private property" of a gang of insiders and manipulators. Nor had that "gang" troubled to enact the socioeconomic and political reforms that had been expected to follow the Sporazum. The European war, which should have served as a spur for the belated implementation of such reforms, became instead the excuse for their indecent burial.

Hence, the state of public morale was fragile when the war finally struck Yugoslavia with the Axis invasion of April 6, 1941: the Croatian troops widely shirked mobilization, mutinied sporadically, and scarcely fought at all, while the Serbs' performance was flabby in comparison to their tenacity of World War I. Though encircled Yugoslavia's ultimate defeat was admittedly a foregone conclusion, yet the feeble performance of her two-million-man army in 1941 was nevertheless a sorry reflection on her people's current sentiments toward the regime and its system. A decade of repressive yet irresolute misgovernment, in the name of national unity, authority, and regeneration, had squandered the confidence of all ethnic communities, even of the Serbs, while the last-minute Sporazum had not purchased even the elementary loyalty of the Croats. The opposition constellations and parties had, alas, reciprocated the regime's failures with their own sorry spectacle of political inconstancy, opportunism, and frivolity. Yugoslav politics had proved no less depressing during the 1930s than it had in the 1920s.

The war engulfed Yugoslavia in the spring of 1941 despite—or, perhaps, because of—the desperate diplomatic gymnastics of Prince Paul's government to keep it at bay. By that time France had fallen, in June, 1940, and Yugoslavia's neighbors, Hungary, Romania, and Bulgaria, had joined the Axis' Tripartite Pact respectively on November 20 and 23, 1940, and March 1, 1941. By that time also, Mussolini's attack on Greece, launched via Albania on October 28, 1940, had been repulsed and Hitler felt obliged to come to the rescue of his foundering partner. Hence he applied strong pressure on Yugoslavia, which was already surrounded by Axis powers and trapped in Germany's economic web, to adhere to the Tripartite Pact so as to secure his diplomatic rear in the

Balkans preparatory to his military assault on Greece and the British contingents bolstering her resistance.

To purchase Yugoslavia's adhesion, Hitler was even prepared to guarantee her territorial integrity and to give assurances that she would not be required to furnish military assistance nor even to let her territory be used for the stationing or transportation of alien troops. Compared to her neighbors, her status within the Axis camp would thus be uniquely privileged. Other more ambiguous bribes were held out by Hitler: a possible Yugoslav territorial corridor to the Aegean Sea with the eventual transfer to her of the Greek port of Salonika; and, on a more personal level, a suggestion of German support for Prince Paul should he wish to postpone the young King Peter's legal coming-of-age from his eighteenth to his twenty-fifth birthday or otherwise to tamper with the royal succession. Simultaneously, Belgrade was given to understand that it would no longer be permitted the luxury of categorical neutrality. Unless the invitation to join the Tripartite Pact were accepted, Yugoslavia would henceforth be regarded by the Axis Powers as an unfriendly state. This meant, at a minimum, that Hitler would authorize his Italian, his Bulgarian, and possibly also his Hungarian allies to present and enforce their irredentist demands to several Yugoslav regions.

Whether or not he was tempted, Prince Paul remained aloof to the personal bait. But the Germans' political arguments and the power behind them impressed him and the Cvetković-Maček cabinet. To repudiate the Axis pressure would have required a degree of domestic consensus and national solidarity that this regime could not then command and that it was reluctant to even try to mobilize lest it be swept aside in the ensuing momentum. In international terms, furthermore, Yugoslavia was now geopolitically surrounded by the Axis and militarily unprepared to resist the Wehrmacht. Quite apart from profound errors in the strategic dispositions of her armed forces which would only be exposed in the course of the April, 1941, campaign, their logistical situation was known to be hopeless ever since Hitler's earlier destruction of Czechoslovakia had interrupted Yugoslav access to the production of the Škoda works, the Yugoslav army's standard supplier of armaments. No anti-Axis power was now able to fill this gap, and her own industrial capacity and transportation network were inadequate to sustain mechanized warfare. The northern frontiers and cities would probably have been indefensible even without the additional aggravation of Wehrmacht concentrations in Romania and Bulgaria. Nevertheless, due to Croatian and Slovene political sensitivities and pressures the Yugoslav armies were unable to concentrate in the mountainous central redoubt of Bosnia and western Serbia. That would have been the logical strategy, given their technical limitations. Instead, they were deployed in shallow and overextended formations all along the long borders.

Aware of Yugoslavia's military weakness and economic vulnerability, which were in some part their own fault, and of the current European balance, or lack of it (France defeated, Britain unable to render effective aid, America remote, and the Soviet Union enigmatic), Prince Paul and his ministers cautiously eased their way toward the formidable Reich and eventually adhered to the Tripartite Pact on March 25, 1941, under the exceptional waivers promised earlier. Though many Western and virtually all Communist historians have deplored this decision as short-sighted—and, in retrospect, it was—and dishonorable, it should be recalled that, unlike Chamberlain and Daladier in 1938 and Stalin in 1939, Prince Paul in 1941 was negotiating with Hitler only over his own country's destiny and not bartering away another's territory or existence, and that German power over Europe had meanwhile vastly expanded. The British were prodigal with exhortations to the Yugoslavs to preserve their honor by rebuffing the Germans, but short on the military assistance that might have given weight to this advice. Simultaneously, Britain was showing greater patience with Sweden, which permitted the movement of German troops and material across its territory to and from occupied Norway, than with Yugoslavia, which had extracted from Germany explicit exemption from such collaboration. It is scarcely surprising that Prince Paul, for all his Anglophilia, came to suspect that London regarded Yugoslavia as expendable.

Had he been leading a united country that was persuaded of the utility of his diplomatic and domestic policies, Prince Paul would have been able to shrug off the foreign excoriators of his accommodation to Germany. Alas for him, the Serbs—ranging from the Orthodox clergy, the secular intelligentsia, the Sokol youth, the veteran organizations, the officer corps, to the masses in general—were already disgruntled by his earlier Sporazum with the Croats and now doubly resented his adhesion to the Tripartite Pact as a betrayal of their national interest, tradition, and honor. What outraged them was not so much the specific terms of the pact—Hitler's waivers, after all, meant that Yugoslavia was giving little away while his record of broken guarantees also implied that she was gaining little in the long run—but rather its deeper significance as capitulation to Teutonic pressure, a capitulation that they abhorred as cutting against the grain of Serbia's finest history. The ink was scarcely dry on Yugoslavia's signature when a bloodless military coup, organized by Air Force Brigadier General Borivoje Mirković, overthrew the regime during the night of March 26-27, 1941, forced "the foreigner" Prince Paul into exile, proclaimed King Peter as having come of age, and replaced "the gypsy" Dragiša Cvetković with General Dušan Simović as premier. Simović had recently served as chief of the general staff (1938-40) in between two terms as commander of the air force (1936-38, 1940-41) and had warned Paul as late as March 23, that the Tripartite Pact might well provoke an air force mutiny.

While the Belgrade street crowds greeted the Mirković-Simović coup with ecstatic and rhymed shouts of *Bolje rat nego Pakt* (Better war than the pact), *Bolje grob nego rob* (Better the grave than a slave), *Nema rata bez Srba* (No war without Serbs), those of Ljubljana and especially of Zagreb were resentful that the Serbs had unilaterally committed the whole country to the very high—virtually the certain—risk of war. Whereas Maček profoundly regretted this development, more extreme Croatian nationalists by now actually craved a German invasion as a catalyst to achieving Croatian independence. For Pavelić, indeed, the Belgrade coup was a godsend, as the Axis promptly took his Ustaša exiles out of mothballs to use them as auxiliaries in the demolition of the Yugoslav state.

Whereas the coup's tactical organizer, General Mirković, was politically too naive to anticipate Hitler's enraged response, the more sophisticated Simović desperately sought to stave off German retribution. Despite the anti-Axis enthusiasm of the Serbian street crowds and the embarrassing applause with which Churchill greeted the coup, Simović frantically tried to make his government and its policies palatable to the Axis Powers. The aged and deaf Momčilo Ninčić, who had been Pašić's foreign minister in the mid-1920s and had since functioned as chairman of the German-Yugoslav, Italian-Yugoslav, and Magyar-Yugoslav friendship societies, was resurrected from political oblivion to resume his old portfolio. He promptly announced that the postcoup government accepted all international obligations contracted by its predecessors. Simović likewise sought to convince the German minister to Belgrade that the coup's causes were exclusively internal, and that he was a friend of Germany and proud of his acquaintance with his fellow aviator, Reichsmarshall Goering. To the resident American minister, Simović and Ninčić confessed that they could not afford to repudiate the Tripartite Pact for fear of infuriating Hitler and provoking Maček.

The Croatian leader, indeed, resumed his vice-premiership on April 4 only after receiving explicit assurances that the new government would honor the Sporazum and would endeavor to placate the Reich. Even then, Maček's step was not popular with his fellow Croats and was largely a hedge since he was also in contact with German agents in Zagreb. He was insuring himself and his constituency against two sets of contingencies: peace or war for Yugoslavia in the immediate future and Western or Axis victory in the longer run. When the onslaught came a few days later, Maček broadcast a weak and ambiguous appeal to his Croats to maintain discipline and do their duty. He then declined to go with the rest of the government into British-protected exile, retiring instead to his farm in what had meanwhile become a Pavelić-ruled, Axis-affiliated Croatia.

As far as Hitler was concerned, all the exertions by the Yugoslav leaders to appease him were *ab initio* futile. Within hours of the coup he directed the Wehrmacht to smash Yugoslavia, without regard to any possible declarations of loyalty that its new government might tender. He simply ignored Nincic's abject pleas to be permitted to come to Berlin for consultations and was undeterred by a last-minute demonstration of Stalin's interest in the form of a Soviet-Yugoslav Treaty of Friendship and Non-Aggression, concluded late on April 5. The next morning the Luftwaffe razed Belgrade and the German army poured across the Yugoslav borders from sundry directions. On April 10 the Ustaša proclaimed an Independent Croatian State in Zagreb; on April 12 Belgrade fell; and on April 17 the remains of the Yugoslav army surrendered, and the government went into exile (first in Athens, then in Jerusalem, and finally in London). Deeply shocked by the Belgrade coup, Hitler had taken swift and devastating revenge on those who had thus dared to cross him. Yet, in the long run, he was to be the biggest loser of the Balkan campaign of 1941, since it postponed his scheduled invasion of the Soviet Union by a month. The loss of that precious month of summer campaigning was to prove irreparable, perhaps even decisive, when his panzers ground to a halt at the outskirts of Moscow that winter. He might have been shrewder to have explored the Simović government's conciliatory gestures.

Judging the Yugoslav events and decisions of March, 1941, remains as difficult and controversial a problem for historians as it was at the time for the participants. Partisans of the Paul-Cvetković-Maček government argue that in reluctantly adhering to the Tripartite Pact, the government was using diplomacy as the necessary substitute for the economic and military power, as well as for the national unity and international assistance, that Yugoslavia lacked at the time; that the exceptional waivers it extracted from Hitler were likely to avert the war from Yugoslavia's borders and hence to preserve the state from annihilation and its peoples from devastation; that this government's policy, in short, was rational and prudent. They proceed then to denounce the Mirković-Simović coup for being exclusively Serbian and for precipitating the Axis invasion and occupation, which in turn led to a devastating cycle of guerrilla resistance and reprisals, ethnic and ideological civil war, reciprocal atrocities and exterminations, and ended in Communist rule over the country. In the light of these consequences, they argue, the coup must be condemned as politically immoral and counterproductive.

Simović's defenders, in turn, retort that even in politics, morality is not simply a matter of weighing material gains and risks and that the coup restored Yugoslavia's self-respect and Serbia's honor after the allegedly shameful abdication of signing the pact. They point to Romania as an example of a country that had "realistically" tacked with every wind of the

1930s and 1940s, yet also ended as a battleground, though admittedly it did not suffer the devastation of Yugoslavia's civil wars. They remind their rivals of Hitler's record of broken commitments, of the unpopularity of the Pauline regime, and of the genuine revulsion of the Serbian masses to the pact. They claim that, despite its putschist origins and its geronto-cratic composition, the short-lived Simović government was interwar Yugoslavia's most authentically representative one. Though uncomfort-ably aware that it was scarcely applauded outside Serbia, they insist that since the Slovenes and Croats had even better reason to fear Italy than the Serbs had to distrust Germany, the coup's rebuff to the Axis expressed the interests of all three Yugoslav state-peoples. Here they accept Hitler's and Churchill's parallel interpretations of the coup as a reversal of the previ-ous government's foreign policy and ignore, or interpret as merely tacti-cal, Simović's failure to repudiate the pact and his abortive endeavor to propitiate the Axis dictators.

To the criticism that its ultimate denouement was but a Communist dictatorship, the coup's non-Communist defenders retort that the Bal-kans would in any event have fallen within the Soviet sphere at the conclusion of World War II and that Yugoslavia's own Tito was, after all, preferable to a Stalinist agent imposed by the Soviet Union. To this, a disinterested observer might add that it was precisely the conditions of guerrilla warfare, which were so deplored by the defenders of Prince Paul's policy, that stimulated a Communist Yugoslav patriotism, a sense of self-reliance, and an effective administrative structure among Tito's Par-tisans and hence provided him with the organizational, psychological, and emotional resources to defy Stalin in 1948. Communist contributors to the discussion make some of the same points as the coup's "bourgeois" defenders, but in general they deemphasize the autonomous role of the putschist officers and insist that these could act as they did only thanks to the revolutionary rage of the masses, incited by the Communist Party, against the Pauline regime's policy of commitment to the Tripartite Pact.

11

Though the politics of ethnicity were more conspicuous than those of class in interwar Yugoslavia, the nation's profound socioeconomic problems also exacerbated her political divisions. A country of pro-found geographic, geological, hydrographic, and climatic variations, Yugoslavia's agricultural output ranged from subtropical fruits to the hardiest cereals, the most important single crop being corn. About 58 percent of the total area was officially defined as arable in 1938, but only 33 percent was actually cultivated as the official definition included mar-ginal land inaccessible to cultivation under prevailing or even more mod-ern agronomic techniques. Twenty-nine percent was forested. Though irrigation was little practiced in the interwar era, there were considerable efforts at water-flow control; many of the country's rivers were navigable and/or feasible for hydroelectric harnessing.

Yugoslavia was also generously endowed with a substantial number of minerals. By 1939, among European countries other than Soviet Russia, she ranked first in the production of lead and antimony, second in copper and chromium, third in silver and magnesite, and fourth in bauxite, lignite, and zinc. There were also significant deposits of coal, iron, asphalt, asbestos, manganese, gold, and salt. She was, indeed, better favored in natural resources than was Italy. But much of her interwar industrial development was either exclusively extractive (mining and logging for export) or confined to food-processing and textiles. The capital, the managerial talent, and even many of the skilled workers were foreign, and Yugoslavia herself was deprived of the benefits of a rounded industrial complex.

It would, however, be a mistake to attribute this stunted pattern exclusively to malevolence on the part of the "colonial" investors or to the venality of the native čaršija. At the time, Yugoslavia's internal market, capital resources, transportation network, skilled labor supply, and entrepreneurial experience were all too weak to render her a likely candidate for general industrialization. In the second half of the 1930s, indeed, the Stojadinović regime did press foreign governments and capitalists to develop the local processing of the country's crude ores. Accordingly, the newly invited Krupp firm built the Zenica iron-and-steel mill in 1936-37, while the long-established French concessionaires opened, in 1938, a copper refinery at Bor, and the British built lead and zinc furnaces at Zvečan and Šabac. In light industry, entire textile factories, including machines and skilled workers, were imported from Czechoslovakia and Poland; cement plants and furniture factories to process the extensive local asphalt and timber resources were also developed under governmental stimulation. As regards transportation, over 1,000 kilometers of new railroad tracks were laid, 40,000 kilometers of roads were built or improved, 1,200 new bridges were constructed and 3,600 repaired, and the merchant marine tonnage was tripled. Nevertheless, the growth of industry and of industrial employment was not adequate to propel Yugoslavia into sustained economic growth or to absorb her stagnant village population, whose immobility had been aggravated by the restrictive American immigration laws of the early 1920s. Emigration had until then served as a double remedy for rural poverty; it reduced the surplus population and it increased financial remittances from abroad.

The politically inspired and politically effective land-reform program of 1919 (see section 2) had indeed expropriated German, Magyar (in Slovenia, Croatia, and Vojvodina), Turkish (in Macedonia), and native (in Bosnia-Hercegovina and Dalmatia) landlords owning more than three hundred hectares of cultivated land or more than five hundred hectares of land in toto, in favor of Southern Slav peasant families. The governments had also sought to dovetail this program of land redistribution into a colonization policy designed to settle politically reliable Serb and Montenegran veterans, and wartime Croatian volunteers to the Yugoslav cause, in those Macedonian and Vojvodinian regions where the indigenous populations were ethnically non-Serbocroat and supposedly warranted surveillance. Predictably, much confusion, friction, and resentment ensued. All in all, 2,484,481 hectares, or one-tenth of the country's total area and one-sixth of her agricultural land, were expropriated between 1920 and 1938 and distributed among 637,328 families, or almost one-third of the country's total number of peasant families. This was, in fact, a major land reform that affected all regions except Serbia and Montenegro (where large estates and servile institutions had been abolished long before or had never existed) and involved twice as much land as the Communists' reforms after 1944. In Bosnia-Hercegovina and Macedonia, indeed, the result was an initial increase in productivity as the peasants no longer paid exorbitant rents to "feudal" landlords and hence had an incentive to produce. In the northern regions the break-up of large estates probably entailed a slight decline in productivity, but this was regarded as a price worth paying to achieve a land-owning Southern Slav peasantry.

Alas, this political desideratum having been achieved, the interwar regimes failed to devote equivalent attention to the economic and agronomic aspects of agriculture. The schedule of compensation was first used by Pašić in 1921 to purchase Bosniak Muslim endorsement of the Vidovdan draft-constitution, and a political football the whole program remained. Its administration was utilized as a lever for party patronage and bureaucratic nepotism and was frequently incompetent and even corrupt. The crucial stratum of the middle peasantry was not strengthened, as too many beneficiaries each received too little land for economic viability. To have given larger plots to fewer peasants, though theoretically preferable, was perhaps politically unfeasible. Credit and capital for the recipients of the new or slightly enlarged dwarf-holdings were not made available by governments confident that the peasants' docility could be purchased with land alone, and the bulk of the rural population soon relapsed into misery. The survival of the zadruga (the extended family-household) until well into the nineteenth century in most regions of Yugoslavia had contributed to rural overpopulation by holding surplus people on the land. Then the sharp decline in infant mortality rates, the inadequate growth of industrial employment, and the throttling of emigration had so aggravated this demographic squeeze, that by 1931 as much as 43 percent of the rural population was surplus even at the prevailing low levels of agronomic technology. At the same time, the percentage of the total population engaged in agriculture had decreased only slightly between 1921 and 1931, from 78.9 to 76.5. Languor and impoverishment in the villages was the result.

Politically, this problem was further exacerbated by the sharp variation in rural overpopulation and poverty among the several regions of Yugoslavia. The range here was as great as between the general Yugoslav average and those of some Western European countries. The governments' efforts, albeit erratic, to narrow regional differences were resented by the better-off Slovenes, Croats, prečani Serbs, Germans, and Magyars of the country's northern half. They charged that such efforts simply defrauded them for the benefit of the allegedly shiftless and/or turbulent and therefore poorer Serbs, Montenegrans, Bosniaks, and Macedonians of the south. Furthermore, the peasants' standard of living was falling precisely as their expectations were rising. This disparity provoked a political mood of rage alternating with gloom, screened by a deceptive veneer of apathy. Ironically, the capacity of the economic system to fulfill rising peasant expectations was now limited precisely by the kind of growth that the interwar urban economy was experiencing; far heavier in service fields, urban housing, and government office buildings than in production, this growth tended to orient the national income in a direction detrimental to the rural sector.

The other potential remedies for rural overpopulation were also hampered by social, political, or natural factors. Birth control was practiced in the relatively richer (albeit Roman Catholic) areas, but in the poorer regions, where children were put to work earlier, large families were sought to insure a labor force. While the cultivated area increased by one-fifth between 1921 and 1938, thanks to water control, reclamation, forest clearance, reforestation, and the exploitation of marginal land, this outlet soon reached its natural limits. Cottage industry, though assigned a high value in Croatian Peasantism, made no significant dent in rural overpopulation and underemployment. Finally, the shortage of capital for investment in agriculture as well as in industry, combined with certain cultural and psychological resistances on the part of the peasant, aborted the improvement in techniques of cultivation and resultant intensification of productivity that, when combined with industrialization, is perhaps the most promising (but admittedly also the most difficult) long-run solution to rural impoverishment.

Loans granted to peasants, and business transacted with them, were generally usurious and exploitative and hence, in effect, further drained the rural economy. The only significant exception here was the Slovene cooperative movement. Endorsed by the local Roman Catholic clergy and affiliated with Korošec's Slovene People's Party, whose economic arm it became, it functioned as a production and marketing as well as a credit agency. In the rest of the country, private banks and especially private money-lenders held over three-fourths of the peasants' debts (32.43 percent and 45.27 percent, respectively, in 1932) at usurious interest rates. In 1932, 35.7 percent of all rural households were in debt (many of the others being too poor to obtain credit), and the sum of their indebtedness amounted to 46 percent of the previous year's gross agricultural income and 80-90 percent of the total cash income of agriculture.[8]

On April 20 of that miasmic depression year, the government proclaimed a moratorium on repayment of peasant debts and on foreclosures; in practice, this also entailed a cutoff of further, urgently needed loans and, indeed, imposed a virtual moratorium on peasant economic activity as such. Hence, these depression years witnessed a fall of total investment in agriculture, as used capital resources were not replaced. Politically, the royal dictatorship may have damaged itself with this moratorium, which injured the resented but powerful village usurers and interrupted a process whereby wealthier peasants and nonpeasant creditors had been gaining economic control over the land and other assets of the indigent peasants. On September 26, 1936, Stojadinović replaced this moratorium with his more dynamic and popular arrangements for the consolidation, reorganization, transfer, reduction, and partial repayment of peasant debts (see section 9). Even thereafter, however, the ability of peasants to obtain credit at reasonable rates remained constricted. Meanwhile, the state was less willing to write off debts owed to itself, i.e., tax arrears, than debts owed to private and commercial creditors.

The balance of labor, land, and technology in Yugoslav agriculture was not typical of either a stable and traditional or of a modern pattern, and it was in some ways irrational even within the available economic limits and possibilities. Crop rotation patterns were poor; too much arable land was plowed for grains, especially corn; farm work peaked during four months (June-July and September-October), when even smallholders craved additional labor, while idleness prevailed much of the rest of the year; the variety of implements led to chaos in repairs and the supply of spare-parts; livestock were grazed in the open, and manure was not readily available; though labor was in over-supply, the type of agriculture practiced was extensive. In turn, the very abundance of labor acted as a brake on the application of technology, as did the fact that modern apparatus had to be imported, was heavily taxed and hence prohibitively expensive. Those sons of peasants who attended agricultural high schools and colleges, supposedly to learn how agronomic science might benefit their villages, generally vaulted directly out of agriculture into the bureaucracy, where they went on to manipulate one of Europe's least reliable systems of agricultural statistics.

Approximately half the output of Yugoslav agriculture was marketed (in Western Europe the proportion was three-fourths). This half did not,

8. Tomasevich, *Peasants, Politics, and Economic Change in Yugoslavia*, pp. 671-73.

however, represent an authentic surplus over a satisfactory consumption level in the villages, but was marketed out of necessity by impoverished and even undernourished peasants to raise cash to pay their debts, taxes, purchases that were indirectly heavily taxed, and lawyers' fees that were a by-product of chronic indebtedness and tax-delinquency. Poor storage and transportation facilities further aggravated the peasants' plight and forced them to compete against each other by selling at glut-season to a small number of collusively organized middlemen at low prices. In their purchases, too, the peasants were again unorganized, under time pressures (a scythe had to be in hand by reaping time, kerosene by winter time), and hence obliged to pay high prices to merchants charging extravagant markups on commodities whose wholesale prices had already been set by cartels and on which the government had levied heavy excise taxes. The cost of the country's extremely high tariff policy, which was extolled by the regime on economic, military, and political grounds, was largely carried by the rural population.

Some of the peasants' own treasured customs and values also injured them. They preserved into the interwar era certain practices from the former zadruga culture, such as a plethora of feast days and ruinous standards of hospitality, which now had a deleterious effect. More serious was the progressive subdivision of their holdings among family sons, a pattern which held surplus labor on the land, increased the number of dwarf-holdings, lowered productivity, and maximized pauperization. Already by the 1931 census, two-thirds of all holdings were smaller than five hectares, the minimum necessary to sustain a peasant family. Ideologically and morally, the peasants also identified with "heroic" values and institutions—a projection of their former *haiduk* and *graničar* traditions as warriors against the Ottomans—to the extent of never protesting, not even through the legal opposition parties, against the fact that about a third of government expenditures went annually to that sacred cow which was to collapse so ignominiously in 1941, the military, while the state scarcely used its economic power at all on behalf of agriculture. Before the Stojadinović ministry, governments had shown little interest in such rural public works projects as the construction of storage facilities, irrigation, pest control, and cattle breeding. The extravagant expenditures on the military, the gendarmerie, and the bureaucracy were sapped from the unresisting peasantry and contributed to its low standard of living. The peasantry annually transferred about half its cash income to the state as taxes while remaining at the bottom of that state's scale of priorities.

A Croatian or Macedonian or ethnic-minority peasant was likely to resent the interwar Yugoslav state and governments as Serb-dominated and hence as ethnically alien. Yet there was also another dimension, not related to ethnicity, to the peasant's resentment: he feared and hated the city as culturally alien and economically exploitative. "God made the country; the Devil made the city," "The nearer to the city, the nearer to the Devil," and "Christ was born in a village and crucified in a city" were characteristic peasant aphorisms. While understandable, such attitudes were not in the peasants' own best interests, for the solution to the problems of agricultural backwardness lay in the development of urban industry and markets. By insisting that the peasantry was not a class but the moral hypostasis of "the whole people," peasantist ideology implied that the urban classes were somehow "outside" the people and would be dealt with accordingly when the peasants achieved power. Such animosity only hardened urban indifference to rural problems and furnished ammunition to demagogic and manipulative politicians, which was used in the same way as ethnic animosities among Yugoslavia's several peoples were.

The ethnic animosities were, indeed, compounded by economic grievances and cleavages. The ex-Habsburg provinces brought to the interwar Yugoslav state many resources—industries, railroads, roads, harbors, mines, forests, taxable revenue, etc.—which, their inhabitants alleged, were then exploited in Serbia's exclusive interest. The Serbs, in turn, felt themselves entitled to compensation for having borne so much suffering in World War I for the South Slav cause. They also reasoned that, but for Serbia's "covering" them with its moral and political credit at war's end, the ex-Habsburgers, as the subjects of a defeated power, would have been saddled with heavy war-indemnity payments; therefore, they ought now to release a part of these "spared" assets to defray the costs of Serbia's reconstruction. When the currency was unified at war's end at an exchange ratio of four Habsburg crowns to one Serbian dinar, the northern population complained that this proportion in effect sequestered twenty percent of its liquid assets. Different direct tax levels survived until the royal dictatorship and were higher north of the Una-Sava-Danube line than south of it, though they were also lower in Bosnia and Dalmatia than in Serbia itself. Though the state drew only one-fifth to one-fourth of its tax revenue from direct taxes, these regional differences contributed significantly to the tensions among the ethnic groups during Yugoslavia's first decade.

Indirect taxes, in turn, had been unified in the early 1920s by extending the Serbian system to the entire country and then raising the rates. A fiscal pattern in which indirect taxes furnished 75-80 percent of tax revenues was politically feasible in interwar Yugoslavia but socially inequitable and amounted to a veiled system of extortion from the entire peasantry, Serbian and non-Serbian alike. Civil service recruitment and assignment as well as allocations of public revenues (in capital investments, social overhead investments, and general governmental services) again favored the urban sector in general and Serbia in particular. Croatian complaints, for example, to the effect that almost two-thirds of state expenditures were spent in old Serbia and that only half the revenue collected in Croatia was spent there, were probably exaggerated but not simply fictitious. The reply of the Serb-dominated regimes was, of course, that Yugoslavia's long-run viability required her development as a unit, entailing the temporary subsidization of her poorer by her more developed regions. Though plausible in theory, this rationale was undermined by the often irrational manner in which public funds were allocated and by the scandalous neglect of the very poorest rural regions in Macedonia, Bosnia, and karstic Dalmatia in favor of Serbia proper, especially its towns.

The depression spotlighted and aggravated all these socioeconomic flaws. From 1930 onward, foreign capital inflow, tourist spending, and emigrant remittances all plummeted—indeed, there was a net outflow of foreign and domestic capital. The fact that Yugoslavia's own harvests remained plentiful was of little avail in the face of a precipitous fall in the international price of her agricultural commodities. Initially she hoped to compensate for this decline in prices by exporting greater quantities of grain, but the protectionist policies of her market-countries soon aborted even this remedy. The currency was then "saved" by a ruthless deflationary policy, but at the cost of the economy as a whole and particularly of its already crippled rural credit system. In the aftermath of a severe drought in 1931 followed by an extraordinarily harsh winter, the desperate peasants resorted to mass slaughter of their cattle in the spring of 1932. The royal dictatorship was now also deep into its slide to political isolation and paralysis, but even with a more prescient and energetic regime, Yugoslavia would probably have been economically too weak to conduct an effective and independent policy to counter the depression.

In theory, Yugoslav governments and elites had always acknowledged that the long-run remedy to their country's socioeconomic problems was industrialization with the aid of foreign capital, in the form of direct investments as well as favorable trade balances, and they had sought to guide her diplomatic, tariff, cartel, and tax policies accordingly. Hence, already during the 1920s, the favorable world prices for Yugoslavia's principal exports and her own hospitality toward foreign capital had permitted modest but significant investments in mining and textile industries, transportation, shipping, lumbering, and tourism. Admittedly, the conventional plight of primitive capital accumulation, such as low wages, long hours, and dangerous working conditions, pertained in the industrializing sectors. Admittedly, also, the economy as a whole became semicolonial. But in spite of the high price paid for the foreign capital and the failure to yoke its distribution to an optimal strategy of national economic development, its influx was on balance necessary and positive.

Certain anomalies, however, in the structure of Yugoslavia's foreign economic relations during the favorable 1920s would then render her particularly defenseless in the depression storm of the early 1930s and hence vulnerable to Nazi Germany's subsequent drive for economic hegemony over the Balkans. France, England, Belgium, and the United States, who supplied Yugoslavia's foreign investment capital, as well as her diplomatic allies, France, Czechoslovakia, and Romania, were inhospitable to her exports and disappointing as trading partners. *Per contra,* her most promising commercial linkages were precisely to those countries with which her political relations were most frictional or aloof—Italy, Germany, Austria—until Stojadinović closed this gap in the aftermath of the depression.

Italy had been Yugoslavia's main foreign market, absorbing over one-fourth the value of her exports, until deep into the depression, when Mussolini decided to favor his Hungarian client. Even after that, trade between them remained substantial for a few more years, until Yugoslavia's participation, at the behest of France and England, in the League of Nations' sanction of Italy for her invasion of Abyssinia in 1935. This became the first year in which less than one-fifth of Yugoslavia's exports went to Italy, and thereafter the fraction shrank rapidly. Such a renunciation of her Italian market might have been economically fatal to Yugoslavia but for Nazi Germany's alacrity at filling the gap. Britain and especially France, on the other hand, were loath to share the economic costs of the political course they had been urging on Yugoslavia and on Italy's other vulnerable trade-partners by any analogous increase in their absorption of these countries' exports. German propaganda thus found it relatively easy to depict her substantial barter arrangements with Yugoslavia in the later 1930s as altruistic, honest, direct, and interest-free in contrast to the allegedly selfish, exploitative, nebulous, and usurious foreign trade policies of the decadent capitalist states.

Germany's readiness to buy up Yugoslav surpluses was, indeed, initially beneficial. But eventually it gave her a stranglehold on the Yugoslav economy, which virtually ceased to earn foreign credits in convertible currencies as Berlin insisted on direct barter: German capital goods (primarily for extractive industries) and industrial commodities in exchange for Yugoslav raw materials and agricultural products. The latter were, to be sure, generously rated at prices far above prevailing world-market prices, and it was scarcely Germany's fault that Yugoslav government agencies and middlemen absorbed much of this difference. In the long run, however, Yugoslavia became dependent on German goodwill for the ongoing flow of spare-parts and replacements to the newly supplied capital equipment. By 1938, 36 percent of all Yugoslav exports (in value) were going to Germany, while 32.5 percent of all her imports came from Germany. But these same goods accounted for only 2 and 2.2 percent respectively of the Reich's total imports and exports in that year. Thus there was little question as to which trade-partner was vital and which one expendable to the other. Yet for Yugoslavia there appeared to be no alternative to this economic dependency, which fact renders her resistance to German political pressure in the spring of 1941 all the more impressive. The Western Powers were relatively uninterested in her exports, expected payment in convertible currencies for her imports, were reluctant to advance long-term credits (except France, and then only for military purchases), and tended to insist on the immediate profitability of any investments. Their foreign economic policy, in short, was planless, sporadic, and hence inferior to the sustained drive of Nazi Germany.

Up to the eve of World War II, Germany had interested herself almost exclusively, apart from some industrial prestige-projects, in the acquisition and stockpiling of the agricultural and mineralogical produce of Yugoslavia and her Balkan neighbors. They reached their capacity to supply these German needs by 1939. In that year, Germany started to encourage the area's industrialization, provided the capital equipment was supplied by herself and provided the local industrial projects complemented her own war economy. Thus, while Germany did not oblige these countries to renounce their industrial aspirations as such, she did constrain them to concentrate on industries that processed raw materials and food products, and punctured their dreams of heavy and machine industries. The political corollary of this German economic policy was the protection of Yugoslavia's territorial integrity. Until Hitler's sudden enraged reaction to the Yugoslav internal crisis of March, 1941, he had consistently rebuffed Mussolini's sporadic intrigues to fragment Yugoslavia. Preferring a wide Yugoslav market and a centralized political administration, he had throughout "bet on" Belgrade and remained aloof from Zagreb.

Interwar Yugoslavia's cultural and social profiles paralleled the above-described economic patterns. Here, too, there were sharp regional variations along a north to south axis of regression and strenuous, but only partly successful, endeavors during the two interwar decades to overcome the country's lag behind average European levels of literacy, culture, health, administrative competence, etc.

Illiteracy above the age of five had been 51.5 percent in Yugoslavia as a whole at the time of the 1921 census, with the following regional diversities: Slovenia, 8.8; Vojvodina, 23.3; Croatia, 32.3; Dalmatia, 49.5; Serbia, 65.4; Montenegro, 67.0; Bosnia-Hercegovina, 80.5; and Macedonia, 83.8. In the 1931 census the base age was raised from five to ten, yet illiteracy was still 44.6 percent, and again greater in the south than in the north. In 1940, at the close of our era, illiteracy above age ten was estimated at 40 percent. Between 1919 and 1940 the number of elementary schools increased from 5,600 to 9,170, their teachers from 11,000 to 31,000, and their pupils from 650,000 to 1,493,000. Despite the high value placed on education by a people resentful of being traditionally disparaged as backward by the neighboring Germans, Italians,

Magyars, and Ottomans, in 1940 there were still some 250,000 Yugoslav children who attended no school at all; Muslim parents were suspicious of modern schooling for girls and schools were simply geographically inaccessible in certain remote areas. Even among those children attending elementary school, only one out of every fifteen proceeded to secondary school. However, a far higher proportion of secondary school graduates went on to university. The educational system, in other words, was top-heavy, and peasants by-and-large had less access to it than did the urban population. A peculiar feature was an abundance—for such a relatively poor country—of special vocational and experimental schools.

Except for the universities, the educational system was centrally controlled and administered from the ministry in Belgrade. Its overt ideology was nationalistic, secular, and religiously tolerant. Many Croatian teachers, however, became Ustaši, and Serbian instructors turned to Communism or socialism. The university youth was also heavily radical, Left and Right. Its preferred fields of study were, in descending order, law, philosophy, and technical fields—scarcely an optimal sequence from the perspective of the country's most pressing needs. Nevertheless, the intelligentsia enjoyed great prestige and sought assiduously to keep au courant with Western cultural movements and "isms."

The press was frequently censored and yet thoroughly slanderous. Personal abuse and political incitement ran at a high pitch while every shade of political opinion and ethnic claim was pugnaciously expressed and attacked. Of the country's many newspapers, journals, and periodicals, which totaled over eight hundred during the Vidovdan era and about two-thirds that number after the Alexandrine coup, only one, the Belgrade *Politika*, published in editions of forty-five to one hundred thousand copies, enjoyed a national readership, and even this clientele was elite.

Public health paralleled education as an area of strenuous but imbalanced government endeavors to tackle interwar Yugoslavia's appalling problems. The death rate from pulmonary turberculosis, a disease directly reflecting inadequate nutrition, sanitation, and housing, was Europe's highest. Other endemic diseases were malaria, syphilis, trachoma, typhoid, typhus, and dysentery. Physicians were maldistributed: the ratio of physicians to population in 1938 was estimated as 1:750 in urban localities but only 1:14,400 in the rural regions. Yet Yugoslavia's organization of public health and her programs of preventive medicine in rural areas, despite major weaknesses, were widely conceded to be superior to those of other East Central European countries with similar socio-economic structures. In the long run, of course, the improvement of health, educational, and administrative standards required the raising of the country's general economic base, and this, in turn, appeared to entail the renovation of her political system.

12

Yugoslavia's interwar history thus closed with her major ethnic communities unreconciled, her citizens' civil liberties violated, her economic unification and development stunted, and her agrarian problems only partially alleviated at the price of economic and political dependence on Germany. The brutality and cynicism of successive regimes had estranged the best of the intelligentsia, while their sheer incompetence and corruption had alienated the peasants and workers. But it was only after the German army had exposed the brittleness of the Yugoslav state apparatus in April, 1941, that the country's pent-up ethnic and social rages exploded into civil and revolutionary war. Until then, only extremists of the Croatian Ustaša and the Macedonian IMRO had sought to achieve separation through violence. Despite endemic ethnic tensions, the idea of a Yugoslav state had been accepted throughout the interwar decades by the influential elements in the several ethnic communities, though the idea itself did not suffice to effect their reconciliation.

While the elites of all of interwar Yugoslavia's ethnic communities were culpable, the srbijanci Serbian politicians and bureaucrats, who were as consistently dominant in the authoritarian 1930s as in the parliamentary 1920s, bear major responsibility for her political fragility. It was primarily they who squandered the moral capital that Serbia's heroic performance in World War I had earned for Yugoslavia. Confusing authority with arbitrariness and administration with police methods, they were insensitive to the other communities' cultural, historic, and provincial sensibilities (while admittedly also riding rough-shod over their own lower classes) and monopolistic in their grip on the levers of power. With remarkable albeit exaggerated self-assurance, they leapt insouciantly and possessively into governing a Yugoslavia four times as populous as their prewar Serb base and many of whose "added" peoples regarded themselves as the srbijanci Serbs' cultural superiors. One need not make a judgment on such claims to cultural superiority to conclude that it was myopic and contrary to Yugoslav *raison d'etat* for the srbijanci Serbs to exclude so many other civil, diplomatic, and military officers from Yugoslav state service merely because these had been trained in the Habsburg Empire and hence were allegedly suspect.

Some statistics will illustrate this Serbian urge for hegemony. Croatian regiments in Habsburg service had over the centuries earned an illustrious reputation for military prowess; of 375 generals and admirals in the Austro-Hungarian armed forces at the outbreak of World War I, 57 (55 generals and 2 admirals), i.e., over 15 percent, were Croats. Yet, on the eve of the second world conflagration, of the 165 Yugoslav generals in active service, 161 were Serbs while the Croats and Slovenes furnished only 2 each; of some 1,500 military cadets, 1,300 were Serbs, 150 Croats, and 50 Slovenes. Only Serbian military traditions were preserved and inculcated in the Yugoslav army; those of the other peoples were ignored or suppressed. As regards the civilian sectors of government, in 1939 the Serbian contingents among senior permanent functionaries in several Yugoslav ministries numbered as follows: (a) Office of the Premier, 13 of 13; (b) Royal (Regency) Court, 30 of 31; (c) Ministry of the Interior, 113 of 127; (d) Ministry of Foreign Affairs, 180 of 219; (e) Ministry of Education, 150 of 156; (f) Justice Ministry, 116 of 137; (g) Transportation Ministry, 15 of 26; (h) State Mortgage Bank, 196 of 200.

To the extent that the Serbs shared responsible administrative posts, it was less with the Croats than with the strategic and hence privileged Slovenes, whose "Central European" standards of order were valuable bureaucratic assets. Within their Drava banovina itself, moreover, the Slovenes enjoyed a virtual administrative monopoly and were thus able to protect their provincial culture from "Balkan pollution." Inferior jobs in certain central ministries, e.g., transportation, were habitually distributed as patronage to Bosniaks.

As regards explicitly political offices, the pattern of Serb preponderance was similar to that in the civil service, though here the Croatian policy of boycott pursued by Radić and Maček through most of the interwar era played into Serb hands. Of the 656 ministers in office between the formation of the state and the conclusion of the Sporazum, 452 were Serbs, 49 were Slovenes, 18 were Bosniaks, 26 were Croats who belonged to Croatian parties, and 111 were Croats regarded as "renegades" for joining Belgrade governments as unrepresentative individuals over the objections of the Croatian Peasant leadership. If one divides interwar Yugoslav political history into the 121 months of the parliamentary era (December, 1918 to December, 1928), and the 147 months of the authoritarian era (January, 1929 to March, 1941), then the number of months during which certain key portfolios were held by Serbs in each of these two eras was as follows: (a) Premiership, 116 and 147; (b) Defense, 121 and 147; (c) Interior, 111 and 129; (d) Foreign Affairs, 100 and 147; (e) Finance, 118 and 98; (f) Education, 110 and 126; (g) Justice, 105 and 132.

Distinct from, though politically related to, the pattern of Serbian domination was that of administrative centralization, which was a heritage of small Serbia's nineteenth-century experience in state-building. But in twentieth-century Yugoslavia administrative centralism implied, as preconditions, an excellent communications network and high bureaucratic competence; both were lacking. Chronic cabinet instability at the top of the administrative hierarchy then further compounded the problems of accountability and authority at the bottom. Confusion, delay, waste, corruption, as well as political favoritism and personal nepotism became the *modus operandi* of an overcentralized, overly expensive, but underpaid and well-nigh irresponsible civil service. And the final irony was that this centralized administrative apparatus was not harnessed to any sustained legislative program of rational national priorities. Instead of pressing a sustained campaign to overcome the country's serious economic and social problems, the čaršija squandered the resources that its inegalitarian tax system extracted from the masses on a speculative residential building spree and other state-protected "investments," on the unresponsive state apparatus which it "owned," and on a hideously expensive but hidebound and obsolescent military establishment. Such were some of the costs of "prestige politics."

For its part, the Croatian Peasant Party shares a heavy responsibility for this false ordering of Yugoslav priorities. Already during the 1920s, under the boisterous and unpredictable leadership of its emotional tribune Radić, it had become so absorbed in ethnic politics that it ceased to be a party of socioeconomic reforms; it sponsored none during its brief experience in government and advocated none from its prolonged posture of opposition. With the passage of Radić's mantle to the weaker shoulders of the more prosaic Maček, real peasants virtually vanished from the directorate and its leadership fell into the hands of the intelligentsia. During its years of ideological and social vigor before World War I, this party had conferred a sense of dignity, security, and citizenship on the peasant and had educated him to pride in his peasant culture; it had then filled the moral and emotional void left in the peasant's world by the disintegration of the zadruga. But in its declining phase of bureaucratic ossification, mere nationalism, and ideological senility of the late 1930s, it permitted itself to be infiltrated by fascist elements and reactionary ideas. Committed to denying the manifest trends of economic and social differentiation in the village, it blinded itself to the need for industrialization. The stillborn Sporazum with which it finally pushed its way into the ministries and the bureaucracy was its swan song. Thereafter, the mantle of Radić slipped off Maček's shoulders and was, in a sense, inherited and shared by Pavelić and Tito.

Chapter Six

ROMANIA

1

ON THE morrow of World War I Romanian society could reasonably anticipate a hopeful future. The prewar Old Kingdom, or Regat, had more than doubled in area and population; from a land of 130,177 square kilometers and 7,160,682 people in 1912, it became Greater Romania, or România Mare, with 295,049 square kilometers and 15,541,424 people in 1920. The new, or restored, regions were: Southern Dobruja, which had first been acquired from Bulgaria in the Second Balkan War of 1913 and then regained at the end of the World War; the Bukovina, which had been under Austria since 1775; Bessarabia, annexed by Russia in 1812; and Transylvania, which had long been politically a part of historic Hungary. All these lands, and particularly Transylvania, were expected to add valuable agricultural and especially industrial resources to the Romanian economy.[1] *Per contra*, the historically dangerous neighbors, Russia and Hungary, had been correspondingly weakened by their defeats in the World War and by the subsequent territorial losses to Romania. Furthermore, the economic potential of the new as well as of the old Romanian provinces was expected to be released and developed to an unprecedented degree by a radical postwar land reform, which was intended also to immunize the Romanian peasantry against the revolutionary fever that at war's end had infected Romania's Russian and Hungarian neighbors. Romania's strategic location at the mouths of the Danube was also thought to have been enhanced by her reannexation of Bessarabia, overlooking the river's northern banks at its egress into the Black Sea. Finally, Romania's governmental and dynastic continuity, unique in postwar Eastern Europe, was also expected to contribute to her international prestige as well as to her domestic stability.

While the problems and hazards confronting interwar Romania were

1. The term Transylvania will be used to denote all the territory acquired from Hungary, i.e., Transylvania proper plus the Romanian Banat and the Crişana-Maramureş district.

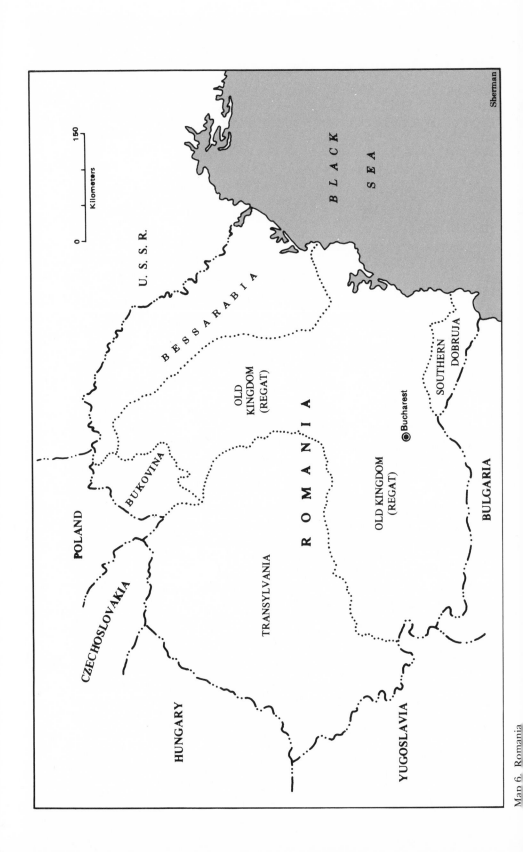

Map 6. Romania

acknowledged, they were nevertheless initially de-emphasized. Like many of their colleagues in other East Central European countries, Romanian politicians tended to delude themselves with exaggerated expectations of the extent to which Russia and Germany had been permanently weakened by war and revolution. They also failed to evaluate realistically the staggering difficulty of modernizing their backward economy and truly integrating a society rent by long historical separations, class divisions, and ethnic tensions.

2

As background to interwar Romania's political history, this is an appropriate point to present and analyze some of her social and economic statistics. The census of December 29, 1930, indicated Romania's population as 18,057,028, rendering her the second most populous country of East Central Europe, after Poland. The regional, ethnic, religious, and economic composition of this population is shown in tables 40-43.[2]

TABLE 40

POPULATION BY REGIONAL UNITS (1930)

	Number	Percentage
Regat and Southern Dobruja	8,791,254	48.7
Bukovina	853,009	4.7
Bessarabia	2,864,402	15.9
Transylvania, the Banat, and Crişana-Maramureş	5,548,363	30.7
Total	18,057,028	100.0

The ethnicity and religion tables reflect certain correlations: Romanians were either Eastern Orthodox (in all regions) or Uniate (a substantial fraction in Transylvania); Russians, Ukrainians, Serbs, and Bulgarians were also Orthodox; Magyars were Roman Catholic, Calvinist, or Unitarian; Germans were Roman Catholic (the Schwabs) or Lutheran (the Saxons); Croats, Slovenes, Czechs, and Slovaks were also Roman Catholic; some Jews-by-religion (Mosaic) indicated their nationality as Magyar or Romanian; the Turks and Tatars were Muslim, except for the

2. Statistical data collated from *Recensământul General al Populaţiei României din 29 Decemvrie 1930* (Bucharest: Imprimeria Naţională, 1938), vols. 2, 3, and 6.

TABLE 41

POPULATION BY ETHNICITY (1930)*

	Number	Percentage
Romanian	12,981,324	71.9
Magyar	1,425,507	7.9
German	745,421	4.1
Russian	409,150	2.3
Ukrainian	582,115	3.2
Serb, Croat, Slovene (Yugoslav)	51,062	0.3
Bulgarian	366,384	2.0
Czech and Slovak	51,842	0.3
Jewish	728,115	4.0
Turk and Tatar	176,913	1.0
Gypsie	262,501	1.5
Gagauz	105,750	0.6
Other (Polish, Greek, Armenian, etc.)	170,944	0.9
Total	18,057,028	100.0

*Based on subjective declaration of respondent.

TABLE 42

POPULATION BY RELIGION (1930)

	Number	Percentage
Eastern Orthodox	13,108,227	72.6
Greek Catholic (Uniate)	1,427,391	7.9
Roman Catholic	1,234,151	6.8
Calvinist	710,706	3.9
Lutheran	398,759	2.2
Unitarian	69,257	0.4
Baptist	60,562	0.4
Mosaic	756,930	4.2
Muslim	185,486	1.0
Other (Adventist, Armeno-Gregorian, etc.)	105,559	0.6
Total	18,057,028	100.0

Gagauz of Bessarabia and Dobruja, whose language was Turkish but whose religion was Orthodox. The bulk of the minorities lived in the new provinces; indeed, minorities formed less than 8 percent of the Regat's population. There were also about 675,000 Romanians in neighboring countries and perhaps 150,000 in the United States, but Romania did not enjoy anything like the flow of remittances from emigrants which enriched, for example, interwar Yugoslavia's economy.

TABLE 43

POPULATION BY ECONOMIC SECTORS (1930), (INCLUDING DEPENDENTS)

	Number	Percentage
Agriculture	13,063,213	72.3
Mining	153,423	0.9
Industry	1,560,061	8.6
Commerce, banking	749,508	4.2
Transportation, communications	508,620	2.8
Public services (civil and military)	863,572	4.8
Free professions and others	1,158,631	6.4
Total	18,057,028	100.0

The overall profile is thus of a country of which the prewar Regat core accounted for slightly less than half of the total population, and in which the Romanian state-nation formed over seven-tenths of that total but in which the ethnic minorities, despite their substantial numbers (28.1 percent), lacked ethnic or religious cohesion. In any event, the Romanians' birthrate was outstripping those of the ethnic minorities. Romania's population was overwhelmingly rural, 79.8 percent living in villages of less than 10,000 inhabitants. It was one of relatively low productivity (Romania's per capita output in agriculture being but 48 percent of the European average) and of low literacy (57.1 percent from age seven upward). Romania had the dubious distinction of having the highest general death rate, the highest infant mortality rate (one out of five dying in the first year of life), and the second highest tuberculosis mortality rate (after Yugoslavia's) in Europe. She also furnished Europe's highest birth rate, with an average annual population increase of 1.4 percent; hence she had a relatively young population (46.4 percent below the age of twenty), a circumstance entailing both hazards and promises.

Romanian society was, finally, also characterized by substantial and debilitating regional variations. Thus, to cite but one characteristic example, whereas the national average of literacy above the age of seven was 57.1 percent, and that of the Regat stood close to it at 56.1 percent, the new provinces varied from 67.3 and 65.7 percent, respectively, in Transylvania and Bukovina, through 45.5 percent in the Southern Dobruja, to a low of 38.2 percent in Bessarabia. Though these and additional, similar, data were not compiled until the 1930 census, the general pattern indicated by them was already apparent a decade earlier, but its danger signals had then been discounted as transitory in the euphoria of Greater Romania's emergence from World War I.

3

The political unification of Greater Romania bore certain parallels to the corresponding processes in neighboring Yugoslavia and Poland. The role of the Regat may be analogized to that of Serbia, and the domineering Liberal Party of the Brătianu family to Pašić's Serbian Radicals. The National-Peasant Party of aggrieved Transylvanian Romanians allied with alienated Regateni forces played, all things considered, a somewhat more pragmatic version of the Radić-Pribičević oppositional game. The attitude of the Transylvanian Romanians toward their Regateni brethren also resembled somewhat that of the Poznanian Poles toward their fellow Poles in Galicia, the Kongresówka, and the *kresy*; the first-mentioned in each case regarded themselves as harder working, better disciplined, more "Western," but felt exploited by the politically adroit, yet economically parasitical, "Levantines" of the southern and eastern regions. Indeed, the Polish analogy to Romania is in one major respect more apposite than the Yugoslav one, since the process of integrating the state-nation of the country's several prewar parts, which was quite a different problem from that of reconciling the ethnic minorities to the state, was, despite frictions and resentments, handled more successfully in these two states than in Yugoslavia. Romanians and Poles, after all, each composed one nation, whereas Croats and Serbs did not feel that they belonged to a single Yugoslav people. Yet another experience shared by the three states was the existence of a particularly backward, refractory, and incendiary region (Bessarabia, Macedonia, or Eastern Galicia and the *kresy*) whose problems were then compounded by its use as a bureaucratic exile for incompetent, corrupt, sadistic, or politically out-of-favor administrators. Not only were the Slavic, Jewish, and Turco-Tatar minorities of Bessarabia unreconciled to Romanian rule, but the province's Romanian majority was considered benighted and reactionary even by prevailing Romanian standards.

To the Transylvanian Romanians, on the other hand, it was the Regat that appeared obscurantist and oriental. Thanks to a strong national solidarity that transcended class lines, they had succeeded better than any other minority of prewar Hungary in protecting themselves against magyarization. But in this endeavor, they had long regarded Vienna rather than Bucharest as their natural political ally. Though maintaining close cultural contacts with the Regat, the Transylvanian Romanians nevertheless had long remained *Kaisertreu*, and it was only after prolonged and bitter experience with Magyar oppression and Habsburg indifference that they redirected their political aspirations toward union with the Regat shortly before World War I. Nevertheless, even after union was consummated at war's end, the Transylvanian Romanians nursed many pretensions and grievances vis-à-vis the politically dominant

Regatenis. Conscious of having once served as the cradle of Romanian nationalism and aware of their currently strong cultural and social institutions, they were proud that they had no native nobility and produced their political leaders from the common people, and they scorned the allegedly feudal-boyar society of the Regat. Toughened and disciplined by their sustained struggle against magyarization, they were more "Central European," more in tune with Germanic styles and habits, more immune to Phanariot and Ottoman influences, more solid and stolid than were the sinuous, theatrical, "Mediterranean" Regatenis. Denied administrative autonomy by the latter, they would complain that the prewar Hungarian administration, though politically hostile, had nevertheless been more honest and competent than that of their supposed brothers from the Regat. But, since they had been so completely without political rights in old Hungary, their complaints never escalated into serious secessionism.

The Regateni politicians, in turn, who were dominated by the Liberal Party, felt their region entitled to compensation for the extensive damage inflicted on it initially during the military operations of 1916-17 and then through the forced deliveries of goods and services during the Central Powers' occupation of 1917-18. More importantly, they were exceedingly sensitive to the supposed centrifugal dangers presented by the new Romanians' occasional nostalgia for the bureaucratic efficiency (although never for the political dominion) of old Austria-Hungary. In Regateni eyes, these dangers were compounded by, and in turn compounded, the allegedly subversive threats posed by the ethnic minorities. Their training in French administrative methods and their current anxiety lest the state disintegrate thus rendered the Regatenis excessive centralizers who were determined to rule Greater Romania as but an extension of the Old Kingdom, despite the new provinces' diverse historic experiences and economic needs. While exaggerated, their fears and responses were not without bases. Romania's communications network, for example, was disconcertingly centrifugal; the railroads and roads of the new provinces had been designed to mesh into the systems of their prewar Austrian, Hungarian, and Russian host-states rather than into the Regat's.

Despite the many difficulties, administrative, fiscal, and monetary unification and centralization were achieved by 1920, and tax legislation was made uniform in 1923, though tax collection, characteristically, was stricter in the ex-Habsburg regions than in the Regat where, however, most of the revenue was spent. Simultaneously, the latter's Liberal-controlled banks were encroaching on the new provinces. Export levies were also employed to discourage trade between the new provinces and the states to which they had formerly belonged and to urge them instead into greater Romanian economic integration. While such integration —political and cultural as well as economic—may indeed have been a manifest desideratum, the Regateni leaders embroiled the process in unnecessary bitterness by monopolizing control over it, and using this control to enhance their region and enrich themselves at the expense of the new provinces, thereby offending the latter's Romanian as well as minority populations.

Despite such frictions within the Romanian community, that community was at one in believing itself to be something special. The only Latin nation of Orthodox rite, the Romanians were both tied to and separated from their neighbors. While their Latin ethnic and linguistic pedigrees separated them from the Slavs and the Magyars and connected them with the West, their Orthodoxy tended to separate them from the West and again from the Magyars and to tie them to the neighboring Slavs. On balance, the Romanians' cultural pretensions, which implied repudiation of Eastern Europe in general and of the Balkans in particular, irritated all their neighbors, especially as their general standards of public behavior and social morality tended to be, if anything, even more "oriental" than these neighbors'. Good linguists, well read, externally westernized, the interwar Romanians, like many other peoples emerging from a colonial or semicolonial condition, tended to lack confidence in their relations with foreigners and to oscillate between extremes of deference and repudiation in their stance toward foreign models and standards.

4

The ethnic minorities, whether those who had been indigenous since medieval times (Magyars, Saxons) or more modern immigrants (Jews, Russians, Ukrainians), were regarded as foreigners. The Magyars, as a former ruling nation, were especially feared on a political level; hence the Germans and Jews of Transylvania were encouraged to recover their own cultural identities by repudiating their prewar magyarization. The Germans complied with alacrity, but many Transylvanian Jews remained touchingly loyal to Hungary and were spurned for their pains by the younger, racist, Magyars as well as by the Romanians. On the one hand, all of Transylvania's minorities, accustomed as they were to the relative efficiency of the old Hungarian administration, chafed under the sloppier bureaucratic styles of their new Regateni masters. On the other hand, this very slackness often attenuated the rigor of antiminority policies. The older Regateni bureaucrats lacked the tenacity of their Czech and the truculence of their Serb equivalents. When, in the 1930s, the Iron Guardist generation of young Romanians rebelled against these lax habits, its purism dovetailed neatly with its xenophobia, and the minorities learned that such idealism could be a bitterer experience than the earlier corruption.

As the Magyars were feared for their political prowess, so the Jews evoked Romanian economic anxieties. They had immigrated to the Romanian lands from Galicia in large numbers during the nineteenth century as lessees and administrators of the estates of the boyars, who were then developing a penchant for luxury and absenteeism in the wake of the economic revolution induced by the Treaty of Adrianopole's free-trade provisions (1829) and by Western Europe's swelling demand for Romanian grain throughout the century. Jews replaced Greeks and Armenians as the commercial class and functioned as "usurers" (and innkeepers, tailors, merchants, etc.) to the peasantry (see section 5).

Upon the achievement of Romanian independence (1856-78), the native intelligentsia was ever more absorbed by state-service, politics, and the free professions, thus leaving the economic realm relatively vacant for massive Jewish penetration. The prewar Romanian statesman Petru Carp conceded that Jewish hegemony over trade and finance was the result, not the cause, of the boyars' aversion to business, the peasants' lack of thrift, and the legal restrictions upon Jewish access to public and professional careers. He warned that "the Jewish question" would be solved only when Romanians worked as hard as Jews at economic activities. By the middle of the interwar era, Jews controlled the bulk of private capital in the export, transportation, insurance, textile, leather, electrotechnical, chemical, housing, printing, and publishing industries. Though their access to the universities was restricted by statutory limitations and extralegal violence, they were also strongly represented in the legal, medical, dental, journalistic, and banking professions. Though only 4.2 percent of the total population, they constituted 30.1, 27, and 23.6 percent, respectively, of the town populations of Bukovina, Bessarabia, and Moldavia, and 14.3 percent of the entire country's urban population. In such cities as Chişinău (Kishinev) and Cernăuţi (Chernovtsy, Czernowitz), where the Jews accounted for 52.6 and 44.9 percent of the population, most store signs were in Hebrew letters.

Excluded, and excluding themselves, from assimilation, the Jews appeared as sinister and exploitative outsiders to the Romanians, and much anti-Semitism was really a variant of xeonophobia. Their readiness to appeal for international intervention against Romanian anti-Semitic legislation that violated the Minorities Protection Treaty of 1919 only deepened their reputation as seditious foreigners. And since they represented commercial and capitalistic values, which were alien to the peasant's inherited life-style, much of the latter's anti-Semitism expressed the reaction of tradition against modernity.

The other minorities were less feared and resented than the Magyars and Jews and did not suffer from such principled discrimination. Their vexation was rather over poor administration. The Russian, Ukrainian, Turco-Tatar, Bulgarian, and Jewish minorities of Bessarabia, the most misgoverned province, were particularly aggrieved. In addition, the Bulgarians and Turks of Southern Dobruja resented the colonization of Romanian veterans and repatriates from Macedonia (Kutso-Vlachs) in their region, and the Saxon Germans of Transylvania similarly regretted the loss of their ancient local jurisdictions of self-government under extreme Romanian centralization. All the ethnic minorities, with the possible exception of the Germans, would eventually welcome the truncation of Romania at the hands of the Soviet Union, Hungary, and Bulgaria in 1940 (see section 13). Thereafter, the half-million Germans who remained in rump Romania were recognized as a public juridical, corporate entity under Nazi control.

5

Peasant land hunger posed a potentially even more explosive problem than did ethnic tensions. In 1864 servile labor obligations had been abolished in the Regat and the arable land divided between peasants and boyars on a 2:1 ratio. In the next half-century, the plots of the highly fecund peasantry were constantly subdivided among succeeding generations until, by the eve of World War I, the disparity in Romanian land distribution between large estates and dwarf-holdings was the greatest in Europe (including Russia). In 1907 the Romanian peasantry had staged modern Europe's most violent *jacquerie*, but upon its brutal repression had relapsed into the traditional postures of depression and deference.

Yet the freshly triumphant ruling establishment of boyars, bourgeoisie, and intelligentsia was soon to learn, during World War I, that peasant passiveness could just as easily express itself in a reluctance to fight a foreign foe or resist a foreign ideology as in docility toward the native rulers. Hence, the crushing military defeats of 1916 and the specter of the Russian revolutions of 1917 prompted this Romanian establishment to save itself by parceling the large estates among the peasantry. A supplementary postwar incentive to such a policy was the nationalistic satisfaction of transferring the agricultural land of the new provinces from Magyar, German, Russian, and Turkish estate owners to Romanian peasants. In the Regat core, however, it was the Romanian boyars who were expropriated while eligible peasants from the ethnic minorities shared in the distribution in the new provinces.

Between March 22, 1917, when the first promise of such land reform was given to the faltering peasant troops of the Regat's army, and January 1, 1927, when the expropriations authorized by the legislation of 1917-21 were concluded throughout Greater Romania, the government claimed to have expropriated 6,008,098.05 hectares from large holders and to have distributed 3,629,824.75 hectares among 1,368,978 hitherto landless peasants or dwarf-holders. The remaining 2,378,273.30 hectares were reserved for communal grazing, communal woodlands, state forests, and general reserve. Though an additional 610,105 smallholders were legally eligible to share in the land distribution, they had till then been passed over as less needy than the favored recipients. During the next decade, through 1938, the number of peasant beneficiaries and of allocated hectares increased slightly by 24,405 and 293,182.25, respectively. This increase, however, could not have modified by much the data for 1930 (see table 44).[3] The reader is here reminded that interwar Romanian statistics, even when official, were rather uncertain. Nevertheless, the Romanian land reform was undoubtedly the most extensive one in interwar Europe (excluding the Soviet Union).

TABLE 44

STRUCTURE OF LAND DISTRIBUTION (1930)

Size of Holdings	Number of Holdings		Agricultural Area		Arable Area	
(In hectares)	Number	Percentage	Hectares	Percentage	Hectares	Percentage
0-1	610,000	18.6	320,000	1.6	275,000	2.1
1-3	1,100,000	33.5	2,200,000	11.1	1,850,000	14.4
3-5	750,000	22.8	3,015,000	15.3	2,475,000	19.3
Subtotal 0-5	2,460,000	74.9	5,535,000	28.0	4,600,000	35.8
5-10	560,000	17.1	3,955,000	20.0	3,110,000	24.2
10-20	180,000	5.5	2,360,000	12.0	1,715,000	13.3
20-50	55,000	1.7	1,535,000	7.8	1,015,000	7.9
50-100	12,800	0.4	895,000	4.5	540,000	4.2
100-500	9,500	0.3	2,095,000	10.6	920,000	7.2
Over 500	2,700	0.1	3,375,000	17.1	950,000	7.4
Total	3,280,000	100.0	19,750,000	100.0	12,850,000	100.0

The land reform had admittedly achieved its intended objective of immunizing the Romanian peasantry against revolution; however, since it was conceived as a political prophylactic, it failed to correct the economic weaknesses of Romanian agriculture or the social problems of rural backwardness. The problem here lay not even so much in the continuing inequalities of distribution, which are indicated in table 44; after all, even a further partition of all arable land in excess of one hundred hectares, or even of fifty hectares, among all landless and dwarf-holding peasants would not have sufficed to transform them into a "healthy" peasantry. Rather it lay in the more general and persistent conditions of rural overpopulation, underemployment, and low productivity. Furthermore, even the existing "healthy" smallholdings tended to degenerate into scarcely viable dwarf-holdings during the 1930s, as peasant property continued to be uneconomically subdivided among the burgeoning number of peasant sons. By the time of the 1941 census, of a Romania that

3. Agricultural statistics in this section are collated from Henry L. Roberts, *Rumania* (New Haven: Yale University Press, 1951), pp. 366-71.

had been shorn the previous year of one-third of her territory but which retained its fertile Regat and Banat breadbaskets, 58.4 percent of all agricultural properties were smaller than the minimum viable size of three hectares, and "healthy" peasant properties of three to five hectares accounted for only 18.4 percent of all agricultural properties and only 16.1 percent of the country's privately owned land. Thus, the statistical average failed to become the predominant type, and the politically motivated land reform of the beginning of the interwar era had failed, by its end, to create a sound, peasant-based, agriculture.

The problem was compounded by the failure of the land reform to consolidate the scattered strips, separated from each other by several kilometers, into which a peasant's property was usually fragmented—not that the tradition-bound peasants were pressing for such consolidation. On the other hand, the break-up of large estates did not necessarily imply a lowering of productivity, since these boyar estates had not previously been farmed as well-managed, highly capitalized, plantations. Rather the latifundia had been leased to peasants who then cultivated them in strips, mostly for cereals, with their own primitive tools, weak draft animals, and shallow plows. Hence the land reform did not entail much change in agronomic techniques. As for the expropriated boyars, they received forty times the average land price of 1917-22. Though later inflation drastically devalued their monetary compensation, they were otherwise well-rewarded with easy bureaucratic and political careers and with sinecures on the boards of Jewish-, foreign-, and state-owned industrial and commercial enterprises.

The Romanian peasant had craved land more than suffrage, the other major, and even more abortive, "reform" of prewar patterns. It had now been granted to him "from above," and the effect was to postpone by a quarter-century the coming of Communism, which, ironically, was then also imposed on him "from above" after 1944. As mentioned earlier, since 1907 he had reverted to deference and had attempted no revolution "from below," despite appalling rural conditions during the interwar era. The political elite, in turn, satisfied to have eased its own political difficulties with the land reforms of 1917-27, thereafter turned its back on the village's continuing socioeconomic problems. Necessary capital was not invested, and rational agronomic techniques were not encouraged. Hence, despite Romania's rich soil, her productivity was low: the wheat yield per hectare after 1928, for example, was less than a third of Denmark's. Indeed, rates of grain yield even slipped below Romania's own prewar levels, as the limited use of manure (due to a decline in the number of cattle) and the virtual absence of chemical fertilizers tended to deplete the soil.

Meanwhile, industry, despite its heavy subsidization by the state, did not expand rapidly or generally enough to rescue agriculture from its burdens of obsolete equipment and overpopulation (over half the available agricultural labor force was estimated as surplus). And so the swelling village population fatalistically expanded the area plowed for grains at the expense of meadows and pastures, absorbing the additional arable into its irrational strip system and killing the cattle deprived of grazings. It also fell ever deeper into debt to the local usurer, who was usually Jewish and filled the gap left open by the absence of an adequate cooperative system and the indifference of the state banks to agriculture.

From these interrelationships there grew a complex set of attitudes. The Romanian intelligentsia and bourgeoisie assuaged their guilt over their neglect and exploitation of the peasant by cheaply celebrating him in literature and propaganda as the archetype of the national character and inciting him to anti-Semitism. The Jew, in turn, regarded the peasant as a lazy and reactionary brute. Finally, the peasant was uninterested in progress and development as long as the fruits thereof were certain to fall to those whom he regarded as outsiders—the Jews as well as the westernized Romanian bourgeoisie, bureaucracy, and intelligentsia. In his view, they were all one vast conspiracy: an "ingenuity culture" parasitical upon his own "toil culture." While they ruled, he "knew" that there would be no just relationship between the intensity of his work and his eventual economic lot.

6

The political parties addressed these social, economic, and ethnic issues with sharply differing programs and they appealed to several distinct clienteles. The Liberal Party of the Regat bore greatest responsibility for the decision to arrange the land reform purely as a political safety valve and thereafter to ignore agriculture except as a resource to be squeezed on behalf of industry. "Liberal" only in the historical sense of being the heirs of the revolutionaries of 1848 and of the revokers of serfdom of 1864, this party's economic ideology was thoroughly Listian. Explicitly rejecting the international division of labor as tantamount to Romania's colonization, the Liberals insisted on her "economic emancipation" through broad industrialization *prin noi înşine* (by ourselves alone). While foreign *loans* to the Romanian state were acceptable as a recognition of the latter's sovereignty, their application was to be an internal decision, and foreign *investments* were suspect. Romania's resources were to be developed by Romanians, preferably by Liberals. This party's leaders were so convinced of the validity of this ideology and so anxious lest other parties forsake it, that they never shrank from such illiberal devices as rigging elections and intimidation in order to retain power so that they could give it effect.

The dominant party of the first interwar decade, the Liberals, together with the upper bureaucracy, the banks, and the corporation boards formed an oligarchy. In practice, the Liberals' commitment to industrialization lacked planning and direction and succumbed to favoritism and corruption. Hence, instead of stimulating self-sustaining development, they simply created a series of overprotected, overbureaucratized, and noncompetitive politico-economic fiefdoms. These fiefdoms were artificially sustained through exorbitant prices, tariffs, and taxes imposed on the peasantry; they were capable of wrecking rural handicrafts but not of supplying the peasant with quality commodities at feasible prices.

Though they sought to utilize the administration of the land reform in Transylvania as a patronage lever, the Liberals failed to develop any reliable clientele outside the Regat. On the other hand, they were consistently abetted by King Ferdinand, who put his considerable constitutional powers at their disposal.

The prewar Conservative Party, which had represented the landed interests, accepted industrialization only as a complement to agriculture, and welcomed foreign investments, had disintegrated under a series of blows: the defeat of its favored Germany, which enabled the Francophile Liberals to reap the credit for the achievement of Greater Romania; the postwar introduction of universal male suffrage; and the accompanying land reform. Most of its survivors eventually found their way into the National-Peasant Party.

The National-Peasant Party, in turn, was formed by the fusion, in October, 1926, of the Peasant Party, a "class" organization of the Regateni and Bessarabian peasants led by members of the intelligentsia, with the National Party, which transcended class lines but was also led by the intelligentsia and had, before the war, represented the Transylvanian Romanians against the Hungarian administration.[4] Though these two parties had periodically cooperated, their merger had been long delayed by the National leadership's aversion to any identification with a single class and had only been catalyzed in 1926 by some particularly egregious Liberal manipulations and brutalities. Nor did the merger altogether resolve their differences; the Peasant component continued to hate the Liberals as exploiters whereas the National leaders merely envied them as monopolizers of power. The united party also drew support from those unskilled workers who still felt themselves to be peasants.

Though interwar Romanian politics was basically a bipolar competition of Liberals versus National-Peasants, there were also some smaller parties. In protest against the Peasants' merger with the more conservative Nationals, a Dr. Nicolae Lupu had, in February, 1927, organized an Old Peasant secession. While Lupu's allegation of a betrayal of peasant interests had substance, and while his rhetoric was impressively radical, his political behavior proved quite fickle and he soon sat in Liberal cabinets.

4. The Peasant Party was itself the product of the merger of its Regateni and Bessarabian components in 1921.

He, too, had some appeal among the workers. The vain, ignorant, and popular war-hero General (Marshal from 1930) Alexandru Averescu led the People's Party, which, he claimed, represented no classes or interests but had simply sprung "from the sufferings of the war." Behind his authoritarian style and demagogic rhetoric, Averescu served as a stalking-horse for the Liberals, who occasionally found it expedient to withdraw from the limelight of government and to transfer nominal ministerial authority to him while retaining intact their own bureaucratic, corporate, and fiscal power.

Professor Nicolae Iorga, a great historian and polyglot but a man of limited political talents, who regarded himself as the incarnation of the nation's conscience, headed the National Democratic Party. Though it was very small and had little popular support, other politicians courted it to protect themselves from the devastating diatribes of the prestigious and irritable Iorga. Professor Alexandru Cuza, a prewar associate of Iorga's, broke away to found the explicitly and exclusively anti-Semitic League of National Christian Defense, whose electoral strength was in the north-east. The Iron Guard movement of the radical Right and its meteoric career during the 1930s will be discussed at the appropriate chronological point (see section 10).

On the opposite side of the political spectrum, the Social Democrats enjoyed some support among the white collar personnel of the railroad administration and the lower rungs of the public services. They functioned politically as an ally of, and pressure-group on, the National-Peasants. The Communists were damagingly identified with the ethnic minorities and with a Soviet Union that refused to recognize Romania's incorporation of Bessarabia. They were driven underground in July, 1924, whence they conducted unimpressive "front" tactics at election time and organized the dramatic, if short-lived and ferociously repressed, miners' strike of August, 1929, and the even more spectacular railroad workers' rebellion in February, 1933. Of the ethnic minority parties, the Magyars were oppositional and the Germans opportunist-governmental.

All Romanian parties were led by members of the intelligentsia and most of them were congeries based on personalities and clans. This was true not only of the minor parties but to a considerable extent also of the Liberals, who were very much the creature of the Brătianu family, and the National-Peasants, whose leaders, such as Iuliu Maniu, Alexandru Vaida-Voevod, Ion Mihalache, and Constantin Stere, each had his own retinue. A leader was followed for the sake of the power, influence, and positions he could command and distribute, and so his death would entail a severe crisis for his party, and perhaps even dissolution. The character of the parties, their multiplicity, and the ferocity of their competition confronted the nation's political youth with the demoralizing choice of careerism or idealism; this dilemma eventually helped fuel the flames of Right-Radicalism.

A corollary of this party system was an extremely corrupt electoral system; Romanian elections were "arranged" by the interior minister of whichever government had been appointed by the king. Thus the cabinet, in effect, designated the parliament by manipulating the electorate rather than, as the formal constitutional theory implied, being itself confirmed or ousted by a parliament that reflected the electorate's preferences. Hence, the universalization of male suffrage at war's end —supposedly the twin to the land reform in the democratization of Romanian political and social life—merely led to the further exploitation and intimidation of the peasant masses, who remained *de facto* excluded from the "political nation" despite all the spurious nostalgia with which the elite sentimentalized their virtues.

7

Interwar Romania's political chronology can be divided into three periods: (1) a decade of Liberal domination, whether in or out of office, from 1918 to 1928; (2) a National-Peasant interlude, from 1928 to 1930; and (3) a Carolist decade, from 1930 to 1940. The third period, in turn, can be subdivided into three intervals: (a) from 1930 to 1933, when King Carol used a series of National-Peasant politicians to govern the country and simultaneously to splinter their own party; (b) from 1933 to 1937, when he applied the same stratagems to the Liberals; and (c) from 1938 to 1940, the years of explicit royal dictatorship which followed logically from Carol's destruction of the two major parties. In 1940 the nation's outrage over Carol's surrender of one-third of the country's territory, after a decade of jingoistic bluster, forced him into exile. He was succeeded by a military dictatorship under Marshal Ion Antonescu, initially in brief alliance with the Iron Guard. Antonescu, in turn, was overthrown by King Michael's domestic coup and diplomatic *volte-face* of August 23, 1944. Such is the broad outline.

Early in the first period, the first elections by universal male suffrage[5] were held, on November 8, 1919. The Peasant and National parties gained at the expense of the Liberals, who were now being punished for their military unpreparedness and chaotic administration during the years 1916-18, and thereupon formed a coalition government, in which the Transylvanian Nationalist Vaida-Voevod served as Premier, and the Regateni Peasantists Mihalache and Lupu respectively as Ministers of Agriculture and Interior. But when this cabinet prepared a comprehensive program of administrative decentralization that respected the peculiarities of the new provinces, and of land expropriation to be ac-

5. Women voted in municipal, but not parliamentary, elections during the 1930s and received the general franchise in 1946.

companied by sustained socioeconomic reforms and agronomic investments in the villages, it was promptly ousted by King Ferdinand acting in
collusion with, and at the behest of, the alarmed Liberals.

General Averescu was designated premier as camouflage for the Liberals on March 15, 1920, "made" new elections to give his People's Party an
overwhelming but fraudulent parliamentary majority on May 25, and
proceeded to impose rigid administrative centralization and to formalize
the exclusively political land reform discussed in section 5. Averescu's
premiership also initiated the era of martial law and censorship that was
to last until 1928 and then again from 1933 until the close of World War
II, as well as the style of government-protected Jew-baiting and strike-
breaking which was to characterize the interwar scene. Having served his
function, he was ousted on December 17, 1921, in the same manner as he
had been installed, through the connivance of the Liberals and the king,
and without comprehending either episode.

After a month's time, during which the Conservative Take Ionescu
vainly sought to stabilize a government, the Liberals openly resumed
office on January 18, 1922, with Ionel Brătianu as premier and his
brother Vintilă as finance minister, and consolidated their grip with the
expected "land-slide" electoral victory in March. Once Averescu had
disposed of the potentially explosive land reform and the postwar turmoil
had abated, the Brătianus had decided to reemerge from the wings. With
but one brief interlude—again a spurious withdrawal behind Averescu
from March, 1926, to June, 1927—they were to hold center-stage for the
next seven years.

Self-confident in their commitment to economic nationalism, secure in
their affinity with the bureaucracy and the banks, unashamed to use
coercion and manipulation, aided by the divisions among their opponents, the Liberals proceeded to govern in the interests of industrial and
commercial wealth in general and of predatory Regateni firms in particular. Such a policy required centralized administration and heavy peasant
taxation. To facilitate it, the Liberals replaced the 1866 constitution with a
new one, on March 29, 1923. The new constitution (a) declared the
country's natural resources, including her subsoil minerals, to be state-
property, thus paving the way for the eventual expropriation of foreign
concessionaires; (b) restricted land ownership to citizens, which was again
an example of xenophobia; (c) severely limited the right of association,
thus cramping the organization of labor and peasant unions; (d) imposed
categorical centralization, thereby showing little respect for the different
traditions of the new provinces; and (e) confirmed the extensive royal
powers and facilitated the invocation of martial law, which was clearly
self-serving as the Liberals had the king in their pocket. Though this was a
patently partisan constitution, rammed through the parliament by an
exclusively Liberal majority against the objections or abstentions of all

other parties, it was nevertheless to be retained by the National-Peasants during their interlude in government, from 1928 to 1930, and to remain in effect until the proclamation of the royal dictatorship in February, 1938.

The Liberals rounded out the constitution with laws on energy exploitation and mining of July 1 and 4, 1924, which implemented the nationalization of natural resources by restricting foreign capital and personnel, and with an authoritarian administrative law of June 13, 1925, organizing the country into seventy-one highly centralized prefectures. They introduced a "bonus" electoral law on March 28, 1926, giving any party that won 40 or more percent of the votes a premium of half the parliamentary seats plus a proportion of the remaining seats corresponding to its percentage of the electoral votes; alternatively, any party that received less than 2 percent of the votes was to have no parliamentary representation. This law was the Liberals' incensed response to their unexpectedly poor performance in communal and municipal elections during February, 1926. It could, in theory, be rationalized as necessary for a healthy, working, governmental majority, but in Romanian practice it functioned as but one more dubious device to concentrate power in self-selected and unrepresentative hands and to provoke small parties that fell under the 2 percent threshhold into extraparliamentary excesses.

To clinch their political hammerlock, the Liberals also forced the exclusion from the royal succession of Crown Prince Carol, known to be ill-disposed toward them. His irregular matrimonial life supplied the pretext for an Exclusion Act of January 4, 1926, which declared Carol's infant son Michael (Mihai) heir to the throne and provided for a Regency Council, to be controlled by Liberals, in the likely event of King Ferdinand's death before Michael's majority.[6]

Having thus secured their interests and commitments with this string of legislation, but also aware of the discontent that their deflationary and

6. During the war, Carol had "deserted" his military post to elope with Zizi Lambrino, daughter of a Romanian general. Their marriage of September 12, 1918, in the Odessa cathedral was annulled by the Romanian government on January 8, 1919, and Zizi and her infant son Mircea were exiled on a pension to Paris. On March 10, 1921, Carol concluded a more appropriate royal marriage with Princess Helen of Greece, which union produced Prince Michael ("Michel Vitesse") on October 25, 1921. Shortly thereafter Carol abandoned Princess Helen for a lifelong liaison with the divorcée Helen (Magda) Lupescu, which provoked the Exclusion Act of January 4, 1926. Lupescu, apparently a shrewd and determined woman, was generally suspected to be of Jewish origin, despite her education at a convent and her previous marriage to a cavalry officer. However, one extraordinary counter-rumor has her as the illegitimate daughter of Romania's first King Carol (which would make her the second Carol's second cousin), for whom the pharmacist Lupescu-Wolff acted as ostensible father in a well-rewarded favor to the embarrassed royal family. Having been divorced by Princess Helen on June 21, 1928, Carol finally married Lupescu in Brazilian exile on June 3, 1947, and died in Portugal on April 3, 1953. The readiness of the otherwise quite cynical Carol to risk his crown on Lupescu's behalf during the 1920s, and to sustain a relationship of virtually "bourgeois" loyalty with her through three decades, remains something of a personal mystery.

anti-agricultural policies as well as their corrupt and brutal methods were arousing, the Liberals now felt it safe and prudent once again to hide behind a second Averescu ministry. Appointed premier on March 30, 1926, the general promptly rigged the elections of May 25, which were considered outrageous even by Romanian standards, and thereafter sustained Liberal policies in principle while deviating slightly from their administration in practice. Thus, he maintained the exclusion of Carol, the primacy of the Regat, and the quest for industrial autarky, but he reduced freight rates and taxes on agricultural exports, negotiated an Italian loan with somewhat lowered "anticolonialist" safeguards, and sought to bring the formally autonomous but Liberal-controlled railroad administration under his own authority. His interior minister, Octavian Goga, was simultaneously flirting with Right-Radicalism. The Liberals' annoyance with these little deviations, together with their nervousness lest their policies and control be seriously jeopardized at the impending death of the cancer-stricken King Ferdinand (Averescu allegedly had a contingency-plan for military administration in that event), prompted Ionel Brătianu and Ferdinand to collude again in "dumping" Averescu on June 3, 1927.

Resuming the premiership on June 22, Brătianu followed up with conventionally rigged elections on July 7. To illustrate the flavor of Romanian electoral statistics, it suffices to note that whereas in his "own" elections of May, 1926, Averescu had claimed 292 mandates on the strength of 1,366,160 alleged votes and had limited the Liberals to 16 seats for 192,399 votes, the Brătianu elections a year later assertedly witnessed a Liberal recovery to 318 seats for 1,704,435 votes, while Averescu was deprived of parliamentary representation because his People's Party supposedly drew only 53,371 votes, which was less than the required 2 percent. Meanwhile, the "bonus" electoral law and the spurious replacement of Brătianu with Averescu in March, 1926, had finally catalyzed the National-Peasant merger of October, 1926, thus creating a credible alternative to the Liberals, which Averescu was manifestly not. Throughout these years the Liberals had resorted to insinuations of Communism to tar their principled opponents, obliging the Peasant movement in particular vehemently to protest its loyalty. This led, alas, to a relative de-emphasis on peasantism and gratuitous avowals of nationalism by the newly united party.

The Liberals resumed office just in time, for Ferdinand succumbed on July 20, 1927. But their victory proved hollow; on November 24, the masterful Ionel Brătianu himself died unexpectedly and was succeeded by his equally tenacious but less adroit brother Vintilă, who now retained the finance portfolio upon assuming the premiership. The two deaths were a heavy blow to the Liberals; lost were the irreplaceable assets of Ferdinand's popularity with the peasants for having promised them land in the dark days of the war, and of Ionel's prestige as the supposedly permanent custodian of the national interest. The king had been a covert ally, Ionel the party's public leader. As if confessing his relative weakness, Vintilă Brătianu now coopted three stalwarts of Lupu's Old Peasant Party into his cabinet, but he also offered the National-Peasants a deal under which new elections would be arranged to give them 45 percent of the votes and seats (to the Liberals' 55 percent) and the same proportion of portfolios in a subsequent two-party cabinet from which the minor parties would be excluded.

Though restricted to but fifty-four seats in the elections of July 7, 1927, the National-Peasants, sensing the Liberals' malaise and their own increasing popularity, rejected this proposal and held out for the novelty of unrigged elections. Simultaneously they sought to hasten their hour by funneling public unrest into a series of mass peasant rallies in the spring of 1928; 100,000 turned out at Bucharest on March 18, 200,000 at Alba Iulia (Gyulafehérvár, Karlsburg) on May 6. Furthermore, they sabotaged Vintilă Bràtianu's desperate efforts to float a Western government loan by warning that a future National-Peasant government would not honor his obligations. They also "seceded" from his "illegitimate" parliament on July 26. Though these National-Peasant tactics were risky—how long, for example, could the peasants be mobilized for such monster marches without becoming either violent or disillusioned?—the Liberals' luck ran out first, as poor harvests in 1927 and 1928 eroded their fiscal as well as their political position.

Vintilă Brătianu was now fatally trapped: his economic and budgetary problems required a foreign loan; negotiations for such a loan were, however, impeded by the domestic turmoil; the turmoil, in turn, was further exacerbated by his inability to secure that loan. Foreign private capital, resenting the Liberals' nationalistic economic legislation of the mid-1920s and hoping for a friendlier reception from the National-Peasants, was content to see him fall. Finally, even the sympathetic Regency Council, nervous lest the impending tenth anniversary of Greater Romania be marred by serious violence, recognized the political omens and, to Vintilă Brătianu's chagrin, accepted as substantive a resignation that he had tendered *pro forma* on November 3, 1928.

Thus ended the Liberals' and Brătianus' decade of domination. They achieved the unification of Greater Romania and the dubious land reform, but they never gained the confidence of the bourgeoisie in the new provinces and were detested by the entire peasantry. Nor were they able to implement their program of national industrialization, for while they were exploitative enough to outrage the peasantry, they lacked the true ruthlessness of totalitarianism to impose the necessary sustained investments on the whole society. Toward the political opposition, their stance had been equally *à la roumaine*: they had applied sufficient chicanery to provoke their opponents but not enough to break them. By now both they and Averescu were too discredited to stage another spurious rotation-of-the-guard.

8

A National-Peasant cabinet headed by Iuliu Maniu took office on November 10, 1928. A Transylvanian Uniate, Maniu was puritanical and keen where Brătianu had been shameless and Averescu obtuse. He started out well, lifting martial law, the censorship, and other restrictions on communication, proclaiming an amnesty, purging the notorious gendarmerie and transferring it from the jurisdiction of the interior ministry to that of defense. He attempted, with only indifferent success, to depoliticize the bureaucracy and pledged himself to administrative decentralization with regional autonomies. His was the first authentically popular Romanian government during the interwar period, and the first to come to office without preliminary deals or intrigues and to be free of Regateni domination.

Under his supervision, genuinely free elections took place on December 12, 1928. However, the subsequent distribution of parliamentary seats was again based on the dubious "bonus" law of 1926. The National-Peasants received 78 percent of the votes and 316 seats and their several allies a total of 33 seats, distributed as follows: Social Democrats, 9; Germans, 11; Magyar Peasantists, 5; Zionists, 4; Bulgarians, 2; and Ukrainians, 2. The Liberals were reduced to 13 seats, almost all of which were from the Regat; Lupu won 5; an Averescu-Iorga joint slate, 5; and the Magyar Nationalists, 15. No seats were won by Cuza's anti-Semitic League or the Communists' Peasant-Labor "front." In February, 1929, Maniu solved the problem that had broken Vintilă Brătianu by negotiating a foreign loan for $102 million, issued at 88 and carrying 7 percent interest. This allowed him to balance his budget and stabilize the currency and make it convertible; he could even subsidize some modernization of railroads.

Maniu now applied himself to implementing his party's pledges and policies. In March, 1929, state monopolies such as ports, railroads, and roads, which were hitherto overbureaucratized and subsidized by the Liberals, were transformed into autonomous bodies and obliged to administer themselves according to sound commercial principles. Later that same month the Liberals' xenophobic, hence counterproductive, mining law of 1924 (see section 7) was revised to abolish the nationality qualifications for sources of investment. Repudiating the Liberals' illusion of economic self-sufficiency and emphasizing the primacy of agriculture over hitherto favored industry, the National-Peasants also lowered industrial tariffs, especially on farm implements and items of peasant consumption, and ended export duties on agricultural produce. Alas, the timing was bad: just when Romania at long last welcomed foreign capital, the depression rendered it unavailable; and when a government finally supported agriculture, the collapse of world grain prices and the European panic into agricultural autarky eroded its efforts.

Nor did Maniu's government, for all its concern for agriculture, regard itself as the specific political instrument of the peasantry in anything like the way the Brătianus had acted for the bourgeois-bureaucratic oligarchy. Within the merged National-Peasant Party, the center of political gravity had steadily shifted away from peasantist commitments. Now that it was in office, the party not only rejected (perhaps justifiably) another round of partition of the remaining large estates as a worthless palliative to rural overpopulation, but also failed to press for the consolidation of the scattered peasant strips into units (which was a surrender to peasant inertia). Instead, it facilitated the sale of land by indigent peasants to purchasers owning not more than 75 hectares. This was a "kulak" measure, perhaps economically rational but morally dubious and politically costly. Industry was unable to absorb the peasants who had been bought out; they vegetated on the land as agricultural proletarians. The peasant masses also found the National-Peasant interest in industrialization *with* foreign capital (in contrast to the Liberals' commitment to industrialization through domestic resources alone) to be too sophisticated. Later in the decade, accordingly, they would shift their emotional support to the thoroughly anti-industrial, antimodernist Iron Guard movement.

In noneconomic spheres of government, the National-Peasants also faltered thanks to internal contradictions and external resistance. On July 14, 1929, their administrative reform, weakly modifying their predecessors' extreme centralism with an intermediary layer of seven provincial jurisdictions and slightly more self-government on the village level, provoked the Liberal and People's (Averescu) deputies into a legislative boycott, which lasted until November 15, 1930. (The reform was eventually rescinded by the Iorga government in 1931.) In the same month (July, 1929), their discovery of a putschist plot by some army officers prompted the National-Peasants to organize their own paramilitary guards, with consequent alienation of the military establishment. The next month, the army—perhaps deliberately overreacting in order to embarrass Maniu—suppressed a coal miners' strike with much ferocity and unnecessary bloodshed. An abortive attempt to assassinate Interior Minister Vaida-Voevod resulted in rabid police excesses against innocent suspects, demonstrating that the tradition of administrative brutality had not been curbed under the new government. Similarly, when one of the three regents died in October, 1929, the National-Peasants promptly replaced him with one of their own men rather than with a neutral.[7] Thus, when in

7. The original Regency Council consisted of Carol's younger brother Prince Nicolae, the Orthodox Patriarch Miron Cristea, and Chief Justice of the Supreme Appeals Court

power they were not altogether above emulating the Liberals' style, as had already been suggested by their retention of the "bonus" clause in the elections of December, 1928.

When Carol, who had been vividly signaling his own availability for the throne since Ionel Brătianu's death, returned suddenly on June 6, 1930, and had himself proclaimed king two days later, relegating his son Michael to the dignity of Grand Voevod of Alba Iulia and abolishing the Regency, the National-Peasants acquiesced by nullifying the Exclusion Act (see section 7) and hence acknowledging Carol's legitimate succession as of the moment of Ferdinand's death. Aware of Carol's relative popularity as a new face at a time of widespread disillusionment, they hoped he would be "their" king as his father had been the Liberals'. The latter party's initial resistance to Carol's return collapsed when Vintilă Brătianu died on December 22, 1930; his younger brother Constantin (Dinu) and nephew Gheorghe (Ionel's adopted son) lacked the two elder brothers' obsessive horror of a non-Liberal monarch.

In spite of his initial welcome of Carol's reign, a tired Maniu chose to utilize the king's quasi-official installation of his mistress Lupescu in Bucharest as grounds for resigning on October 6, 1930, precisely four months after Carol's return. An ascetic bachelor, Maniu was indeed personally offended by Carol's matrimonial irregularities, but his decision to make them a political issue in the absence of any general outrage (Romanians are nicely tolerant of such a life-style) suggests that he, too, like several other leaders of the one-time ethnic minorities of prewar Hungary (e.g., the Slovaks' Hlinka, the Croats' Radić) actually felt more comfortable in righteous opposition than in the harness of governmental responsibility. On the other hand, Maniu may also have been disconcerted by Carol's quickly surfacing reluctance to be led by his prime minister.

Whether or not Carol had reneged on prior promises to abandon his mistress, to be reconciled to his royal ex-wife, and to reign strictly constitutionally, as insinuated by Maniu's partisans, he soon exposed his itch to dominate. The National-Peasants wished to replace Maniu with their vice-president and second strongest leader, the peasantist ideologue Ion Mihalache. Mihalache, however, was too radical and especially too inde-

---

Gheorghe Buzdugan. The first two were considered Liberal agents, the third neutral. Two days after Buzdugan's death on October 7, 1929, Maniu replaced him with Constantin Sărățeanu, also a jurist but a nonentity, related to two current cabinet ministers, and very much a representative of the Transylvanian wing of the National-Peasant Party. His designation accordingly disquieted the party's Regateni and Bessarabian wings, offended the opposition parties, and lowered the Regency Council's repute in general. Other candidates had been the prestigious diplomat Nicolae Titulescu, the wartime chief of staff, General (Marshal from 1930) Constantin Presan, the Dowager Queen Mother Marie, Princess Helen, and even the exiled Carol, whose "standing" of course gained at the Regency's expense. The issue was important, as the Council potentially exercized the extensive royal powers.

pendent for Carol's taste and hence was obliged to defer to the king's preferred choice, Gheorghe Mironescu, a wealthy lawyer who now retained the foreign affairs portfolio upon his elevation to premier. This was the opening shot in Carol's campaign to fragment and subvert the parties as such—a campaign actually facilitated by his deceptive reputation as a mere playboy who need not be taken seriously. Mironescu was now retained only until his successful conclusion of the negotiations for a French loan of $53 million—the last major one before the depression shut down the Western money markets. He was then dropped on April 4, 1931, having been undermined by the unpopular obligation (imposed by the foreign bankers) to pursue a drastically deflationary budgetary policy, including the fatal requirement to dismiss many bureaucrats.

Thus ended in vast disappointment the once-hopeful experiment in National-Peasant government. Its one undeniable achievement was the authentic unification of Greater Romania: the reconciliation of the Regatenis with their brethren of the new provinces. The rest was disappointment. The democratization of provincial administration proved superficial; little was done for the peasantry; though Maniu's personal probity was beyond reproach, it was given an aura of hypocrisy by his failure to curb the tradition of corruption, a tradition which his own followers, tempted by the numerous foreign loans and concessions that were floated during these years, adopted. Bribery and brutality seemed to cling to office no matter who held it. Furthermore, the bureaucratic, financial, and industrial establishment remained a Liberal bastion, while the army viewed itself as a royal instrument, and Carol was determined to rule as well as reign. But while acknowledging that these domestic obstacles, as well as the world depression, sabotaged Maniu's intentions, it must also be conceded that he was too aloof, fastidious, and sanctimonious to come to grips with his political problems. In short, he was weak and evaded his responsibility to govern; for all his rectitude, he proved to be yet another of the "brilliant ineffectuals" of the interwar East European peasant movement. That his failure was but an episode in the general European failure to render democracy effective is a fact, but it is no excuse.

9

Romania's two major parties thus discredited themselves during the 1920s, and the Right-Radical movement being as yet immature, the 1930s was to be a transitional decade of gradually increasing royal domination. King Carol's tactics in his quest for control were to divide and conquer the main parties, to isolate the Right-Radicals and yet simultaneously to incite them against the established parties, and eventually to create his own monoparty with auxiliary youth and paramilitary groups. Though ultimately the domestic repercussions of external pressures would destroy him in 1940, Carol's tactical success was initially brilliant. Barely tolerated upon his return from exile, he quickly gained full mastery, as is suggested by the large number of cabinets, premiers, and ministers who were rotated in and out of office at the king's whim between 1930 and 1940: 25 cabinets, 18 different premiers with 61 ministers and 31 undersecretaries in the premier's office; 390 departmental (portfolio) ministers with 213 undersecretaries; also 9 chiefs of the general staff. During the first third of his decade, when he was fragmenting the National-Peasants, Carol provoked eight cabinet crises and gyrated as many premiers between mid-1930 and the end of 1933: Maniu to October 6, 1930; Mironescu, October 6, 1930, to April 4, 1931; Titulescu, from April 4 to 17, 1931; Iorga, from April 18, 1931 to May 31, 1932; Vaida-Voevod, June 6, to October 17, 1932; Maniu, October 20, 1932 to January 12, 1933; Vaida-Voevod, January 16, to November 12, 1933; Duca, November 15 to December 29, 1933.

The diplomat Titulescu having failed to construct a viable coalition cabinet upon Mironescu's dismissal in April, 1931, Carol then called on the academician Iorga to form a supposedly nonpolitical government of experts. Rather ineptly, Iorga proceeded to put together a cabinet composed exclusively of Regateni Romanians together with one German undersecretary of state for minorities (see below). The professor then proceeded to earn the dubious distinction of arranging interwar Romania's most brutal, corrupt, and rigged elections on June 1, 1931, from which his coalition (his own National Democrats, a Liberal faction led by Ion Duca, and the Germans) claimed to emerge with 49.88 percent of the valid votes. This entitled it to 287 of the 387 chamber seats, which he divided as follows: 205 for himself, 70 to Duca, and 12 to the Germans. The Opposition Liberals were allowed 12 seats; the National-Peasants, 30; Averescu, 10; Lupu, 7; Cuza, 8; the Anti-Usury League of the Bessarabian populist Constantin Stere, 6; the Social Democrats, 7; the Magyars, 11; and the Jews, 4. A Communist "front" received 5 seats, which were later annulled and redistributed among Iorga (2), Averescu (1), National-Peasants (1), and Social Democrats (1).

This election was also distinguished by the first participation of the Right-Radical Iron Guard movement. Since it received less than 2 percent of the votes, it did not gain a seat. Nevertheless, its leader Corneliu Zelea Codreanu and his father were shortly afterward to win bi-elections in Moldavia.

Even had he been less vain and more astute, Iorga's government would probably have been wrecked by the depression, which forced him into unpopular economies, the peasants into crushing debt, and a number of banks into bankruptcy in the aftermath of the collapse of the Vienna Kreditanstalt in May, 1931. Yet his own measures were often poorly conceived. Instead of putting the administrative apparatus on a more rational basis, Iorga simply reversed the National-Peasants' tentative decentralization efforts, purged his personal and political enemies, and reduced salaries of civil servants so drastically that graft became a virtual necessity. Characteristically, he paid the bureaucrats residing in Bucharest and a few other major Regat cities but defaulted on the salaries of those in the provinces. Not until early 1932 did he belatedly bring two Transylvanian and two Bessarabian ministers into his hitherto pure Regateni cabinet. In the spring of that year this renowned academician responded to student unrest by closing the universities.

On the other hand, he merits some credit for establishing an undersecretaryship for minorities—which subsequent governments, alas, abolished—and for the creation of chairs for minority ethnic studies in their several languages at the universities of Bucharest, Cernăuţi, Cluj (Kolozsvár, Klausenburg), and Iaşi. He also ordered that agricultural debts be reduced by 25-50 percent for owners of less than ten hectares and by 40 percent for owners of more than this. (A later government was to slash all agricultural debts antedating December, 1931, by 50-70 percent on April 7, 1934.) Yet these measures were but palliatives for the minority and peasant problems. The deeper social tensions, aggravated now by the depression, baffled Iorga. After little more than a year in office, Carol replaced him with Vaida-Voevod, who had hitherto appeared to be Maniu's loyal lieutenant but now allowed himself to be used as the most malleable royal instrument for fragmenting the National-Peasant Party.

In the elections of July 17, 1932, Vaida-Voevod barely managed to squeeze out the 40 percent plurality necessary to operate the "bonus" clause, while the Iron Guard made a break-through to five seats. Shrewdly anticipating the drift of popular opinion, Vaida-Voevod soon moved to reinsure himself with the radical Right, whereupon Carol, objecting less on principle than resenting his premier's unwelcome autonomy, imposed the revolving-door game between him and Maniu whose chronology was itemized above and which by the end of 1933 had irredeemably broken their party.

Dusting off his hands, Carol now proceeded to apply the same tactics to the Liberals. On November 15, 1933, he made their Ion Duca premier, thereby excluding the wing of the party led by Gheorghe Brătianu. Enjoying the reputation of being a strong, conscientious, and personally honest man (he was one of the rare Romanian politicians to die poor), Duca proceeded to assign himself 50.99 percent of the votes and 300 of the 387 seats in new elections rigged on December 20, 1933. He rigorously suppressed the Iron Guard, having about 18,000 arrested, several hundred beaten and one or two dozen killed by the gendarmerie. On December 29, however, this toughness cost him his life. He was murdered by the Guard under suspicious circumstances that suggested police, and possibly royal, complicity. His assassins were acquitted by a military tribunal. In any event, the elimination of the strong Duca, who had opposed Carol's return in 1930 and was hostile to the royal mistress Lupescu, crippled the Liberals' capacity to resist Carol's manipulation as effectively as the engineered feud between Maniu and Vaida-Voevod had enfeebled the National-Peasants.

Gheorghe Tătărescu was appointed on January 3, 1934, in a royal gambit that irrevocably split the Liberals between Tătărescu and Brătianu camps. He was destined to last longer than any of Carol's other premiers, until December 27, 1937, and was the only one to sit out a full parliamentary term. Compliant and optimistic, he governed by martial law, tapped telephones, and rotated his ministers. Clandestinely, but with Carol's connivance, he spurred the Iron Guard on against the other parties politically while Carol's favorite industrialist, Nicolae Malaxa, was subsidizing it financially. Yet at the same time the regime was also competing with the Iron Guard through such newly fashionable proto-totalitarian trappings as its official youth organization and a vividly advertised armaments program, both of which were launched in 1934, and compulsory '"strength through joy") labor brigades, unveiled in 1936.

The rapidly reviving European demand for Romanian petroleum after 1934, together with the good harvests of 1936 and 1937, allowed the Carol-Tătărescu government to enjoy budget surpluses and favorable trade balances. The government put its fiscal house in order and, in a reversion to neo-Liberal economic policy, subsidized native industries. Especially favored were metallurgy and heavy industry, and cartellization was encouraged. Yet the state's prosperity was not shared with the village which remained starved of capital but swollen with a surplus labor force. Tătărescu was thus unable to capitalize politically on his substantial but partial economic successes as the neglected and alienated peasants either revived their faith in Maniu or, more ominously, transferred it to Codreanu. Under the apparent stability of the mid-1930s, the political atmosphere was becoming quite volatile, and the government's own attitude toward the extremist trend increasingly equivocal.

10

The Right-Radical Iron Guard (or Legionary) movement, founded in 1927 by Corneliu Zelea Codreanu, which functioned under different names at different times and was frequently banned but always re-emerged, was spawned by the impact of modernization upon a rural society and was the interwar Romanian expression of a general European spiritual and political crisis. Reacting to the exploitation, corruption, indolence, and incompetence rampant in public and economic life, and to the deep cynicism and superficial cosmopolitanism of the established elite, the Iron Guard demanded a revolution of justice, honesty, energy, idealism, and nativism. Its rhetoric and symbolism appealed to the mythical, the instinctive, the primitive, and the spontaneous in man against the allegedly decadent, subversive, and "judaic" pseudo-values of logic, rationalism, secularism, and materialism. Yet its own ideologists, like fascist leaders elsewhere, tended to be self-conscious and well-educated would-be intellectuals.

Promising equity to the peasantry, a new world to the youth, and order to the bourgeoisie, the Guardists subtly appealed to the xenophobic, chauvinistic, anti-Semitic, anticapitalist, and anti-Marxist attitudes and anxieties of the various sectors of Romanian society. Religious, evangelical, ascetic, and somewhat necrophilic, the Guardists impressed the peasants and the influential village priests not only with their sincerity and piety, but also with their altruistic and disciplined readiness to help bring in the harvest, to build rural roads and dams, and summarily to punish corrupt officials. This was authentic "propaganda by work and deed" and elicited a warm response in many villages where disillusionment with the National-Peasants' exhaustion and remoteness prevailed. Less expected, and hence more interesting, were the substantial inroads that the Guard, despite its anti-urban and anti-industrial propaganda, made after 1933 —a year of labor turmoil—among the Romanian proletariat, disgusted with the weak and docile trade unions. Unemployable university graduates, dismissed or transferred civil servants, and underpaid army officers were other, more obvious, adherents. Yet the Guard's toughest vigilante-executioners—and it proudly practiced "righteous violence"—were recruited by Codreanu from among the Macedo-Vlach (or Kutso-Vlach) postwar refugees repatriated to Romania from Greece and Yugoslavia.

Spiritual and political heir, via Bessarabia, of the Tsarist Black Hundreds, with whom it shared the cult of the Archangel Michael, the Guardist movement soon extended its ideological commitments from anti-Semitism to a general critique of modernism as such. Indeed, the occasion of Codreanu's break in 1924 with his original mentor, Professor Cuza (see section 6), had been precisely over the latter's "mere" anti-Semitism and "soft" parliamentarism. In contrast to the pagan enthusiasms of West European fascist movements, the Guard courted the Orthodox religiosity of the as yet unsecularized Romanian masses. Shrewdly declining to articulate a specific, and therefore vulnerable, program, Codreanu emphasized the primacy of organization and dedication, retorting that "this country is going to ruin not for lack of programs but for lack of men."[8] And his demand that the conventional mendacity, sloth, and verbosity be replaced by honesty, stamina, and stoicism, together with his frequent evocations of discipline and martyrdom, did indeed inspire his cohorts and impress the nation.

Two theories have been advanced to explain and to pinpoint the

8. Corneliu Z. Codreanu, *Eiserne Garde* (Berlin: Brunnen, 1939), p. 273.

Guard's popularity. Henry L. Roberts sees it as a function of rapid social change, magnetizing particularly the interstitial and déclassé social groups, and hence growing as the depression reduced ever larger sectors of Romanian society to déclassé status. Eugen Weber, on the other hand, locates its appeal in retarded areas of stable poverty, among social strata consistently neglected by other parties, and thus as filling a vacuum rather than capitalizing on change.[9] Both agree that the Guard fed on social marginalism, though they define that marginalism differently, and that its greater dynamism and generality account for its pulling rapidly ahead of the old-fashioned, exclusively anti-Semitic, rightist groups. Indeed, by the mid-1930s it was tacitly endorsed by all the enemies of the Carol-Tătărescu regime.

Yet for all its antiregime philippics and its revolutionary postures, there was, as suggested earlier, something ambiguous about the movement's relations with the authorities. Except for Premier Mironescu and his Interior Minister Mihalache in 1930-31, successive governments tolerated, used, and surreptiously encouraged it, and even these two ministers may have acted more out of deference to Western expectations at a time when they were negotiating for loans than out of principle. Duca's personal determination to crush the Guard in 1933 appears to have been authentic, but the fact that his assassination at its hands was so easy and went unpunished reflects suspiciously on the rest of the ruling oligarchy, as does the Guard's consistent financial affluence. Its inroads on the older parties were certainly useful to Carol's authoritarian ambitions. At the same time, the Guard was sporadically also the victim of violence at the hands of the gendarmerie, which was more widespread than the violence that it, in turn, inflicted on allegedly culpable officials, politicians, and apostates, though these latter cases excelled in ghastliness. Whereas the 1920s had been relatively free of political murders, the 1930s witnessed an orgy of them as the Guard and the regime, having pulverized the established parties, now competed to capture the increasingly extremist national mood. Ideological idealism thus exposed itself as potentially more frightful than the earlier corrupt cynicism, and most frightening of all was the fact that the masses as well as the elite indulged and applauded the violence.

11

The inconclusive elections of 1937 and their tangled aftermath provided Carol with the opportunity to establish his royal dictatorship early the next year. As the quadrennial term of the parliament "arranged" by Duca in December, 1933, and then retained by Tătărescu approached its

---

9. Henry L. Roberts, *Rumania*, pp. 226-33, and Eugen Weber, "The Men of the Archangel," in Walter Laqueur and George L. Mosse, eds., *International Fascism 1920-1945* (New York: Harper and Row, 1966), pp. 101-26.

expiration, the premier, conscious of his unpopularity, fashioned an electoral bloc of his own wing of the Liberals, Vaida-Voevod's hypernationalistic defectors from the National-Peasants, Iorga's National Democrats, and the Germans, in an effort to wrest the necessary 40 percent of the vote. Simultaneously, Maniu, Codreanu, and Gheorghe Brătianu concluded an electoral nonaggression pact precisely to frustrate this aim. The Communists, then underground, endorsed the latter pact, though after World War II they would berate Maniu for his association with Codreanu. The fact that Maniu, who had hitherto disdained all "deals," now felt constrained to conclude this pact was a measure of his National-Peasants' demoralization, notwithstanding his assurances to some uneasy followers that the arrangement was exclusively electoral and connoted no political agreement or dilution of his own democratic commitments. In any event, the rough balance between the two blocs produced relatively free elections from which, for once, the government failed to extract its conventional "bonus" premium.

Held on December 20, 1937, the elections gave Tătărescu's coalition 35.92 percent of the votes and 152 seats. Of the three counterbloc partners, who had run separate lists, Maniu was credited with 20.40 percent and 86 seats, Codreanu with 15.58 and 66 (rumor claimed that he had actually done better), and Gheorghe Brătianu with 3.89 and 16. Cuza's one-issue anti-Semitic National Christians, to which the talented Transylvanian poet Octavian Goga had recently been coopted as fellow leader, received 9.15 percent and 39 seats. A splinter group from the National-Peasants led by former Justice Minister Grigore Iunian took 2.25 percent and 9, and the Magyars 4.43 percent and 19 seats. None of the seven other competing parties won the 2 percent of votes necessary to achieve parliamentary representation. The low turnout—66 percent of registered voters in contrast to 77.4 in the other significant interwar elections of 1928—was symptomatic of disillusion with parliamentarism.

Carol cleverly finessed the results. Conceding that his Tătărescu protégés had been rebuffed, but unreconciled to Maniu and fearful of Codreanu's radicalism, he was aware that the Right demanded some satisfaction. He summoned the Goga-Cuza team to form a cabinet on December 28, 1937, and played this pair off against Codreanu as he had earlier played Vaida-Voevod against Maniu and Tătărescu against Brătianu. It took but forty-five days for these two ideologically sterile, politically incompetent, and rabidly anti-Semitic old men to provoke paralysis in business, a run on the banks, the collapse of the stock exchange, governmental chaos, and an international uproar. So thoroughly had they discredited themselves, that the probably unsurprised and satisfied Carol had a pretext to oust them, suspend the constitution, and inaugurate his royal dictatorship on February 10, 1938. The final catalyst may have been a belated effort by Goga-Cuza to widen their appeal through a *modus vivendi* with Codreanu on February 8. Though Goga shouted "Israel has triumphed" on his dismissal, the episode suggests that Jew-baiting alone was not a sufficient program to govern Romania.

12

The figurehead for the royal dictatorship was the premier, the vain and hypernationalist Orthodox Patriarch Miron Cristea, but Carol's reliable agent within the cabinet was the tough, one-eyed Armand Calinescu. A former National-Peasant, Calinescu held the posts of vice-premier and minister of interior and of education (to control the students). For window dressing, every former premier was invited to become a minister-without-portfolio, and all but Maniu and Goga, who died on May 5, accepted. On February 24, 1938, a new, corporatist constitution was "approved" by 4,289,581 to 5,483 in a plebiscite in which voting was open and compulsory. The anxious and disenchanted public would probably have given a similar endorsement even in a secret ballot. The independence of the judiciary and the autonomy of the universities had been suspended a few days previously, and all political parties were now dissolved by law. An administrative reorganization reminiscent of King Alexander's in neighboring Yugoslavia (see Chapter 5, section 7) consolidated the seventy-one prefectures into ten regions. Its purpose was to improve central control and to dilute provincial loyalties. Civilian prefects were replaced with military ones, royal powers were extended, and the legislature emasculated. The propaganda myths of this royal dictatorship were organic nationalism, family, church, and the gospel of work—its rubber-stamp parliament, for example, being selected from the three work-categories of agriculture, industry and commerce, and the professions of the intelligentsia. All in all, it was a pseudo-radical, semifascist burlesque, intended to stymie the Iron Guard and steal its ideological appeal.

Codreanu's reaction was fatally passive. On February 22, 1938, he had compliantly dissolved his party, released his followers from their allegiance, and announced his own political retirement and intention to go into temporary exile in Italy. When the government confiscated his passport, he spurned flight and on April 19 resignedly let himself be sentenced to six months' imprisonment for slandering Iorga. Iorga was pathologically jealous of Codreanu's popularity and had ranted, "Who is this young man who is saluted like a Roman emperor by the youth of this country, who have forgotten their old teachers?" Codreanu had charged him with "intellectual dishonesty."[10] In revenge, Iorga had procured his indictment. While serving his term, Codreanu was also tried for treasonable conspiracy and sentenced on May 27 to ten years' hard labor. During

---

10. Quoted from Michel Sturdza, *The Suicide of Europe* (Boston: Western Islands, 1968), pp. 113-14.

the night of November 29-30, 1938—the night of the vampires in Romanian folklore—he and thirteen fellow Guardist prisoners were garroted to death by the regime, which falsely announced that they had been shot while attempting to escape.

Codreanu's inertia during his final year was a mystifying anticlimax from a political point of view and invites a psychological explanation. Perhaps he had a theomanic craving for *Imitatio Christi* or, at any rate, for martyrdom—a frequent theme in his ideological exhortations. His relations with Carol had throughout oscillated between mutual appeasement and reciprocal coercion as Codreanu waited for the king to jettison his camarilla and redeem the nation while Carol, in turn, kept probing to ascertain Codreanu's price for collaboration. In the end, it was Codreanu's quite "un-Romanian" ideological and political incorruptibility that led their relationship to its violent end.

Economically, the Carolist dictatorship was a neo-Liberal period that was characterized by rapid, state-directed industrialization at the expense of agriculture, and endowed Carol and a few industrialist-cronies with huge fortunes from the accompanying rearmament program. Yet prosperity also became more general, if still precarious, as Britain, France, Germany, and Italy competed for Romania's foreign trade, especially her oil exports.

Diplomatically, therefore, the Carolist dictatorship turned into an interval of straddling, as Romania edged away from her hitherto categorical identification with a now weakening France and sought to balance between the Western and the Axis Powers. This quest involved the delicate task of affirming Romania's own particular postwar acquisitions, but without ruffling a generally revisionist Germany, and it came closer to success than is often appreciated. Enjoying many ready markets for her oil, Romania could stave off German economic hegemony longer than her neighbors could, while her generous treatment of her German minority, relative to Hungary's, gratified Hitler. But in the long run the effort to straddle failed; Germany's political and economic drive into the Balkans compelled Romania to accommodate. Their trade treaty of March 23, 1939, recognized the Reich's predominance not only in Romania's foreign trade but also in her general economic development, for which mixed binational companies were to be organized. Yet, though it put her raw materials at Germany's disposal, this and subsequent economic agreements were not ipso facto disadvantageous to Romania, as her agricultural surpluses were henceforth absorbed at high prices by Germany and her industrial economy was modernized and rationalized by German capital and expertise over the next six years.

The ideological affinity between the Nazis and the Iron Guard had caused some strain between the two governments at the time of Codreanu's murder, which had reportedly enraged Hitler and prompted

German dignitaries to return their Romanian decorations, but considerations of *raison d'état* prevailed on both sides. Indeed, to compensate Hitler for his provocation, Carol prudently became more accommodating in the trade negotiations and, combining flattery with self-service, he thereafter also aped totalitarian styles and trappings more assiduously. On December 15, 1938, the Front of National Renaissance was founded as the regime's monoparty, and on June 21, 1940, in a step which Carol advertised as an advance from the Corporate to the Totalitarian State, it was reorganized as the Party of the Nation, with membership compulsory for all holders of public and of corporate office and with the Iron Guard's now rehabilitated remnant quite prominent. But all this rigmarole never developed any authentic dynamism.

Carol's relations with the post-Codreanu Iron Guard make intriguing reading. Initially demoralized, the Guard's élan was revived by Hitler's *Blitzkrieg* in Poland, and on September 21, 1939, it avenged Codreanu by assassinating Calinescu, who had succeeded to the premiership upon Patriarch Miron Cristea's death the previous March. On the one hand, Calinescu's murder deprived Carol of his only resolute minister; on the other, it freed him of a liability that had stood in the path of full rapprochement with Hitler. The assassins had returned from Germany only a few days previously and, following their movement's standard procedure of accepting political responsibility for its actions, now turned themselves in to the authorities after committing the murder. A massacre of Guardists and others nevertheless immediately ensued, but early in December Carol dismissed his police and secret-police chiefs, allegedly for having failed to protect Calinescu but in fact as a gesture of appeasement toward the Guard and Hitler. Several hundred imprisoned Guardists were then quickly released in January, 1940, and another thousand or so permitted to return from German refuge in the course of the spring, on condition that they enter Carol's monoparty. Among these returnees was Horia Sima, who had succeeded to the movement's leadership through the violent attrition of all other candidates. He was now to be alternately arrested and courted by Carol; he, in turn, was to join the royal cabinet and then to denounce the king, as the Guard and the regime groped toward a nervous and brittle détente. On balance, however, Carol's was the stronger hand, and he could have controlled the Guard had not a series of fiascos in foreign policy in the late spring and summer of 1940 utterly discredited him among all sectors of the Romanian public.

13

Carol's understandable but increasingly unrealistic hopes to continue straddling among the now-warring Great Powers was symbolized by his recall of the arch-juggler Tătărescu to the premiership on November 24, 1939, after the dust from Calinescu's assassination had somewhat settled.

Tătărescu fashioned a cabinet delicately balanced between surreptitiously pro-Ally neutralists and overt pro-Germans. His effort was to no avail. In the aftermath of Germany's destruction of France, which was a psychologically devastating blow to a Romanian elite always self-consciously Latin in culture, Stalin decided to collect the pledges secretly given him the previous August by Hitler in return for Soviet neutrality at war's outbreak. On June 26, 1940, he issued an ultimatum to Romania to cede Bessarabia and the northern half of the Bukovina to the Soviet Union. The Romanian Crown Council was advised by Berlin to comply and did so two days later, with Iorga vehemently dissenting. On July 1, 1940, Romania renounced an Anglo-French guarantee that dated from April 13, 1939, and three days later Tătărescu yielded the premiership to the pro-German engineer and businessman Ion Gigurtu, who on July 11 took Romania out of the League of Nations and on July 13 announced her desire to join the Axis camp.

Such desperate endeavors to purchase German protection against further revisionist demands upon Romanian territory came too late. At the spectacle of Romania's yielding to the Kremlin, the Hungarian and Bulgarian governments decided to present their claims as well. The latter's was settled relatively easily with the retrocession to Bulgaria of Southern Dobruja, whose population was admittedly almost 80 percent non-Romanian, under an agreement concluded on August 21 and formalized by the Treaty of Craiova on September 7, 1940. But the Hungarian demand for Transylvania failed of a bilateral accommodation and was reluctantly arbitrated by Germany and Italy in the so-called Second Vienna Award of August 30, 1940, by which Hungary regained approximately two-fifths of her 1919 territorial losses to Romania (see Chapter 4, section 7). Altogether, these three amputations cost Greater Romania one-third of her total territory, two-fifths of her arable area, more than two-fifths of her forests, most of the lands on which promising new industrial crops were being cultivated, and a third, or over six million, of her people, of whom about half were ethnically Romanian.[11]

These losses were more than even the generally docile Romanian people were prepared to forgive Carol. For a decade he had extracted painful political and economic sacrifices from the society in the name of national defense, and over the past several months he had repeatedly sworn that "not a single furrow" (nici o brăzda) of "eternal" Romanian territory would be yielded. And now he had supinely allowed his country to be truncated without a shot being fired in its defense. In neighboring Poland, the Piłsudskist regime, which also had extracted sacrifices and

11. The cession to Hungary was to be reversed after World War II but those to the Soviet Union and Bulgaria to be confirmed, thus negating Romania's attempted recovery, between 1941 and 1944, of the lands she had in 1940 yielded to the Soviet Union and leaving her with a current post-World War II area of 237,502 square kilometers.

emasculated parliamentary government in the name of national mobilization, had at least fought and thus sustained national honor in its own extremity the previous year. Execrated by the entire nation, and pursued by the bullets of the Iron Guard—which, true to its spasmodic record, now bungled a belated attempt to apprehend him—Carol fled into exile on September 6, 1940, first to Spain, then to Latin America, and finally to Portugal. He left his nineteen-year-old son Michael to reign over an army-Iron Guard duumvirate led by General Ion Antonescu and Horia Sima.

Even making full allowances for the limitations that the historic and structural weaknesses of Romania's society imposed upon all her political leaders, it is nevertheless difficult to be generous in judging Carol's stewardship of power. Though energetic, alert, and clever, he was also vindictive, suspicious, and unscrupulous. Well-informed and gifted with a superb memory, his deficiencies were those of character, not of intellect. Finding the elements of incipient political and moral degeneration at hand on his return in the midst of the depression in 1930, he took advantage of them over the next decade to aggrandize not only his personal political power but also his own and his cronies' personal wealth, immune from even those minimal restraints of press or parliamentary exposure which had occasionally inhibited the Liberals in the 1920s.

In addition to thus indulging the endemic tradition of financial corruption, Carol conducted public affairs in a politically hollow and superficial manner. Jealous of anyone with greater popularity or authority, which in part accounts for his ultimate persecution of Codreanu, he preferred to surround himself with political mediocrities. Having destroyed the established parties by the middle of the decade, he was unable to replace them with any instrument of creditable political legitimacy. Preferring intrigue over consensus, moral authority, or terror, his dictatorship proved to be merely "Balkan" rather than seriously reformist, sustainedly modernizing, or authentically totalitarian. Compared to Piłsudski, Atatürk, or even Gömbös or King Alexander, Carol was a light-weight. Having for a decade cheated all, he was now appropriately abandoned by all.

In the duumvirate that succeeded Carol, the army, demoralized by its inactivity during the recent surrenders of national territory, initially appeared to be weaker than its Iron Guard partner, basking now in the heady atmosphere of open alliance with Nazi Germany. The Guard was declared the sole legal party of the National Legionary State proclaimed on September 14, 1940, and assigned responsibility for the nation's moral and material regeneration. Adventurers and opportunists now flocked to it. Starting with the second anniversary of Codreanu's murder, the Guard went on a sustained rampage, slaughtering scores of political opponents (including Iorga and the only slightly less prestigious National-Peasantist economist Virgil Madgearu), massacring Jews, and hinting ominously at the coming "popularization" of the officers' cadre. This protracted radicalism in the style of Roehm's "night of the long knives," however, proved its undoing; Hitler, on the eve of his Russian campaign, required a disciplined and stable Romania, productively harnessed to the German war effort. Accordingly, he allowed army chief General Ion Antonescu to suppress the ideologically sympathetic but turbulent Iron Guard in three days of ferocious street fighting, January 21-23, 1941. At the same time he granted Horia Sima and a few fellow Guardists political asylum in Germany and kept them in reserve as reinsurance for Antonescu's reliable behavior for the rest of the war. Thus, ironically, was an authentic fascist movement emasculated with Nazi connivance at a moment when Germany's power in Europe and over Romania stood at its zenith. As at the time of Carol's royal dictatorship two years earlier, so now once again the Iron Guard collapsed when confronted with a strong hand. By carrying its negative radicalism to uncompromising, and hence irrational, lengths, it had thrown away repeated opportunities to achieve power. As a symptom of the ills of Romanian society, and as the nemesis to the falsehoods of Romanian politics, the Iron Guard was a serious phenomenon; but as a remedy for these very ailments it was trivial.

General Antonescu dismantled the National Legionary State on February 15 and replaced Iron Guard functionaries with military personnel. He elicited public endorsement in a lopsided (99.91 percent) plebiscite of March 2-5, and took Romania into the war against the Soviet Union as Germany's most valuable and valued ally on June 22, 1941. Though originally a professional disciple of French military models, Antonescu's reading of the European balance had led him to recommend a German association for Romania well before the war. As a "political" general, Antonescu had also for a time cultivated the Iron Guard and, after serving as war minister in the Goga-Cuza and the first Cristea cabinets of 1937-38, had incurred Carol's displeasure by appearing as a character witness for the defense at Codreanu's treason trial in May, 1938. But he had also kept on good terms with the now passive Maniu, with whom he shared a puritanical disdain of the royal camarilla. Indeed, it had been Antonescu's probing into some dubious armaments contracts awarded to Carol's crony Malaxa which had prompted his relief as war minister on March 30, 1938, and transfer to a corps command in Bessarabia. In "exile" his popularity was only heightened. When he interceded on behalf of the Guardists subjected to the regime's terror after Calinescu's assassination in September, 1939, Antonescu was relieved of this assignment as well. Still later, as Carol desperately sought to secure himself against the expected national outrage over his territorial cessions to the Soviet Union on June 28, 1940, he arrested Antonescu, who was by now the logical leader of such a backlash, on July 9. This was to no avail: in the aftermath of the Second Vienna Award, Antonescu vaulted straight from detention to power while Carol slid from power into exile.

Courageous and incorruptible, but also peevish and egotistical (he spoke of himself in the third person), Antonescu had the support of a united public for his attempted and initially successful recovery of Bessarabia and the northern half of the Bukovina from the Soviet Union—a feat for which he was designated Marshal by King Michael on August 23, 1941. And Romania's contribution to the Axis war effort against Russia, which Antonescu sustained even after Romania's own irredentas had been recovered, was far more substantial than that of any other German partner. As a result, Antonescu became Hitler's favorite ally, the first foreigner to be awarded the Knight's Cross of the Iron Cross, the only one to be solicited for military advice, and probably the only person—German or foreign—permitted to out-talk and contradict the Führer. Within the Axis, Antonescu defended Romania's sovereignty and national interest with much stubbornness, though during the triumphant first half of the war he joined eagerly in the genocide of the Jews. When after Stalingrad, which was a Romanian as well as a German military debacle, the Romanian public and elite became skeptical of a continued war effort, Antonescu replied, (a) that the recent recovery of Bessarabia and northern Bukovina would prove ephemeral unless Russia were categorically defeated, and (b) that Romania could only hope to recover the lost fraction of Transylvania by out-performing Hungary for Hitler's favor and thus inducing him eventually to reverse the Second Vienna Award. The first part of his analysis proved correct, the second false, as it was to be the Allied Powers that eventually returned all of Transylvania to Romania as a reward for having abandoned the Axis before Hungary had.

This about-face was achieved through a *coup d'état* by the hitherto figurehead King Michael against Antonescu on August 23, 1944, when Soviet armies, having already reconquered all of northern Bukovina and part of Bessarabia, were poised to overrun the Regat. Antonescu, too, was by now prepared to sue for an armistice, but not without loyally informing Hitler beforehand; this would have aborted the enterprise. Already from the end of 1943, his foreign minister had sought to avert the need for the royal coup by initiating secret peace feelers through various Romanian legations abroad, especially those in Ankara, Madrid, and Stockholm. But Romania's reluctance to concede the Soviet-claimed territories and Antonescu's personal scruples about deserting Hitler protracted these contacts until they were overtaken by King Michael's decisive action, taken on his own responsibility but with the endorsement of the leaders of the long illegal National-Peasant, Liberal, Social Democratic, and Communist parties. The next day, August 24, the Germans belatedly produced Horia Sima as head of a puppet government in Viennese exile, and their Luftwaffe began a futile three-day bombardment of Bucharest.

Antonescu was now arrested (and eventually executed on June 1, 1946), and an armistice was concluded with the Allied Powers on September 12, 1944, which reconfirmed the 1940-41 Soviet-Romanian border but, in compensation, indicated restoration of the 1920-40 Hungaro-Romanian border. Already on August 25, 1944, Romania had joined the Allies against Germany, and on September 7 she also declared war on Hungary. Having earlier fielded twenty-seven divisions and suffered half a million casualties (of whom three hundred thousand died) in Hitler's war against Russia, having fueled and fed his armies with her oil and grain, having then pulled off the most decisive *volte-face* of the war—one which turned the Wehrmacht's southeastern hinge and opened the Balkans to the Soviet army—Romania was now to contribute another twenty-seven divisions and suffer a further 170,000 casualties (among whom 111,000 died) in the final Allied campaigns against Hitler. Her military prowess on both sides, from 1941 to 1944 and from 1944 to 1945, was an impressive contrast to the spineless surrenders of 1940.

14

During the early war years, the urban and industrial prosperity of the second half of the 1930s had finally spilled over into the villages and the agricultural sector. This was not, be it said, due to any structural reform of the latter, but simply thanks to massive German procurements of Romania's agricultural produce and to the recruitment of surplus rural manpower into Romania's own army. During the war's last year, however, this brittle prosperity vanished as the countryside became an object of both German and Soviet looting. The logic of military requirements had impelled Antonescu, until his overthrow, to seek the functional rationalization of the economy but, as regards agriculture, his success in this quest was but slender. The Germans, in turn, were recommending a neo-National-Peasant economic policy: Romania would develop processing industries organically connected with her agriculture, and diversify the latter from grains to industrial crops as well, but she would rely on Germany for her heavy and secondary industrial needs. This was a reversal of the neo-Liberal economic ambitions of the Carolist era.

That earlier recovery from the depression, while impressive in some industrial sectors, had again—as with the Liberals' predepression industrialization—failed to generate sufficient momentum, or to become general enough, even to begin to solve the chronic problems of Romanian agriculture. Concentrated in such capital-intensive sectors as metallurgy and armaments, petro-chemicals, timber, and textiles, the industrialization of the late 1930s had scarcely made a dent in rural overpopulation or in effectively alleviating the peasantry's hunger for commodities. It did, however, bring to prominence a new type of monopolistic entrepreneur, who usually operated with Carol as a silent but richly rewarded partner.

In contrast to the Brătianu types of the 1920s, who were basically politicians influencing industrial policy through their control of the government and of the banks, these new men of the 1930s—"xenocrats" such as the Romano-Greek Nicolae Malaxa or the Jew Max Auşnit—were essentially captains of industry who would intervene in politics to protect and enhance their economic stakes. The fact that the index of Romanian industrial production rose during the 1930s by 56.3 percent but per capita income rose by only 8 percent (even in neighboring Bulgaria—also an agrarian society—this latter figure was 35 percent) serves as an oblique indicator that the Carolist regime had been as neglectful as its Liberal predecessors of the country's vast peasant majority. That majority's level of consumption continued to stagnate; its indebtedness, which was incurred for consumption and not for investment, remained staggering; and its levels of health, housing, welfare, and education stayed squalid. Inevitably, such profound rural poverty amidst manipulated, subsidized, graft-ridden, and often alien-owned industrial opulence undermined the social and psychological bases of parliamentary government.

15

Before we proceed to our conclusions on interwar Romania, some technical and cultural issues merit brief discussion. Her railroad network was the Balkan Peninsula's densest, but it was poorly integrated between the Regat and the new provinces: the lines of Transylvania and the Bukovina were oriented toward Budapest, Fiume, and Vienna, and those of Bessarabia toward Odessa. Until 1923 the Bessarabian lines were broad-gauged according to the Russian pattern. The 11,206 kilometers of track in 1919 had been but slightly expanded by the eve of the truncation of 1940 to 11,815 kilometers; of these a mere 405 were double-tracked, a distinct handicap in a situation where most railroad traffic consisted of heavy goods trains. Indifferent administration and political boon-doggling compounded the deficiencies deriving from inadequate physical assets. Every politician appeared to have his favorite line to extend in his favorite direction. The result was many false starts and incompletions in railroad construction as successive ministers interrupted each other's projects. At harvest time an oil-train might require two weeks to travel the two hundred kilometers from the refineries at Ploeşti to the port of Constanţa. The ports, incidentally, handled 80 to 90 percent of Romania's exports (oil, grain, timber), while the railroads carried half her imports (industrial equipment and products).

As pointed out above, oil was the asset that allowed Romania to maintain favorable trade balances, budget surpluses, and fiscally profitable railroads. But this industry employed relatively little labor and was heavily foreign-owned, hence it brought no relief to rural overpopulation and rather aggravated xenophobic frustrations. Furthermore, Romania never produced a sufficiently high percentage of the world's petroleum output to exert influence over its international price. This vulnerability to such price fluctuations is illustrated by the following: whereas her 1,886,000 tons of oil production in 1926 were then worth 9,500 million lei, her nearly quintupled production of 8,700,000 tons in 1936 was worth only 9,000 million lei. Other mineral resources, which were never as intensively exploited as oil during the interwar era, were lignite coal, chromium, manganese, mercury, mica, copper, iron, lead, antimony, bismuth, molybdenum, and pyrites, and, in Transylvania, methane gas, bauxite, gold, and silver. Whereas the timber industry of the Bukovina and Transylvania had employed the greatest number of nonagricultural workers in the 1920s, it was overtaken in this regard during the Carolist era by the heavily subsidized metallurgical-engineering and textile industries, concentrated in the Regat. Nevertheless, Transylvanian industries on the whole survived Regateni economic competition and administrative discrimination far more successfully than, for example, did the infant Slovak industries survive Czech pressures in that neighboring fused state (see Chapter 3, section 7). While the total number of Romanian industrial workers nearly doubled between 1930 and 1939, from 157,000 to 294,000, the simultaneous expansion of surplus and unabsorbed rural manpower was between one and two million people. Industry thus sadly failed to fulfill the Liberal and Carolist promises of functioning as a *deus ex machina* for the ills of agriculture.

At peak periods in the farming cycle, the peasants nevertheless felt they needed their children for field labor and preferred to pay fines for withholding them from classes rather than surrender them to the schools. The weakness of the elementary educational system was suggested by the low literacy statistics already cited (see section 2). The secondary school system, in turn, was frankly designed to develop servants of the state, not the talents of individuals. The universities, finally, bred a surplus academic proletariat of lawyers and classicists whom the economy was insufficiently developed to absorb and who thus swelled the ranks of a too numerous, powerful, underpaid, and hence corruption-prone officialdom. In 1929, when modern, industrialized Germany was training 1.7 university students per 1,000 inhabitants, backward, agricultural Romania was presuming to train 2 per 1,000. Romania's students were always an active, and usually a disruptive, political cohort. While the interwar Bucharest bar numbered more lawyers than the Paris bar, Romania's ratio of rural doctors to rural population was no better than India's, i.e., 1.1 per 10,000. Nothing came of occasional National-Peasant calls to shift educational priorities from the classical and humanistic curriculum favored for prestige reasons by the Liberals toward the scientific, technical, vocational, and trade schooling for which there was far more urgent social need.

In 1930 the press numbered 709 dailies and weeklies (of which 505 were in the Romanian language, 112 in Hungarian, 72 in German, and the rest in Yiddish, Russian, Bulgarian, and French) and 554 periodicals (of which 433 were Romanian, 69 Magyar, 30 German, and the rest scattered). As in several neighboring countries, it was venal, defamatory, and extravagant. A number of the Romanian-language papers were Jewish-owned and most of the journalists appear to have been Jews. After the Goga-Cuza government had outlawed the specifically Jewish press early in 1938, the royal dictatorship went on to suppress all party-affiliated newspapers a little later in the year.

16

Against the early background of her hopeful expectations on the morrow of World War I, Romania's political and socioeconomic history in the interwar era presents a disheartening spectacle. The peasantry was, in effect, excluded from the nation's political life and treated as an inert object to be manipulated; hence, it mistrusted all authority. The oligarchic, bureaucratic ruling elite behaved simultaneously as nationalistic modernizers and as prospective emigrants, salting away in foreign banks the wealth squeezed out of the peasantry under the device of jingoistic banners. The "alien" middle class was economically essential but politically resented and socially unassimilated; nationalist and class hatreds could easily be mobilized against it, but Romanian society was still incapable of replacing it. It was precisely this absence of an autonomous and civically responsible Romanian *economic* middle-class, in contrast to the all-too-numerous "intelligentsia-bureaucratic" middle-class, that largely accounts for that lack of structure in the country's politics, of which the extreme if spurious electoral oscillations of the 1920s and the plethora of political assassinations in the 1930s were the most vivid expressions. That absence also accounts for the many conspiracy theories bred in interwar Romania to rationalize the failure of the numerous reformist promises to make any dent in the pervasive poverty, and to explain away the incompetence of the innumerable state-owned and state-partnered corporations, which were created for reasons of economic nationalism rather than economic rationality to replace the despised Jewish and other "foreign" merchants, manufacturers, and moneylenders. In no other European country of the interwar era was the moral and psychological chasm between the oligarchic, bureaucratic elite and the lower classes as wide and deep; even its cultural infatuation with France and its fetishistic fascination with foreign affairs and foreign politico-legal models was a kind of flight from its own people on the part of that elite.

Paralleling the transitions from the triumphant atmosphere of the early interwar years, through the anxious mood of the depression era, to the paralyzing despair at the time of the territorial amputations, was the constitutional-political shift from the French-modeled pseudo-democracy of the 1920s, through the fragmentation of the political parties in the first half of the 1930s, to the eventual fascist-modeled pseudo-corporatism of the late-1930s—with the pseudo-totalitarian Iron Guard both exposing and itself embodying the manifold weaknesses and deceptions of Romanian public life. Such sharp fluctuations were, of course, a likely consequence of extremely rapid socioeconomic change. Romania had in less than a century passed from a pastoral society to one producing grain exports for a capitalistic, world wide market, but its own society was still characterized by neoservile relations. At the same time, it was seeking to endow itself with a modern industry. A transition that had taken a millennium in the West the Romanian elite was now seeking to achieve in haste and without permitting a politico-social revolution. That potent, if dormant, energies had accumulated during the unimpressive interwar era is, however, indicated by the performance of Romanian society during and since World War II. And that interwar Romania produced her own most perceptive critics of the contradiction between the reality of her public life and its alleged aims is suggested by the following pair of quotations, which may serve as a fitting eulogy to this unfortunate era:

> We have introduced liberal commercial laws, but with anti-Semitism at their base; we have introduced universal suffrage, but with ballot-stuffing; we have ruined rural households in order to increase credit institutions, but we have not permitted free competition among these institutions . . . we have encouraged national industry, but not for the benefit of the rural population . . . [who] made the sacrifices, but for the benefit of politicians who are pensioners of this national industry; we have centralized the administration of the country, but not in the hands of a trained bureaucracy but in the hands of . . . party . . . partisans; in a word, we have aped the European bourgeoisie in form, but at bottom we have persisted in the sycophantic habits of the past. In this way we have transformed political life into a hopeless turmoil.[12]

> The greatest and most fruitful revolution which could be accomplished in Romania would be simply to apply the existing laws.[13]

---

12. C. Rădulescu-Motru, quoted in Henry L. Roberts, *Rumania*, p. 116.
13. *Adevărul* (The Truth), February 25, 1937, quoted in Eugen Weber, "Romania," in Hans Rogger and Eugen Weber, eds., *The European Right* (Berkeley: University of California Press, 1966), p. 539.

· *Chapter Seven* ·

BULGARIA

1

THE study of interwar Bulgarian politics tends to puncture the conventional myth that political violence and political radicalism are functions of socioeconomic inequality and/or of the existence of large and unassimilated ethnic minorities. Bulgaria had the most egalitarian society in interwar East Central Europe in terms both of property distribution and of status flexibility; it had no nobility, and its educational system was accessible, prestigious, and of high quality and was quite effective in facilitating social mobility. She also had one of the area's ethnically most homogeneous societies. Yet Bulgaria's politics were particularly violent, and her extremist movements—of both the "right" and "left" variety—were exceptionally strong. Frustrated nationalism, and specifically the presence within her borders of a large and well-organized community of irredentist Macedo-Bulgarians, which was ever ready to smite any political figure suspected of laxness in the pursuit of Bulgaria's aspirations to all of Macedonia, accounted for most of interwar Bulgaria's domestic violence, though powerful and sporadically active Anarchist and Communist movements also contributed to the phenomenon of frequent assassinations, bombings, riots, and quasi-insurrections.

In addition to evicting her from all but a small fraction of Macedonia, the Neuilly Peace Treaty of November 27, 1919, deprived Bulgaria of her granary in the Southern Dobruja, which had accounted for only 8 percent of the area she had held before the Balkan and World wars but for 20 percent of her cereal production, and of her Aegean maritime access and some rich tobacco fields in Western Thrace, which she had only recently acquired from Turkey during the Balkan Wars of 1912 and 1913 but was now obliged to surrender to the Allied Powers for transfer to Greece. Finally, she lost a few small but strategic border salients to Yugoslavia. Her total area was thus reduced from 111,836 square kilometers at the close of the Balkan Wars in 1913, to 103,146 square kilometers after Neuilly. She

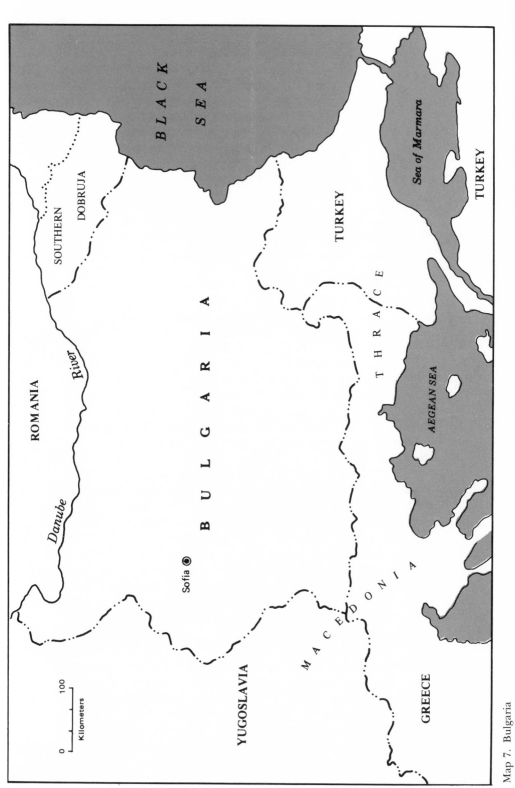

Map 7. Bulgaria

was also saddled with heavy indemnity, restitution, and reparations payments and with a ceiling on her armed forces of 20,000 troops serving twelve-year enlistments, 10,000 gendarmes, and 3,000 border policemen.

Thus came to naught Bulgaria's prodigious and almost continuous military efforts of 1912-18, in the course of which her armies had suffered approximately 155,000 killed and over 400,000 wounded, apart from 150,000 civilian dead in the course of cholera, typhus, and influenza epidemics, and not to mention the several hundred thousand "unborn" of these war years or the loss of a third of her livestock and farm inventory. The military dead alone numbered more than a fifth of the male population between the ages of twenty and fifty.

Bulgarian nationalists subsequently contended that the Neuilly Treaty's territorial sacrifices left as much as one-third of their countrymen outside the state's frontiers, in neighboring Romania, Yugoslavia, and Greece. Such a claim rested in part on the controversial, indeed dubious, identification of all Slav Macedonians as Bulgarians and was exaggerated, though the interwar boundaries undoubtedly did violate the principle of nationality at Bulgaria's expense. While public opinion was most outraged by the separation of the major parts of Macedonia, yet the losses of the Aegean littoral and tobacco fields in Western Thrace and of the South Dobrujan breadbasket were economically more painful and significant. The Southern Dobruja, on the other hand, alone of the Neuilly losses, was destined to be recovered from Romania at the close of the interwar era, on September 7, 1940, and to be then retained by Bulgaria after World War II (see Chapter 6, section 13).

In inflicting the settlement of 1919 on Bulgaria, the Allied powers were presumably determined to reduce the significance of a state that, though small, had cost them much strategic anguish during the war by bringing German power to the Straits, thereby helping to sever the supply of Western reinforcements to Russia, and nearly destroying Serbia. Yet the harshness and vindictiveness of the Neuilly terms left Bulgaria not only an angrily revisionist state, isolated from and hostile toward her neighbors, but also a rancorous society, which was characterized, as mentioned above, by much internal violence. Some of this domestic acrimony stemmed from a frustrated sense that the decision to support the Central Powers in 1915 had, like the previous one to launch the Second Balkan War in 1913, been a gratuitous miscalculation, and that shrewder diplomacy could have brought Bulgaria onto the victorious bandwagon and hence into possession of all her irredentas. The conduct of the war effort had, furthermore, been inept and poorly organized. Neither the society nor the army were prepared for a sustained, three-year-long effort. Desertions, strikes, bread riots, fatigue, and resentment finally culminated in a major mutiny of the peasant troops during the second half of September, 1918. Alternatively termed the "Radomir Rebellion" or the

"Vladaya Uprising," after the two southwestern localities near which it peaked, it forced the speedy conclusion of an armistice on September 29 and the abdication of Tsar Ferdinand in favor of his son Boris on October 3, though it failed to achieve its proclaimed goal of replacing the monarchy with a republic.

Under any circumstances the Macedonian problem would have weighed heavily on interwar Bulgaria's politics. Bulgaria now held but 6,789.2 square kilometers (10.1 percent) of a region to which her nationalist sensibilities were strongly attached, while the lion's share was divided between Greece (34,602.5 square kilometers, or 51.5 percent) and Yugoslavia (25,774 square kilometers, 38.4 percent). Additional irritants were Yugoslavia's arbitrary and neglectful administration of her fraction of Macedonia, and Greece's decision to resettle onto her share of the region about half of the million Greek refugees from Turkey who swarmed into the country after the Greek military debacle of 1922 in Anatolia. In Bulgarian domestic politics, the Macedonian problem posed itself not merely in the form of extensive public identification with the cause of Macedonian revisionism. An even stronger expression was in the ability of the highly cohesive, committed, and energetic Macedo-Bulgarians to penetrate and, indeed, for a long time almost to dominate her political, administrative, military, commercial, academic, and free professional cadres. Thus, the 206,814 Macedonians of Bulgaria's fraction of Macedonia (1934 census), together with the 101,144 refugees from the Yugoslav and Greek shares who fled into Bulgaria after the Balkan and First World wars (1926 survey), exercised a degree of power far out of proportion to their numbers and came close to functioning as a state-within-the-state.

Their paramilitary arm, the Internal Macedonian Revolutionary Organization (IMRO) not only intimidated the Bulgarian elite by terrorizing personalities suspected of softness on the irredentist issue, but also engaged in raids across the border and assassinations in the Yugoslav and, less frequently, the Greek parts of Macedonia. The result was to further isolate Bulgaria from her neighbors. In the later 1920s, IMRO's violence turned inward as rival factions decimated each other, and in the early 1930s its remaining members degenerated to gangsters, extortionists, and drug smugglers. It also took to hiring out its professional killers to other European extremist movements. The assassin of Yugoslavia's King Alexander and of French Foreign Minister Barthou, for example, was an IMRO gunman in the service of the Croatian Ustaša (see Chapter 5, section 8). Before it was eventually broken up by a "new broom" regime in 1934, IMRO had imposed one and a half decades of intimidation and terror on a Bulgarian society that had been both victim and collaborator. The ease of its final destruction suggests that previous Bulgarian governments had lacked the will, rather than the power, to curb IMRO's excesses.

2

As background to the later analysis of Bulgaria's political history, some of her social and economic statistics are presented and examined here, particularly those pertaining to agriculture, the basic sector of her economy. Interwar Bulgaria took three censuses, on the last day of the years 1920, 1926, and 1934, which cumulatively convey an impression of rapid population growth absorbed within a remarkably stable pattern of urban/rural, religious, and ethnic ratios and of divisions by economic sectors (see tables 45-48).[1]

TABLE 45

POPULATION BY URBAN/RURAL RESIDENCE

	1920		1926		1934	
	Number	Percentage	Number	Percentage	Number	Percentage
Urban	966,375	19.9	1,130,131	20.6	1,302,551	21.4
Rural	3,880,596	80.1	4,348,610	79.4	4,775,388	78.6
Total	4,846,971	100.0	5,478,741	100.0	6,077,939	100.0

TABLE 46

POPULATION BY RELIGION

	1920		1926		1934	
	Number	Percentage	Number	Percentage	Number	Percentage
Eastern Orthodox	4,061,829	83.8	4,568,773	83.4	5,128,890	84.4
Muslim	690,734	14.3	789,296	14.4	821,298	13.5
Roman Catholic	34,072	0.7	40,347	0.7	45,704	0.8
Protestant	5,617	0.1	6,735	0.1	8,371	0.1
Israelite	43,232	0.9	46,431	0.9	48,398	0.8
Armeno-Gregorian	10,848	0.2	25,402	0.5	23,476	0.4
Other	639	0.0	1,757	0.0	1,802	0.0
Total	4,846,971	100.0	5,478,741	100.0	6,077,939	100.0

1. Having earlier slogged his way through the morass of interwar Yugoslav and Romanian statistics, the author had pleasure, on coming to this Bulgarian chapter, in dealing with the data of a country whose statisticians knew how and what to count. All the demographic, socioeconomic, and electoral statistics in this chapter are from sequential annual volumes of the official *Statisticheski Godishnik na Tsarstvo Bŭlgariya* (Sofia: Glavna Direktsiya na Statistikata), except for the agricultural data for 1946 in section 2, which are from S. D. Zagoroff *et al., The Agricultural Economy of the Danubian Countries 1935-45* (Stanford: Stanford University Press, 1955), pp. 381-82. In Bulgaria, an urban locality was defined legally, and not in terms of size. Some towns had less than ten thousand inhabitants and a few villages had more. Hence the urban/rural ratio here is not exactly comparable to those of other countries, where size was the criterion.

TABLE 47

POPULATION BY ETHNICITY (LANGUAGE)

	1920		1926		1934	
	Number	Percentage	Number	Percentage	Number	Percentage
Bulgarian	4,041,276	83.4	4,585,620	83.7	5,274,854	86.8
Greek	46,759	1.0	12,782	0.2	9,601	0.1
Jewish	41,927	0.8	41,563	0.8	28,026	0.5
(Hebrew or Ladino)						
German	3,515	0.1	5,110	0.1	4,171	0.1
Russian	9,247	0.2	19,590	0.4	11,928	0.2
Serb	1,259	0.0	647	0.0	172	0.0
Turkish	542,904	11.2	607,763	11.1	618,268	10.2
Gypsy	61,555	1.3	81,996	1.5	80,532	1.3
Other	98,529	2.0	123,670	2.2	50,387	0.8
Total	4,846,971	100.0	5,478,741	100.0	6,077,939	100.0

On the whole, the figures for religion correspond to those for ethnicity. The number of Muslims is throughout higher than the number of Turks and Gypsies combined (most of the latter also being Muslim), thanks to the statistical weight of the Pomak mountaineers, who were Bulgarian by race and language but in the seventeenth century converted to Islam. The decline in the number of Hebrew and Ladino speakers between 1926 and 1934 without a corresponding reduction in the number of professing Jews is due to a change in the official census criterion from "mother tongue" to "language of usual discourse," the latter being declared as Bulgarian by two-fifths of the Jews in 1934. The decline of the Greek population after 1920 reflects a Greco-Bulgarian population exchange, while the growth in Russian population is due to the arrival of a portion of the counterrevolutionary Wrangel army upon its defeat in the Russian Civil War. On balance, Bulgaria's ethnic minorities were small and did not pose the difficult problems for national political integration that plagued most other interwar East Central European countries. In turn, her treatment of their civil rights and cultural-pedagogical institutions was just and generous.

As shown in table 48, any shift from agriculture toward other economic sectors was so minute as to be barely perceptible. Furthermore, the structure of land distribution was remarkably stable and quite egalitarian. But the average size of holdings declined, as the rural population not only increased more rapidly than the amount of land under cultivation, which was close to its agronomically feasible maximum, but was also obliged by the dearth of alternative employment opportunities to remain on the land and partition its plots into ever smaller sizes. Thus, whereas the agricultural population grew between 1926 and 1934 by 8.8 percent, the area

TABLE 48

POPULATION BY ECONOMIC SECTORS
(INCLUDING DEPENDENTS)

	1920		1926		1934	
	Number	Percentage	Number	Percentage	Number	Percentage
Agriculture	3,655,800	75.4	4,087,810	74.6	4,446,784	73.2
Mining	12,047	0.3	15,733	0.3	23,197	0.4
Industry, handicrafts	484,509	10.0	576,293	10.5	616,110	10.1
Communications, transport	102,123	2.1	117,088	2.1	137,933	2.3
Commerce, banking	205,260	4.2	223,400	4.1	219,328	3.6
Armed forces	59,036	1.2	52,399	1.0 ⎫	162,749	2.7
Civil service	81,988	1.7	90,835	1.7 ⎭		
Free professions	106,185	2.2	124,503	2.3	82,184*	1.3
Rentiers, Pensioners	69,645	1.4	67,720	1.2	219,448*	3.6
Others	70,378	1.5	122,960	2.2	170,206*	2.8
Total	4,846,971	100.0	5,478,741	100.0	6,077,939	100.0

*In 1934 several categories were rearranged: medical personnel, for example, were shifted from "Free professions" to "Personal services," and certain "inexactly determined" professions were added to "Rentiers and pensioners."

under cultivation increased during this same period by only 1.8 percent. As a result of this demographic pressure on the land, the number of agricultural holdings swelled by 17.9 percent while the average size of these holdings shrank by 14.0 percent. Relevant data for earlier and later interwar years, such as 1920 and 1940, is unfortunately not available. But one can extend the comparison from 1926 to 1946 for the same territory, i.e., excluding the Southern Dobruja which was reacquired in 1940. Over this longer period, the percentage changes are as follows: growth of agricultural population, 18.4; increase in area under cultivation, 3.4; rise in number of agricultural holdings, 38.4; shrinkage in average size of holding, 25.0.

Such declines in the average size per holding, 14 percent over an eight-year interval and 25 percent over a twenty-year span, are serious but need not necessarily be disastrous provided agriculture can be rendered more intensive and productive. This, indeed, was to happen to a considerable extent in the 1930s, as many peasants shifted from cereal production to remunerative garden, fiber, and industrial crops (see section 10). Furthermore, *average size* per holding is a purely statistical concept and tells nothing about the *predominant types* of holdings (e.g., dwarf, medium, large). In spite of the fact that land distribution was, in fact, quite egalitarian in interwar Bulgaria, as will be illustrated presently, there is no denying that the data do indicate heightening population pressure on the available agricultural land and hence an increase in surplus agricultural population.

It should also be noted that the statistics refer to *holdings*, not to *properties*; the former were operational-farming units, the latter legal-ownership units. As Bulgaria did not have hordes of sharecroppers and tenants leasing land from absentee latifundists, such as plagued interwar Hungary and Poland, there is a congruence between properties and holdings in the various size-categories of her agriculture, although some of both the smallest and the largest owners, owning under two and over thirty hectares, leased land to medium peasants who owned from five to thirty hectares. While 98 percent of all farmers owned their own land in 1934, 31 percent leased some additional land. Still, only 10 percent of the agricultural area consisted of such leased land in 1934. Our statistics also incorporate agricultural land that was technically located within town limits (gardens, vineyards, etc.) and whose cultivators were numbered with the urban population.

The earlier contention that the structure of interwar Bulgarian agriculture was both stable and relatively egalitarian, i.e., an agriculture of small and middle peasants, is supported by a break-down, in percentages, of the proportion of all holdings and of agricultural area in each of the size-categories (see table 49). In studying it, the reader should bear in mind that most of the smallest holdings of less than one hectare were either

TABLE 49

STRUCTURE OF LAND DISTRIBUTION

Category (Hectares)	Percentage of Holdings			Percentage of Agric. Area		
	1926	1934	1946*	1926	1934	1946*
0—1	11.9	13.5	14.9	1.0	1.3	1.7
1—2	12.4	13.5	14.9	3.2	4.0	5.1
2—3	12.0	13.2		5.1	6.6	
3—4	11.0	12.2	38.8	6.7	8.5	30.7
4—5	9.7	10.7		7.6	9.6	
0—5	57.0	63.1	68.6	23.6	30.0	37.5
5—10	28.0	26.2	24.5	34.5	36.9	39.3
10—20	12.6	9.2	6.2	29.3	24.3	18.6
20—30	1.8	1.1	0.6	7.3	5.2	2.9
30+	0.6	0.4	0.1	5.3	3.6	1.7
Total	100.0	100.0	100.0	100.0	100.0	100.0

*The data for 1946 subtract the recently recovered Southern Dobruja and thus refer to the same area as those for 1926 and 1934.

vineyards and gardens cultivated by persons for whom agriculture was a secondary occupation, or intensive tobacco farms. Hence, they are not evidence of agricultural pauperism.

Even though interwar Bulgarian agriculture was happily free of an indigent proletariat, it was burdened with serious problems stemming from: (a) the uneconomic system of scattered strip distribution, which was once a venerable form of insurance against hail but by this period obsolete and irrational; (b) the primitive level of agronomic technology, as indicated by the inventory in 1934 which numbered 149,465 wooden plows without metal parts, 545,216 wooden plows with metal plowshares, 279,368 metal plows, and 285,740 antiquated threshing-boards as against only 14,900 threshing machines and 1,523 tractors; (c) the high level of rural overpopulation and underemployment (37 percent of the 1934 agricultural population being redundant even at the then prevailing level of agronomic technology). Low productivity, low consumption, and low capital formation in agriculture fed each other in a tight cycle. The peasant lived on bread, potatoes, cheese, yogurt, onions, and paprika, and by the eve of World War II only one-ninth of his villages had electricity. Yet, though his per hectare yield rates were low compared to the European average, the Bulgarian peasant, partially compensating with sheer diligence for his poor technology, produced the Balkan Peninsula's highest yield rates, while scarcely cultivating its best soil. Nor did he cleave to old techniques even when change would have benefited him, nor flatly mistrust the urban-based state-apparatus no matter what its policies, as did the Romanian peasant. He turned with alacrity to industrial crops in the 1930s, when both the market and the government suggested that diversification would be to his interest. For all his relative poverty, he was neither abject nor inert, and he knew himself to be a full member of the Bulgarian polity, capable of bringing his interests to bear in the determination of its socioeconomic policies.

3

As noted earlier the society was, indeed, relatively homogeneous in political and economic as well as ethnic, religious, and linguistic terms. The Bulgarians had accomplished all their major revolutions simultaneously, with the expulsion of the Ottomans in the 1870s, when at one blow they achieved independence, eliminated the alien nobility, and distributed the land to the peasantry. Their political, bureaucratic, and military elites were thereafter recruited from the peasantry and artisans, and since the educational system was more open and widespread than in most other interwar East Central European countries, the psychological alienation of the peasantry from the elite of bureaucrats and intelligentsia was milder in Bulgaria than in the area's other states.

Frequently dubbed "the Prussians of the Balkans" or "the Slavic world's

Japanese," the Bulgarians were considered by outsiders and by themselves to be the most diligent, frugal, sober, orderly, systematic, and correct, as well as practical and alert, people of the peninsula. They prided themselves on sustaining a *robota*-work culture, in contrast to the Serbs' *haiduk*-hero culture or the Romanians' and Greeks' alleged mercantile-ingenuity culture. Conversely, their very stoicism supposedly also rendered them indifferent to coercion and cruelty inflicted on, or by, themselves or others. While such generalizations about national character may be overdrawn, the Bulgarians are, on balance, rather impressively utilitarian and hardheaded, with little of the romanticism or mysticism of other Slav peoples. Yet, while they innovatively adapted many Western technical and institutional devices to create and exploit opportunities for economic rationalization in the interwar era (refrigerator ships on the Danube, for example, to export their fruit, eggs, and dressed fowl to Germany), on the other hand the Ottoman spirit also long survived: time was never urgent in those pre-Communist days.

Interwar Bulgaria's social security and insurance systems were the Balkans' most advanced, and they encompassed peasants and artisans as well as workers and employers. Of course, the fact that virtually the entire rural and a significant fraction of the urban population owned some productive land provided a certain amount of additional security. Similarly, Bulgaria's cooperative movement was the peninsula's most flourishing one (if Slovenia be here regarded as non-Balkan), and the public health program was also stronger than her neighbors'. The ready availability of credit to the peasants through their cooperatives and the state's banks rendered private usurers superfluous and hence allowed Bulgaria's largely Sephardic Jewish community to function in far less controversial roles and with greater acceptance than, for example, Romania's (see Chapter 6, section 4).

Finally, and most importantly, the educational system was sound and accessible. It was free and compulsory to age fourteen, and cheap and with fee-waivers for the poor; hence, it was conducive to an open and mobile society. Though teachers were underpaid and the schools' physical plants often inadequate, education enjoyed enormous prestige in this society that was craving to catch up with the rest of Europe after the long Ottoman stagnation. Bulgarian literacy levels were the highest of any Balkan country: 79.6 percent for males and 57.2 percent for females above the age of seven in 1934; 97 percent for military recruits in the late 1930s. They would have been still higher but for the Muslim minority's low rates. The fact that literacy was sustained after the end of formal schooling is indicated by the prevalence of public reading rooms. In 1934 there were 2,356 such rooms, of which 1,208 were in villages, with just short of a million books. It is also evidenced by the interesting statistic that the number of privately written letters per inhabitant handled by the postal authorities in 1931 was 31 in Bulgaria, in contrast to 23 in Romania, 25 in Yugoslavia, and 18 in Greece.

At the secondary and university levels the Bulgarian educational system did, alas, also produce the same kind of academic proletariat that burdened all of the interwar Balkan countries and partly accounted for the bloated size and spasmodic behavior of their political and bureaucratic cadres. But the Bulgarian students, to judge from their faculty enrollments, were less disdainful of technical and engineering and science programs and less prone to the mania for law, classics, and literature than were their colleagues in neighboring countries. The Bulgarian state, in turn, reflected and reciprocated the society's high esteem for education by allocating almost three-tenths of its budget to the education ministry. Less happily, it also felt obliged to absorb much of the otherwise unabsorbable academic proletariat into its competent but rigid, poorly paid, yet politically privileged, administrative apparatus.

4

In contrast to her relatively stable, egalitarian, open, and quite progressive society, Bulgaria's political life was extraordinarily turbulent. The proliferation of parties and their very nature also contributed heavily to the ferocity of political life. Though the "bourgeois" political spectrum derived from two quite delimited and authentic sets of issues, the conservative-liberal differences of the constitutional debate of 1879 and the controversy of the 1880s over association with or independence from Russia, it soon splintered into a plethora of parties based on personalities, which were constantly fusing and splitting according to the relations and aspirations of their leaders. Whereas in classical parliamentary theory party leaders supposedly form governments, in Bulgaria the royal ministers would create parties to sustain their portfolios. Though designating themselves by prestigious adjectives such as liberal, democratic, progressive, radical, and populist—but never conservative—these parties lacked any ideological or social rationale and were predicated exclusively on the office-hunger of their leaders and cohorts. Forty such parties achieved legislative representation at various times. Next came the Marxists, whose activities began in the mid-1880s and who soon split into what eventually would crystallize as the Communist (stronger) and Socialist (weaker) parties. Ironically, the Peasantist Party was the last to be founded in this overwhelmingly peasant country, in 1899, and even then it was at first more a social than a political movement. After the mid-1920s, it too splintered into sundry factions. Bulgaria being relatively small and homogeneous, it had no regional parties. Nor was the turmoil of its partisan life attenuated by a permanent pivot party such as the Czechoslovak Agrarians, by a "Government Party" analogous to Bethlen's or Piłsudski's in Hungary and Poland, or by a formal monoparty such as King Carol founded in Romania. Participation in interwar parliamentary elections varied between 54 and 87 percent of the eligible electorate and 12 and 23 percent of the total population; married women with children achieved the suffrage in 1934.

Bulgaria's first interwar parliamentary elections, held on August 17, 1919, in an atmosphere of national weariness and revulsion after the vain sacrifice of so much blood, saw all the "bourgeois" parties defeated by the two articulate antiwar parties, the Agrarian Union (hereafter the Peasant Union) and the more radical of the two Socialist parties, which had just restyled itself in May as the Community Party. The Peasantists won 85 seats in the Sŭbranie, the unicameral national legislature, on the strength of 203,630 votes (31.0 percent); the Communists, 47 on 119,395 votes (18.2 percent); the moderate Social Democrats, 38 on 84,185 (12.8 percent). The 11 "bourgeois" parties received only 66 of the chamber's 236 seats and but 237,436 votes (36.2 percent); not one of these parties won as many seats or votes as even the Social Democrats, let alone the two front runners. There were 11,708 (1.8 percent) invalid ballots. After protracted but abortive negotiations with the Social Democrats, the Peasantist leader Aleksandŭr Stamboliski formed a coalition government with two minor parties on October 6, 1919.

An intensely ideological and emotional man, Stamboliski had transformed his originally rather apolitical movement into a political one shortly before and during the war. In the process, he had wrested the leadership away from its original founder, Dimitŭr Dragiev. An authentic, if somewhat demagogic, agrarian radical, he was unique among the various peasantist leaders of interwar East Central Europe in his militancy. Stamboliski was no political "broker" like Witos, no "statesman" like Švehla, no "betrayer of trust" like Szabó, no Proteus like Radić, no "conscience" like Maniu, no office-seeker like Lupu, and no "pragmatist" like Korošec; he was determined to impose the dictatorship of the village and its peasants upon Bulgaria, and, indeed, upon all East Central Europe, and to destroy the hitherto dominant power and values of the hated cities, or "Sodoms," and their allegedly denatured and parasitical inhabitants.

The Communists promptly, albeit unintentionally, played into his hands. Euphoric from their own success in the Sŭbranie elections, and from an even more emphatic triumph in local elections on December 7, 1919, and from the general social ferment of the time, they underestimated Stamboliski as a "mere Bulgarian Kerenski." At the turn of the year 1919-20, they sought to break him through a transport and general strike in which about twenty thousand railroad, postal, and telecommunications workers as well as thirteen thousand general workers in private industry participated. Stamboliski smashed it with great vigor and some brutality, mobilizing the Peasant Union's paramilitary Orange Guard to cow the strikers, calling some into the army, and evicting others from their state-owned residences.

The peasant leader then capitalized on the momentum of this severe but impressive performance by dissolving the only recently assembled Sŭbranie on February 20 and scheduling new elections for March 28, 1920, at which the latent power of the peasantry would be realized by making the suffrage compulsory. As a result, the percentage of eligible voters who cast ballots jumped to 77.3 from the 54.5 of the previous year. The postwar leftward tide was still running strongly. The Peasant Union took 110 Sŭbranie seats on the strength of 349,259 votes, or 38.2 percent of the total; the Communists 50 seats for 184,616 votes (20.2 percent), while the Social Democrats slipped to 9 seats and 55,452 votes (6.1 percent). The 12 "bourgeois" parties won a total of 60 of the chamber's 229 seats and 316,291 votes (34.5 percent). Two of these parties had polled more votes than the Social Democrats, though none had done as well as the Communists. The invalid votes numbered 9,554 (1.0 percent). Undaunted by his failure to achieve an absolute majority, Stamboliski arbitrarily invalidated 9 Communist, 3 Democratic, and 1 Populist mandate to give his party a Sŭbranie majority of 110 versus 106, and proceeded to organize an all-Peasant Union government. He was now ready to implement his vision of a peasantist policy and a peasant society.

Stamboliski, who had been imprisoned from 1915 to 1918 for his antiwar stance and had then been involved in the Radomir Rebellion at war's end (see section 1), was agreeable to abiding by the territorial severance of Macedonia, as he expected this condition to be transcended by a general restructuring of international relations in East Central Europe, specifically by a Bulgar-Yugoslav federation and by a more general confederation of all the area's agrarian states. He intended this "Green International" of peasantist parties and peasant societies to be a politico-ideological alternative to both the capitalist West and the Communist East, and his commitment to it was of such sincerity as to devalue in his eyes conventional irredentism and revisionism. Alas, this was as utopian as his hopes for the more limited association with Yugoslavia, which the exclusively Serb-oriented Pašić did not reciprocate or even understand. Stamboliski's vision of reconciliation earned him nothing but the suspicion of Tsar Boris, who feared that his own foreign dynasty would be the one to be jettisoned in any union with a Yugoslavia ruled by the native Karadjordjević family, and the mortal hatred of IMRO, which was determined to wreak vengeance on this "betrayer" of Macedonia. Against this enmity, it availed Stamboliski nothing that Bulgaria became, thanks to his stance, the first ex-enemy state to achieve acceptance and even some popularity in Allied capitals, or that he assiduously, albeit vainly, sought to trade on this good reputation to regain for Bulgaria access to the Aegean through Western Thrace—an issue of far lower emotional saliency with his own public than was Macedonia.

In domestic policy, the application of Stamboliski's concept of peasantism entailed a number of interesting social and political experiments. On May 9, 1921, legislation was passed for a thirty-hectare maximum for peasant properties, with five additional hectares for every member of a family beyond the fourth. For land not cultivated directly by its owners, the maxima were to be four hectares per individual and ten per family. Land beyond these maxima was to be expropriated (with compensation) and placed in a special fund, to which would also be added surplus monastic land, underutilized communal grazings, reserve land owned by the state, and unexploited but arable land; these lands were for eventual distribution to landless and dwarf-holder peasants. Though it reflected Stamboliski's fervent belief that no man is genuinely free unless he owned and tilled land and hence that such properties had to be small if all men were to be free, this legislation was actually of relatively little practical significance. The preponderant number of properties were already well within its limits, and it was destined to be gutted by legislation of August 1, 1924, passed by a successor regime, which expanded the maximum for "scientifically organized" farm holdings to 150 hectares and returned to the previous owners about two-thirds of the private land expropriated by Stamboliski, while retaining the former monastic, communal, and state lands. But the legislation of 1924 was also destined to have but limited consequences; holdings larger than thirty hectares continued to be of little and declining significance (see section 2), and Bulgaria was to remain what she had been before—the classic East European country of small and evenly distributed land holdings. The postwar loss of the Southern Dobruja, where large estates abounded, had removed precisely that area in which the legislation of 1921 would have had some "bite." In any event, experience has shown that land maxima such as Stamboliski's, though reflecting an egalitarian and agrarian ideology, can not by themselves cure the socioeconomic problems of rural overpopulation, underemployment, underconsumption, etc. Interestingly, Stamboliski's original legislation, which was amended three times during his own term of power, had not been particularly controversial, had received the assent of several urban-based parties, but had been most vehemently attacked by the Communists as "petit-bourgeois."

As for distribution from the state's land fund, 64,288 landless and dwarf-holder families and 28,576 Bulgarian refugees from beyond the Neuilly frontiers had been resettled by the end of 1929 on about 240,000 hectares. But only a fraction of this land had come into the state's fund through expropriations under the legislation of 1921 and 1924; a substantial part had been realized through consolidations of strips and reclamation of previously unused land. That the state interested itself in such consolidation despite the peasantry's partiality for strip-cultivation is again evidence that Bulgarian governments were more solicitous of agriculture, more diligent in exploring ways of improving it, and more ready to invest capital and technology in it than were neighboring governments.

A more original expression Stamboliski's ideological commitments was his compulsory labor legislation of June 14, 1920, requiring every male between the ages of twenty and forty to perform eight months of physical labor for the state, and an additional twenty-one days annually within his home commune; for unmarried women between the ages of sixteen and thirty the requirement was four months' service. Due to Allied demands, it was possible to purchase exemption after November 9, 1921, for a substantial fee. But no more than 20 percent of those designated for the call-up could take advantage of this in any one year. In fact, an average of only 10 percent annually availed themselves of this opportunity, and the privilege was repealed in the late 1930s as a violation of the spirit and purpose of the program. Though designed in part as a substitute for universal military conscription, which was now prohibited to Bulgaria under the terms of the Neuilly Treaty—indeed, the laborers were uniformed and subject to discipline—this compulsory service was also intended to exemplify the egalitarian value of universal physical labor and the moral and pedagogical value of social service for the public weal. Finally, it also absorbed some excess labor-power and effectively, if crudely, built some important public works. Hence, subsequent regimes retained the system but exempted females. Between 14,500 and 29,000 men were called up annually, and they built and repaired several thousand kilometers of road, laid several hundred kilometers of railroad track, built a few hundred bridges, planted millions of saplings, drained swamps, dug canals, raised dams, strung telephone wires, etc. Though much labor was wasted due to faulty organization, the program's achievements were considerable and impressive. And as important as its physical achievements were the moral, psychological, and political benefits that came from instilling in the young a sense of solidarity, sacrifice, and service.

The less happy side of Stamboliski's egalitarian peasantist ideology was a vehement, almost irrational, hatred of cities and their social modes. He divided society into six estates: agricultural, artisanal, hired-labor, industrial, commercial, and administrative-bureaucratic. Of these only the first two were virtuous, while the last pair were condemned to be liquidated as parasitical. Implementing this social theory, he restricted the political activities of lawyers, the profession which had traditionally dominated Bulgarian political life but was resented by the peasantry as the incarnation of alien and negative values, and curbed and intimidated journalists. He sought to destroy the grain merchants by organizing, on December 5,

1919, a monopolistic State Cereal Consortium intended to assure high peasant returns while eliminating middlemen. (The Allied Control Commission forced its abandonment on September 24, 1921.) Stamboliski also gleefully authorized the compulsory quartering of poor people on the "excessively large" residences of the prosperous, and abused a law of December 9, 1919, which authorized the punishment of those who had prepared for, prolonged, or profited from the war, as a club to settle scores with politicians of the opposition and with businessmen.

Other interesting manifestations of Stamboliski's ideological passions were his exclusion of the intelligentsia from membership in the Peasant Union, his flooding of the state bureaucracy with enthusiastic but inexperienced Peasant Union stalwarts, his revision of the tax system in favor of the peasants and his expansion of their credit facilities, his pressure to shift—or to unbalance, as his detractors would have it—educational priorities toward the elementary schools and "practical" subjects at the expense of the higher levels and of theoretical subjects, and, finally, his mobilization of the peasantry's Orange Guard cadres to molest the opposition. Though many of his measures were plausible, they were marred by Stamboliski's erroneous evaluation of the nonpeasant classes of the society. Regarding "the city" and its inhabitants as sinful and parasitical, he misunderstood the interrelationship between urban and rural prosperity and axiomatically believed that the latter required the former's destruction. At times, indeed, he almost appeared to be less interested in benefiting the peasants than in harassing the other classes. A trenchant polemicist and compelling orator, a man of considerable, though incomplete, education, Stamboliski's actions often degenerated into a brutal and myopic externalization of hitherto frustrated peasant resentments. Hence, despite his laudable efforts for intra-Balkan and East Central European reconciliation, and his sympathetic commitment to egalitarian peasantism, Stamboliski's regime must be reckoned a failure, predicated as it was on a static and irrational vision of society and on the implementation of that vision through ruffianism and demagoguery.

That the bourgeois-intelligentsia parties and class, whom Stamboliski quite explicitly proposed to expel from the political and social body of the nation, and whose nationalist and irredentist passions he deliberately "betrayed," should conduct a life-and-death battle against him was a foregone conclusion. More ambivalent and interesting were his relations with the second strongest party, the Communists. Here the two protagonists misunderstood and misjudged each other. Stamboliski would neither take seriously a party committed to an urban, industrialist, proletarian ideology nor regard as a major enemy this movement whose rhetoric was as antibourgeois as his own yet sneered at his idolized village utopia. He came to view the Communists as "toothless bears," who were useful for frightening the middle classes but were neither dependable nor desirable political allies. They, in turn, failed to understand this peasantist enthusiast and his movement, whose revolutionary militancy and chiliastic self-righteousness more than matched their own despite an "objectively reactionary" ideological base, and into whose mass support they were unable to make significant inroads despite their supposedly infallible Leninist strategy of inciting the poor and middle peasants against the wealthier kulaks. Though they might rhetorically dismiss him as a "mere Kerenski," the Communists in fact feared and hated Stamboliski. Thus each regarded the other as an instrument to be manipulated during a temporary period of parallel struggle against the bourgeoisie, but then to be discarded and destroyed. When the country's nationalist elite (the military, intelligentsia, and bourgeoisie) supported by IMRO launched a *coup d'état* against Stamboliski's regime on June 9, 1923, the Bulgarian Communist Party simply stood by, to Moscow's fury, falsely and fatefully alleging that this episode was merely an internal quarrel between the rural and urban bourgeoisies within the bourgeois enemy camp, and that the working class and its Communist cadres had no stake or interest in the outcome.

5

The background to this coup, whose success demonstrated the political superiority of the city over the village even in as overwhelmingly agrarian and peasantist a country as Bulgaria, is the story of Stamboliski's increasing euphoria and isolation in his last year of power. His pacific international stance, together with his militant domestic policy, had always affronted the nationalistic bourgeoisie and intelligentsia in general and the Macedonians in particular. In the spring of 1922, the White Russian Wrangelite officer-expatriates were added to the ranks of his enemies when Stamboliski expelled a number of their officers on the charge, which was probably valid, of abusing their Bulgarian sanctuary by intriguing both against him and against the Soviet authorities. In mid-September, 1922, his Orange Guard ruffians almost lynched a group of leading bourgeois politicians whom Stamboliski then placed in "protective custody" in a provincial jail. On November 19, 1922, he conducted a demagogic national plebiscite on the question of whether twenty-two cabinet ministers of the 1912, 1913, and 1918 wartime governments should be tried as war criminals; this group heavily overlapped with the group who were to be lynched in September. Stamboliski having previously intimated that the country's reparations burden would be geographically distributed in proportion to the number of negative ballots cast in the various districts, this plebiscite produced 647,313 votes for and 223,584 against the proposed trial (there were also 55,593 blank and invalid ballots). The trial, however, never took place, and the prospective defendants remained in their "protective" imprisonment until

Stamboliski's overthrow the following June. That the issue of alleged war criminality was but a pretext is suggested by the fact that in 1919-20 Stamboliski had served in coalition cabinets with a number of the "war criminals." It was probably after this episode, which indicated that he would stop at nothing to destroy all opposition, that the conspiracy to overthrow Stamboliski was launched. In December, 1922, following an IMRO-Orange Guard clash in a nearby provincial townlet, the Guard invaded Sofia ("Sodom") to sack the offices of opposition parties and then to loot quite indiscriminately.

Following up this escalation of Peasant Unionist violence during 1922, Stamboliski conducted new Sŭbranie elections on April 22, 1923. He prepared for them by purging his own Peasant Union of moderates, jailing a number of Communist leaders, unleashing the Orange Guard to wreck opposition meetings, again making voting compulsory, and in general enveloping the electoral campaign in an atmosphere of intimidation. The turnout was 86.5 percent of those eligible to vote. As a result of the above pressures, his Peasant Union won 212 of the Sŭbranie's 245 seats on the strength of 571,907 votes, or 53.0 percent of the total; the Communists were reduced to 16 seats though their 203,972 votes (18.9 percent) were only a shade under their proportion of three years earlier. The Social Democrats slipped to 2 seats representing 27,816 votes (2.6 percent), and the bourgeois parties were relegated to but 15 seats. A coalition of most of the last-named parties, significantly styling itself the Constitutional Bloc, had polled 166,909 votes (15.5 percent), and the National-Liberals, who ran independently, had received 55,963 (5.2 percent). In some districts the Constitutional Bloc and the Social Democrats had nominated joint lists, which polled 31,768 votes (2.9 percent). A mere 141 ballots were scattered among lists that failed to achieve representation, and 20,532 (1.9 percent) were invalid.

These seemingly triumphant results actually proved fatal to Stamboliski: he was seduced into megalomania while, on the other hand, the bourgeois opposition became convinced that there no longer existed any possibility of defeating him through legal political means. The Communists, in turn, concluded that the bourgeois parties had now been effectively eliminated and that Stamboliski was henceforth their main, indeed their only serious, enemy. He likewise inferred that the bourgeoisie was now finished and that only the Communists remained to be similarly humbled. Thus, both fatefully exaggerated the significance of the election results and underestimated the resilience, power, and desperation of the phalanx composed of the military, the intelligentsia, the bourgeoisie, and the Macedonians.

Stamboliski now lost all sense of political reality. During May, 1923, he alarmed the royal court with hints of establishing a republic; he offended the military by shuffling its command structure and elevating the Orange

Guard into a semiofficial paramilitary body; he provoked IMRO by outlawing a number of its "cover" organizations, confiscating their journals, and arresting their leaders; and he vexed the Communists by arresting and beating some of their provincial functionaries. In mid-May, Stamboliski scheduled a monster rally of a quarter million Peasant Unionists, to be held in September in Sofia, and announced that his regime would last for decades. Alas, all these excesses simply set the stage for his own destruction scarcely seven short weeks after his stunning, but deceptive, electoral triumph of April 22. Mesmerized by the fact that three-fourths of the nation's population consisted of "his" peasants, Stamboliski deluded himself that this provided both the justification and the guarantee of his rule. He forgot that political power does not automatically grow out of demographic statistics.

Though he strenuously sought Balkan peace, Stamboliski's regime proved, on balance, a disappointment. The ideological postulates of his policies, and their moral intentions, were often interesting and worthy, but they were debased in their implementation by his irrational anti-urban prejudices and the approved rowdyness of his cohorts. Much of his legislation was but the short-sighted and static codification of peasant grudges. Instead of establishing a model peasant democracy in Bulgaria, he discredited the vision of government by the rural masses throughout East Central Europe.

6

The *coup d'etat* that overthrew Stamboliski on June 9, 1923, was executed by army units under the command of officers belonging to the Military League, a small conspiratorial body of active and reserve officers. Founded in 1919, the league was dissolved the following year by Stamboliski, but it was clandestinely and illegally reorganized in 1921. It was at the political disposal of the National Concord (Naroden Sgovor), also a small but legal organization of politicians, businessmen, intelligentsia, and reserve officers, founded early in 1922. The membership of these two bodies partly overlapped through the reserve officers in each, and their activities complemented each other. The actual plot to overthrow Stamboliski was necessarily confined to a minority of initiates even of these two bodies, but it appears to have enjoyed the passive protection—at any rate, the suspiciously prompt endorsement upon its success—of Tsar Boris. IMRO bands assisted the army units in destroying the scattered and ineffectual Orange Guard resistance to the coup, and it was they who, after inflicting horrible mutilations, actually beheaded and dismembered Stamboliski on June 14. Their participation symbolized the coup's international significance as signaling Bulgaria's reversion to a revisionist and anti-Yugoslav stance; hence her switch from a French to an Italian Great Power orientation.

Professor Aleksandŭr Tsankov, an economist and the leader of the National Concord, assumed the premiership on June 9, 1923, and proceeded to organize a cabinet in which all parties except the Peasantists and Communists were initially represented. The exclusion of these two parties was a measure of the bitter polarization that had crystallized in the Stamboliski era. Eager to transform his small and clubby National Concord into a comprehensive organization of all the bourgeois groups, Tsankov persuaded the Populist-Progressives and the bulk of the Democrats and Radicals to join with it in the formation, on August 10, of the rather misnamed Democratic Concord (Demokraticheski Sgovor), a body impressive in size but not in cohesion. The Liberals and Social Democrats, though outside this phalanx, also served in his cabinet. Indeed, the Social Democratic minister of transportation played an indispensable role in the Tsankov regime's suppression of a Communist uprising in September, 1923, by effectively mobilizing the railroad system and its workers for the speedy despatch of army units to the trouble spots. Not until February 15, 1924, did the Social Democrats withdraw this minister from the Tsankov cabinet. Even then it was only after the premier had rebuffed their importunings for a second portfolio and after they had been repeatedly prodded by the West European leaders of the Socialist International, who were embarrassed and appalled by Tsankov's reputation for ruthless "white terror," which had been well-earned in the course of his regime's systematic decimation of Peasantist and Communist cadres after the crises of June and September. The Social Democrats' motives for going into formal opposition were thus less than estimable, and the party was soon to atrophy for the rest of the interwar era into a small, stable, passive coterie with some influence over teachers and communications workers. It was valued by other politicians chiefly for its access to European Socialist statesmen, such Western contacts always conveying "respectability" in Bulgarian eyes.

The Communist insurrection to which allusion has just been made was also a response to external prodding by Soviet and Comintern leaders, who were outraged by their Bulgarian comrades' passivity in the face of Tsankov's coup against Stamboliski. Moscow correctly judged that that clash was not an internal quarrel within the bourgeois camp in which the proletariat had no stake, as the Bulgarian Communists had alleged, but rather a portentous confrontation between the peasant masses and a bourgeois-military elite in which the Communists' political interest and ideological obligation was to support the former, à la the Bolsheviks' own "Kornilov policy" of 1917. Furthermore, in terms of its international implications, Tsankov's regime was suspected by the Soviet leaders of being another link in the chain of a British-inspired encirclement of Soviet Russia, whereas Stamboliski, for all his "utopian peasantist nonsense" and his repudiation of the Bulgarian Communists, had always maintained a correct and even cordial stance toward Moscow.

With impressive obedience to their international headquarters, the Bulgarian Communists thereupon reversed themselves and launched the insurrection of September 19-28, 1923. They were too late. Stamboliski's Orange Guard, which would have been a potential ally on June 9, had since been destroyed, and Tsankov had then proceeded substantially to preempt the Communists' belated blow by suddenly arresting over two thousand of their members on September 12. Here he acted on the basis of intercepted communications between Moscow and its Bulgarian adherents. Politically, too, his preparations for the confrontation were more effective than the Communists'; he had fashioned the Democratic Concord coalition and secured a Social Democratic minister of transportation who held the crucial railwaymen to their work. The Communists, on the other hand, despite earnest entreaties in several directions, failed to enlist any organized allies and only managed at the last minute to recruit some scattered provincial survivors of Stamboliski's once-powerful cohort, now politically demoralized and motivated only by an understandable but primitive craving to wreak vengeance upon the cities for their martyred leader. All in all, the insurrection was poorly conceived, hastily prepared, and sloppily executed, and the Communist cells in the capital and several other cities did not participate. Yet it did achieve a ten-day toehold in the country's extreme northwestern corner, whence some of its survivers managed to withdraw into Yugoslavia and from there into subsequent Comintern careers.

This brief but violent episode earned the Bulgarian Communists a lasting reputation for "Bolshevik" discipline and toughness in the eyes of the Communist world's Soviet leaders. It also allowed Tsankov, for a brief period, to ingratiate himself in the West as a "bulwark" against Communism. Capitalizing on this image, he prosecuted a "white terror" of such ferocious intensity against surviving Peasantists and Communists (real and alleged), that it eventually proved counterproductive. Bulgaria's repute in European eyes was tarnished, and, ironically, Tsankov's attempt to isolate morally the country's authentic Communists was nullified. Despite and because of this persecution, the latter developed into an impressive and eventually polar opposition force. Though outlawed on April 4, 1924, the party functioned through a series of "fronts" and became the strongest interwar Communist movement in the Balkans.

The Communists' dexterity and recuperative powers were first demonstrated in the legislative elections of November 18, 1923, when they fashioned a complex electoral arrangement with the Peasantists, nominating joint lists in some districts and endorsing the Peasant Union lists in others. Despite being prohibited from nominating candidates in these two parties' traditional strongholds and from campaigning at all, this partner-ship collected 221,777 votes (20.3 percent of the total), and 30 Peasantist and 8 Communist seats. The government coalition of the Democratic Concord, which was itself a coalition, and the Social Democrats received 639,881 votes (58.3 percent) and 201 seats, of which the Social Democratic share was 29, in a Sŭbranie of 247. The National-Liberals, the "war hawks" of 1915-18, who had almost been wiped out in the initial postwar revulsion against that slaughter, recovered with 120,640 votes (11.0 per-cent) and 8 seats. Minor lists that earned no parliamentary representation received 21,215 ballots (1.9 percent). It is probable that a substantial proportion of the ballots officially declared invalid (92,964 or 8.5 percent) had also been intended as protest votes against the Tsankov regime's repressiveness. Compulsory voting had again brought 86.2 percent of the eligible electorate to the polls.

7

The next several years witnessed an ongoing vendetta. The govern-ment periodically outlawed one after another of the "front" organizations which the hydra-headed Communists were able to form, and also toler-ated, or even arranged, the frequent assassinations of radical Peasantist leaders at the hands of IMRO and police agents. On the other hand, these two movements successfully strove to isolate and to blacken Tsankov. There were occasional fiascos. In 1924 the Communists made an abortive effort to persuade IMRO to switch sides; this hardly sat well with the Peasantists. In 1925 their terroristic bombing of the Sofia Cathedral, a "sectarian deviation" that killed 128 people, gave Tsankov a temporary propaganda windfall. But over the long run the premier's position was indeed eroded by his reputation for grimness and ferocity and by the chillingly methodical savagery with which he reacted to these Communist provocations. Embarrassed politicians who had originally hastened to jump on the Democratic Concord's bandwagon soon jumped off with the same alacrity. In addition, Tsar Boris took umbrage at the government's unexpected flirtations with Belgrade in 1925.

On January 4, 1926, Tsankov was obliged to yield the premiership to Andrei Lyapchev, also of the Democratic Concord, who on the one hand eased the repression of Communists and Peasantists, but on the other gave full license to IMRO's activities at home and abroad. Tsankov was relegated to the speakership of the Sŭbranie, from where he led the "internal opposition" to Lyapchev on the basis of three primary charges: the new premier's "softness" toward the Communists, his hospitality to foreign investors under terms that allegedly undermined the nation's sovereignty, and his permissiveness toward IMRO, which also damaged Bulgaria's interests by isolating her from her Balkan neighbors and ren-dering her a cat's paw of Italian diplomacy. In the 1930s and 1940s

Tsankov was destined to become an overt Nazi with a limited and exclusively urban following; no peasant would endorse "Stamboliski's butcher."

The Communists and Peasantists responded in different fashions to these changes in the regime. The Communists took advantage of the milder Lyapchev era to hone to a fine edge their skills at "front" activities. While their own party remained banned, they were enabled to engage in activities of trade unions and youth organizations, to float a number of journalistic ventures, and, on February 24, 1927, to found a legal Labor Party, which they discreetly but effectively controlled. For the once-imposing Peasant Union, on the other hand, the alternating experiences of persecution and toleration proved too much. It fragmented into several competing factions whose stances were dictated as much by personal and tactical as by ideological and strategic differences.

As a result of the above fragmentation, the Sŭbranie elections of May 29, 1927, were particularly intricate and confusing. The electoral atmosphere, while no longer as nakedly terroristic as in the immediate aftermath of the putschist and insurrectionary crises of 1923, was still intimidating, especially in the villages. Hence the participation of 84.3 percent of the eligible electorate was a reflection of pressure as much as of commitment. At stake were 273 seats. The Democratic Concord, allied with a fraction of the National-Liberals, received 522,592 votes or 44.1 percent of the total, and 168 seats, of which 33 belonged to Tsankov's "internal opposition." A coalition of Social Democrats, Artisans, and Peasant Union "centrists" polled 285,758 votes (24.1 percent) and 56 seats which were divided among 10 Social Democrats, 4 Artisans, and 42 Peasantists. The "front" Labor Party, allied with a smaller faction of Peasant Union "leftists," earned 29,210 votes (2.5 percent) and 4 seats. Still another coalition composed of dissident Democrats, a different fraction of National-Liberals, and Peasant Union "rightists" drew 179,491 votes (15.2 percent) and 32 seats. A fourth Peasant Union splinter, the "Dragievites," presented a joint list with dissident Radicals which was credited with 29,637 votes (2.5 percent) and 2 seats. IMRO virtually hand-picked the 11 deputies from the southwestern, i.e., Macedonian, districts, to whom 37,854 votes (3.2 percent) were tabulated. Other fractions of Peasantists, Democrats, National-Liberals, and minor groups ran separate slates that drew a total of 69,771 votes (6.0 percent) but achieved no representation. The number of invalid ballots was 28,809 (2.4 percent).

The Social Democrats, who had earlier collaborated with the Democratic Concord while always spurning the Peasantists and Communists and had in the course of recent years become, *de facto*, one of the parties of the "establishment," were now outraged by the fact that in these elections the machinery of government had been mobilized against them as efficiently as against the opposition parties. Smarting under the reduction of their parliamentary representation from 29 to 10, they now proposed the alliance of all "left" and "labor" groups that they had hitherto fastidiously disdained. Ironically, the Communists, who had wanted precisely such a united front ever since the preparations for their insurrection of 1923, now also reversed course and repudiated the Social Democrats' offer because of the world-Communist movement's new "social fascist" line. That line defined non-Communist parties of the Left, and especially Socialists, as tools of fascism; hence they were the major enemy.

While the Social Democrats stagnated, torn between their craving for domestic leverage and their desire for international Socialist approval, and while the Peasantist movement was still hamstrung by its internal divisions, the underground Communists and their legal Labor Party fed on the social unrest and radicalism engendered by the depression. They could now capitalize on their reputation as the opposition movement par excellence. The Labor Party's membership rose from 6,000 at the end of 1930 to 35,000 two years later, when its youth organization numbered 18,000 and its trade unions 10,000 members. In communal elections of November 9, 1930, it drew 11 percent of all votes; this was more than any other single opposition party, though the combined portions of all Peasant Union factions would admittedly have been higher. In municipal elections held between November 1, 1931, and February 14, 1932, the Labor Party achieved majorities on two city councils and pluralities on ten others. Its press and other propaganda activities were also vastly expanded at the turn of the decade, and it organized many strikes.

Simultaneously, the Labor Party's controlling Communist cadres, having but 3,000 members at the end of 1932 with another 2,250 in the youth section, escalated their acts of violence against the authorities, who reciprocated in kind. The temptations and the risks of this confrontation helped to induce an apocalyptic fervor within these underground ranks, which was abetted by Moscow's "social fascist" line of the day, and to which subsequent Communist historiography alludes deprecatingly as the "left-sectarian" deviation. The authorities, for their part, were most alarmed in their prosecution of this vendetta by disconcertingly successful Communist conspiratorial infiltrations of army garrisons. Hence the ferocity of both their formal-juridical and their unofficial-homicidal pursuit of the Communist cadres.

The Sŭbranie elections of June 21, 1931, came in the midst of this inveterate and escalating feud, but had no discernible impact on it. At stake were 274 seats; 85.2 percent of the eligible electorate participated. Despite a superficial Lyapchev-Tsankov reconciliation the previous year, their long quarrel had weakened the Democratic Concord, Premier Lyapchev's permissiveness toward IMRO's violence had tarnished its image, and the economic "predepression" since 1928 had undermined its acceptability. It went down to a narrow defeat at the hands of a competing coalition, formed just two months before the election, after Lyapchev had rejected as exorbitant the price of five cabinet portfolios which its leaders were demanding to spare him this contest.

Consisting of dissident Democrats and Radicals, i.e., those outside the Concord, part of the National-Liberals, and that "centrist" wing of the Peasant Union named, after the address of its headquarters, the "Vrabcha" faction, this victorious coalition received 625,553 votes, or 47.6 percent of the total, and 150 seats divided among 41 Democrats, 7 Radicals, 29 National-Liberals, and 73 Peasantists. The Democratic Concord, allied with another National-Liberal faction, drew a combined vote of 403,686 (30.7 percent), good for 65 seats for itself and 14 for its partner. The Labor Party was third, with a spectacular leap to 167,281 votes (12.7 percent) and 31 seats. The regular Democrats leveled off at 27,323 votes (2.1 percent) and 5 seats. The handpicked Macedonian candidates were this time assigned to run on the lists of the Democratic Concord and of a proregime defection from the Social Democrats that styled itself the Socialist Federation and was led by Tsankov's brother and his former transportation minister from the days of the 1923 Communist insurrection (see section 6). This latter group polled 26,501 votes (2.0 percent), of which 24,654 were officially credited to the Macedonian candidates, 8 of whom were seated in the Sŭbranie. Many minor parties and splinter groups, at least three of which were Peasantist, totaled 43,385 votes (3.2 percent); their 1 seat went to a member of one of the Peasant factions. The number of invalid votes was 21,778 (1.7 percent).

These elections inaugurated the only peaceful and constitutional governmental transition that Bulgaria was to experience in the interwar period, as the Democratic leader Aleksandŭr Malinov formed a cabinet on June 29, 1931, consisting of four Democrats, one Radical, two National-Liberals, and three "Vrabcha" Peasantists. The last-mentioned party grumbled that this distribution of portfolios did not reflect its numerical strength at the polls, and technically this was a legitimate claim. Nevertheless, it owed a substantial, non-numerical debt to Malinov for covering it with his own unimpeachable "respectability" and thus enabling the Peasant Union, or at least its major faction, to become once again a governing party. On October 13, 1931, Malinov, citing reasons of health, turned the premiership over to his fellow Democrat Nikola Mushanov and took the less demanding speakership of the Sŭbranie. Mushanov was tougher but less prestigious than his predecessor, and this change, on balance, weakened the government and whetted still further the appetite of its Peasantist contingent for more portfolios and patronage. The Democratic Concord, for its part, had no rationale other than the exercise of office and proved too heterogeneous to survive out of power; it soon disintegrated.

The Communists were understandably elated by their Labor Party's impressive showing in these elections, and interpreted it as justifying their "social fascist" line of spurning alliances with other leftist parties and groups. Their strength was to be reconfirmed the following year by municipal elections in Sofia on September 25, 1932, when they captured nineteen of the capital's thirty-five council seats. Their apocalyptic revolutionary expectations were thus confirmed and their "sectarian" deviation correspondingly strengthened. The number of strikes, riots, and conspiracies multiplied. The authorities responded by redoubling their own anti-Communist terror, regardless of the political freedom and juridical fastidiousness that the new government claimed to exemplify. On February 11, 1933, fifteen of the Labor Party's nineteen seats on the Sofia City Council were invalidated, and on April 12 twenty-nine of its thirty-one Sŭbranie deputies were expelled; the remaining two repudiated their Communist connections. Riots and mass arrests ensued. Such harassments were accompanied by frequent killings of Communist and Labor Party activists "while under interrogation" or "while attempting flight." This violence on the part of the government appears to have been relatively effective; the wave of strikes and riots subsided during the second half of 1933 and the Labor Party, if not yet the "harder" underground Communists, showed signs of the exhaustion that usually follows euphoria.

Simultaneously the government rather effectively immunized the masses of the peasantry against "radicalization through proletarianization" with a program that included reduction of debts (up to 40 percent) and postponement of their repayment (up to fifteen years), prohibition on foreclosures of holdings of five hectares and less, state purchase of cereals at high prices, and tax reductions. Such emergency steps were, of course, but temporary and deceptive palliatives for the government's own problems. Indeed, they rather aggravated those problems over the long run in that age of internationally imposed orthodox economic standards. Only later was Nazi Germany to teach the Balkan countries how to shake off these standards. But the measures did help Bulgaria to slip through the depression without crippling peasant unrest.

8

Though it did not culminate in mass peasant violence, the depression nevertheless had a severe impact on Bulgaria's economy and provoked profound political changes. The economic aspects were almost as depressing in Bulgaria as in the rest of East Central Europe and can be summarized briefly. With the loss of the grain-growing Southern Dobruja and the acquisition of some tobacco-bearing regions along her southern border in the course of her three wars of 1912-18, tobacco had replaced cereals as interwar Bulgaria's chief export crop. Even in the core parts of the country many peasants shifted cultivations. By 1926 tobacco exports accounted for 41 percent of the value of the country's total exports and 90 percent of this crop's production. In that year, the international price of tobacco dropped precipitously, and Bulgarian agriculture was plunged into a predepression malaise a few years before the rest of the world. Grain and other agricultural export prices followed into the slump after the collapse of the Vienna Kreditanstalt in May, 1931, on the eve of the elections that turned the Democratic Concord out of office. To compensate for the disasterous decline in the prices of her agricultural exports, Bulgaria sought to increase their volume, at tremendous domestic effort and cost.[2] By 1934 the country's national income was but 61.4 percent of what it had been in 1929.

Though this crisis was not as disasterous as in some neighboring countries—Yugoslav and Romanian national incomes, for example, were down to 46.5 and 49.4 percent of 1929 levels and Bulgaria's peasants, while heavily indebted, at least owed their debts to their own cooperatives and to the state's banks rather than to urban and Jewish usurers—it sufficed to erode peasant confidence in the Malinov-Mushanov government. That government's formation after the pivotal elections of 1931, and particularly its inclusion of Peasant Union ministers, had initially elicited considerable optimism among peasants and other "little folk"; but by 1934 this had withered into disillusionment. The situation resembled the history of the Maniu regime's reputation in Romania between 1928 and 1930. Not only was the new government saddled with the inevitably frustrating task of coping with the economic consequences of a world depression over which it had little control, but it gratuitously undermined itself by its continued toleration of IMRO's murders and extortions, by the chronic bickering among its constituent parties over the distribution of portfolios and patronage, and by the unsavory behavior of many of its ministers. The Peasantist politicians, having finally pushed their way back to the "trough" of pecuniary and administrative rewards after eight long years in the wilderness, exploited their opportunities with abandon—to the disgust of the peasantry at large.

This dismaying complex of Communist-incited labor and street unrest, which had recently somewhat abated, endemic IMRO violence, police excesses, economic depression, helplessness of government, administrative corruption, and ministerial "betrayal of ideals" helps explain the background of, and the lack of popular resistance to, a second *coup d'état*, executed on May 19, 1934, by middle-rank army officers and technocrats. The immediate trigger was another of the many crises over portfolios within the Mushanov cabinet, resulting from Peasantist hunger for office. This time, Tsankov and his Nazis were about to intervene with ominous

2. For details, see Joseph Rothschild, *The Communist Party of Bulgaria* (New York: Columbia University Press, 1959), p. 281.

demonstrations and parades. The officers and technocrats thereupon struck to preempt his and the Peasantists' bids for power, either of which might well have unleashed a civil war.

The coup's colonels came from the Military League, which had already participated in the earlier putsch against Stamboliski (see section 6); its civilians were from a "supra-partisan" club named Zveno (Link), which had been founded secretly on June 27, 1927, and had started to publish a weekly of the same name on January 1, 1928. The inner club had about three hundred members, the public journal about twenty-five hundred subscribers. It preached "national regeneration" through "strong government" and the vigorous application of "expertise" and "science." Hence, like their military associates, the Zveno-ists were authoritarian modernizers but not demagogues or fascists. Nor did either set of partners represent any particular class. Indeed, this lack of a social base was to prove the Achilles heel of these Bulgarian putschists. Their regime's strongman was Colonel Damian Velchev, who enjoyed much influence among younger officers thanks to his former command of the Cadet School, but he now declined formal cabinet office, preferring the less visible but powerful role of "advisor." Its premier was Kimon Georgiev who, as a colonel in the reserves and a leading member of Zveno, served as a link between the regime's military and civilian components.

Whereas the coup d'état of 1923 had been well-prepared both technically and politically, and was directed toward a concrete and feasible purpose (namely, the destruction of Stamboliski's regime and the reversal of some of his policies), this coup, though well-prepared from a technical point of view and bloodless in its execution, was too general and impracticable in its aims—the "regeneration" of the country through the "cleansing" and "rationalization" of all its institutions and habits. Its perpetrators lacked an effective ideology to mobilize the people and thus were unable to build a mass base under themselves. They proved, in short, to be better conspirators and technicians than politicians. Their political naiveté played into the hands of the astute Tsar Boris who, with the support of senior generals, pushed aside these enthusiastic young colonels and technocrats early in 1935.

Boris repudiated as too radical these enthusiasts' socioeconomic program of rapid, étatist development, but he happily retained their authoritarian innovations. The innovations that were destined to become permanent were: the suspension of the constitution, which, despite many crises, had been in continuous effect since its adoption in April, 1879; the prohibition of political parties without replacing them by any "official" government-sponsored movement such as was imposed in many other authoritarian states; the transformation of the Sŭbranie into a body of up to 160 deputies to be selected from lists approved by the government and indicating no political affiliations; the limiting of the cabinet's responsibility exclusively to the monarch; the purging of the bureaucracy and the reform of the administration through the amalgamation of certain ministries (those of agriculture and commerce and industry into a new ministry of the national economy, and those of transportation and public works into a new ministry of communications); the simplification of local government and its transformation from an elective to an appointive character; the destruction of the free press and of independent trade unions and their replacement by government-sponsored successors; the revision of educational priorities toward engineering, technology, and science; and the surprisingly easy suppression of IMRO. This last-mentioned step was a logical corollary of the Zveno-ists' wish to be reconciled to Yugoslavia and to replace Italy with France as Bulgaria's major international base of support. These last preferences, however, failed to survive the later German drive for hegemony in the Balkans and that country's eventual purchase of Tsar Boris' accommodation with the bribe of territorial revisions at Yugoslavia's and Greece's expense. On the other hand, Boris never repudiated the Velchev-Georgiev regime's establishment of diplomatic relations with the Soviet Union on July 23, 1934.

9

Boris' coup had been staged on January 22, 1935. Though he ruled thereafter through a series of military and civilian ministers and avoided any ostentatious display of his personal power, he was now the controlling and decisive force in Bulgarian politics until his sudden death at the early age of forty-nine on August 28, 1943, shortly after a difficult conference with Hitler. Until 1938 he dispensed with the Sŭbranie and in March of that year allowed one to be "elected" under the Velchev-Georgiev rules of prohibiting political labels and identifications. Nevertheless, 56 of its 158 deputies were known to be more or less in opposition, and 11 of these (Communists and "left" Peasantists) were shortly expelled. Boris repeated the electoral experiment during December, 1939, and January, 1940, once again staggering the voting so as to permit maximum police concentration in the various districts. This time the opposition was reduced to about 20 of 152 deputies, 9 of whom were actually Communists. Thereafter Boris enjoyed a docile Sŭbranie, though the various political parties managed to survive in a shadow existence throughout the war years. The nine Communist deputies were expelled and arrested on July 10, 1941, shortly after the German invasion of the Soviet Union.

Managing the legislature was, however, the least of Boris' problems. The destruction of the Velchev-Georgiev team was more critical. Here he was aided, as mentioned above, by their lack of political sophistication, which contrasted sharply with his own shrewd and finely honed skills. For underneath his propaganda image of a frugal, unassuming, simple man, who would have preferred to indulge his hobby of driving locomotives over immersing himself in affairs of state, and allegedly did the latter only out of a sense of royal duty, Boris was in fact a cynical, intriguing, and quite ruthless operator. He was adept at using others and playing people off against each other; he did this with his own officers and ministers and even with Hitler, Mussolini, and Molotov. The cabinet of generals that had succeeded the Velchev-Georgiev colonels on January 22, 1935, lasted until April 18, when the army was sent back to its barracks and excluded from politics. Though he now reverted to civilian premiers, Boris simultaneously announced that there would be no backing away from the authoritarian *faits accomplis* of the previous year. On July 26, 1935, Velchev was exiled to Yugoslavia. His clandestine return on October 2 played into Boris' hands, and he was arrested on charges of treason and plotting against the monarchy. (He and Georgiev were indeed Platonic republicans.) Simultaneously, about one hundred "left" Peasantists were arrested as his alleged accomplices. A death sentence of February 22, 1936, was commuted to life imprisonment on March 28.[3]

In addition to destroying the power of the Velchev-Georgiev team, Boris wished to cancel its semiradical social programs. One of his first decisions after installing the conservative civilian ministers in mid-1935, for example, had been to abolish a Directorate of Social Renovation which the pair had founded as a hybrid propaganda, labor, and youth organization. It was an ideologically primitive and politically artless experiment, yet to Boris the egalitarianism, idealization of the workers, and flattery of the young in its rhetoric were implicitly socialistic, revolutionary, and dangerous.

In international diplomacy, Boris reverted to a more pro-German and pro-Italian course, while maintaining the Velchev-Georgiev détente with Yugoslavia, until the temptations of territorial loot proved irresistible in the spring of 1941. These temptations also prompted Boris to reverse a détente he had reached with Greece on July 31, 1938, whereby that country remilitarized Thrace while allowing Bulgaria to rearm beyond the limits set by the Neuilly Treaty. But then Boris went on to capitalize on the Axis destruction of Greece in the spring of 1941 and occupy her Aegean coastal strip and some islands.[4]

While Boris thus identified Bulgaria with the Axis cause, this was again as cold and calculated (or rather, in this case, miscalculated but still cold)

3. Released from jail in 1940 but kept under surveillance, Velchev was to reemerge into brief but vivid prominence as war minister in the early Communist-dominated governments that followed Bulgaria's diplomatic about-face in September, 1944. Georgiev simultaneously resumed the prime ministry. Both were to be shunted off into lesser posts when the Communists decided to assume complete and open control toward the end of 1946.

4. The territorial acquisitions from both Yugoslavia and Greece were to be reversed at the close of World War II, though Bulgaria was then permitted to retain the Southern Dobruja, which had reverted to her from Romania in 1940 (see Chapter 6, section 13).

as were all his decisions. He was neither intoxicated nor intimidated by Hitler and declined collaboration beyond the limits of what he viewed as strictly Bulgarian interests. The absence of a Volksdeutsche minority in Bulgaria, in turn, deprived Hitler of a lever with which to extract further concessions. Thus, for example, Boris allowed Bulgaria to be used as a Wehrmacht staging area for the invasions of Yugoslavia and Greece, and he participated in their subsequent occupation, but not directly in the invasions. He declared token war on the Western Allies in December, 1941, but never on the Soviet Union, which many of his people viewed as their "big Slavic brother." He deported the Jews of the occupied Greek and Yugoslav areas for eventual extermination but confined the persecution of the Bulgarian Jews to a level short of deportation and death.

In September, 1944, a year after Boris' death, Bulgaria followed Romania in switching alliances. Her armies thereafter fought along with the Soviets through the Balkans, Hungary, and up to Vienna, suffering 31,360 killed and wounded. Though Bulgaria's previous participation in Hitler's war effort had been relatively minimal, though it had entailed fewer sacrifices for her own people than was the case with other Axis satellites, and though her Communist Partisans had fought and suffered comparatively little, yet the subsequent postwar purge by the Communists of royal Bulgaria's political elite was to be particularly savage. Her somewhat mystifying tradition of apparently gratuitous political violence was thus maintained into the postwar era.

10

In economic as in diplomatic relations, Tsar Boris had aligned his country with Nazi Germany. Here the benefits to Bulgaria proved lasting, in terms both of palpable results and of the less tangible, but equally important, factor of experience and know-how. As has been mentioned, tobacco cultivation was promoted over grains in the 1920s; in the 1930s, under German encouragement and tutelage, this shift was to be generalized into a broad-scale expansion of intensively cultivated fiber, oil-bearing, industrial, garden, and other specialized and highly profitable crops. Though neighboring Yugoslavia and Romania experimented with the same policy, Bulgaria pursued it more vigorously. By 1937, 15.8 percent of her agricultural lands were devoted to such crops, as compared to 6.9 percent in Yugoslavia and 10.5 in Romania. The five-year period between 1935 and 1939 was marked not only by the highest level of production in Bulgaria's history, but also, and more significantly, by a qualitative transition to a higher stage of agriculture that involved more intensive use of labor and capital. This expanded development of high-priced industrial and specialty crops helped bring about a rather extraordinary situation: in Bulgaria, the price scissors during this five-year span opened in *favor* of agriculture, entailing an increase in the real income of the peasantry despite rising prices for the commodities it bought.[5]

In industrial policy, too, Boris' regime accepted the sensible, though scarcely altruistic, German advice to concentrate on the expansion of light industrial branches that complemented the country's agriculture rather than to develop heavy industry. The history of Bulgarian industrialization here presented an interesting background to such a policy decision. Bulgarian crafts had once been the Ottoman Empire's most highly developed, but had succumbed to competition from Western factory-made products during the nineteenth century. The achievement of national independence in 1878 could neither halt nor reverse this decline. While subsequent Bulgarian governments repeatedly granted native industry such favors as temporary tax exemptions, duty-free import of capital equipment, reduction of railroad freight rates, free allocation of land for factory construction, and preference in government purchases, no Bulgarian government had ever supported industry at the naked and brutal expense of agriculture the way Liberal governments in neighboring Romania had. Stamboliski obviously would not have wished to adopt such a course, and his successors were inhibited from doing so by their fear of provoking a *jacquerie*. Thus, peasant values and peasant power, which was latent but real, limited the extent of effective state subsidization of industry to rather modest proportions. Even these efforts had been denounced as exorbitant by peasant spokesmen in times of economic hardship such as the depression years of the early 1930s. Thus the German advice to concentrate on agriculture-related and agricultural-processing industries did not, in contrast to the Romanian case, contradict the established tradition of promoting general industrialization. By the eve of World War II, there were approximately forty-five thousand authentic industrial proletarians in Bulgaria (compared to seventeen thousand in 1921), with about the same number engaged in the largely seasonal semi-industrial activity of tobacco-processing. The index of industrial production had climbed in the period 1934/35–1939 from 100 to 164.1.

The capital equipment for this growth had come largely from Germany. Through her "New Plan," unveiled in September, 1934, of deliberate economic expansion into southeast Europe through such arrangements as her purchase of the entire exportable surplus of the local countries' raw materials and agricultural output, and her blocked-currency-clearing devices, she had achieved virtual domination of

5. Otto von Frangeš, *Die Bevölkerungsdichte als Triebkraft der Wirtschaftspolitik der südosteuropäischen Bauernstaaten* (Jena: Fischer, 1939), p. 23; Zagoroff, *Agricultural Economy of the Danubian Countries*, pp. 370, 379-80; Janaki Molloff, ed., *Die sozialökonomische Struktur der bulgarischen Landwirtschaft* (Berlin: Weidmann, 1936), pp. 105-25.

Bulgaria's foreign trade. From 42.7 percent of the value of Bulgaria's exports and 40.1 of her imports in 1934, Germany's share leaped to 67.8 and 65.5 percent, respectively, of the value of Bulgarian exports and imports in 1939. Since in this latter year Austria was included in the German sum recorded in the official Bulgarian statistics, for strict comparison one should also add the Austrian to the German share of Bulgaria's foreign trade in 1934; the figure would then be 48.0 percent of exports and 44.9 percent of imports. In terms of physical volume, Germany took 52,994 tons of Bulgarian exports in 1934 and Austria 23,206 tons; by 1939 this had more than tripled to 272,071 tons for their combined total. As for Bulgaria's imports, in 1934 Germany supplied 63,431 tons and Austria 8,060 tons; by 1939 this had almost tripled to 184,463 tons. Simultaneously, Bulgaria's trade with the West atrophied and her intra-Balkan trade was all but confined to some oil imports from Romania. France held three-fifths of Bulgaria's state debt but scarcely traded with her.

As might have been expected from her changes in the lines of agricultural production, and her strategy of complementary industrialization, the profile of Bulgarian foreign trade altered in the interwar era: her exports shifted from grains to tobacco, eggs, fruits, and other specialized industrial and garden crops; her imports shifted somewhat from finished consumer products toward capital goods and additional raw materials for her budding textile, leather, pottery, woodworking, and paper industries.

In "social overhead" capital investments such as transportation facilities, land reclamation, reforestation, and water control, Bulgaria achieved much by combining imported German equipment with native manpower mobilized under the terms of the compulsory labor program (see section 4).

All in all, while Bulgaria's interwar *political* experience conformed to the general East Central European trend of degeneration from parliamentary to authoritarian solutions, her *social* institutions were more egalitarian and open, her *demographic* profile more homogeneous and integrated, and her *economic* efforts more rational and hopeful than in most of the other states in the area.

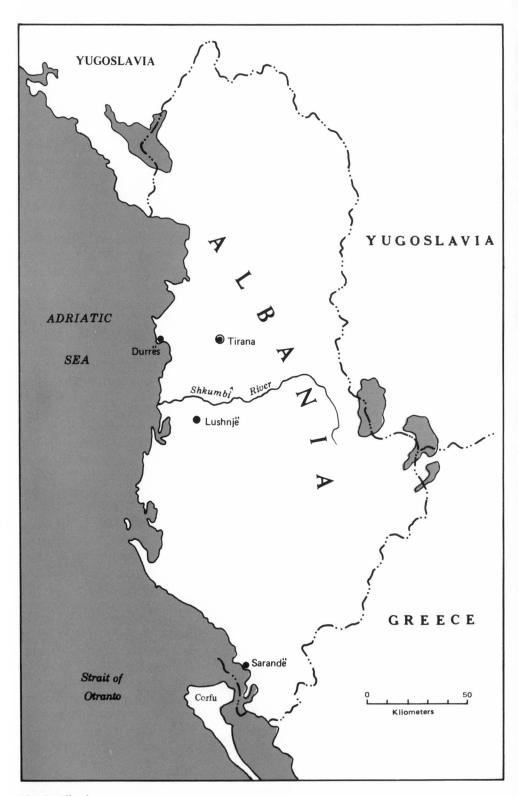

YUGOSLAVIA

YUGOSLAVIA

A L B A N I A

ADRIATIC

SEA

Durrës

Tirana

Shkumbi *River*

Lushnjë

GREECE

Strait of
Otranto

Sarandë

Corfu

0   50
Kilometers

Map 8. Albania

· Chapter Eight ·

ALBANIA

1

THE Albanians were the only interwar European nation with a Muslim majority. Seventy percent of them were Muslim, while 20 percent were Eastern Orthodox, and 10 percent Roman Catholic. They were also the last to opt out of the Ottoman Empire, whose elite structure had always been open to their talented and ambitious sons, which had generally not oppressed them, and toward whose Caliph-Sultan most of them felt genuine religious reverence. Indeed, the Albanians' decision finally to bid for full independence late in 1912 was, in a sense, provoked only by the fear that otherwise they would be partitioned amongst Montenegro, Serbia, and Greece, then freshly victorious (with Bulgaria) in their First Balkan War against the Ottoman Empire. Hitherto the Albanian political aspirations had never exceeded a moderate degree of autonomy. Now, however, they felt obliged to preempt their possible partition by quitting the Ottoman ship before it sank under them. Their decision was eased by the affronts dealt to their conservative and religious sensibilities by the brashly centralistic and secularistic policies of the current Young Turk regime in Istanbul (Constantinople, Byzantium). Their late bid for independence was now also endorsed by Austria-Hungary and Italy, each reluctant to see either a South Slav state or Greece astride the strategic Otranto Strait at the exit of the Adriatic Sea into the Mediterranean. Hence international recognition of Albanian independence came promptly in 1913.

Independence was almost lost again in the turmoil of World War I and the confusion of the ensuing peace settlements, when Albania's Yugoslav, Greek, and Italian neighbors sought, through such varying stratagems as military occupation, diplomatic trade-offs, and the subsidization of internal mutinies and *frondes*, to achieve her territorial partition or truncation or else her political reduction to the status of a protectorate. The obstinacy of President Wilson and, even more decisively, the political and military resistance of the Albanians themselves averted such fates and restored their country's independence in 1920. It is an interesting comment on the then prevailing stage of Albanian society that the crucial Lushnjë Congress of her political leaders, which met from January 21 to February 9, 1920, to plot her strategy of countering the predatory intentions of her neighbors, could only assemble after the solemn proclamation of a *besa*, or truce of several weeks' duration, suspending the blood-vegeance and vendetta obligations of her still heavily clan-based social structure. Though independence was restored when the foreign armies were evacuated from Albanian territory later in 1920, a price had nevertheless to be paid for the earlier Albanian tardiness in demanding independent statehood. The price came in the form of compressed frontiers that left very large Albanian irredentas in neighboring Yugoslavia and Greece, totaling about two-thirds as many ethnic Albanians as inhabited the Albanian state itself.[1]

The interwar Albanian state had an area of 27,539 square kilometers and a population, according to a census of May 15, 1930, of 1,003,097, divided more-or-less evenly between the still largely clan-structured Geg mountaineers of the country's northern half and the more agrarian Tosk villagers of the south. The Shkumbî River was the dividing line between these two subcommunities of the Albanian nation, which were differentiated by dialects as well as by social patterns. In the interwar decades, the Gegs were still ruled by their tribal chieftains in a patriarchal but egalitarian style and were also still prone to brigandage to supplement their pastoral economy. Tosk society, on the other hand, was both less primitive and less egalitarian, being characterized by landlord-peasant class divisions based on land ownership and tenancy relations. The Tosk-populated areas were less rugged than the northern mountains, hence more easily invaded and occupied, and hence had always been more subject to the political, legal, cultural, and economic controls and influences of the Byzantine and Ottoman empires. The Tosk peasants regarded themselves as more civilized and hard-working than the Geg shepherd-brigands, while the latter believed themselves to be freer men and braver warriors.

Religious differences contributed less to political and social tensions in interwar Albania than did such tribal and class differences. The Gegs were Muslim and Roman Catholic; the Tosks were Muslim and Eastern Orthodox; but religion sat relatively lightly on the faithful of all denominations, and if clans of different religions prosecuted vendettas against each other, or if peasants of one faith rebelled against latifundists of another, the religious aspect was always epiphenomenal to the real ter-

1. The Albanians in Greece have since then been largely assimilated into Greek society, while those in Yugoslavia have preserved their identity and in the current political system enjoy a degree of cultural and administrative autonomy.

ritorial or social or "honor" issue at stake. Some families and even individuals, indeed, cultivated two religions: they would practice both baptism and circumcision, and then use Christian or Muslim names and honor Christian or Muslim festivals as the circumstances of any particular occasion might warrant.

Finally, it must be borne in mind that while tribal and social divisions were indeed more significant than religious ones, Albanian nationalism proved stronger than any of these cleavages. The Albanians proudly regarded themselves as the oldest autochthonous ethnic entity on the Balkan Peninsula, descendent from the Illyrians and/or Thracians, hence probably antedating even the Hellenes and certainly the much more recent Slavs and Turks. The cult of Skënderbeg, who was reinterpreted as the leader of a national rather than a feudal or a Christian resistance movement to the Ottoman conquest in the fifteenth century, gave a particular symbolic focus to their national pride. This pride was enhanced again in 1908, on the eve of independence, when the Albanian intelligentsia standardized a modified Latin alphabet, thus both easing communications between Gegs and Tosks and, as a political gesture, differentiating the Albanian from the Greek and Serb-Cyrillic alphabets.

Though they might regret the large irredentas of their kinsmen left in neighboring countries, the Albanians could, on the other hand, take political comfort from the fact that their own state's consolidation was not hampered by any significant, alienated ethnic minority. The state-nation accounted for 92 percent of the population; the remainder was scattered among Greeks, Slavs, Vlachs, and Turks. Albania, in other words, was one of the most ethnically homogeneous states in interwar East Central Europe.

Economically, she was a country of meager and still largely undeveloped resources. Her mountains were bare, her lowlands marshy, her agricultural yields low, and her industry barely existent. By the end of the interwar era, only 9 percent of her land area consisted of cultivated arable and orchard land; 33 percent was woodland, which was either potentially valuable but still largely untapped forests or else marginal scrubs; 25 percent was open pastureland; and 33 percent was totally unproductive. Of the population, 80 percent depended on agriculture or herding, only 15 percent lived in localities of over five thousand people, and 80 percent above the age of seven were illiterate.[2]

Such economic development as took place during the interwar era was heavily subsidized by Italy. All the oil pumped, which by 1937 had reached 72,000 metric tons, was absorbed by and refined in fuel-poor

2. Statistics in this section are from Stavro Skendi, ed., *Albania* (New York: Frederick A. Praeger, 1956), Part I; Otto Ronart, "L'Evolution Economique de l'Albanie," *Revue Economique Internationale* 4, no. 3 (December, 1936), pp. 581-97; Richard Busch-Zantner, *Albanien* (Leipzig: Wilhelm Goldmann Verlag, 1939), pp. 171-92.

Italy. All the road construction, which totaled 1,200 kilometers between 1926 and 1939, the several hundred new bridges, and the extensive harbor improvements at Durrës (Durazzo) and Sarandë (Santi Quaranta) were financed by Italy, as were a cement mill, some cigarette factories, tanneries, mills, a brewery, a soap factory, and many public buildings. The last-named were less productive but visually impressive and hence symbolically reassuring. The major need was capital and, for international political reasons, the only available source of capital was Italy, whose claim to exclusive patronage over Albania was respected by the other Great Powers.

Italy, in turn, viewed her stake in Albania not as a "normal" economic one, but as basically political and strategic. Hence she charged little interest and tolerated heavy losses on her investments there and consistently absorbed far higher proportions of Albania's exports (about three-fifths) than she supplied of her imports (about two-fifths), while covering Albania's resultant payments gap with generous, though hardly altruistic, subsidies. Thus even at the economic level, and disregarding for the moment the military implications of the road and harbor developments which Italy constructed in Albania, Rome viewed her small trans-Adriatic protégé more as a source of essential raw materials than as a potential market for commodities.

Despite such pockets of economic investment, Albania remained interwar Europe's least developed state, partly because, due to the mores and values of her society and of her political culture, much potentially productive investment was absorbed into the traditional "Ottoman" consumption patterns of the ruling establishment. This establishment, an interlocking network of politicians, bureaucrats, latifundists, merchants, and clan chieftains, in turn was divided into two political camps.

The more traditional and politically quite experienced camp, composed primarily of chieftains, beys from the former Ottoman imperial service, and rentier-landlords, was led by Ahmed Zogu, a young warrior-chieftain of the Muslim Mati clan. The more westernized, but politically less tested, bourgeoisie and intelligentsia were led by the Harvard-educated Orthodox Bishop Fan S. Noli. The competition between them was, however, quite uneven. Noli, though an occasional foreign minister for European display during the early interwar years, was prime minister for only six months, in the second half of 1924; that was long enough to demonstrate his political incompetence to both his supporters and his adversaries. After that, many realists in his entourage forsook him for a marriage of convenience with Zogu, while the idealists retreated with Noli into highly principled but ineffectual exile.

Ahmed Zogu (the name had recently been re-nativized from the erstwhile Turkic construct Zogolli) had made his political reputation as a resourceful and bold commander in the period of confusion immediately following World War I, when he had coolly led his clan retinue of hill-warriors against foreign invaders and native *frondeurs* at a time when many senior political leaders had sunk into panic or paralysis. As frequent minister of the interior and occasional premier in subsequent cabinets, he insinuated his clansmen into the gendarmerie and through this instrument effectively dominated the governments of the day, whether he formally presided over them or not. But his pasha-like political style in general, and his preference for ex-Ottoman officials and for his clansmen in state employment in particular, and—most specifically—his penchant for collecting state revenue from the agricultural south but spending it among the central and northern hill tribes, provoked resentment and opposition. Despite considerable chicanery and pressure on the part of the police, Zogu's partisans won only a plurality of 40 seats in the legislative elections of November 26 and December 27, 1923, with 35 going to Noli's opposition camp and 20 to independents. In a crime which was also a blunder, Zogu's retainers then assassinated a young and talented opposition leader named Avni Rustem on April 20, 1924. This act, in turn, galvanized his exasperated enemies into a successful insurrection between May 25 and June 10. Zogu fled to Yugoslavia, and on June 16, 1924, Noli formed his only government.

Noli's regime, composed both of principled reformers as well as of "feudal" elements who actually shared Zogu's values but felt themselves short-changed by his particular distribution of patronage, lacked unity. Noli announced a sweeping reform program but did little to implement it. Seeking to make a favorable impression on European public opinion, he proclaimed many liberal and modernistic commitments that were quite irrelevant to Albanian reality. At home, meanwhile, he constituted a politically packed special court to condemn his exiled opponents to death and confiscate their property, when he might have been shrewder to issue an amnesty or at least to refrain from political intervention in the judicial process. Moreover, though he had come to power in a formally unconstitutional, insurrectionary manner, Noli refused to regularize or legitimize his position through a plebiscite or a general election. Instead, he imposed rigid censorship and appeared to concede by implication that he doubted he enjoyed the public's confidence. Finally, he recognized the Soviet Union and solicited her support at a time when she was still an international quasi-pariah, whereupon the Wrangelite army of Tsarist Russian émigrés in Yugoslavia, with the endorsement of that country's government, put its resources at the exiled Zogu's disposal. Reinvading Albania on December 14, 1924, and quickly rallying his own and allied hill clans to his banner, Zogu triumphantly reentered the capital of Tirana on December 24. Noli fled into exile, from where he composed a valid, albeit incomplete, epitaph on his brief exercise at dabbling with power: "By insisting on agrarian reforms, I aroused the wrath of the landed aristocracy; by failing to carry them out, I lost the support of the peasant masses."[3]

Operating mainly out of Switzerland and Austria, Noli and his followers organized a National Liberation Committee, generally known by its acronym Konare. In 1925 it sent several Albanians to the Soviet Union for political training and by 1928 was utterly dependent on international Communist financial subventions. In that year Konare purged those of its members who opposed its transformation into a Communist Trojan horse. Having lost control of his own movement, Noli abandoned politics in 1930 to resume his interrupted ecclesiastical and literary career in America. The conservative, "feudal," merely personal enemies of Zogu, though also driven into exile at the end of 1924, had remained aloof from Konare and instead organized themselves into the National Union, or Bashkimi Kombëtar, which turned to Yugoslavia and France for support.

Meanwhile, the victorious Zogu gave evidence of having learned from Noli's and from his own earlier mistakes. After initially liquidating or exiling his most dangerous foes, he proclaimed and honored an amnesty for the middle-ranking and rank-and-file oppositionists in 1925. Over time, he also persuaded a substantial portion of the modernizing intelligentsia to serve the nation by putting its talents at the disposal of his regime, thereby simultaneously rendering himself less exclusively dependent on his tribal and ex-Ottoman retinue. Zogu also took fastidious care to obtain formal, albeit rigged, constitutional and parliamentary legitimation for all his political acts, including his election to the presidency on January 31, 1925, and his assumption of royal status as "Zog I, King of the Albanians" on September 1, 1928. On this latter occasion, significantly, his Arabic first name of Ahmed was abandoned just as he had earlier dropped the Turkic suffix to his surname, which now, as a purely Albanian word meaning bird, became his royal appellation.

The Yugoslav government, incidentally, took alarm at Zog's styling himself King of the Albanians rather than King of Albania, thereby, it charged, laying an irredentist and illicit claim on the political loyalties of its own large Albanian minority. This Yugoslav protest was actually an excessively nervous misreading of Zog's intentions and must be understood in the light of the fact that, though he had returned to power with Yugoslav connivance in December, 1924, Zog soon realized that only Italy was in a position to grant him the generous financial subsidies needed to consolidate his regime; accordingly, he had promptly and unsentimentally switched his diplomatic allegiances.

As king, Zog now relinquished to subordinate appointees the office of prime minister, which he had kept in his own hands during the years of his presidency, 1924-28. But he retained command and control of the

---

3. Quoted from Joseph Swire, *Albania: The Rise of a Kingdom* (London: Williams and Norgate, 1929), p. 444.

armed forces and supplemented this source of power by disarming all tribes other than his own Mati warriors and one allied clan. Simultaneously, he bought off the other chieftains with generous subsidies and the conferral of remunerative and undemanding military reserve ranks. The style as well as the substance of Zog's regime, in other words, was hybrid "feudal"-modern, and it was, in its own terms, quite effective.

Whereas in the first half of the 1920s there had been at least one serious mutiny or regional insurrection annually in Albania, these ceased after 1926 when Zog smashed a final one subsidized by his erstwhile Yugoslav patrons. Admittedly, he achieved this relative political tranquillity through punitive razzias and martial law, but henceforth the country was spared its earlier chronic civil wars and later episodes of political violence were little more than crude efforts by disappointed office-seekers to assassinate or ambush Zog. Indeed, his assumption of royal title in 1928 may well have been intended as a signal that no crisis of transition, which could possibly reopen the doors to civil war, would be permitted in his lifetime.

Zog had similar success in gradually curbing the institutions of vendetta and blood-vengeance and replacing these primitive legal instruments with modern civil (1929), penal (1930), and commercial (1931) codes. Traditional brigandage was suppressed, and fiscal and tax policies were reformed to reassure potential foreign investors and to encourage the nascent native bourgeoisie. Land reform, on the other hand, proceeded extremely slowly and cautiously; only about 8 percent of state-owned land and 3 percent of the area of privately owned estate land was redistributed among landless peasants. On balance, therefore, Zog apparently concluded that the landlords, the chieftains, the bureaucrats, and the businessmen were more essential pillars of his regime than was the still basically inarticulate peasant majority.

The same assumption underlay Zog's cultural policy. He made only a very modest dent in mass illiteracy, which was reduced from 90 to 80 percent, but he did support a number of high-quality lycées for the elite, whose alumni gained ready admission into Western universities where they were sustained by generous royal scholarships. In religious affairs, Zog's policy was secularistic and nationalistic. Already in 1923, during his earlier term of unofficial but nonetheless effective power, the Albanian Muslims had severed themselves from the Caliphate a year before that supranational Muslim institution was ended by the Turkish authorities, and had abolished the women's veil as well as the old Ottoman title of "bey." On resuming power after 1924, Zog encouraged the efforts of the Albanian Orthodox community to achieve autocephalous status. This campaign was constantly sabotaged by the government of Greece but ultimately triumphed with the granting of a *tomos* of autocephaly by the Patriarch of Constantinople in April, 1937. The liturgy and hierarchy had been albanianized well before this culminating event. The school system of the Roman Catholic Church was closed in 1933, when Zog nationalized all education, but then reopened in 1936 upon the Franciscan Order's reluctant acceptance of state control and inspection. This nationalization of education was an assertion of Albanian national pride specifically vis-à-vis Italian and Greek "paternalism," as the supervisory and pedagogical staffs of most religious and private schools were citizens of these two states and the ideological thrust of their teaching programs was felt to be the inculcation of their own national values into Albanian children.

2

While Zog's domestic policy was thus effective in mastering the problems of internal political and administrative consolidation and in making slow but palpable progress toward economic and cultural modernization, his foreign policy failed, in the short run, to anchor Albania's independence firmly in the European state-system. Here, however, his problems were quite beyond Albania's or his own capacities to control or effect, even with the astutest diplomacy. As mentioned earlier, the other Great Powers acknowledged Italy's claim to a hegemony over Albania, thus depriving Zog of any realistic possibility of obtaining effective international support to end this dangerous and humiliating dependence on Rome. Furthermore, Italy was undoubtedly very generous in economic and fiscal assistance. Finally, her political protectiveness toward this Balkan protégé served to deter the ever-latent and occasionally overt Yugoslav and Greek desires to partition Albania between them. On balance therefore, Italy's interest in Albania, while undoubtedly imperialistic, was not without benefit to the client state. Zog's problem was to strike a balance between his need for Italian capital and patronage on the one hand, and on the other hand the restiveness of his own people, particularly of the new intelligentsia which resented the Italian patronage as a national humiliation. His personal pride and determination to be his own man was a third factor in this balancing act.

Zog's overt political ties to Italy began with the First Treaty of Tirana of November 27, 1926, which he concluded in understandable reaction to Yugoslavia's subsidization of the serious and possibly secessionist insurrection of earlier that month (see section 1). The two partners pledged mutual support in maintaining Albania's territorial, juridical, and political status quo, and Mussolini further pledged himself unilaterally to give such support only in response to an explicit Albanian request. A year later, on November 22, 1927, the Second Treaty of Tirana widened these commitments into a defensive alliance—again with Yugoslavia and Greece implicitly in mind—entailing the despatch of a large Italian military mission to train and develop the Albanian army. (The gendarmerie, on the other hand, remained under Zog's personal control through individually hired retired British officers.)

Though Italian investments now flowed into the Albanian economy and direct Italian subsidies allowed the Albanian government to balance its budgets, Zog presently came to fear for his and his country's independence and to resist further Italian encroachments. In 1931 he refused to renew the First Treaty of Tirana; in 1932 he rejected Mussolini's offer of a customs union; and in 1933 his nationalization of religious and private schools was also, as mentioned earlier, an implicitly anti-Italian gesture. Zog now dismissed some of his Italian advisers and sought both a rapprochement with his immediate neighbors, Greece and Yugoslavia, as well as diplomatic support from the more remote, but more powerful, governments of France and Britain. Here, however, he came up against a blank wall. By the mid-1930s Belgrade had tacitly disinterested itself from Albania in return for Mussolini's curbing the Croatian Ustaša (Chapter 5, section 9), and neither Paris nor London was prepared to offend Rome over what was to them the tertiary Albanian issue. They advised Zog, who had meanwhile stood firm despite a cutoff of Italian subsidies and a menacing Italian naval demonstration in Albanian waters, to capitulate. By now, however, his own elite's nationalistic sensitivities were a factor to be reckoned with, and he could no longer simply revert to the status of an Italian client, even had he been personally so inclined, which he was not. Indeed, in 1935 and 1936 Zog liberalized his regime, allowing a moderate degree of freedom to the press and to political life in an effort to secure firmer domestic anchorage in compensation for his current diplomatic isolation. Strikes, however, were firmly crushed even during this liberal interlude; the proletariat had not yet achieved the power that the intelligentsia and the businessmen had recently acquired and the chieftains and landlords had always had. On balance, Zog's resistance to Italian pressure won him increased popularity.

Mussolini's mid-decade preoccupation with Austrian independence, then with his Abyssinian campaign, and, finally, with the Spanish Civil War gave Albania and Zog an extended and heady, but ultimately illusory, reprieve. A temporary compromise was reached in 1936; the terms were something of a defensive triumph for Albania, considering the imbalance of power between the protagonists, and even though Italy retained a strong stake in the smaller country's economy and administration. But when the other claims on his international attention no longer distracted him, Mussolini moved swiftly and ruthlessly. On March 25, 1939, he delivered an ultimatum demanding a formal Italian protectorate over Albania and the stationing of Italian garrisons on its soil. When Zog stalled, his country was swiftly bombarded, invaded, and occupied between April 7 and 10, 1939, and he, driven into exile.

The precipitating stimuli to Mussolini's sudden and peremptory crackdown appear to have been (a) anxiety lest the new Yugoslav regime might repudiate Stojadinović's earlier acknowledgment of Italian hegemony over Albania, and (b) a wish, born of wounded vanity, to emulate Hitler and at the same time repay him in kind for having occupied the rump Czech state on March 15 without consulting his Axis partner. A similar motive also prompted Mussolini's invasion of Greece from Albania on October 28, 1940, under the pretext of recovering Albanian, not Italian, irredenta in Epirus. Here, however, the Greek army soon turned the tables, first halting the Italians and then pushing them back into southern Albania. Italian military morale never recovered from this fiasco, which in the spring of 1941 precipitated the German invasion of the Balkans as a rescue operation for the embattled and weakening Italians. As for the Albanians, they had initially applauded the victories of the Greeks but then changed their attitude when Athens signaled its (eventually unrealized) intention to annex southern Albania (northern Epirus to Greek nationalists). Then, between 1941 and 1944, the Germans almost doubled Albania's territory and population by assigning to her large parts of occupied Yugoslavia and Greece. This, too, was reversed at war's close.

3

The politics of interwar Albania—which is to say the rule of Zog—is an intriguing subject. His regime was an interesting and evolving mixture of the styles of a tribal chieftain, a haiduk brigand, an Ottoman pasha, and a modernizing despot. It was authoritarian as a result of the drives and requirements of his own tough personality, of the intricate complex of domestic interests, and of Albania's precarious international position. It was corrupt and oppressive, yet it also unified and modernized the country and was accepted by the nation as preferable to the preceding anarchy and chaos. In foreign affairs, Zog was both cautious and pragmatic. Indeed, he vexed some Albanian nationalists by never pressing irredentist grievances against Yugoslavia and Greece beyond styling himself King of the Albanians. As regards Italy, whose economic assistance his underdeveloped country desperately needed, Zog "yielded when he had to, resisted when he could, and made a good thing out of both."[4] On balance, to have in two short decades consolidated the new Albanian state against the pulls of regionalism and tribalism, against the pressures of the frondeur and brigand tradition, against the corrosions of mass poverty and illiteracy, and against the hazards of an international system that allowed predatory neighbors to deny the very legitimacy of an independent Albania was a creditable political achievement.

4. Robert L. Wolff, *The Balkans in Our Time* (Cambridge: Harvard University Press, 1956), p. 143.

· Chapter Nine ·

ON THE PERIPHERY OF
EAST CENTRAL EUROPE:
THE BALTIC STATES

1

ONE might question the inclusion of Estonia, Latvia, and Lithuania, whose brief period of independence did not survive World War II, in this book. Soviet writers and scholars, indeed, regard the Soviet Union's reabsorption of these three southern Baltic states in 1940 as constituent Socialist republics as final, and they tend to suspect and resent any discussion that locates these three countries within the system of interwar East Central Europe's independent nation-states. As far as they are concerned, these three countries' two decades of separation from Russia between 1920 and 1940 was an unnatural interlude, suitably closed with the Baltic littoral's reversion to its supposedly more appropriate destiny of integration with its Russian hinterland. It is, indeed, correct that before World War I the nationalist movements of the Baltic peoples had originally called for autonomy within, not independence from, the Russian Empire and had only extended their goals to full independence during the war, under the stimuli of Russian collapse, German occupation, and final German defeat—three developments of world magnitude of which the Baltic peoples could take alert advantage but which had been beyond their power to cause or to prevent. Thereafter, however, during the interwar period they had welcomed the status of independence and had thoroughly integrated their countries into the European state-system and the world economy. Their achievements and successes during their two decades of interwar sovereign independence render the inclusion of these three states in this book appropriate and even necessary.

They were, of course, quite small countries in terms both of population and size: in the mid-1930s there were under one and a quarter million people in Estonia (47,549 square kilometers), just short of two million in Latvia (65,791 square kilometers), and just over two and a half million in

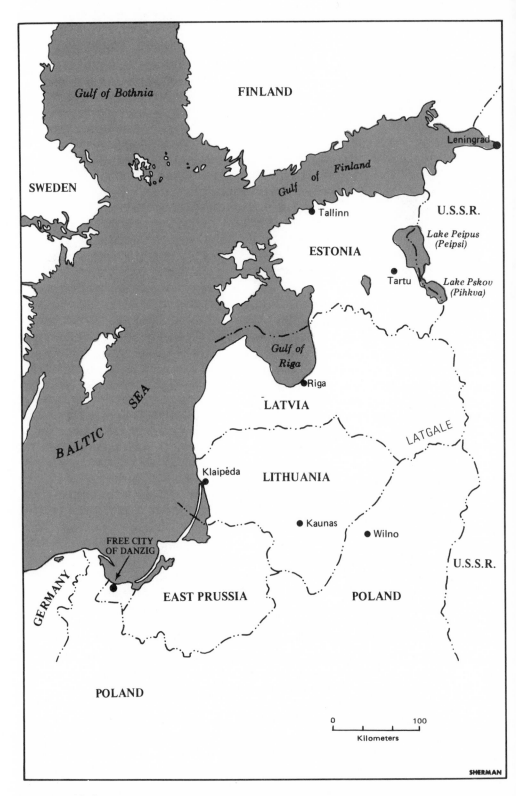

Map 9. Baltic States

Lithuania (55,670 square kilometers), of which the proportions engaged in agriculture were, respectively, three-fifths, two-thirds, and over three-fourths. Urban/rural ratios, at the same time, were 33/67 (Estonia), 36/64 (Latvia), and 15/85 (Lithuania)—"urban" being here officially defined as a locality of over two thousand people.[1] Illiteracy rates at age ten and above also reflected the declining north-to-south scale of socioeconomic achievement, being in the mid-1930s less than 4 percent in Estonia and just over 10 percent in Latvia, but approximately 30 percent in Lithuania. The proportions of the total populations belonging to ethnic minorities were, in turn, one-tenth (Estonia), one-fourth (Latvia), and one-fifth (Lithuania). Russians formed the largest single minority in the first two countries (and accounted for most of their illiterates) and Jews in the third. No minority exercised significant political influence, though Germans, Jews, and Poles initially enjoyed substantial economic power in the urban, commercial, and professional sectors of Lithuania's economy, as did Germans in Estonia's and Latvia's. But this, too, was of declining importance during the two decades of strenuous economic advance by each country's state-nation majority, determined to develop its own economic and professional middle class.

By the time they settled down to full sovereignty and peace in 1920, the Baltic states had experienced six years of military campaigns, invasions, occupations, economic and administrative turmoil, and wastage of manpower and equipment at the hands of the Russian and German armies, but on the other hand they were free of the legacy of indebtedness inherited from prewar regimes that so heavily burdened the other "successor states" of interwar East Central Europe. When originally acknowledging the Baltic peoples' secession from Russia and recognizing their independence by a series of treaties in 1920, the Bolshevik government had shown them remarkable financial generosity. Not only had it formally relieved them of any share of the Tsarist Empire's debts, but it had also paid them quite high indemnities for destruction inflicted on their territories during the war.

While the victorious Western Powers originally wished to regard the newly independent Baltic states as part of a *cordon sanitaire* buffering the rest of Europe from Soviet Russia, and while Germany eventually came to regard them as candidates for economic penetration and the Soviet Union as crucial to its security, the objects of all this interest were reluctant to become an arena for the strategic and ideological competition of the Great Powers. They would have preferred to have been members of a pacific Scandinavian-Baltic bloc. However, such a constellation was ren-

1. All statistics and statistical generalizations on the Baltic states are from the official publications of their central bureaus of statistics: *Estonia: Population, Cultural, and Economic Life* (Tallinn, 1937); *Annuaire Statistique de la Lettonie* (Riga, 1939); *Annuaire Statistique de la Lithuanie* (Kaunas, 1935).

dered impossible by Scandinavian isolationism and by the chilly attitude of Germany and the Soviet Union, who suspected that such a bloc would be but a screen for Poland's international ambitions. Hence, the other prospective members of a Scandinavian-Baltic bloc were reluctant to risk the ire of these two Great Powers and the plan was stillborn. The more limited alternative of a tripartite association among Estonia, Latvia, and Lithuania came to naught, as the first two were loath to be drawn into Lithuania's quarrels with Poland and Germany over Wilno (Vilnius) and Klaipėda (Memel), respectively.

While relations among the three Baltic states were correct, they were not nearly as close as outsiders often assumed from their mere geographical propinquity and identical fates. Their languages differed radically, and their histories before the nineteenth century varied considerably. Whereas the Estonians were overwhelmingly Lutheran with a small Eastern Orthodox minority (the Setukests), the Latvians were preponderantly Lutheran with a somewhat larger Roman Catholic minority; the Lithuanians were almost entirely Roman Catholic. The economies of the three states were more competitive than complementary. All three were basically agrarian, though Estonia and Latvia also boasted modest maritime and industrial activities. On the other hand, Lithuania was almost landlocked and, as a vulnerable frontier region of the Tsarist Empire bordering on East Prussia, had been deliberately deprived of industries by the Russian governments. Hence, she entered the interwar era quite poor, with a preponderantly agricultural economy and some timber resources. The educational systems of Estonia and Latvia were also more advanced than that of Lithuania. Thus political, economic, and cultural experiences and levels differed considerably among these three countries. While the protestation of one interwar Estonian statesman to the effect that they had little in common except similar memories of ethnically alien and resented "feudal" landlords was a testy hyperbole, it was nevertheless intended as a well-meant corrective to the widespread assumption that these countries were virtually identical simply because they shared a number of problems.

The most salient of these shared problems was the land-hunger of the native peasants, who resented the ownership of most of the land by ethnically alien, though long-settled, gentries—mainly Baltic Germans in Estonia and Latvia and Poles in Lithuania. The Baltic Germans, in particular, had traditionally placed their military, diplomatic, and administrative talents at the service of the tsarist governments and received, in turn, a free hand to exercise virtually feudal authority over the native peasants toiling on these Germans' estates. Indeed, this land-hunger, together with its accompanying political resentments, had been a major propellant to the prewar nationalist movements of the Baltic peoples, and it was one of the first issues that their new governments tackled on the morrow of independence.

The land reforms in all three states were quite radical, and the former German, Polish, and occasional Russian landlords received little or no compensation. Initially some decline in agricultural production resulted from the break-up of these gentries' estates, which had been farmed quite efficiently. But thanks to the native cooperative movements and the general economic competence of the local peasantries, productivity was quickly raised to even higher than prewar levels. The Baltic states' land reforms thus achieved several goals with one swoop: they satisfied peasant land-hunger, thereby immunizing the peasantries against the appeals of Bolshevism, to which the Latvians had originally been rather receptive; and they eliminated the non-native elites, of which the Baltic Germans had been the most powerful and resented.

A second economic problem shared by the three Baltic states was the need to redirect their trade patterns and outlets. Their prewar agricultural, industrial, and transportation ties had all been with the adjacent St. Petersburg (Petrograd, Leningrad) metropolitan region in Russia. With the Soviet economy's virtual departure from the world market, the three Baltic states found it necessary to reorient their own economic patterns. They succeeded in opening the British and German markets for their dairy and truck-farm products, bacon, poultry and eggs, as well as flax, timber, paper, cellulose, plywood, glass, and ceramics. Estonia also exported high-quality cement and shale oil, which was of particular interest to the German navy. Though the depression dealt a severe blow to their international trade, the Baltic economies managed to adjust better than those in most of the other East Central European countries and to recover from it more quickly. They had not previously been overindebted to foreign creditors, and they now successfully associated their mature cooperative movements with newer government export monopolies to protect both the volume and the prices of their relatively specialized and high-quality exports. Budget deficits, exchange restrictions, alternations in currency parities, and recourse to increased state-capitalism, as well as strenuous efforts to be self-sufficient in cereal production, also cushioned the blow of the depression and facilitated early recovery from its effects.

As regards constitutional and political structures, each Baltic state originally organized itself as a democratic republic, with a unicameral, sovereign legislature elected triennially by universal, equal, direct, secret, and proportional suffrage, and supplemented with extensive provisions for plebiscites on popular referenda and initiatives. A plethora of political parties, however, and the general political inexperience that was one of the unhappy heritages of Tsarism, promoted extreme cabinet instability. This, in turn, degenerated into parliamentary paralysis, and eventually provoked *coups d'etat*. In Lithuania the coup occurred in 1926, hard on the heels of Piłsudski's seizure of power in Poland, and in Estonia and Latvia in the depression year of 1934. In each case, interestingly, the coup was to a certain extent a preemptive one, staged by established heroes of the wartime struggle for independence (as was the case with Piłsudski) and designed to avert bids for power by younger Right-Radical elements. Because they, too, feared the Right-Radicals above all else, some leaders of the parliamentary Center and even of the Left as well as the conservative Right endorsed these coups. The putschist regimes avoided extremism or terrorism, though they did encourage a certain degree of demagogic chauvinism and toyed with corporativist experiments.

The party systems against which these coups were staged, though extremely convoluted, can be roughly schematized as follows. In Estonia and Latvia, the moderate Left was led by the Social Democrats, who started out strong but gradually weakened as land reform satisfied the rural part of their original constituency and as their increasing reluctance to hold office and accept responsibility in coalition governments cost them public prestige. The moderate Right and the Center were composed of a large number of Agrarian and Populist parties—so numerous, in fact, that many of them were actually specific interest groups dressed up as political parties. The highly nationalistic intelligentsia, also organized in parties as well as in nonpartisan veterans' and social societies, oscillated between Center and Right and gradually gained in strength. In Lithuania, this scheme, though basically also applicable, was complicated by the clerical issue, which split the peasantry, the intelligentsia, and even the small proletariat. Most Baltic politicians, whatever their political commitment, were peasants' sons, the first educated generation of their families and thus symbols of the recent unlocking of their nations' reserves of talent.

Despite these many common features of the Baltic party systems and the coups that overturned them, there were also significant differences in the stances and strategies of the postcoup regimes. These differences suggest that at this point our general Baltic survey might appropriately be replaced by brief separate discussions of the particular interwar experiences of each of the three states.

2

Between 1919, when she launched herself into independent political life after wartime turmoil, and the eventual coup of March 12, 1934, Estonia had experienced twenty-one different cabinets, all at the mercy of an undisciplined legislature and its heterogeneous parties. Though a serious but abortive Communist insurrection on December 1, 1924, did briefly galvanize the other parties into forming a broad coalition government, this shock proved insufficient to end the country's chronic cabinet instability.[2] The gradual rightward shift of electoral strength over six elections (1919, 1920, 1923, 1926, 1929, 1933) failed to induce greater stability, as the Social Democrats, who remained a substantial and crucial party, were increasingly reluctant to participate in coalitions. Simultaneously, the Right-Radical League of Freedom Fighters, which was originally a veterans organization and now was generously subsidized by industry, threatened the moderate parties from the opposite direction. An additional, and quite unusual, factor that contributed to this instability was the constitutional provision that the cabinet's premier be the chief of state. Hence, a useful element of continuity and solidity was missing, and the state as such was shaken by every cabinet crisis.

During 1932 and 1933 the Left and the Radical Right defeated several moderate constitutional and political reform projects in several referenda. Simultaneously, the depression was playing into the hands of the Freedom Fighters. In October, 1933, they secured plebiscitary endorsement of their own more radical project for constitutional revision: a popularly elected president with extensive powers of legislative dissolution and veto; a legislature drastically reduced in size and authority. In the early months of 1934 the Freedom Fighters sustained this success with a series of victories in municipal elections. Their conduct became increasingly violent, and they indicated waxing confidence in winning the upcoming elections for the newly established office of president. In vain. On March 12, 1934, Konstantin Päts, a leader of the Agrarian Party and hero of the independence movement, who had again become premier for the fifth time on October 21, 1933, staged a preemptive and bloodless *coup d'état* with the support of the senior army officers and the assent of the leaders of the established parties, including the Social Democrats. A state of emergency was proclaimed, the impending presidential elections were suspended, and the Freedom Fighters as well as other radical organizations were immediately banned. A year later, on March 5, 1935, all political parties were dissolved and replaced by a mass organization, the Patriotic League.

On December 7, 1935, Päts smashed a planned insurrection by the now underground Freedom Fighters and followed up this success with a victorious plebiscite, on February 23-25, 1936, which endorsed in principle his proposals for a new constitution and authorized him to convene a

2. On the Communist side, the motive for this hopeless Estonian uprising may have been a desperate effort by Zinoviev, then head of the adjacent Leningrad CPSU (b) organization and of the Comintern, to enhance his standing in the Soviet Union's succession struggle for Lenin's mantle through a demonstration of international revolutionary vigor. Alternatively, the affair may have been the work of an OGPU-affiliated terror or military group operating on the fringes of the Soviet party apparatus. Cf. E. H. Carr, *Socialism in One Country*, vol. 3, pt. I (London: Macmillan & Co., Ltd., 1964), p. 285, note 1.

national assembly to draft it. His popularity was greatly enhanced by a remarkable postdepression economic revival that Estonia was experiencing during the middle 1930s.

The authorized constituent assembly was elected, not without some pressure and chicanery, in December, 1936, and, under Päts' "guidance," it drafted a new constitution during 1937. Entering into effect on January 1, 1938, this charter authorized a powerful president, to be elected indirectly for a six-year term, and a weaker, bicameral legislature with a five-year span of office. Nominations were to come from communities and not from the banned political parties, and elections were to be on the basis of single-member districts, not the old proportional lists. The legislature's upper house was to consist partly of ex-officio members and partly of presidential appointees. A number of corporativist features also characterized the constitution.

On February 24, 1938, the twentieth anniversary of Estonia's proclamation of independence, which had also occurred under Päts' leadership, the new legislature was elected, with 90 percent of eligible voters participating and chosing fifty-five supporters of the government and twenty-five oppositionists. Two months later, on April 24, Päts was formally designated president. By and large, the country's peasant majority was well satisfied with "his" prosperity, the workers less so due to the miserable housing conditions resulting from a steady migration from village to town, and the intelligentsia most alienated by the increasing restrictiveness of the regime. Though mild compared to totalitarian models, this nevertheless took the form of the perpetuation of martial law after the coup of 1934 and the suspension of the civil liberties formally enumerated in the constitution of 1938. The resultant alienation of the intelligentsia was politically damaging to Päts, because in interwar Estonia, with the world's then highest ratio of university education (1 student per 220 citizens), the academic intelligentsia, centered on the old and excellent university of Tartu (Dorpat), enjoyed a particularly high moral authority.

3

Latvia's parliamentary politics were even more fragmented and intricate than Estonia's, due to the peculiar social configuration of her southeastern region of Latgale, where not only most of her ethnic minorities were concentrated but where even the local Latvian majority was Roman Catholic rather than Lutheran, spoke a distinctive dialect, and nursed a somewhat aggrieved sense of regional particularism. Under the Russian Empire, Latgale had been administered separately from the rest of Latvia and only here did the collective village, or *mir*, take root. In the interwar period, Latgale duplicated and complicated the general Latvian party system with a regional one of its own and was socioeconomically the country's most underdeveloped region.

As many as forty-four political parties competed in the Latvian legislative elections of 1920, 1922, 1925, 1928, and 1931; of these between sixteen and twenty-eight achieved representation in any one parliament, and many had but one or two seats each. Indeed, virtually all the so-called Latvian parties other than the Social Democrats and the Agrarians were actually special interest groups. Their proliferation—in effect to one party per 45,000 inhabitants—was fatally encouraged by the exceedingly easy requirements for official nomination: a mere hundred signatures, whereupon the state was obliged to place its resources at the nominee's disposal. Although between 75 and 85 percent of the eligible voters participated, the parliamentary system worked poorly. There were eighteen cabinets up to the coup of 1934; those with a broad base lacked direction, and those with a narrow base could not rely on majorities. The prolonged negotiations necessary to construct each cabinet conveyed an impression of chronic crisis which undermined the parliamentary system *per se.*

The political trend over the five Latvian elections was away from the Left and toward the Agrarians. Though the Social Democrats remained the largest single party, they lost the rural part of their political base through land reform and became increasingly reluctant to participate in coalition governments. This enabled the Agrarians to furnish twelve of the eighteen precoup prime ministers. Though the Agrarians were emphatically nationalist, the initial economic hardship and social turmoil of the depression energized highly chauvinistic and radical organizations on their rightward flank.

These Right-Radicals designated themselves with such characteristic appellations as "National Revolutionaries," "National Socialists," "Legionnaires," "The Fire Cross," and "The Thunder Cross." The last-named was the largest and most menacing of their organizations. These groups were led by veterans and lumpen-intelligentsia, appealed to popular jingoism and peasantism, and developed cults of romantic primitivism and of blind fealty to their leaders. But for their overt paganism, their style and policy otherwise resembled those of the Romanian Iron Guard. Partly under their pressure and partly from independent conviction, the Agrarians, who regarded themselves as the particular bearers and protectors of the Latvian state, proposed certain constitutional revisions in October, 1933, intended to strengthen the president. In place of his current designation by the legislature for three years, he was to be elected for a six-year term, and he was to be endowed with authority to suspend laws and rights and to dissolve the legislature. Simultaneously the legislature itself was to be halved in size and reduced in power. The Agrarians also sought to steal the Right-Radicals' thunder by endorsing the curtailment of the cultural rights and economic power of the ethnic minorities.

Though these Agrarian constitutional proposals were moderately authoritarian rather than categorically dictatorial, and though their intent was to preempt rather than imitate the Right-Radicals, the Social Democrats resisted them. It appears that they feared the Agrarians would use the enhanced executive powers exclusively against the Left. This suspicion was understandably strengthened when in November, 1933, seven crypto-Communist deputies were deprived of their legislative mandates and arrested, while the Thunder Cross still remained untouched despite the professed determination on the part of the Agrarians to resist all subversion from any direction. On the other hand, as regards the proposed restrictions on the ethnic minorities, the Social Democrats proved surprisingly acquiescent. They were probably disturbed and disgusted by the inroads of nazism into the local German community.

As the constitutional revisions remained stalled in the legislature, the Agrarian leader Kārlis Ulmanis—like Päts in Estonia, the "grand old man" of the independence movement—personally assumed the premiership for the fifth time on March 17, 1934, displacing a weaker ally. Early in May, the legislature finally adopted a watered-down, and hence to Ulmanis unacceptable, version of his proposed constitutional reforms. Utilizing his own party's paramilitary organization and the army, he thereupon staged a *coup d'etat* during the night of May 15-16, 1934, suspended the legislature, proclaimed martial law, and this time suppressed the Thunder Cross as well as the Communist Party. This blow against the radicals of Right and Left now allowed Ulmanis, like Päts two months earlier, to claim that his coup was intended to save rather than overthrow democracy and had been rendered necessary to preempt putsches planned by the two political extremes. Be that as it may, he never presented evidence of such alleged, though possible, intentions to seize power, and his own subsequent political behavior renders his professions of commitment to basic democratic principles less plausible than Päts'. Furthermore, Ulmanis was also tainted by prevailing, if vague, rumors of corruption, and this circumstance, together with certain doubts concerning his explanation for the coup and his political intentions, resulted in the Latvian Social Democrats' decision to withhold from his coup the assent that their Estonian colleagues had given Päts'.

In contrast to Päts, Ulmanis never solicited endorsement of his coup and his regime through a plebiscite, though both were definitely popular. Perhaps he wished to avoid possible charges of imitating Hitler. Again unlike Päts, he never organized a mass party. Instead, he soon dissolved all political parties, his own included, and ruled through the bureaucracy and the army, supplemented by certain advisory but powerless corporativist bodies. On April 11, 1936, he combined the offices of president and premier in his own person but he never formally replaced the now disregarded constitution.

In foreign policy Ulmanis introduced no changes. He continued to depend primarily on British support but was careful not to offend either Germany or the Soviet Union, and he held Latvia aloof from Lithuania's quarrels with Germany and Poland. In domestic affairs, however, he energetically and successfully promoted economic recovery from the depression through etatist measures and sought to arouse public enthusiasm with demagogic programs of social mobilization, which seem to have impressed the youth and the peasants. The workers were less impressed. Indeed, one of the decisive reasons why Ulmanis later succumbed to Soviet pressure in June, 1940, without seeking to mobilize the Latvian public was his fear that the workers were too alienated and resentful to defend his regime. He also appealed to nationalistic emotions, which were always somewhat cruder and more chauvinistic here than in Estonia, by pursuing antiminority (especially anti-German and anti-Jewish) educational and economic policies and by pressing the "Latvianization" of Latgale.

4

Unfulfilled territorial claims to Poland's Wilno, a city that Lithuanians regarded as their historic capital though they were but a small minority of its interwar population, together with chronic anxiety lest Germany reclaim their only port of Klaipėda, gave Lithuania's interwar politics a far more explicitly and shrilly nationalistic tinge than was the case in Estonia and Latvia. These two countries, whatever their concern over Soviet and German aspirations, at least harbored no territorial-revisionist pretensions of their own. As independence had brought neither fulfillment nor security to Lithuania, her interwar nationalism waxed to a rather frenetic and truculent intensity, particularly against Poland and the local Polish ethnic minority. She refused to establish diplomatic relations with her southern neighbor, closed the frontier, and insisted on regarding herself in a formal state of war (but without fighting) with Poland, despite the fact that her own economy suffered in consequence. Indeed, while Poland's own hands were scarcely clean in the Wilno dispute, there appears to be some validity to the suspicions of Polish analysts that the Wilno grievance was deliberately nursed and inflamed by the Lithuanian nationalist elite as a pretext to raise a barrier against Polish cultural and political influence upon their still "young" and "impressionable" peasant people. The same need to assert Lithuanian nationalism against the historic cultural and socioeconomic hegemony of the local Polish gentry animated interwar Lithuania's land reform.

Ethnic and class cleavages compounded each other: peasants and workers were Lithuanian; landlords were Polish or of polonized (i.e., "renegade") Lithuanian noble stock; merchants were German and Jewish. As only the Jews were unidentified with any hostile or feared neighbor-state, and as they represented no conceivable threat to the developing national culture, and, finally, as they were not yet economically replaceable by the still immature Lithuanian middle class, they were relatively the best-treated of the country's interwar minorities. The Poles fared the worst.

Lithuania's precoup domestic politics over four parliamentary elections (1920, 1922, 1923, and 1926) did not manifest that clear a drift from Left toward Center and Right as had characterized Estonia's and Latvia's. Here, the three major political camps were the Catholic, Populist, and Socialist ones; the first two competed for the same rural clientèles and promoted similar right-center socioeconomic policies but were divided over the issue of secularization. While there were oscillations in electoral strength among the numerous parties within each large camp, the balance among them was relatively stable until it was eventually upset by a traumatic external event. The Catholic camp, which had from the beginning of independent statehood been the largest and most powerful one, and had shaped the constitution and the state structures to its ideology, proved unable to prevent Vatican recognition of Polish sovereignty over Wilno in the Papal-Polish Concordat of February 10, 1925. The national revulsion over this humiliation then cost the Catholic camp its absolute legislative majority in the next elections (May 8-9, 1926) and brought a coalition cabinet of Populists and Socialists into office.

Although the Catholic camp had hitherto enjoyed a legislative plurality and ministerial power, it had not succeeded in endowing Lithuania with a government that functioned smoothly and effectively. Ten cabinets had succeeded each other at frequent intervals over the short span of seven-and-a-half years since the achievement of independence; parliamentary interpellations and debates were both petty and ferocious and conveyed a sense of perpetual, albeit latent, crisis; most of the bureaucracy was inexperienced and not a few officials were guilty of irregularities, corruption, and abuse of authority; the tax and social security systems were primitive and inequitable. Upon these long-smoldering embers, the newly installed Populist-Socialist coalition government of mid-1926, in which the Socialist partner took over the ministries of interior and education, now poured still more incendiary fuel. It amnestied a number of imprisoned Communists, showed benevolence toward strikes, concluded a nonaggression treaty with the Soviet Union (September 28, 1926), inaugurated a secularistic educational policy that its enemies denounced as not only anti-Christian but also pro-Polish, used the police to break up protest demonstrations by Roman Catholic and nationalistic student groups, offended the military establishment by curtailing its budget and arresting two officers for subversive, i.e., right-wing, incitement, and launched a probe into the previous regime's fiscal and administrative malfeasances.

While the new government's urge to purge its predecessors' legacy was understandable, it proved fatal, especially as the country was currently passing through an economic crisis for which the current political incumbents were naturally, if unfairly, blamed. Furthermore, Piłsudski's recent seizure of power in neighboring Poland had set a vivid and enticing example for the Lithuanian enemies of the parliamentary system in general and of the incumbent government in particular. Accordingly, during the night of December 16-17, 1926, a junta of ultranationalistic officers and intelligentsia, with the connivance of vested economic interests and of the Catholic camp's political leadership, staged a successful and bloodless coup. Two veteran heroes of the independence movement were installed in power: Augustinas Voldemaras as premier and Antanas Smetona as president. In terms of their earlier political biographies, this pair at this juncture were Lithuania's analogues to Estonia's Päts and Latvia's Ulmanis.

The original Catholic involvement in this coup was myopic and proved a political blunder. The Populist-Socialist government was obviously crumbling and, what was equally obvious, it was about to be replaced by a Catholic-Populist one if only the logic of the parliamentary system was to be allowed to run its course. The coup, however, relegated the Catholics from the position of senior partner in an impending parliamentary government to a minor position in the Voldemaras-Smetona regime. By the time the Catholics recovered from their misjudgment and joined the Socialists and Populists in opposition in the spring of 1927, it was too late. The ultranationalists were already solidly entrenched.

To show that it meant business, the Voldemaras-Smetona regime inaugurated its rule by executing four leading Communists ten days after it seized power. It was also quite repressive against the "respectable" opposition, imprisoning a number of Socialist and Populist leaders and obliging others to flee to (Polish) Wilno. In response to the Catholics' passage into opposition, the regime simply dissolved the legislature and ruled thereafter through the army, the bureaucracy, the nationalistic intelligentsia, and its own paramilitary and youth organizations. On May 25, 1928, it decreed a new constitution that provided for a powerful president popularly elected for a seven-year term, and a weak, quinquennial legislature, which in fact never met. Vigorously applying censorship and martial law, this regime was the most dictatorial of those in the Baltic states, though still not nakedly terroristic.

In 1929 Voldemaras began to overreach himself. He used a secret cabal of extremist younger officers, known as the Iron Wolf, as his personal retinue for intimidating opponents. On April 30 he smashed the Social Democrats in revenge for the activities of their Wilno exiles. On May 6 an abortive attempt on his life, in which his aide was killed, provoked him into threatening unlimited vengeance. His megalomania and political extremism became a threat to President Smetona, who dismissed Premier Voldemaras on September 19, 1929, and shortly afterward suppressed the Iron Wolf. This episode was the Lithuanian version of a similar pattern in other interwar East Central European and Baltic states, whereby the authoritarian elites preempted, repelled, or expelled their Right-Radical challengers. Its decisiveness was confirmed when Smetona smashed a second coup attempted by Voldemaras and his extremist cortege on June 6, 1934.

In the five years between his two triumphs over Voldemaras, President Smetona had somewhat relaxed his regime's political repressiveness, only to revert to a tougher style from the mid-1930s on. This shift was in part a response to peasant and worker unrest which, in turn, was provoked by the economic deprivations ensuing from the territorial disputes with Poland and Germany, and in part a reaction to his deteriorating relations with the Catholic Church. The Social Democrats having already been outlawed in 1929, Smetona now dissolved all the other political parties except his own Nationalist League in the autumn of 1935; at the same time he redoubled the severity of press censorship. In the spring of 1936 he ordered tightly controlled elections for an "advisory" legislature, but as the single list of candiates had been handpicked by the government, public interest was minimal. On May 12, 1938, Smetona decreed yet another presidential constitution, this time separating Church and State. Meanwhile, he had fused the free trade unions and youth organizations into government-controlled fronts, strengthened his personal paramilitary retinue which supplemented the state organs of surveillance and control, and tightened the curbs on civil liberties. Smetona's rhetoric became ever more hyper-nationalistic and corporativistic, and he proceeded to encourage his own "cult of the individual," arranging to have himself adulated and addressed as The Nation's Guide (*Tautos Vadas*).

Smetona's prestige and authority had been adequate to ride out the depression and its attendant political repercussions. But when he yielded to a Polish ultimation of March 17, 1938, for the immediate establishment of diplomatic relations and opening of the border without reference to the Wilno question (an ultimatum which the Polish regime intended as a parallel and quasi-competitive emulation of Hitler's Anschluss of Austria four days earlier), and again when he capitulated a year later to the German ultimatum of March 22, 1939, for the instant retrocession of Klaipėda, his position—after so many years of intransigent rhetoric and diplomacy—was severely shaken. On March 27, 1939, public backlash obliged him to coopt some Catholics, Populists, and even partisans of Voldemaras into the government. But World War II intervened before any substantial democratization or even systemic reform could unfold.

The fact that the Nationalist regime was humbled through the nemesis of Lithuania's two open territorial disputes entailed a certain element of historic irony. The Wilno issue, on the one hand, had throughout helped that regime to consolidate its grip on the public; on the other hand, the persistent refusal to compromise on Klaipėda had stirred the peasants to the uneasy suspicion that their basic interest in trade with Germany was being sacrificed on the altar of symbolic prestige. Hence Smetona had always enjoyed proportionally less peasant support than had Päts and Ulmanis and had been more exclusively dependent on the army and the intelligentsia. On balance, Smetona's regime, for all its illiberal features and its integral nationalism, remained an authoritarian, rather than a totalitarian, one. The same judgment applies to its immediate Baltic neighbors as well as to interwar East Central Europe in general.

5

Unlike the rest of East Central Europe, however, the Baltic states lost even their formal independent statehood in the course of World War II. They were absorbed into the Soviet Union as constituent socialist republics in the summer of 1940, when Stalin decided to shore up certain strategic Soviet vulnerabilities on the heels of Hitler's triumphant Blitzkrieg in the West. Though overrun by the Wehrmacht a year later, the Baltic states' fate was then reconfirmed by the war's outcome. Ironically, within the Soviet Union, the Lithuanian S.S.R. now finally possesses Vilnius (Wilno). Though Europe is thus today poorer by these three states, and though the Kremlin has diluted their ethnic integrity by settling many Russians in them, yet they are still regarded within the Soviet Union—by their own peoples as well as by the Russian public—as a piece of "Europe." Though much of their native intelligentsia was deported into the Soviet interior in 1940, the experience and memories of the two interwar decades of independent statehood today sustain resistance to Russification, even by the native Communist cadres, and oblige the authorities to tread with some care of local nationalistic sentiments.

· *Chapter Ten* ·

SURVEY OF CULTURE

1

As REGARDS the formal academic expression of culture, the area's interwar universities maintained a high level. In particular, they cultivated the study of their respective countries' national institutions, history, and literature. These subjects were frequently taught in a romantic, rather than an analytic, manner. Though such legal, social, and humanistic studies drew far greater student interest than did scientific and technological disciplines—a phenomenon that contributed to and resulted from the earlier mentioned hypertrophy of politics and underdevelopment of industry—several areas of pure science were enriched by discoveries of universal significance. The contributions of the Polish mathematicians Zygmunt Janiszewski, Wacław Sierpiński, Stefan Mazurkiewicz, Kazimierz Kuratowski, Stefan Banach, Hugo Steinhaus, and Tadeusz Ważewski, for example, to set-theory, topology, the theory of functions of a real variable, functional analysis, and probability theory established the universities of Warsaw and Lwów as world centers of mathematics during the interwar period. The work of these Polish mathematicians, in turn, and of the Polish philosophers Jan Łukasiewicz, Stanisław Leśniewski, Tadeusz Kotarbiński, and Alfred Tarski had a profound and revolutionary impact upon such areas of philosophy as symbolic and mathematical logic, epistemology, semantics, and the philosophy of science.

Similarly, mathematicians, physicists, chemists, and physiologists of Hungarian origin and early training, such as John von Neumann, Eugene Wigner, Leo Szilard, Edward Teller, Theodore von Kármán, György Hevesy, György Békesy, and Albert Szent-György, advanced their fields through work of remarkable originality. Many of this latter group were obliged to pursue their mature work outside their homeland, as political or ethnic émigrés or simply because interwar Hungary was too small and limited to absorb and support them. The faculty of arts and sciences at the university of Budapest, for example, funded only two chairs of mathematics as contrasted to eleven of history in the interwar period.

In "softer" sciences, the Prague school of structural linguistics, which was founded by Vilém Mathesius, had several Czech disciples, and was enriched by the Russian émigrés Roman Jakobson and Nikolai S. Trubetskoi, was a universally acknowledged pioneer in its field. The Polish and Romanian sociologists and anthropologists Bronisław Malinowski, Florian Znaniecki, Ludwik Krzywicki, and Dimitrie Gusti received similar acclaim.

As international intellectual repute enhanced national prestige, the area's governments were financially generous to their universities and to other institutions of higher learning. They also, for double motives of need and national pride, made strenuous and successful efforts to reduce illiteracy levels through the extension of primary education. While impressive in general terms, the results here still left considerable regional differentiation within each country, as well as among the area's several countries. This, in turn, entailed political grievances as the regions of particularly high or low literacy were usually those where ethnic minorities were concentrated. The educational systems were also somewhat marred by a tendency to advance too many secondary-school graduates into universities in proportion to the number of elementary-school children admitted to secondary schools. Their structures, in other words, tended to be cylindrical after elementary school and therefore top-heavy in general, rather than pyramidal and balanced. The result was an economically superfluous and politically dysfunctional academic proletariat.

This problem was least acute, though not altogether absent, in interwar Czechoslovakia, especially among that country's Czech and German populations. A law of 1922, establishing a compulsory minimum of eight years of elementary education, did much to raise the hitherto low literacy and cultural levels of that country's Slovak and Ruthenian peoples, who had long been neglected by their prewar Magyar rulers. The Czechoslovak governments also adopted a more tolerant policy than their neighboring regimes toward education, at all levels, in the languages of the country's ethnic minorities. Also enlightened was the strategy of seeking to contain the above-mentioned danger of a burgeoning academic proletariat by vigorously promoting vocational training programs, particularly at the secondary level. By 1938 there were 763 vocational secondary schools in Czechoslovakia with 75,522 students.

In Poland, on the other hand, vocational education, while endorsed by the governmental elite, was undervalued by a social prestige system heavily biased toward classical humanities. Here a program of seven years of compulsory schooling, decreed in 1919, was finally implemented only in 1932; even thereafter it was not always fully applied in the countryside. Furthermore, beyond the sixth grade, interwar Poland had, in effect, a dual educational system, which tended to sustain the existing stratification and separation of social classes, or at least to slow down changes therein. Children of peasants and workers constituted less than 14 percent of the secondary-school pupils and about 7 percent of students in higher educational institutions in a country where these two classes accounted for approximately four-fifths of the total population. Poland's educational system was thus a less effective funnel of upward social mobility than were those of her neighbors (excepting Romania's). It also suffered from extensive wartime destruction of school buildings and teacher cadres and thereafter from insufficient material and human investments relative to the country's swelling number of children. Toward the close of the era it was still forty-five thousand classrooms short of minimal needs and over the whole span of that era the pupil/teacher ratio actually worsened somewhat, from 42.3 elementary school children per teacher in 1922 to 61.3 in 1938.

It must, however, be conceded that interwar Poland faced a particularly difficult problem in unifying and polonizing the three different educational systems inherited from the partitioning powers.Only in her ex-Habsburg areas had the system hitherto been authentically Polish in culture, and the formerly Russian one was of low calibre. Indeed, whereas eight years of elementary education (in German) had been compulsory in the ex-Prussian partition since 1825 and six years in the ex-Habsburg one since 1895, the prewar Tsarist regime had never fully implemented a compulsory four-year curriculum legislated by the Third Duma as late as 1908. In an understandable, but nevertheless unfortunate, overreaction to the disabilities inflicted on her national culture by the authorities of the prewar German and Russian empires, interwar Poland herself now chose to be niggardly in the educational facilities she made available to her large ethnic minorities in their own languages. This policy, and the resentments that it provoked, soon compounded into a festering and highly charged irritant.

Hungary's educational policy, while also highly nationalistic and emphatically hostile to any cultural claims by her ethnic minorities, sought to steer a sociopedagogical middle course between the relatively open Czechoslovak system and the relatively intelligentsia-dominated Polish one by experimenting with so-called "continuation schools," of which there were 395 by 1938, for lower-class children whose parents' economic situation prevented their attending the regular schools beyond the age of twelve. Even so, it was still unusual for any but the most gifted offspring of peasants and workers to squeeze through the system's bottlenecks into higher educational institutions.

As for the Balkan countries, a Yugoslav law of 1929, requiring universal elementary education for eight years, was never fully implemented; most peasant children left school after four years. Inadequate attention to vocational schooling at the elementary level was somewhat compensated by official recognition of its importance at the secondary level. Admissions standards for Yugoslavia's varied institutions of secondary and higher education were academically extremely selective. This was an admirable policy in terms of maintaining intellectual standards, but its social consequences in a developing country desperately in need of a technical intelligentsia were questionable. Romanian institutions of higher education, on the other hand, were numerically swollen, academically rather lax, and politically overheated. They were veritable incubators of surplus bureaucrats, politicians, and demagogues. Elementary education, in turn, was scandalously underfunded and neglected; only 5.4 percent of children, among whom but a trickle came from peasant families, continued beyond the fourth grade during the decade of 1929-38. An additional handicap to social mobility for the peasant and working classes as well as to national economic development was the paucity of vocational schools. Bulgaria's educational system, on the other hand, was a particularly effective one, as reflected in that country's high literacy levels and in its seven-year compulsory curriculum which reflected the country's socioeconomic levels and needs. Albania, in turn, established a state school system only in 1933, with the nationalization of religious and private schools, which, as noted above, had often been founded and administered by foreigners. By the school year 1937-38 her 642 elementary schools with their 1,350 teachers (an average of 2 teachers per school) were educating 54,000 pupils, while 261 secondary school masters were teaching 5,677 students. Interwar Albania lacked institutions of higher education, but generous government scholarships were available for study abroad.

The number of institutions of higher education (including universities, polytechnics, and specialized academies but not independent theological seminaries) existing in the other East Central European states by the close of the interwar era was: Poland, twenty-four; Czechoslovakia, seventeen; Hungary, thirteen; Yugoslavia, thirteen; Romania, eighteen; Bulgaria, seven; Estonia, five; Latvia, four; Lithuania, six. The main thrust of educational policy in these three last-mentioned Baltic countries, with their relatively egalitarian, mobile, and progressive societies, was to utilize compulsory schooling as a lever to emancipate their national cultures from the historically conditioned and politically enforced former German, Polish, and Russian cultural and educational hegemonies.[1]

1. The data for the several preceding paragraphs on education are from Martena T. Sasnett, *Educational Systems of the World* (Los Angeles: University of Southern California Press, 1952), passim; from the several chapters on education in the series *East-Central Europe under the Communists*, edited by Robert F. Byrnes (New York: Praeger, 1957); and from the periodic Bulletins and Reports on comparative education published by the Office of Education, U.S. Department of Health, Education, and Welfare (Washington, D.C.: U.S. Government Printing Office).

Quite often, of course, the social and ideological results of the area-wide commitment to education went quite beyond the sponsoring governments' control or intention. While the officially inculcated values were nationalistic and liberal-conservative in the conventional central European legal-political style, and while the influence of organized religion upon the curricula of primary, secondary, and normal (teacher-training) schools was vivid and considerable, the younger intelligentsia nevertheless often emerged from its educational experience highly radicalized. Here some interesting national variations were apparent. While the academic institutions of every interwar East Central European country generated clusters of students manifesting commitments all across the political spectrum, as well as apolitical attitudes, one can nevertheless speak of prevalent national "tilts" in this matter. Thus, whereas Bulgarian and Serb university students tended to lean toward Communism (when they were not simply career-oriented), their Croatian, Romanian, Slovak, and Polish counterparts preferred Right-Radical political stances, which were often explicitly hostile toward their states' regimes and "Establishments." Czech and Hungarian students, while sharing the emphatic nationalism of the second group, did not generally adopt its, or the Communists', vividly oppositional stance. Yet, the relative political moderation of the Czech and Hungarian *academic* intelligentsias was counterbalanced by the intense political radicalism of these two nations' *literary-artistic* avant-gardes, who maintained particularly close ties to the Communist and Right-Radical political movements. One need cite here but two exemplary pairs: the Czech poet Stanislav Kostka Neumann exchanged his early individualism for collectivism and revolutionary pathos, while the talented and esthetically innovative poet, dramatist, and novelist Viktor Dyk allowed his name to grace the small Czech Fascist movement; the analogous Hungarian cases are the brilliant, obsessed, proletarian poet Attila József and the volatile, bellicose novelist Dezső Szabó, who was a nativist, populist, and primitivist.

Distinct from, though related to, the question of the intelligentsia's ideological radicalization stands the consideration that, on balance, the area's secondary and higher schools functioned as funnels of upward mobility for a significant, though insufficient, number of ambitious candidates from the lower classes. Though the newly risen *arrivistes* often adopted the values of the established elite and severed their moral and psychological ties, though not their political, propagandistic connections, to the villages and milieux of their origin, their very numbers at least weakened the former power monopoly of the traditional ruling strata. And even though the great majority of the children of peasants and workers and ethnic minorities did not advance beyond elementary education, nevertheless their horizons were sufficiently broadened to undermine the immemorial and fatalistic assumption that their lot was inevitable and ordained. Here too, the political consequences were unsettling.

The pursuit of intellectual and cultural prowess as an expression of national greatness was particularly deliberate and political in defeated and revisionist Hungary, where it served as something of a compensation mechanism. Her energetic minister of education and cults, Count Kunó Klebelsberg, operated on the proposition that, having been reduced to third-rate military and economic status, Hungary must henceforth make her weight felt internationally by becoming a first-rate cultural power.[2] This strategy called for the restless pursuit of Nobel prizes, Olympic medals, and other vivid symbols of international achievement. It also entailed the extension of educational opportunities so as to train the country's best young minds and talents, irrespective of class origin, to absorb, extend, and deepen international "high culture," and, in turn, to impress the international community with Hungary's political case at a high and subtle level of persuasion. In this craving to subsidize cultural excellence and then translate it into political prestige, the Hungarian government differed from its neighbors only in its systematic intensity, not in basic expectations.

2

In the artistic realms of culture outside academia, interwar East Central Europe was also highly creative. Here the area's finest representatives, though deliberately rooted in their respective national idioms, were nevertheless so original as to transcend mere national charm. Hence the innovative achievements of Czechoslovak and Hungarian composers (Leoš Janáček, Bohuslav Martinů, Béla Bartók, Zoltán Kodály), of Romanian and Yugoslav sculptors (Constantin Brâncuşi, Ivan Meštrović), of modern painters of Czechoslovak origin (Oskar Kokoschka, Otakar Kubín-Coubine, František Kupka), and of many performing vocal and instrumental virtuosos (too numerous to identify individually) from the area have earned recognition as powerful and lasting contributions to universal culture. Similarly, its bold innovations in stage-production, set-design, and the imaginative integration of language, light, music, and acting, made the interwar Polish theater (producers Stefan Jaracz, Juliusz Osterwa, and Leon Schiller) a cultural herald of trends that were subsequently absorbed into international drama and cinema. The experimental thrust in all these arts was away from traditional romanticism toward new forms, styles, and expressions. Indeed, the atmosphere was one of restless ferment.

Literary creativity is, of course, more difficult to appreciate and

2. Graf Kunó Klebelsberg, "Ungarische Kulturpolitik nach dem Kriege," *Ungarische Jahrbücher* 5 (1925): pp. 343-63.

evaluate across language barriers, as many qualities and nuances do not lend themselves to translation. Nevertheless, the very frequency of translations of the works of East Central European poets and novelists into western languages is a partial index of their universality and quality. As regards literary, artistic, and political trends among writers, it is of some interest to note that in those nations that had not enjoyed independent statehood before World War I, and whose writers had consequently felt themselves responsible for sustaining national identity, integrity, pride, and hope during the era of partition or subjugation, the achievement of emancipation and statehood elicited a *volte-face* on the part of many writers. They now felt that their earlier national patriotic responsibilities could now be assumed by their new states' politicians, soldiers, and diplomats, while they themselves were henceforth entitled to pursue strictly artistic goals or to sponsor radical political causes. Many writers of the newly defeated or of the still aggrieved nations and of the ethnic minorities, on the other hand, now often accepted or continued to feel an obligation to put their talents to the political education and service of the nation. Here, too, some believed that the nation was best served by Communism or Right-Radicalism.

All the general European literary and artistic trends of the interwar era—expressionism, futurism, constructivism, cubism, surrealism, formalism, functionalism, primitivism, abstractionism, religious neopietism, existentialism, peasantism, Marxism—were echoed in East Central European belles lettres and arts, and some were even anticipated. Poets were, on the whole, more enthusiastically experimental and, surprisingly, more acclaimed by the reading public than were prose writers. It was the poets in particular who turned away from nostalgia for the countryside and the past and now celebrated the city both in theme and in their very metaphors. Perhaps this enthusiasm of the poets was psychologically and culturally related to the bold work of their contemporary East Central European, and especially Polish, architects and town planners, who were committing themselves simultaneously—though not always successfully —to simplification, functionalism, and monumentalism.

Though interwar Polish literature boasted a number of novelists and dramatists of considerable talent, none of these could be said to have marked a whole era with his or her genius, such as their prewar predecessors Stefan Żeromski, Władysław Reymont, or Stanisław Wyspiański had done. Rather, they maintained this established tradition on a generally high level. Interwar Polish poetry, on the other hand, was truly innovative and creative in thematic as well as linguistic terms. The Skamander circle, which, adopting an allusion by Wyspiański, named itself after ancient Troy's river to symbolize Poland's ties to classic culture, was led by Julian Tuwim, Jarosław Iwaszkiewicz, Antoni Słonimski, Kazimierz Wierzyński, and Jan Lechoń (pen name of Leszek Serafinowicz). Its members reveled in daring metaphors, startling similes, bold assonances, colloquial idioms, and an enthusiastic celebration of urbanism. Though rejecting the hitherto characteristic historical romanticism of Polish letters in favor of a sometimes deliberately shocking commitment to the present and the future, and while indulging in their doctrine of linguistic spontaneity and raciness, the Skamanderites nevertheless wrote poetry of extraordinary lyrical beauty. Though their original artistic program had been deliberately apolitical in the 1920s, they were nevertheless drawn into social issues and political polemics during the 1930s.

Stylistically to the left of the Skamander circle stood the looser "Awangarda" (Vanguard). This movement was more expressionistic and sometimes surrealistic, more prone to "catastrophism," less lyrical, than the former. Its most influential poets were Julian Przyboś, Adam Ważyk, Józef Czechowicz, and Czesław Miłosz, and they had an impact in the postwar era as well. To its political, though not necessarily stylistic, left, in turn, emerged a group of young Communist poets led by Władysław Broniewski, Witold Wandurski, Stanisław R. Stande, and Bruno Jasieński—several of whom went as political refugees to the Soviet Union, only to be liquidated there in the Stalinist terror.

Mention must also be made of the "regional" school of Polish poetry, best represented in the interwar era by Kazimiera Iłłakowiczówna's celebration of the Wilno countryside, which though nostalgic in theme was often literally fantastic in style and imagery. Also meriting notice is a traditional Polish literary genre which entails its own peculiar kind of creativity, that of translation from other languages. Here the indefatigable Tadeusz Boy-Żeleński's translations from all eras of French literature into the corresponding Polish literary style were the most outstanding and were often as brilliant as the originals.

With the towering and popular exception of Karel Čapek, Czech writers had less international impact than had Czech composers, painters, and scientists. Indeed, though it was represented by poets and novelists and dramatists of considerable talent—one thinks here of the mystical poet Otakar Březina, the Catholic neoromanticist Jaroslav Durych, the esthete and critic F. X. Šalda, and the playwright František Langer—Czech interwar literature was, by cosmopolitan standards, somewhat underdeveloped. This may, in part, have been an effect of its prewar commitment to political rather than esthetic endeavors and, in larger part, also a result of excessive receptivity to foreign influences, which it tended to ape rather than transform and creatively merge with its own native idiom. The combination of her Slavic tongues, her Western political orientation, and her geographic centrality rendered Czechoslovakia highly susceptible to powerful cultural cross-currents. The result was an interwar literature that tended to echo universal literary trends rather than to develop them. Even Čapek, though he was a subtle stylist and passionate moralist,

owed his fame more to the political and social significance and interpretation that his themes and symbols suggested, than to their literary and
esthetic qualities. His robot powerfully expressed the utopian potential of
the machine to liberate man from toil, as well as its sinister threat to de-
humanize him by mechanizing his civilization. Both were equally plausible results of removing conflict from life.

The generation of Slovak writers that first revealed its talents during
the interwar era was emphatically radical, in both nationalistic and
socialistic terms, in its ideological commitments. In its effort to prove the
maturity of Slovak literature it was often even more receptive to cosmopolitan influences than was its Czech counterpart. Thanks to a massive
assault of government on illiteracy, it enjoyed a rapidly expanding readership. Its most durable talent proved to be the lyricist Laco Novomeský,
who combined Communist ideology with a pure and formal literary style.

Any discussion, however brief, of Czechoslovak cultural figures and
their contributions invites at least a passing reference to the tremendous
impact of German and Jewish luminaries hailing from the Czech lands of
Bohemia and Moravia upon German literature and international culture
and science of the interwar era. Among the best known of these were the
novelists, poets, and critics Franz Kafka, Rainer Maria Rilke, Franz
Werfel and Karl Kraus, the architect Adolf Loos, and the philosopher
Edmund Husserl. One might also recall in this connection that Sigmund
Freud and Gustav Mahler stemmed from these lands, and that Ernst
Mach and Albert Einstein had in prewar days taught physics at the
German (Ferdinand) University of Prague.

There is a parallelism between the artistic psychology of the composers
Bartók and Kodály, on the one hand, and that of interwar Hungarian
writers, on the other. Music and literature each sought to be both cosmopolitan and national, to face westward and inward, to be technically
innovative, yet rooted in folk rhythms of song and speech. Scornful of
nineteenth-century platitudes, even the ideologically conservative writers
sought to explore the emotive possibilities of the Magyar tongue through
experimentation in structure and prosodic dissonances reminiscent of the
techniques of their composer colleagues. Though their efforts were
sometimes spoiled by mannerisms, the writers nevertheless achieved a
high general standard of stylistic clarity. They also had moral and political
integrity. Once again, as often before in Hungary's history, her men of
letters now injected imagination and criticism into a politically constrained environment. The regime, in turn, eager for the reasons expressed earlier to impress the West with the quality of Hungarian culture,
tolerated a wide spectrum of artistic and ideological latitude on the part of
the country's writers.

One aspect of the writers' program was superior translations into the
Magyar tongue from other literatures. To these translations even the

most talented and prolific writers devoted a considerable proportion of their time and energy. Thus, for example, Hungary's leading man of letters of the 1930s, the gifted poet, novelist, and essayist Mihály Babits, translated Sophocles, Dante, Shakespeare, Goethe, and Baudelaire into superior Magyar verse. On the other hand, the difficulty and remoteness of their own Finno-Ugric language made it hard for the Hungarian literati to project their own culture to the outside world.

A number of literary trends, often associated with particular periodicals, can be identified in interwar Hungary. The liberal-cosmopolitan *Nyugat* (West) group, though lacking its original prewar élan and combativeness, still maintained high standards of esthetic finesse and social conscience. Its leading lights during this era were the above-mentioned Mihály Babits and Zsigmond Móricz, a prolific novelist who wrote about provincial and rural life and is regarded by many as Hungary's greatest prose writer. These two "liberal humanists" became the leaders of the interwar "moderns" after Endre Ady's premature death in 1919. They defended culture against vulgarization by the Right or the Left; yet they were also sensitive to social issues and were determined to explain and protect the exploited classes of Hungarian society, especially the peasantry. Like this pair of leaders, the *Nyugat* group as a whole sought to straddle the two commitments to art as pure esthetic experience and as serving a social function. But even when most vividly political, it never sank to crude didacticism and always remained cultivated and creative.

The conservative-nationalist writers congregated around the reviews *Napkelet* (East) and *Új Idők* (New Times). Their leader Ferenc Herczeg was apotheosized by the regime as a kind of author laureate of interwar Hungary, but he was not a mere hack; he was a disciplined dramatist and short-story writer. Nor, in general, did this school spawn the era's racist-fascist literature; it was far too self-consciously civilized and restrained for such excesses. Rather, it was radical populism that, out of passionate devotion to the supposedly pure Magyar peasantry, occasionally degenerated into racism.

Populism's literary prophet was the brilliant and polemical novelist Dezső Szabó, who as a young man had come under the influence of the French popularizer of "integral nationalism," Maurice Barrès. The self-appointed guardian of the Magyar soul, for whose future he quaked apocalyptically, Szabó identified Magyardom exclusively with the peasantry, all other classes being venomously denounced as Judaized, Germanized, or internationalized and hence psychologically and morally deracinated. A master of diatribe, a literary brawler who proclaimed himself destiny's messianic choice to purge Hungary of infamy and "foreignisms," yet gifted with a superb prose style, Szabó's torrential example released many younger populist writers, such as Gyula Illyés, László Németh, János Kodolányi, Péter Veres, Pál Szabó, and József

Darvas, from their social and ideological inhibitions. Several of these worked with the semisociological, semipolitical "village explorers" movement of the 1930s which recorded and criticized the depressed condition of the peasantry. In the ideological crisis of populism toward the close of that decade, some of them were to gravitate to Right-Radicalism, some toward Marxism. Their periodical was *Válasz* (Answer).

Lajos Kassák was the first worker to achieve a recognized niche in Hungarian literature with his expressive blank verse and candid, often moving, autobiography. He was, however, too much of a literary and political maverick to remain consistently identified with any ideological camp. Hence the accolade of leading proletarian writer has gone to the high-strung, tragically short-lived, angry yet tender poet Attila József, the master of a severely intellectual yet magically melodious genre. His expulsion from the Communist Party in the early 1930s for "premature" anti-Hitlerism and for partiality to psychoanalysis is an embarrassment to the current regime.

Though only a fraction of his attention was devoted to Hungarian literature, the great Marxist critic and philosopher György Lukács also merits mention in this discussion of interwar Hungarian culture. He, too, had occasional difficulties toeing the frequently fluctuating party line. Like some, but not all, of his fellow Communist, and several non-Communist, writers, Lukács worked in exile during the interwar era. Those Marxist writers who remained in Hungary had Kassák's periodical *Munka* (Labor), the Communists' *100%*, and the Social Democratic daily *Népszava* (Voice of the People) available as publishing outlets. The simultaneous Catholic literary revival clustered around *Vigilia* (Vigil). Regional writers in the territories lost at Trianon sustained local Magyar culture in Romania, Czechoslovakia, and Yugoslavia, respectively, on the pages of the literary organs *Erdelyi Helikon* (Translyvanian Helicon), *Magyar Irás* (Hungarian Letters), and *Kalangya* (Sheaf).

The particular severity of the horrors of World War I in the Serb lands ended any "art for art's sake" type of estheticism in interwar Yugoslavia's literature, while the subsequent vehemence of the political quarrels among the ethnic groups likewise rendered hollow the earlier stances of "cult of form" and "aristocracy of sensibility" within her cultural intelligentsia. Indeed, the strains among Yugoslavia's ethnic communities were such that the writers regarded themselves as the preservers and developers of three separate literatures—Slovene, Croatian, and Serb —rather than a single Yugoslav one. The fact that the Croats and Serbs wrote in the same language, the most phonetic and vocalic of all the Slavic tongues, one that is devoid of the difficult consonant combinations of many of the others and is a remarkably graceful and precise vehicle of expression, did not suffice to instill a sense of cultural unity. In historical retrospect, it is nevertheless possible and necessary to identify certain trends and shifts that were common to all three of these supposedly distinct literatures of the Yugoslav peoples.

The first interwar decade saw an explosion of self-consciously bold and expressionistic writing, which articulated and released basic, often raw, emotions, and frequently spilled over into stylistic surrealism. Language was used freely, spontaneously, with unrestrained lyricism and psychological self-revelation. Institutionally, it was a decade of many, often short-lived, cultural programs and periodicals. With the 1930s, however, came a sharp turn toward concern with the social content and the claimed political responsibility of literature, even at the cost of form (a harbinger of post-World War II developments). The cultural "socialists" now attacked the stylistic "moderns" as frivolous, and a number of sur-realists converted to Marxism. The political background of this shift was the depression, the sharpening of Croatian-Serb tensions, and the Nazi offensive against the European security system—all of which prompted Yugoslav intellectuals to take a stand on the issues and hence to reveal, adopt, or change their ideological commitments, occasionally in narrowly sectarian and esthetically defective terms. Interestingly, however, some of the best writers now also celebrated particular geographical regions in their work. This was not an expression of mere old-fashioned folklorism, still less of the regime's official "Yugoslavism," but rather of their own pessimistic projections of the disappearance of local cultures under the pressures of interethnic and international conflict.

The most widely appreciated authors of Yugoslavia's three interwar literatures are easily identified. The rich metaphors, lively rhythms, guile-less style, and linguistic versatility of the Slovene poet and translator Oton Župančič, who creatively fused his heritage of folk poetry with his cos-mopolitan education, perfected the Slovene poetic language and pro-foundly influenced contemporary and later Slovene writers. The re-markable talent of his younger countryman Srečko Kosovel, whose poems explore the pains of living and dying, was prematurely silenced by an early death in 1926. Toward the end of the 1930s the stylistic versatility and the psychological insights of the autodidact Prežihov Voranc (pen-name of Lovro Kuhar), a radical and sarcastic observer of Carinthian village and small-town life (and at the time a political exile from his country), blossomed into maturity and received critical and public ac-claim.

Vladimir Nazor had been regarded as the outstanding modern Croa-tian national lyricist before World War I and continued to stamp his stylis-tic and critical seal on many interwar Croatian writers. A connoisseur of European, and especially of Italian, literature, a romanticist influenced by Heine, Hugo, Pascoli, and d'Annunzio, his poetry abandoned rigid metrical rules for flowing, apparently irregular, verses. In his interwar writing, prose came to predominate over poetry, but in both categories Nazor found in myth, legend, and fable his most congenial themes. More modernistic and less optimistic was his versatile and prolific younger colleague Miroslav Krleža. A poet, novelist, dramatist, writer of short stories, essayist, and journalist, Krleža was the most forceful and unsettling interwar Croatian writer; the thrust of his work was a mordant dissection of the era's upper and middle classes.

A large proportion of interwar Serb writers were members of Yugoslavia's diplomatic corps, which fact reflected the leisured life-style enjoyed by that profession in those years. Among the most highly regarded were: the stylistically meticulous, "westernizing," individualistic, and aristocratic poet, aphorist, and travel-writer Jovan Dučić; the pessimistic poet of decadence and intellectualism, Milan Rakić; and the eventual Nobel laureate Ivo Andrić. Andrić's novels and short stories, often set in his native Bosnia and of epic sweep, are crafted in measured, limpid, polished language that is full of tenderly expressed humanity and compassion, yet characterized by an absolute artistic integrity in which traditionalism and modernism are successfully united. Though his work exudes an aura of sadness stemming from his sense of the transience of life and the indifference of nature, Andrić apparently wishes to believe that courage in the face of nothingness is its own reward.

The self-taught Communist poet Kosta Racin was the only interwar writer to express himself in the Macedonian language. His style was inspired by traditional folk-lyrics and his theme was the hard fate of the poor. He was killed in battle in 1943.

Romanian literature, habitually oscillating between receptivity to foreign influences and self-revivification from native sources, was preoccupied with the social and moral upheaval that resulted from the assault of urbanization and commercialization upon traditional rural culture. It now depicted man in a state of disintegration while uncomprehended fates destroy his freedom. There is a pervasive sense of injustice without apparent object or end. Mihai Sadoveanu, Liviu Rebreanu, and Cezar Petrescu were the leading novelists of this era and mood. Their language is consistently appropriate to this theme—in turn liturgical, velvety, cadenced, and brutal—though their characters are occasionally mere stereotypes.

Poetry, and especially lyrical poetry, retained into the interwar era its traditional place as Romania's most cultivated literary genre. Here towered the superbly talented Transylvanian Octavian Goga, whose reputation had already been solidly established in the prewar years, and who now became deeply involved in nativist anti-Semitic politics that logically, albeit disasterously, complemented his antimodernist esthetics. Many younger interwar poets, the most gifted of whom was Ion Pillat, also assumed a traditionalist stance. They adopted pastoral, patriotic, and religious themes and, for all their contacts with foreign, especially French, cultural movements, denied the possibility of good cosmopolitan literature.

Interwar Bulgarian literature was particularly rich in the psychological treatment of peasant and artisan characters. Many of the writers were themselves village schoolteachers or provincial functionaries of peasant origin; in this country the capital was less a center of cultural life than elsewhere. The literary styles, however, were anything but merely rustic and reflected the full gamut of contemporary European trends. Representatives of these styles often clustered around particular journals. Thus *Strelets* (Archer) was the focal organ of the expressionists, *Hyperion* of the symbolists (and toward the close of the era of the non-Communist political Left), while those writers emphasizing technical form and the narrative tradition remained with the somewhat older *Zlatorog* (Golden Horn). Other cultural and political trends represented in interwar literature, but without specific foci in journals were historicism, mysticism, futurism, and proletarianism. The most popular interwar writer was Elin Pelin (*nom de plume* of Dimitŭr Ivanov), whose short stories depict the corrosion of traditional village life under the impact of modernization. He also wrote superb children's stories and poems. Even more restrained and, on balance, somewhat more gifted was Iordan Iovkov, who also analyzed village life, observing everything but sentimentalizing nothing: a pure artist. In poetry, the work of Elisaveta Bagryana perfectly fused traditional and experimental styles and was the culmination of the strong Bulgarian tradition of women writers.

At opposite corners of East Central Europe, the interwar literatures of the Albanians and of the Baltic peoples were, in each case, esthetically shaped on the one hand by native folklore, folksong, and epic traditions, and on the other by contemporary European stylistic influences, especially symbolism, expressionism, futurism, and formalism. In terms of subject matter, they again shared certain dominant themes: the contemplation of nature and of man's problematic relationship to her; the memorialization of the historic travails and triumphs of the nation, which were usually treated romantically and sometimes in terms of biblical analogies; and, especially in the 1930s, the analysis of contemporary social issues and fates, which were generally treated neorealistically and often pessimistically in the Baltic literatures but romantically in the Albanian. The market for their respective literatures differed, however, quite radically. The high Albanian illiteracy rate sharply restricted that country's potential reading public, and the lower but still extensive Lithuanian rate also had a moderately depressing effect on that society's "consumption" of literature. By contrast, the per capita ratios of book publication and possession in Estonia and Latvia were among the world's highest. In one final respect, however, Albanian and Baltic literatures shared similar fates: the potential international appreciation for the literary creativity of these four little nations on the geographical margins of Europe was, and remains, limited by the relative inaccessibility of their difficult languages.

3

Though the political and diplomatic orientations of most interwar East Central European governments were, until the second half of the 1930s, toward France and Italy, it appears that the area's cultural intelligentsia was throughout the interwar period at least equally, if not more, impressed by the intellectual authority and creative vitality of Weimar German academic and artistic circles. The alleged grip of Francomania upon East Central Europe has often been exaggerated even as regards the local cultural elites, with the possible exception of the Romanian one, while the peasant masses remained quite immune to it.

On balance, one may conclude that the best representatives of interwar East Central European culture, both academic and artistic, were the equals of any other nation or area. But average levels of culture and literacy were, as a result of complicated historic and socioeconomic factors, lower than West Europe's, though the gap was being closed. The problem, which here as elsewhere was not always fully recognized, was to assure that in this drive to catch up with the West, the average and the merely good would not destroy the best in East Central Europe's culture.

BIBLIOGRAPHICAL ESSAY

1

THE FOLLOWING is neither a comprehensive bibliography nor a list of sources used for this book. It is an annotated selection of materials in Western languages that students wishing to probe certain problems more deeply will find particularly useful. Students who have a command of East Central European languages have at their disposal the extensive historical and bibliographical output of the several countries' scholars and Academies of Arts and Sciences, as well as the burgeoning number of memoirs published by political figures prominent during the interwar era in East Central Europe.

Particularly useful are the following periodicals, some of which are no longer published: *East European Quarterly, Journal of Central European Affairs, Polish Review, Slavic Review, Slavonic and East European Review, Le Monde Slave, Les Balkans, Osteuropa, and Südosteuropa-Jahrbuch*. Furthermore, in the 1960s the Academies of Arts and Sciences of several East Central European countries began to publish periodicals or yearbooks carrying translations in Western languages of what is regarded as the most exemplary local historical research, including that on the interwar era. To signal their universal linguistic accessibility, these series, while published in the modern languages, are often endowed with Latin titles. Thus the Polish one is *Acta Poloniae Historica*, the Czechoslovak one *Historica*, the Hungarian pair *Acta Historica* and *Studia Historica Academiae Scientiarum Hungaricae*, while the Romanian and Bulgarian ones carry the French titles *Revue Roumaine d'Histoire* and *Études Historiques*. Also available are the many research papers presented by Eastern and Western scholars in the fifth volume of the *Acts du Premier Congrès International des Études Balkaniques et Sud-Est Européennes* (Sofia: Académie Bulgare des Sciences, 1970), dealing with the period since 1848.

Interwar East Central European statistical data are also readily available to the reader confined to Western languages. The official annual statistical yearbooks were published by each state in bilingual editions: in the language of the given state and in either English, French, or German.

For books and monographs, the following are the most useful and comprehensive bibliographies: Paul L. Horecky, ed., *East Central Europe: A Guide to Basic Publications* (Chicago: University of Chicago Press, 1969); Paul L. Horecky, ed., *Southeastern Europe: A Guide to Basic Publications* (Chicago: University of Chicago Press, 1969); Charles Jelavich, ed., *Language and Area Studies, East Central and Southeastern Europe; A Survey* (Chicago: University of Chicago Press, 1969); Gertrud Krallert-Sattler, ed., *Südosteuropa-Bibliographie* (Munich: Oldenbourg, 1956-71), four volumes of which have been published to date. For articles as well as books, there is the useful and thorough *American Bibliography of Slavic and East European Studies* (Bloomington: Indiana University Press, 1957-71; Columbus: Ohio State University Press, 1972-).

There are two earlier general surveys of interwar East Central Europe. Hugh Seton-Watson, *Eastern Europe between the Wars, 1918-1941* (3d ed., Hamden, Conn.: Archon Books, 1962) was written during World War II under the erroneous assumption that the West and the Soviet Union would cooperate to modernize and democratize the area at war's end. This assumption led to misjudgments of the roles of the local Peasantist and Socialist movements and of the anxieties of some of the local governments. Though Seton-Watson has long since acknowledged his mistake, he has made only minimal revisions in the later editions of his work, preferring to let it stand as originally written to serve as evidence of the spirit of his wartime generation. Despite its weaknesses, this remains a comprehensive and rich survey. C. A. Macartney and A. W. Palmer, *Independent Eastern Europe* (London: Macmillan, 1962) concentrates overwhelmingly on foreign policies and diplomacy; institutional, political, and socioeconomic developments are neglected. It is also marred by an excessive number of factual errors on dates and names and by its strong revisionist bias, particularly in favor of Hungary.

For the several general themes taken up in the first chapter, the following are the most useful or intriguing studies. The interwar international system is traced in the many volumes of the *Survey of International Affairs* edited by Arnold Toynbee and his colleagues for the Royal Institute of International Affairs in London. France's original efforts to underwrite that system in East Central Europe are studied by Piotr Wandycz, *France and Her Eastern Allies 1919-1925* (Minneapolis: University of Minnesota Press, 1962). The eventual failure of that system to contain Nazi Germany in the 1930s has been well analyzed by Gerhard L. Weinberg, *The Foreign Policy of Hitler's Germany: Diplomatic Revolution in Europe 1933-36* (Chicago: University of Chicago Press, 1970). An interesting collaborative effort by seventeen American-based scholars is Gordon Craig and Felix Gilbert, eds., *The Diplomats 1919-1939* (Princeton: Princeton University Press, 1953). The specifically economic aspect of Nazi Germany's ambitions in

East Central Europe is analyzed by Antonín Basch, *The Danube Basin and the German Economic Sphere* (New York: Columbia University Press, 1943). A basic and statistically rich study of the Great Depression, which forms the economic background to the disintegration of the interwar political and diplomatic systems and the related rise of Nazi Germany, is Ingvar Svennilsen, *Growth and Stagnation in the European Economy, 1913-1945* (Geneva: UN Commission for Europe, 1954). The generally unimpressive efforts of the East Central European states to protect themselves against these economic and political erosions through some intra-area cooperation are pithily discussed in a number of essays in Henry L. Roberts, *Eastern Europe* (New York: Knopf, 1970). Earlier and more sanguine studies of these efforts are Robert Machray, *The Little Entente* (1929; reprint ed., New York: Fertig, 1970), and Robert J. Kerner and H. N. Howard, *The Balkan Conferences and the Balkan Entente, 1930-1935* (Berkeley: University of California Press, 1936). More journalistic but quite solid in its conclusions is Josef Hanč, *Tornado across Eastern Europe* (New York: Greystone, 1942).

The ethnic tensions that largely account for this failure of the interwar East Central European states to achieve area-wide solidarity vis-à-vis their aggressive Great Power neighbors have been analyzed comprehensively in a number of books by C. A. Macartney: *National States and National Minorities* (1934; reprint ed., New York: Russell and Russell, 1968); *Hungary and Her Successors* (London: Oxford University Press, 1937); *Problems of the Danube Area* (London: Cambridge University Press, 1944). Other general surveys of this problem are two volumes by the German economist Walter Hoffmann which, though clearly revisionist, are still free of excessive Nazi propaganda: *Südost-Europa* (Leipzig: Lindner, 1932), and *Donauraum-Völkerschicksal* (Leipzig: Meiner, 1939). Also useful is the American survey by the contributors to *Nationalism in Eastern Europe* edited by Peter F. Sugar and Ivo J. Lederer (Seattle: University of Washington Press, 1969).

The several studies on East Central European peasantist ideology and politics are generally written with much greater enthusiasm or nostalgia than I can bring to this overrated subject. The best of these are: David Mitrany, *Marx against the Peasant* (New York: Collier, 1961); G. M. Dimitrov, "Agrarianism," in Felix Gross, ed., *European Ideologies* (New York: Philosophical Library, 1948); and some of the essays in Ghiţa Ionescu and Ernest Gellner, eds., *Populism* (New York: Macmillan, 1969). More sentimental are H. Hessell Tiltman, *Peasant Europe* (London: Jarrolds, 1936), and Milan Hodža, *Federation in Central Europe* (London: Jarrolds, 1942). Helpful monographs dealing with particular aspects of the peasant question in several countries are: Otto von Frangeš, *Die Bevölkerungsdichte als Triebkraft der Wirtschaftspolitik der südosteuropäischen Bauernstaaten* (Jena: Fischer, 1939); S. D. Zagoroff et al., *The Agricultural Economy of the Danu-*

bian Countries 1935-45 (Stanford: Stanford University Press, 1955); Sigismund Gargas, *Die Grüne Internationale* (Halberstadt: Meyer, 1927); and George D. Jackson, Jr., *Comintern and Peasant in East Europe 1919-1930* (New York: Columbia University Press, 1966). Gargas and Jackson complement each other. An attempt to deal with all the area's interwar land reform programs in one symposium is O. S. Morgan, ed., *Agricultural Systems of Middle Europe* (New York: Macmillan, 1933). It was, however, undertaken too early; most of the essays were written in 1931 when the intent of these several programs could be clearly presented but their results were still unclear. Hence, it is no substitute for later monographs, many of which postdate World War II, on these land reforms in individual countries.

Studies of the area's Right-Radical, or Fascist, movements are generally more skeptical than those of peasantism, and often more insightful. Three books that include East Central Europe in more sweeping surveys of this phenomenon are: Hans Rogger and Eugen Weber, eds., *The European Right: A Historical Profile* (Berkeley: University of California Press, 1966); Walter Laqueur and George L. Mosse, eds., *International Fascism 1920-1945* (New York: Harper and Row, 1966); and S. J. Woolf, ed., *European Fascism* (New York: Random House, 1968). All these are collaborative efforts, and some of the authors have essays in two of these three volumes. A study concentrating exclusively on East Central Europe and interestingly organized as a series of parallel essays by contemporary Western and East Central European historians, country by country, is Peter F. Sugar, ed., *Native Fascism in the Successor States 1918-1945* (Santa Barbara: ABC-Clio, 1971). An officer of the Nazi German intelligence services (RSHA) whose assignment included the observation and evaluation of East Central European Right-Radical movements and groupings was Wilhelm Hoettl, who has written about this subject under the pseudonym of Walter Hagen in *Die Geheime Front* (Linz: Nibelungen, 1950). A stimulating interpretative essay on the relationship between the native Right-Radicals and Nazi Germany, which was often more complex than initially assumed, is Martin Broszat, "Faschismus und Kollaboration in Ostmitteleuropa Zwischen den Weltkriegen," *Vierteljahrshefte für Zeitgeschichte* 14 (July, 1966): 225-51. Related to the activities of these native Right-Radicals were those of the increasingly Nazified local Volksdeutsche communities, on which see G. C. Paikert, *The Danube Swabians* (Hague: Nijhoff, 1967).

The transition from parliamentary to authoritarian political systems has drawn the attention of several German scholars. Werner Conze, "Die Strukturkrise des östlichen Mitteleuropas vor und nach 1919," *Vierteljahrshefte für Zeitgeschichte*, vol. 1, no. 4 (October, 1953), pp. 319-38 and especially the several papers collected in Hans-Erich Volkmann, ed., *Die*

Krise des Parlamentarismus in Ostmitteleuropa Zwischen den Beiden Weltkriegen (Marburg/Lahn: Herder, 1967) shed light on this subject. Also stimulating despite its misleading title is the long essay by Andrew C. Janos, "The One-Party State and Social Mobilization: East Europe Between the Wars," in Samuel P. Huntington and Clement H. Moore, *Authoritarian Politics in Modern Society* (New York: Basic Books, 1970). Surveys of the earlier parliamentary systems are the two volumes by Malbone W. Graham: *New Governments of Central Europe* (London: Pitman, 1924) and *New Governments of Eastern Europe* (New York: Holt, 1927). A helpful survey of interwar Communism in the area is the encyclopedic but controversial third volume, part one, of E. H. Carr, *Socialism in One Country* (London: Macmillan, 1964).

The demographic and economic backgrounds to these political trends are examined in several excellent books. Dudley Kirk, *Europe's Population in the Interwar Years* (Geneva: League of Nations, 1946) is heavily statistical. Wilbert E. Moore, *Economic Demography of Eastern and Southern Europe* (Geneva: League of Nations, 1945) is more interpretive. Reservations about Moore's method for calculating surplus agricultural population have been expressed by Nicholas Spulber, *The Economics of Communist Eastern Europe* (Cambridge, Mass.: MIT, 1957), pp. 275-76. Spulber also has a long essay on "The Role of the State in Economic Growth in Eastern Europe Since 1860," in G. J. Aitken, ed., *The State and Economic Growth* (New York: SSRC, 1959). Two anonymous staff studies by the Royal Institute of International Affairs are *South-Eastern Europe: A Political and Economic Survey* (London: Oxford University Press, 1939) and its sequel, *South-Eastern Europe: A Brief Survey* (London: Oxford University Press, 1940). Another report was prepared by the Political and Economic Planning Organization: *Economic Development in South East Europe* (London: PEP, 1945). A specialized study of an area-wide problem is Paul de Hevesy, *World Wheat Planning and Economic Planning in General* (London: Oxford University Press, 1940). From the area itself we have *L'État Économique des Pays Balkaniques* (Belgrade: L'Institut Balkanique, 1938), which, though rich in statistics, presents an overly optimistic interpretation of the situation in an effort to attract foreign investments. An impressive geographical study that elucidates some of the reasons for the area's disappointing economic performance is H. G. Wanklyn, *The Eastern Marchlands of Europe* (London: Philip, 1941).

As of this writing there exists no synthesis or interpretation of cultural developments throughout the area as a whole, and we must still rely on literary and cultural histories for individual countries. However, a radical improvement may be expected to result from the launching by the Nürnberg (Germany) publishing house Glock und Lutz of its new series "Kultur der Nationen: Geistige Länderkunde." Already two fine encyclopedic studies of modern Polish and Bulgarian "high culture" have appeared in this series (see below for details), and more are presumably in progress.

Before concluding this survey of materials pertaining to several countries, mention should be made of the helpful calendar series in six slim volumes entitled *Chronology of Political and Economic Events in the Danube Basin, 1918-1936* (Paris: International Institute of Intellectual Cooperation, 1938) and of the wartime United Nations series under the general editorship of Robert J. Kerner, published by the University of California Press at Berkeley. In this latter series three East Central European countries were given uneven treatment in *Poland* (1947), *Czechoslovakia* (1949), and *Yugoslavia* (1949).

2

Turning to the scholarly literature on individual countries, we find exhaustive treatment of the experiences of the area's several countries at the hands of Great Power diplomacy during World War I and at the subsequent peace conference in: Titus Komarnicki, *Rebirth of the Polish Republic* (London: Heinemann, 1957); Dagmar Perman, *The Shaping of the Czechoslovak State* (Leiden: Brill, 1962); Francis Deák, *Hungary at the Paris Peace Conference* (New York: Columbia University Press, 1942); Ivo J. Lederer, *Yugoslavia at the Paris Peace Conference* (New Haven: Yale University Press, 1963); Sherman D. Spector, *Rumania at the Paris Peace Conference* (New York: Bookman, 1962); Georgi P. Genov, *Bulgaria and the Treaty of Neuilly* (Sofia: Danov, 1935); and Jürgen von Hehn, ed., *Von den baltischen Provinzen zu den baltischen Staaten* (Marburg/Lahn: Herder, 1971). Though important, this genre of detailed diplomatic history tends to be tedious.

Three comprehensive and excellent surveys of interwar Polish political, economic, demographic, and cultural experiences and contributions are: *La Pologne 1919-1939*, 3 vols. (Neuchâtel: Baconnière, 1946); Werner Markert, ed., *Polen* (Cologne: Böhlau, 1959); and Alexander Gieysztor et al., *History of Poland* (Warsaw: PWN, 1968). Briefer but also fine narratives are: Adam C. Rosé, *La Politique Polonaise entre les Deux Guerres* (Neuchâtel: Baconnière, 1945); Ferdynand Zweig, *Poland between Two Wars* (London: Secker and Warburg, 1944) which is exclusively economic; Hans Roos, *A History of Modern Poland* (New York: Knopf, 1966); and V. L. Beneš and N. J. G. Pounds, *Poland* (New York: Praeger, 1970). Relations between the Polish state-nation and the country's ethnic minorities are well analyzed by Simon Segal, *The New Poland and the Jews* (New York: Furman, 1938), Nicholas P. Vakar, *Belorussia* (Cambridge, Mass.: Harvard University Press, 1956), Volodymyr Kubijovyč, ed., *Ukraine*, 2 vols. (Toronto: University of Toronto Press, 1963-71), and Adam Żółtowski,

Border of Europe (London: Hollis and Carter, 1950), which presents the Polish National Democratic point of view. A description of the formal governmental system is B. Mirkine-Guetzevitch and A. Tibal, *La Pologne* (Paris: Delagrave, 1930). Analyses of Polish domestic politics in the 1920s and 1930s are, respectively, Joseph Rothschild, *Piłsudski's Coup d'État* (New York: Columbia University Press, 1966) and R. L. Buell, *Poland* (3d ed., New York: Knopf, 1939). Complementing these is Jack Taylor, *Economic Development of Poland 1919-1950* (Ithaca: Cornell University Press, 1952). Cultural contributions are itemized and evaluated by Karl Hartmann, *Polen* (Nürnberg: Glock und Lutz, 1966). Among the many careful studies on interwar Polish diplomatic problems are: Piotr Wandycz, *Soviet-Polish Relations 1917-1921* (Cambridge, Mass.: Harvard University Press, 1969); Bohdan Budurowycz, *Polish-Soviet Relations 1932-1939* (New York: Columbia University Press, 1963); Christoph Kimmich, *The Free City* (i.e., Danzig) (New Haven: Yale University Press, 1968); Harald von Riekhoff, *German-Polish Relations 1918-1933* (Baltimore: Johns Hopkins Press, 1971); and Hans Roos, *Polen und Europa* (Tübingen: Mohr, 1957). The edited papers and memoirs of several Polish diplomats have also been published: Jan Szembek, *Journal 1933-1939* (Paris: Plon, 1952); Wacław Jędrzejewicz, ed., *Diplomat in Berlin: Papers and Memoirs of Józef Lipski* (New York: Columbia University Press, 1968); and from the same editor, *Diplomat in Paris: Memoirs of Juliusz Łukasiewicz* (New York: Columbia University Press, 1970).

Czechoslovak scholars in exile have published three massive volumes of papers presented at symposia on their country's cultural, political, socioeconomic, and jurisprudential history, all edited by Miloslav Rechcigl, Jr.: *The Czechoslovak Contribution to World Culture* (Hague: Mouton, 1964) and *Czechoslovakia Past and Present*, 2 vols. (Hague: Mouton, 1968). A good brief survey is Jörg K. Hoensch, *Geschichte der tschechoslowakischen Republik* (Stuttgart: Kohlhammer, 1966). An early economic and geographical study by a skeptical Swiss is Hugo Hassinger, *Die Tschechoslowakei* (Vienna: Rikola, 1925). A close yet friendly scrutiny of the political system is Harry Klepetař, *Seit 1918* (Moravská Ostrava, 1937). More formal and legalistic are Karel Hoch, *Les Partis politiques en Tchécoslovaquie* (Prague: Orbis, 1935) and Edward Táborský, *Czechoslovak Democracy at Work* (London: Allen and Unwin, 1945). The difficult relations between Czechs and Germans are best handled by: Elisabeth Wiskemann, *Czechs and Germans* (London: Oxford University Press, 1938); the Sudeten German Socialist Johann Brügel, *Tschechen und Deutsche* (Munich: Nymphenburger, 1967); Radomír Luža, *The Transfer of the Sudeten Germans* (New York: New York University Press, 1964); and the several authors in E. Lemberg and G. Rhode, eds., *Das deutsch-tschechische Verhältnis Seit 1918* (Stuttgart: Kohlhammer, 1969). Negative and positive Slovak assessments of that people's interwar relationship with the Czechs are, respectively,

Joseph A. Mikuš, *Slovakia* (Milwaukee: Marquette University Press, 1963) and Jozef Lettrich, *History of Modern Slovakia* (New York: Praeger, 1955). A recent symposium on the current state of research is Karl Bosl, ed., *Aktuelle Forschungsprobleme um die erste tschechoslowakische Republik* (Munich: Oldenbourg, 1969). An important survey of political and economic history published since my manuscript went to press is Victor S. Mamatey and Radomír Luža, eds., *A History of the Czechoslovak Republic 1918-1948* (Princeton: Princeton University Press, 1973).

The most comprehensive history of interwar Hungary, sympathetic toward the Horthy-Bethlen elite, is by C. A. Macartney, *A History of Hungary 1929-1945*, 2 vols. (New York: Praeger, 1956-57). Shorter surveys are Walter Schneefuss, *Ungarn* (Leipzig: Goldmann, 1939), Otto Isbert, *Ungarn* (Berlin: Junker und Dünnhaupt, 1941), and Nandor Dreisziger, *Hungary's Way to World War II* (Astor Park, Fla.: Danubian Press, 1968). The Károly and Kun episodes have received massive coverage by the participants and scholars: Michael Károlyi, *Memoirs* (London: Cape, 1956); Oszkár Jászi, *Magyariens Schuld, Ungarns Sühne* (Munich: Kulturpolitik, 1923); Wilhelm Böhm, *Im Kreuzfeuer Zweier Revolutionen* (Munich: Kulturpolitik, 1924); A. Kaas and F. de Lazarovics, *Bolshevism in Hungary* (London: Richards, 1931); Rudolf Tökés, *Béla Kun and the Hungarian Soviet Republic* (New York: Praeger, 1967); and Iván Völgyes, ed., *Hungary in Revolution 1918-1919: Nine Essays* (Lincoln: University of Nebraska Press, 1971). The diplomatic aspects are clarified by Alfred Low, *The Soviet Hungarian Republic and the Paris Peace Conference* (Philadelphia: American Philosophical Society, 1963) and Arno Mayer, *Politics and Diplomacy of Peacemaking* (New York: Knopf, 1967). There are many laudatory articles on the Horthy system in the interwar *Ungarische Jahrbücher*, while postwar Hungarian scholars have sought to blacken that regime's reputation by publishing *The Confidential Papers of Admiral Horthy* (Budapest: Corvina, 1965). Hungarian Right-Radicalism is discussed in the general surveys of this phenomenon itemized earlier and in two monographs: M. Lackó, *Arrow-Cross Men, National Socialists* (Budapest: Akadémiai Kiadó, 1969) and Nicholas Nagy-Talavera, *The Green Shirts and the Others* (Stanford: Hoover, 1970). Certain cultural contributions are evaluated by T. Erdey-Grúz and I. Trencsényi-Waldapfel, *Science in Hungary* (Budapest: Corvina, 1965).

The most sweeping survey of interwar Yugoslav politics is Gilbert In der Maur, *Die Jugoslawen Einst und Jetzt*, 3 vols. (Leipzig: Günther, 1936-38). Splendidly supplementing it for economic and social problems are Werner Markert, ed., *Jugoslawien* (Cologne: Böhlau, 1954) and Jozo Tomasevich, *Peasants, Politics, and Economic Change in Yugoslavia* (Stanford: Stanford University Press, 1955). Finely distilled recent surveys are the opening essay in Wayne S. Vucinich, ed., *Contemporary Yugoslavia* (Berkeley: University of California Press, 1969) and the second chapter of

Stevan Pavlowitch, *Yugoslavia* (New York: Praeger, 1971). The parliamentary system of the 1920s is analyzed sympathetically by Charles Beard and George Radin, *The Balkan Pivot* (New York: Macmillan, 1929) and Albert Mousset, *Le Royaume Serbe Croate Slovène* (Paris: Bossard, 1926). The authoritarian politics of the 1930s are viewed critically by Svetozar Pribičević, *La Dictature du Roi Alexandre* (Paris: Bossuet, 1933), but rationalized by Erich Richter (Erich Reimers), *Das Neue Jugoslawien* (Leipzig: Goldmann, 1939). Apart from Maček's memoirs, *In the Struggle for Freedom* (New York: Speller, 1957), the most articulate statements of the Croats' case are Emil Gärtner, *Kroatien in Südslawien* (Berlin: Junker und Dünnhaupt, 1944), and Rudolf Kiszling, *Die Kroaten* (Cologne: Böhlau, 1956). The diplomatic drift toward Germany is analyzed by J. B. Hoptner, *Yugoslavia in Crisis 1934-1941* (New York: Columbia University Press, 1962) and Johann Wuescht, *Jugoslawien und das Dritte Reich* (Stuttgart: Sewald, 1969). Its nemesis is described by D. N. Ristić, *Yugoslavia's Revolution of 1941* (University Park: Pennyslvania State University Press, 1966). "Low" (folk) and "high" (literary) culture, respectively, are studied by Ruth Trouton, *Peasant Renaissance in Yugoslavia* (London: Routledge and Kegan Paul, 1952) and Antun Barac, *A History of Yugoslav Literature* (Belgrade: Committee for Foreign Cultural Relations, 1955). An anthropological monograph is A. Balagija, *Les Musulmans Yougoslaves* (Algiers: Maison des Livres, 1940).

By far the wisest analysis of the interrelationship of Romania's political and socioeconomic problems is Henry L. Roberts, *Rumania* (New Haven: Yale University Press, 1951). Also useful for economic issues are André Tibal, *La Roumanie* (Paris: Rieder, 1930), Alfred Malaschofsky, *Rumänien* (Berlin: Junker und Dünnhaupt, 1943), and Henri Prost, *Destin de la Roumanie 1918-1954* (Paris: Berger-Levrault, 1954). The land reform of the 1920s is analyzed in great detail by David Mitrany, *The Land and the Peasant in Rumania* (London: Oxford University Press, 1930). The political developments, parties, and personalities of that decade are given somewhat overly optimistic and friendly surveys by C. U. Clark, *United Roumania* (New York: Dodd, Mead, 1932) and Joseph S. Roucek, *Contemporary Roumania and Her Problems* (Stanford: Stanford University Press, 1932). More jaundiced views of the 1930s are the Communist Lucretiu Patraşcanu, *Sous Trois Dictatures* (Paris: Vitiano, 1946) and Andreas Hillgruber, *Hitler, König Carol und Marshall Antonescu* (Wiesbaden: Steiner, 1954). The ideology and flavor of the Iron Guard leadership is conveyed in Corneliu Z. Codreanu, *Eiserne Garde* (Berlin: Brunnen, 1939). A recent specialized monograph is Maurice Pearton, *Oil and the Roumanian State* (Oxford: Clarendon Press, 1971).

The best and most concise survey of interwar Bulgaria is Richard Busch-Zantner, *Bulgarien* (Junker und Dünnhaupt, 1943). Windy, but highly informative, is G. C. Logio, *Bulgaria: Past and Present* (Manchester:

Sherratt and Hughes, 1936). The current authorities have also published a useful section on the interwar era in the *Short History of Bulgaria* (Sofia: Foreign Language Press, 1963). Economic and demographic problems and developments are well analyzed in a number of specialized studies: G. T. Danailov, *Les Effets de la Guerre en Bulgarie* (Paris: Presses Universitaires, 1932); Henri Prost, *La Bulgarie de 1912 à 1930* (Paris: Roger, 1932); Janaki Molloff, ed., *Die sozialökonomische Struktur der bulgarischen Landwirtschaft* (Berlin: Weidmann, 1936); and Oskar Anderson, *Struktur und Konjunktur der bulgarischen Volkswirtschaft* (Jena: Fischer, 1938). The politics of the Macedonian question and the IMRO movement are discussed by Joseph Swire, *Bulgarian Conspiracy* (London: Hale, 1939), and by Elisabeth Barker, *Macedonia* (London: RIIA, 1950). Bulgaria's Marxist and Peasantist parties are studied in the monographs of Joseph Rothschild, *The Communist Party of Bulgaria 1883-1936* (New York: Columbia University Press, 1959), and Nissan Oren, *Bulgarian Communism 1934-1944* (New York: Columbia University Press, 1971). A sensitive sociological study of peasant life is Irwin Sanders, *Balkan Village* (Lexington: University of Kentucky Press, 1949). Folk and literary culture, respectively, are encyclopedically studied by Christo Vakarelski, *Bulgarische Volkskunde* (Berlin: de Gruyter, 1969) and Christo Ognjanoff, *Bulgarien* (Nürnberg: Glock und Lutz, 1967).

A good survey of interwar Albania is the initial chapter of Nicholas Pano, *The People's Republic of Albania* (Baltimore: Johns Hopkins Press, 1968). The current official interpretation of that era is in the second half of Kristo Frasheri, *The History of Albania* (Tirana, 1964). A balanced review is Stavro Skendi, *The Political Evolution of Albania* (New York: Mid-European Studies Center, 1954). Two detailed studies on the domestic and foreign policies of the 1920s are Joseph Swire, *Albania: The Rise of a Kingdom* (London: Williams and Norgate, 1929), and Albert Mousset, *L'Albanie Devant l'Europe* (Paris: Delagrave, 1930). For the second interwar decade the best survey is Richard Busch-Zantner, *Albanien* (Leipzig: Goldmann, 1939), though the more journalistic and anecdotal Vandeleur Robinson, *Albania's Road to Freedom* (London: Allen and Unwin, 1941) is also informative.

Of several good studies on the interwar Baltic region as a whole, the best and richest in statistical data is that sponsored by the Royal Institute of International Affairs, *The Baltic States* (London: Oxford University Press, 1938). Also informative on political developments are E. Walter, *Estland, Lettland, Litauen* (Berlin: Hobbing, 1939) and Georg von Rauch, *Geschichte der baltischen Staaten* (Stuttgart: Kohlhammer, 1970). For Estonia the best surveys are: Louis Villecourt, *L'Estonie* (Paris: Rieder, 1932); J. Hampden Jackson, *Estonia* (London: Allen and Unwin, 1941); and Artur Mägi, *Das Staatsleben Estlands während seiner Selbständigkeit* (Stockholm: Almqvist & Wiksell, 1967). For Latvia the best studies are: Alfred Bilmanis, *A History of Latvia* (Princeton: Princeton University Press, 1951); Jürgen von Hehn, *Lettland Zwischen Demokratie und Diktatur* (Munich: Isar, 1957); and Edgar Anderson, ed., *Latvia 1918-1968* (2nd ed., Waverly, Iowa: Latvju Grāmata, 1969). Three works on Lithuania are especially useful: Manfred Hellmann, *Grundzüge zur Geschichte Litauens* (Darmstadt: Wissenschaftliche Buchgesellschaft, 1966); Alfred E. Senn, *The Great Powers, Lithuania, and the Vilna Question 1920-1928* (Leiden: Brill, 1966); and Leonas Sabaliūnas, *Lithuania in Crisis 1939-1940* (Bloomington: Indiana University Press, 1972).

In addition to the occasional titles pertaining to culture which were listed above with the individual country-résumés, the following books contain selected chapters of helpful summaries and critiques of interwar literary creativity. For Poland see Maxime Herman, *Histoire de la Littérature Polonaise* (Paris: Nizet, 1963), Manfred Kridl, *A Survey of Polish Literature and Culture* (The Hague: Mouton, 1967), and Czesław Miłosz, *The History of Polish Literature* (New York: Macmillan, 1969). For Czechoslovakia see Paul Selver, *Czechoslovak Literature* (London: Allen and Unwin, 1942), René Wellek, *Essays on Czech Literature* (The Hague: Mouton, 1963), Josef Mühlberger, *Tschechische Literaturgeschichte* (Munich: Ackermann-Gemeinde, 1970), Andreas Mráz, *Die Literatur der Slowaken* (Berlin: Volk und Reich, n.d.). For Hungary see Miklós Szabolcsi, ed., *History of Hungarian Literature* (Budapest: Corvina, 1964) and Joseph Reményi, *Hungarian Writers and Literature* (New Brunswick: Rutgers University Press, 1964). Anton Slodnjak, *Geschichte der slowenischen Literatur* (Berlin: de Gruyter, 1958), Ante Kadić, *Contemporary Croatian Literature* (The Hague: Mouton, 1960), and Ante Kadić, *Contemporary Serbian Literature* (The Hague: Mouton, 1964) are good for Yugoslavia. For Romania see Basil Munteano, *Modern Rumanian Literature* (Bucharest: Curentul, 1939). Georges Hateau, *Panorama de la Littérature Bulgare contemporaine* (Paris: Sagittaire, 1937), Clarence A. Manning and Roman Smal-Stocki, *The History of Modern Bulgarian Literature* (New York: Bookman, 1960), and Charles Moser, *A History of Bulgarian Literature 865-1944* (The Hague: Mouton, 1972) are good surveys for Bulgaria. Helpful are Stuart E. Mann, *Albanian Literature* (London: Quaritch, 1955), and Koço Bihiku, *An Outline of Albanian Literature* (Tirana: N. Frashëri State Publishing House, 1964). Literary developments in the Baltic States are treated in: Henno Jänes, *Geschichte der estnischen Literatur* (Stockholm: Almqvist & Wiksell, 1965); Endel Nirk, *Estonian Literature* (Tallinn: Eesti Raamat, 1970); Jānis Andrups and Vitauts Kalve, *Latvian Literature* (Stockholm: Goppers, 1954); Victor Jungfer, *Litauen* (Leipzig: Breitkopf und Härtel, 1938); and Jean Mauclère, *Panorama de la Littérature Lithuanienne contemporaine* (Paris: Sagittaire, 1938).

INDEX